INVITATION TO AN EXECUTION

▼▼

A HISTORY OF THE DEATH PENALTY IN THE UNITED STATES

Edited by Gordon Morris Bakken

UNIVERSITY OF NEW MEXICO PRESS

ALBUQUERQUE

© 2010 by the University of New Mexico Press
All rights reserved. Published 2010
Printed in the United States of America
15 14 13 12 11 10   1 2 3 4 5 6

Library of Congress Cataloging-in-Publication Data

Invitation to an execution : a history of the death penalty in the United States
/ edited by Gordon Morris Bakken.
    p. cm.
  Includes bibliographical references and index.
  ISBN 978-0-8263-4856-2 (cloth : alk. paper)
  1. Capital punishment—United States—History. 2. Capital punishment—
United States—States. 3. Executions and executioners—United States.
4. Executions and executioners—United States—States. I. Bakken, Gordon Morris.
  HV8699.U5.I58 2010
  364.660973—dc22
                                            2010010258

To Richard B. Bilder

and

the memory of Gordon B. Baldwin

Admirals of the University of Wisconsin Law School

Contents

Preface

In November 2004, Evan J. Mandery of the John Jay College of Criminal Justice in New York wrote, "It is meaningless, really, to speak about the death penalty in America without being geographically specific. Each death penalty state, as well as the federal government, has its own system of determining who shall be subject to capital punishment. These systems share some basic features, but they are each unique, and some are more problematic than others."[1] This book focuses on these differences and many of the similarities among the states and with the federal government. I must thank all of the librarians who wrote for this project and who gave so many hours helping the scholars researching this most difficult topic. Without the librarians, the research would be virtually impossible given the bulk of material available to researchers. Further, the librarians helped to separate the law review material from the social science scholarship for many of the authors. Thank you!

Gordon Morris Bakken
California State University, Fullerton

Note

1. Evan J. Mandery, "Foreword," in Jon Sorensen and Rocky Leann Pilgrim, *Lethal Injection: Capital Punishment in Texas during the Modern Era* (Austin: University of Texas Press, 2006), ix.

Part One

Introduction

INVITATION TO AN EXECUTION

INVITATIONS TO executions were very much a part of the ritual of death concluding a criminal proceeding in the United States. Until the early twentieth century, lawmen issued printed invitations to executions. These invitations were the last gasp of public executions in death penalty states.[1] These volumes are an invitation to readers to an understanding of the death penalty in America. The goal of the essays is to put death penalty statutes and practices in particular contexts. Moreover, these original essays use history to illuminate the circumstances of law and politics. Stuart Banner persuasively argues, "Many aspects of capital punishment today appear paradoxical without an appreciation of its history."[2] Some of those paradoxes include the United States' commitment to human rights worldwide amid executions not practiced in the industrialized western world. The death penalty was to serve as a deterrent, yet executions have been moved from the public square in front of crowds of thousands to the confines of prisons, hidden from public view. Some say the death penalty should be retributive, but we have come to the position that death must be relatively painless. History, particularly American cultural history, facilitates understanding of this movement in time and place.

An emphasis on place in time and history provides another dimension helping us to understand the evolution of American cultural attitudes about crime and the death penalty. In November 2004, Evan J. Mandery of the John Jay College of Criminal Justice in New York, wrote, "It is meaningless, really, to speak about the death penalty in America without being geographically specific. Each death penalty state, as well as the federal government, has its own system of determining who shall be subject to capital punishment. These systems share some basic features, but they are each unique, and some are more problematic than others."[3] One part of this work is devoted to a regional analysis in the scholarly context of regionalism and regional studies. The split of the American Civil War commonly defines the North and South. The Midwest emerged from the settlement of the Old Northwest. The Great Plains was first the "Great American Desert" and was later marked by aridity, dry-land farming, and irrigation. The Northwest of Washington and Oregon also was part of a settlement pattern, but now in the influence of the Pacific rains, coastal mountains, and arid interiors. The regional essays put death penalty issues in this geographic and cultural context.

The American West is less well defined. Readers of Gordon Morris Bakken and Brenda Farrington, editors, *The American West: Interactions, Intersections, and Injunctions* (2001), will find the question of "Where is the West?" debated by fourteen scholars.[4] Parts of this West are included in the essay on the Great Plains because of physiographic characteristics. California, Montana, and Texas have separate chapters because of their unique histories and the centrality of the death penalty in the criminal justice systems of the three states.

The death penalty is part of the criminal justice system and the system is frequently the target of criticism as part of the death penalty abolition movement. Criminal punishment was a product of English tradition, liberal democracy of the early national period, and the creation of the penitentiary.[5] In addition to reforming deviants, the prison as well as the death penalty was to be a deterrence of people from crime. Lawrence Friedman argues that deterrence works, but "the relationship between punishment and behavior is not a straight line but a curve; it flattens out as more and more people are, in fact, deterred."[6] Yet if murder is a crime of passion in some cases, how can the death penalty deter such behavior?

Some argue that race is a factor in the criminal justice system with African Americans "accused, arrested, tried, and jailed out of all proportion to their numbers."[7] Black defendants were sentenced to death at higher rates than white defendants.[8] This was particularly true in the American South.[9] But southern justice was not solely in black and white. American Indians suffered similar discrimination in state criminal courts.[10] Racism was "not merely a psychological response driven by irrational gut instinct, nor solely a collective symbolic construction to define American whiteness," it served white economic and political interests.[11] Racial stereotypes were transported into jury boxes.[12] The nature of the jury was part of criticism of the system as unfair.

The jury, the democratic protector of liberty and the foundation of justice, was only one part of the system. Lawrence Friedman sees crime as national in scope, but criminal justice "is as local as local gets."[13] It is not a system but a "jigsaw puzzle with a thousand tiny pieces." Legislators write statutes, police enforce the rules of the statutes, district attorneys prosecute the criminally accused, defense lawyers defend the accused, and in the courtroom "judges and juries go their own way."[14] It is easy to argue that the system is flawed.

It is even easier to find fault through specific cases. For example, Bill Neal's *Getting Away with Murder on the Texas Frontier: Notorious Killings & Celebrated Trials* (2006) demonstrates that many of the criminally accused slipped through the criminal justice net for a wide variety of reasons.[15] David R. Dow's *Executed on a Technicality: Lethal Injustice on America's Death Row* (2005) tells many tales of justice failing to function in Texas. Among those cases is that of Randall Dale Adams. A jury found Adams guilty of the murder of Robert Wood, a Dallas police officer, gunned down in 1976. Adams, a man without a criminal charge or a criminal conviction on his record, lost at trial due to the testimony of David Harris, a career criminal, who lied to avoid the death penalty. Harris did even better based on his testimony. He was not charged with anything. Adams went to death row and Harris went free only to murder. This time the jury sent him to death row and Texas ended his life in 2004. Harris admitted to the Wood murder long before his execution, but that did not get him off death row. Rather a documentary filmmaker, Errol Morris, produced *The Thin Blue Line*, it gained public notice, Adams's lawyers went to the Texas Court of Criminal Appeals and won a new trial. The prosecution did not move to trial and Adams was a free man. He returned to his law-abiding lifestyle.[16] The system had flaws on both sides.

The flaws give abolitionists academic fodder. Hugo Adam Bedau launched a series of death penalty books in 1964 warning his readers that he was "opposed to the death penalty in all its forms, no matter how awful the crime or how savage the criminal."[17] William R. Long's *A Tortured History: The Story of Capital Punishment in Oregon* (2001) focused on the history of a single state.[18] Long's history of Oregon's death penalty law concluded that the 1984 death penalty statute's costs outweigh its benefits in that post-conviction litigation was more expensive than life sentences. This anti-death-penalty message ran into the pesky problem of direct democracy. The people at the polls simply wanted the death penalty as the flood tide of voter sentiment washed away opposition in 1984.

The people of Oregon in prior years abolished the death penalty twice. Long focused on four periods in Oregon history to tease out the legal and political issues surrounding the death penalty. First, 1901–1903 was of interest because executions were taken from the public view and tucked away in the Oregon State Penitentiary in Salem. Second, the Progressive Era, 1912–1920, when voters gave the state direct democracy, abolished the death penalty, and then changed their collective mind on executions. Third, 1958–1964, when the voters return to the execution ban; and fourth, 1978–1984, when the flood tide swept the death penalty back into the statute books. In the process of analysis, attorney Long provided frequent historical and political linkages to Texas. Most revealing was his footnote on page 15: "Texas didn't began [*sic*] to execute people in earnest until the late 1980s. Now the flood is coming there, and the rest of the nation is standing back rather nonplused at the reality of sending a person to death every month in that state."

Long's historical treatment of the four eras was balanced and demonstrates extensive primary source and legal research. For example, in dealing with the Progressive Era debates, Long correctly balanced the contrary views of the advocates. Those against the death penalty saw the march of progress in science, social science, and civilization leading to only one conclusion, the abolition of the death penalty. On the other side, advocates believed themselves to be the true bearers of civilization. True civilization was ordered liberty, certain punishment for crime, and the elimination of the "everlasting meddling with the straightforward and certain operation of the law by weak-kneed Governors and by the higher courts through quibbles, technicalities, evasions and hair-splitting."[19] So it was. The contours of the debates have not changed much since then with the exception of the costs of justice.

Long's treatment of the rise of social science and prisoner therapy is important. Social science could rehabilitate and safely release convicted murderers back into Oregon society, or so we thought. The paroled and rehabilitated murderers of the 1970s did not cooperate. They killed again with the same brutality and the people looked to the death penalty for protection. Texas law seemed to hold an answer and an initiative petition started the process forward leading to the 1984 statute. Long carefully chronicled the numerous state supreme court and United States Supreme Court cases that cropped up in the 1970s and 1980s further complicating the legislative and political process. Between initiative petitions and judicial declarations of principle, the therapy argument was lost. Oregon death penalty opponents were left with calls for the Oregon Supreme Court to revisit questions of the recent past in hopes of killing death for convicted murderers.

John D. Bessler's *Legacy of Violence: Lynch Mobs and Executions in Minnesota* (2003) tells another story with an abolitionist victory in 1911.[20] Minnesota experienced nineteenth-century traditions of executions and a parallel abolition movement as early as 1864. Executions moved from the public square to the local jail with written invitations to attend. The fact that local sheriffs used these printed invitations motivated abolitionists to stop the practice. In turn, the state legislature forbade newspapers to print notices of executions. Finally, in the Progressive Era the death penalty was buried. Less than a decade later, Minnesota passed an antilynching law directed at racially motivated lynching in Duluth.

Eliza Steelwater's *The Hangman's Knot: Lynching, Legal Execution, and America's Struggle with the Death Penalty* (2003), like Bessler, explores the national relationship between lynching and the state execution of the criminally accused.[21] Steelwater cofounded Project HAL, Historical American Lynching, focused on the long-term practice of lynching. She deploys data from the Capital Punishment Research Project to demonstrate that historical practices are at the root of the politics of punishment. Based on the data and historical studies, she argues that executions, legal and extralegal, were the product of the political and economic aspirations of the people in power. She implicates western vigilante movements as well as modern lethal injection advocates in historical power alliances. Her message is clearly for the abolition of the death penalty. Fittingly, her last citation is to Michel Foucault's *Discipline and Punish: The Birth of the Prison*.[22] Thomas L. Dumm's *Democracy and Punishment: Disciplinary Origins of the United States* (1987) focused on the linkages of Foucault's observations and the American experience. The American prison system as well as the death penalty was what Tocqueville termed "democratic despotism."[23] Dumm and Long both acknowledged the power of the people at the polls.

Regardless of democracy, there are committed advocates for the abolition of the death penalty. Anthony G. Amsterdam, an extraordinary attorney, has labored for more than a half-century for abolition. In addition to numerous appellate appearances, Amsterdam has written extensively since the 1970s against the death penalty.[24] Advocates like Bryan Stevenson, the celebrated death penalty defense lawyer and professor, carry on Amsterdam's legacy.[25] Amsterdam and Stevenson are men committed to saving the lives of the condemned. They make the arguments that become media headlines and appellate cases.

The media keeps the issue of the death penalty before the reading public. When the United States Supreme Court blocked the execution of Scott Louis Panetti in 2007, it was headline news in the Milwaukee (Wisconsin) *Journal Sentinel*.[26] The majority of the court took the position that Panetti was too delusional to be put to death. The case was part of an ongoing debate over whether the mentally retarded could be executed. The *Los Angeles Times* gave the issue front-page coverage after the Panetti decision noting that defining the group was difficult as experts disagreed about the nature and extent of mental retardation.[27] State cases reveal inconsistency in exactly what constitutes mental retardation. Sara Catania argues that "the inconsistency may stem from confusion about what, exactly, defines mental retardation." The American Association on Intellectual and Developmental Disabilities says it consists of "significant limitations both in intellectual functioning and in adaptive behavior as expressed in conceptual social and practical adaptive skills." She notes that there are IQ standards, "but these are not legal parameters, and the U.S. Supreme Court left state legislature and courts to wrestle with the definition." Definitions, if they exist in statute, vary among the states.[28]

Courts and juries find for and against the death penalty and the media keeps the issue before the reading public. The California Supreme Court threw out a death penalty finding because the accused was not afforded the "right to represent himself."[29] The United States Supreme Court, reversing the Ninth Circuit Court of Appeals, restored the death penalty of a Washington man because the appellate court erred by intervening in the case and second-guessing the determination of the trial court judge.[30] A Los Angeles jury decided that death was appropriate for a murderer of ten women. Chester Dewayne Turner "thus joined the roster of L.A. area's infamous killers: Charles Manson, Night Stalker Richard Ramirez, Freeway Killer William Bonin and the Hillside Strangler."[31] Also of note, Sacramento Superior Court Judge Gary E. Ranson sentenced death penalty foe Kathleen Culhane to five years for producing fake documents to try to delay four executions. Prosecutors termed her actions "one of the largest frauds against the legal system in California history." Culhane termed capital punishment "a brutal legacy of lynching" and declared, "I cannot have remorse for a government that kills at midnight and invests millions of dollars in the process."[32] In contrast, Oklahoma District Court Judge Twyla Mason Gray set Curtis E. McCarty free because a police chemist who had been fired for fraud and misconduct six years prior had acted in bad faith. Innocence Project attorney Colin Starger observed, "Every piece of evidence [that] was used improperly to secure convictions, now shows Curtis McCarty's innocence." The chemist's false and misleading testimony in twenty-three other cases helped send him to death row and eleven had been executed by 2007.[33] The stakes are high and it is clear that the criminal justice administration system has flaws.

Abolition advocates argue that one of the flaws is lethal injection. On May 4, 2007, U.S. District Judge Todd J. Campbell blocked the execution of Philip Ray Workman on the grounds that Tennessee's lethal injection protocol would expose him "to a foreseeable and likely unnecessary risk of unconstitutional pain and suffering in violation of the Eight Amendment."[34] It was Workman's sixth stay of execution in over twenty years. On May 9, 2008, Workman's time was up after a three-judge panel of the Sixth Circuit Court of Appeals lifted the temporary restraining order and the Tennessee

Supreme Court rejected defense motions.[35] On September 25, 2007, the United States Supreme Court agreed to hear another challenge to lethal injection in a Kentucky case.[36] The U.S. Supreme Court stopped a Mississippi inmate's execution on October 30, 2007, signaling to some that executions should be halted pending the court's decision.[37] That did not stop Florida's supreme court from ruling lethal injection was constitutional.[38] Eric Berger, a University of Nebraska College of Law professor, wrote, "It is outrageous that statues and the federal government have elected to carry out executions with dangerous, painful chemicals and then abdicated responsibility for the procedures to untrained, unqualified personnel. Government owes its citizens a transparent, careful reconsideration of this deeply flawed procedure that, as currently constituted, is bound to fail."[39] This argument was one offered to the high court on January 7, 2008.[40]

While high court legal jousting continued, others questioned the jury and other aspects of the criminal justice system. The high court agreed to hear a Louisiana case of a man sentenced to death by an all-white jury constituted by keeping African Americans off the jury.[41] On February 11, 2008, the Pentagon announced that it would seek the death penalty for six of the 9/11 conspirators.[42] The United Nations called for a worldwide moratorium on the death penalty on December 18, 2007.[43] Maureen Faulkner wrote a book to counter the death penalty abolitionist support for Mumia Abu-Jamal who was convicted of her husband's murder a quarter-century ago.[44] It was a victim's voice seldom heard. Another voice unheard except in trial was that of the county district attorneys. A report to the California Commission on the Fair Administration of Justice noted that only fourteen of the state's fifty-eight counties explained the criteria used to determine whether the death penalty would be requested.[45] On February 20, 2008, the commission held hearings in

Los Angeles and "defense lawyers and prosecutors agreed . . . that California's death penalty system was deeply troubled but split over the causes and solutions."[46] On March 14, 2009, the *Los Angeles Times* ran a story about the costs of capital punishment focused on New Mexico, Louisiana, and California. New Mexico's legislature voted on March 13 to abolish the death penalty; California found that it could not afford a new $395 million death row prison; and Orleans Parish was next to bankruptcy because of a death penalty trial.[47] On March 19, 2009, the *Los Angeles Times* triumphantly announced that New Mexico governor Bill Richardson had signed the bill abolishing that state's death penalty.[48] The death penalty debate is current and solutions are hotly contested.[49]

In the chapters that follow in this work, our authors offer extensive analysis of the issues surrounding the death penalty. As you can tell, this is a developing field of inquiry and a hot-button political and legal issue. You will find extensive research advice and tools for your personal research. *Invitation to an Execution* is an invitation to you to understand a most complex historical, political, and legal question with more facets revealed over time.

Part one focuses on politics, legal history, multicultural issues, and the international aspects of the death penalty. Whether discussed in the realm of law or politics, remember the death penalty is a highly charged moral, legal, and cultural issue. Changes in time and place are rapid or incredibly stable depending upon the factors explored in these chapters. Part two is a regional analysis with authors analyzing the rule of law and capital punishment in a regional setting.

Notes

1. See Stuart Banner, *The Death Penalty: An American History* (Cambridge: Harvard University Press, 2002), 144–68; Lawrence M. Friedman, *Crime and Punishment in American History* (New York: Basic Books, 1993), 168–71; and Louis P. Masur, *Rites of Execution: Capital Punishment and the Transformation of American Culture, 1776–1865* (New York: Oxford University Press, 1989).
2. Banner, *Death Penalty*, 3.
3. Evan J. Mandery, "Foreword," in Jon Sorensen and Rocky Leann Pilgrim, *Lethal Injection: Capital Punishment in Texas during the Modern Era* (Austin: University of Texas Press, 2006), ix.
4. Gordon Morris Bakken and Brenda Farrington, eds., *Where Is the West: Interactions, Intersections, and Injunctions* (New York: Garland Publishing, Inc., 2001).
5. Thomas L. Dumm, *Democracy and Punishment: Disciplinary Origins of the United States* (Madison: University of Wisconsin Press, 1987).
6. Friedman, *Crime and Punishment in American History*, 458–9.
7. Ibid., 459.
8. Banner, *Death Penalty*, 289.
9. Edward L. Ayers, *Vengeance and Justice: Crime and Punishment in the 19th-Century American South* (New York: Oxford University Press, 1984). Also see Ariela J. Gross, *Double Character: Slavery and Mastery in the Antebellum Southern Courtroom* (Princeton: Princeton University Press, 2000).
10. Deborah A. Rosen, *American Indians and State Law: Sovereignty, Race, and Citizenship, 1790–1880* (Lincoln: University of Nebraska Press, 2007), 38–46.
11. Ibid., 103. Also see Clare V. McKanna Jr., *White Justice in Arizona: Apache Murder Trials in the Nineteenth Century* (Lubbock: Texas Tech University Press, 2005); and Vanessa Ann Gunther, *Ambiguous Justice: Native Americans and the Law in Southern California, 1848–1890* (East Lansing: Michigan State University Press, 2006).
12. On whiteness, a very expansive literature, see David R. Roediger, *The Wages of Whiteness: Race and the Making of the American Working Class*, revised edition (New York: Verso, 1999); Ronald Takaki, *Iron Cages: Race and Culture in 19th Century America* (New York: Oxford University Press, 1990); and Thomas A. Guglielmo, *White on Arrival: Italians, Race, Color, and Power in Chicago, 1890–1945* (New York: Oxford University Press, 2003).
13. Friedman, *Crime and Punishment in American History*, 461.

14. Ibid.

15. Bill Neal, *Getting Away with Murder on the Texas Frontier: Notorious Killings & Celebrated Trials* (Lubbock: Texas Tech University Press, 2006).

16. David R. Dow, *Executed on a Technicality: Lethal Injustice on America's Death Row* (Boston: Beacon Press, 2005), 98–108.

17. Hugo Adam Bedau, ed., *The Death Penalty in America: Current Controversies* (New York: Oxford University Press, 1997), vii.

18. William R. Long, *A Tortured History: The Story of Capital Punishment in Oregon* (Eugene: Oregon Criminal Defense Lawyers Association, 2001).

19. Ibid., 29.

20. John D. Bessler, *Legacy of Violence: Lynch Mobs and Executions in Minnesota* (Minneapolis: University of Minnesota Press, 2003).

21. Eliza Steelwater, *The Hangman's Knot: Lynching, Legal Execution, and America's Struggle with the Death Penalty* (Boulder, CO: Westview Press, 2003).

22. Ibid., 272.

23. Dumm, *Democracy and Punishment*, 128–40.

24. Nadya Labi, "A Man against the Machine," *The Law School: The Magazine of the New York University School of Law* (Autumn 2007):10–19.

25. Paul M. Barrett, "Bryan Stevenson's Death-Defying Acts," *The Law School: The Magazine of the New York University School of Law* (Autumn 2007):32–41.

26. Derrick Nunnally, "Hayward native's execution blocked," *Milwaukee Journal Sentinel*, June 29, 2007.

27. David G. Savage, "IQ debate unsettled in death penalty cases: The Supreme Court ruled against executing the mentally retarded, but defining that group has proved difficult," *Los Angeles Times*, June 11, 2007.

28. Sara Catania, "Death row's IQ divide," *Los Angeles Times*, May 8, 2007.

29. "State Court throws out a death sentence," *Los Angeles Times*, August 31, 2007.

30. "High court restores man's death sentence: In a 5–4 vote, justices support a trial ruling that excluded a juror who expressed some reservations about capital punishment," *Los Angeles Times*, June 5, 2007.

31. John Spano, "Jury votes execution for serial killer: The former L.A. crack cocaine dealer who murdered 10 women is to be sentenced July 10," *Los Angeles Times*, May 16, 2007.

32. "Death penalty foe gets five years: Former defense investigator Kathleen Culhane faked documents to try to delay four executions," *Los Angeles Times*, August 17, 2007.

33. Henry Weinstein, "Judge frees man facing execution: Police misconduct tainted the case against an Oklahoma convict who did 22 years," *Los Angeles Times*, May 12, 2007.

34. Henry Weinstein, "Tennessee killer's execution is blocked: A lethal injection set for Wednesday is stayed. Attorneys argue the condemned could face torturous pain," *Los Angeles Times*, May 5, 2007.

35. "Convicted cop-killer is executed: Tennessee's highest court denies pleas for further delay to study protocol," *Los Angeles Times*, May 10, 2007.

36. David G. Savage, "Supreme Court to hear lethal injection case: Justices could ban commonly used chemical concoctions that may cause dying inmates to suffer," *Los Angeles Times*, September 26, 2007.

37. Joan Biskupic, "Executions likely on hold until high court ruling: Reprieve in Miss. case signals more stays as justices review lethal injection," *USA Today*, November 1, 2007.

38. Paul Flemming and John Torres, "Florida top court rules lethal-injection method constitutional," *USA Today*, November 2, 2007.

39. Eric Berger, "Unfit to execute," *Los Angeles Times*, November 26, 2007.

40. Henry Weinstein, "High court takes up lethal injection: States have kept the execution process shrouded in secrecy," *Los Angeles Times*, January 7, 2008.

41. Henry Weinstein, " Jury to come under justices' scrutiny: The Supreme Court will hear a Louisiana case in which a black man was sentenced to die after African Americans were kept off the panel," *Los Angeles Times*, December 3, 2007.

42. Carol J. Williams, "9/11 suspects may face death penalty: The Pentagon brings murder and conspiracy charges against six detainees accused of plotting the attacks," *Los Angeles Times*, February 12, 2008.

43. Louise Arbour, "A world without executions: The United Nations addresses its voice to ending capital punishment," *Los Angeles Times*, December 19, 2007.

44. Catherine Sillant, "Still her husband's voice: In a new book the widow of a policeman gunned down in 1981 questions the high-profile support for his killer," *Los Angeles Times*, January 7, 2008.

45. Henry Weinstein, "Death penalty survey spurned: Many California D.A.s refuse to explain their decision-making on seeking executions," *Los Angeles Times*, February 20, 2008.

46. Henry Weinstein, "Lawyers divided on problems of the state's death penalty system," *Los Angeles Times*, February 21, 2008.

47. "States weigh cost of capital punishment," *Los Angeles Times*, March 14, 2009.

48. "N.M. Repeals Death Penalty," *Los Angeles Times*, March 19, 2009.

49. The debate in California has been a long one. See Theodore Hamm, *Rebel and a Cause: Caryl Chessman and the Politics of the Death Penalty in Postwar California, 1948–1974* (Berkeley: University of California Press, 2002).

CHAPTER 1

Politics and Capital Punishment

THE ROLE OF JUDICIAL, LEGISLATIVE, AND EXECUTIVE DECISIONS IN THE PRACTICE OF DEATH

Stacy L. Mallicoat

Introduction

SINCE THE first execution in 1630, America's use of the death penalty has evolved significantly. From its historical roots to the modernized practices of contemporary society, these changes are seen in the legislative decisions on death eligibility and criminal procedure, to the executive functions of clemency, to the judicial interpretations of constitutional validity. This essay examines the role of the legislative, judicial, and executive functions in the practice of capital punishment.

Judicial Issues

While constitutional challenges in death penalty cases may reflect Fifth and Sixth Amendment procedural concerns such as racial bias in jury selection or Fourteenth Amendment habeas corpus challenges. Such challenges have questioned the application of the death penalty to certain offender classifications, the methods by which executions are carried out, as well as the administration of the system as a whole. Successful challenges resulted from Eighth Amendment challenges to the practice of death as a violation of the protection against cruel and unusual punishment.

Fixing a Broken System

Prior to 1968, the Supreme Court cases on the death penalty challenged the constitutionality of the practice. Instead, these cases focused on specific issues related to the process of the death penalty as violations of due process under the Sixth and Fourteenth Amendments. These attempts failed to make significant changes to a system where disproportionate and arbitrary sentencing practices were not uncommon. While the denial of *certiorari* in *McGautha v. California* (1971) summarily approved a process whereby the guilt and sentencing phases of the death penalty process were determined within a single trial, and permitted unregulated jury discretion, these decisions were made on the basis of the Fourteenth Amendment rather than an Eighth Amendment challenge. One year later, the Court heard arguments in the case of *Furman v. Georgia* (1972) to address the question of whether the administration of the death penalty constitutes cruel and unusual punishment under the Eighth and Fourteenth Amendments. In the 5–4 decision, the majority opinion of the Court held that the current statutes under which the death penalty was administered amounted to cruel and unusual punishment on the grounds that the current practice illustrated patterns of arbitrary and discriminatory sentencing decisions. While Justices Brennan and Marshall gave concurring opinions declaring the death penalty as unconstitutional per-se under the Eighth Amendment, the majority opinion (to include Justices Stewart, White, and Douglas) maintained that it was the current administration of the death penalty and not the concept of death as the ultimate punishment which violated the protections of the Eighth and Fourteenth Amendments. The majority opinion held that the current laws allowed for arbitrary applications of death sentencing. Justice Stewart suggested that the pattern of "death sentences are cruel and unusual in the same way that being struck by lightning is cruel and unusual."[1]

The majority opinion also held that the current laws were discriminatory as their implementation was biased against minority defendants. In referencing several studies indicating that the death penalty is disproportionately imposed on blacks and the poor, Justice Douglas held that "these discretionary statutes are unconstitutional in their operation. They are pregnant with discrimination and discrimination is an ingredient not compatible with the idea of equal protection of the laws that is implicit in the ban on 'cruel and unusual' punishments."[2] While the majority decision left open the door that new laws could resolve these concerns, the effect of the *Furman* decision overturned 629 death sentences in 32 states.[3]

Following the *Furman* decision, several states developed new death penalty statutes to address these constitutional violations and bring the death penalty back to life. In an attempt to resolve the issue of arbitrary administration, North Carolina and Louisiana designed laws requiring mandatory death sentences for capital crimes. These states posited that such laws would eliminate the unregulated discretion of the jury's decision-making process that concerned the *Furman* court. The justices held that mandatory death sentences would violate "the fundamental respect for humanity" and declared these laws unconstitutional.[4] However, the Court approved the statutes presented in the cases of *Gregg v. Georgia* (428 U.S. 153), *Jurek v. Texas* (428 U.S. 262) and *Proffitt v. Florida* (428 U.S. 242). Known as the *Gregg* decision, these cases developed a new system by which offenders could be sentenced to death. The provisions in these cases created four new procedures that dramatically altered the administration of capital sentences. First, the *Gregg* decision created a bifurcated process for capital crimes, and separated the guilt and sentencing decisions into two separate trials. Second, a system of automatic appeal was created, which mandated that the highest court of each state review all convictions and death sentences to protect against constitutional errors. Third, proportionality reviews were suggested to protect against sentencing disparities. While the Court felt that proportionality review was a desirable protection, they later held that such a practice was not mandatory to pass constitutional muster.[5] The fourth provision hinged on the concept of guided discretion. The most common form of guided discretion statutes requires the jury to weigh the effects of aggravating and mitigating factors in applying a death sentence. Aggravating factors are circumstances which increase the severity of the crime, such as torture, excessive violence, or premeditation. Mitigating factors include references to the defendant's background which may explain the defendant's behavior, but which do not constitute a legally relevant defense.

In order for a death sentence to be handed out under these guided discretion statutes, a jury must determine that the value of the aggravating factors outweighs any mitigating factors. If the value of the mitigating factors exceeds any aggravators, then a life without the possibility of parole (or a similarly designated sentence of incarceration) is given. Today, thirty-seven of the thirty-eight states that have the death penalty also offer life without the possibility of parole (LWOP) as a sentencing alternative.[6] The process of guided discretion created a standard for systematically evaluating the application of sentencing options for different cases across the nation. These practices returned the death penalty to the national stage and many states soon reinstated the death penalty in theory and practice.

Methods of Execution under the Eighth Amendment

Recent execution history in the United States has involved five methods of execution: hanging, firing squad, electrocution, lethal gas, and lethal injection. While each had its day of popularity, most of these methods have drifted into obscurity in light of constitutional challenges and evolving standards of decency. With the exit of one method, another form of execution arrives to take its place and each cycle attempts to bring in a cleaner and, ideally, more humane method of execution. The Supreme Court's struggle with Eighth Amendment interpretations on execution methods began in 1878, when they specified that particular forms of torture such as "drawing and quartering, embowelling alive, beheading, public dissection and burning alive and all other in the same line of . . . cruelty, are forbidden."[7] While this ruling was explicit in its discussion regarding which specific forms would be unconstitutional, later decisions allowed for greater flexibility and interpretation. *Weems v. U.S.* (1910) stated that

execution methods should be subject to interpretation and change, and *Trop v. Dulles* (1958) set forth the precedent that the definition of cruel and unusual "must draw its meaning from the evolving standards of decency that mark the progress of a maturing society."[8] Together, these opinions created the opportunity for future discussions on the constitutionality of cruel and unusual punishments.

In *Wilkerson v. Utah* (1878), the U.S. Supreme Court held that the firing squad was not cruel, nor unusual.[9] While the firing squad is available in Idaho, Oklahoma, and Utah, these states limit their application, as Idaho and Oklahoma only permit the use of the firing squad if lethal injection is declared unconstitutional and Utah allows this method as a choice only in cases sentenced prior to 2004.[10] The use of the firing squad was made famous in modern times with the execution of Gary Gilmore in January 1977, the first execution following the reinstatement of the death penalty in *Gregg v. Georgia* (1976).[11] With the introduction of lethal injection in Utah in 1980, the state legislature retained the choice of the firing squad in an effort to balance their historical tradition with the evolving standards of decency. While only Gilmore[12] and John Albert Taylor[13] elected to die by firing squad in Utah, the legislature reasoned that it should be kept as an option "in case the man who was going to die wanted his blood to be shed, as a bid for salvation."[14] In 2004, the Utah legislature enacted a provision that eliminated the option of the firing squad for future death row inmates but that inmates sentenced prior to 2004 could retain the firing squad as an option.[15] The decision by the State of Utah to end the use of the firing squad came not from constitutional Eighth Amendment challenges by prisoners, but rather from an effort to eliminate the negative public relations circus that has accompanied the modern-day use of the firing squad whereby media reports from around the world of such executions made celebrities of the offender and ignored the suffering of the victims and their families.[16]

Like the firing squad, hanging remains a constitutionally valid method of execution, even as many states have eliminated its use. Historically, hangings account for the majority of all executions throughout the history of the United States.[17] Today, hanging is utilized as an option for execution in New Hampshire and Washington. In 1994, Charles Rodman Campbell was executed via hanging, the second and last man to die by hanging since the reinstatement of the death penalty in Washington.[18] While the Court acknowledged that risks such as strangulation and decapitation did exist with the use of hanging, the Ninth Circuit opinion in *Campbell v. Wood* (1994)[19] held that Washington's protocol for hangings did not violate the Eighth Amendment and that since the offender chose the method of hanging for his execution, he was barred from then challenging the method. In 1996, the Washington state legislature clarified their laws on execution methods and made lethal injection the default method unless the offender specifically chooses the gallows.[20]

Electrocution represents the last challenge to the methods of execution that the Supreme Court has issued an opinion on to date. In 1890, the Court upheld the use of the electric chair in *In re Kemmler* (1890). The Court also indicated that the use of successive electrocutions due to failure does not constitute cruel and unusual punishment. In their review of the constitutionality of the electric chair, the Court indicated that the level of pain experienced by the offender formed the basis for their decisions on whether the use of the electric chair constitutes an Eighth Amendment violation.[21] Since *Kemmler*, several decisions have noted the need to preserve the dignity of humanity as a protective factor of the Eighth Amendment.[22] While once seen as the wave of the future for quick and painless executions, today's

use of the electric chair has been reduced to only ten states. Nebraska is the only state that requires the use of electrocution while the remaining nine states allow offenders to choose electrocution or maintain the option in case lethal injection is unavailable. While several defendants have recently raised concerns regarding the constitutionality of the electric chair, the Supreme Court has yet to hear a case and issue an opinion. The Court has denied *certiorari* in two cases involving the constitutionality of the electric chair: *Glass v. Louisiana* (1985) and *Poyner v. Murray* (1993). As an opponent of capital punishment, Justice Brennan (joined by Justice Marshall) argued in his dissenting opinion for *Glass* that not only are all methods of execution inherently cruel and degrading, but that the specific practice of electrocution is

> a cruel and barbaric method of extinguishing human life, both per se and as compared with other available means of execution. As in this case, such claims have uniformly and summarily been rejected, typically on the strength of this Court's opinion in *In re Kemmler* (1890), which authorized the State of New York to proceed with the first electrocution ninety-five years ago. *Kemmler*, however, was grounded on a number of constitutional premises that have long since been rejected and on factual assumptions that appear not to have withstood the test of experience. I believe the time has come to measure electrocution against well-established contemporary Eighth Amendment principles.[23]

In recent history, several cases of botched executions via electrocution have made headlines. In the state of Florida, the executions of Jesse Tafaro in 1990 and Pedro Medina in 1997 ended in flames erupting from their heads due to the improper use of sponges designed to conduct electricity to their brains.[24] In both cases, the men did not die quickly and the media accounts for both cases made international headlines. The state responded to these issues, stating that the botched executions were a result of human-related error. During the execution of Wesley Allen Dodd, witnesses noted several audible displays of pain and a medical review following the execution noted significant burns on his head. Based on this evidence, Thomas Harrison Provenzano filed a petition that the electric chair constitutes cruel and unusual punishment. The Florida State Supreme Court held that the electric chair is a constitutionally permissible method of execution.[25] While the U.S. Supreme Court granted *cert* to hear this challenge in 1999, they later vacated their decision in light of the decision by the Florida state legislature in 2000 to reflect lethal injection as the default method of execution.[26] This policy change rendered the case that challenged the constitutionality of the electric chair moot.[27] In 2001, the Georgia Supreme Court declared the electric chair unconstitutional following their legislature's decision to make lethal injection their state's primary execution method.[28]

As the public grew concerned with the potential for pain in execution methods, several states looked toward technological advances in their search for a humane execution. For many states, the movement to lethal gas was the answer. Introduced in 1921 by the state of Nevada, officials believed that the introduction of cyanide gas into the cells of death row while the inmates were sleeping would equate to a peaceful death.[29] However, several documentations of botched executions challenge this premise of a simple, pain-free death.[30] While lethal gas is an option in Arizona, California, Maryland, Missouri, and Wyoming, the practice is rarely utilized today. In 1996, the Ninth Circuit Court of Appeals in the case of *Fiero v. Gomez* held that the use of the gas chamber was unconstitutional.[31] Following this decision, the

state of California amended their statute to make lethal injection the primary method of execution unless the inmate chooses lethal gas. Like many other challenges to the Court, this decision was never affirmed by the U.S. Supreme Court as no case has had the legal standing in light of such legislative changes.

Currently, the primary method of execution is lethal injection. First adopted by the state of Oklahoma in 1977 (with the first execution by lethal injection by the state of Texas in 1982), lethal injection represents the concept of the most humane medicalized method of execution to date. The process of lethal injection involves the introduction of three separate prescriptions through an intravenous drip: (1) sodium thiopental, to render the inmate unconscious; (2) pancuronium bromide, to paralyze the nervous system and stop the breath; and (3) potassium chloride to introduce cardiac arrest and stop the heart.[32] Since its acceptance as a method of execution, lethal injections have accounted for the majority of all executions carried out during the modern era of the death penalty.[33]

While lethal injection has been presented to the public as the most humane form of execution, accounts of well-known botched executions indicate that lethal injection was the method utilized in twenty-eight of the forty examples from the modern era.[34] The constitutionality of the use of lethal injection is currently being challenged in the courts and involves not only the petitions of death row inmates, but also the opinions of medical professionals. This challenge is based on the administration of the drugs used during the execution process and inquires whether (1) the chemicals cause unnecessary pain, and (2) whether the lethal injection "cocktail" masks the true levels of pain experienced by the inmate during the execution. Previous decisions by the Court have paved the way for inmates to challenge the injection process as a civil rights violation (*Hill v.*

McDonough[35]) and to allow inmates to challenge the "cut-down procedure" occasionally utilized when prison personnel are unable to find a suitable vein for an intravenous drip to administer the medications (*Nelson v. Campbell*[36]). The American Medical Association and the American Society of Anesthesiologists have issued statements that such participation would compromise their Hippocratic Oath to "do no harm," and has led most medical professionals to refuse to participate in the execution process.[37] Consequently, many states have shifted their execution protocols to use prison personnel, rather than medical professionals, to carry out the prep work for executions.

The U.S. Supreme Court granted *certiorari* in 2007 in the case of *Baze v. Rees* which challenges the lethal injection process in the state of Kentucky. This case allows the court to address the question of whether the drugs used in executions constitute cruel and unusual punishment. This challenge was made possible by the Court's earlier decision in *Hill* which allowed inmates to challenge the constitutionality of lethal injection. While Hill was granted the ability to challenge the constitutionality of the lethal injection process, he never received an evidentiary hearing in Federal Court and was executed in Florida on September 20, 2006. Since the decision in *Hill*, twenty-nine inmates received a temporary stay of execution, seven of whom have since been executed. In related cases, California has ruled that their practice of lethal injection is unconstitutional while other states are reviewing their execution protocols. As a result, many states have voluntarily halted their executions and an additional thirteen inmates have received stays in anticipation of the Court's ruling in *Baze*.[38] In effect, this temporarily resulted in a moratorium on executions across the United States. *Baze v. Rees* was argued before the Court on January 7, 2008. During oral arguments, several justices appeared to grapple with the lack of a standard to evaluate the issue of the constitutionality of lethal injection. Justice Stevens, a noted opponent of the death penalty, appeared to urge the justices to make a declaration regarding the case at hand rather than simply return the issue to the lower courts for future discussions, while Justices Roberts and Kennedy questioned the consistency of the issues presented in *Baze*. In contrast, Justice Scalia showed signs that he may uphold the process of lethal injection, stating "this is an execution—not surgery."[39] The Court's decision on April 16, 2008, upheld Kentucky's lethal injection process with a 7–2 vote. Writing for the majority, Chief Justice John G. Roberts stated the Court held that Kentucky's lethal injection protocol does not create a "substantial risk of wanton and unnecessary infliction of pain."[40] In his concurring opinion, Justice Stevens, a strong opponent against the death penalty, argued that rather than ending the debate on the death penalty, the decision of the Court in *Baze* will not only perpetuate future discussions on the lethal injection process, but may call in to question the practice of death in its entirety.[41]

Chipping Away at the Death Penalty

Since the reinstatement of the death penalty in 1976, the Court has addressed many cases relating to the administration of the death penalty and have included discussions on what makes a capital crime, the definitions and applications of aggravating and mitigating circumstances, the appellate process, the role of capital juries, and other procedural issues.[42] Recent years have seen a gradual shift toward prohibiting the death penalty for special populations such as the mentally ill, mentally retarded, and juvenile offenders. While these decisions have not dramatically altered the sizes of death rows across the nation, they have indicated a willingness of the Court to insure that the application of the death penalty is consistent with its theoretical intent. The Court developed a two-prong test to assess whether death penalty statutes were constitutionally acceptable under the Eighth Amendment: (1) is there a national consensus against the practice of capital punishment? and (2) is the punishment proportional to the crime? In assessing proportionality, the Court held that the death penalty should only be applied to the worst of the worst offenders and utilized to reinforce the correctional philosophies of deterrence and retribution.[43] These decisions reinforce the Court's commitment toward maintaining practices in accordance with the evolving standards of decency.

Mental Retardation and the Death Penalty

In 1989, the Supreme Court addressed the constitutionality of the death penalty for the mentally retarded. In *Penry v. Lynaugh*, the Court held that since only two states[44] had laws on the books specifically barring the execution of the mentally retarded, such a practice did not "mandate a categorical exception,"[45] even though polling data indicated that a majority of individuals opposed the practice. The Court had raised concerns in other cases over the acceptance of public opinion as an indicator of national consensus[46] and believed that such data was more appropriate as an influence of legislative processes, rather than judicial actions.[47] Thirteen years later, the Court returned to the question of mental retardation and the death penalty. In a 6–3 decision, the Court held that the death sentence for Daryl Atkins, a Virginia inmate who possessed an IQ of 59, violated the Eighth Amendment.[48] In assessing whether a national consensus had developed against the death penalty for the mentally retarded, the Court looked for objective indicators of change such as legislative activity, jury discretion, and execution patterns.

During the thirteen years between *Penry* and *Atkins*, fifteen states created new laws banning the execution of the mentally retarded. While some jurisdictions voted to reintroduce the death penalty after a period of absence, the reinstatement of the death penalty in New York and the federal government specifically did not include provisions allowing for such executions at the time of *Atkins*, and both Virginia and Nevada had bills pending that demonstrated signs of promise for change. It was these patterns that led Justice Stevens as the voice of the majority to remark that "it is not so much the number of these States that is significant, but the consistence of the direction of change."[49] The Court also noted that even those states that had laws on the books permitting the execution of the mentally retarded used them infrequently, as only five states had executed individuals with documented IQ scores less than 70,[50] and that juries were generally reluctant to exercise their discretion in sentencing such offenders to death. Additionally, the Court felt that the execution of the mentally ill did not fit with the theoretical intent of the law, stating that "the impairments of mentally retarded offenders make it less defensible to impose the death penalty as retribution for past crimes and less likely that the death penalty will have a real deterrent effect."[51] While the Court did outlaw the execution of the mentally retarded, they left it up to the states for each to determine their own standards in defining the legal standard for "mental retardation."[52]

The *Atkins* decision also relied, at least in part, on the statements by professional and public opinion data. The review of over twenty opinion polls indicated high levels of opposition by the public to the use of the death penalty for the mentally retarded. The Court also weighed expert opinion from groups such as the American Psychological Association and the American Association on Mental Retardation[53] as well as international perspectives on the issue. While the majority opinion does reference that public opinion polls are "by no means dispositive,"[54] dissenting justices voiced concern over the use of public opinion data in determining the constitutionality of a given punishment.[55] Despite these concerns, the Court acknowledged that the use of public opinion serves as an objective indicator in determining the national consensus, particularly given its concurrent agreement with trends of legislative activity.

Juvenile Executions

During the late 1980s, the Court also dealt with questions regarding the constitutionality of the death penalty for juvenile offenders. At the time of *Thompson v. Oklahoma* (1988), thirty-seven jurisdictions had death penalty statutes on their books. Eighteen of these death penalty jurisdictions set a minimum age of death eligibility at sixteen while nineteen other states did not have a specific minimum age. The Court overturned the sentence of William W. Thompson, deciding that the execution of a juvenile who was age fifteen at the time of the crime constituted cruel and unusual punishment. However, the Court upheld the constitutionality of the execution of persons sixteen and seventeen years of age at the time of their offense in *Wilkins v. Missouri* (1989) and *Stanford v. Kentucky* (1989). At the time of these decisions, the Court held that since a national consensus had not been established against the use of the death penalty for juveniles, such a practice could not be labeled as cruel and unusual.

Based on the reasoning of the *Atkins* decision, the Court indicated a willingness to revisit the issue of juvenile executions. In denying *certiorari* in 2004 for a case where the offender was seventeen years old at the time of the crime, Justices Souter, Ginsburg, and Bryer joined with Justice Stevens in his dissent where he argued that "the practice of executing such offenders is a relic of the past and is inconsistent with evolving standards of decency in a civilized society. We should

put a shameful end to this practice."[56] However, the Court did not have to wait long for a second chance to revisit the issue of juvenile executions. In 2005, the Court issued its opinion in *Roper v. Simmons* (2005) which ruled that the execution of offenders under the age of eighteen constituted a violation of the Eighth Amendment protections against cruel and unusual punishment. This decision resulted in the invalidation of nineteen state laws and the commutation of seventy-one sentences of juvenile offenders on death row.[57]

The *Roper* decision closely followed the logic of the *Atkins* court and held that the evolving standards of decency of a maturing society had moved to a national consensus against the practice of death for juveniles. The Court noted that since its ruling in *Stanford*, seven states created new laws prohibiting the execution of anyone under the age of eighteen, bringing the total number of states to eighteen that prohibited the practice. In addition, the carrying out of executions was rare, as only Texas, Oklahoma, and Virginia had done so in the past ten years.[58] Drawing from the social, behavioral, and biological literatures on adolescent development, the Court agreed that to classify juvenile murders as "the worst of the worst" failed to acknowledge the immaturity and irresponsible nature that is often consistent with adolescence, and therefore results in a diminished capacity toward the "adult" understanding of their criminal actions.[59] The justices also agreed that the execution of juveniles does not appropriately serve the interests of retribution and deterrence. Like the *Atkins* court, the *Roper* court felt that this was enough to warrant that the shift to abolition indicated "sufficient evidence that today our society views juveniles . . . as categorically less culpable than the average criminal."[60] They also noted the lack of acceptance of juvenile executions around the world as countries such as Iran, Pakistan, Saudi Arabia, Yemen, Nigeria, the Democratic Republic of Congo, and

China had abolished the juvenile death penalty in either law or practice. These actions led the Court to conclude that "the United States now stands alone in a world that has turned its face against the juvenile death penalty"[61] and called for its abolition.

Executing the Mentally Ill

The Court has also explored the constitutionality of executing the mentally ill, though they have yet to make a similarly definitive decision like that of *Atkins* and *Roper*. The decision in *Ford v. Wainwright* (1986) prohibited the execution of the insane. Here, the Court looked at the issue of competency at the time of execution and focused on the current state of the inmate's mental health and held that the State could not execute someone if they developed a mental illness while on death row. However, states have constructed their definitions of competency quite narrowly. Take the example of Rickey Ray Rector, who was executed in Arkansas in 1992. While he made several statements that he knew he would die that night, he later told guards that he was going to vote for Bill Clinton for president and even saved the pecan pie from his last meal for later,[62] which questions whether Rector truly understood what it meant to be executed.

Since *Ford*, the Court has continued to address the issue of competency. In the denial of *certiorari* for *Singleton v. Norris* (2002), the Court upheld a prior decision by the Eighth Circuit Court of Appeals which held that states could forcibly administer antipsychotic medication once an execution date has been set in order to maintain competency for execution.[63] However, the Court continues to avoid setting forth a specific definition of competency. In *Panetti v. Quarterman* (2007), the Court reaffirmed their decision in *Ford* and argued that the retributive and deterrent goals of capital punishment are not served by executing the mentally ill. In the case of Scott Panetti, the Court believed that if an offender cannot appreciate the relationship between their criminal actions and the punishment handed down, then to carry out an execution would be a violation of the Eighth Amendment. However, the ruling did not set out a specific definition of competency and instead returned the case to the lower court for a new hearing to assess whether Mr. Panetti is competent for execution.[64]

Legislative and Executive Issues

The work of legislatures on the death penalty is often a response to decisions enacted by the judiciary. Throughout history, these actions have led to revisions in the laws that allow for the death penalty as a sentencing option, criminal procedures during the trial and appellate phases, as well as challenges to the methods of executions. While separate branches of government, the legislative and executive branches of government often work together in the development and implementation of the law.

The decision by the Court in *Furman v. Georgia* (1972) had legislatures in many states rushing back to the drawing board to create new laws that would pass constitutional muster. Indeed, the efforts by several states including Georgia, Florida, and Texas created aspects of the system that we follow today. Once these test cases satisfied the concerns of the judiciary, additional state legislatures followed their lead and proceeded to develop appropriate statutes for their state. While many states created such laws in the late 1970s and early 1980s, others delayed their process and did not immediately enact statutes permitting the death penalty. In the case of New York and Kansas, it took until the twenty-first century for the Court to consider legal challenges to these statutes.

On June 24, 2004, the State Supreme Court

of New York declared their death penalty statute unconstitutional. Enacted in 1995, New York jurors were given the option of sentencing eligible defendants to either the death penalty or life in prison without the possibility of parole. On the surface, this distinction is in line with most other death penalty states. However, New York's law has a unique consideration in that it requires the jury's decision to be unanimous. Referred to as a "deadlock instruction," jurors are told that if they cannot come to an agreement, the judge will sentence the offender to a lesser sentence of life with the eligibility of parole after 20 years.[65] The case of *People v. Stephen LaValle* (2004) argued that the concerns regarding the future dangerousness of the offender may push them to a sentence based on fear rather than the facts of the case. The New York Supreme Court held that such a sentencing structure and its potential results equal a violation of an offender's rights and rendered the statute unconstitutional.[66] While three offenders currently on death row were sentenced under this law, no executions were carried out and it is likely that these offenders will be sentenced to life without the possibility of parole. Following the ruling, the State of New York Codes Committee of the Assembly voted not to pursue new legislation during the current term to reinstate the death penalty.[67]

The constitutionality of Kansas's death penalty law has also recently been challenged in the courts. Created in 1994, Kansas's death penalty law states that if the jury gives equal weight to the value of the aggravating and mitigating factors, a sentence of death can be imposed. The case of Steven Marsh challenged Kansas's death penalty law, arguing that the weighing equation violated the Eighth and Fourteenth Amendments. While the Kansas Supreme Court agreed, the U.S. Supreme Court did not and held that the statute was constitutionally permissible in *Kansas v. Marsh* (2006).[68] In the dissenting opinion,

Justice Souter[69] advocated that the use of a tie-breaker philosophy in death sentences is unconstitutional as it did not reserve the death penalty for the worst of the worst. The opinion also noted that the process by which juries weigh the value of aggravating and mitigating factors fails to take into account the details of the crime and the individual characteristics of the offender.

In addition to responding to the general constitutionality of capital punishment, judicial decisions have also forced legislatures to redesign the process by which offenders are sentenced to death. Since the reinstatement of the death penalty, several states have moved from a jury sentencing process to having a judge or judicial panel make the final sentencing decision. The state of Colorado adopted the three-judge panel in 1995 in response to public opinion and legislative concerns that juries had not been aggressive enough in the sentencing of death-eligible offenders. Proponents believed that the three-judge panel would lead to more death sentences in a time when several high-profile death-eligible inmates were sentenced to life without the possibility of parole.[70] At the time of *Ring v. Arizona* (2002), five states relied on a single judge or a panel of judges. Under these practices, 168 individuals were sentenced to death.[71] Applying the rule of law established by *Apprendi v. New Jersey* (2000), the Court in *Ring v. Arizona* held that any fact that extends a punishment beyond the maximum sentences must be decided by a jury and held to the "beyond a reasonable doubt" standard. Under Arizona law, the maximum punishment for first-degree murder at the trial stage is life without the possibility of parole. Since the facts of the case that make an offender eligible for the death penalty are heard during a sentencing trial and not the guilty/not guilty stage, the jury never have the opportunity to render a decision on these elements "beyond a reasonable doubt" as required by the Sixth Amendment. *Ring* declared the process of judicial sentencing to violate the defendant's right to trial by a jury and determined that judicial sentencing in death penalty cases was unconstitutional. Some states returned to their legislative sessions to redesign sentencing schemes that would remand these cases back to the trial courts for a resentencing hearing to life in prison without the possibility of parole, since ex post facto clauses forbid the administration of a new punishment that is harsher than the one that was proscribed under the law at the time the crime was committed.[72] The Court later ruled in *Schiro v. Summerlin* (2004) that the *Ring* decision was not retroactive.

In recent years, state legislatures have been active in discussions on death penalty reform and moratoria. Responding to concerns regarding wrongful convictions and the risk of executing the innocent, several states have established independent review commissions designed to assess the issues surrounding the administration of capital punishment in their states. Typically, these commissions are established by either a legislative or executive action. One example of such a commission is that of the California Commission on the Fair Administration of Justice. Created by the California State Senate in 2004, the members of the commission represent a bipartisan collaboration of academics, attorneys, police chiefs and sheriffs, judicial officers, and government officials. Together they are charged with investigating issues related to wrongful conviction (both generally and in regard to specific issues related to the death penalty) and to make legislative recommendations to the governor for reform. To date, the commission has made several significant recommendations on the issues of eyewitness identification, false confessions, and use of jailhouse testimony. Each of these recommendations has passed legislative sponsorship and bills for reform have reached the governor's desk. Despite significant efforts by the

commission and the legislature, these bills were vetoed by the governor. The commission has also made recommendations on the problems with scientific evidence and professional responsibility and accountability of prosecutors and defense lawyers and will be addressing the topics of wrongful conviction compensation and the fair administration of the death penalty in the near future.[73] However, not all state commissions have seen inaction as a result of their research. The Illinois Commission on Capital Punishment made eighty-five separate recommendations to the governor in April 2002 which spanned the entire criminal justice system and included every aspect of the death penalty sentencing process.[74] Several of these recommendations have been approved by the Illinois legislature.[75]

Many states, often in conjunction with the appointment of a study commission, have declared moratoriums on the death penalty. While this declaration typically does not stop the process of handing out death sentences or limit judicial review, it has halted the carrying out of executions. As mentioned previously, the majority of state moratoriums today are a reflection of the U.S. decision of *Baze v. Rees* on the constitutionality of the lethal injection process. However, several states have declared a moratorium in their state as a result of concerns regarding the system of capital punishment as a whole. As part of the Illinois Commission on Capital Punishment, Governor George Ryan declared a moratorium on the death penalty in his state in January 2000 following the execution of twelve inmates and the release of thirteen wrongfully convicted in the post-*Furman* era.[76] Following Ryan's departure from office, incoming Governor Rod Blagojevich stated that he would continue the moratorium, stating no significant reasons exist to mandate its removal.[77] Governor Parris Glendening of Maryland issued a moratorium to study patterns of racial bias in 2002. However, the most significant effort toward a moratorium was the recent action by the New Jersey state legislature, whereby the State Assembly and Senate overwhelmingly passed legislation to replace the current death penalty law with the sentence of life without parole.[78] Governor Jon Corzine signed the bill on December 17, 2008, making New Jersey the first state to abolish the death penalty in over thirty years.[79]

The most significant impact of the executive role in the death penalty process involves a highly political process: clemency. Since 1976, 245 death row inmates have been granted clemency. These include three broad commutations of state death sentences in Illinois, New Mexico, and Ohio. The most prominent of these reforms was the commutation of 167 death sentences by Governor George Ryan on January 12, 2003, effectively emptying out Illinois's death row.[80] In 1986 Governor Toney Anaya of New Mexico issued a blanket commutation of the five offenders on death row due to his personal beliefs on capital punishment. Ohio Governor Richard Celeste commuted the sentences of eight inmates in 1998, citing concerns of racial bias.[81] In addition to commutations based on humanitarian reasons such as remorse for the victim, or concerns regarding systemic errors about the death penalty, governors have granted clemency following legal decisions, such as *Atkins v. Virginia* and *Ring v. Arizona*. These commutations are done more to ease the burdens placed on a state that, by virtue of a judicial declaration, must resentence offenders under new laws. While these resentencings are done under the power of the clemency process, their intent is not for humanitarian value and therefore they are not included in the traditional records of clemency.[82]

While there are several different forms of clemency that are utilized by the government to indicate leniency for actions under the law, the use of reprieves, commutations, and pardons are appropriate examples of clemency in death penalty cases. Reprieves are the most common form of clemency issued in death penalty cases. These forms of clemency are typically narrow in scope and their effects are usually temporary, often pending a judicial decision or legislative action. Commutations do not remove the offender's guilty status, but are used to change the sentence handed down by the Court. The most common form of sentence commutation in death penalty cases is the removal of the sentence of death with a replacement of the next harshest sentence, usually life without the possibility of parole. For many offenders, a clemency hearing and request for commutation is the last step prior to execution, notwithstanding any relevant legal challenges which may delay the execution. Pardons offer the greatest demonstration of political power and are the least common form of clemency utilized in death penalty cases. The effect of a pardon not only erases the sentence handed down to an offender, thereby setting them free, but it also eliminates any legal declaration of guilt and restores the civil liberties of the offender. Pardons are typically found in cases of death row offenders who have been released from death row on evidence of innocence.[83]

The process of clemency varies from state to state and involves either the governor or a board of advisors who make recommendations to the governor.[84] Fourteen states give the sole authority to the governor, while eighteen utilize advisory boards to give recommendations (binding and nonbinding) to the governor.[85] In an additional six states, the advisory group makes the decision whether to grant clemency.[86] Outside of a legal injunction to halt an execution at the eleventh hour, clemency is traditionally the offender's last chance to avoid execution. Most clemency hearings involve statements by the offender's attorney for mercy and statements by the victim's family members. As noted by the number of commutations compared to the number of executions that have been carried out in the post-*Furman* era, the granting of clemency is a rare experience. Indeed, political pressure often plays a significant role in the rejection of clemency. During the six years he served as governor of Texas, George W. Bush presided over 152 executions, more than any other state in the post-*Furman* years.[87] Perhaps the most famous of these was the execution of Karla Faye Tucker. The Tucker case received international media attention and pressure for clemency from all walks of life, including Pope John Paul, Reverends Pat Robertson and Jerry Falwell, and even one of Bush's own daughters.[88] Her execution in 1999 came during Bush's campaign for the 2000 presidential election. Just a few years prior, Bill Clinton found himself in a similar situation regarding a high-profile execution: Rickey Ray Rector. In order to demonstrate his "tough on crime" position on the death penalty, Clinton returned from the campaign trail in 1992 to his home state of Arkansas, where he was currently serving as governor, to preside over Rector's execution. While it was certainly not the first execution in Arkansas with Clinton as governor, it was an opportunity to demonstrate his enforcement of the punishment on a very public stage.[89] These actions represent the world of politics in the clemency process, otherwise described as "election year pressure" from pro-death-penalty voters.

The Future of the Death Penalty

Since the first execution in 1630, the practice of capital punishment has evolved dramatically in the United States. Changes to the system of capital punishment have called upon all three branches of the government to maintain the death penalty, from the creation of administrative policies and practices of death eligibility, to the judicial interpretation of the constitutionality of such laws and the executive authorities under which the death sentence is carried out. The impact of public opinion has seeped its way into the politics of capital punishment, as many legislative, executive, and judicial actions have referenced these shifts in public opinion as part of their decision-making process. While the majority of Americans still indicate support for the death penalty compared to alternative sentences, this gap continues to decrease. Recent polls have demonstrated that when asked if they prefer the death penalty over life without the possibility of parole, 47 to 54 percent of respondents indicate a preference for the death penalty, given the LWOP alternative.[90] Indeed, public opinion data demonstrates that the public is growing increasingly concerned with death penalty issues such as the risk of executing the innocent as well as concerns over the fair administration of capital punishment. Indeed, the majority of Americans (58 percent) express support for a moratorium on the death penalty while the process is taken under review.[91]

Certainly the shifts concerning the death penalty from all three branches of government indicate a general trend in the lessening of the popularity of the death penalty, if not a shift toward abolition. As several states study their administrations of capital punishment, others have suspended its use and still others have abolished its use entirely. Even in those states that permit the practice of capital punishment, the administration is limited to a few select jurisdictions responsible for the majority of death sentences and executions, as many states have exercised their implementation of capital punishment for only a small minority of offenders. Yet, while we seem content to chip away at the death penalty or at least limit its use, we fall short of abolishing the practice across the board for all jurisdictions. While much of society remains convinced that the death penalty is the best sanction for murder, the politics of capital punishment as illustrated by the decisions of the legislative, executive, and judicial branches of government do indicate an evolving shift in its practice toward reform.

Dr. Stacy L. Mallicoat is an associate professor of criminal justice with the Division of Politics, Administration, and Justice at California State University, Fullerton, where she teaches courses in capital punishment, women and crime, and juvenile justice administration. Her work, titled "The Growing Significance of Public Opinion for Death Penalty Jurisprudence" and coauthored with Michael L. Radelet, was published in the *Journal of Crime and Justice* in 2004. Her current work on capital punishment focuses on issues of rationale for support and the mutability of death penalty opinion among college students and has been published in the *Southwest Journal of Criminal Justice* in 2008 (with Scott Vollum and Jacqueline Buffington-Vollum) and the *Journal of Ethnicity in Criminal Justice* in 2009 (with Gregory C. Brown). Outside the realm of capital punishment, her research has focused on issues of feminist criminology such as issues for women exiting prostitution and the differential processing of male and female offenders in the juvenile court.

Suggested Readings

Acker, James R., Bohm, Robert M. and Lanier, Charles S. (eds.). (2003). *America's Experiment with Capital Punishment: Reflections on the Past, Present, and Future of the Ultimate Penal Sanction.* 2nd edition. Durham, NC: Carolina Academic Press.

Banner, Stuart. (2002). *The Death Penalty: An American History.* Cambridge: Harvard University Press.

Bedau, Hugo A. (ed.). (1997). *Death Penalty in America: Current Controversies.* New York: Oxford University Press.

Bedau, Hugo, and Cassell, Paul (eds.). (2004). *Debating the Death Penalty: Should America Have Capital Punishment: The Experts from Both Sides Make Their Case.* Oxford, UK: Oxford University Press.

Bohm, Robert M. (2007). *DeathQuest III: An Introduction to the Theory and Practice of Capital Punishment in the United States.* 3rd Edition. Newark, NJ: Lexis-Nexis.

DelCarmen, Rolando V., Vollum, Scott, Cheeseman, Kelly, Frantzen, Durant, and San Miguel, Claudia. (2005). *The Death Penalty: Constitutional Issues, Commentaries and Case Briefs.* Newark, NJ: Lexis-Nexis/Anderson Publishing.

Patternoster, Raymond, Brame, Robert, and Bacon, Sarah. (2008). *The Death Penalty: America's Experience with Capital Punishment.* Oxford, UK: Oxford University Press.

Robinson, Matthew B. (2008). *Death Nation: The Experts Explain American Capital Punishment.* Upper Saddle River, NJ: Prentice-Hall.

Notes

1. *Furman v. Georgia* 408 U.S. 238, 307 (1972).
2. Ibid. at 257.
3. Data obtained from the Death Penalty Information Center, http://www.deathpenaltyinfo.org.
4. *Woodson v. North Carolina* 428 U.S. 280, 304 (1976).
5. *Pulley v. Harris* 465 U.S. 37 (1984).
6. Data obtained from the Death Penalty Information Center, http://www.deathpenaltyinfo.org.
7. *Wilkerson v. Utah* 99 U.S. 130 (1878).
8. *Trop v. Dulles* 356 U.S. 86, 101 (1958).
9. *Wilkerson v. Utah* 99 U.S. 130 (1878).
10. http://www.deathpenaltyinfo.org.
11. Cutler, Christopher Q. (2002), Nothing Less than the Dignity of Man: Evolving Standards, Botched Executions and Utah's Controversial Use of the Firing Squad, 50 Clev. State L. Rev. 335.
12. Executed by the State of Utah, January 17, 1977.
13. Executed by the State of Utah, January 26, 1996.

14. Gilmore, Mikal (1994), *Shot in the Heart* (New York: First Anchor Books), 351.

15. http://www.le.state.ut.us/%7E2004/htmdoc/hbillhtm/hb0180.htm.

16. http://www.internationaljusticeproject.org/utah.cfm.

17. Espy Files available for download at http://webapp.icpsr.umich.edu/cocoon/ICPSR/STUDY/08451.xml.

18. National Association for the Advancement of Colored People, "Death Row USA," January 1, 2007. Retrieved from http://www.naacpldf.org/content.aspx?article=297.

19. *Campbell v. Wood* 18 F.3d 662 (1994).

20. http://www.historylink.org/essays/output.cfm?file_id=5555.

21. *Louisiana ex rel. Francis v. Resweber* 471 U.S. 1080 (1985).

22. *Furman v. Georgia* (1972); *Gregg v. Georgia* (1976); *Estelle v. Gamble* (1976); *Atkins v. Virginia* (2002).

23. *Glass v. Louisiana* 471 U.S. 1080, 1082 (1985).

24. Radelet, Michael L., "Post Furman Botched Executions," http://www.deathpenaltyinfo.org/article.php?scid=8&did=478.

25. *Provenzano v. Moore* 744 So 2d 413 (1999).

26. Fla Stat 922.105 (2000).

27. *Bryan v. Moore* 99–6723 (2000).

28. 554 SE 2d 137 (2001).

29. Robinson, Matthew B. (2008), *Death Nation: The Experts Explain American Capital Punishment* (Upper Saddle River, NJ: Prentice-Hall).

30. Radelet, "Post Furman Botched Executions."

31. *Fiero v. Gomez* 77 F. 3d. 301 (1996).

32. Robinson, *Death Nation*.

33. Patternoster, Raymond, Brame, Robert, and Bacon, Sarah. (2008). *The Death Penalty: America's Experience with Capital Punishment*. Oxford, UK: Oxford University Press.

34. Radelet, "Post Furman Botched Executions."

35. *Hill v. McDonough* 547 U.S. 573 (2006).

36. *Nelson v. Campbell* 541 U.S. 637 (2004).

37. See http://www.ama-assn.org/ama/pub/category/16007.html and http://www.asahq.org/news/asanews063006.htm for statements by the American Medical Association and the American Society of Anesthesiologists.

38. http://www.deathpenaltyinfo.org/article.php?did=1686&scid=64.

39. Stout, David, "Justices Hear Arguments in Lethal Injection Case," *New York Times*, January 7, 2008. Retrieved from www.nytimes.com/2008/01/07/washington/07cnd-scotus.html?ex=1357362000&en=aed5689099613032&ei=5088&partner=rssnyt&emc=rss.

40. http://supreme.justia.com/us/553/07–5439/.

41. *Baze v. Rees* 553 U.S. 35 (2008).

42. For a detailed review of these cases, see Bohm, Robert M. (2007), *DeathQuest III: An Introduction to the Theory and Practice of Capital Punishment in the United States*, 3rd Edition (Newark, NJ: Lexis-Nexis).

43. *Gregg v. Georgia* 428 U.S. 153, 183 (1976).

44. Georgia and Maryland were the two states at the time of *Penry* who had laws on the books prohibiting the execution of the mentally retarded.

45. *Penry v. Lynaugh* 492 U.S. 302, 334 (1989).

46. *Stanford v. Kentucky* 492 U.S. 361, 377 (1989).

47. *Penry v. Lynaugh* 492 U.S. 302, 334 (1989).

48. *Atkins v. Virginia* 536 U.S. 304 (2002).

49. Ibid. at 315.

50. Death Penalty Information Center, http://www.deathpenaltyinfo.org.

51. *Atkins v. Virginia* 536 U.S. 304, 319–320 (2002).

52. Patternoster, Brame, and Bacon, *The Death Penalty*.

53. In an effort to move away from the stigmatic term of "mental retardation," the AAMR changed their association name to the Association on Intellectual and Developmental Disabilities (AAIDD) in January 2007.

54. *Atkins v. Virginia* 536 U.S. 304, 317 (2002).

55. See Justice Rehnquist's dissenting opinion, *Atkins v. Virginia* 536 U.S. 304, 322 (2002).

56. *In re Kevin Nigel Stanford*, 537 U.S. 968 (2002).

57. Streib, Victor L. (2005), "The Juvenile Death Penalty Today: Death Sentences and Executions for Juvenile Crimes, January 1, 1973–February 28, 2005" (Issue #77). Available at http://www.law.onu.edu/faculty/streib.

58. Ibid.

59. *Roper v. Simmons* 543 U.S. 551, 569 (2005).

60. Ibid. at 567.

61. Ibid. at 577.

62. Frady, Marshall, "Death in Arkansas," *The New Yorker*, February 22, 1993.

63. *Singleton v. Norris* 540 U.S. 832 (2003).

64. *Panetti v. Quarterman* 551 U.S. 930 (2007).

65. New York's Criminal Procedure Law 400.27 (10).

66. *People v. Stephen LaValle* 3 N.Y.3d 88 (2004).

67. http://www.deathpenaltyinfo.org/article.php?scid=38&did=1413.

68. *Kansas v. Marsh* 548 U.S. 1037 (2006).

69. Joined by Justices Stevens, Ginsberg, and Breyer.

70. Lutz, Robin (2002), "Experimenting with Death: An Examination of Colorado's Use of the Three Judge Panel in Capital Sentencing," 73 U. Colo. L. Rev. 227.

71. http://www.nacdl.org/sl_docs.nsf/freeform/DeathPenalty_Ring?OpenDocument.

72. Peters, Colette (2003), "Colorado's Death Penalty—Back in the Hands of a Jury," Colorado Legislative Council Staff Issue Brief 03–14. Retrieved at http://www.state.co.us/gov_dir/leg_dir/lcs.htm.

73. http://www.ccfaj.org.

74. http://www.idoc.state.il.us/ccp/ccp/reports/commission_report/index.html.

75. Illinois Senate Bill 472 (2003).

76. http://www.deathpenaltyinfo.org/timeline.pdf.

77. http://www.deathpenaltyinfo.org/article.php?did=2183.

78. Majority vote on December 13, 2007 (NJ Assembly),

and December 10, 2007 (Senate), to replace the current death penalty law with LWOP only option.

79. http://www.deathpenaltyinfo.org/NJpressrel.pdf.

80. Bedau, Hugo, and Cassell, Paul (eds.). *Debating the Death Penalty: Should America Have Capital Punishment: The Experts from Both Sides Make Their Case.* Oxford, UK: Oxford University Press.

81. www.deathpenaltyinfo.org/article.php?did=126&scid=13.

82. Radelet, Michael L., and Zsembik, Barbara A. (1993), "Executive Clemency in Post-*Furman* Capital Cases." *University of Richmond Law Review* 27: 289–314.

83. Kobil, Daniel T., "The Evolving Role of Clemency in Capital Cases," in Acker, James R., Bohm, Robert M., and Lanier, Charles S. (eds.), *America's Experiment with Capital Punishment: Reflections in the Past, Present and Future of the Ultimate Penal Sanction* (Durham, NC: Carolina Academic Press), 673–92.

84. In the federal system, clemency is granted by the president.

85. For a list of states, see http://www.deathpenaltyinfo.org/article.php?did+126&scid=13.

86. In Nebraska, Nevada, and Utah, the governor sits on the board or advisory group that determines clemency.

87. Prejean, Helen, "Death in Texas," *New York Review of Books*, 52, no. 1 (January 13, 2005).

88. Ibid.

89. Frady, Marshall, "Death in Arkansas," *The New Yorker*, February 22, 1993.

90. http://www.gallup.com/poll/101863/Sixtynine-Percent-Americans-Support-Death-Penalty.aspx.

91. Dieter, Richard C. (2007), "A Crisis of Confidence: Americans Doubts about the Death Penalty," Death Penalty Information Center. Available for download at http://www.deathpenaltyinfo.org/CoC.pdf.

CHAPTER 2

Conflicts of Interest

BUSINESS, DEATH, AND THE BIRD COURT

Michael A. Pierson

Introduction

OTHER SECTIONS of this accumulated narrative, written by other authors, will delve into several of the individual controversies of the Rose Bird Court—that being, as the title implies, the subject of this book. The main purpose of my contribution is threefold: sections 1 through 3 describe the context in which Rose Bird arrived as the Chief Justice of California's highest court in early 1977, and dwells primarily on her predecessor, Chief Justice Roger Traynor, the Federal Supreme Courts of Earl Warren and Warren Burger, and the rich legacy of activism these courts left behind. Sections 4 and 5 present what I believe to be the convergence of forces that worked against Bird and her colleagues Grodin and Reynoso in the 1986 election precipitating their demise. Finally, I will conclude with a critique of the Rose Bird Court, including a brief critical analysis of Justice Grodin's autobiography, *In Pursuit of Justice.*[1]

Before Chaos Arrived in the Courthouse

Those of us coming of age during the sixties often attempt to relate the mythology of the period to those who were not participants. We remember and retell our stories of the era with some fondness: the sit-ins on our various college campuses; the turmoil in Chicago at the 1968 Democratic National Convention; Watergate, and Nixon climbing aboard that helicopter in front of the White House as Gerald Ford looked on. I say "mythology" because our minds have woven what we saw then, what we know now, what we were told later, and what we remembered to remember, into a relatively seamless narrative. It usually begins sometime in high school and ends around the time of Nixon's resignation, or perhaps a little later with the election of Jimmy Carter.

The sixties were hardly seamless; chaos always creates seams, schisms, fissures, and fractures, and it was a most chaotic time. Maurice Isserman and Michael Kazin subtitle their survey of the period "the Civil War of the 1960's"[2] and make a convincing argument that only the conflict of a century before represented a period of greater chaos for most Americans.[3] Like many myths, the memories and events we evoke as having taken place during that period do, in fact, have a basis in fact. Thus, we may wax nostalgic about the eloquence of Martin Luther King, the assassination of the Kennedys, or the events surrounding any of the epoch's mythical icons. We can be quite selective in our recollections—remembering events without ever having participated in them. However, unlike *Beowulf* and other sagas of our more ancient myths, these actually happened. Just not in the way we remember or retell them.

College campuses, the White House, and city streets were not the only scenes of chaos. Beginning nationally in 1952 with the successive Supreme Courts of Earl Warren and Warren Burger, and California in 1944 with the state supreme court of Roger Traynor, a near revolution was occurring in *juris prudence*. Professor Gary Schwartz, in his 1991 presentation to the faculty and alumni of the University of Georgia School of Law, and (because of my relative ignorance of the subject at hand) a source to whom I will refer often, stated:

> The Warren Court was the paradigm of judicial activism. Its 1954 decision in *Brown v. Board of Education*, for example, initiated the revolution in race relations in the United States; *Brown* was the first of what turned out to be dozens of decisions by the Court addressing questions of racial equality.[4]

The Warren Court did not limit itself to issues of racial equality. *Baker v. Carr* in 1962 "set the stage for a revolution in legislative reapportionment" by extending the constitutional concept of "one person, one vote" to both the state and national domains.[5] The Court moved further and "initiated a thoroughgoing reconceptualization of the law" in its 1964 decision of *New York Times Co. v. Sullivan*, so that the First Amendment issues involved might be brought into account. In referencing that particular case to the greater body of law created during the years of the Warren Court, Schwartz concludes that

Sullivan was only one portion of a larger transformation of the First Amendment that was effectuated during the Warren Court era. Indeed, during that era, one area after another of federal and constitutional law was subjected to renovation.[6]

State courts, especially the various courts of appeal, quickly adopted the initiatives proposed by this yeasty, vital Court to their own canon. They began ignoring the *stare decisis* theory that "courts should not feel free to overturn precedents that have come to seem unwise,"[7] choosing instead to act as their mentor Court had done when it overturned the racially motivated, *ergo* unwise *Plessy v. Furgeson* decision of six decades earlier.

The California Supreme Court under Chief Justice Traynor was one such court. It was already activist, but it quickly embraced this federal mantra of revolutionary change as its own and began incorporating it into interpretations of what the role of law in California would be during the next several decades and, perhaps, into the next century. For example, in 1968 the court invalidated Proposition 14, a 1966 ballot initiative approved 2-to-1 by the electorate, and which would have allowed racial discrimination in the sale and rental of real property. In *Mulkey v. Reitman*, the state court held that the Equal Protection Clause of the Fourteenth Amendment made the initiative unconstitutional, meaning that "realtors and apartment managers could not discriminate on the basis of race in the sale or rental of housing."[8] This decision was later upheld when it was appealed to the Warren Court. Justice Grodin, in an anecdotal aside, quipped that Traynor, who was reconfirmed by a relatively narrow margin in that year's election, "had his bags packed in anticipation of an adverse vote."[9] Another controversial decision rendered by the Traynor Court in 1971 declared education to be a "fundamental interest"; the state legislature was therefore required to "equalize expenditures per public school child throughout the state."[10]

Arguably the most radical of these incorporated changes occurs in the arena of negligence, liability, and tort law, for it is during the entire Traynor epoch that tort law essentially discards its old models and assumes the modern face of negligence and liability theory evident today.

The liabilities created by negligent acts are most easily understood as sanctions against those who would "egoistically give more weight to their own welfare than to the welfare of their possible victims."[11] As a cause of action, negligence theory is not new. Its roots are well established in English Common Law, predating even the advent of the nineteenth-century Industrial Revolution. In the United States, state judges using common-law precedent and a great deal of creativity weaved together a hodge-podge of laws that came to represent tort theory in the nineteenth century. Between 1911 and 1917 the various state legislatures reduced to a trickle the myriad of employee on-the-job injury torts by enacting Workers' Compensation legislation, and in the early twentieth century, cases like *MacPherson v. Buick Motor Co.* "affirmed the negligence liability of manufacturers" by declaring that "where danger is to be foreseen, liability will follow."[12] Thus, although admittedly a legal patchwork, liability caused by one's acts assumed a doctrine of fairness. Americans accepted as Natural Law "the idea of liability for harm caused by one's unexcused errors and mistakes [as] both straightforward and intuitive."[13]

By the time Traynor assumed the mantel of California's chief justice, American tort law had maintained a general stability since before the turn of the century. Negligence and monetary sanctions for negligent acts "had been the primary

(though not the exclusive) standard of tort liability in the United States for over a century."[14] This period of relative stability had lulled manufacturers—and the casualty companies insuring them—to sleep. In short order they would receive their wake-up call.

Chaos in Black Robes

There are infinite ways in which any one person might understand the meaning of any word. How you comprehend the word, how you employ it, is based upon the community using it and in which it is being used. The California Court during the Traynor years "was regarded as an innovative, independent, and activist tribunal"[15] by many, if not most, in the legal community. The insurance and manufacturing communities saw this innovative activism as a series of "judicial attitudes which favor the plaintiff" that were "swelling the court dockets across the nation" with product liability suits, the costs of which would ultimately "be borne by everyone who participates in the marketing system" including, "finally, the consumers who purchase the products."[16]

One part of the legal community's innovation and the manufacturer's nightmare was the "doctrine of strict liability" moving at will between the Warren Court and the various states. Under this doctrine, all the plaintiff has to do to win a case is "show that the product involved was in some way defective when it was produced."

> [The plaintiff] does not have to prove that the manufacturer was negligent in the preparation of the product. . . . [T]he manufacturer can be subject to potential liability even if he shows that he has exercised all reasonable care in preparing the product and has used the best material available in its production.[17]

Through these activist courts, *strict liability* began replacing the *contributory negligence* theory under which a plaintiff during the preceding fifty years had to prove a defendant knowingly placed a defective product on the market. Assuming the plaintiff could attain this nearly impossible plateau of evidence, the defendant could then claim that part of the liability issue was the plaintiff's misuse of the product; monetary damages would be reduced by whatever proportion the plaintiff had contributed to his or her own mishap.

A second legal theory placed under close scrutiny by the Traynor tribunal was the doctrine of *privity*. Simply stated, privity provided implied manufacturer's warranties only to the original purchaser. Thus, when Lewis, a man injured on a defective bed purchased by his landlord, sued the bed manufacturer Terry, the case was dismissed because it was not Lewis who had purchased the bed.[18] However, just as they had prudently accepted the Warren Court's decree that "separate was inherently unequal" when it overturned *Plessy*, the Traynor Court addressed the privity issue by carefully analyzing *Burr v. Sherman Williams*, a suit brought about by a farmer, Burr, whose crops had been damaged by a Sherman Williams insecticide purchased by his farming cooperative and sprayed onto his fields by a pilot contracted by them. Sherman Williams argued that, since it was the cooperative, not Burr, who had purchased the insecticide, damage done to his property was not covered by any implied warranty, citing as precedent the 1896 decision of *Lewis v. Terry*. The Traynor Court dismissed this argument by addressing the question of who was the obvious ultimate consumer:

> [T]here was no requirement of privity of contract between the manufacturer and the ultimate consumer and the manufacturer would be liable, regardless of negligence, for the damage caused by any breach of this warranty.

... [T]he persons to whom the insecticide was delivered were obviously [plaintiffs'] agents for purposes of the spraying operation.[19]

Privity theory would be tested again in a 1955 industrial accident that would not find its way onto the California Supreme Court calendar for five years. In June of 1955, Ervin Peterson, a machinist, was working to remove burrs from a piece of metal using a large disk sander provided by his employer. He was severely injured when the sanding disk shattered in his face. Lamb Rubber Co., manufacturer of the disks, stated in their defense that Peterson had no cause of action because it was his employer who had purchased the disk. The lower courts agreed; at each point Peterson had to appeal their decisions. Justice Schauer, referring to the recent privity decision in *Burr*, wrote the state court's final, unanimous opinion, stating:

> it is a matter of common knowledge [to manufacturers] that most businesses are carried on by . . . employees and that equipment or supplies purchased by employers will in actual use be handled by the employees, who in this respect may be said to stand in the shoes of the employer . . . we believe [the employee] be considered to be in privity to the vendor-manufacturer with respect to the implied warranties of fitness for use and of merchantable quality upon which recovery is here sought.[20]

Such insidious reasoning in both arenas—strict liability and privity—sent shudders through the insurance and manufacturing communities; the stability of fifty years of never having to consider or express any concern whatsoever for an ultimate consumer went the way of *Plessy*, and in the same year, no less! Now insurers would have to evaluate and adjust the actuarial assumptions of risk formulae to take into account an assessment of what damages a product held strictly liable could do to an unknown *and unknowable* final consumer at some unknown future date. The chaos of product liability in the courtroom was just beginning for both insurers and manufacturers. For consumers, however, the courts would swiftly come to represent the voice of what Justice Grodin would eventually call a "legislature at the retail level"[21] and whose obligation Justice Tobriner said should be to represent and protect "the plight of the economically downtrodden,"[22] a force of considerable power which could place the consumer and the manufacturers of the products they consumed on a relatively level playing field.

The Death Part

From the spectacle of Puritan colonists hanging witches from gallows built in their "City on a Hill" to the *Judge Judy Show*, the often dramatic conflicts between the sunlight of right and the midnight of wrong have been a staple of American culture. High tension and drama are constant factors whenever two lawyers meet before the bar of justice to plead their cases. It stems from the "winner take all" dynamics of the courtroom and the messages of good and evil, right and wrong, produced by and through the narratives of trial participants: the DA, defendants and their attorneys, spectators and witnesses, judges and juries. As the narratives change, the truth—a relative truth at best—takes on its unique and often distorted shape. The audience sometimes applauds when the results confirm their paradigm of truth, but often they seem to ignore such confirmations and move quietly along with other business. It is when the results assault the paradigm that society erupts: only the good should win.

Courts, especially criminal courts, represent high drama, the cosmological play of good against evil, order against chaos. "Crime, particularly violent crime, is at or near the top of everyone's list of social concerns."[23] It is the spectacle of order staving off chaos, the stuff of Aeschylus and Euripides, that gives criminal law its aura. It is also "a high public priority . . . not for reasons of deterrence alone," that makes criminal law such a compelling part of our lives. "Even those of us who have not experienced crime directly can empathize" with victims of violent crime; for "victims and their families it is a matter of personal vindication" that some grief fall upon the head of the perpetrator.[24]

For nearly a quarter of a century Americans had been changing, or at least reprioritizing, their beliefs of what should happen to people who murder other people. Beginning in the 1960s, polls consistently found that less than half felt the death penalty appropriate. In a 1953 Gallup poll asking, "Are you in favor of the death penalty for persons convicted of murder?" 64 percent answered yes, another 4 percent qualified their yes, and only 6 percent did not have an opinion.[25] The same question posed in 1960 found the 68 percent reduced to 53 percent,[26] although this particular poll did not have a "qualified yes" category. By 1971 only 49 percent answered in the affirmative, continuing the trend.[27]

A new trend emerged in the mid-1970s however, and lasted into the 1980s. *Time* magazine's first 1976 issue provides clues to the new narrative. The *World* section leads with the headline, "Terrorists: Kidnapping in Vienna, Murder in Athens":

An epidemic of political violence and murder shattered the peace of a week in which millions of people throughout the world honored the birth of Christ. The most dramatic incident was the kidnapping of eleven oil ministers in Vienna. Then, in Athens, the chief of the CIA office in Greece was slain by three gunmen as he returned home from a Christmas party. In

Lebanon, an estimated 250 people were killed and another 400 kidnapped in that country's civil war.[28]

Much later, in the third week of April 1976, the Boston Courthouse was bombed by the New World Liberation Front, a California-based terrorist group, and eighteen people were injured, one seriously enough to require the amputation of a leg.[29] In reality American newspapers and magazines in 1976 spent the greatest amount of their news space covering the upcoming Bicentennial, primaries, and presidential elections, yet the illusion at the time was that specters of skyjackings, bombings, and chaos were appearing almost daily.

These chronically rare, always random spectacular acts of global violence and mayhem may have provided the gigavoltage necessary to push the death penalty meter consistently into the seventieth percentile. It seemed to "coincide with a sharply rising fear of crime on the part of the American people"; many were "fearful of venturing out after dark," even in their own neighborhoods.[30] Thus, in an April 1976 poll conducted by *Time* magazine, only 22 percent did not believe the death penalty, which had been declared unconstitutional in most states—including California—by the immediate post-Warren court of Justice Burger, should ever be used.[31] However, the 78 percent balance either fully or partially agreed it was appropriate *to restore the death penalty as punishment for kidnappers and hijackers.*[32]

For more than a century there had been a substantial amount of debate over the deterrent efficacy of the death penalty; it still raged unabated within legal, academic, and religious communities. By 1976, however, there could be little doubt about the belief most American communities had in the right of a state to take the lives of its most notorious citizens. Californians, using an initiative followed quickly by enabling legislation

consistent with federal court guidelines, reinstated the death penalty in 1974 by a 3-to-1 margin.[33] It was obvious that efficacy was not the real issue. Instead, it was the matter of spectacular vindication *both personal and social*, in the courtroom, that kept (and probably still keeps) the death penalty alive in our justice system.[34] Such a presumption would make it "seem reasonable to hold [the court] responsible to do its job."[35]

This is particularly the case when we observe a trial court dismiss a prosecution or exclude evidence on what appear to be technical grounds, or impose a sentence that appears overly lenient, or when we observe an appellate court overturn a jury's guilty verdict for reasons we do not entirely understand or accept.[36]

Rarely had it been held in a judge's defense that "one person's technicality is another person's constitutional right," thus any who provided such a *deus machina*, especially for acts of mayhem and murder, would be labeled "soft on crime" at election time.[37] In California, in 1976, it remained the constitutional right of the community to remove judges from the bench in hopes that the next would stage a more rewarding, if not more entertaining, presentation.

A Confluence of Various Rages

In the spring of 1976, Kenneth C. Tyler, past-president of the Western Insurance Information Service, concluded in a brusque response to a *Los Angeles Times* letter from the president of the California Trial Lawyers Association published a few days earlier:

As a lawyer, a businessman and a private citizen, I am alarmed at what could happen to our whole system of reparations without substantial tort reform.[38]

This letter appears in the same issue as a brief article citing the growth of support for the death penalty,[39] and five days after an article in which the death penalty of Vaughn Greenwood, convicted of the eleven so-called "Slasher" slayings between 1964 and 1974, had been voided for the two murders committed in 1964. The reason for the dismissal, the article goes on to say, is that "the current death penalty law in California, which became effective in 1974, could not be applied retroactively to the 1964 murders."[40]

As a reminder of the nation's recent and still festering wounds, *All The President's Men*, starring Robert Redford and Dustin Hoffman, was scheduled to premier in Hollywood in late spring of 1976. The movie chronicles the sullied Watergate scandal. It labeled itself as "the most devastating detective story of the century."[41] During the second week of April, *U.S. News & World Report* released two articles short enough to be placed on the same page. The first is entitled "Judges, Lawyers Speak Out—U.S. Court System Under Fire"; the second, "Chief Justice Burger: How to Simplify Justice."[42] Both address the concerns of another crisis beginning to chafe the nation's already badly blistered economic skin: the rising cost of liability and malpractice insurance, and the effect a flood of new litigation was having on the court system.

It is a concern that had moved from professional journals like *Journal of American Insurance*, *Best's Review*, and *Risk Management* into mainstream weeklies like *Newsweek*, *Time*, and *U.S. News & World Report*. The most scholarly of the three journals, *Risk Management*, while discussing the new Financial Accounting Standards Board commentaries on "accrual of future loss" accounting methods, declared that "the most significant impact could be that certain accounting

procedures now being employed for . . . catastrophic losses of property and casualty insurance companies"[43] may no longer be acceptable under generally accepted accounting principles; one reason given is that, at best, "there is a tenuous relationship between past and present losses."[44] Bernard J. Daenzer, CPCU, writing for *Best's Review*, says that his "look into the future begins with a 'foul weather' report for the first three [years] of the next five: 1976, 1977, and 1978":

Some companies are losing as much as $20 on every $100 premium they write. There may be a substantial number of failures, and there may be some big ones. . . . Depending on the distribution of premium volume by state, [state insurance guarantee solvency fund] assessments could trigger the failure of other companies which had been only slightly impaired, not mortally wounded, by the present trend.[45]

The *Journal of American Insurance* assumed "the growing surge of patient lawsuits is commanding serious attention by all concerned," because

as medical technology grows, becomes more complex . . . the patient finds it easier to be disappointed and dissatisfied . . . [and] his desire for "satisfaction" leads to the next step. Why not sue?

"In former years," the article laments, "a patient wouldn't think of suing his family doctor," but the impersonalization of medical arts, and the tsunami of lawsuits that results, means that "the doctor cannot practice, the hospital cannot admit the patient, and the host of other health care providers cannot function."[46]

Americans started to become aware of the medical malpractice problem in 1973 when the U.S. Department of Health, Education and Welfare acknowledged, with some alarm, that a "decreasing availability of medical malpractice insurance and the increasing frequency and costs of medical malpractice litigation" was making the cost of health care soar out of sight; in some areas, it was nearly unavailable.[47] Whether the crisis was caused, as noted above, by the impersonalization of the medical arts, or by insurance companies unable to cope with the actuarial vagaries and potential losses they augured, or the floodgates opened by greedy patients and their greedier lawyers, the California state legislature acknowledged that

> there is a major health care crisis in the State of California attributable to skyrocketing malpractice premium costs and resulting in a potential breakdown of the health delivery system, severe hardships for the medically indigent, a denial of access for the economically marginal, and depletion of physicians such as to substantially worsen the quality of health care available to citizens of this state.[48]

This extraordinary legislative session was called in 1975 specifically to address the problem and find a solution. After the battles were fought between these titans, they adopted a "public policy favoring the use of arbitration as a means of resolving medical malpractice disputes" and created the Medical Injury Compensation Reform Act of 1975, or MICRA. Essentially an agreement between groups of medical practitioners, insurance companies who contract with them for medical services, and the employers who purchase medical coverage from the insurance companies, it required employees to arbitrate any malpractice claims they may have and placed a $250,000 limit on damages. The solution, then, is reactionary, one imposed through political, financial, institutional, and bureaucratic pressure upon the employee, the common man.

The legislature, however, hailed MICRA as a reform, a progressive solution not dissimilar to the landmark worker's compensation programs enacted during the Progressive Era sixty years earlier.

As if there weren't enough conflicting legal currents washing out the banks of what had been a trickling, lazy stream of friendly decisions, into this raging torrent dropped, first, the *coup d'etat le juris femme* up to that moment—"You Can Sue, Judge Rules":

> A federal court judge has ruled that a worker who resists the boss' sexual advances may sue for sexual discrimination if the worker loses his or her job or is denied advancement. . . . [The] decision came in a case involving a female Justice Department worker who lost her job in 1972. . . . [T]he decision is apparently the first in which the 1964 Civil Rights Act has been successfully invoked by a worker charging sexual discrimination.[49]

Then, quite late in 1976, "Governor Moonbeam" Jerry Brown escorted the nomination of Rose Elizabeth Bird as the first woman chief justice of the California Supreme Court through the legislature; she was confirmed in February of the following year. Not since Clara Shortridge Foltz became a candidate for governor nearly six decades earlier had a woman gained so much political prominence in the Golden State. California's eclipse into complete chaos and utter pandemonium was now, in the eyes of some segments of the community, complete. To others, of course, it was a new day.

Roses, Moonbeams, and "Flipping the Bird"

Perusing the table of contents should assure you that the years between the entrance and exit of

Rose Elizabeth Bird will be thoroughly examined in great detail. I would like to leap ahead to the twelve to eighteen months preceding, and leading immediately up to, her hubristic, ignoble fall from grace at the hands of a furious, highly inflamed electorate. Many tales about the source of that inflamed electorate abounded at the time, and they continue to the present time in the retelling. All indications are that she and her story will become mythology, hovering in that netherworld between what probably was real and what probably was not.

There are several discourses and infinite versions about the events that unfolded from the spring of 1985 to the fall of 1986, and of Rose Bird. Stipulations between factions would be rare. Appointed by Brown, himself sandwiched as governor between the Republican administrations of Reagan and Deukmejian, Rose Bird was a target for Republicans almost from the day of her confirmation in February 1977. The California Supreme Court halted sixty of the sixty-four executions to have taken place on her watch, and had it been up to her alone, she would have halted all sixty-four. These barren, stripped statistics are perhaps the only stipulations, for it is at this point the discourse patterns diverge at near right angles. Depending upon your particular worldview, she was a "political pariah, a symbol of a liberal anti-death penalty philosophy that was out of touch with an increasingly conservative public,"[50] or "a trailblazer as the first woman to serve on the Supreme Court";[51] "soft on crime and tough on the taxpayer,"[52] or the leader of an activist, Traynoresque court with a "liberal bent in civil suits: siding with tenants against landlords, with the poor against taxpayers and with the injured against holders of liability insurance."[53]

Perhaps no greater illustration of these universally polar and mutually exclusive, zero-sum views is more evident than two versions of *Bell v. Industrial Vangas*, one as told by the *Journal of American Insurance*,[54] the other in the California Supreme Court opinion written by Justice Staniforth in the court's 5–3 decision.[55] The undisputed facts are these:

> William Bell, a salesman for Industrial Vangas, Inc., of Fresno, California, was making a delivery of gas when a fire broke out as he was transferring propane from his truck to several small tanks. He was badly burned. Bell collected $30,000 in workers compensation settlements.[56]

Under normal circumstances, Workers' Compensation as it was established in 1911 provides "compensation to workers injured or killed on the job regardless of who is at fault," and is considered the exclusive remedy for work-related injuries. Bell, however, sued his employer, not as an employer but as a manufacturer, for Vangas "had assembled the propane truck, and had even sold four"[57] it had manufactured to other propane dealers. As a manufacturer it could be held under the *dual capacity* doctrine adopted by the Traynor court in 1952.[58] This doctrine

> assumes a logical, rational and legally self-evident premise. An individual can act in two or more different, distinct capacities, either simultaneously or sequentially, giving rise in law to separate and distinct sets of obligations. There is no fictional character, no need to create any "Doppelganger" to support the rule as long applied in California; only a recognition of a simple fact—one person can have separate and distinct legal personalities.[59]

The dual capacity doctrine is among the "areas of greatest concern to insurers and employers alike" because it allows "workers to bring product liability and other suits against their own employers" even if they have already collected worker compensation benefits.[60]

> Workers are gaining the right to sue their employers without giving up any of the benefits the system already provides: the certainty that a worker whose own negligence contributed to a work injury will still receive benefits. . . . Employers, on the other hand, must not only shoulder the cost of workers compensation, but also the bill for these newly-created liabilities.[61]

Both the journal article and the court opinion use *Mercer v. Uniroyal*, a case heard in the Ohio Court of Appeals, in their arguments. Mercer, an employee for Uniroyal Tires, was hurt when a tire blew out while he was driving a truck; the truck was mounted at the factory with Uniroyal tires. The Ohio court allowed Mercer to continue his product liability suit against Uniroyal, declaring that "[i]t was only a matter of circumstance that the tire on the truck in which the plaintiff was riding was [the employer's] tire rather than a Sears, Goodyear or Goodrich."[62] The *Journal* article says, however, that it was "*because Uniroyal also made the tire*, [the] Ohio court ruled that the employee could both collect workers' compensation and file a product liability suit."[63]

Although ultimately the decision was made on behalf of Bell, it was not unanimous. Justice Mosk, a holdover from the Traynor Court and considered liberal, joined the consistently conservative Justice Richardson and provided an impassioned dissent incorporating concerns similar to those expressed in the *Journal*:

> The majority opinion . . . emphasizes the social policies favoring adequate recovery by injured employees such as Bell. There is no reason to believe that the Legislature is insensitive to these policies . . . [but] it is not our function

to tinker with these laws for the purpose of "improving" them . . . [thus] if policy considerations were relevant here, surely the exclusivity rule is founded upon a sound policy of "reciprocal concessions" underlying the entire workers' compensation scheme [which provides] an assured protection from [income loss and medical expenses]. . . . [A]ny broad exceptions . . . would undermine the underlying premise upon which the workers' compensation system is based . . . the advantage to the employer of immunity from liability at law against the detriment of relatively swift and certain compensation payments. Conversely, while the employee receives expeditious compensation, he surrenders his right to a potentially larger recovery in a common law action for the negligence or willful misconduct of his employer.

The majority, however, immediately seized upon the logical fallacy seemingly not grasped by the *Journal* and not addressed in the dissent: If the tire had been made by Sears, Goodyear, or Goodrich, then Mercer could have sued any of them for product liability, *and he still would have collected workers' compensation from Uniroyal.* Justice Staniforth declared as much in his *Bell* opinion:

> If the injured individual had not been an employee, he would have had a cause of action against the defendant. To deny Bell such a cause of action because he is an employee, gives the employer more protection than envisioned by the 1911 [Workers' Compensation] Act. *In effect, a manufacturer would [be permitted] to test new products, utilizing his employees, and limit his liability from resulting injuries from a defective product to workers' compensation remedies.* This is unsound social engineering grossly unfair to the worker.[64]

Once again, words took on new meanings once community vocabularies were considered. The employer gaining "more protection than envisioned" under workers' compensation became the "erosion of an employer's legal immunity in the sticky product liability area."[65]

The *Journal* brandished its conclusion over the head of the various legislatures with an admonition that they "need to examine closely the changes wrought in workers compensation laws by the court." Echoing the Richardson and Mosk dissents, they said:

> Clearly, any legislative solution would have to restore the health of the exclusiveness of remedy provision and prevent suits against employers. Such a move would also restore the intent of workers compensation laws, and preserve the equitable balance of the system.

The article also discussed possible legislative changes that manufacturers and insurers were wont to pursue, all of which would preclude an employee suing his employer and thus allowing an employer to

> escape full liability for the defective manufacture of goods simply by using those goods in his own plant . . . the employee, an intended and foreseeable user, must, therefore, bear the full loss . . . while the non-employee party can force that loss onto the manufacturer.[66]

While manufacturers and insurers may certainly *ask* the courts "to look past the individual case, and consider its impact on the workers compensation and civil justice system as a whole,"[67] they have little power to force change in that political venue. It is, however, the ability of these industries to exert such tremendous political and financial pressure on legislatures—essentially arm-twisting them into doing the same things that can only be nicely asked of the courts—that allowed Chief Justice Bird to remain so passionate about the plight of those voices unheard or ignored by others, and led Justices Tobriner and Grodin to consider the court system as the "Working Man's Congress."

Unlike the federal courts, California's Supreme Court does not have lifetime tenure; periodically each justice must stand for an uncontested reconfirmation.[68] In most election years the race is accompanied by extended yawns and a series of ho-hums; 1986 was not going to be such a year. As I mentioned at the beginning of this section, one fact uncontested is that the Republicans did not like Justice Bird. Male chauvinism has been suspect,[69] and it could certainly be well argued considering that Ms. Bird had absolutely no track record, judicial or otherwise, that could have offended the GOP, yet there was *such* an immediate, almost knee-jerk, dislike that she instantaneously became "the most powerful hate figure for right-wing direct mail fund-raisers since Tom Hayden started wearing a tie."[70] During her first confirming election in 1978, an opposition campaign launched by the ultraconservative state senator from Orange County, H. L. "Wild Bill" Richardson, nearly cost her the election; she only garnered a bare 51.7 percent and "narrowly missed becoming the first justice in the state's history to be rejected at the polls."[71] Since she did not have to stand for confirmation again until 1986, it became "only natural . . . for underemployed Republican political consultants to think about ginning up the anti-Bird committees" for her next appearance on the ballot.[72] Thus, from 1978 until the spring of 1985, Republicans of all shapes and sizes took periodic potshots at those members of the court who had been appointed by Governor Moonbeam; at the same time they began to accumulate munitions, primarily in the form of the sixty commuted death penalties handed down by her court, in preparation for a full frontal assault.

Barely had the flowers from the 1986 Rose Parade wilted than the opposition opened fire. On January 8, San Diego County Sheriff John Duffy, speaking in the shadow of the Capitol dome, equated Justice Bird to "the head of a snake," and launched a campaign against the three Brown appointees by enlisting the aid of on- and off-duty deputies to distribute anti-Bird material. He had recently received several thousand postcards asking for Bird's resignation, leaving adequate space and a nice line for a signature. While declaring that "he doesn't want on-duty officers 'going out door-to-door'" to pass out the blue-and-white cards, he added that, "I wouldn't get too excited if they gave them to a citizen [while] in a patrol car." The ACLU and the California Attorneys for Criminal Justice took exception to this action, the latter stating emphatically that "if in fact we learn that an officer [is] using taxpayer time or resources . . . we will take some action."[73]

The following week, U.S. House of Representatives member William Dannemeyer, a conservative Orange County Republican and possible Senate candidate, announced the formation of "Bird Watchers," another group hell-bent on unseating the three justices. Sheriff John Duffy and long-time Bird opponent Bill Roberts, past campaign manager for Ronald Reagan's successful gubernatorial bid and currently serving as executive director of "Crime Victims for Court Reform," joined him in the attack. Using resources provided by Roberts, Duffy enlisted Lucile Ulrich, whose seventeen-year-old son was murdered in 1967 by William Archie Fain. She and others "collected 62,000 signatures on petitions in an effort to prevent Fain from being paroled in October 1983."[74] Deukmejian wanted Fain's parole revoked, but . . . well, there are two sides to this story. Deukmejian submitted a petition "that the Supreme Court refused to review," yet Grodin discusses in some detail the parole of Fain, who had originally been scheduled for parole in 1976. "His impending parole drew bitter and vocal opposition . . . from the citizens of Stanislaus County," where the crime had been committed and where he would presumably be released. Because of this maelstrom of opposition, and pursuant to a decision by the court of appeals, the Board of Prison Terms moved his new parole date to 1982. As the date once again approached, bitter protestations began arriving at the offices of the board; they included not only Lucille Ulrich's 62,000 signatures and the governor's petition, but "resolutions of four city councils and three boards of supervisors, a petition of the attorney general, and a concurrent resolution of the California Senate," requesting that Fain's parole be revoked. After initially granting parole, the board bowed to such "extraordinary public outcry" and revoked it. Fain petitioned for a *habeas corpus* to the Marin County Superior Court. Judge Breiner, in his opinion, declared that

unlike the Roman circus, where the roar of the crowd would determine the life or death of the gladiator, our community cannot serve without rules, and whether the object of the justice system is the best of us or the worst, those rules must apply fairly to all.[75]

Justices Grodin, Rouse, and Miller heard the expected district attorney's appeal. Grodin acknowledges that, today, Fain's sentence would probably be "Life Without Possibility of Parole," but such law could not be applied because the law under which Fain had been convicted had since been deemed unconstitutional and, therefore, could not allow such an amendment. Two of the three did not disagree with Breiner's opinion and sent it back to the Board of Prison Terms for final disposition;[76] thus Fain was eventually released and the anti-Bird coalition accumulated one more piece of ammunition.

Jim Nielsen, GOP state senate floor leader, declared that "it is very important that the campaign against Rose Bird be as non-partisan as possible," while at the same time, in the same article, taunting that "the case against Rose Bird is sound":

Rose Bird has left her mark on other areas of the law as well. Decisions that have subverted the intent of Proposition 13, hampered law enforcement investigations, and denied basic rights to property owners in the name of rent . . . the Bird Court has ruled qualified initiatives off the ballot before the people could vote on them. In 1983, it was the Sebastiani reapportionment initiative; last August, it was the balanced federal budget initiative.

Both decisions overruled the will of the people as expressed through the initiative process.[77]

Thus in January of 1985, fully eighteen months before the election, the entire battery of anti-Bird artillery was engaged, preparing for a long, brutal campaign in which there would be no prisoner taken, no quarter given, and no holds barred.

On August 8 Jim Lehrer led off his segment of the *MacNeil/Lehrer NewsHour* with a segment he called "Improper Advice":[78] "There is a most unusual, most heated election campaign underway in California," he began. It would not, he opined, be the congressional, gubernatorial, or senatorial races that would gain national attention, it would be "Rose Bird and two fellow justices . . . running against their own record" that would steal the limelight. His "guests" via sound bite and taped interview spliced into an almost seamless dialogue included virtually all opposing parties: Justices Bird, Grodin, and Reynoso, and Governor George Deukmejian; Justice Bird's campaign manager Bill Zimmerman and GOP consultant Bill Roberts; UC Berkeley law professor

and "national authority on criminal law" Louis Schwartz, and Kern County District Attorney Edward R. Jagels; and finally activist actor Warren Beatty and San Luis Obispo County Sheriff George Whiting.

Justice Bird started the dialogue, saying, "We're an easy target":

We basically don't answer charges. We basically don't come out and defend decisions, we let them speak for themselves. And as a result sometimes we are a relatively easy target because we don't fight back.

Elizabeth Farnsworth, KQED-TV (San Francisco) political commentator and guest narrator for this segment, expressed how the Bird Court had "won the praise of lawyers and scholars for [their] well-reasoned opinions," but also brought into focus the contentious subject which had come to dominate an election still more than a year away. "She has also been unwilling," Farnsworth said, "to implement the death penalty. Now her opponents were out to remove her from the bench," along with Reynoso and Grodin. Like modern-day Hester Prynns, the three were emblazoned with "Soft on Crime" in scarlet.

To be sure, capital punishment was still on the minds of Californians in 1985 and 1986; Harris, Gallup, ABC, and other polls taken during the period still show those in favor to be well into the sixty-fifth to seventy-fifth percentiles. Of equal importance, the "No Opinion" category usually amounted to between 4 percent and 6 percent; while opinions were obviously polarized, the death penalty was more incredibly popular than at almost any time in the past.

Sheriff Whiting, speaking in the tones and voice of the seeming Everyman, also expressed these sentiments. "I think they should get rid of them," he comments with some great disdain. "I think they are hurting law enforcement, they're hurting the people of California, and they're hurting the victims of the crimes."

Bill Zimmerman, a partner in the firm bearing his name, had begun to manage Bird's campaign in February of 1985. "She came to us," he says in a campaign *post mortem* article published in the *Los Angeles Times* a few days after the election, "because we have a reputation for effectively representing progressive candidates" and because they could craft both positive and negative campaigns.[79]

"Conservatives and the Moral Majority types want to take over the courts," he commented through sound splice to Farnsworth, "because they haven't gotten decisions out of the courts that they feel they can live with on a number of issues that are important to them."

Bill Roberts agreed with his own conservative twist, emphatically declaring, "I think the implications for the judicial process throughout the nation could be enormous, because the public will awaken to the fact that the judicial process is as accountable as the legislative and the administrative process."

Deukmejian, author of the new and improved 1977 death penalty law (the one that had replaced the 1974 version declared unconstitutional by the Burger Court) had his own political agenda. Some observed that he "all but drools in public at the prospect of making four court appointments."[80] Although he insisted that he was "not involved in the anti-Bird effort," he left little doubt about his position that evening. "The most recent California field poll indicates that many Californians have disturbing doubts about our judicial system," he proclaimed.

"One of the principal reasons that many people have lost confidence in the supreme court," he continued to elaborate, "is because they're dissatisfied with the court's refusal to implement the death penalty. The juries by unanimous decisions have imposed the penalty, and it's long past the

time for our California supreme court to act on enforcing capital punishment."

The camera moved quickly to the still face of Bill Zimmerman as Farnsworth added in a voice-over, "at this point, she is letting others argue her case. Zimmerman says an election of this type poses special problems."

Zimmerman's face came alive; he responded, saying, "I think this is probably the toughest job in American politics this year. There's never been a judicial confirmation election of this magnitude, where millions of dollars will be spent on both sides." Besides these vast amounts of money, he added that "we have the problems of the office being a unique one in electoral politics." Rephrasing Bird's earlier comment, he admonished the audience that "a chief justice cannot run around the state saying, 'I've done a great job, vote for me.'"

Justice Reynoso's meme echoed these sentiments, reminding the invisible audience that "judges are constrained by the Constitution and by the statutes and by the traditions of the common law. Indeed, it can't really be a campaign in a traditional sense" because judges are unable to make any promises.

"You have one of the toughest judiciaries in the entire United States," Bird added through the editing process, emphasizing an undisputed fact: "We forget about the vast majority of people who are tried, who are sentenced, and who are sent to state prison."

Edward R. Jagels of Kern County disputed the obvious, however, declaring that "Bird votes in favor of the criminal and against the people and the victim 88% of the time," without citing his source or questioning its accuracy. "It has become an intolerable situation," he hissed.

"Jagels' views," observed Farnsworth, "are representative of California's district attorneys." The district attorneys had taken it upon themselves to issue a White Paper "which reviews 96 Supreme

Court opinions the DA's consider to be soft on crime." Farnsworth then introduced UC Berkeley Professor Louis Schwartz, "a national authority on criminal law," who was there to "object to the district attorneys' campaign."

"It is really unethical," Schwartz said, "to make individual decisions a basis for retiring a judge who has behaved as a judge, even though you may differ with the results."

Farnsworth added to the professor's comments, emphasizing that he "believes a judge should be unseated only for incompetence or unethical conduct." Even among Republicans, "there are no such allegations in Rose Bird's case."

But even as the campaign was beginning to heat up, Farnsworth concluded by saying that "California's voters seem to be turning against her. In February a statewide poll indicated that 35% of the electorate would vote against the chief justice; by May the figure had risen to 46%."

MacNeil and Lehrer would visit the campaign again almost exactly a year later; many of the same personalities espousing the same frantic litany would be on the program, but with the added tragic personality of Darrel Fredrickson, father of sixteen-year-old Karen Green, a girl murdered by her estranged husband; the man had shot her in the face with a shotgun.

A parole official declared grimly to the *Mac-Neil/Lehrer* camera, "This was a cold blooded, senseless and extremely cruel act demonstrating the prisoner's total disregard for the law, human dignity, human suffering, and ultimately for human life."

"I had to make the identification," the father said painfully. "I had to come home and tell her mother, 'Yes, that's Karen.'" He paused for a moment, sighed, and continued on. "She never got to see any part of our daughter. She saw a closed casket."

Groups like Bill Roberts' Crime Victims for Court Reform had selected a few tragic cases such as that of Green and Ulrich, cases guaranteed to enrage and inflame the public. Like those few other cases, Green's murderous husband had initially been sentenced to death, and like the pre-ordained climax in an ancient Greek tragedy, the end was known before the first actor had stepped onto the stage.

Thus, the chorus of Mr. Fredrickson's narrative continued: "First we heard he was guilty. We've been told that by Sutter County. And then we heard about the death penalty. And it was like just a weight being lifted off. I thought, 'Good. That will settle it.'"

Green's sentence, however, was predictably appealed to the Bird Court; he was, again, predictably offered the *deus machina* when the court overturned his death sentence, pending a new trial. The prosecution decided against retrying him, leaving Green to serve his life sentence at the California Medical Facility in Vacaville. What is not mentioned is that the retrial was for the penalty phase only; the murderer would not be let out to roam our mean streets. He was to remain incarcerated.

"Now," however, lamented the reporter, "every two years, the couple comes to Vacaville to plead that their daughter's killer not be paroled."[81]

Unfortunately, by this time Zimmerman was no longer managing Rose Bird's campaign; she had taken complete control. More accurately, according to Zimmerman, whatever control she had, she lost; like doomed Elektra walking across a stage in ancient Athens, the audience hushed in tense anticipation, aware that whatever her fate would be, it would be sealed by her own hand. Everyone in the audience knew what her fate would be.

It did not have to be that way, Zimmerman proclaimed, undoubtedly with some anger. "It wasn't hers to lose."[82] She had been reluctant to engage a political consultant, but once convinced, decided that "the cornerstone of the campaign would have to be television commercials, and that she was prepared to fight fire with fire."

Offensively there were many possibilities. The public responded favorably to arguments that Gov. George Deukmejian was guilty of court-packing, that the Bird court had protected the public against infringements of rights held dear by a majority—including those having to do with abortion, clean air and water, labor and housing discrimination—and finally, that the drive to unseat the court was fueled by a combination of powerful corporate special interests and extreme right-wingers trying to shape decisions for their own benefit.

Additionally, as Kaus reminded his readers and a fact alluded to by Bird herself, "a reading of [her] opinions themselves does not back up Deukmejian's charge that Bird is cynically twisting the law to avoid capital punishment," implying that even her stand on the death penalty might not withstand the bright light of the truth.

The contradictions within the campaign quickly became apparent: While the state constitution "mandates that the judiciary not only remain independent of other branches of government," and that it "reach decisions on the basis of law, without regard for political pressure and the changing tides of public opinion," polls commissioned by Zimmerman found that voters "felt they had every right to reject sitting Supreme Court justices if they disagreed with their decisions" by a 68 percent to 24 percent margin. Thus, while he knew that "public opinion could be moved on this issue to blunt the attack of our opponents," the one strategy they could not use was one based "on the independence of the judiciary"; to do so would be to "commit political suicide."

Yet this is precisely the strategy the chief justice decided to use. When she demanded that Zimmerman have no further contact with the press,

they severed their relationship; Bird then went to another consultant who outlined a similar offensive strategy, and Bird severed that relationship, also. "Thus did Bird," Zimmerman laments, "launch herself on the remarkably inept effort that became her campaign," one that was always uncoordinated and at times "bordered in the bizarre," trying to move forward on the "one message that would not work."

He asks, somewhat rhetorically, "Did she really want to win?" to which the answer is, he feels, "a resounding and unequivocal yes." Never, he says, had he met a candidate who wanted more than to win. By mid-1986, however, "she took the ultimate step" by writing and producing her own commercials which "not surprisingly . . . had no effect on the vote." With only weeks left in the campaign, her only remaining strategy was to "rail publicly against political consultants for polluting the electoral environment and subverting the democratic process."

Fin le Guerre and the Body Count

During the 1985 airing of *MacNeil/Lehrer*, actor and liberal activist Warren Beatty called those who would remove Justices Bird, Grodin, and Reynoso from the Supreme Court "the direct descendants of Joe McCarthy, the John Birch Society and the far right of the 1950s that said impeach Earl Warren."[83] Like so many of the angry words mouthed in the polarized worlds of the Bird confirmation, within it could be found a grain of truth. In recalling the halcyon days of the Civil Rights Movement and antiwar protests, we forget that the far-right, ultraconservative factions of American society did attempt to make a case for the impeachment of Chief Justice Earl Warren. Although doomed to failure from the outset, had such a faction been able to exercise their prerogative at some point in his tenure, basic shifts in jurisprudence like

Brown, *Sullivan*, *Burr*, and *Baker* might never have happened.

In that same report, Justice Grodin reiterated as much when he chastised the far right, saying "the minute we start calling the shots the way some of the crowd at any particular time wants them called, then we're in trouble, and the game is in trouble. The system depends upon judges who call them as they see them according to principle." He, Justice Bird, and all those who sat, had ever sat, now or will ever sit, on the Supreme Court benches know of the titanic battles going on between industrial and financial conglomerates and every individual man and woman who must, at some point in time, oppose them. With such powerful forces controlling the Capitol buildings and various congresses of the assorted states arrayed against every interest but their own, Justice Bird and her Governor Moonbeam-appointed cohort stood as the only political defense against such megalithic tyranny. While it is true that these forces may bicker between themselves like the gods on Olympus, their forces allied against interests contrary to their overall goodwill can, and most often do, roll over opposition like a millstone over so much flour.

Grodin in his book, and Reynoso in his comments to *MacNeil/Lehrer*, argue that often both the trial and appeal judges are bound by constraints beyond their control and which are only dimly understood by the audience—if they are understood at all. Decisions discussed by the other writers herein, as well as those like *Miranda*, *Carlos*, and *Johnson* discussed in *In Pursuit of Justice*, do create opportunities for reversible error that compel the state to retry a defendant. The press, a most confounding and mistrusted component for Justice Bird and her cohort caught in the crosshairs of nemesis Bill Roberts and his Crime Victims for Court Reform, had both a right and duty to question the Court's torturous convolutions in decisions like the one which forced Mr. and Mrs. Fredrickson to face the murderer of their daughter once every two years.

Can blame, if blame is the right word, for the murderer living instead of dying be placed at the foot of the Bird Court, or should the district attorney have sought a new penalty phase? Is it the DA's fault that a family so devastated by the savage slaying of their daughter must see over and over again the face of the man who did it, until the end of their days? Or is it the fault of the Bird Court? I find the reasoning behind the Grodin and Reynoso Gorgonian Knot legal theory disturbing, severely taxing to my sense of reality, and verging on a pathetic, self-serving apologia. There is no question that, in spite of rhetoric to the contrary, their court was as harsh on criminals as other courts had been[84]—except for its prosecution of the death penalty. The fact also remains that Bird and her court, after seeking out *in certiorari* decisions which had not been sent to them on appeal (or even reappeal), did return sixty capital cases for penalty phase retrial at great expense and/or social stress to the public, and with little or no public return for the expenses incurred. As important as their continued presence on the bench was to the common man, I for one do not understand why they not only chose to stand in harm's way, but also seemed to freeze there like rabbits caught in the headlights of an oncoming truck.

A critical public respects the rule of law because it provides order, and the price of that respect is the spectacle order creates in the courtroom when chaos threatens in the streets. The Bird Court worked at cross purpose with the message perceived by the public, threatening to create chaos in the criminal courtroom. Political opposition extrapolated this threat to include chaos in the civil courtroom, a place where the playing field was level enough and the monetary veins large enough that lawyers could feed almost at will. It was also the only place in which the Goliath of big business was periodically given a split lip from the commoner's slingshot.

There is hubris in the community of citizens who pilloried the 1986 Supreme Court because it was done by our own hands; in this way, we are all much like Rose Bird. We all wanted to win but someone got us to take our eye off the real prize: the integrity of our courts—or more accurately, a *return* of integrity to our courts. While it appears that the Bird Court had all of the integrity of the Gibson and Traynor courts preceding them, the argument defies appearance. This is our tragedy, for within this cohort was the embryonic advancement of consumer rights. These rights, as the Supreme Courts of Warren and Burger consistently write in their opinions, are only implied in the Constitution, yet the implications are clear. The Bird cohort was needed to shepherd a new theoretical canon of consumer case law and precedence through the legal maze, as Roger Traynor had done a quarter century before. Instead the cohort allowed a political opposition made up of those interests whom they rightfully alienated to seize the political initiative. Manufacturers, insurance companies, and the morass of other entities within the general rubric of Big Business thereby were allowed to grasp as an issue the still-existing and very healthy death penalty paradigm and, through skillful media manipulation, allowed the public to become:

> Convinced that the [California Supreme Court judges'] view of the law and its relationship to society is so extreme that it lies outside the mainstream of legal thought and community values.[85]

Reinvigorating opposition to the death penalty proved to be a knight-errant's job; the cohort tilting at windmills. It was in the area of tort reform, strict liability, privity, and dual capacity the cohort's message was writ large, and in which it incurred the wrath of big business and its minions, the Republican right wing. It was on the slopes of capital punishment made slippery by those minions that the hopes of consumers were set back by decades, subject to the ravages of tribunals less tolerant to the foibles of the common man. As Grodin observed about the creation of law and the dichotomy between the judicial and legislative branches of government:

> There are certain areas of the law in which development is best left to the judicial branch. The legislature, when it does act, necessarily takes wholesale action, making broad rules of general application. Courts, on the other hand, act typically at the "retail" level [and] although legislatures are expected to give voice to the interests of the people as a whole, they are inclined to listen most carefully to the voices of politically powerful people and groups.[86]

The courts have too many important battles to fight; they must be most judicious in the ones they chose. If, as the members of this cohort believed, the court is the legislature of the common man, then laws of greatest value to the most people should be of the highest priority. Because the Bird Court chose to battle on behalf of a group of sixty-four murderers in relatively meaningless debates over, among other things, whether lower courts had given the jury proper instructions about applications of the death penalty—and in no case actually overturning the verdict itself—millions of consumers today do not have the protection they might have otherwise received from the Bird Court, assuming she remained on the bench until her death. This is a case where the well-crafted myth of one position betrayed the truth of another of equal or greater social importance.

The question posed herein involves the courts as both spectacle and *juris practica*. While we would all like to believe in the sober application of law by all factions of the legal establishment, circus and entertainment remain an important and viable part of the process. *Judge Judy* and *The People's Court*, *Family Law* and *Ally MacBeal* do not survive season after season, and then survive indefinitely through reruns, because people cannot find value in their entertainment. In a perfect world the Bird Court's reconsideration of death penalty cases would not have ultimately had an effect on consumer rights, but in a perfect world there would never have been capital cases to rehear, and the audience would have no need of the ensuing high courtroom drama.

Michael A. Pierson CLU, ChFC, served in the United States Air Force during the Vietnam War. He received his Bachelor's degree in history from San Jose State University, with a minor in English. He spent twenty years as a registered investment advisor in his financial planning practice before returning to California State University, Fullerton, for his Master's degree in American Studies. He has written articles about financial planning, insurance, and investments in magazines such as *Your Money*, and has served on the editorial board, and as an editor of, Cal State Fullerton's history department publication, *The Welabaethan*. He is a member of the California Democratic Party Central Committee. He currently teaches American Government, U.S. History, and English in the Anaheim Union High School District. His poetry has been published nationally, and his latest effort, *Left Click*, is a cultural study of liberal political activism in cyberspace since 2004.

Works Cited

Books and Essays

Culver, John H. "The Transformation of the California Supreme Court: 1977–1997," *Albany Law Review*, Albany, NY, 1998.

Grodin, Joseph R. *In Pursuit of Justice: Reflections of a State Supreme Court Justice*, University of California Press, Los Angeles, 1989.

Isserman, Maurice, and Kazin, Michael. *America Divided: The Civil War of the 1960's*, Oxford University Press, New York, 2000.

Kaus, Mickey. "Flipping the Bird," *The New Republic*, April 15, 1985.

Schwartz, Gary T. "The Beginning and the Possible End of the Rise of Modern American Tort Law," *Georgia Law Review*, University of Georgia, Spring, 1992.

Magazines

The Economist, 10/4/86.
Journal of American Insurance
——— Spring, 1976
——— Winter, 1981–82
Risk Management: The Journal of the Professional Risk Manager, January, 1975.

Time Magazine
——— 1/5/76
——— 4/12/76
U.S. News & World Report, 4/19/76.

Newspapers

Los Angeles Times
——— 4/24/76
——— 4/26/76
——— 4/29/76
——— 11/9/86
The Orange County Register, 4/22/76.
The San Diego Union-Tribune
——— 1/16/85
——— 2/2/85
——— 2/8/85

Government and Miscellaneous Publications

California Government Press Release, 12/6/99, "Chief Justice Rose Bird dies, Supreme Court to hold memorial session."
Gallup Organization
——— 11/5/53

———— 3/7/60
———— 11/2/71
The MacNeil-Lehrer NewsHour
———— August 8, 1985

———— August 17, 1985
WWW/SFBG.COM/NEWS/34/10/EDBIRD.HTML, 12/8/99

Notes

1. Joseph R. Grodin, *In Pursuit of Justice: Reflections of a State Supreme Court Justice* (Los Angeles: University of California Press, 1989).
2. Maurice Isserman and Michael Kazin, *America Divided: The Civil War of the 1960's* (New York: Oxford University Press, 2000).
3. They are also generous in the period allotted for this decade, at times allowing the late 1940s to be included. While I would not be quite so generous in the allocation of time, I would agree with their assessment of the period from 1954 to 1976 as a period of great social upheaval and cultural change, a period generally acknowledged as being "the sixties" inclusively.
4. Gary T. Schwartz, "The Beginning and the Possible End of the Rise of Modern American Tort Law," *Georgia Law Review*, University of Georgia (Spring 1992):5.
5. Ibid.
6. Ibid.
7. Ibid.
8. John H. Culver, "The Transformation of the California Supreme Court: 1977–1997," *Albany Law Review* (1998):3.
9. Grodin, p. 105.
10. Ibid. Culver, "Transformation," *Albany Law Review* (1998).
11. Schwartz, p. 47.
12. Ibid., p. 3. See also Grodin, *supra*, p. 76.
13. Schwartz, quoting from his own work, "The Character of Early American Tort Law," 36 UCLA L. REV. 641, 678–79 (1989).
14. Schwartz, p. 4.
15. Culver, "Transformations," *Albany Law Review*, p. 2–3.
16. "Product Liability: The Bill Everyone Pays," *Journal of American Insurance* (Spring 1976):8.
17. Ibid.
18. *Lewis v. Terry* (1896), 111 Cal. 39 [43 P. 398, 52 Am.St. Rep. 146, 31 L.R.A. 220].
19. *Burr v. Sherman Williams Co.*, 42 Ca1.2d 682, p. 695–97 (1954).
20. *Peterson v. Lamb Rubber Co.*, 54 Cal. 2d 339; 353 P.2d 575; Cal. Rptr. 863 (1960).
21. Paraphrased from Grodin, p. 83.
22. Mickey Kaus, "Flipping the Bird," *The New Republic*, April 15, 1985, p. 25.
23. Grodin, p. 86.
24. Ibid.
25. Gallup Organization, 11/5/53, QUESTION ID: US GALLUP.53–522, Q07A.
26. Ibid., 3/7/60, QUESTION ID: USGALLUP.60–625, Q003A.
27. Ibid., 11/2/71, QUESTION ID: USGALLUP.839, Q011. An additional poll summarizing the years between 1953 and 1976 appears in the Los Angeles *Times*, 4/29/76, Pt. 1, p. 29, "More Support the Death Penalty, Poll Says."
28. *Time* magazine, 1/5/76, p. 40.
29. *Los Angeles Times*, "Liberation Front 'Combat Unit,'" 4/26/76, Pt. 1, p. 2.
30. Ibid., *Times*, 4/29/76.
31. *People v. Anderson*, 493 P.2d 880, 893 (Cal. 1972), the Burger Court finding "public acceptance of capital punishment is a relevant but not controlling factor in assessing whether it is consonant with contemporary standards of decency."
32. *Time* magazine, 4/29/76, poll conducted by Yankelovich, Skelly and White, QUESTION ID: USYANK.768510, Q04AC. An ABC News/Washington Post poll taken in 1981 asked the original question posed by Gallup in 1953. Even in this later (and presumably more enlightened) decade, 73 percent of Americans polled thought the death penalty appropriate for the simple crime of murder, without posing any of the possible causatives— as had been done in prior polls. One might deduce from this that the deaths caused by terrorists, hijackers, and kidnappers had so heightened the awareness of the act, making it so spectacular, that *all* murderers were painted with the same broad brush and thus deserved the same punishment. ABC News/Washington Post 6/8/81, QUESTION ID: USABCWP.34, R37.
33. William Farr, "Death Penalty Ruled Out in 2 Slasher Cases," *Los Angeles Times*, 4/24/76, p. 30.
34. *Time* magazine of 4/12/76 discusses this dialectic in some detail. See "Reconsidering the Death Penalty," p. 49.
35. Grodin, p. 86.
36. Ibid.
37. Ibid., p. 92.
38. "Insurance Costs and Tort Reform," *Letters to The Times*, 4/29/76.
39. Ibid., Pt. 1, p. 29.
40. Ibid., Farr.
41. *Time* magazine, 4/12/76. Advertisement, p. 31.
42. *U.S. News & World Report*, 4/19/76, p. 43.

43. Richard J. Keintz and J. Finley Lee, "Accounting for Future Losses: The Risk Management Problem," *Risk Management: The Journal of the Professional Risk Manager* (January 1975):7.

44. Ibid., p. 9.

45. "A Look into the Future," *Best's Review: Property and Casualty Edition* (December 1975):26.

46. "Malpractice Insurance: A Medical-Legal Dilemma," *Journal of American Insurance* (Spring 1975).

47. Weldon E. Havins, M.D., and James Dalessio, "Limiting the Scope of Arbitration Clauses in Medical Malpractice Disputes Arising in California," *Capital University Law Review*, 28 Cap. U.L. Rev. 331 (2000).

48. Ibid., p. 3.

49. "Boss Amorous? It's Safe to Resist," *The Orange County Register*, 4/22/76, p. 1.

50. Editorial, "Rose Bird, 1936–1999," 12/8/99, www/SFBG.com/news/34/10/ edbird.html.

51. California Government Press Release, 12/6/99, "Chief Justice Rose Bird dies, Supreme Court to hold memorial session."

52. Kaus, p. 21; he is quoting from Republican direct mail pieces.

53. "Birdshot in California," *The Economist*, 10/4/86, p. 30.

54. "When Your Employee Takes You to Court," *Journal of American Insurance* (Winter 1981–82):1.

55. 30 Cal. 3d 268; 637 P.2d 266; 179 Cal. Rptr. 30; CCH Prod. Liab. Rep. P9109 (1981). Judge Kaus did not participate in this decision.

56. "When Your Employee . . . ," *Journal*, p. 1.

57. Ibid.

58. *Duprey v. Shane*, 39 Ca1.2d 781 [249 P.2d 8](1952).

59. *Bell*, footnote N4.

60. "When Your Employee . . . ," *Journal*, p. 2.

61. Ibid., p. 2–3.

62. *Mercer v. Uniroyal, Inc.* (1976) 49 Ohio App.2d 279 [3 Ohio Ops.3d 333, 361 N.E.2d 492, 496].

63. "When Your Employee . . . ," *Journal*, p. 3. My italics.

64. *Bell*, p. 8. My italics.

65. "When Your Employee . . . ," *Journal*, p. 3.

66. *Bell*, p. 9.

67. "When Your Employee . . . ," *Journal*, p. 4.

68. Justices must run in the next gubernatorial election after they are appointed, then at the end of the unexpired term for which they were appointed, then finally for a full twelve-year term.

69. "Improper Advice?" *The MacNeil-Lehrer Newshour*, August 8, 1985.

70. Kaus, p. 21.

71. Ibid.

72. Ibid.

73. Ron Roach, "Bird, 2 Other High Court Justices Targets of New Ouster Campaign," *The San Diego Union-Tribune*, 1/16/85, p. A3; Roy Schneider, "Sheriff Drafts Deputies for War against Bird," *The San Diego Union-Tribune*, 2/8/85, p. A1.

74. Ibid., Roach.

75. Grodin, p. 44–45.

76. Ibid., p. 45.

77. Jim Nielsen, "A Case against Rose Bird," *The San Diego Union*, 2/2/85, p. B3.

78. In order to simplify reading and reduce the confusion of looking down to the bottom of the page every third line, I will adopt the convention that this entire dialogue took place on the evening in point, thus reducing my footnotes to this single entity.

79. Bill Zimmerman, "The Campaign that Couldn't Win: When Rose Bird Ran Her Own Defeat," *Los Angeles Times, Opinion*, 11/9/86, p. 1.

80. Kaus, p. 21.

81. "Death Penalty Politics," *MacNeil/Lehrer Newshour*, 9/17/86, Transcript #2863.

82. Unless otherwise cited, all quotations used in this particular section will be from the Zimmerman article cited above.

83. "Improper Advice?" *MacNeil-Lehrer Newshour*, August 8, 1985

84. A more detailed discussion is beyond the scope of this essay. For a more thorough comparison of decisions involving the Bird, Lucas, and George Courts, see *Albany Law Review*, ibid., Section II, "Decisionmaking on the California Supreme Court."

85. Grodin, p. 186. The quotation refers to a judge—singular. For clarification of my argument I have changed it to paraphrase Grodin's admonition to a student's question, and to which he was responding.

86. Ibid., p. 82, 83.

CHAPTER 3

Fear, Capital Punishment, and Order

THE CONSTRUCTION AND USE OF CAPITAL PUNISHMENT STATUTES IN EARLY MODERN ENGLAND AND SEVENTEENTH-CENTURY NEW ENGLAND

Patrick Callaway

THE GREATEST hopes and greatest fears of a ruling class are reflected in the legal codes that they create to fight disorder. The nature of the threat to society changes in nature over the course of time and is a reflection of the values of that society. The fears of a society evolve over time based on economic and class structures, religious beliefs, and perceived threats to the social order. Capital punishment was a tool at the disposal of society to enforce conformity with the expected economic and moral order while protecting property and propriety.

Throughout the early modern legal system, there were important differences between the enactment of capital punishment legislation, the enforcement of this legislation, and the practical structures of law enforcement. By modern standards, this process was a haphazard one that oftentimes depended on informal structures. The eighteenth-century process of law creation was unsystematic and resulted in laws that served at cross-purposes to one another, provided a scale of punishments that bore little resemblance to the seriousness of crime committed, and functioned as a remedy for alleged social disorders that were a direct threat to members

of Parliament. Law creation at this time was an intensely personal process; the resulting legislation oftentimes reflected the deeply seated fears of individual legislators rather than a systematic system of law. Law enforcement was also unsystematic. Although the written law statutes were exceptionally brutal and recommended the mass employment of the hangman's rope, in practice, capital punishment was not universally enforced. Capital punishment was a tool of terror; theoretically, that terror inspired by the law maintained order. In practical usage, capital punishment could only be used in a selective balance between terror, mercy, and the preservation of the majesty of the law.

Colonial law evolved in a different social and economic context than English law. The social conflicts of the colonies varied from those of the mother country. As a result, the nature of the legal system in the colonies differed in important aspects from those of England. Generally, English legal codes sought to maintain an order based on the protection of property and wealth while the New England colonies placed an emphasis on the preservation of a religious moral order. Although each system had different features, the ultimate result of the law, and the role of capital punishment in law enforcement, remained consistent: to keep the social and economic control of society in the hands of the elite classes within that society.

Early Modern English Law and Capital Punishment

The rise in the number of capital statutes during this time period was influenced by the evolution of English society as a whole. The seventeenth and eighteenth centuries were a time of upheaval in society. A significant change in English society was the Glorious Revolution of 1688. This revolution brought a new governing mentality and justifications for power to the forefront of the political and legal process. In *Albion's Fatal Tree*, Douglas Hay argues that this revolution "established the freedom of not men, but men of property."[1] The political system was effectively controlled by people of property without any serious interference from the crown or the citizenry. The class interest of property owners was the domestic platform of the British government throughout the eighteenth century. Hay argues that the imposition of a new basis of government based on the open display of power was not sufficient, unless there was an accompanying change in the basic ideological relationship between property and governmental legitimacy. Hay writes that "there was little pretense that civil society was concerned primarily with peace, or justice, or charity. Even interests of the state and divine will had disappeared. Property had swallowed them all."[2] John Locke was the clearest ideological voice on the new relationship between property and power. According to Hay's interpretation of Locke's *Second Treatise of Government*, the government is transformed into a body whose only concern is the preservation of property. Further, political power can be

defined through the government's ability to inflict the death penalty as well as lesser punishments.[3] This ideological shift, accompanied by the shift of political power into the hands of the property-owning class left the lower classes of society trapped in a maelstrom of social, economic, and demographic change under a governing structure that professed little concern for easing the people's adjustment into an increasingly uncertain world.

In his book *Colonists in Bondage*, Abbot Emerson Smith argues that "crime, as a social problem, did not exist until great numbers of poor people had been turned away from their manoral occupations and set adrift into a society that was learning to disclaim responsibility for their support."[4] As a result of this economic and social revolution, a brutal criminal code was created by those who "viewed them with alarm" in order to maintain authority over these newly migratory populations.[5] The mobile nature of poor persons during this time period was an evolution in societal organization that undercut many of the informal legal customs that were common in rural England. With the collapse of many of the traditional structures of order such as the church and to some degree the family, the law became the ideological safeguard for the protection of power and property for the upper classes.[6]

The legal structure of early modern England was hierarchical and increasingly specialized in nature. In his book *Crime and the Courts in England, 1660–1800*, J. M. Beattie writes that the lowest level of legal authority was the office of the justice of the peace. The justices of the peace had some summary powers to adjudicate minor infractions of the law without recourse to a trial or a jury. Offenses that fell under the summary purview of the justice of the peace included offenses against game and the theft of minor amounts of wood and agricultural produce.[7] Beattie argues that the most important type of court pertaining to capital punishment during this period was the assizes.[8] The assizes were designed to handle serious offenses "that were subject to capital punishment under common law."[9] These offenses included homicide, especially when committed against a criminal's "natural superiors" such as masters and husbands, coinage, and "other homicides, infanticide, rape, burglary, larceny, and arson."[10] The number of specific offenses that were subject to the death penalty and nonclergyable steadily increased throughout the seventeenth and eighteenth centuries, tripling in number from about 50 in 1688 to about 160 in 1760.[11] Quarter sessions, according to Beattie, dealt with less serious offenses such as assault, riot, and fraud. Quarter sessions had ceased to deal with capital offenses by the early seventeenth century.[12] Many legal cases or potential legal cases never reached the formal legal system at either the assize or the quarter session courts. Oftentimes, conflicts were settled informally through extralegal social networks that helped to check deviant behaviors.

Informal social controls over behavior are only effective in a stable society. Even the formal law was an intensely personal affair in rural England, as many possible legal cases were settled out of court. Under the early modern system, the victim of a crime was responsible for initiating a legal case against a defendant.[13] If a victim chose not to prosecute, then no legal case was formed. The victim also had the right to settle any grievances with a perpetrator informally. Character and reputation were vitally important to the public standing of an individual, especially in a rural setting. Potential prosecutors found themselves in the unenviable situation of weighing the potential social costs of a prosecution against the potential social disruption a prosecution might cause. Beattie argues that informal sanctions were often as useful in regulating behavior as an appeal to the court system.[14] Supplications to the courts were usually reserved for repeat offenders, as a

last resort, or in regard to those outside of the local community structure who held no standing in the community.[15] In this informal setting, it is impossible to speculate precisely how many crimes were not reported to the authorities, and what impact that might have had on the administration of or the statistics about capital sentences. It also reveals the personal nature of society and of the legal system.

Prosecutions were not the only element of the justice system that was intensely personal in nature. Mercy was also an inherent part of the legal system. Mercy was also thought of in personal terms. As Douglas Hay argued in *Albion's Fatal Seed*, "mercy was part of the currency of patronage."[16] Networks of patronage and obligation formed a vertical bond through society that influenced the legal system as it was applied to all levels of society. In one case that Hay presents, a chain of patronage linked a defendant to the prison chaplain, who in turn was connected to a London minister, who was in turn linked to Member of Parliament William Wilberforce, who in turn applied to the Home Secretary to consider the case. A pardon was subsequently granted.[17] This type of informal extralegal social connection and its impact on a legal case is not the product of a rational, consistent legal system. However, it formed an important element in the mental construction of a paternalistic state in which there was a quasifeudal relationship between the lower classes and their social superiors based on the exchange of loyalty for protection.[18] The apex of this system of mercy was the king, who could commute sentences entirely or on some condition, such as the commutation of a capital sentence in favor of transportation.[19]

In his book *Albion Ascendant*, Wilfrid Prest contends that "the conceptual poverty of English criminal law" helped spur the continued growth of capital statutes in early modern England.[20] This intellectual poverty is reflected in the process of law formation. In *A History of the English Criminal Law*, Leon Radzinowicz argues that "practically all capital offenses were created more or less as a matter of course by a placid and uninterested Parliament."[21] The law code was not the result of a carefully constructed system of governance; rather, it was the product of an accumulation of various intricate statutes over the course of time. Ideology, rather than conscious aforethought, drove the process of law making. This trend became increasingly prominent after the Glorious Revolution of 1688 and the rise to power of the great Whig lords. This ideology "encouraged the Whig oligarchy to regard one of the chief objects of government to be the protection of their own rights of property."[22] Property and the protection of property became the ideological framework of the legal system. There is a significant overlap between this ideology and the actual function of law creation and enforcement. Members of the government were hardly dispassionate or disinterested onlookers to the expansion of capital punishment for property crimes. The property that they sought to protect was their own.

Many law codes reflected this personal and class interest of the Whig oligarchy. For example, the Waltham Black Acts were a series of wide-ranging statutes that were "designed to meet a purely local emergency" but subsequently evolved into template for many other capital punishment statutes.[23] The Black Act was a response to poaching near Waltham. According to Leon Radzinowicz, the act applied to "persons armed and having their face blackened, armed and otherwise disguised persons, having their face blackened, otherwise disguised, any other person or persons, principals in the second degree, and accessories after the fact (in certain cases)."[24] The broad expanse of this act made many new capital offenses; for example, an act as simple as having a blackened face was subject to the death penalty without benefit of clergy whether or not

any law was being broken at the time.[25] This effectively expanded the capital statutes to include the potential conspiracy to commit a crime as a punishable offense under the law. This legislation was embedded in the context of the social upheaval of the early eighteenth century, and reflects the fears of the upper classes of Georgian society that any person in disguise or possessing weapons was a direct threat to the safety of the realm; the requirement that proof was needed that there was actually some malfeasance taking place fell by the wayside.

In his book *Whigs and Hunters*, E. P. Thompson argues that there was a direct link between the rise of Walpole to political prominence and the start of a regime of retributive justice.[26] The system of retributive justice, as encoded by the Black Act, "could only have been drawn up and enacted by men who had formed habits of mental distance and moral levity towards human life—or, more particularly, towards the lives of the loose and disorderly sort of people."[27] Although Parliament was acting as a body to defend the abstract ideal of property, there was a personal element to the construction of the Black Act. Some of the victims of the Black Act were well connected to the government. Thompson argues that the Black Act could be understood as a "severe measure of government business, serving first of all the interests of the government's own closest supporters."[28] The close alliance between the government as a structure and the interests of property owners materially impacted the course of capital statutes throughout the eighteenth century. Law codes that were as broadly written as the Black Act could be expanded in scope to cover almost any type of social discontent, thereby subjecting defendants to a set of capital statutes that had little or nothing to do with any activities that they might have been involved in.

The law code was not a unilateral imposition of statutes by Parliament onto the public.

Parliament was bound to some degree by public opinion, and the need to ensure that the public would actually obey the statute without causing irreparable damage to the mystique of the law. Public opinion formed an informal power structure that often exerted as much influence on the course of law enforcement as did the statute law. Many activities that were defined as crimes had a wide base of social approval. An example of this is smuggling. In his article *Sussex Smugglers*, Cal Winslow writes that a virtual state of war existed between governmental authority and smugglers in Sussex and Kent.[29] Government authority was checked not only by the size and violent capacity of a potential mob, but also by the general support for the mob within the community. The authorities could not control the illegal smuggling trade because there was too much profit for too many people.[30] Winslow writes that the smugglers "increasingly found their crimes adding to the swelling list of capital offenses designed to protect property of Georgian England."[31] Smuggling undercut the legitimate movement of trade goods such as wine and tea throughout the country, thereby denying the treasury tax revenue and undermining the link between the possession of property and class status.

Smuggling was often a source of violence between smugglers and authority structures. In 1740 Thomas Carswell, an officer in the customs service, was shot and killed in a battle with smugglers. No witnesses could be found to testify against the perpetrators for ten years after the event.[32] The Carswell case is not unusual either in offense or in the lack of immediate consequences for the guilty. The lack of witnesses can be attributed to two factors: There was a level of public support for smuggling and the smugglers that impeded investigation into crimes of this nature; as well as intimidation.[33] One informer by the name of Harrison faced the wrath of the entire community of Hastings for his activities as an informer;

he barely escaped with his life.[34] As the 1740s progressed, the rampant lawlessness in Sussex came to the attention of the government. By 1748, the eyes of the nation were focused on Sussex due to the murders of William Galley and Daniel Chater, a customs officer and an informant, respectively.[35] This act sparked the outrage of the Duke of Richmond, a powerful local landowner. He convinced the government to convene a special court of Oyer and Terminer for Essex in order to restore order. As a part of this series of trials, he determined that the liberal use of capital punishment for smugglers, both for their role in the smuggling trade as well as their role in the illegal economy. By the end of Richmond's campaign two years later, thirty-five people had been hung, with another ten dying in gaol.[36]

The case of the Essex Smugglers illustrates many of the elements and conflicts over the law. Douglas Hay wrote in his article "Property, Authority and the Criminal Law" that gentlemen were sensitive to the public opinion in their area "for there might be serious consequences if the show of force was either not quite impressive enough, or so brutal that it outraged men and destroyed the mystique of justice."[37] Although Richmond's campaign against smuggling could have imposed obedience onto the population by force, the mystique of justice effectively limited the extent to which the court of Oyer and Terminer could change the actions of society as long as there was widespread popular support for crimes such as smuggling. The court of Oyer and Terminer was a special judicial body dedicated to the adjudication of exemplary cases in a forum outside of the standing court structure in order to produce an exemplary trial and probable capital sentence.[38] Although the Richmond court could not force the public to accept smuggling as a crime, it could inflict punishment on the perpetrators of that crime in a fashion that would gain the notice of the widest possible audience.[39] An example was needed in order to encourage obedience to the laws of trade and property as the law was set forward by Parliament. The Sussex Smugglers' court of Oyer and Terminer was designed to provide that example, but the success of that example in producing behavioral changes is very questionable.

Although the penal code became increasingly dependant on capital punishment statutes, the use of capital punishment declined as new alternative means of punishment became more popular. One of the most popular of these alternative sentences was transportation to the colonies for a term of seven or fourteen years. In *Colonists in Bondage*, Abbott Emerson Smith estimates that from 1719 to 1772, no fewer than 17,000 convicts were transported under Treasury contracts; perhaps as many as 30,000 convicts were transported to the American colonies by the British government.[40] Of the 17,000 that Smith can confirm as defiantly transported, it is estimated that only 14,000 to 15,000 actually reached America.[41] The impacts of this mass deportation are reflected in the statistics gained from an examination of session papers from the Old Bailey prison. For a typical year from 1729–1770, an average of 560 people stood trial at Old Bailey. Of these, 352 (63 percent) were convicted of a felony or misdemeanor. Of that number, 60 were condemned to the death penalty while 235 were sentenced to transportation. He further estimates that approximately half of the 60 condemned to execution were subsequently pardoned entirely or had their sentence reduced to transportation. Calculating only those convicted of felonies, Smith estimates that only about 7.5 percent of the convicted felons in his study were actually executed.[42] The time period of his study is of particular interest. The 1720s saw the growth of the capital punishment statutes in force through the Black Act and other legislation, while the percentage of criminals actually executed was small. The existence of a reasonable alternative to the noose materially decreased the number of actual executions.

The jury system also mitigated the severity of the formal penal code. In his book *The London Hanged*, Peter Linebaugh argues that the jury could influence the use of capital statutes based on their own valuations of goods.[43] According to the law, theft above the value of 5 shillings from a shop, stable, or warehouse was subject to capital punishment without benefit of clergy. If the value of goods stolen was below 5 shillings, the crime was subject to capital punishment, but with the benefit of clergy.[44] In his research of the January 1715 Old Bailey sessions, Linebaugh found that many defendants were charged with stealing goods worth 4 shillings 10, an amount that saved the defendant from a potential capital sentence.[45] The deliberate undervaluing of stolen goods by the jury (pious perjury) helped mitigate some of the harshness of the penal code. Linebaugh complicates this picture of a willfully merciful jury, however. He argues that the term *pious perjury* is misleading because it assumes that there was a universal means of valuing goods that a jury should have followed.[46]

A trial by jury for felony cases is one of the most prominent features of the common law. However, the composition of the jury is of interest during the study of the legal system. By law, jurors were required to meet certain property qualifications in order to serve.[47] In 1692, the property qualification was set at ten pounds per year "above reprises of freehold or copyhold land or tenements."[48] Linebaugh argues that this property qualification, in a society where two-thirds of the population was too poor to even pay taxes, ensured that the administration of justice would remain in the hands of the propertied interest.[49] By this system, most of the people who were judged in a court setting could not have served on the jury that judged them. What impact the composition of the jury as it was set forth in statute had on the use or nonuse of the capital punishment statutes is uncertain.

The benefit of clergy was perhaps the most important structure that curtailed the actual use of capital punishment. The benefit of clergy was a remnant of a middle ages custom that split jurisdiction over members of the clergy between religious and secular authority. At its root, the benefit of clergy was a literacy test. If the condemned could prove that they were literate (usually by reading Psalm 51, or the neck verse), then the sentence was reduced.[50] After 1705, the literacy test for claiming the benefit of clergy was abolished; the benefit of clergy was extended to all capital sentences except for those that were directly exempted by Parliament.[51] While the benefit of clergy tradition did inject some measure of mercy into the legal system, Parliament continued to pass laws establishing an increasing number of capital punishments, many of which were passed with the proviso that the offense was nonclergyable. By 1769, there were about 169 felonies that were deemed nonclergyable.[52]

Despite the many loopholes in the capital statutes and the growth of alternative punishments such as transportation, many executions still took place. These executions were used as a public spectacle and morality tale in order to warn the public of the potential consequences of crime. In *A History of English Criminal Law*, Leon Radzinowicz wrote that the public execution of a criminal was designed to produce a "salutary" effect on the onlookers while the journey to the place of execution would give the condemned an opportunity to appreciate the enormity of his crime.[53] While the procession to Tyburn and the execution did attract a great deal of attention, the lesson that the judicial system intended to deliver to the lower sort by the spectacle was oftentimes lost. The condemned was usually met with cheers, flowers, and fruit on their journey to their end.[54] The sympathy of the crowd was openly with the condemned in most cases. The scene at Tyburn itself was also far from solemn. A hanging did not invoke the feelings of terror, majesty, and dread intended by the state; rather, a hanging became a scene of disorder, conflict, and near riot.[55] The spectacle of a public execution was a part of a great public morality play; however, the message that was received was much more ambiguous than the authority structure had intended.

The lack of an execution did not necessarily mean that a very public message concerning the law and authority was not delivered through the legal system. Those who were sentenced to transportation to the American colonies were often publically shamed and reviled as they were marched from prison to the ships that would carry them to their new homes across the Atlantic. During these marches, crowds would occasionally throw stones and mud upon the prisoners.[56] Even in its mercy, the law still required that an example be made of malefactors in order to encourage socially correct behavior in the larger population.

In *Albion's Fatal Seed*, Douglas Hay argues that a legal system that was "precise, consistent, and wholly enforced was alien to the thought of most eighteenth century Englishmen."[57] Authority at this time was "embodied in direct personal relationships" rather than any universal adherence to an abstract ideal such as justice.[58] The law was a pragmatic exercise that sought to govern a rapidly changing society, not a consciously formatted series of statements about abstract principals. Sometimes statements of principal were codified into the law, either by intentional design within the law itself or by a subsequent ruling within the courts. However, the law was a reflection more of an ideology that supported the rights of property and hierarchy. The rigid legal code built around capital punishment was softened by personal interactions that could result in a private settlement to a legal dispute, mercy, or an alternative punishment such as transportation. This brutal but in many ways informal legal code was a reflection of seventeenth- and eighteenth-century English society. If capital statutes are designed to assuage the fears of the ruling classes of society, the code functioned through a pragmatic blend of terror and a brand of mercy that enforced the vertical hierarchy of society.

The Most Holy Experiment

Puritan New England

The English colonies in New England were settled in the early seventeenth century by Puritan religious separatists seeking a place for the establishment of a society based on biblical traditions. The social structures, as well as the law codes, reflected the pursuit of biblical purity within the society. Although there are some distinctions between each colony in the exact legal codes and judicial formats, the law was generally consistent throughout the region in following religious ideals to a degree that was exceptional by English standards. This was shown not only by what types of statutes were included in the legal code, but also by what statutes were not included. Although the establishment of the Massachusetts colony predates by some sixty years the Glorious Revolution of 1688 which figured prominently in the history of the English penal code, it was clear that from inception the colony did not share the basic underlying assumptions about class and property that drove the creation of a capital punishment system based on property and crimes against property. Legal codes reflect the fears of society; laws that stipulate death as the penalty for violation of the statute are especially reflective of a mentality of fear. The use of capital punishment under Massachusetts law reflected not only the fears of the society, but also the hopes of a biblically based

society by providing punishments for those who trespassed against the image of the perfect society. Instead of the property divisions of England, the primary fear of the Puritan hierarchy in the early years of settlement was religious and moral in nature.

Kathryn Preyer's article "Penal Measures in the American Colonies: An Overview" details some of the differences between the penal systems of Massachusetts and England. Preyer notes that the Massachusetts statutes lacked many of the capital punishment statutes for crimes against property.[59] This is in stark contrast to the English tradition that placed an increasing emphasis on the prevention and punishment of crimes against property. Instead, Massachusetts law focused on the enforcement of moral codes. The 1648 statutes laid out fifteen capital statutes. Included within these statutes was a host of moral offenses that carried a potential capital sentence, such as blasphemy, murder, bestiality, disobedience toward parents, and treason against the commonwealth. Each of these statutes was directly drawn from the Bible.[60] By 1684, there were only twenty-five capital laws on the books, with twenty-one of them providing no penalty but death.[61] The other four statutes provided for "other grievous punishment," which is an echo of the benefit of clergy tradition in England.[62] Preyer concludes that only nine of the capital punishment statutes were actually used between 1630 and 1692, encompassing the execution of only fifty-six people. Quantitatively, of these fifty-six criminals, twenty-three were hung for witchcraft, eleven for murder, six for piracy, four for rape, four for the defiance of banishment by Quakers, and two executions each for the crimes of bestiality, adultery, arson, and treason.[63] These statistics stand in stark contrast to the daily carnage inflicted on the English population through the judicial system.

The structure of Massachusetts' seventeenth-century court system was not an identical copy of

England's, but there were important similarities in both the form and the function of the legal system. In his article "Crime and Law Enforcement: The British Colonies," Peter Hoffer writes that "the lowest officer with colonial criminal jurisdiction was the justice of the peace."[64] In Massachusetts, the justice of the peace had jurisdiction over minor offenses. To ensure the community peace and to encourage obedience to the laws, justices of the peace could impose fines and extract sureties from the people that they oversaw.[65] County courts were established in 1643 in order to hear relatively minor cases that were outside the scope of responsibility for the justices of the peace. By 1650, the county courts' jurisdiction extended to "all civil and criminal cases not expressly reserved to the Court of Assistants or to some other inferior court or to a single magistrate."[66] From 1629 to 1635, the Court of Assistants consisted of the governor, assistant governor, and eighteen assistants that formed both a judicial body and the legislature.[67] The assistants acted as a court of appeal for the county courts. The general court was the lower house of the legislature.[68] In 1686 the Superior Court was created. This court consisted of "a majority of the Governor's councilors."[69] The legal structure also included statutory authority to call special courts of Oyer and Terminer in order to adjudicate situations of special interest or notability, such as the Salem Witch Trials.[70] The hierarchical court structure is similar to the English system of courts. However, the courts of Massachusetts tended to be more directly linked to the political structure than English courts.

Property crime was not as prevalent in colonial Massachusetts as it was in England. The social structure of seventeenth-century Massachusetts lacked the gross disparity of wealth and the grinding poverty that was the norm in England. Informal social connections also served to reduce the prevalence of property crimes. In his article "Crime and Social Control in Provincial Massachusetts," David H. Flaherty writes that provincial Massachusetts was "remarkably free of serious crime (and probably of all crime) because of the efficiency of the instruments of social control."[71] Flaherty further writes that a homogeneous population with low population density "reinforced the traits of order and stability in community and family life."[72] This is a comparable model of informal law with the English tradition of informal social networks and interconnections governing behavior, especially in smaller communities. In his article "Crime, Law Enforcement, and Social Control in Colonial America," Douglas Greenburg speculated that the efficiency of informal social controls over behavior in Massachusetts aided the efficient operation of the formal law by explicitly linking formal penalties with informal social penalties for violating social norms.[73] Law enforcement was generally efficient in provincial Massachusetts; if a malefactor was "unresponsive to these general modes of social control an efficient system of law enforcement further discouraged deviant behavior," then formal legal sanctions would be employed in order to secure the peace.[74] This is a separation from the general state of English justice, which was certainly expansive but oftentimes inefficient.

Even though Massachusetts was generally free of serious crime, executions still took place. Executions in Massachusetts were public affairs, much like the common practice in England, but the spirit behind and the public reception of the execution was vastly different. An integral part of the Massachusetts execution was the execution sermon. In the execution sermon, a minister "berated condemned criminals of their misconduct, explained how they arrived at so terrible a fate, warned others against similar wickedness, and sought to turn the awful spectacle at the gallows into an occasion for the saving of souls."[75] That gallows were a scene a public theater and an opportunity for the encouragement of righteousness, much like the example of Tyburn in England. However, there is little evidence to suggest that the Massachusetts gallows became a scene of social conflict and disorder. In a strange twist of fate, the sobering effect that was the goal of public capital punishment in England found its most effective expression in Puritan New England.

The English tradition of selectively enforcing capital statutes was also a feature of Massachusetts law. Many sexual crimes that carried the penalty of death were not enforced with any degree of regularity. In his article "Things Fearful to Name: Sodomy and Buggery in Seventeenth-Century New England," Robert F. Oaks writes that "despite the harsh penalties for sodomy and buggery, Puritan leaders often refused to apply them, especially for homosexual activity."[76] In 1636, the colony of Plymouth held the first trials for homosexuality; John Alexander and Thomas Roberts were "found guilty of lude behavior and unclean carriage one with another, by often spending their seede on upon another."[77] Despite clear-cut nature of both the offense and the law, sentence was reduced from execution to whipping and banishment in the case of John Alexander and just whipping and a ban on owning property in the case of Thomas Roberts.[78] Oaks speculates that "Plymouth officials prosecuted with some reluctance" and that law was "meant only as a warning, and no one seriously thought of using it."[79]

The last execution for buggery in Puritan New England was Benjamin Goad in 1673. In his case, he was convicted of committing buggery on a mare on the evidence of one witness and his own retracted confession.[80] While buggery was the stated reason for execution, the Reverend Samuel Danforth conceived of the case in different terms. In his execution sermon, he emphasized "the youth's chronic misconduct had actually forced that hand of public justice."[81] In his framework, the case was not necessarily about the act of buggery itself, but an extended

career of wickedness—including prior offenses of sexual misconduct, as well as charges of Sabbath breaking, lying, and stealing—of which buggery was merely the final act.[82] Although Goad's series of legal troubles was essentially social in nature, open social deviancy could not be ignored by society. Part of the Puritan mindset was the ever-present fear of divine retribution upon the entire community for Goad's actions. Goad's execution, then, was not just an effort to enforce the law, to set an example for the rest of society, or even to uphold social order. There was also a divine audience to the execution.[83]

In practice, most of the capital statutes from the 1648 code were seldom if ever used. In his book *Early American Law and Society*, Stephen Botein wrote that no one was ever executed for the abuse of a parent, despite that law's place in the formal criminal code.[84] Executions for homosexuality and bestiality were also relatively rare, despite the perceived threats that those activities posed to the creation of a holy Puritan state. The selective application of capital punishment in order to encourage morally correct social behavior without recourse to the full weight of the penal code is also a feature of English law. From this perspective, the cases of Benjamin Goad, Thomas Roberts, and John Alexander fulfill the same legal and social function as did the case of Lord Ferrers in England: an example was made for the encouragement of the larger society without causing the social upheaval that would occur if the law was fully enforced.

The close relationship between the law, moral codes, and society in Puritan New England impacted not only the laws that dictated capital punishment, but the justification for executions as well. Justifying an execution, such as the case of Benjamin Goad, in terms of a religious act was an evolution from English practice that justified executions as a sin against that law itself. The audience for the execution pageant was not just the community or other potential malefactors in the audience; the audience was also the Lord, and the execution of Benjamin Goad was as much a statement of public piety as exercised through the law as it was a social legal case.

The use of the legal system as a vehicle of piety forms part of the background of the most infamous exercise of capital punishment in colonial history of Massachusetts: the Salem Witch Trials of 1692. The broad outlines of this event are familiar to most audiences through a host of published works based on the events of that year, such as Arthur Miller's play *The Crucible*. Although the human drama is familiar, the social and political backdrop is much less well known. From the perspective of the law and court structures, the trials were not an evolution or a revolution. All of the legal activities of the trials took place under the law as it existed and through the legal structures as they existed prior to 1692. In her book *In The Devil's Snare*, Mary Beth Norton writes that the visible and invisible worlds were both seen as real.[85] Setbacks in the visible world could often be attributed to the influence of supernatural forces, such as witches. The last quarter of the seventeenth century was a time of crisis for the Massachusetts colony. Indian conflicts such as King Philip's war rocked the colony to its foundations by drawing the special relationship between the Lord and Massachusetts into question.[86] In a worldview that saw the signs of the Lord's displeasure through natural events, the outbreak of a witchcraft crisis in Salem had an incendiary impact on the colony.

In May of 1692, Sir William Phips, the new governor of the colony of Massachusetts, established a court of Oyer and Terminer to manage the spiraling crisis in the town of Salem. According to both English and colonial law, it was a capital offense to use witchcraft to kill, maim, or lame another human being.[87] The first conviction under the court of Oyer and Terminer was Bridget Bishop. Under the standards of evidence for capital trials, it was necessary for there to be two witnesses to the same act of witchcraft. Bishop had been charged with witchcraft for tormenting, torturing, and afflicting six women. Through the evidence of the six women, along with three other villagers, the standards of evidence for a capital conviction had been met.[88] She was subsequently convicted and hung. According to Eve LaPlante's book *Salem Witch Judge*, the conviction of Bridget Bishop was enabled by her poor reputation in town. The tavern that she ran was allowing gambling and was often open after curfew.[89]

It was relatively easy to convict and execute a peripheral member of society such as Bridget Bishop without a serious question being raised about the court or how the court operated. As more and more of the better sort of people were brought before the court, serious questions were raised about the court, particularly concerning the use of spectral evidence. The court allowed the use of spectral evidence, although that sort of evidence had no standing or tradition in common law.[90] In June of 1692, the court asked the opinion of many of the leading clergymen in the colony over the merits of spectral evidence. Their reply expressed support for the goals of the court, but also concern about the interpretation of spectral evidence.[91] This ambiguous response had little immediate impact on the court. The link between religious thought and the law is revealed by the "Return of the Several Ministers." A duly empanelled criminal court was in the position of asking various ministers in the colony to opine on the standards of criminal evidence and the use of evidence in capital trial. The network of ministers functioned as an informal religious court of appeal for the court of Oyer and Terminer.

Much as was the case in England, the will of the people was an important part of the course of justice. LaPlante writes that the courts came to an end not because of a change in the law or a change of heart on the part of the judges. The court came to a close "because the tide of public opinion had turned."[92] Two factors influenced public opinion. The standards of evidence used by the court were severely criticized. The specter of witchcraft had expanded too far to remain socially sustainable. While it was easy for society to suspect a character like Bridget Bishop of witchcraft, society could not support the indefinite expansion of the defendants. One historian wrote that if the trials had lasted much longer, "everybody in the colony except for the magistrates and the ministers would have been charged with witchcraft."[93]

The penal codes of a society reflect the fears of the upper classes of that society. These fears are constructed in the economic and social realities of their place and time. The social efforts to mitigate these fears form the basis of the capital punishment statutes. In late seventeenth- and eighteenth-century England, the control over property was the central conflict in society. As a part of that conflict, the number of capital statutes expanded to an incredible level that, if all of them had been enforced in their totality, would have caused the collapse of civil society. A complex ideological web of mercy, justice, and terror found expression in the legal codes of England. The fears of society in seventeenth-century Massachusetts did not revolve around ideas of property. The prominent fear in this society was moral in nature. The capital statutes were written to help enforce a moral code, rather than to govern access to material goods. The capital statutes were relatively unused in colonial Massachusetts, indicating that an ideology that took a very different view of the value of human life than that of England was common in Massachusetts. While numerous causes have been attributed to the behavior in Salem, the structure of the legal system and its workings are centered in this chapter. Despite the differences in ideology and social conditions, the capital statutes in both England and Massachusetts centered on the same goal: the use of the law to defend against the fears of the upper classes of society in whatever form that fear appeared.

Patrick Callaway is currently completing his Master of Arts degree in history at Montana State University. His research interests include the economy of colonial America in the Atlantic world and the connection between religion and politics in the Early Republic.

Notes

1. Douglas Hay, "Property, Authority and the Criminal Law," in *Albion's Fatal Tree: Crime and Society in Eighteenth-Century England* (New York: Pantheon Books, 1975), 18.
2. Ibid.
3. Ibid., 18–19.
4. Abbot Emerson Smith, *Colonists in Bondage: White Servitude and Convict Labor in America, 1607–1776* (Gloucester: Peter Smith, 1965), 89.
5. Ibid.
6. Wilfrid Prest, *Albion Ascendant: English History, 1660–1815* (Oxford: Oxford University Press, 1998), 202.
7. J. M. Beattie, *Crime and the Courts in England, 1660–1800* (Princeton: Princeton University Press, 1986), 17–18.
8. Ibid., 5.
9. Ibid.
10. Ibid.
11. Prest, 202.
12. Beattie, 5.
13. Ibid., 8.
14. Ibid.
15. Ibid.
16. Hay, 45.
17. Ibid., 46.
18. Ibid., 47.
19. Leon Radzinowicz, *A History of English Criminal Law* (London: Stevens and Sons, 1948), 108.
20. Prest, 202.

21. Radzinowicz, 85.

22. Ibid., 84.

23. Ibid., 51.

24. Ibid.

25. Ibid., 57.

26. E. P. Thompson, *Whigs and Hunters: The Origin of the Black Act* (New York: Pantheon Books, 1975), 23.

27. Ibid., 197.

28. Ibid., 206.

29. Cal Winslow, "Sussex Smugglers," in *Albion's Fatal Tree: Crime and Society in Eighteenth-Century England* (New York: Pantheon Books, 1975), 119.

30. Ibid., 147.

31. Ibid., 131.

32. Ibid., 128–29.

33. Ibid., 130.

34. Ibid., 145.

35. Ibid., 136.

36. Ibid., 166.

37. Hay, 50.

38. Ibid., 31.

39. Winslow, 164.

40. Smith, 116–17.

41. Ibid., 118.

42. Ibid., 117.

43. Peter Linebaugh, *The London Hanged: Crime and Civil Society in the Eighteenth Century* (Cambridge: Cambridge University Press, 1992), 82.

44. Ibid.

45. Ibid.

46. Ibid.

47. Ibid., 78.

48. Ibid.

49. Ibid.

50. Ibid., 53.

51. Smith, 90.

52. Ibid.

53. Radzinowicz, 165.

54. Ibid., 172.

55. Peter Linebaugh, "The Tyburn Riot against Surgeons," in *Albion's Fatal Tree: Crime and Society in Eighteenth-Century England* (New York: Pantheon Books, 1975), 66–7.

56. Smith, 124.

57. Hay, 39.

58. Ibid., 39.

59. Kathryn Preyer, "Penal Measures in the American Colonies: An Overview," *The Journal of American Legal History* 26, no. 4 (October 1982):333.

60. Alden T. Vaughan, ed., *The Puritan Tradition in America, 1620–1730* (Hanover, London: University Press of New England, 1972), 166–67.

61. Preyer, 334.

62. Ibid.

63. Ibid.

64. Peter Hoffer, "Crime and Law Enforcement: The British Colonies," in *Encyclopedia of the North American Colonies*, Volume 1, ed. Jacob Cooke (New York: Charles Scribner's Sons, 1993), 392.

65. Ibid.

66. George Lee Haskins, *Law and Authority in Early Massachusetts: A Study in Tradition and Design* (New York: Macmillan Company, 1960), 33.

67. Anton-Herman Chroust, *The Rise of the Legal Profession in America, Vol. 1: The Colonial Experience* (Norman: University of Oklahoma Press, 1965), 66.

68. Virginia Dejohn Anderson, "British Settlements: New England," in *Encyclopedia of the North American Colonies*, Volume 1, ed. Jacob Cooke (New York: Charles Scribner's Sons, 1993), 160.

69. Chroust, 67.

70. Ibid.

71. Daniel H. Flaherty, "Crime and Social Control in Provincial Massachusetts," *The Historical Journal* 24, no. 2 (June 1981):355.

72. Ibid., 356.

73. Douglas Greenburg, "Crime, Law Enforcement, and Social Control in Colonial America," *The American Journal of Legal History* 26, no. 4 (October 1982):297.

74. Flaherty, 356.

75. Daniel A. Cohen, "In Defense of the Gallows: Justifications of Capital Punishment in New England Execution Sermons, 1674–1825," *American Quarterly* 40, no. 2 (June 1988):148.

76. Robert F. Oaks, "Things Fearful to Name: Sodomy and Buggery in Seventeenth-Century New England," *Journal of Social History* 12, no. 2 (Winter 1978):269.

77. Ibid., 270.

78. Ibid.

79. Ibid.

80. Ibid., 277.

81. Cohen, 150.

82. Ibid.

83. Ibid.

84. Stephen Botein, *Early American Law and Society* (New York: Alfred Knopf, 1983), 26.

85. Mary Beth Norton, *In the Devil's Snare: The Salem Witchcraft Crisis of 1692* (New York: Alfred A. Knopf, 2002), 6.

86. Ibid., 296.

87. Ibid., 200.

88. Ibid., 205.

89. Eve LaPlante, *Salem Court Judge: The Life and Repentance of Samuel Sewall* (New York: Harper, 2007), 153.

90. Ibid., 154.

91. Norton, 213.

92. LaPlante, 175.

93. Ibid., 177.

CHAPTER 4

Murder Most Foul

NATIVE AMERICANS AND THE EVOLUTION OF THE DEATH PENALTY

Vanessa Gunther

THE ISSUE over how to treat native people in the United States was a problem that vexed Europeans since their first attempts at colonization in the sixteenth century. Early settlers who arrived on the shores of what would become America were simultaneously repelled by and curious about the indigenous people they came into contact with. Despite their fascination, however, the assumption of their own cultural superiority colored all interactions between the two groups. Coming from a tradition where life was harsh and short, and transgressions against social norms were punished with unstinting barbarity, it would hardly seem surprising that the early colonists were not paragons of liberalism. The early settlers reflected a culture that sought to impose control, by any means necessary—a trait that they extended not only to their judicial traditions, but to their settlement patterns and interactions with the native people they encountered as well. The decision to endure an arduous journey across the Atlantic to escape privation or persecution did not imbue the settlers with a great deal of empathy for the people they encountered. On the contrary, in America it seemed the more persecuted an individual was in the Old World, the more likely he was to persecute in the new.

The social traditions of the Europeans contrasted sharply with those of the native people of the New World. While each of the more than five hundred estimated native groups in America at the time of contact were uniquely distinct from each other, they also shared many similarities. One of those similarities was a perpetual striving for balance—a balance between members of the tribe, and between the tribe and the world that surrounded it. Since the majority of native people lived in small, interdependent groups, the benefits to be gained from inter- and intratribal cooperation were obvious. Harmonious relations could make life safer, more profitable, and certainly more pleasant. Tribal bands that averaged fifty to a hundred individuals were interdependent on each other for protection and the continuation of their shared culture. The loss of even one individual could negatively impact the survival of the whole group by denying the tribe not only the protection that individual offered, but the goods he or she made or the knowledge of tribal history and custom that he or she held. To deal with these issues, Native Americans developed legal traditions that show a remarkable similarity across all regions in what would become the United States of America. In dealing with what many would consider the most antisocial of crimes—murder—tribes focused not on punishment of the perpetrator, but on restoration of harmony within the tribal group.[1] This does not mean that native people did not value life—quite the opposite was true. Murder was the one crime that could threaten the safety and longevity of the tribal society from within. Dealing with it required the Indians to both exact punishment and maintain social integrity, something the larger European societies at the time seemed unable to comprehend. The early colonists mention this "restorative justice" in their encounters with many of the native groups they dealt with. One such account, which occurred in 1719, dealt with the Dakota people.[2] According to Dakota legal tradition, when a murder occurred the nearest relative(s) of the victim was expected to take revenge. However, this exercise in private justice could have resulted in a perpetual feud among the bands of the Dakota and severely disrupted the harmony within the tribe. To prevent further bloodshed, the elders of the families involved ordered the capture of the murderer and presented him to the victim's family. It was here the victim's family was presented with a choice: kill the offender or settle on a blood price, or compensation for the loss of their family member. A blood price was agreed upon and a feud was avoided.[3] The Dakota were not alone in their treatment of murderers within their tribal groups. However, there were some variations in how strongly tribes viewed the crime of murder. Among the Cheyenne, murder was considered such a heinous crime that it brought shame not only on the criminal, but on the tribe as a whole. Such antisocial behavior resulted in what many Cheyenne considered fair punishment, expulsion from the tribal group for up to five years.[4] To the American mind, such a penalty seems paltry in comparison with the loss of a human life, but we need only consider the actions of Socrates when we judge the importance of communal life among small groups of people.[5] For the Native Americans there truly was a fate worse than death, the shame that the crime of murder brought upon the murderer and his family as well as the entire tribe. For someone who lived within a tight-knit group, the taint of their crime was not one easily erased and sometimes living with the shame was worse than putting the murderer to death. For this reason Native Americans, when faced with a murder within their tribal groups, did not immediately call for revenge. However, penance was demanded and a blood price would be offered to the family of the victim by the family or individual who caused the death. At times respected members of the tribal group would serve as intermediaries and negotiators between the two families. If the blood price was accepted, no further punishment was exacted. However, it was significant for both the victim's family and the murderer's family to come to terms. Any lasting resentment over a price that was too low could fester into discontent and destroy the harmony of the tribal group. The price paid by the murderer's family was not merely the payout in goods to cover the antisocial behavior of one of their members. The loss of the property could literally threaten the survival of the family itself, and negotiations were not taken lightly. This also does not mean that Indians had such little regard for human life that they could easily translate the value of a person into moveable goods. Quite the opposite, while restoration of tribal harmony was important, punishment was based on signs of contrition and the punishment exacted by the offending member was not insignificant.[6] One of the rare instances when the payment of a blood price was rejected comes from the Assiniboine tribe. In the nineteenth century a single murder ignited a "Hatfield and McCoy"–style feud that resulted in a cycle of violence that decimated the respective clans until a smallpox epidemic destroyed the remaining members of one clan and ended the bloodshed.[7]

Since actions of aggression seldom occur out of the blue, and their ramifications were felt beyond the two families involved, many tribes established peacekeepers who assisted in maintaining social harmony. These tribal police often came from particular clans or families and bore the burden of ensuring tribal members did not stray from social norms. The formalization of this practice was most commonly noted among the Plains Indians, although all tribes had respected individuals who served as a governing force within the band.[8] Within the Menominee tribe, warriors who were designated as "pipe holders" were responsible for preventing discord within the tribe from reaching the point of murder. For many tribal groups, the peace pipe was a traditional symbol of peace and diplomacy. The interjection of this powerful symbol by a pipe holder during a heated quarrel had a sobering effect on those involved. Other tribal groups used respected warriors to police the tribe and to ensure social norms were being maintained. Their status among their people as protectors and providers gave these policemen the added respect they needed to exercise their authority during a time of dispute. Despite the best efforts of mankind, even the most advanced societies will one day need to deal with the actions of those who step outside social norms.

To the Indians of North America, murder was a heinous crime, one that disturbed the natural balance of harmony within the tribal group and as such needed to be dealt with harshly. Like the European legal system that would eventually come to dominate the hemisphere, there was no statute of limitations. Despite the seemingly infinite expanses of the American continent, there was no place an individual could escape to in order to avoid punishment. If distance was not sufficient to protect a murderer from his crimes, neither was time. An illustrative case occurred among the Crow Indians in the middle of the nineteenth century. Although the reasons for the murder have been lost, one Crow warrior killed another, after which the murderer abandoned his tribe to escape punishment. For twelve years the Crow warrior avoided contact with his people and resided with the Shoshone Indians. On the supposed belief that time heals all wounds, the Crow warrior returned, whereupon he was recognized and "obliged again to leave." The Crow warrior was never heard from again.[9]

To the European mind the lax punishment imposed on individuals who committed serious crimes made no sense.[10] In the European judicial tradition, the Crow warrior should have been arrested and put to death, not banished from the tribe for life. This cultural misunderstanding came from two fundamentally different judicial traditions and resulted in confusion and prejudice between the Europeans and the Indians. For the Indians of North America, survival was not a singular activity, either within the tribal groups or without. Tribes sought alliances with other like tribes in order to ensure the mutual survival of both groups. These alliances between Indian nations also colored their ardor to seek revenge. If a murderer belonged to a rival tribe, then vengeance was sought. However, if a murder was perpetrated by a member of an allied tribe, then "covering" the death with a blood price was common, just as though the murder had occurred among tribal members.[11] The only difference would be that instead of families negotiating for a blood price, leaders of the tribe would be involved along with the family members. To the Europeans who were unaware of tribal legal traditions, alliances, and obligations, this practice might seem as though someone could literally get away with murder. During the colonial era this native practice came up against the differing worldview of the French. When French trappers killed two members of the Iroquois Nation the Indians presented themselves before the French military commander in charge of the region and demanded restitution for the loss of their men. To the Iroquois, this restitution could be either a blood price, or the victim's family could claim the life of the murderer. Since the French only maintained a small military presence in the region and were dependent on friendly relations with the Indians for the fur trade, the French commander acquiesced to their demands. He arrested five men who had been involved in the altercation, tried and then sentenced them to hang. To prove his fidelity to the Indians, the commander then invited the Iroquois to watch as the men were executed. Once aware of the French commander's intention, the Iroquois pleaded unsuccessfully for the pardoning of three of the men. The Iroquois reasoned that since they had only lost two men in the skirmish, only two of the trappers should pay the price.[12] For the Anglo-Europeans who encountered native forms of law and justice, what seemed to be tolerant attitudes among the Indians toward crime resulted in sound condemnation and helped to seal within the European mind the concept that the Indians were lawless and uncivilized. However, while only anecdotal information exists, it consistently shows that the murder rate among Indians was exceptionally low, especially when compared to European rates. Several American and European writers noted that "murder seldom occurs" among the Indian nations.[13]

In European legal tradition the private justice of the Indians had been replaced with the public justice of an impartial judicial system. While the legal traditions of the various European nations who established settlements in the New World were similar, their response to the Indians they encountered was more nuanced. Among the French a greater degree of cooperation existed between the colonists and the Indians. The same could not be said of the English colonies. After less than twenty years of settlement, the Puritan colonists insisted that Indians conform to the English legal tradition.[14] In 1638, Arthur Peach and three indentured servants came upon an Indian who was returning after successfully trading in Boston. Peach and his cohorts seized the unfortunate man, robbed and stabbed him, and then left him for dead. Despite the best efforts of Peach and his cohorts, the Indian did not die, but lived for the next few days and in that time identified his attackers. Based on this deathbed testimony, Peach and his cohorts were arrested and held over for trial. On 4 September 1638, Peach and his cohorts were convicted of the Indian's murder and eventually hung for the offense. Many of the colonists at the time protested the execution of an Englishman for the murder of an Indian. As with the Iroquois, the Indian sachem, Massasoit, also protested the sentence. Massasoit viewed the trial and execution from a different cultural milieu. The English were his allies, while the Indian who was killed belonged to another tribe. The colonists' decision to execute the four Englishmen for a single Indian was not "worthy" of the crime. In Massasoit's world a price should be paid for the death of the individual but the price demanded by the English judicial system was too high, one that would likely breed discontent and result in further bloodshed. Massasoit was not far wrong in his assessment, as the execution of Peach was strenuously protested by the English colonists. It is possible that the inability of the English colonists to fully appreciate the Indian view of murder may have partially led to the eruption of King Philip's War in 1676. Fourteen years before the war that bore his name erupted across New England, Philip's brother Alexander was ordered to appear before the colonial magistrates to answer to rumors that he was behind a conspiracy to attack the colony. When Alexander did not respond to the rumors or the demand to present himself to the court, he was tracked down and arrested by Major Josiah Winslow.[15] While escorting the sachem to the court, Alexander became ill and died. Philip remained convinced that Winslow had murdered his brother.[16] The ill will that festered between the colonists and the Pokanoket could well have been the type of blood feud that tribal tradition attempted to circumvent with the blood price. To be sure, the colonists often used their courts against whites who victimized the Indians, but equally as obvious is the realization that the Indians were also still fully beholden to their traditional legal system. An example of which would be the case of Nathaniel York who, in 1664, struck an Indian named Obediah. York subsequently "satisfied him (the Indian) by half a bushel of corn, and his fine is left to the town's determination."[17] However, it must have appeared to the Indians that as time passed and the number of colonists grew, their ways and their very lives evoked scant consideration among the colonists.

Before the outbreak of King Philip's War, the colonists had been warned of Philip's plans for war by John Sassamon, a converted Indian.[18] The information, however, was ignored until the body of Sassamon was found floating beneath the ice of Assawompsett Pond. His head and neck were bruised and swollen and, when pulled from the water, no water issued from his mouth. According to white authorities, Sassamon had been murdered and they demanded Philip come before the court to answer questions. Philip, by now a sachem in his own right, as his father and brother had been before him, denied any involvement in Sassamon's death and insisted that this was a matter outside the jurisdiction of the colonial court. His response was fully in keeping with the tradition of his tribe, which would have had the members of the families involved—not nonrelated individuals—gathering to iron out a solution.[19] When it seemed as though the case would go nowhere, an Indian named Patuckson appeared and claimed to have been hiding in the woods just as the murder occurred. He insisted he witnessed three Indians coming upon Sassamon

as he fished in the pond and that they eventually killed him. One of these men was Tobias, a senior counselor to King Philip. According to English law at the time, in order to convict an individual of murder, the testimony of two witnesses was needed. The singularity of Patuckson's testimony, however, did not dissuade the colonial authorities. Tobias, his son, and another Indian were arrested and charged with murder. The case proceeded with eight English judges, twelve English and six praying Indian jurors.[20] This overwhelming display of authority was one way of reiterating to the Indians that they would be subject to the authority of the Europeans who ironically enough they had helped to establish on their lands only a few years previously.[21] Despite the fact that the case violated the laws of the colony because only one witness was available, the three men were found guilty and two were hung on 8 June 1675.[22] The hanging of Philip's trusted advisor and friend further damaged Indian/white relations on several levels. It openly challenged the authority of the sachem (Philip), denied the Indians redress through their traditional customs, and asserted the dominance of the Anglo-Europeans in the region, at the expense of the tribal culture. Other factors that most assuredly impacted the growing hostility between the colonists and the Indians included the usurpation of the land's natural resources by the colonists and the colonial habit of taking Indian lands. The puzzle is not that the colonists and the Pokanoket went to war, but what took them so long.

As Europeans continued to migrate to the Americas, their presence pushed the tribes that had once occupied the coastal lands farther into the interior where wars erupted between once friendly tribal groups. The warring over the ever-shrinking natural resources was made easier for the Europeans by the introduction of disease. In some cases tribes that had once flourished were decimated or completely destroyed by diseases brought over from Europe. The allied tribes in Massachusetts who greeted the Puritans in 1620 had recently lost as much as 90 percent of their population because of what many believe was a smallpox outbreak left behind by earlier explorers.[23] As Indians became a minority within their own lands, the growing dominance of European legal traditions filtered into their lives. However, the interest among Anglo-Europeans was less in the introduction of what Europeans may have considered a superior legal tradition, than in exacting punishment when the two cultures collided. In most instances when only Indians were involved, Anglo-Europeans were content to let the tribes handle their own affairs. This tradition extended beyond the forests of the East and well into the territories of the trans-Mississippi West. As the nation evolved from a colony of Great Britain into an independent nation with its own peculiar identity, little changed in the attitudes Anglo-Europeans held toward the Indians.[24]

As the new American nation entered into its independence, the issue of regulating interactions between tribal groups and U.S. citizens took on several forms. Because the new government was weak and ill-equipped to fight the Indians for legal and territorial concessions, treaties became the dominant way in which the fledgling nation and native peoples established judicial boundaries. Under the Articles of Confederation, the colonists were already following in the well-trod path of the British by establishing treaty agreements with the Indians. In the Wyandot Treaty of 1785, the new government asserted that if any person attempted to "settle on the lands allotted to the Windot and Delaware . . . such person shall forfeit the protection of the United States, and the Indians may punish him as they please." However, if any Indian committed a murder or robbery on a citizen of the United States, the tribe was to deliver up that individual for punishment.[25] This reciprocal treaty, while it granted some respect to

the Indians and their sovereignty, would be short-lived. The limitations of the Articles of Confederation and its inability to address the massive number of problems faced by the new nation led to the adoption of the Constitution in 1789, and a series of federal laws and treaties to regulate relations between the Americans and the Indian nations.[26] The 1790 Act to Regulate Trade and Intercourse with the Indian Tribes stated that

> if any citizen or inhabitant of the United States, or of either of the territorial districts of the United States, shall go into any town, settlement or territory belonging to any nation or tribe of Indians, and shall there commit any crime upon, or trespass against, the person or property of any peaceable and friendly Indian or Indians, which, if committed within the jurisdiction of any state, or within the jurisdiction of either of the said districts, against a citizen or white inhabitant thereof, would be punishable by the laws of such state or district, such offender or offenders shall be subject to the same punishment, and shall be proceeded against in the same manner as if the offence had been committed within the jurisdiction of the state or district to which he or they may belong, against a citizen or white inhabitant thereof.[27]

The Trade and Intercourse Act clearly stated that the laws of the nation would exceed those of the Indians when it came to American citizens on Indian land. Indian-on-Indian crime merited no mention in the act. The Trade and Intercourse Act would be renewed by the U.S. Congress every two years until it was made permanent in 1802. However, the permanency of the act did not mean that it was stagnant. In 1817 another Trade and Intercourse Act was passed that established federal jurisdiction over Indians and non-Indians alike who committed federal crimes in Indian territory.[28] The act still recognized the preeminence of tribal law for Indians who committed crimes within their own cultural group. However, with the flourish of a pen Indians who committed crimes against whites or violated federal laws now found themselves under the jurisdiction of the new nation. The extraterritoriality of this act provided a great deal of protection for Anglos within Indian country, but virtually none for the Indians. While the practical application of this act would take years to recognize in some regions, the massive expansion of the nation at the beginning of the nineteenth century and the constant challenge for lands made conflict inevitable. In 1834 a final Trade and Intercourse Act was passed. In this act the 1817 act was repealed and a more restrictive law was applied to the Indian tribes.[29] Under the 1834 act, the laws of the United States extended into Indian territory, but only when a white man was involved. Indian-on-Indian crime would be dealt with by the tribes.[30] In the congressional report that accompanied the 1834 act, the United States government noted that "it is rather of courtesy than right that we undertake to punish crimes committed in that territory by and against our citizens."[31] While the government recognized the limitations of the new government to extend its laws over the Indian nations, clearly the legislators believed the laws of the nation to be superior to those of the Indians. By the early national period, Indians were frequently seen as the "miserable remnant of a broken race given up to all sorts of degradations."[32] Such a "degraded" people were often not considered human, let alone civilized enough to have developed a legal tradition that rivaled the European traditions.

An unfortunate case that illustrates the brewing conflict between the judicial traditions of the Anglo-Europeans and the Indians can be found in a murder committed within the Cherokee Nation and by a member of the Cherokee tribe. Under Cherokee legal tradition, murder was a very personal affair. Demands for redress for the crime, as with other tribes, came from within the clan to which the victim belonged. According to historian John Philip Reid, "Vengeance is the right of the victim's clan—a privileged act which evens the score and cannot be revenged." The difference between the Cherokee domestic and international law for homicide was that when an individual from outside the tribe was killed—either intentionally or unintentionally—the result was usually war.[33] When a Cherokee was murdered either from within or without, the clan or tribe was owed another life. While the clan could demand a life for a life, it was not a requirement. However, if the murderer fled from the tribe after the commission of his crime, another member of his clan would be held accountable for his actions. This unique feature within Cherokee law kept even the most cowardly murderers from fleeing and burdening their clans with payment for their actions. The Cherokee recognized the increasing threat presented by the incursion of Americans into their territory early on, and attempted to assimilate as much as possible to the dominant Anglo-European culture without sacrificing the significant elements of their traditional culture. To that end the Cherokee clans united in 1839 and produced a written constitution to protect their laws and customs.[34] The Cherokee patterned their constitution and their government on the United States government, creating three branches of government, executive, legislative, and judicial. The legislative branch was composed of the National Committee and the tribal Council, and courts were established which mirrored the federal courts of the day. One of the first cases heard by the newly organized Cherokee courts was for the murder of John MacIntosh by Archilla Smith in the fall of 1839. Since both men were members of the Cherokee nation there was no struggle over jurisdiction in the case. According to court proceedings as recorded by

John Howard Payne, Smith, long associated with robbery and mayhem within the region, was accused of stabbing John MacIntosh following a dispute over MacIntosh's rowdy behavior. In the trial that ensued, the privileged position of the clan to seek justice was replaced by a jury. In the end Smith was found guilty and sentenced to hang, despite attempts by Smith's supporters to have the principal chief, John Ross, intercede and grant him a pardon. Smith was hung the first week of January 1841.[35]

To the mind of the dominant society, white individuals within Indian territory were entitled to the protection of American law; Indians, however, were not granted this same privilege when in Anglo territory. Nor did it extend to Anglos who voluntarily abandoned the American culture and wholly adopted native culture. The 1846 case of *U.S. vs. William Rogers* exemplifies this point. For a decade William S. Rogers had lived, married, and raised children within the customs of the Cherokee people and on their designated reservation. His tenure with the tribe had earned him the distinction of being a member of the tribe with full rights and privileges. He retained those privileges even after his wife died in September 1843. However, in 1845 Rogers became involved in a dispute with another white man, Jacob Nicholson, who "although a native-born free white male citizen of the United States, had settled in the tract of country assigned to said Cherokee tribe of Indians west of the State of Arkansas, without any intention of returning to said United States; that he intermarried with an Indian Cherokee woman, according to the Cherokee form of marriage; that he was treated, recognized, and adopted by the said tribe as one of them, and entitled to exercise, and did exercise, all the rights and privileges of a Cherokee Indian," Rogers and Nicholson's dispute resulted in the death of Nicholson and Rogers was brought before the white authorities and charged with murder. Rogers challenged the jurisdiction of the federal courts to try him as he was no longer a citizen of the United States. In a decision written by Chief Justice Roger Taney, the U.S. Supreme Court ruled that jurisdiction for the case lay in the federal courts since the crime involved two white men and that any punishment confirmed by those courts would be binding.[36] For William Rogers, his petition to have his case determined within the traditions of the Cherokee people was preferable to the near certain death he would face within the American courts. It should be noted that Rogers did not deny his involvement in the murder, nor did he seek to escape punishment. Both of these were attributes that were valued among the Cherokee and which had been culturally instituted in order to prevent the innocent from suffering for the crimes of the guilty. The American system offered an avenue for the guilty to escape responsibility for their actions. The issues that surrounded the jurisprudence of the Cherokee Nation, and their attempts to accommodate the traditions of the Anglo-European culture to their own, proved to be impossible in the aftermath of the Cherokee Removal in 1838.[37] The two Cherokee factions, which eventually reunited in Indian Country in 1839 following what became known as the Trail of Tears, greeted each other with such hostility that thirty-three murders occurred from 1 November 1844 to 28 August 1845 according to the Indian agent, John McKissick. Most of these murders went unpunished by the courts and the old traditions of vengeance began to rear up. In order to control the rapidly deteriorating situation, the United States government invited the two factions to Washington in 1846 and a new treaty was approved. Within this treaty the laws of the Cherokee would hold sway over all their people and those on their reservation lands.[38] Eventually this treaty would be called into court when an Indian stood accused of murdering a white man who had been adopted into the tribe. The federal district court ruled in *U.S. v. Ragsland* that the murder was "fully and absolutely pardoned."[39]

As the space between the Indians and the Americans dwindled as a result of westward expansion, the forced intimacy did not result in greater cultural understanding. As the dominant cultural group, Americans viewed the traditions of the Indians with increasing contempt. In 1854, the popular concept of the Indian as a lawless savage compelled Congress to ameliorate relations between Indians and settlers on the far-flung frontier with the General Crimes Act. The act "removed from the jurisdiction of the federal courts the offenses committed by Indians against non-Indians in Indian Country" who had been punished by the local law of the tribe.[40] The only exceptions to this act were the crimes of arson and assault with intent to maim or kill—crimes which could impact the growth and safety of the burgeoning white communities. The General Crimes Act proved to be ineffective in curbing the growing animosity between Indians and whites on the frontier, and for the next thirty years Congress attempted to regulate interaction between the differing national groups by occasionally amending its previous acts.[41] However, while the nation extended its laws over the nation, even into areas controlled by the Indians, it still excluded Indians who committed crimes against Indians from punishment under American law. All this would change in 1881.

On 5 August 1881, the Brule Sioux warrior Crow Dog shot and killed another Brule Sioux chief named Spotted Tail on the Sioux Reservation in Dakota Territory. In order to prevent a blood feud from erupting, a council meeting was called and the respective families were encouraged to negotiate for a mutually acceptable price for the family of Crow Dog to pay to the family of Spotted Tail. The price was six hundred dollars in cash, eight horses, and one blanket. Satisfied with the price, both families allowed the issue to

fall behind them and peaceful relations returned to the Sioux Reservation.[42] The facts of the case were never in dispute as Crow Dog never denied his actions. Bad blood had existed between the two men over public and personal matters for many years. The more assimilated Spotted Tail had often served as a buffer between the growing white community and the Sioux Indians. He counseled peaceful relations and had proven to be among the most supportive of the Indian agents who worked on the reservation. As a reward for his support of the Indian agents, and by extension the dominant white culture, Spotted Tail had been rewarded with a new home and had begun to extend his authority within the tribe to included previously taboo areas, like assuming the right to wives of other tribal chiefs. For the more traditional Sioux, Spotted Tail was little better than a collaborator who willingly sold out his people and his culture for his own pleasure and enrichment.[43] When the Anglo community learned of the death of Spotted Tail, and that Crow Dog had seemingly escaped punishment, they responded with outrage. The treatment of the murderer of Spotted Tail was proof in the eyes of the white community of the backward, savage nature of the Indian and served as a clarion call for greater accordance within the tribes to the legal mores that had been established by the white community. The result of the friction was a technical disregard for America's Common Law principle of double jeopardy, when Crow Dog was ordered to be tried for Spotted Tail's murder in a territorial court.[44] Crow Dog was convicted of the murder of Spotted Tail in 1883, but challenged his conviction to the Supreme Court and was later released as the territorial court, and for that matter any white court, had no jurisdiction over the tribes within the borders of the United States. The uproar among the members of the white community eventually resulted in the passage of the Major Crimes Act in 1885.[45] The Major

Crimes Act established seven crimes that would be removed from the jurisdiction of the tribes and would instead be tried in the federal courts.[46] The list of crimes would be extended over the years, slowly eroding any claims of sovereignty the tribes once claimed. The Major Crimes Act serves several functions here, to exemplify the different views toward murder among the indigenous tribes in America and the Anglo-European community. Additionally, the case serves to elucidate how one culture impacts the traditions of another. The native challenge to the Major Crimes Act would come within the same year of its passage. In August, Kagama, and his accomplice Mahawaha, were arrested and charged with the murder of another Indian, Iyouse, on the Hoopa Valley Indian Reservation in California. Kagama and Mahawaha argued that the laws of the United States did not apply to Indians on Indian reservations and subsequently that they should be punished in accordance with tribal tradition, not American law. The Supreme Court determined that "[t]he power of the general government over these remnants of a race once powerful, now weak and diminished in numbers, is necessary to their protection, as well as to the safety of those among whom they dwell."[47] As such, the ultimate authority in the nation resided with the federal government, under the terms of the Major Crimes Act, and the Kagama case, while an abrupt transition, clarified without question where tribal jurisprudence stood in relation to American law, especially in regard to cases of murder.

The settlement patterns of Anglo-Europeans within the boundaries of the United States were uneven from the inception of the nation. While the traditions of the common law of England held sway in the East and Midwest, the legal traditions of Spain dominated the lands along the western coast. However, despite the differences in the European legal traditions, the legal traditions among the Indians remained relatively constant. The ideal of social and environmental harmony was no different among the Indians of the West. In the event of a murder the offending individual was expected to show remorse for his actions. However, this did not exempt him (or his family) from the payment of a blood price. As with the eastern tribes, it was in the interest of the tribal group as a whole to ensure the peaceful resolution of the crisis. A blood feud would have destroyed the fragile harmony that existed within the social group and potentially ruined the tribe's chance for survival.[48] Negotiators were used to help the two families come to terms and settle the matter. For this they were often paid a token fee for their efforts. However, if an individual was killed by a member of a rival group the actions would result in war.[49] The exception to the blood price for murder occurred when an individual, usually a shaman, was considered to be evil and whose presence or spells had brought privation or disease to the tribe. In this case the tribe was responsible for the assassination of the individual and no blood price was paid. The tradition of putting to death individuals considered to be witches occurred in dramatic fashion when Narcissa Whitman, the nineteenth-century missionary, was murdered by the Cayuse Indians when she and other white missionaries were suspected of practicing witchcraft.[50] As the Indians of the Pacific Coast encountered the Spanish culture, a gradual change in how a tribe viewed and punished murder began to change. As the mission system came to dominate, not only the early economy, but the very lives of the Indians within the mission system, they developed tribal traditions that, like the eastern tribes, began to mirror those of the Spanish and later the Americans. An oration by the Cahuilla chief Juan Antonio to the American authorities in 1861 exemplifies the transition that occurred in California. Sadly, the words of Juan Antonio echo similar sentiments the Cherokee expressed thirty years earlier when they attempted to maintain their cultural integrity by creating their own tribal constitution.

> I come not here as a child to play, but as an old grey-haired chief to transact business and talk with the white man. I come because my people asked me; they sent for me. I was far away from my village when they came and told me that murders were being charged upon my people. I took some of my old men who do not steal and murder, and came a long way to meet you. On our way we caught an Indian who murdered a Sonorian named Antonio. But we being few in number, last night he made his escape. But my Indians are on his trail, and he cannot escape if he remains in Indian country. He is a bad Indian and should be hung. I am an American—my people are all Americans, although we are Indians. . . . He alone should be punished who murders and steals. . . . Now I want when one of my people commits a crime, to have him punished. I will deliver up any white man who commits crime to be dealt with by his people, and I wish to punish my people my own way. If they deserve hanging I will hang them. If a white man deserves hanging, let the white men hang him.[51]

By the end of the nineteenth century the traditions that had governed the behavior of Indians across the continent in regard to punishment for murder had begun to change radically. As the American nation continued to unify culturally from two distinct eastern and western regions, the native people caught in the middle of this transition continued to fair poorly. The passage of the Major Crimes Act in 1885 and the Kagama decision in 1886 sounded the death knell for an independent Indian judicial.[52] After the passage of the disastrous Dawes Allotment Act of 1887, Indian culture and tradition were relegated to the trash heap of history by the dominant American society. Children were often taken from their parents and enrolled in government-run schools that diligently erased any evidence of their cultural uniqueness.[53] Those children, indoctrinated into the dominant culture (although not as equals), lost their appreciation for the culture of their ancestors. It would not be until the Indian Reorganization Act was passed in 1934 and later the Indian Rights Movement of the 1960s that Indians would begin to recognize all they had lost and attempt to reassert their tribal authority over their members. The Indian Civil Rights Act of 1968 attempted to increase the sovereign rights of tribes, but only superficially. It limited their ability to regulate activities on tribal land to misdemeanors and established guarantees for petitioners.[54] While this has resulted in the establishment of numerous tribal courts and a greater attempt to exercise sovereignty over their lands, American Indian tribes are still denied the full ability to govern their members in accordance with their traditions. This inability has also prevented the tribal governments from exercising their sovereign rights over their lands.

In March 1984 Albert Duro, a Torres Martinez Desert Cahuilla Indian, moved in with his common-law wife on the Pima-Maricopa Indian Reservation near Scottsdale, Arizona. Duro worked for the tribe's construction company from March until June of that year, but remained enrolled as a member of the Torres Martinez Cahuilla tribe. On June 15, Duro shot and killed a fourteen-year-old boy from the Gila River Indian tribe on the Pima-Maricopa Reservation. Duro was arrested by federal authorities and charged in district court with murder and aiding and abetting, but the U.S. Attorney later dismissed the case without prejudice. Once released from federal custody, the Pima-Maricopa tribe arrested Duro but because their authority was limited to misdemeanor offenses, Duro was charged with the illegal discharge of a firearm. Duro challenged his arrest due to a lack of jurisdiction on the part of the Pima-Maricopa tribe. In deciding the case in 1989 the Supreme Court ruled that "Indians like all other citizens share allegiance to the overriding sovereign, the United States. A tribe's additional authority comes from the consent of its members, and so in the criminal sphere membership marks the bounds of tribal authority."[55] Duro was not subject to the authority of the Pima-Maricopa tribe despite his actions on their reservation.[56]

While the Indian tribes in America have slowly been forced to bend to the authority of the United States government, murder still remains the one crime in which they are capable of exercising some control. Under a special provision of the 1998 Federal Death Penalty Act, it is up to the individual tribes to choose whether they want to "opt in" to capital punishment.[57]

The decision to put an individual to death for the commission of an offence considered to be so heinous that to allow that person to live would be an affront to the very existence of that society is one that has occupied civilized societies since people first banded together in social groups. The punishment itself forces the society to adopt the very same antisocial behavior assumed by the criminal. The decision of any society to take the life of an individual is fraught with problems, as the action deprives the condemned of their very existence, forfeiting any chance of reprieve, pardon, or rehabilitation, while also denying these things to the society as well. The debate over the death penalty draws its support and its detractors largely from the same Judeo-Christian camp.

As such, the death penalty has resulted in fierce national debates within civilized nations up to the present day. Yet without punishment for crime, societies would break down and be lost amid the ensuing chaos. While the debate over the ultimate punishment has been reconciled as too gruesome a punishment by most western nations, America remains one of the few holdouts in administering this punishment. Criticism over whether the death penalty tradition in American jurisprudence has had an impact on crime overall remains to be seen. However, it has had a marked impact on the lives of Native Americans. According to the U.S. Bureau of Justice Statistics, from "1976 to 2001 an estimated 3,738 American Indians were murdered. Among American Indians age 25 to 34, the rate of violent crime victimizations was more than 2 1/2 times the rate for all persons the same age. Rates of violent victimization for both males and females were higher for American Indians than for all races."[58] Such statistics bring to question whether the western judicial system could have benefited from learning from the very groups they once considered to be savage.

Vanessa Ann Gunther holds a Ph.D. from the University of California, Riverside, and is the author of *Ambiguous Justice: Native Americans and the Law in Southern California, 1848–1890* (East Lansing: Michigan State University Press, 2006). She teaches at Chapman University in Orange, California.

Suggested Readings

Calloway, Colin C. *New Worlds for All: Indians, Europeans and the Remaking of Early America*. Baltimore: Johns Hopkins University Press, 1997.

Cawley, Jared B. "Just When You Thought It Was Safe to Go Back to the Rez: Is It Safe?" *Cleveland State Law Review*, 52 Clev. St. L. Rev 413 (2004/2005) 413–40.

Greenberg, Douglas. "Crime, Law Enforcement and Social Control in Colonial America." *The American Journal of Legal History* 26, no. 4 (Oct 1982):293–325.

James, Harry C. *The Cahuilla Indians*. San Bernardino: Malki Museum Press, 1995.

Lujan, Carol Chiago, and Adams, Gordon. "US Colonization

of Indian Justice Systems: A Brief History." *Wicazo Sa Review* 19.2 (2004):9–23.

MacLeod, William Christie. "Police and Punishment among Native Americans of the Plains." *Journal of Criminal Law and Criminology* 28, no. 2 (Jul–Aug 1937):181–201.

Mooney, James. *The Ghost Dance Religion and the Sioux Outbreak of 1890.* Lincoln: University of Nebraska/Bison Books, 1991.

Payne, John Howard. *Indian Justice: A Cherokee Murder Trial at Tahlequah in 1840.* Norman: University of Oklahoma Press, 2002.

Philbrick, Nathaniel. *Mayflower: A Story of Courage, Community and War.* New York: Viking Press, 2006.

Reid, John Philip. "A Perilous Rule: The Law of International Homicide." In *The Cherokee Indian Nation: A Troubled History*, ed. Duane H. King, 33–45. Knoxville: University of Tennessee Press, 1979.

Rotenberg, Daniel L. "Special Issues and Topics: American Indian Tribal Death—A Centennial Remembrance," *University of Miami Law Review*, 41 U. Miami L. Rev. 409 (Dec 1986).

Sears, Louis Martin. "The Puritan and His Indian Ward." *The American Journal of Sociology* 22, no. 1 (July 1916): 80–93.

Notes

1. Restorative justice, with its intent to restore the harmony of the social group and return to social norms, is easily contrasted with the punitive justice common at the time which called for sometimes extremely harsh punishment for relatively minor infractions of social norms. In punitive justice an individual is separated from society, a condition which has often been seen to encourage further antisocial behavior among some individuals. One need only look at the U.S. Department of Justice recidivism statistics which for criminals released in 1994 (the last year for which statistics are available) show 67.5 percent of criminals in a fifteen-state study were returned to prison within three years. See *Bureau of Justice Statistics*, "Reentry Trends in the US," (2002). In comparison, Carol Chiago Lujan and Gordon Adams noted that between 1835 and 1879 only sixteen murders occurred among the Cheyenne. See Lujan and Adams, "US Colonization of Indian Justice Systems: A Brief History," *Wicazo Sa Review* 19.2 (2004):9.

2. In 1719, the Dakota Indians had not yet moved from their woodland homes into the Great Plains.

3. William Christie MacLeod, "Police and Punishment among Native Americans of the Plains," *Journal of Criminal Law and Criminology* 28, no. 2 (Jul–Aug 1937):197–98.

4. The practice of banishment from the tribe was not unique to the Cheyenne; many other Plains tribes including the Omaha and Ponca shared the same tradition. For the Cheyenne this appeared to be the punishment of choice, while other tribes considered the nature of the murder itself, whether intentional or unintentional, in making decisions for banishment. For those tribes, banishment might still be resorted to, but only for a limited period of time. MacLeod, 196.

5. After being accused and convicted of corrupting the minds of the youth of Athens, Socrates was sentenced to die by drinking poison. Despite being presented with the opportunity to escape his prison, Socrates chose instead to stay and suffer his punishment. While the reasons for his choice have been expounded upon for ages, one chief reason was that death was preferable to abandonment of his cultural group. According to Vine Deloria and Clifford Lytle, "banishment, not execution, was regarded as the most serious punishment since an individual without a community or relatives literally did not exist as a human being for many groups." See Deloria and Lytle, *American Indians, American Justice* (Austin: University of Texas Press, 1983), 162.

6. In a murder involving a Crow Indian man who killed a boy, historian William Christie MacLeod writes that the murderer "chopped off his own fingers, gashed his own legs, and cut off his own hair." In addition to these acts of contrition, the murderer's family also gave property to the victim's family. See MacLeod, 194.

7. MacLeod, 199. Before the smallpox epidemic one of the clans had been reduced to only two members. One can hardly believe that a single act of violence could have resulted in the systematic annihilation of an entire family group. The Hatfield and McCoy feud, which has become an iconic image of a blood feud, occurred in the late nineteenth century along the border between Kentucky and West Virginia. The initial reason for the feud is unknown, although many believe it started in 1873 when Floyd Hatfield and Randolph McCoy both claimed ownership of the same hog. McCoy lost his petition in court and the feud was on. For almost the next two decades more than a dozen members of both families were killed. By 1891, with several family members sentenced to hang or serve life terms in prison for murder, the families finally agreed to end the feud.

8. The Plains Indians, while not a culturally distinct group, did share many cultural similarities. These tribal groups would include the Crow, Ojibway, Cree, Dakota, Cheyenne, Omaha, Shoshone, Arikara, and Kiowa, to name

but a few. Within these tribes the tradition of blood revenge was still practiced.

9. MacLeod, 194.

10. It should be noted that among Anglo-European tradition an individual could still be executed for stealing or for a host of other relatively minor offenses well into the nineteenth century.

11. Colin C. Calloway, *New Worlds for All: Indians, Europeans and the Remaking of Early America* (Baltimore: Johns Hopkins University Press, 1997), 118.

12. Deloria and Lytle, 162–63. In accordance with Iroquois tradition, the French trappers (and by extension the French) had refused to pay a blood price for the warriors they had killed. Without restitution, the only solution was the execution of the guilty party.

13. MacLeod, 195.

14. Twice during the thirty years he served as governor of the Plymouth colony, the colonists attacked the Indians they perceived as being a threat to the colony itself. That said, under the direction of Bradford, recalcitrant colonists who murdered Indians were held to account. However, there is enough evidence to suggest that this occurred because the individual was disruptive to the colony as a whole, not because of his offense against the Indians. Nor were the Puritans so convinced of their own superiority that they were comfortable in assessing and insisting upon punishment alone. In the Pequot War of 1637, the Puritans ordered the death of Canonchet, but ensured that the Indian groups that had supported them in the conflict also took part in the murder.

15. Oddly enough, Winslow's father, Edward, had once been credited with saving the life of Massasoit, the father of Alexander and Philip. Alexander is also known by his Indian name Wamsutta and Philip is known as Metacom. For a highly readable text on the early Plymouth Colony, see Nathaniel Philbrick, *Mayflower: A Story of Courage, Community and War* (New York: Viking Press, 2006).

16. Philip's belief that his brother had been poisoned by Josiah Winslow is often cited as one of the leading causes of the war that bears his name. Since Winslow never admitted to the murder or offered compensation for Alexander's death, Philip believed justice had been denied his brother. Within Indian tradition, it was his right as the nearest relative to retaliate against those who had caused his brother's death.

17. Louis Martin Sears, "The Puritan and His Indian Ward," *The American Journal of Sociology* 22, no. 1 (July 1916): 85.

18. The story of John Sassamon exemplifies the distrust and conflict that developed between the Indians and the colonists in New England. Sassamon was likely adopted by a Puritan family as a child and subsequently learned to speak and read in English. He later converted to Christianity and briefly attended Harvard College. During his lifetime Sassamon was a man who proved to be of incalculable value to both the Indians and the Puritans because of his linguistic skills. However, the tightrope he walked between each culture prevented him from fully devoting himself to either group and as a result he was not fully trusted by either group.

19. While a blood price was paid by the respective families, it should also be noted that respected members of the tribes would also be used to facilitate discussions (and resolutions) in order to maintain peace within the group.

20. A praying Indian was one who had converted to Christianity. Generally they lived apart from their tribes in what became known as praying towns and allied themselves with the settlers.

21. The importance of the assistance meted out by various Indians and tribes to Euro-Americans cannot be understated. Without the expertise, protection, and guidance of the native groups in America, the chance of survival in the strange new world of the western hemisphere would have been significantly reduced. Individuals like Tisqunatum (Squanto) of the Patuxet tribe, Matoaka (Pocahontas) of the Powhatan Confederacy, and Sacagawea of the Shoshone are all examples of the largess displayed by the native people of the land. There is a sad irony that their generosity and humanity would often be repaid with greed, murder, and theft.

22. Philbrick, 220–23. Of the three Indians convicted that day, only two were hung. The third was the son of Tobias, and by design or divine intervention, his rope snapped as he fell through the gallows and he was spared the hanging. Confused and frightened, he confessed that indeed his father had killed Sassamon. This confession was not enough to save his life. A month later as King Philip's War erupted across the land, he was taken from his cell and shot to death by colonists. None were ever brought to trial for the murder.

23. When disease followed the appearance of Europeans, tribes, not understanding the transmission of disease, often looked upon these strangers as witches who had cursed their people. For native people, witchcraft was one of the few incidents of murder that could be justified as the individual was a reprobate.

24. The government of Great Britain largely regulated its intercourse with the native people of the Americas through individual treaty agreements that regarded the tribes as sovereign entities. These treaties, like the treaties that would be entered into by the United States, were frequently ignored, amended, or upheld when convenient. England's willingness to enter into treaties with the Indians is often seen as the mark of a progressive nation. However, the limited time that England had in the colonies (after 150 years British colonies had still only advanced to the Appalachian Mountains) and thus their impact on the interior tribes had not been fully

realized yet. Given more time as a colonial power there is little doubt that England would have proven herself to have shared many of the same attitudes as her former subjects.

25. Vine Deloria and Clifford M. Lytle, *American Indians, American Justice* (Austin: University of Texas Press, 1983), 164. The Wyandot Treaty is significant in the evolution of criminal jurisdiction between the United States and the Indian tribes. It is the first instance in which the government recognized the rights of the tribes.

26. As America became independent many of its citizens engaged in what can only be termed rapacious and dishonest relations with the Indians. A series of treaties forced land concessions from tribes or at times included tribes that were not present during the treaty negotiations. These treaties led to a sharp decline in the relations between the new government and the Indians. Had the states been allowed to continue, the situation would have devolved into an all-out war between the former colonists and the Indian nations. The new nation was ill-equipped to fight a war from within and this partially prompted the establishment of the Constitution.

27. An Act to Regulate Trade and Intercourse with the Indian Tribes, Section 5 (22 July 1790).

28. An Act to Regulate Trade and Intercourse, March 3, 1817, ch. 92, 3 Stat. 383.

29. Daniel L. Rotenberg, "Special Issues and Topics: American Indian Tribal Death—A Centennial Remembrance," *University of Miami Law Review*, 41 U. Miami L. Rev. 409 (Dec 1986), 412.

30. The Intercourse Act, 30 June 1834. ch. 161, § 29, 4 Stat. 734.

31. Deloria and Lytle, 166.

32. John Howard Payne, *Indian Justice: A Cherokee Murder Trial at Tahlequah in 1840* (Norman: University of Oklahoma Press, 2002), xxi. John Payne would become one of the most sympathetic American supporters of Indians and their traditions following his exposure to their culture in the early national period.

33. John Philip Reid, "A Perilous Rule: The Law of International Homicide," in *The Cherokee Indian Nation: A Troubled History*, ed. Duane H. King (Knoxville: University of Tennessee, 1979), 34.

34. The eastern Cherokee had codified their laws as early as 1808, but their effect was not globally applied to all the Cherokee clans until the tribe wrote its formal constitution in 1839.

35. Payne, 91–93.

36. *U.S. v. Rogers*, 45 U.S. (4 How.) 567 (1846).

37. The Cherokee Indians had once occupied lands in the American Southeast, in present-day Georgia. However, as the white population increased in the region, challenges over ownership of the land were fought within the state and in the courts. The eventual result was the dispossession of the majority of the Cherokee Indians.

While some of the bands determined to stay and fight for their traditional lands, several of the bands abandoned their claims to the land and moved to Indian Country. For a thorough discussion of the events and the legal issues surrounding the dispossession of the Cherokee, see Lindsay G. Robertson, *Conquest by Law*, New York: Oxford, 2006.

38. While the Cherokee would struggle to maintain control over their nation and their unique status in a rapidly changing America, the tribal courts they established in the early nineteenth century would be all but abandoned following the Dawes Allotment Act (1887) and Curtis Act (1898), which divested the Indians of their land and proved to be an equally devastating threat to the culture of the Cherokee and other tribes.

39. *U.S. v. Ragsland*, Hemp. 497.

40. Deloria and Lytle, 167.

41. General Crimes Act (Federal Enclaves Act), 18 U.S.C. § 1152. The General Crimes Act established federal jurisdiction over more than a dozen crimes. If an Indian while in Indian Country violated federal law against a non-Indian, he could be tried in federal court. However, the act did not extend to Indian-on-Indian crime. Those offenses were still dealt with by the tribes.

42. *Ex Parte Crow Dog*, 109 U.S. 556, 3 S.Ct. 396, 27 L. Ed. 1030 (1883).

43. Deloria and Lytle, 168.

44. Since the Constitution prevents an individual from being tried twice for the same crime, Crow Dog's willingness to submit himself to American authorities when the issue had already been settled by tribal authorities resulted in his being judged twice for the same crime. Had the white authorities had their way, Crow Dog would have also paid twice for his crime, first with the blood price settled by the respective families and second by his conviction and sentence to die in the white courts in 1883. Many would dispute this position by maintaining that the council met with the intent to reconcile the two affected parties, not to adjudicate the murder of Spotted Tail. What is clear is that the conceptual differences between the Common Law traditions of America rely on punishment for infractions against society, while Indian tradition focuses on reconciliation and redress in order to maintain tribal harmony, and thus to ensure the survival of the group.

45. Crow Dog would continue to promote the traditional ways of his people over the assimilationist stance of others. He would be one of the individuals who introduced the Ghost Dance to the tribe in the 1890s. This distinction would prove to be disastrous among the Brule when federal troops were called in because whites increasingly viewed the Ghost Dance as a threat and would indirectly lead to the slaughter at Wounded Knee. For an extended discussion of the Ghost Dance events, see James Mooney, *The Ghost Dance Religion*

and the Sioux Outbreak of 1890 (Lincoln: University of Nebraska/Bison Books, 1991).

46. The Major Crimes Act, U.S.C. § 1153, reads: (a) Any Indian who commits against the person or property of another Indian or other person any of the following offenses, namely, murder, manslaughter, kidnapping, maiming, a felony under chapter 109A, incest, assault with intent to commit murder, assault with a dangerous weapon, assault resulting in serious bodily injury, arson, burglary, robbery, and a felony under section 661 of this title within the Indian country, shall be subject to the same law and penalties as all other persons committing any of the above offenses, within the exclusive jurisdiction of the United States.

47. *U.S. v. Kagama*, 118 U.S. 375 (1886).

48. Among the Indians of California, the families of all those who died within the previous year must receive some compensation from the tribal chief in order to allow the annual dance rituals that ensured peace and prosperity to the whole tribe to take place. The only exceptions to this were those families who had lost a family member to murder. They were given no compensation because they had already received compensation. See R. E. Heizer and M. A. Whipple, *The California Indians: A Sourcebook*, 2nd edition (Berkeley: University of California Press, 1971), 409.

49. Among the California Indians who practiced slavery, the exception to the familial rule of compensation arose. If a slave was killed, compensation was owed to his master, not to his kin group. See Heizer and Whipple, 405.

50. The Whitman Massacre, which has been written about in several texts on the settlement of the Pacific Northwest, occurred in November 1847 when several members of the Cayuse and Nez Perce tribes became convinced that a measles epidemic was evidence of the evil intentions of the whites. In the epidemic, whites appeared to suffer less and recovered from the disease while the Indians, who lacked immunity, died. Since the disease had not occurred within their communities prior to the appearance of the missionaries, they were blamed for the outbreak.

51. Harry C. James, *The Cahuilla Indians* (San Bernardino: Malki Museum Press, 1995): 124–25.

52. Rotenberg, "Special Issues and Topics: American Indian Tribal Death," 409–27.

53. Those parents who protested the removal of their children and attempted to have them remain on the reservations could be arrested and incarcerated in federal penitentiaries.

54. Indian Civil Rights Act of 1968 (25 U.S.C. §§ 1301–03).

55. *Duro v. Reina*, 495 U.S. 676 (1990).

56. Jared B. Cawley, "Just When You Thought It Was Safe to Go Back to the Rez: Is It Safe?" *Cleveland State Law Review*, 52 Clev. St. L. Rev 413 (2004/2005), 420–21.

57. Ken Murray and Jon M. Sands, "Race and Reservations: The Federal Death Penalty and Indian Jurisdiction," 14 Fed. Sent. R. 28. The federal death penalty legislation contains "opt-in" provisions for the Indian tribes. n4 Title 18 U.S.C. § 3598 reads: Not withstanding §§ 1152 and 1153, no person subject to the criminal jurisdiction of an Indian tribal government shall be subject to a capital sentence under this chapter for any offense the federal jurisdiction for which is predicated solely on Indian country (as defined in § 1151 of this title) and which has occurred within the boundaries of Indian country, unless the governing body of the tribe has elected that this chapter have effect over land and persons subject to its criminal jurisdiction. No Indian tribe other than the Sack and Fox of Oklahoma has "opted in" for the death penalty pursuant to this provision. The government can, however, seek the death penalty for those murders that occur under general federal jurisdiction under the Federal Enclaves Act. This can include murders under drug offenses, murders of public officials or government law enforcement, and possibly the murder of tribal police officers. The government can also still seek the death penalty for federal capital offenses that are based on noncapital Major Crime offenses, such as conspiracy to commit a substantive offense for which a death occurs and witness homicide. Finally, the government has also aggressively sought to include capital punishment for murders that were committed under any conspiracy committed under the Major Crimes Act or related to a Major Crimes Act offense.

58. Bureau of Justice Statistics, "American Indians and Crime: A BJS Statistical Profile, 1992–2002."

CHAPTER 5

The Death Penalty in Federal Law

Lonnie Wilson

SINCE THE adoption of the Constitution, the Congress of the United States has made a number of crimes punishable by death. The Constitution itself only specifies one crime, treason, but does not specify a penalty. The maximum penalty chosen by Congress for the ultimate federal crime is death. However, many other statutes have been added to the list of federal capital crimes. Due to the nature of the American system of law, relatively few death penalty cases are now prosecuted in federal court. This has not always been the case, and the number of federal death penalty cases has waxed and waned throughout the history of the United States.

Treason, as defined in the United States Constitution in Article 3, Section 3, "shall consist only of levying War against them, or in adhering to their Enemies, giving them Aid and Comfort. No Person shall be convicted of Treason unless on the testimony of two Witnesses to the same overt Act, or on Confession in Open Court." This definition of treason is very narrow in comparison to the crime of treason under the English law from which the founding fathers derived their experience and knowledge. Treason under English law included sex with the wife of the sovereign by anyone other than the sovereign, or with the unmarried eldest daughter of the sovereign. Should the sex be consensual, then the female was guilty of treason as well.

Furthermore, in English law, in addition to death, the traitor was "attainted." The principal of "attainder" held that all of the property of the attainted was forfeit to the Crown, and the heirs to the traitor were barred from inheritance. In effect, the family of one guilty of treason was punished as well.

The former revolutionaries that framed the Constitution consequently limited the scope of treason to making war on the United States and providing aid and comfort to an enemy. They also restricted the punishment in regard to attainder. No doubt the attitudes of the framers of the Constitution were influenced by the knowledge that they had been, under English law, guilty of treason themselves when they had fought for the independence of the United States.

The Congress of the United States imposed the death penalty as the maximum penalty for treason. However, since the adoption of the Constitution there have been no executions for violations of the federal crime of treason. There have been convictions for treason, and there have been open acts of rebellion, the largest being the American Civil War. There are several reasons for the absence of federal executions for treason.[1]

In several cases of rebellion, the offenders were tried in state court instead of answering to federal charges of treason. For example, Shays Rebellion took place in Massachusetts in the years 1786 to

1787, shortly after the conclusion of the Revolutionary War. Armed clashes occurred between state militia and armed farmers led by Daniel Shays. The intent of the farmers included the prevention of the state supreme court from convening. They feared that more farmers would be evicted from their land, which had been occurring frequently at the time. Militia loyal to the state government eventually succeeded in defeating the farmers who had risen in armed rebellion. Shays was tried in absentia in Massachusetts after the rebellion was defeated. Though sentenced to death, he was granted clemency and pardoned by the newly elected governor, John Hancock.

It may have helped Shays's case that Governor Hancock had personal knowledge and experience in armed rebellion, having helped incite the War of Independence and been indicted for treason by English authorities for doing so. Shays could not have been prosecuted by any other authority than the state of Massachusetts because the federal Constitution had not yet been adopted. In fact, Shays rebellion may have helped shape attitudes that led to the Constitutional Convention and the definition of treason contained in the product of the convention, the Constitution of the United States. The outcome of the criminal charges of treason against Shays is still of interest because it illustrates the political nature of the charge and how that affects the application of the law. The law provided for a sentence of death, and that is what the court imposed on Shays. However, his execution would have created a martyr for his cause and incited his followers to further acts of violence. Instead, he was granted clemency, and the situation was diffused.

Though Shays Rebellion occurred during the period of the Articles of Confederation, other acts of rebellion were also prosecuted under state law rather than federal law after the federal Constitution took effect on March 4, 1789. In 1841 a crisis known as Dorr's Rebellion erupted over

voting rights in the state of Rhode Island. At that time Rhode Island retained the colonial requirement of land ownership for enfranchisement. As the state was becoming more industrialized, that left nearly 60 percent of white males in the state unable to vote. Irish immigrants composed most of the disenfranchised, the local militia, as well as the followers of Thomas Wilson Dorr, the leader of the faction advocating an expansion of suffrage. Dorr's followers attacked an arsenal in Providence unsuccessfully, and rival militia sought out the perpetrators with an equal lack of success. Dorr left the state and the rebellion fizzled. However, the rebellion accomplished the political goal of increased white male suffrage when the state legislature framed a new state constitution that took effect the following year.[2]

Dorr returned to Rhode Island in 1843 after the adoption of the new constitution, and was tried under Rhode Island law for treason against the state. He was found guilty of treason, but instead of the death penalty, he was sentenced to solitary confinement at hard labor for life. However, he was released from custody the following year, and eventually the conviction was set aside.

President John Tyler carefully avoided intervention at the federal level, preferring that the conflict over a state constitution be resolved within the state. He only offered to intervene should the state authorities fail to find resolution, but he did not detail what criteria would determine the state civil authority's success or failure. Since the rebellion was suppressed, no federal intervention occurred. By avoiding federal intervention, Tyler avoided the possibility of federal charges of treason being brought against a popular leader of political opposition. Had Dorr been executed, he, like Shays, would have become a martyr to his cause and incited his followers to greater acts of rebellion. The death penalty for treason was already becoming problematic due to the political nature of the charge.[3]

A different sort of rebellion, the slave rebellion in the Louisiana Territory in 1811, resulted in the execution of sixteen slaves. Little information is available on this episode or the prosecution of the slaves. However, since Louisiana was a territory and not organized as a state, the prosecutions and executions occurred under color of federal authority. Since they were slaves, they were not charged with treason but executed as rebellious slaves.[4]

Far more dramatic was the attack on Harper's Ferry Arsenal by John Brown on October 16, 1859. Brown planned to incite a spontaneous slave rebellion, and hoped to use the weapons he anticipated capturing at the federal arsenal to arm slaves in a general insurrection. Brown and his followers easily overwhelmed the solitary guard at the arsenal. Skirmishing with local militia followed, and Brown fortified himself and his nineteen followers in a position within the arsenal. Two days later, on October 18, United States Marines arrived by train from the barracks in Washington, D.C., led by U.S. Army Lieutenant Colonel Robert E. Lee. The Marines assaulted the position held by Brown and his followers. John Brown was captured during the assault.

Though the attack occurred on a federal facility, and Brown was captured by federal forces on federal property while committing federal crimes, he was not prosecuted in federal court. Instead, he was prosecuted under state charges of murder, conspiring with slaves to rebel, and treason against the State of Virginia. The trial began on October 27, slightly more than a week after his capture. On November 2 a jury returned a verdict of guilty on all three charges. John Brown was executed by public hanging on December 2, 1859.

Though murder, or at least conspiracy to commit murder, would have been easily justifiable in state court even though it occurred on federal property and the state of Virginia had no

jurisdiction, the other two charges are problematic. Brown did not conspire with slaves to rebel; he had incorrectly anticipated that a spontaneous rebellion would occur. Brown was not a citizen of Virginia, had never taken an oath of loyalty to Virginia, and therefore could not commit treason against the State of Virginia. It would have been more proper to charge Brown with treason against the United States, if he were to be charged with treason at all.

There is no record of the reason for the decision by the governor of the state of Virginia, Henry Wise, to try Brown, and the complicity in the decision by the federal authorities who more properly had jurisdiction. It is hardly surprising that President James Buchanan, who later failed to react to southern secession, did not assert federal authority in this case. Clearly, Brown's actions were directed at a federal facility, and he was apprehended by federal authorities. Virginia had no jurisdiction in the case and no justification for removing Brown from federal custody and transferring his custody to Virginia authorities. President Buchanan entrusted the command of the federal forces in a southerner, Robert E. Lee. This no doubt facilitated the transfer of Brown to state authority. Subsequent actions on the part of Lee in the American Civil War proved where his loyalties lay.[5]

It is impossible to determine what difference in outcome a federal trial might have produced. In any case, the federal government once again avoided the possibility of prosecuting a federal treason case, possibly carrying the death penalty, by instead allowing a state to prosecute under its own laws. Unlike the two previous examples, in this case the accused was found guilty, sentenced to death, and promptly executed. And, as expected under the circumstances in the politically superheated atmosphere of 1859 over the issue of abolition, Virginia managed to create a martyr for the coming conflict, the American Civil War.

Not all rebellions could be handed off to state courts. The American Civil War is a case in point. After the war was won by the Union forces, several of the Confederate leaders, such as Jefferson Davis and Robert E. Lee, were indicted for treason. However, nobody was ever convicted for participation in the rebellion of southern states. This was in large part due to political considerations regarding reconstruction. President Andrew Johnson favored leniency in reconstruction, advocating only the wealthy leaders of the Confederacy be punished, hence the treason charges against the senior leaders. However, due to the rancorous relationship Johnson had with Congress, by the end of his term in office he abandoned his class-based prosecution strategy, and granted amnesty to all who had participated in the rebellion.

The Whiskey Rebellion of 1794 did not produce the only federal cases of treason prosecuted and resulting in sentences of death, but it did produce the first. The rebellion was the result of a tax on liquor passed by the Congress of the United States at the instigation of Alexander Hamilton, secretary of the treasury for President George Washington. The residents of western Pennsylvania did not take well to the new tax, especially coming from the new authority of the federal government of the United States. When they rose in rebellion against the tax, it provided a test of the new authority of the central government.

President George Washington raised an army of approximately thirteen thousand men and placed the Revolutionary War cavalry officer Henry "Light Horse Harry" Lee (the father of Robert E. Lee) as commander, though both Washington and his wartime aide-de-camp, Hamilton, accompanied the force into the field. The federal army was able to beat the bush and demonstrate Washington's resolve without causing or incurring much damage or any casualties. Approximately twenty suspects were rounded up, but only two were tried for treason. Both were convicted and sentenced to death. However, George Washington issued a blanket pardon for the rebels, including the two convicted of treason.

These rebellions illustrate the political nature of the charge of treason and illustrate why no one has ever been executed by the federal government for treason in the United States. The death penalty, in this case, is largely symbolic. In the particular case of the Whiskey Rebellion, Washington demonstrated the newly created power of the central government by mustering and sending overwhelming force to quash the insurrection, and using the charge of treason to overawe the public while demonstrating that the central, federal government had real authority and real power. Once the point was made, the need to diffuse the situation outweighed the need to actually execute the perpetrators. The tax, having gone largely uncollected, was repealed in 1802. However, open rebellion against the central government had been quashed without creating a martyr or generating resentment toward the central government.[6]

The only other federal prosecution for treason resulting in a sentence of death occurred after World War II. Tomoya Kawakita, a United States citizen, traveled to Japan in 1939, prior to the two countries engaging in war. Kawakita remained in Japan and eventually secured a job in China with a Japanese mining company acting as an interpreter with American prisoners of war that were forced to work at the mine. Though only required to interpret, Kawakita participated in several acts of physical abuse of prisoners at the mine. After the war, Kawakita attempted to return to the United States, was recognized by a former prisoner, arrested, and charged with treason. A jury found that he was still a United States citizen, and that he had committed at least eight overt acts, each witnessed by at least two United States citizens, and he was therefore guilty of treason, and the court sentenced him to death. The U.S.

Supreme Court affirmed the decision. However, in 1953 President Dwight D. Eisenhower commuted the sentence to life imprisonment. Then, in 1963 President John F. Kennedy pardoned him on condition he was stripped of his U.S. citizenship, deported to Japan, and barred from re-entry to the United States.[7]

Though treason has not resulted in any federal executions, the federal government has conducted many executions as a result of enforcing federal law. The federal government applies the death penalty in both the primary federal codes and in military law as well. Federal civilian jurisdiction applies to those areas of the law specifically reserved to the federal government and to lands or areas not under the jurisdiction of a state.

A specifically federal crime that is a close cousin of treason and the sole purview of the federal government is espionage. During the American Revolution, espionage had been practiced by both the revolutionaries and the forces of King George. Famous cases of espionage from that war include the capture and execution of Nathan Hale in New York City in 1776. He was a captain in the Continental Army sent by General Washington behind British lines to report on troop movements. By international law at the time, he was an unlawful combatant by conducting espionage in civilian clothes. In other words, he was a spy.

The far more substantial case from that war was the attempt by General Benedict Arnold to hand over the defenses at West Point, New York, to the British. During the course of negotiations, American forces captured the British Army officer conducting the negotiations with Arnold, Major John Andre. Like Hale, Andre was captured in civilian clothes, carrying incriminating evidence that he was conducting espionage. He was tried and convicted of espionage, and hanged by American forces. General Arnold escaped capture and left a legacy in American history, making his name synonymous with betrayal and treason.

In contrast with the swift pursuit of execution in the cases above, the federal government under President Abraham Lincoln released the most notorious Confederate spies that were identified and captured during the American Civil War. The fact that they were women almost certainly saved them a trip to the gallows. The sensitivities of the time, the deferential treatment given women by the justice system of the time in general, and the political context of the crimes contributed to their avoiding the death penalty, or in this case, any prosecution at all.

Rose O'Neal Greenhow used her social position in Washington, D.C., to collect intelligence for the Confederate forces. She provided invaluable information to General Pierre G. T. Beauregard that enabled southern forces to mass at Manassas Junction in time to stop the first federal invasion of Virginia at the first Battle of Bull Run. Eventually identified, arrested, and imprisoned, she continued her intelligence gathering from inside custody by gleaning intelligence from conversations with well-wishing visitors, using her daughter as a courier. Instead of being prosecuted for espionage and hanged as a spy, she was "deported" to Richmond, Virginia.[8]

The other notorious Southern spy who was caught and subsequently released was Maria Isabella Boyd, also known as Belle Boyd. Her first encounter with federal authority involved her killing a union soldier for insulting her mother. She was arrested, but released without trial. A guard was placed on her residence, and she romanced a union officer, Captain Daniel Kiely, who was part of the force meant to keep her under surveillance. Information she obtained from him was used to assist Confederate forces in the Shenandoah Valley. Arrested twice more for spying, she was never tried for espionage, and each time was simply released without any action being taken against her.[9]

The only two people who ever received the

death penalty for espionage in the United States were Julius and Ethel Rosenberg. During the 1930s they had become associated with the American Communist Party, which is where they had met. Julius worked for the federal government as an electrical engineer. More importantly, Ethel's brother, Sergeant David Greenglass, worked as a machinist at the Los Alamos National Laboratory in New Mexico with the Manhattan Project.

The Manhattan Project was the code name for the massive wartime program by the United States to develop a nuclear weapon. President Franklin Delano Roosevelt initiated the project at the urging of many scientists, including Albert Einstein, for the purpose of researching the potential power of splitting atoms, and utilizing this power as a weapon. The originally intended target of the weapon was Nazi Germany. However, the program did not produce the weapons in time to be used against Germany, and instead, the first two operational uses of nuclear weapons occurred in Japan in August 1945, followed shortly after by the surrender of Japan and the end of World War II. After the war, the United States enjoyed a monopoly of nuclear military power until the Soviet Union successfully detonated a nuclear device in 1949. By this time, the confrontation between the Soviet Union and the United States and its western allies, known as the "Cold War," was in full swing. The Cold War tension, combined with fear of nuclear attack, following the successful conquest of China by the communist forces led by Mao Tse Tung in 1947, generated the second "Red Scare" in United States history.

Added to this volatile situation in 1948, Whittaker Chambers, a senior editor for *Time* magazine, testified to the House Un-American Activities Committee (HUAC) that Alger Hiss, a state department official and protégé of Supreme Court Justice Felix Frankfurter, was a communist spy. Under oath, Hiss denied being either a communist or a spy. A young freshman representative

from California, Richard M. Nixon, set out to prove Alger Hiss committed perjury. Nixon and the prosecution team that tried Hiss succeeded in convincing a jury that Hiss had committed perjury, and he went to prison. Nixon parleyed his success into a Senate seat in 1950 and the vice-presidency from 1952 to 1960; he was elected president in 1968 and re-elected in 1972, only to resign from office in disgrace for the Watergate scandal and its subsequent cover-up. The significance of the Hiss case comes from the intense media coverage it generated, and the public perception that communists had infiltrated all levels of the government and posed an imminent threat to national security.

Julius Rosenberg not only belonged to the communist party, but he worked for Soviet intelligence, providing information to the Soviets on the projects he was working on, such as radar and proximity fuses. Julius also aided in the recruitment of additional spies. One spy he helped recruit was his brother-in-law, David Greenglass.

Also working on the Manhattan Project was a German refugee physicist representing the British on the project, Klaus Fuchs. Fuchs was a brilliant theoretical physicist who made significant contributions to the design of early nuclear weapons. British MI5 identified Fuchs as a Soviet spy, and after interrogation in January 1950, Fuchs confessed, and among the information he revealed was the name of his courier contact, Harry Gold, an American chemist who also worked on the Manhattan Project. Fuchs was punished by British authorities, sentenced to fourteen years in prison and stripped of his British citizenship. Gold confessed to being a Soviet spy since 1934, and in 1951 he was sentenced to thirty years in prison for espionage. He also identified David Greenglass, a machinist sergeant in the United States Army assigned to work on the project, as another espionage contact.

The FBI arrested David Greenglass in June of

1950. He quickly implicated Julius Rosenberg in an effort to obtain leniency. He also implicated his sister, Ethel, by claiming she had typed his notes for transmission to the Soviets. Julius and Ethel Rosenberg did not cooperate with investigators, and when on the witness stand, each sought protection from self-incrimination by invoking the Fifth Amendment. In *U.S. v. Rosenberg*, 192 F. 2nd 583 (Second Circuit, 1952), they were both tried and convicted on March 29, 1951, of violations of the 1917 Espionage Act, and sentenced to death. In pronouncing the sentences, the judge clearly linked the severity of the sentence to the perceived magnitude of revealing nuclear secrets to the Soviets, stating that they shouldered much of the responsibility for the Korean War and future conflicts and the deaths those conflicts involved. They were executed in Sing Sing State Prison in New York by electrocution on June 19, 1953, leaving their two sons orphans. Ironically, though the Rosenbergs were "godless communists," their defense counsel sought a stay of execution because it would have occurred on the Jewish Sabbath and would have violated their religious sensitivities. To avoid such a conflict, they were executed before sundown.[10]

Even more ironic, it was the information provided by Fuchs, the theoretical physicist initially identified by British intelligence, that was the most important provided to the Soviets. Furthermore, the Soviets did not use any of the information obtained by espionage directly in the development of their own nuclear weapons. Rather, they used it to check and compare the work by their own engineers and scientists. By attacking the criminal conspiracy by identifying the most important member of the ring first, in this case law enforcement officials, granted leniency to the most important targets and worked their way down the organization until they got to the Rosenbergs. Julius and Ethel had no one to hand over to authorities, though they had the

least important part to play in the criminal espionage scheme.

There were several factors, beyond the simple application of law, that contributed to Julius and Ethel being executed. They were unfortunate in being the last members of the ring identified. Identity may also have been a disadvantage, the Rosenbergs being Jewish. Clearly the most important factor was the superheated political situation. Their case came on the heels of the start of the Cold War, China falling to the communists, the Berlin crisis, the Korean War, and the Alger Hiss scandal and trial. The timing of the case, during the nascent beginnings of McCarthyism, could not have been worse. Subsequent espionage trials in the United States have not resulted in anyone being sentenced to death. The threat of the death penalty, combined with the example of the Rosenberg case, could provide an inducement for negotiation for those accused of espionage. Counterintelligence agencies have a vested interest in avoiding the death penalty and obtaining the cooperation of the accused in identifying other subjects and determining what information has been compromised. In most cases the system itself works against the use of the death penalty.

Another closely related activity to espionage that has led to the federal government of the United States using the death penalty is sabotage. The primary case in U.S. history involving the execution of saboteurs occurred during World War II. It is of interest not only because of the federal use of the death penalty, but also for the manner in which the case was prosecuted. The eight German defendants were tried as unlawful combatants before a military tribunal, found guilty, and sentenced to death.

In June of 1942 two German U-boats each landed four saboteurs as part of Operation Pastorius. The first group landed in New York, and the second in Florida. The New York group was spotted on the Long Island beach they landed on by a Coast Guardsman, John C. Cullen, who confronted the men. The Germans offered Cullen a bribe; he took the money and reported the incident anyway, though shortly after the confrontation the four saboteurs left the area and took a train into New York City. The four agents who landed in Florida traveled to Chicago and Cincinnati. The mission was to sabotage war industries and commit acts of terror within the United States.

All eight of the men had lived in the United States previously and relocated to Germany prior to the outbreak of war. The head of the team, George John Dasch, and Ernest Burger decided to abandon the mission. Dasch attempted to turn himself in to the FBI in Washington, D.C. After some difficulty in convincing officials of the veracity of his story, he was eventually arrested, and he informed the FBI of the whereabouts of the other seven German agents.

Both Dasch and Burger provided information to the FBI in order to obtain more lenient treatment. President Franklin Delano Roosevelt ordered the eight tried by a military tribunal. All eight were tried and convicted of sabotage. All eight were also sentenced to death. However, President Roosevelt commuted the sentences of Dasch and Burger. Roosevelt reduced the sentence for Dasch to thirty years in prison, and Burger received a sentence of life in prison.

An appeal of the case, titled *Ex parte Quirin*, 317 U.S. 1 (1942), was heard by the U.S. Supreme Court. The seven defendants, Dasch not being one of the petitioners, filed writs of habeas corpus in federal court, and their petitions were denied. The Court's decision affirmed the convictions and sentences. The ruling determined that the president had by proclamation declared that enemy saboteurs and spies would be tried under the Articles of War (the precursor to the Uniform Code of Military Conduct now used for military law) by military tribunals. The Court further

determined that they were unlawful combatants, subject to prosecution under the Articles of War and denied the right to access to the courts via habeas corpus. The six German saboteurs who did not have their sentences commuted were executed on August 8, 1942, less than three months after their arrival on U.S. shores.[11]

The fate of the German saboteurs is in stark contrast to the sentences received by the members of the Duquesne Spy Ring. Through the services of William G. Sebold, a double agent, the FBI conducted a two-year-long investigation that culminated in the arrests in June 1941 of thirty-three German spies working within the United States. The leader of the ring was Frederick (or Fritz) Joubert Duquesne.

Duquesne was a South African Boer who harbored significant resentment and hatred for Britain as a result of the war. His accomplishments included teaching shooting to Theodore Roosevelt and claiming credit for the sinking of HMS *Hampshire* in World War I, thereby killing Field Marshal Lord Kitchener. This second act prompted Germany to award him the Iron Cross. He was arrested twice by the FBI for extradition to Britain. The first time he escaped from custody, and the second time the presiding judge dismissed the extradition as the statute of limitations had run out.

William Sebold had been blackmailed into working for the German Abwehr intelligence service, reported to American authorities what he had become involved in, and the FBI used him as a double agent. Using the information Sebold provided, the FBI conducted a two-year investigation of the spy ring, and in 1941, before the United States had entered World War II, arrested thirty-three members of the "Duquesne Spy Ring" in the largest espionage sweep ever conducted by the FBI. All thirty-three members were convicted of a variety of charges, but none received the death penalty. Duquesne received the longest sentence, eighteen years for espionage. Sentencing occurred in January of 1942. Compare this to the six executed saboteurs arrested just months later.[12]

The differences between cases and outcomes of the saboteurs and the spies result from the timing and the nature of their offenses. The FBI arrested, charged, and began the prosecution of the spies in 1941, months before the attack on Pearl Harbor and the declaration of war by Germany on the United States. They were here to collect information, not to directly commit violent acts. Though their actions could cause even greater damage to national security in the long run, they did not generate the same emotional responses of hatred and fear because of the timing of their arrest and the nature of their offense. The saboteurs had secretly infiltrated the United States after the surprise attack on Pearl Harbor with the specific intent of committing acts of terror to generate yet more fear. Their intent and purpose created a far more emotional reaction when public emotions and belligerence, as well as those of public officials, were running as high as they could ever be. They were executed as a result.

The traditional crimes that normally carry the death penalty, such as murder, rape, and extreme forms of larceny, are the crimes that are the legal basis for most federal executions since the adoption of the Constitution. Typically these sorts of social crimes are proscribed by state law and prosecuted in state courts. However, in territories and possessions that are unorganized and do not possess any locally organized civil authority, the federal government must enforce these laws to preserve social order. Consequently, during the westward expansion of the United States, frontier justice was the responsibility of the federal government. Criminals guilty of social crimes, such as murder, or other offenses had to be brought to justice by federal authorities in federal courts. As unorganized territories became states, the federal

government's law enforcement role in these areas diminished, and consequently, it isn't surprising that the number of federal executions dropped precipitously after 1892, when Frederick Jackson Turner announced that the American frontier was "closed."

The peak in the number of federal executions happened during the period of the 1870s through the 1880s. Of the 343 federal civilian executions, 118 occurred during this period, or roughly 34 percent. There are a number of reasons for the statistical spike that occurs during this period. The situation was precipitated by westward territorial expansion in the first half of the nineteenth century. The first big expansion came with the Louisiana Purchase. Napoleon Bonaparte sold the remaining French holdings in North America to the United States in order to insure that the United States would be able to thrive sufficiently to be a rival to Great Britain, his perennial nemesis in Europe.

The expansion to the west coast of North America was completed by conquest. First, the Republic of Texas, which had fought a war of independence from Mexico, was annexed by the United States. Then President James Polk used border disputes between Texas and Mexico to instigate the Mexican-American War of 1846–1848. The United States then annexed what is now the southwestern portion of the United States, including states such as California, Nevada, Arizona, and New Mexico.

The territorial expansion itself, completed by 1850, did not produce the spike in executions by the federal courts. All of the annexations occurred prior to the American Civil War, and the statistical spike in executions occurred long after the annexations. Territory devoid of euro-American settlement does not generate criminal offenses, and most of these territories, with the exception of California, remained populated predominantly by American Indians until after the Civil War.

California was an exception because of the extermination of most of the native American Indian population by the Spanish, the 1849 Gold Rush, and its coastal location. The mission system implemented by the Spanish concentrated the native population, who were then subject to European diseases for which most had no immunity. The resulting catastrophic epidemics decimated their population, almost exterminating them. After annexation of the area following the Mexican-American War, the discovery of gold at Sutter's Mill provided a powerful stimulus for migration to California. Its location on the coast facilitated the migration. A traveler could reach the area by water route, which at the time was far easier and more rapid than travel by land. Consequently, California was organized as a state and admitted to the Union prior to the Civil War. Much of the remaining area was difficult to access as there were no major, easily navigable east-west watercourses to facilitate the movement of people and goods to the newly acquired territories, which lacked the incentive and lure of gold to overcome these limitations.

Therefore the next event that contributed to the situation was the completion of the transcontinental railroad in 1869. The railroads dramatically reduced the time necessary to travel west, enabling many more people to migrate westward, and into areas not accessible by water transportation. The federal government also provided the railroad developers generous land grants to facilitate and encourage the building of a national rail network. In order to capitalize on the immense potential value of the land, the railroads needed to encourage people from the eastern United States to move west.

The success of stimulating migration to the west resulted from several factors. The American Civil War contributed by making a significant portion of the American population more mobile in fact and outlook. Soldiers who had left the family farm and "seen the elephant" had broader horizons than they otherwise might have. Rapid industrialization of the United States created equally rapid social changes. Cities grew, encroaching on pastoral areas, and populations swelled with massive levels of immigration. The lure of new beginnings and cheap land that was now accessible drew waves of migrants westward. Until the territories were organized and admitted into the Union as states, the federal government exercised judicial responsibility and jurisdiction for maintaining order.

The influx of euro-American migrants into areas populated by American Indians resulted in frequent conflicts. The federal government followed a policy of removal and relocation of native populations to lands reserved for them, called "reservations." Many such reservations existed, but by far the largest area reserved for American Indian removal and relocation was the area originally known as Indian Territory, most of which is now part of the state of Oklahoma.

Social crimes, such as murder, that occurred in the Indian Territory and involved nonmembers of resident tribes came under federal jurisdiction. The tribal authorities within Indian Territory had no authority over persons not belonging to the tribes located there. The federal court in Fort Smith, Arkansas, for the Western District of Arkansas had jurisdiction for the Indian Territory during most of the period of the spike in federal executions of the 1870s through the 1880s. The presiding judge, Isaac Parker, earned the sobriquet of "Hanging Judge" due to the immense number of capital crime trials he presided over and the large number of executions that they produced. Judge Parker presided in over 300 capital trials, sentencing 160 defendants to death. Of those, 79 were executed by the federal government by hanging. Of the 118 federal executions during the 1870s and 1880s, Judge Parker accounted for approximately 67 percent of that number, and

23 percent of all federal executions to date. Clearly no nickname has ever been more accurate.[13]

Migration westward and the federal policy of removal and relocation of American Indians to reservations generated a constant stream of conflict until nearly the end of the nineteenth century. When the conflicts involved whole tribes or large numbers of American Indians, and involved the United States Army, they were usually considered military actions, and the only deaths resulting from the conflict came in combat. However, in 1862 a violent conflict occurred in Minnesota resulting in hundreds of deaths. When the dust settled it led to the largest mass execution in United States history.

The Lakota Sioux of Minnesota, at times called Dakota or Santee Sioux, were by treaty removed and relocated to reservation lands in southwestern Minnesota. The United States Senate removed key sections of the treaty before ratifying it. Corruption within the Bureau of Indian Affairs resulted in the theft of compensations owed to the Lakota by treaty obligation. By 1862, the Lakota of Minnesota were not able to convince a government distracted and encumbered by a major civil war to make good on its treaty obligations. Euro-American settlement further exacerbated the situation as settlers stripped the area of natural resources necessary for the Lakota to survive.

Placed in a desperate situation, beginning on August 17, 1862, the Lakota attacked the new settlers with considerable violence. Militia and units from Minnesota volunteer infantry regiments participated in the fighting, commanded by Colonel Henry Hastings Sibley, a distant relative of the Confederate general Sibley and the first governor of the state of Minnesota. On September 6, 1862, President Lincoln ordered Major General John Pope, recently defeated at the First Battle of Bull Run, to take command of U.S. forces in the northwest, and directed him to suppress the uprising.

However, Colonel Sibley retained field command. Fighting continued until the end of September. Sibley decisively defeated the Lakota at the battle of Wood Lake on September 23, 1862. Over the next several weeks Lakota surrendered and released hostages taken during the uprising.

Five days after his victory, on September 28, Colonel Sibley appointed a military commission to begin trials of captured Lakota. Eventually, forces under Colonel Sibley arrested thousands of Lakota, and 393 are tried by military tribunal for murder and rape. The military tribunals denied the Lakota legal representation during the proceedings. Out of 393 charged, 323 were convicted, and 303 were sentenced to death. General Pope informed President Lincoln of the trials, and Lincoln ordered that none of the executions were to be conducted without his review.

Lincoln reviewed the cases and commuted most of the sentences, only allowing 38 executions to proceed. Three other captives of the original 303 condemned Lakota died when the Army transported the prisoners through New Ulm, Minnesota, the scene of heavy fighting. Bitter, angry residents attacked the column, and many of the captives were injured, in addition to the three that died. The day after Christmas, in Mankato, Minnesota, the Army executed all 38 Lakota by hanging, simultaneously from a single scaffold. It was the largest mass execution in American history. Conducted in public, the crowd of local citizens cheered as the scaffold fell out from under the men. One rope broke and the condemned was successfully executed on the second effort.

There are numerous questionable aspects to the trial and execution of the Lakota stemming from this rebellion. Though the Lakota were nominally treated as a foreign entity and as combatants, and trials for war crimes by a military commission were reasonable under the circumstances, it is questionable that the military trials met constitutional muster. To begin with, the

Lakota did not receive legal counsel, nor were the proceedings translated for them. The members of the commission were officers from the Minnesota volunteer regiments that not only participated in the fighting, but were locally recruited and therefore local residents. Considering the hundreds of settlers and soldiers who died in the conflict, it would be ridiculous to expect anyone to be a fair and impartial judge under the circumstances. The conduct of the trials appears inadequate, some lasting less than five minutes, and evidence was conspicuously absent.

Lincoln was well aware of the political situation in Minnesota, and feared that if all the executions were prevented, or not enough Lakota were executed to satisfy the citizens of Minnesota, all could die in an act of mob violence, as had already happened when three of the condemned were killed as they were being transported through New Ulm. Lincoln's staff had difficulty in completing the review of the cases due to the incomplete and inadequate records made by the commission. Lincoln's review initially looked for cases that included rape, and only two could be found. Apparently two Lakota were considered insufficient to satisfy the public demand for vengeance, and another review produced a total of 39 cases that contained evidence of rape or attacks against settlers not related to a "battle," and Lincoln authorized the execution of these 39 prisoners. Exculpatory evidence for one defendant later dropped the number to 38, which was the actual number of executions that the Army carried out. Those not executed were held in custody until 1866 when President Andrew Johnson ordered the remaining 177 survivors released.

Later conflicts with a variety of Indian tribes resulted in criminal trials and executions. However, nothing ever approximating the simultaneous execution of thirty-eight Lakota had ever occurred during an Indian conflict with the United States, nor would it again. Many violent clashes between rebellious tribes and the Army occurred, but the Indian participants were never again prosecuted en masse after these clashes. Many instances occurred during the Indian Wars of acts of violence committed by euro-American civilians, troops, and American Indians which, judged by European standards, would be considered atrocities. However, it must be borne in mind that the Indian participants did not conduct war by European standards, and the distinctions between combatants and noncombatants did not have the same clear distinctions for tribal warriors. Furthermore, western European history is replete with examples of atrocities and deliberate military attacks against civilian populations. During World War II millions of civilians died due to deliberate aerial bombing of civilian population, such as the firebombing of cities like Dresden and Tokyo. No one was punished for those actions because they were perpetrated by the victor. The Lakota suffered the mass execution in 1862 because they lost. North American European settlers had practiced wars of extermination against American Indians since the Pequot War and King Philip's War in the seventeenth century. Sensitivities about waging such wars changed in large part because of the American Civil War. The sanguinary nature of the war, still the bloodiest war in American history in terms of deaths of Americans, had a traumatic impact on American society. The sort of blood lust for vengeance that spurred the 1862 demands for retribution would diminish after the horrible acts and devastation that would be wrought within the United States as a result of the war. Consequently, the sort of shocked outrage about civilian casualties caused by the nature of tribal warfare paled in comparison to the shock of the Union campaigns in the Shenandoah Valley, and Sherman's March to the Sea. Furthermore, the military leaders during most of the following Indian Wars were General Phillip Sheridan and General William T. Sherman, the commanders of those two campaigns, respectively. Their experience in the Civil War certainly tempered their posture toward Indian actions after the war. The Army never again conducted trials by military tribunal of tribal warriors who had participated in open hostilities against the United States.[14]

However, the American Civil War also produced another set of controversial trials by military tribunal, those of the Lincoln assassination conspirators in 1865. John Wilkes Booth, an actor with Southern sympathies in the war, shot President Abraham Lincoln in the back of the head at Ford's Theater in Washington, D.C., on April 14, 1865. President Lincoln died the following day. Federal authorities cornered and killed Booth in a Virginia tobacco barn on April 26, precluding any judicial punishment for the first presidential assassin in United States history. However, the post-assassination investigation resulted in the prosecution of eight coconspirators.

The conspirators had acted without any known connection to the Confederate government or military forces. Hence, their actions constituted a violation of civil criminal law. However, they were tried by military tribunal by order of President Andrew Johnson, Lincoln's successor, and the military commission for the trial was formed on May 1, 1865. Former U.S. Attorney General Edward Bates and Secretary of the Navy Gideon Welles opposed the use of a military commission to try the conspirators, arguing for trials in civil court, but the administration went ahead with the military tribunal trials.

The investigation revealed that originally the conspiracy had formed for the kidnapping of President Lincoln, but in the end Booth had decided on murder. The intent of the assassins was to disorganize the federal government, possibly causing its collapse, by killing President Lincoln, Vice-President Andrew Johnson, and Secretary of State William H. Seward. Booth

succeeded in killing Lincoln. However, the assassination attempt on Seward was unsuccessful, though violent and resulting in the wounding of Secretary Seward and several other people, and the death of one person. The would-be assassin of Vice-President Johnson gave up when he discovered the vice-president wasn't home.

The military tribunal found all eight conspirators guilty. Mary Surratt, Lewis Powell, David Herold, and George Atzerodt were all sentenced to death, while the other four received prison terms for their part in the assassination. On July 7, 1865, the Union Army executed the four condemned in Washington, D.C., making Mary Surratt the first woman executed by the federal government, as well as one of the first four people executed for the assassination of a president of the United States. Two others since then have been executed for presidential assassination. Charles J. Guiteau was executed by federal authorities for the murder of President James A. Garfield, and Leon Czolgosz was likewise executed for assassinating President William McKinley. No one was ever prosecuted for the murder of President John F. Kennedy. His accused killer, Lee Harvey Oswald, was in turn murdered by Jack Ruby prior to trial.[15]

The American Civil War and the year 1862 saw yet another unique event in the history of the use of the federal death penalty. The federal government executed Nathaniel Gordon for illegally participating in the slave trade. He was the only slave trader ever executed by United States.

The slave trade had been outlawed in 1809. However, enforcement of the ban on the slave trade was not just lax, it was nonexistent. The U.S. Customs Service insisted that it was an immigration issue that should be handled by anyone else but them, preferably the U.S. Navy. The navy felt it was a customs issue. Abolitionist and international pressure, primarily from Great Britain, led to an amendment in 1820 by Congress to the 1790 Piracy Act that included participation in the slave trade as an act of piracy punishable by death, and allowing for the payment of rewards for informing on slave traders. The payments for informing could be substantial. The amendment did not, as it had been hoped by abolitionists, increase the level of enforcement by the federal government in a substantial way.

Some took advantage of the new informant provisions to aggrandize themselves. James Bowie, of later Alamo fame, entered into a criminal smuggling scheme with a notorious pirate, Jean Lafitte. Lafitte smuggled the slaves into Galveston, Texas, and Bowie transported them through Texas, mixing them with legal slaves and thereby hiding their origin. It was effectively a "slave laundering" business. Bowie increased his profit margin by reporting Lafitte to federal authorities and collecting the informant fees, while still doing business with Lafitte. Enforcement was so lax that nothing ever happened to either of them.

In addition to amending the law, the United States Navy dispatched two small warships to attempt to intercept American flag slavers off the coast of Africa. Captain Robert Stockton was one of only two U.S. Navy captains that demonstrated any initiative at intercepting slavers, the other being a Quaker (the abolitionist movement in the United States began with and was strongly supported by Quakers). In doing so he managed to cause several international incidents by dueling with and killing officers from other navies and unlawfully seizing a Portuguese slaver, which led to a U.S. Supreme Court case (*The Marianna Flora*, 24 U.S. 1 (1825)), claiming it had committed an act of piracy, which the court held was in fact justifiable self-defense. Stockton's motivation derived from his racist convictions that all blacks should be returned to Africa, and he was a major supporter of the creation of Liberia. With these controversies as justification, President James Monroe, a Southerner, recalled the aggressive young officers who were seizing American slavers

that the administration had been ardently claiming didn't exist. Significantly, none of the slavers intercepted during this period resulted in the death penalty being imposed.

The federal administrations continued to insist that American vessels were not participating in the slave trade. International and abolitionist pressure in the 1840s led to the dispatch of Commodore Mathew C. Perry to the coast of Africa to intercept American flag slavers. Seemingly proving the point that the administration was correct in its estimation, Perry failed to find any American slavers operating in the area. However, the American slave trade was headquartered in Rhode Island, Perry's home state. In fact, the most successful known American slaver of the era was Perry's father-in-law. The conflict of interest could not have been missed by President Tyler, another Southerner.

From 1820 to the outbreak of the American Civil War, there were no cases of anyone being sentenced to death for piracy related to the slave trade. Then, on August 8, 1860, the U.S.S. *Mohican* intercepted the *Erie* commanded by Nathaniel Gordon carrying nearly nine hundred Africans with the intent of selling them as slaves. In November of that year, Abraham Lincoln was elected president of the United States, and the following spring the American Civil War began. On November 9, 1861, after several major battles had already been fought in the Civil War, Nathaniel Gordon was convicted of piracy for participating in the slave trade. In February of 1862, Gordon was sentenced to death. After the Supreme Court refused to intervene, he was executed on February 21, 1862—the only person ever executed in the United States for participation in the slave trade.[16] Most of his fellow slave traders found more lucrative employment shortly after Gordon's arrest. With secession, and the imposition of a blockade of the Confederacy by the United States Navy, blockade running of war materiel became more lucrative than smuggling slaves. The skills and the vessels needed for success in blockade running did not differ in the least from slave running. The primary difference was the amount of effort federal authorities exerted in enforcing the blockade during the war.

Another major source of federal death penalty cases derives from the application of military law. The Congress of the United States originally codified military law in what were called the Articles of War. They applied to both the army and the navy. Modified through the years, they were replaced in 1951 with a new code called the Universal Code of Military Justice (UCMJ), and applied to all branches of the United States military forces. Both sets of codes contained provisions for the death penalty to be imposed by courts martial or, as explained earlier, by military commissions such as in the Sioux Rebellion of 1862. The jurisdiction of military law is limited, though in recent years efforts have been made to expand those limits. In general the capital violations mirror those in civil law, but in addition there are crimes specified in military law that are specifically military in nature, are not among the social crimes that normally merit the death penalty but are capital crimes nonetheless.

Mutiny is one such crime. In 1842, aboard the U.S.S. *Somers*, three men were executed for conspiring to commit mutiny. They are the only executions in the history of the U.S. Navy for mutiny.

The U.S.S. *Somers* was an experiment in naval education in 1842. Commodore Mathew C. Perry had lobbied for a special ship to be commissioned to train midshipmen in a uniform manner. Until that time the navy scattered midshipmen among the various vessels of the fleet and their education suffered the vagaries of whatever degree of interest their particular ship's captain showed toward educating them. The navy designated the *Somers* to conduct a cruise under Perry's scheme

as an experiment to determine the value of such an enterprise. Commander Alexander Slidell Mackenzie, brother-in-law to Perry, commanded the *Somers*.

During the cruise, Midshipman Philip Spencer, along with Boatswain's Mate Samuel Cromwell and Seaman Elisha Small, were accused of conspiring to commit mutiny. Spencer was named the ringleader, though he claimed in his defense he was only joking. No ordinary midshipman, Spencer was the nineteen-year-old son of Secretary of War John C. Spencer. He had been expelled from two colleges and from two warships. When initially assigned to the *Somers*, Mackenzie had refused to accept Spencer, but the Navy Department overruled his decision in the matter.

On December 1, 1842, Mackenzie convened a board of inquiry composed of the officers from the *Somers*. The ship's captain felt insecure in holding the three mutineers for two weeks on a small vessel, unable to prevent contact with other crew members, and their presence constituting a hazard for operating the ship, a small brig. The board found the three guilty of conspiring to commit mutiny, and recommended they be hanged immediately. Ten minutes later, the three were hoisted and swinging from the main yardarm, Spencer to port and the other two to starboard.

To no surprise, the execution at sea of the son of the secretary of war for conspiring to commit mutiny did not go unnoticed. Mackenzie faced both a board of inquiry and courts martial for the incident. He was exonerated by both, but the incident effectively terminated his naval career. One positive result from the incident was that the idea of training midshipmen at sea was abandoned, and the Congress established the U.S. Naval Academy at Annapolis to train midshipmen.[17]

Another strictly military offense subject to the death penalty is desertion in the face of the enemy. Since 1865, only one soldier has been executed for this offense, during World War II. Though some may argue that the crime is victimless, that is not accurate. A soldier who deserts has to be replaced, so his aversion to danger and his duty exposes someone else to fulfill his obligations. His absence could also mean the difference between living and dying for the other members of his unit, diminishing the unit's combat capability and collective ability to survive. Consequently, military commanders demanded harsh punishment for deserters, especially during World War II, with one caveat: after trial, conviction, and sentencing, should the soldier agree to return to his unit, the sentence would be stayed or reduced. Private Edward "Eddie" Slovik refused to return to his unit, and became the only soldier executed for desertion since 1865.

Initially exempt from the draft, after reclassification Slovik was drafted into the United States Army in January of 1944. In August of that year he was assigned as a replacement infantryman. While en route to his unit, Slovik became separated from the detachment due to artillery fire. He attached himself to a Canadian military police unit, and eventually turned himself in to his own unit roughly six weeks after deserting. He promptly deserted again, and was caught. Slovik informed superior officers in writing that he would not return to his unit, and if taken back, he would desert again.

Slovik was charged with desertion and given the opportunity to have all the charges dropped if he would return to his unit. He refused. The court found him guilty and sentenced him to death. He appealed for clemency to General Dwight Eisenhower. However, Slovik still refused to return to his unit, and his criminal record factored against granting clemency. Consequently, he was executed on January 31, 1945, approximately five months from the time he was assigned to his unit and five months before the end of the war in Europe. Many other soldiers were charged with desertion, tried, found guilty, and sentenced to death, but all the others returned to their units and whatever fate combat had for them. Slovik, having had experience with the civil criminal justice system, apparently did not believe that the army would execute him for just running away.[18]

Efforts to curb, restrict, or abolish the death penalty resulted in a Supreme Court–ordered moratorium on executions in 1972 with their ruling in *Furman v. Georgia*, 408 U.S. 238 (1972). Beginning in the 1930s, an effort to stop lynchings began, supported by, among others, Eleanor Roosevelt. As efforts to curb unlawful executions by mob violence grew, it brought closer scrutiny to inequities in lawfully conducted executions. The Supreme Court turned away from economic issues and spent more time and effort ruling on civil rights issues following the court-packing scheme and "sick chicken" case in the 1930s. The civil rights movement gained momentum throughout the 1960s, leading to the Supreme Court ruling on Furman in 1972.

The Furman ruling resulted in a universal national moratorium on executions and the application of the death penalty. The Court found that inequities in the application of the law, and excessiveness in assigning the penalty to crimes other than murder, violated the constitutional prohibition against "cruel and unusual punishment." The ruling didn't find that execution itself was cruel or unusual punishment, referring to the 1890 ruling in the case *In Re Kemmler*, 136 U.S. 436 (1890), in that a penalty of death was cruel and unusual if the means of execution was "inhuman and barbarous." The Court cited, among other things, the Magna Carta and the English Bill of Rights of 1689 when defining the scope and nature of cruel and unusual punishment. In citing the English Bill of Rights of 1689, the Court pointed out the identical language in that act to the language in the Constitution. In the context of the English Bill of Rights, a defining cause for the use of the phrase "cruel and unusual" punishment derived from selective or irregular application of harsh penalties in English Common Law. The implication drawn by the Court concluded that the inequities in the application of the death penalty in the United States violated the Eighth Amendment prohibition against cruel and unusual punishment. Language in the Magna Carta proscribed disproportionate punishment, and according to the Court fell within the scope of the cruel and unusual punishment clause of the Eighth Amendment. The dissent in the case primarily concluded that the Court exceeded its authority in striking down the death penalty and abused state's rights by using the Fourteenth Amendment to apply the ruling to the states.[19]

The decision in Furman effectively required the federal government as well as state governments to revise their capital statutes to prevent the excessive or arbitrary application of the death penalty. Further refinements in the basic decision in Furman came with *Woodson v. North Carolina*, 428 U.S. 280 (1976), and *Roberts v. Louisiana*, 428 U.S. 325 (1976), 431 U.S. 633 (1977). In those decisions, the Court ruled that statutorily mandatory death penalties would also be unconstitutional. The Supreme Court decision in *Coker v. Georgia*, 433 U.S. 584 (1977), barred the use of the death penalty for cases of rape in the absence of murder, arguing that the punishment was disproportionate to the crime.[20]

Currently, capital crimes must be tried by a bifurcated system. In the first proceeding a determination of guilt is made. If a guilty verdict is returned by the jury, the second proceeding, usually referred to as the "sentencing phase," then considers aggravating and mitigating circumstances to determine if the death penalty is appropriate or not. This system came into existence as a result of a Supreme Court decision in *Gregg v. Georgia*, 428 U.S. 153 (1976).[21]

Since these court decisions, the United States Congress revised U.S. statutes in 1988, 1994, and 1996 to reflect the legal requirements imposed by the Supreme Court, and to expand the crimes that carry capital punishment. The U.S. Code currently provides for capital punishment for murders with specific special circumstances as designated by their specific code. In addition, there are three violations that can result in the death penalty under federal law that don't involve murder. Treason (18 U.S.C. 2381) and Espionage (18 U.S.C. 794) are still capital crimes. In addition, crimes related to large drug-smuggling operations have been added to this very short list: Trafficking in Large Quantities of Drugs (18 U.S.C. 3591(b)) and the related "Attempting, authorizing, or advising the killing of any officer, juror, or witness in cases involving a Continuing Criminal Enterprise, regardless of whether any such killing occurs" (18 U.S.C. 3591(b)(2)). It is problematic if any cases ever happen in which the last two statutes are applied, it is dubious if either will pass constitutional muster. As discussed earlier, treason and espionage, for practical and political reasons, are unlikely to produce any more death sentences in the future than they have produced in the past.

Only three federal executions have occurred since 1963. All three executions have occurred during the presidency of George W. Bush. However, they originated from crimes and convictions predating the election of President Bush. Timothy McVeigh, convicted for the terrorist bombing of the federal building in Oklahoma City, Oklahoma, resulting in the deaths of 168 people, was executed on June 11, 2001, exactly three months before his death toll record was exceeded by Islamic terrorists on September 11, 2001. Just eight days later, Juan Raul Garza met his end by lethal injection for the murder of three fellow drug traffickers. The last federal execution to date occurred on March 18, 2003, when federal authorities executed Louis Jones for murder.[22]

The federal application of the death penalty is

more conspicuous in how it hasn't been applied than how it has been applied. Treason, the only constitutionally defined crime, has to date never resulted in an execution. The reason it hasn't resulted in an execution is the same reason some of the other remarkable executions have or have not occurred, the application of political pressure. Nathaniel Gordon and the Rosenbergs, Julius and Ethel, were executed as much for when they were convicted as for the severity of their crimes. The 38 Lakota executed en mass in 1862 died to appease the vengeance of the residents of Minnesota. Prior to the Furman decision by the U.S. Supreme Court, the federal application of the death penalty could be as capricious and arbitrary as any state, but the reasons were different. Racial discrimination seemed to be a prime reason for the arbitrary nature of the application of the death penalty in 1972. Political considerations have played a greater role in the arbitrary application of federal capital punishment. Though an argument could be made that the Lakota mass execution was racially motivated, it really had more to do with political pressure from Minnesota residents and their threatened and attempted efforts at mob violence. The future direction of federal capital punishment should mirror the course of national political developments. Should public sentiment, through fear, terror, or anger, rise to the occasion it would probably raise the number of death penalty convictions. However, the courts and the process of review now in effect go a long way to mitigate public cries for blood.

Lonnie Wilson holds a bachelor's degree in history from the University of California, Berkeley, and a master's degree in history from California State University, Fullerton. He served in the U.S. Army as an infantry officer and Special Forces paratrooper. He worked as a special agent for the Department of Justice, Immigration and Naturalization Service, for sixteen years. Since the creation of the Department of Homeland Security, Immigration and Customs Enforcement in 2003, he was a special agent with that agency. His previous publications include the history of the Miranda decision, published in *Law in the Western United States*, edited by Gordon Bakken, and three articles on immigration history for the *Encyclopedia of Immigration and Migration in the American West*, edited by Gordon Bakken and Alexandra Kindell: "Asian Immigration Law," "Chinese Immigration," and "Immigration and Naturalization Service (INS)."

Notes

1. Lawrence M. Friedman, *A History of American Law*, 2nd ed. (New York: Simon & Schuster, 1985); James Madison, *Notes of Debates in the Federal Convention of 1787 Reported by James Madison* (New York: W. W. Norton & Company, 1987).

2. George Richards Minot, *The History of the Insurrections in Massachusetts, in the Year Seventeen Hundred and Eighty Six, and the Rebellion Consequent Thereon*, 2nd ed. (Cranbury, NJ: Scholar's Bookshelf, 2007).

3. George M. Dennison, *The Dorr War: Republicanism on Trial 1831–1861* (Lexington: University of Kentucky Press, 1976).

4. Federal data, accessed on October 28, 2007, from http://users.bestweb.net/~rg/execution/DATA%20FEDERAL.htm, Internet.

5. Ken Chowder, "The Father of American Terrorism," *American Heritage Magazine* 51, no. 1 (February/March 2000), accessed on October 28, 2007, from http://www.americanheritage.com/articles/magazine/ah/2000/1/2000_1_81.shtml, Internet.

6. William Hogeland, *The Whiskey Rebellion: George Washington, Alexander Hamilton, and the Frontier Rebels Who Challenged America's Newfound Sovereignty* (New York: Scribner, 2006).

7. *Kawakita v. United States*, 343 U.S. 717 (1952).

8. Philip Van Doren Stern, *Secret Missions of the Civil War* (New York: Wings Books, 1990), 54–64.

9. Ibid., 96–107.

10. "The Trial of Ethel and Julius Rosenberg," *Famous Trials*, retrieved on October 23, 2007, from http://www.law.umkc.edu/faculty/projects/ftrials/rosenb/ROSENB.HTM, Internet.

11. *Ex Parte Quirin*, 317 U.S. 1 (1942).

12. *Frederick Duquesne: Interesting Case Write Up*, FBI website recovered on October 25, 2007, from http://foia.fbi.gov/duquesne_frederick_interesting_case_write_up/duquesne_frederick_intersting_case_write_up_part01.pdf, Internet.

13. S. W. Harman, *Hell on the Border: He Hanged Eighty-Eight Men* (Lincoln: University of Nebraska Press, 1992).

14. S. L. A. Marshall, *Crimsoned Prairie: The Indian Wars*, reprint paperback edition (New York: Da Capo Press, 1984), 24–28; Alan Axelrod, *Chronicle of the Indian Wars: from Colonial Times to Wounded Knee* (New York: Prentice Hall General Reference, 1993), 190–195.

15. James L. Swanson, *Manhunt: The Twelve-Day Chase for Lincoln's Killer* (New York: HarperCollins, 2006).

16. *Ex Parte Gordon*, 66 U. S. 503 (1861).

17. Nathan Miller, *The U.S. Navy: An Illustrated History* (Annapolis, MD: United States Naval Institute Press, 1977), 128–129.

18. Uzal W. Ent, *The Sad Story of Private Eddie Slovik*, retrieved on October 27, 2007, from http://28–110-k.org/sad_story_of_private_eddie_slovi.html, Internet.

19. *Furman v. Georgia*, 408 U.S. 238 (1972).

20. *Woodson v. North Carolina*, 428 U.S. 280 (1976); *Roberts v. Louisiana*, 428 U.S. 325 (1976), 431 U.S. 633 (1977); *Coker v. Georgia*, 433 U.S. 584 (1977).

21. *Gregg v. Georgia*, 428 U.S. 153 (1976); Kermit L. Hall, ed., *The Oxford Guide to United States Supreme Court Decisions* (New York: Oxford University Press, 1999), 60, 97–98, 112–113, 338–339.

22. "Federal Death Row Prisoners," *Death Penalty Information Center*, retrieved on October 29, 2007, from http://www.deathpenaltyinfo.org/article.php?scid=29&did=193, Internet.

CHAPTER 6

Ovines and Bovines

Ion Puschila

T HERE IS much to be said about the settlement of the area west of the Mississippi in the middle to latter part of the nineteenth century. The first thing that strikes any visitor who has bothered to tour the land is its vastness. One can drive along the many odd- and even-numbered freeways and marvel at the gall of those who attempted to traverse any part of it. Barren vistas, with gullies and arroyos that could swallow wagons whole, magnificent mountains that could daunt the most enterprising, and seemingly endless, apparently inhospitable deserts are all one sees.

Occasionally, there is a storm that covers the entire horizon, Armageddon itself inexorably creeping its way toward the observer. And that is in the summer. Winter is fatal if one is not prepared. The comfort of one's car affords the time to ponder that Willie Nelson could have written "The Redheaded Stranger" into any one of these settings.

The West was a battleground between man and nature, be it against the earth's caprices or against the nature of man. Pitted against one another were also law-abiding people and criminals, social norms of the period and immigrants, tension between different political entities that reflected the impending carnage that would consume the nation, as well as varied economic

interests. The importance of law in the American spirit is evidenced by looking at how individuals dealt with each other in an environment where there was no law.[1]

At the same time, the wave of reform of the antebellum period can be seen, as can the divisiveness that the country suffered until well after the Civil War. Popular sovereignty and the profitability of the West in the industrial expansion of the late nineteenth century further contributed to the larger picture. In the latter half of the century, there was also the question of integration into the nation. Some of the inimical interests, such as fights between Republicans and Democrats, also spurred vigilante violence.[2]

Only hardy, some at times ruthless, self-reliant characters could have taken it upon themselves to seize the opportunity that at first glance may have seemed the road to perdition. Mainly the young, brash, naïve, and full of hope came. The gold rush prompted many to move as quickly as possible to find wealth. Entire families clambered upon furniture-filled wagons to cross the western expanse, strewing behind a trail of household items, carcasses, and crosses along the ruts they called roads on the way to El Dorado.

Many did not make it, and of those who did few made any money from gold. The majority turned to other occupations, and populated the West.

Perhaps disingenuously to those who look at a map and may imagine that the entire West was settled by people moving in gradually after crossing the Mississippi, many of the Argonauts moved east from California into new mining towns along the Rockies, and settled in unpopulated territories as far away as Montana and Wyoming. Once the gilded dream turned to rust, most former miners settled into other occupations, and found golden opportunities in the dusty lands. There were farmers, ranchers, smiths of all types, professionals, and business owners who wrought civilization out of a mostly inhospitable expanse.

Only a few areas in this vast terrain had any semblance of law. Aside from a territorial marshal, county sheriff, and a deputy or two, much of this land had not yet been visited by a judge, and any legal infrastructure was usually distant, too far for impatient, busy men to transport an offender and await the outcome of a trial. Not only was there a concern about the distant and slow wheels of justice, or a witness moving to a new camp, but the risk that the criminal might flee the poorly built jailhouse, outrun the arm of the law which then was rather short, or in some other way escape justice. For these reasons, there was further motivation to have a speedy, local trial.[3] There was nearly limitless opportunity for miscreants.[4]

The amount of crime is perhaps remarkably small, given the potential for it that presented itself in the presence of a population not foreign to arms, witnessed by a large number of Mexican and Civil Wars veterans, along with others who had a criminal record. Some of the latter sought to mend their ways, and the former wanted opportunity, but guns were indispensable to any frontiersman, cattle driver, and settler. Perhaps it was a healthy respect for another armed human being, or maybe it was a sense of what is legal, fair even, that prevented more nefarious deportment. Even along the wagon trains, when a crime had been committed an ad hoc jury, judge, and if some felt competent, attorneys would be summoned up, and the guilty party tried and punished. Summary justice was commonplace in areas where a legal system did not exist.[5]

Vigilante movements have two generally characteristic traits: they are organized, and they exist for a limited amount of time.[6] They could be socially constructive and socially destructive. The former not only fought crime, but usually sought to reform the status quo.[7] Of the myriad groups that sprang up in the West, we shall look at three specific examples. In Montana, there was a need for crime fighters in the frontier communities, such as Bannack, while in San Francisco there was a sense of popular sovereignty.[8] On the other hand, in Wyoming the movement was socially destructive because it led to backlash, and fighting against the vigilantes, such as the Johnson County War and the later Ten Sleep incident.

Murder was a common reason for a capital sentence to be handed down, but rustling and theft often brought about a similar verdict. In what was termed as a fair fight, one between a couple of gunslingers who had been drinking, as well as perhaps gambling, and had a dispute between them, there would be no consequences for the survivor. On the other hand, when a man was killed without the chance to put up a fair fight, it was termed murder. As so often is the case, there are many reasons for so heinous an act, be they business affairs, crimes of passion, or simply larceny. In the latter case, stagecoaches were the target of many a holdup. Usually the robbers were polite and only took the lock box, containing some cash and gold.

The list of justifications for criminality has since grown to include psychological and socioeconomic factors, which we today employ to look at the past. Our recent ancestors often were endowed with a more straightforward view on life, whose surroundings provided little time to ponder a criminal's motivation through a Marxist philosophic paradigm. Occasionally perhaps the wrong man suffered the ultimate punishment, and a swift injustice happened upon an apparently hapless victim. As we shall see, there were also times when a man was hanged simply because "he needed killin."

There was a generally understood and prescribed way to administer justice among the vigilantes that preserved a mantra of legality. They were well organized into companies and squads, with a clear chain of command, often a written constitution put together by the leaders, and with great organization. A lot of the men had been in some militia, or the regular army, and had been battle-hardened by war with Mexico, the Native Americans, or the internecine struggle. Sometimes when a perpetrator was caught, there was a judge, and from time to time a jury, sometimes selected with some deliberation. Most often the judge and jury were the leaders, or the executive committee, of a vigilante group. The accused was not always present, and occasionally had already been hanged. A hanging would have been considered improper by many contemporaries absent the decorum of a trial to make an otherwise odious murder palatable.[9]

Unsurprisingly, the leaders of the vigilante committees were local business leaders. One may have surmised this because crime disrupts business, the most obvious of conclusions. Not as obvious is the fact that in some cases, such as California and Wyoming, there were different political and business interests that came into conflict, and vigilantism was used to intimidate opponents, occasionally kill some of them, and strengthen one's position. Associations that purportedly fought crime were at times also highly organized political and economic machines.

The precise figures for the number of deaths at the hands of the more than two hundred vigilance committees from 1850 to 1910 may vary

depending upon the interpretation of such a committee, but there were just over five hundred dead during that period.[10] Whippings and expulsions were ulterior punishments, but there were few of these. On average, after at most four deaths committees would disband, having accomplished their goals. There were exceptions, most notably in Montana. By and large most committees were under six hundred members, though there were a few exceptions, such as the one in San Francisco in 1856.[11]

The advent of the discovery of gold in California led to the rapid settlement of the area, which is why California was never a territory, having become a state too rapidly. San Francisco grew with each new shipload of forty-niners. The instant metropolis did not have the infrastructure to handle police duties. There were a couple of vigilante groups formed in the city, one in 1851, and one in 1856. Each one hanged a total of four men, but more importantly they became the model for most western states' committees.

By 1851, San Francisco became a hub of capitalism. So much so in fact that there was an oversupply and business was slow. Inventories remained large, and insufficient orders came in to fill them. In its history, since the arrival of the Argonauts and up to the earthquake of 1906, the city was plagued by fire. Furthermore, there evolved a growing three-way political battle going on among the Democrats, Whigs, and growing numbers of independent-minded citizens. The latter thought themselves to be a force of reform and change, mirroring the sentiments of a polarized nation slipping into the cauldron of war. Indeed, it appears the former two more-established political entities had reached a level of stagnation.[12]

A decrease in business provided the idle hands. Frequent fires and greater demand for reform led many to believe in the existence of some nefarious criminal element, a thought that was the devil's work. The misfortune befell many arriving

Australians, who bore the brunt of the blame of the campaign to stamp out crime. They were generally poor, probably no more criminal, or more innocent, than other elements of the population, but gained a reputation from newspaper accounts of the southern continent's penal colony role. A small percentage of them were former convicts, but the great majority was like all other newcomers, people seeking opportunity.[13]

It was not difficult to discover perpetrators, and then Jensen's store robbery in February 1851, along with some fire alarms and criticism of local law enforcement by some loyal newspapers, led a number of citizens to come together at Samuel Brennan's store, a leading merchant and landowner who was an avid advocate of summary hangings. They created the Committee of Vigilance in June of that year. Nearly two hundred leading citizens attended a third meeting, wrote a constitution immediately, and started looking for the thieves. Inevitably, one was found and hanged. Jenkins's wounds were consistent with strangulation, and the authorities sought the arrest of some vigilantes. When a list of eight emerged, 180 vigilantes swore in a published statement to have collectively partaken in holding the rope. No legal action ensued.[14]

There would be three more hangings. James Stuart, a man with a lengthy criminal record, hanged in July. The remaining two had been taken into custody by the sheriff, who collected Robert McKenzie and Samuel Whittaker from the vigilantes' headquarters and put them in the county jail. They had just been sentenced to death by the committee, and were to be hanged soon. Four days later, incensed vigilantes stormed the jail on Sunday morning during service, took them back to the headquarters, and hanged them both on the spot.[15]

Aside from those executed, of the ninety-one people brought to justice, forty-one were set free, fifteen were given over to the marshal, one was

flogged, fourteen were deported under the threat of death, and the same number were encouraged to leave town. They were predominantly Australian, though the man who was flogged was Mexican. Furthermore, the vigilantes' campaign against foreigners led to one incident of mob frenzy resulting in the lynching of two purported arsonists who were not hanged, but stomped to death, and the whipping of another Mexican on the same night.[16] Xenophobes or crime fighters, the 1851 committee did not succeed in stopping fires in San Francisco or making crime much less of a problem. They would try again.

Unlike the immigrant Aussies, Catholicism has deep roots in California, and in the early 1850s there was an influx of Irish from the East Coast. David Broderick's Democratic Party machine in San Francisco counted a large number of them in its ranks, in part explaining the support for the Know Nothings. Mirroring national politics, the party was itself increasingly split into Tammany (northern) and Chivalry (southern) factions. The American Party, or Know Nothings, had established a branch in the bay area in 1854. Contemporary San Francisco was an ideal location for a nativist party.[17]

The newcomers had elected a mayor in 1855, and the governor of the state was elected the same year. It seems likely that all three political organizations, to lesser or greater degrees, used thugs, stuffed ballots, and generally did whatever it took to win elections. But the Tammany Democrats had more experience because they brought highly adept people in from New York, and had gained the support of the poorer elements of society.[18] To the extent that there was graft and corruption there is no doubt, as the results of the American Party's reforms would bear out in the end.[19]

On the opposite end of the spectrum were the erstwhile Committee of Vigilance members, reform-minded merchants, almost all of whom belonged to the Know Nothing Party. Among the more colorful characters was James King, who took it upon himself to stir things. After a stint of looking for gold, he had come to town on business and became a banker, lost his money to crooks, and opened a newspaper. Newspapers of that era are entertaining to read, as they were nothing like the modern press. Vitriolic, partisan, full of accusations and innuendos, the press editorialized and speculated broadly. James King of William (a reference to his father's name, not a location or title) was aptly named, as his *San Francisco Daily Evening Bulletin* gained immense success and popularity for the critical broadsides it fired upon all leading citizens, but especially Democrats and Irish.[20]

How true to his mark King was by inferring corrupt bargains among the keepers of the port, the marshal, the local Catholic Church leaders, and David Broderick who allegedly ran Tammany Democratic politics as well as Mayor Van Ness's office, is subject to speculation. Yet there was some doubt about the validity of Van Ness's election, as well as some who sat on the Board of Supervisors. Needless to say, he rattled some cages. The last straw came when the *San Francisco Daily Evening Bulletin* attacked a rival publisher, James Patrick Casey, the recent owner of the *Sunday Times* and a Chivalry Democrat. As a side note to the impending crisis the nation would suffer, the latter newspaper offended one of the city's bankers, William Tecumseh Sherman (of later fame), who swore to throw Casey out the window of his third-story office. He was spared the effort.[21]

King dug up Casey's background in New York and published it. Among the biographical highlights were: enforcer for the Democrats, jail time in Sing Sing, and the fraudulent election that put Casey on the Board of Supervisors in San Francisco without his name ever appearing on any ballot. Casey wished to appear a respectable

citizen, and he disliked having his past brought up. He stormed into King's office and demanded an apology on May 15, 1856. None was offered as no libel took place, and Casey left. That evening, as he left his office, James King was shot down in the street by James Casey. The citizens arrested Casey and had him thrown in jail.[22]

James Patrick Casey was of Irish descent, along with Marshal Mulligan, a former enforcer for the Tammany Democrats and now in charge of enforcing the law, to the skepticism of many citizens. So William Coleman took charge, and the call went out to assemble the vigilantes, and within a couple of days there were nearly seven thousand, ten times more than in 1851. Events unfolded rapidly.[23]

Despite the arrival and clemency pleas of the Know Nothing governor of California, J. Neely Johnson, and the call to arms of a hundred militia led by William Tecumseh Sherman, some three thousand vigilantes stormed the jail. They dragged a cannon and pointed it at the entrance, where Sheriff David Scannell stood. Not far off was Mayor Van Ness, who was equally helpless. Sherman may have been one of many bankers who tacitly supported the vigilantes, as well as donating money to the committee. Regardless of his covert actions, overtly he did nothing to stop the proceedings.[24]

The sheriff quickly handed over two prisoners—James Casey and another Irishman, Charles Cora. Cora had shot William Richardson, the federal marshal of the Northern District of California and a hero of the Mexican War, over an argument about a remark made by Richardson's wife and daughter at the theater regarding the reputation of Cora's girlfriend, Arabella Ryan.[25]

Neither Cora nor Ryan were the most upstanding of citizens, he a gambler, and she the most famous madam in town. Both also happened to be Papists in the eyes of well-bred Protestants. Cora found the incident humorous, but Richardson did not. As the argument heated up outside a saloon, Cora claims he feared Richardson would shoot him because he had his hands in his pockets. The former then pulled out a derringer and shot the marshal dead. He had been tried and the jury was hung, seemingly finding that Richardson was the aggressor. The gambler awaited a retrial, and got a very speedy one, but not from the legal system he anticipated.[26]

The two prisoners, Casey and Cora, were taken to Fort Gunnybags, as the vigilantes termed their headquarters. They were tried on the eighteenth. During the proceedings it was discovered that James King had died of his wounds. Now Casey would also be tried for murder. Inevitably both were found guilty and hanged from the façade of the two-storied Fort Gunnybags, but not before Charles Cora married Arabella Ryan. He was granted his last request, and an Italian Catholic priest was brought into the midst of the Know Nothings to perform the wedding. It does seem that Cora had a sense of humor to the very end. They were inanimate witnesses to James King's funeral procession later in the day.[27]

Shortly thereafter, the committee sought out a number of Democratic appointees, such as Marshal Mulligan, and a number of others in different city offices. All were deported. A former Democratic mayor and judge left town on business and vacation, and the vigilantes pondered charging David Broderick with crimes. Instead he was brought in for questioning and released, whereupon he left town. The following year he was sent to the senate by the state legislature. It seems he was too well connected to go after, but Broderick's political machine was destroyed.

The governor of California declared San Francisco County in a state of insurrection and ordered Sherman to form a militia force. Sherman raised a few hundred men, whom he found deplorable, refused to get weapons, and resigned his command after his proposed compromise with the vigilantes was refused by the governor. The next commander, Volney Howard, did get some arms from the federal government, but the shipment was confiscated by the Committee of Vigilance and the boatmen arrested. David Terry, a former Chivalry Democrat turned Know Nothing who pleaded unsuccessfully with Sherman to put an end to the vigilantes, devised another scheme to topple the merchants' hold over San Francisco.

Terry, a state supreme court justice, called miners down from the mountains to rid the city of vigilantes. The element of surprise was lost, and the vigilantes met the miners. In the ensuing scuffle, lost by the invaders, Terry stabbed a Know Nothing operative. Vigilantes arrested the judge and put him on trial for five weeks. By then the committee had disbanded, and Terry was freed. He, too, was too well connected to hang. That was not the case for Philander Brace, a low-level Democrat enforcer who was to be deported but was charged with two murders that had occurred during the elections of the past year, and Joseph Hetherington who shot and killed Dr. Andrew Randall. They were put on trial and hanged on July 29. This was the last of the Committee of Vigilance's acts, and it adjourned on August 18.[28]

There were many consequences to the brief rule of the committee. In three months they changed the political landscape of San Francisco, dismantled the Democratic Party machine, and created a new political organization, the People's Party. It would rule the city for eleven years uninterrupted. There is no evidence that the new administration was any more adept in handling city finances and managing the town. But politics are a matter of perception, and quite often humans are easily mollified by a government that gives them the sense of reform, even if such reform may be insignificant. The committee's reputation spread quickly, and became an inspiration to other westerners who sought to eliminate crime in their own backyards. Some contemporary

Californians also moved, ending up all over the West, and more specifically Montana, where vigilantism peaked later.

To this day Montana honors its vigilantes with markings on police cruisers, 3-7-77, the numerical mark of warning originally posted on residences in Helena. One of the men who moved from California was a very interesting character, Henry Plummer. His journey to Montana provides a microcosm for many whose wonderings landed them in the same territory. Nevertheless, Plummer's story is an adventurous travail to the gallows.

Raised in Wisconsin, he had gone west to seek his fortune in the gold fields, found none, but was able to get into business in Nevada City, California. Plummer was a sociable man; he made friends quickly, and joined the Democratic Party. In 1854 the affiliation seemed a sound decision. By 1856, as he ran for the office of sheriff of Nevada County, the Democratic Party was on the wane because of the San Francisco Committee of Vigilance's work.[29]

The Democrats were seen as corrupt, and the Know Nothings made great inroads in taking power from them. But his popularity got him the seven-vote edge he needed for the office. This event, and another incident where a posse of vigilantes sought to arrest the same party at the same time as he and began a gun fight, made Plummer wary of vigilantes. As in San Francisco, the Know Nothings launched a head-on campaign to rid the county of Democrat office holders. Plummer's reputation as a bar fly, and his failure to prevent violence on a couple of occasions, together with his killing of John Vedder, with whose wife he was alleged to have had an affair, only made it easier to unseat him in September 1857. The Vedder affair would ultimately land him in the newly built San Quentin prison, having gone from sheriff and potential Democratic candidate for state office to inmate in a little over one year.[30]

As divorce procedures began, Plummer and one of his men took turns protecting Lucy Vedder from her violent husband. One night, during Plummer's shift, John Vedder came into the house, and if the sight of Plummer with his wife in front of the fireplace did not slay him, the sheriff's bullets did. In his first trial he was found guilty, but Justice Terry of the Supreme Court of California explained in a majority decision that the jury had been tainted. Plummer's second trial took place in September 1858. He was again found guilty and sentenced to twelve years hard labor. There was plenty of doubt, and he probably should not have been convicted, but juries in small towns were not always impartial, and at times swayed by politics.[31]

In prison Plummer's robust health plummeted to the former frailty of his youth. Due to that, his friendship with the prison doctor, as well as much support from friends, he won an early release in the form of a pardon from the governor in August 1859. Free and healthy, he turned up in Nevada City once again. It is possible he faked the severity of his pulmonary illness in the San Quentin hospital because he would recover rather miraculously from a couple of horrid wounds in the next four years. The marshal appointed him constable, and Plummer was back in business. However, the townspeople were loath to have him back and he lost his job when the marshal was not re-elected. He wandered over to the Nevada gold fields, and back to California, then in 1861 returned to Nevada City and got into trouble again. He fought a man, who died of the gash inflicted upon him by Plummer's gun butt, over patronage of a particular prostitute in Irish Maggie's whorehouse (the Know Nothings apparently did not want all Papists banished).[32]

No charges were filed, but then he killed a knife-wielding Confederate sympathizer in Ashmore's brothel and was jailed again. A gravely wounded Plummer escaped jail and made his way to Carson City, where his friend Billy Mayfield provided him with a safe place to recover. When Mayfield killed Sheriff John Blackburn, who suspected him of harboring Plummer, both men left town. Mayfield was captured but escaped, and Plummer ended up in the Idaho mining camps, where he and two former San Quentin inmates he met up with killed a saloon keeper. It seems that the seeds of the robbery gang he reputedly led were sown here.[33]

Plummer wandered into what was at that time Idaho, and in May 1863 he left Fort Benton and settled in Bannack. These settlements would become part of a new territory, Montana, in 1864. There he helped catch and kill Jack Cleveland, a former associate who had robbed and killed a man. Vehemently opposed to vigilantism as Plummer was, he saw no conflict of interest in shooting Cleveland, especially after the latter, drunk, began talking about old times and was about to divulge Plummer's checkered past. No charges were filed, and though a trial was later held, he was found innocent. After another altercation, where he was shot from behind and wounded in the arm, a wound that he miraculously recovered from with both life and limb, he had become a popular man. There being no government anywhere near Bannack, the elders decided to start one, and fill the positions of judge, sheriff, and coroner. Plummer won the election for sheriff.[34]

At first glance he was a pleasant, civilized man, seemingly without reproach, who wanted to start his life over. He was also made a member of the local Masonic Lodge, consequently earning Plummer the dubious distinction of being the only Mason hanged by the vigilantes.[35] He left immediately to propose to a woman he had met along his pilgrimage to Fort Benton. In his absence, he appointed some deputies, men of dubious character of whom two were San Quentin escapees. Mining towns are a magnet for myriad characters, and his choices may have been limited as most men were engaged in the diggings, with few

idle hands about. In his absence, the Alder Gulch discovery was made, and half of Bannack and its deputies promptly went prospecting for treasure licitly or otherwise.

Sheriff Plummer returned to a completely different town. He married Electa Bryan, of a good family background from Ohio, on June 30, 1863. In early September she left for Iowa, having grown weary of a lonely, log cabin life, and her husband planned to follow her in autumn. He would never see his wife again. Though his own town had grown quieter, and some of his more questionable deputies left for the rapidly burgeoning towns of Nevada City and Virginia City where the new claims were staked, trouble loomed. An increase in crime, more about his own past coming to light, and the overall state of affairs in a territorial government that had little control over a vast space conspired to get in the way of Plummer's apparent efforts to start a new life.[36]

Idaho Territory, as it still was until a year later, was rather sparse and barren, not only in landscape, but also in any governmental and legal infrastructure. There was a federal marshal in Lewiston whose territory was too vast for him to police alone, and there were local sheriffs, like Plummer, along with judges and coroners, elected and paid by the inhabitants at their own expense and organization. Plummer himself made twice weekly trips to Virginia City, about eighty miles away from Bannack, not an inconsiderable distance. Under these circumstances, the law was already in the hands of the locals, and trials were haphazard affairs. At times there were even attorneys, like H. P. A. Smith, who successfully defended Charley Forbes (aka Richardson), in the murder of Deputy D. H. Dillingham.[37]

To be sure, there were a few hangings in the territory, one of which was conducted by Plummer himself in Bannack, loath as he may have been to summary justice. Peter Horan had shot his mining partner over the dividends of their efforts. Judge B. B. Burchette presided over the trial and meted out the sentence.[38]

Many of the miners were not planning to spend the winter in Alder Gulch. The majority went back to the states for the winter to see family, pay debtors, invest some of the money, and returned in the spring to mine their claims again. As they made plans to leave, they could go through Bannack toward Salt Lake City, or head to Fort Benton for a ferry down the Missouri. On the road to Bannack, many were robbed by masked men. These robbers were at times identified and reported to the sheriff. It seemed increasingly to many locals, however, that since Plummer caught none of them he may have been part of the gang.[39]

Moreover, a couple of leading citizens could swear they had seen him, one in the dead of a winter night emerging from some willows beside the wagon trail with three accomplices, and another who supposedly recognized his gun and a small piece of the red lining of the sheriff's vest as he held up a wagon with his masked accomplices. Neither of these stories is particularly plausible, but perception is paramount, and some colluded to cast aspersions and doubt upon Plummer.

In the meantime, a copy of the *Sacramento Union* was delivered to Samuel Hauser, wherein there was an article about Plummer's California days. Hauser was the man who did not like Plummer from the very beginning and who tried to block his appointment to deputy federal marshal, a promotion that arrived by mail shortly after Plummer hanged.[40] It is difficult to understand a small town mentality, the rumors, machinations, and the generally petty disputes that can lead to one's ostracism, or loss of favor, unless one has lived in such an environment.

Plausibly, it is the fate that befell Plummer. On the other hand, the sheriff was a staunch Democrat and leading vigilantes were Republican at a time when the nation was at war.[41] In defense of the vigilantes, the road to Bannack had become too dangerous to travel by December, and the sheriff appeared to have a way of making himself scarce each time a stagecoach would set off. Instead of fighting crime, he was too preoccupied with other affairs of which nobody had any idea.[42]

The event that triggered the beginning of the vigilante committees was the murder and robbery of a young man on an errand. Nicholas Thiebolt was sent to purchase a couple of mules from George Ives. Ives and two alleged accomplices were accused of the crime. All three were arrested, after Ives tried to make an escape on a fast pony, and brought to trial. Ives came from a well-to-do family from Wisconsin, but he left home, in spite of his father's advice, to seek his fortune in 1852. From California he drifted among gold fields and army bases, from job to job. He found little in the way of riches, settling in Bannack, then moving to Adler Gulch where he bought weary animals, nursed them back to health, and sold them.

Once in Nevada City, Ives hired all the lawyers in an effort to prevent the prosecution from getting one. Wilbur Sanders, a civil lawyer who had never handled a criminal trial, acceded to represent the prosecution. There were two judges present, Byam from Nevada City and Wilson from Junction. The latter advised Sanders to enlist the help of an eloquent speaker, a local miner who was a great orator. Sanders had a difficult time believing that the apparition before him could do anything of the sort, but Charles Bagg spoke intelligently, despised Ives, and could easily relate to the miners who made up the jury.[43]

The jury consisted of two dozen men from Nevada City and Junction, despite the fact that Ives had sought to have his friend, Virginia City sheriff "Buzz" Caven, insist on a list of men who were friends with the accused. The trial was held outdoors and there was the danger that Ives's friends may try to rescue him. Sanders wished to portray the accused as a man with an inclination toward crime. He enlisted the help of anyone in the crowd who felt they had suffered an injustice at the hands of Ives, and asked them to be witnesses on the spot. The judges allowed this spontaneous testimony. The night before closing arguments, Sanders went to a meeting with his host, Nicholas Wall.[44]

The back room of Nye and Kenna's store in Virginia awaited John Nye, Alvin Bookie, and Paris Pfouts. One vigilante committee was born that night, and Pfouts became its president. There had been talk of vigilantism for over a month, and the San Francisco example came to many of the locals' minds. They agreed that if a guilty verdict were reached, they would hang Ives immediately without waiting for his lawyers to issue pleas, try to file appeals, or in any way disturb the outcome as had been done in the Dillingham case. Another, less organized group had its start during the trial and consisted of John Lott, a storekeeper, and "Old Man" Clark, the man in whose employ Thiebolt had been. They had the support of James Williams, commander of the guards at the trial.

On December 21, closing arguments were made and the jury took half an hour to decide. One man did not believe there was proof of guilt beyond reasonable doubt. Sanders then asked the crowd what the verdict should be based on the jury's findings, and the crowd found Ives guilty. Judge Byam asked the crowd to vote on the sentence of hanging, and there was an enthusiastic approval of the motion. It took a short time to fashion a makeshift gallows, and despite his pleas to wait until the morning so that he might write some letters to his family, Ives was hanged after proclaiming his innocence and blaming the murder on Aleck (Alex) Carter.[45]

The following day was the trial of the other two accused, but neither was lynched, though one was banished in the dead of winter. Following the trial, there was much discussion as to the procedural aspects. The jury was not unanimous, and there was little order of witnesses, but these facts were not part of the debate, and most men agreed that it took entirely too long and something had to be done to more swiftly bring perpetrators to justice. The first brief constitution of the vigilantes was penned on the twenty-third by the Lott committee. They formed a posse that included many of the men on the Ives raid, and went after Carter.[46]

A few days later, the two groups joined forces and wrote a proper constitution at Jeremiah Fox's house in Alder Gulch, with the help of some veterans from the San Francisco committee. Unlike the California vigilantes, in Montana there was no power struggle, and members had a wide range of political sympathies—Republican, Copperhead, Confederate, and Masons. There was no overt, underlying political agenda, or xenophobia, simply a wish to eradicate crime. They agreed to hand down only one sentence—death—once someone was found guilty. Just over a hundred men joined up,[47] and though most were businessmen, there were miners and laborers among them. Their zeal would become legendary, establishing a tradition in Montana that would last into the twentieth century.

There would be twenty-one executions related to the gang of thieves purportedly led by Sheriff Plummer before the end of January 1864, and thirty total for the Bannack and Virginia City committees.[48] In the next twenty-year period, Helena vigilantes hanged ten men. The most deaths at the hands of a vigilance committee came in 1884, however, in the Musselshell area, when thirty-five rustlers hanged at the hands of Stuart's Stranglers.[49] They were thus named because the man who owned most of the land and cattle, as well as leading the committee, was Granville Stuart.

Theoretically, the executive committee would weigh the evidence and decide what action to take in any case where a man was accused. Summary hangings, with decisions sanctioned by the executive committee only after the punishment, took place as well. Plummer himself was hardly an angel, but the extent of his guilt is questionable, and based only on the confession of a man who was soon to hang, as well as on a dubious eyewitness account wherein the witness saw a small patch of red on a vest.[50]

One man hanged because he was a public nuisance. Slade liked to drink and ride his horse down the main street, guns ablazing, and go into a saloon. A bit of a hell-raiser, and a member of the vigilantes, he was a married man but had a drinking problem. Virginia City grew tired of his alcoholic antics and summarily hanged him. It seems "he needed killin." Patience was not a virtue when it came to justice, and the vigilantes killed James Brady before his victim made a full recovery from his wounds. John "The Hat" Dolan had the unusual distinction of being kidnapped from Utah Territory by the vigilantes, brought back to Nevada City, Montana, and hanged for having stolen a bag of gold dust from his partner. Dolan offered to make restitutions, but was denied the chance. R. C. Rawley, a drunk who had been banished in January and returned by October, complained about the vigilantes in a letter. People looked up to him on Halloween morning, only to see a man without feet dressed in rags.[51]

After Montana became a territory in May 1864, there arrived judges, marshals, and at least the trappings of government, a proper code of law, both civil and criminal. There was an effort by the authorities to stop vigilante justice, particularly by Chief Justice Hezekiah Hosmer. It was of little avail.[52] The governor, Sidney Edgerton, was a standpatter and a radical Republican.[53] He had been a territorial judge in Bannack when the vigilantes began operating there, who could have taken the initiative to lead those men toward more lawful resolutions but did nothing to stop their activities. Indeed he loaned the committee the small cannon he had in his home to go after Jose Pinzanthia, "the Greaser," another suspected

of membership in the Plummer gang and a notorious drunk. Pinzanthia resisted arrest, shot and killed a vigilante, and had his cabin bombed by three shells before he was captured, barely alive, and hanged.[54]

Gold fields continued to crop up, such as in Helena, and crime accompanied the prospectors despite the creation of the Committee of Safety. Even while James Ashley, the Ohio representative and head of the House Committee on Territories, visited Helena, the locals hanged a thief. A new territorial secretary came to Montana in September 1865 to serve in the role of acting governor until one was appointed. Edgerton wished to leave the territory to bring his young daughter up in a more urbane environment. In stark contrast to the laissez-faire Edgerton, Thomas Meagher sought to reign in the vigilantes, but had a severe drinking problem that affected his credibility. It would drown him, literally, as he drank too much and fell off a boat in 1867.[55]

The Committee of Safety hanged James Daniels from the "Hanging Tree" in Helena even though in his pocket there was an official pardon from Secretary Meagher. Montana vigilantes even sent a posse to Denver, Colorado, to lynch a stagecoach driver, whom they thought complicit in a robbery that resulted in four deaths.

Notwithstanding the increased presence of federal authority and complaints by citizens from Montana and adjacent territories, membership in the committees grew yearly. Though activity should have decreased, it did not. Authorities did little to stop vigilantes, and the many citizens who objected feared reprisals. Anyone could find a note with the numbers 3-7-77 on their door for any reason. The committees terrorized whomever they felt deserving of attention, but nobody had the power, the will, or the gall to stop the vigilantes. As the population stabilized by the early twentieth century, crime decreased dramatically. The bloodiest episode in American vigilantism ended, but not the practice itself, as the latter part of the nineteenth century saw it flare up in other nearby areas, such as Wyoming.

The territory of Wyoming came into being as rails began to cross the continent, and it became a state in 1890. The country lends itself to ranching mainly, and there were large cattle herds since the late 1860s. Big Horn Basin, a county as of 1896, could count only one white inhabitant in 1879, J. D. Woodruff, in an area three times the size of Connecticut. Cattlemen began to appear around that time, and most of the cowboys who arrived with the herds were young, rash, rowdy, and tough, not foreign to violence. In the early 1880s, some trading posts cropped up, like that of the popular Frenchman Victor Arland, one of many miners coming out of the Black Hills. Law, on the other hand, was distant and very slow to act in this region.[56]

Vigilante activity in Wyoming began in the frontier town of Cheyenne, with the committee established there in 1868. They claimed to have patterned themselves after the San Francisco example as well, and eradicated crime in the year-old town. Proper authorities arrived and the need for Judge Lynch decreased.[57] This is an example of socially constructive vigilantes. On the other hand, there were those movements that ruined communities, if not permanently, then only temporarily.

That same year, in November, Bear River City had two vigilante groups, arbitrarily one consisting of the upstanding citizens, and the other of ruffians. The former lynched three criminals, leading to riots by the latter. Then the good citizens arrested some of the thugs. The other vigilantes sent a couple hundred men to free the arrested. They burned the jail and were intercepted by their enemies. A large gun battle ensued, with a dozen dead and a couple score wounded until the cavalry came to break it up. No one was charged for anything. Bear River City ended up abandoned as

Union Pacific changed its mind about a railroad switch there.[58]

There were many incidents of sporadic violence as well. In 1885, twenty-eight Chinese scabs were murdered by striking miners. No charges were brought against anyone. Two years after admission into the union in 1890, Wyoming had another bloodbath, named the Johnson County War, where big ranchers fought against perceived encroachments on the land by small ranchers. The big ranchers accused the new settlers of rustling, and, backed by the Wyoming Stock Growers' Association (WSGA), they first sought economic measures to drive out competition. When that failed, they lynched and hired guns to remedy what they regarded as encroachment.[59] On the other hand, small ranchers and sheepmen formed their own organization, along with the homesteaders, the Northern Wyoming Farmers' and Stock Growers' Association.[60]

In collusion with big cattle, a secret Union Pacific train full of Texans, carrying an arsenal with them, passed through the state on its way to Johnson County.[61] The staunchly Republican WSGA controlled much of state politics from Cheyenne to such an extent that even Governor Amos Barber supported the assault with weapons and a call to the militia to do nothing if reports of violence came out of Johnson County.[62] Until the federal cavalry arrived, the mercenary force of fifty Texans that assembled to kill the newcomers succeeded in killing two men, but were encircled, vastly outnumbered by their intended victims who took up their guns in self-defense.

Once arrested, a note was discovered in the pockets of their leader, ex-sheriff Frank Canton, with a few dozen names of people who were to die, and the price the WSGA would pay for each dead rustler.[63] Despite the damning evidence, all were released on bail, and most disappeared. No serious effort was made to prosecute any of them, or any of the men in Cheyenne whose names had been divulged by some of the hired guns. They were too well connected, and none of the witnesses showed up for the trials.[64] The raid having failed, Tom Horn, a hired gun, was employed subsequently and covertly to get rid of the rustlers. He seems to have been successful because resistance ceased by 1901.[65] Johnson County's neighbor to the west is Big Horn County, and the violence spread to that area.

Vigilantism in Big Horn Basin differed from San Francisco and Bannack in that the perpetrators were out to protect the investments of one portion of the population at the expense of another. Buffalo's Bill Cody's Shoshone Land and Irrigation Company sought to build canals and attract settlers to the area in the 1890s. Some trickled in, but not enough for the company to make money.[66] The interest of local vigilantes was to terrorize and exclude from the territory all parties inimical to the cattle business. The WSGA used the local newspapers to publish articles about the land's inhospitability for farming to keep out homesteaders, to paint the small ranchers as rustlers, and to discredit the "woolies" at every turn. The cattle community organized itself and sought by any means possible, violence if necessary, to keep the land for their herds.

Basin became Big Horn County's seat. In 1903, there was the lynching of James Gorman and Joseph Walters, who were shot to death in their jail cell after the mob could not break down the bars to hang them. In the process of keeping the crowd from the prisoners, Deputy Earl Price died, and George Mead the jailer suffered a wound. Were it not for a respected young man's shooting death, the matter would have ended there. Price's death led to an investigation, arrests, trials, and acquittals for all involved.[67]

Much as in Johnson County, the 1880s led to an influx of settlers upon what the cattlemen perceived as their country. Though the Big Horn Basin was federal land, open to use by all, ranchers had a proprietary outlook on the land. Homesteaders came and staked claims. Worse, by 1881 there were more sheep than cattle, and ovines multiplied faster. As happened in all other areas from Texas to Oregon, the sight of sheep struck the ranchers as a vision of Satan. These grazing range wars would be waged in the West until the 1920s, resulting in the loss of over fifty lives, and tens of thousands of sheep.[68] Friction between the different Wyoming livestock raisers increased, such that in 1897 the two sides met and decided to draw a boundary separating the pastures. The feeble effort to divvy up land belonging to all and none who sought to raise stock predictably failed.[69]

The trouble started with Ben Minnick's death in 1897, killed because his sheep seemed to have crossed the line. At the end of the range wars, culminating in the raids of 1908, more than six men died, countless thousands of sheep, valuable sheep dogs, horses, and inestimable amounts of property belonging to the sheepherders destroyed. Sheepherder S. A. Guthrie, with the help of the Wyoming Woolgrowers Association, did hire an able detective, Joe LeFors, and a team of attorneys to bring the fight to the cattlemen, and though the perpetrators were not brought to justice, he did win some civil damages and concessions over the right of "woolies" to share the range.[70] The climax of the struggle would come in the 1909 Ten Sleep raid.

Two new Joes, Allemand and Emge, bought into the area and started raising sheep. They trekked to a new pasture along Spring Creek, along with their employees, Jules Lazier, Pete Cafferal, and Charles David "Bounce" Helmer. Ambushed by cattlemen at night, the wagon they slept in was set on fire. It burned so quickly that Emge and Lazier did not get out. Allemand stumbled out and was shot when he got to his feet. The other two were captured and tied but left to live after witnessing part of the massacre. This was too much for the authorities, as well as the local population, to stomach despite the fact that the cattlemen had thus far been able to operate with impunity. Governor Bryant Brooks, though a Republican who had been backed by the WSGA, expressly wanted all involved prosecuted.[71]

County Attorney Percy Metz had a notion to subpoena all cattlemen in the basin if necessary. Sheriff Felix Alston capably built a list of suspects and focused on them. Eventually, there was a grand jury indictment of seven men: George Saban (who had also been among the leaders in the Gorman and Walters lynchings), Milton Alexander, Bill Keyes, Charley Faris, Ed Eaton, Herb Brink, and Tommy Dixon. Keyes and Faris testified for the prosecution, and quickly left Wyoming in fear after the trial and conviction of the other five. The trial was a turning point because despite the efforts of the cattlemen, who pulled all the strings possible, bought the two local papers, attempted to pack the jury, and brought in expert legal help, they failed to keep the defendants out of jail.[72]

When the trial ended, before going to prison, the sentenced men were feted by the cattle-ranching community who threw them a magnificent party, honoring them as heroes. Saban would later escape and disappear, while the only one who served most of his sentence was Bink, who would participate in a jailhouse lynching. The net effect was a loss of power by the cattlemen, for by now mutton and wool formed a greater share of the economy.[73] Change also reflected in the elections of 1910, where Democrat Joseph Carey became the new governor. It was the end of vigilantism in Wyoming. The law had arrived even in the remotest corners of the state to assert its authority. *The Man Who Shot Liberty Valence* comes to mind here.

There were a number of reasons for the creation of a vigilante committee. Some of these committees were allowed by the local agencies of the law to operate with relative impunity, either because

they were the local establishment, or because the vigilantes vastly outnumbered marshals and sheriffs. In the absence of uniform statutes properly enforced by a strong legal infrastructure, crime is merely a perception relative to the majority, and there were those who on occasion were found on the side of the few. When vigilantes operated in urban areas they created powerful organizations that wielded political influence.

What we see in these groups of men is the effort, misguided and flawed as it often was, to create a better environment for the community they were a part of. Many later rose to prominent positions if they had not yet attained them. The microcosms of activity in California, Montana, and Wyoming are illustrative of a nation that changed rapidly over the sixty years following 1850. Evidenced in them are popular sovereignty at work in antebellum reform efforts, the divisiveness brought on by the Civil War, and the populist struggle of the small farmer against big business.

There are perhaps more conclusions about ourselves that we can draw from this. Certainly by looking at a period of time we discover that the humans who lived then were shaped by their environment, physical and cultural, and that in the end we are only too human. More so, however, Americans have had a dauntless sense of fairness and justice, be it before the law or in politics. They can be seen in our indignation at injustice. Our disgruntled acceptance of politics at times veils an undercurrent of change that surfaces when we become sufficiently nauseated, as was the case with that admirer of the Montana vigilantes and progressive leader, Teddy Roosevelt. Even though shunned by Granville Stuart,[74] Teddy went trust-busting against those corporations he thought bad, a parallel to vigilantism.

An enterprising capitalist spirit continues to drive Americans. Modern Argonauts continue to act on economic interest, which leads us into unchartered waters of finance, new investment opportunities, and at times flawed foreign policy. Yet in spite of our difficulties, the weakness of the dollar, or the price of oil, Americans have a resilience that makes us the envied pariah of the world. Most importantly, the impetuousness of the young man heading west, symbolic of a nation, is still in our character because Americans rarely sit still. We are always looking for the next opportunity, the hope that the next lode is just around the bend, like the miners of old from California, to Nevada, Montana, Colorado, the Dakotas, and Alaska.

Ion Puschila is a high school history teacher in Pomona, California. He emigrated with family in 1981 from then-communist Romania on a 747 rather than a wagon, and saw a much smaller elephant from a different perspective than the Argonauts. His incredible luck has brought him into contact with myriad people of excellent character and intelligence. He is the author of "Dummies before the Court: Stockholders in Western Enterprise," in *Law in the Western United States* (Norman: University of Oklahoma Press, 2000), 408–412.

Bibliography:

Allen, Frederick. *A Decent, Orderly Lynching: The Montana Vigilantes.* Norman: University of Oklahoma Press, 2005.

———. "A Rashomon Night: Montana Vigilantes and the Subjective Question of Guilt." *American History and Life* 54, no. 3 (2004): 34–43.

Anonymous. *Banditti of the Rocky Mountains and Vigilance Committee in Idaho: An Authentic Record of Startling Adventures in the Gold Mines of Idaho.* Minneapolis: Ross & Haines, 1964.

Bakken, Gordon M. *Practicing Law in Frontier California.* Lincoln: University of Nebraska Press, 1991.

Bossennecker, John. *Guns and Gunsmoke: Tales of Gold Rush Outlaws, Gunfighters, Lawmen, and Vigilantes.* New York: Wiley, 1999.

Brown, Richard M. *Strain of Violence: Historical Studies of American Violence and Vigilantism.* New York: Oxford University Press, 1975.

———. "Western Violence: Structure, Values, Myth." *Western Historical Quarterly* 24, no. 1 (1993): 4–20.

Burns, John F., and Richard J. Orsi, eds. *Taming the Elephant: Politics, Government, and Law in Pioneer California.* Berkeley: University of California Press, 2003.

Burrows, William E. *Vigilante!* New York: Harcourt, Brace, Jovanovich, 1976.

Carrigan, William D. *The Making of a Lynching Culture: Violence and Vigilantism in Central Texas, 1836–1916.* Chicago: University of Illinois Press, 2004.

Davis, John W. *Goodbye, Judge Lynch: The End of a Lawless Era in Wyoming's Big Horn Basin.* Norman: University of Oklahoma Press, 2005.

Dimsdale, Thomas J. *The Vigilantes of Montana.* Ann Arbor: University Microfilms, 1966.

Edgerton, Keith. *Montana Justice: Power, Punishment, and the Penitentiary.* Seattle: University of Washington Press, 2004.

Ethington, Philip J. "Vigilantes and the Police: The Creation of a Professional Police Bureaucracy in San Francisco, 1847–1900." *Journal of Social History* 21, no. 2 (1987): 197–227.

Gard, Wayne. *Frontier Justice.* Norman: University of Oklahoma Press, 1949.

Gonzales-Day, Ken. *Lynching in the West: 1850–1935.* Durham, NC: Duke University Press, 2006.

Hewitt, William L. "'Cowboyification' of Wyoming Agriculture." *Agricultural History* 76, no. 2 (2002): 485–501.

Hutton, Harold. *Vigilante Days: Frontier Justice along the Niobrara.* Chicago: The Swallow Press Inc., 1978.

Jolly, Michelle. "The Price of Vigilance: Gender, Politics, and the Press in Early San Francisco." *Pacific Historical Review* 73, no. 4 (November 2004): 511–579.

Kelly, Joseph M. "Shifting Interpretation of the San Francisco Vigilantes." *Journal of the West* 24 (January 1985): 39–46.

Little, Craig B., and Christopher P. Sheffield. "Fighters and Criminal Justice: English Private Prosecution Societies and American Vigilantism in the 18th and 19th Centuries." *American Sociological Review* 48 (December 1983): 796–808.

Love, Nat. *The Life and Adventures of Nat Love Better Known in the Country as "Deadwood Dick."* Lincoln: University of Nebraska Press, 1995.

McConnell, William J., and Howard R. Driggs. *Frontier Law: A Story of Vigilante Days*. New York: AMS Press, 1974.

McGrath, Roger D. *Gunfighters, Highwaymen, and Vigilantes: Violence on the Frontier*. Berkeley: University of California Press, 1984.

Mather, R. E., and F. E. Boswell. "Henry Plummer in Idaho." *American History and Life* 29, no. 2 (1985): 26–31.

———. *Hanging the Sheriff: A Biography of Henry Plummer*. Missoula: Historic Montana Publishing, 1998.

Pisani, Donald J. *To Reclaim a Divided West: Water, Law, and Public Policy 1848–1902*. Albuquerque: University of New Mexico Press, 1992.

Reid, John P. *Policing the Elephant: Crime, Punishment, and Social Behavior on the Overland Trail*. San Marino: Huntington Library, 1997.

———. *Law for the Elephant: Property and Social Behavior on the Overland Trail*. San Marino: Huntington Library, 1980.

Senkewicz, Robert M. *Vigilantes in Gold Rush San Francisco*. Stanford: Stanford University Press, 1985.

Souther, James Otto. *Legend into History: Fact and Fiction of the Lookout Lynching*. New York: Vantage Press, 1968.

Spitzzeri, Paul R. "Popular Justice in Los Angeles, 1850–1875." *Southern California Quarterly* 87, no. 2: 83–122.

Starr, Kevin, and Richard J. Orsi. *Rooted in the Barbarous Soil: People, Culture, and Community in Gold Rush California*. Berkeley: University of California Press, 2000.

Notes

1. Reid, *Law for the Elephant* and *Policing the Elephant*.
2. Brown, "Western Violence," 12.
3. Bakken, 109.
4. Burrows, 16.
5. Reid, *Policing the Elephant*, 28.
6. Brown, *Strain of Violence*, 97.
7. Ibid., 118.
8. Brown, *Strain of Violence*.
9. Allen, *A Decent, Orderly Lynching*, xviii.
10. Both Brown and Gonzales-Day have precise numbers, but imprecise definitions for a committee. The latter's research is more recent as well. Thus the number is somewhere above 511 given by Brown in *Strain of Violence*, 108–110.
11. Brown, *Strain of Violence*, 108.
12. Senkewicz, 39.
13. Ibid., 79.
14. Gard, 156.
15. Ibid., 159.
16. Senkewicz, 85.
17. Starr, 254.
18. Burrows, 111.
19. Brown, *Strain of Violence*, 140.
20. Senkewicz, 159.
21. Ibid., 166.
22. Burrows, 116.
23. Brown, *Strain of Violence*, 137.
24. Senkewicz, 168.
25. Burrows, 164.
26. Senkewicz, 160.
27. Ibid., 172.
28. Ibid., 175–176.
29. Mather, *Hanging the Sheriff*, 115.
30. Allen, *A Decent, Orderly Lynching*, 48.
31. Mather, *Hanging the Sheriff*, 154.
32. Allen, *A Decent, Orderly Lynching*, 50.
33. Anonymous, 53–57.
34. Mather, "Henry Plummer in Idaho," 28.
35. Burrows, 146.
36. He may well have intended to start a new life, as Mather and Boswell argue based on his behavior. Sources from the time are all vigilante committee participants, Dimsdale, and an anonymous account, wholly one-sided.
37. Allen, *A Decent, Orderly Lynching*, 105.
38. Ibid., 117.
39. Burrows, 142.
40. Ibid., 159.
41. Mather, *Hanging the Sheriff*, 5.
42. Allen, *A Decent, Orderly Hanging*, 157.
43. Ibid., 177.
44. Ibid., 195, to discuss potential outcomes of the trial, and the need to punish Ives.
45. Burrows, 150.
46. Ibid.
47. Brown, *Strain of Violence*, 313.
48. Brown puts the total at thirty, while Allen lists all the vigilante and lynching deaths in the Bannack, Virginia City, and Helena areas, and mentions twenty-one associated with the Plummer gang.
49. Burrows, 159.
50. Allen, *A Decent, Orderly Lynching*, 148.
51. Ibid., 305.
52. Allen, "A Rashomon Night," 37.
53. Mather, *Hanging the Sheriff*, 5.
54. Allen, *A Decent, Orderly Lynching*, 231.
55. Ibid., 348.
56. Davis, 15.
57. Ibid., 103.
58. Ibid., 104.
59. Gard, 127.

60. Ibid.
61. Hewitt, 491; Pisani, 245.
62. Gard, 128.
63. Davis, 106.
64. Pisani, 246.
65. Brown, "Western Violence," 19.
66. Pisani, 258–259.
67. Davis, 117.

68. Gard, 101.
69. Davis, 119.
70. Ibid., 121.
71. Ibid., 140.
72. Ibid., 152–153.
73. Gard, 101.
74. Allen, *A Decent, Orderly Lynching*, 362.

CHAPTER 7

Amnesty International and the Death Penalty

TOWARD GLOBAL ABOLITION

Alexander Karn

Background

FOUNDED IN 1961 by a British barrister, Peter Benenson, Amnesty International (AI) has established itself as the world's largest grassroots human rights organization. With more than 2.2 million members and supporters in 150 countries, no other organization compares in terms of global scope or international recognition.[1] Described in one study as a "super democracy,"[2] AI is a self-governing movement divided into national sections that pursue their work, with different degrees of autonomy, under the banner of an International Secretariat (IS) and an International Executive Committee (IEC). The organization's stated mission covers research, education, and direct action, all with the aim of exposing and ending grave abuses of the rights described in the articles of the Universal Declaration of Human Rights (UDHR), which was adopted by the United Nations in December 1948. While much of Amnesty's early work focused on the plight of political prisoners, Benenson's earliest writing for the movement already included a clear statement of opposition regarding the use of the death penalty against "prisoners

of conscience."[3] In 1977, Amnesty received a Nobel Prize for its work, a distinction that significantly elevated the profile of the organization. AI has since expanded its work on the death penalty and today is the largest of ninety-nine organizations which belong to the World Coalition Against the Death Penalty.[4]

Amnesty's Position on the Death Penalty

Amnesty's current position on capital punishment is unambiguous. Calling it "the ultimate denial of human rights," *AI opposes the death penalty in all cases without exception* "regardless of the nature of the crime, the characteristics of the offender, or the method used by the state to kill the prisoner."[5] Seeking the complete abolition of its practice, Amnesty maintains an unwavering position on the death penalty in all of its literature and press communiqués. However, while the current stance can be described as hard-line and straightforward, there is a relatively long and complex history to consider. Looking at the past five decades, one sees that Amnesty did not arrive at its position on the death penalty all at once, nor did the organization develop its current abolitionist stance without internal difficulties.

First Steps:
Toward Unqualified Opposition, 1961–1974

Amnesty's position on capital punishment evolved gradually through a process that both informed and reflected the emergence of a new human rights paradigm. In the first years of Amnesty's existence, international norms prohibiting the use of the death penalty were nonexistent. While Article 3 of the UDHR states that all humans enjoy a fundamental "right to life," not even the members of this landmark document's drafting committee could agree on whether to address the death penalty in explicit terms. Most commentators in the 1950s and early 1960s were inclined to read Article 3 simply as a prohibition against large-scale killing by states.[6] That is, the right to life described in the UDHR was commonly understood as an invocation against mass atrocities on the scale of the Holocaust; it was not yet viewed as a universal prohibition against the execution of criminal offenders prosecuted fairly under the rule of law.[7] Among UN member-states and even within the nascent community of human rights scholars and activists, most conceded that governments retained a legitimate claim on the use of lethal force in a variety of scenarios, including police actions to control crowds, in times of war, and in the assessment of the death penalty against convicted criminals provided due process.[8] Although Benenson had raised the specter of political executions in his 1961 appeal, there was little impetus at that time, even within the ranks of Amnesty's International Secretariat, to question or criticize the state's monopoly on the use of lethal force.

This began to change in 1968 when members of AI attending the group's Sixth International Assembly once again linked the use of the death penalty to the question of political imprisonment just as Benenson had seven years earlier.[9] In the statutes adopted at this meeting, AI members pledged to "oppose by all appropriate means the imposition and execution of death penalties for political prisoners."[10] This marked a major step toward unqualified opposition, although there was still no mandate extending to nonpolitical cases.

Amnesty expanded its opposition to the death penalty in 1971 when representatives for the group requested that the UN and the Council of Europe take concrete steps toward universal abolition. Coming on the heels of the Sixth International Assembly, this was a critical moment for the organization, as it marked the first time that AI had framed its opposition to the death penalty in such broad and uncompromising terms. No longer limiting its scope to political prisoners, AI now sought a prohibition against the use of the death penalty *in all instances*, regardless of any circumstances surrounding individual cases, *and without exception*, even for those who had committed mass murder and other similarly heinous crimes. Since 1971, then, AI has categorically opposed the death penalty, describing it across all of its institutional literature as "the ultimate denial of human rights." In 1974, Amnesty's International Executive Council amended the organizational statutes to include unconditional opposition to the death penalty among its principal objectives.[11] By doing so, Amnesty committed itself to a potent brand of idealism. At the time, the number of countries that had abolished the death penalty for all crimes stood at just sixteen. The new mandate reflected an extreme vision for which there was still no solid basis of support and for which Amnesty would have to develop new strategies and tactics.

Seeking Traction:
The Stockholm Conference (1977)

Though AI officially expanded its mandate in 1974 to include unqualified death penalty opposition, the organization continued working to solidify its platform and build a consensus on the most effective route toward this objective. A major step toward this end unfolded in 1977, when AI organized the Stockholm Conference on the Abolition of the Death Penalty. With more than two hundred delegates attending from fifty-seven countries, the Stockholm Conference had a profound effect on Amnesty's death penalty aspirations. A declaration issued at the conference on December 11, 1977, cemented Amnesty's "total and unconditional opposition" to the death penalty, reiterated its condemnation of all executions, regardless of their legal status, and signaled a renewed commitment to work toward universal abolition.[12] At the conference's conclusion, participants called on nongovernmental organizations (NGOs) to generate and disseminate public information materials oriented toward death penalty abolition. In addition to lobbying national governments directly for an immediate and comprehensive ban on the death penalty, AI also sought a strong statement from the United Nations that the death penalty could not be legally implemented under international law. In sum, the Stockholm Declaration sought to give added political traction to the position that Amnesty had staked out in 1971–1974.

Besides substantiating the position Amnesty had staked out earlier, the Stockholm Conference opened some new ground, too. While acknowledging that attitudes toward death and "the taking of life" were subject to broad cultural differences, AI concluded its 1977 conference on an optimistic note, citing "clear and encouraging proof that it is indeed possible for people from very different backgrounds to be totally united in opposition

to the death penalty in any form and in all circumstances."[13] The Stockholm Declaration, thus, sought to place the death penalty debate in a new context, one that accepted cultural variability yet refused to be limited by these differences.

Another key conclusion from the conference was that judicial executions and extralegal killings, which had been treated together in Amnesty's earlier work, would require different strategies henceforth. Six work groups drafted summary reports, which were then submitted for approval at a plenary session. In one report, strategists noted the tension between public opinion regarding the death penalty and the question of effective deterrence: "Governments tend to justify the use of the death penalty on the grounds that public opinion is in favor of it for certain crimes. They do not, in general, offer proof that public opinion is correct in assuming the death penalty to be an effective deterrent: they simply reiterate the statement that it is so."[14] The suggestion here, i.e., that no deterrent effect had ever been sufficiently demonstrated, subsequently emerged as a fixed point in Amnesty's arguments against the death penalty along with concerns about discrimination, irrevocability, and the potential for error. These key points, together with what Amnesty described in its Stockholm Declaration as a "brutalizing effect" on all who are involved in the process, led the organization to characterize the death penalty as nothing less than "the ultimate cruel, inhuman and degrading punishment and [violation of] the right to life."[15]

The Stockholm Declaration delves deeply into several other issues that Amnesty has continued to pursue, including questions of judicial error and the effects of political pressure on the legal systems that oversee the implementation of the death penalty. Key to Amnesty's arguments against the death penalty are cases involving well-documented instances of inadequate legal representation,[16] concerns over the "personal sensibilities and prejudices" of both judges and jurors, the politically charged climate in which decisions regarding clemency are made, and the competence of psychiatric services used to evaluate the fitness of defendants to stand trial. The Stockholm report also charged that the death penalty is used as an instrument of state-sanctioned repression against racial, ethnic, and religious minorities, as well as political dissidents and members of economically disadvantaged groups. Amnesty's report framed the death penalty, not only as a direct violation of existing human rights norms, but also as a demonstration of *a priori* unfairness inherent to the legal systems which do not adequately represent minority groups either in their judiciary, in the legal profession, or in their jury pools. The Stockholm Conference report included appeals to the Council of Europe and to the governments participating in the Sixth United Nations Congress on the Prevention of Crime and the Treatment of Offenders to insert language into their covenants that would explicitly prohibit the introduction (or reintroduction) of the death penalty and mandate its total and worldwide abolition.[17] The report goes on to state: "The death penalty justifies the intercession by one government with the appropriate authorities in another for executive clemency in any case where the death penalty has been imposed." Aware of the broad protections afforded to state sovereignty, but also insistent that the defense of human rights effectively trumped such concerns, Amnesty made its appeal for abolition following the Stockholm Conference in the most urgent and uncompromising terms possible. Driven by the moral authority provided by its Nobel Prize, Amnesty has attempted since 1977 to pull the abolitionist cart forward rather than push from behind.

The majority of Amnesty's death penalty work since Stockholm has been aimed at realizing (and publicizing) the uncompromising demands

detailed in the conference report and in the declaration it spawned. In keeping with its overall strategy, Amnesty urged new activity on three fronts: research, education, and activism. The report also suggested cooperation between Amnesty sections in countries that retained the death penalty and those in countries where its practice had been abolished.[18] Among the specific recommendations made in the report, Amnesty promised to weigh what level of emphasis its presentations and programs ought to give to the question of physical cruelty[19] as well as what kinds of images would be appropriate for specific audiences (e.g., in presentations given to schoolchildren). One can read in the Stockholm Declaration not only a clear desire to keep the Amnesty message on point and uncluttered, but also a determination to acknowledge and address the complexities of the death penalty in its various forms and contexts of practice. Readily adopted as a "statement of principle" on the death penalty, the Stockholm Declaration of 1977 laid much of the groundwork for Amnesty's future work. While the United Nations seemed to be stuck in place, despite its scattered pronouncements in favor of abolition, Amnesty pressed ahead energetically with its mission.

Amnesty USA:
The Program to Abolish the Death Penalty

While Amnesty's officers were busy organizing the Stockholm Conference, events related to the death penalty took an important turn in the United States. After a four-year interval during which capital punishment had been suspended (1972–1976), the Supreme Court of the United States reinstated the death penalty in *Gregg v. Georgia* (428 U.S. 153).[20] The execution of Gary Gilmore in Utah by firing squad on January 17, 1977, prompted a press statement from Amnesty's headquarters in London, but there was no official response from Amnesty USA (AIUSA), which, like other national sections, had been discouraged by the International Secretariat from commenting on human rights abuses occurring within its own borders. Although London imposed these restrictions on the national sections to circumvent partisan politics, a faction within AIUSA felt obliged to undertake a new campaign to address the reinstatement of the death penalty in their own country.

Still a relatively small organization with limited funding, AIUSA had done little work on the death penalty prior to 1979. The conviction and capital sentencing of John Louis Evans III in Alabama for first-degree murder changed this.[21] When the International Secretariat requested information on Evans's case from AIUSA, Larry Cox, the organization's press secretary at the time (and executive director since 2006), traveled to Alabama on a fact-finding mission. Meeting with members of the Southern Coalition on Jails and Prisons[22] and working to acquaint himself with the details of Evans's upcoming execution, Cox has since described this trip as "a life transforming experience."[23] After witnessing the "planning and plotting"[24] the state prison system and state government performed prior to executions, Cox returned to the AIUSA offices determined to accelerate and intensify the organization's opposition to the death penalty. As Cox has said, "This had been a neglected aspect of the mandate. Pursuing it with full conviction proved to be a matter of great controversy."[25] Not only were some AIUSA members reluctant to divert resources from the campaigns to support political prisoners, work which many regarded as the organization's core mission, there was also deep resistance to the idea of Amnesty working on behalf of individuals who had committed violent and disturbing crimes. According to Cox, many members had joined without even knowing of Amnesty's opposition to the death penalty, and AIUSA lost the support of several high-profile advisors and

board members when it became clear that a vigorous abolition project was being contemplated.

Another turning point for AIUSA came in May 1979 when Cox and a group of death penalty opponents traveled to Florida to protest the scheduled execution of John Spenkelink, the first inmate to be executed in that state following the reinstatement of the death penalty and the first "nonconsensual" case in the country for that period.[26] Cox and others chained themselves to a fence outside the governor's mansion in Tallahassee, and in a dramatic gesture which appeared in local newspapers the following day, Cox refused to shake the governor's hand after the two exchanged words, saying he would not take hold of a hand "stained with blood."[27] Though his tactics had not received approval from the AIUSA board, the photograph of Cox spurning the governor's handshake nevertheless garnered important and useful publicity.[28] Not only did the issue of the death penalty begin to attract new members after that point, but strategic partnerships also emerged with several key groups, including the American Civil Liberties Union (ACLU). AIUSA soon attached itself to the National Coalition to Abolish the Death Penalty (NCADP), and while there still existed tension between the International Secretariat in London and the AIUSA section in New York over the question of country rules (i.e., the prohibition against allowing national sections to work on cases from their own countries), ultimately domestic pressure to confront the death penalty in the United States overshadowed London's insistence that the organization's action campaigns should originate from "neutral" sections. Within a year of Cox's trip to Florida, and in spite of the fact that many of its members still opposed the death penalty work on principle, AIUSA had hired its first coordinator for the newly established Program to Abolish the Death Penalty (PADP).

Cox describes the early years of the PADP as "dark days" and admits that the goal of universal abolition often "seemed hopeless." While the PADP managed to organize a handful of energetic rallies, there were continuing difficulties convincing large segments of the Amnesty membership that the death penalty was a legitimate concern for human rights activists, and public opinion in the United States remained decidedly in favor of the death penalty throughout the 1980s.[29] For AIUSA, the tide only began to turn in 1984, when successes in the international arena gave American abolitionists new impetus to take their message to the public. Within its own ranks, AIUSA saw a marked increase in support for the PADP following the 1984 Annual General Meeting in Chicago, where Cox gave a speech to the general membership in which he linked the death penalty to the practice of torture. Addressing the widespread perception that the death penalty did not belong to the core human rights agenda and taking aim at his own country, Cox sought to describe a double standard:

> It is apparent that many Americans, even some members of Amnesty International, are genuinely horrified at the thought that in places like Chile or South Korea prisoners are taken, strapped down, and electric shock is applied to their bodies until they are in excruciating pain, but find it acceptable, or at least less alarming, that in a place like Florida prisoners are taken, strapped down, and electric shock is applied to their bodies until they are dead. Many Americans, it is clear, are shocked and horrified that drugs are used in a place like the Soviet Union, not to cure people, but to cause pain to prisoners, but find it acceptable, in fact find it humane, that in a place called Texas drugs are used not to cure prisoners, but to poison prisoners to death.[30]

Calling legal executions a "public dress rehearsal" for other human rights violations, Cox maintained

that the struggle against the death penalty was fundamentally linked to the struggle against torture and that both infringements relied on the same justification: the sacrifice of the individual for what governments claim to be a higher purpose. His speech also included what was by then a familiar refrain for the organization, that human rights are not rewards dispensed by governments for good behavior or privileges that can be revoked for bad behavior. The resumption of executions in the United States in 1977 proved to be a mobilizing factor for AIUSA. Over the next several years, the emergence of a discourse that reasserted the inalienable and universal nature of human rights (as seen in Cox's 1984 speech to the AGM), even for criminals whose behavior deeply offended public conceptions of social decency, helped to initiate a highly effective and galvanizing phase in Amnesty's abolition work.

Rising Commitment:
The International Secretariat, 1978–1989

While the PADP was taking shape in the United States, the International Secretariat was devoting increased energy to its global abolition work. In June 1978, representatives from five national sections (Britain, Holland, Germany, Sweden, and the United States) met in London with staff from the IS to pursue plans for a formal campaign aimed at universal abolition. Emphasizing the importance of membership education and the need for a large-scale, but also focused, publicity blitz, attendees swapped general ideas for the new campaign as well as specific tactics that had worked (or not) in previous years.

One of the most interesting aspects of the discussion concerned the use of the term "adopted" in Amnesty's prisoner action appeals.[31] In its work on behalf of political prisoners, Amnesty encouraged local chapters to "adopt" a specific prisoner and channel their collective efforts toward him or her so as to nurture a sense of personal connection and solidarity. The idea was to make these "prisoners of conscience" as real as possible to the people who worked on and watched their cases, often from thousands of miles away. With respect to nonpolitical prisoners who had been sentenced to death for violent crimes, AI campaign planners decided that "adopted" would be confusing to members and onlookers who might mistake Amnesty's attempts to intervene on the behalf of violent criminals for misguided acts of sympathy rather than a principled defense of core human rights. This emotional dissonance, the tension between abstract rights and real individuals, would become a recurrent issue in the emerging abolition campaign. On the one hand, the protection of human rights implied not only the defense of vulnerable individuals whose rights had been infringed, but also a spiritual solidarity with the victims themselves. On the other hand, the death penalty conjured images of depraved offenders with whom such solidarity was impossible. In the mainstream, where support for the death penalty still ran strong, these condemned inmates had forfeited their rights when they committed the crimes for which they were sentenced to die. Whereas Amnesty had previously worked to "give a face" to the victims of human rights abuses, the campaign to abolish the death penalty required a different approach, one that focused attention on abstract principles of justice rather than on the socially marginalized individuals whose violent acts (and bodies) cried out for punishment in the eyes of many.

Notes from the 1978 meeting also mention a forthcoming report that Amnesty aimed to publish the following year. *The Death Penalty* (1979) offered a country-by-country report on capital punishment and outlined the status of the abolition movement around the world. In his preface, Thomas Hammarberg, the chairman of Amnesty's International Executive Committee, recalled

the success of the Stockholm Conference and urged the United Nations to take immediate action on what the General Assembly had once described as "the desirability of abolishing capital punishment."[32] Alongside Hammarberg's call to action, one of the primary goals of the 1979 report was to dispel the notion that the abolition movement reflected only the values of Western cultures and that calls for universal prohibition against the death penalty amounted to a form of cultural imperialism.[33] This had been a struggle for Amnesty since the 1977 conference in Stockholm, and Hammarberg was eager to highlight how the new report broadened the context in which abolition was considered and how it addressed the legal systems in Africa, Asia, and Latin America, as well as those in North America and Europe. Beyond this, the report stuck to the main points outlined in Amnesty's prior work: the possibility of error, the invalidity of deterrence arguments, and the inherent cruelty of the death penalty, etc.

Although *The Death Penalty* broke little new ground, its comprehensive scope helped to lay the groundwork for the worldwide abolition campaign that Amnesty launched a decade later. Already in July 1979, members of the International Executive Committee recognized the need for something "big and bold," however there were also concerns that Amnesty might be overreaching if it were to pursue a major campaign without adequate preparation.[34] According to the notes from the IEC's July 1979 meeting, program coordinators felt it was still too early for a global campaign, given the ambivalence that existed on the death penalty at the grassroots level. Even as some of the national sections were ramping up their work on the death penalty, the IEC worried that the organization was too far ahead of the curve to make a global campaign effective. At the same time, they were adamant in their belief that AI could activate a large swath of their membership by highlighting capital punishment as a core human rights issue. The main task, as the IEC saw it, was to convey to its members "a sense of something international and dynamic combined with the personal approach that has always been at the heart of AI's work."[35] Calling on the United Nations to recommit to death penalty abolition was seen as a way to provide "an overall framework" that could support the "personal" work of members devoted to country-specific situations. Again, there was a recognition that opposition to the death penalty in the context of Amnesty's record of standing up for the innocent and wrongly persecuted could lead to difficulties where calls for clemency were extended to "criminals whose acts have been far from heroic." Even still, the IEC saw a possibility for strengthening the organization as a whole by supporting collaboration between national sections. Groups were encouraged to study the 1979 report and use it in their letter-writing campaigns so that members could identify country-specific links between their work on behalf of prisoners of conscience and the plight of death row prisoners facing execution in those same countries. Above all, the IEC preached the importance of working out a consistent approach for dealing with executions and death sentence verdicts so that members could be persuaded to support the abolition platform regardless of their feelings about individual death row inmates or the crimes for which they had been sentenced to die. The IEC also decided that it would wait to see how the United Nations dealt with the death penalty in 1980 before determining whether to devote more of Amnesty's resources toward a global abolition campaign.

Given the cautious note on which the IEC ended its meeting, it is somewhat surprising to chart Amnesty's rising commitment to death penalty abolition over the next decade. While the United Nations required ten years to pass an *optional* measure aimed at abolition,[36] Amnesty expanded its death penalty program by appealing directly to its members and by sponsoring new publicity campaigns to bring the issue to a wider audience. Instead of waiting for public opinion to catch up, Amnesty looked for ways to influence and inform the international norms to which public opinion would then (hopefully) align itself. The work proceeded haltingly at times. For example, the IEC voted in December 1980 to cut resources for its death penalty work "to a stable level" after it became clear that its appeal to the UN had failed to gain support. In the wake of these cuts, the IEC planned to focus instead on disappearances and extrajudicial killings, a decision which, according to one member of the executive committee, was not meant to imply a decrease in the importance of abolition to Amnesty's overall mission, but merely a "structural shift" to ensure that the death penalty remained part of the organization's everyday work rather than an isolated issue.[37]

In spite of this pull-back and despite receiving more discouraging news from the United Nations, the IS sponsored another international meeting on the death penalty in April 1981 where representatives from national sections discussed ways to bring added consistency to the AI platform. At the suggestion of Eric Prokosch, the International Secretariat's death penalty coordinator, attendees considered the idea of a short-term campaign on the political use of the death penalty, though there was concern that this approach might make universal abolition more difficult in the long term.[38] While some who attended the 1981 meeting remained hopeful that the United Nations might consider another resolution on the death penalty in its next session, there was also discussion of whether Amnesty could be more effective by working outside the framework of intergovernmental organizations. A representative for the Swedish section suggested that Amnesty should consider staging "shadow conferences" rather than wait for signs of progress from the

UN. Others offered that Amnesty should pursue regional initiatives in the absence of a clear consensus for a new UN covenant. All of the attendees agreed that the organization had reached a critical juncture where the choice of tactics would prove decisive.

While there was a consensus at this meeting that Amnesty could do more to publicize its case for abolition, some warned that pressing ahead too aggressively on the death penalty could jeopardize other aspects of Amnesty's work. A representative for the U.S. section suggested that Amnesty would have difficulty attracting new members in his country if the organization were seen as being stridently anti-death penalty.[39] Others reported that their national sections appeared divided on the question of the death penalty and that difficulties engaging the full membership had been demoralizing to those who wished to pursue the issue more energetically. Many of the representatives reaffirmed their commitment to the work, but a fair number also expressed uncertainty about what kinds of training and education might best mobilize the general membership. In one discussion on the second morning of the conference, section representatives lamented that death penalty opposition was seen as an "optional task" by some of the local groups, and there was brief consideration of whether to include abolition work on a list of "minimum tasks" that local groups would have to abide by to maintain their affiliation with Amnesty. As the meeting concluded, attendees strongly supported Prokosch's recommendation that Amnesty should develop a comprehensive death penalty handbook which national program coordinators and local groups could consult for guidance. Though Amnesty had staked out a strong position on the death penalty, the practical aspects of developing effective and consistent tactics proved difficult, and uniform commitment throughout its membership remained elusive.

The difficulties that characterized this period of Amnesty's abolition work (1981–1987) mirror the more general growing pains the organization experienced during that time. Despite being recognized with a Nobel Prize in 1977, Amnesty, as a highly democratic, transnational, and grassroots organization, was still learning how to harness its idealism. On the one hand, Amnesty reacted to events on the ground, raising the alert where gross human rights violations otherwise went unnoticed and/or unpunished. On the other hand, the organization struggled to bridge the gap between aspirations and practice, as the inability to get strong UN support for death penalty abolition revealed. Seeking a way in from the margins, Amnesty's death penalty activists began to think more deeply about how to effect demonstrable change, and much of the conversation relating to the death penalty shifted from appeals to principle to strategic goals and tactics. Unable to win commitments solely on the basis of a moral pinprick, AI took up a new set of questions aimed at understanding how countries actually come to abolish the death penalty. In time, this shift would help to produce many of the group's most important gains toward abolition. Whereas twenty-six countries had abolished the death penalty by the end of 1976, the total had reached eighty by the end of 1988.[40] While this increase cannot be attributed solely to the work of Amnesty activists, their evolving tactics emerged as a key factor in the rising trend toward abolition.

In a paper presented to Amnesty's European death penalty coordinators in 1985, Eric Prokosch detailed how abolition had been achieved in a variety of national contexts.[41] Prokosch's overview suggested that AI could be most effective in the context of political transition, when repressive regimes gave way to new governments committed to human rights in general and abolition in particular. Though somewhat obvious in retrospect, this turned out to be an important recognition at the time, particularly as Eastern Europe headed toward democratization. Prokosch's analysis suggested that Amnesty could make early preparations so that the abolitionist agenda appeared clearly in countries that suddenly faced a regime change. At the same time, Prokosch's report demonstrated that regime change was not strictly necessary to achieve abolition if governments could be persuaded that the death penalty had become an obsolete punishment or a political liability. Prokosch reviewed cases from Liechtenstein, the Netherlands, and Japan (countries where the death penalty had been abolished or where its use had been restricted between 1982 and 1984) to show that constitutional revisions were possible even in the absence of wholesale regime change. The abolition movement could be especially effective, Prokosch ventured, where official commissions were convened to provide an authoritative record of judicial error and to compile evidence documenting the use of the death penalty as an instrument of political repression.[42] Taken as a whole, Prokosch's report suggested that active political engagement on two fronts (i.e., with new governments coming into power after periods of repression and with ruling governments where detailed studies elaborated the ineffectiveness and unfairness of the death penalty) could effectively set the stage for new abolition measures. Pressing political candidates and parties for commitments on abolition, especially those waiting in the wings for an opportunity to govern, became standard practice for Amnesty after this time, as did lobbying influential members of the legal profession who might be called upon to draft revised legislation. In the interim, Amnesty's staffers and officers continued to think about new ways to cultivate public support for abolition so that politicians and officials could pursue abolition initiatives with the backing of their constituents, or at least without substantial opposition. By March 1986, the IEC had decided

to organize an international campaign against the death penalty, culminating in the publication of another major report.

Plans for a global death penalty campaign gained momentum at the end of 1987. Whereas program coordinators had worried in 1980 that Amnesty might be overreaching by supporting a worldwide initiative, they were now ready to proceed with full commitment. Keeping in mind their earlier disappointments at the UN, Amnesty campaign coordinators worked to develop a multipronged initiative to ensure that organizational resources would be deployed along a broad front. Most important, the IS deliberately located the new campaign within the emergent human rights movement to capitalize on (and amplify) the energy it had generated during the 1980s. Abolition was no longer presented as an underground movement looking for inroads to the mainstream, but rather as a critical test case unfolding at the center of a burgeoning human rights movement which had been gaining stature since the end of World War II. The overall tone of AI's work changed from apologetic and pleading to uncompromising and self-assured, with an emphasis not only on the urgency of the vision, but also on the practicality of the plan. Working to distill their message into something actionable, Amnesty's coordinators developed a proactive and positive tone for the new campaign:

Abolition of the death penalty is linked to growth in protection of human rights. While several countries abolished the death penalty last century, international standards tending toward restriction and abolition of the death penalty grew out of the atrocities of the Second World War and have been steadily evolving since then. More and more countries have abolished the death penalty out of consideration for human rights and justice. Where it has been abolished there have not been negative effects. Abolition of the death penalty is an attractive and viable proposition on both moral and pragmatic grounds.[43]

The confidence and optimism in this internal document reflected the growing strength of the human rights movement and signaled Amnesty's determination to set a more demanding pace for reform. Instead of waiting for the UN to invite further testimony or for public opinion polls to swing in their favor, the campaign's strategists decided to position Amnesty at the front of the abolition movement and to exercise the moral authority that the overall rise of the human rights movement had earned them.

Of course, Amnesty could not afford to ignore public opinion altogether, and the campaign planners remained keenly aware of the public relations battle confronting them, even as they began to operate with more bravado. In general, Amnesty aimed to present a consistent and principled argument against the death penalty, while at the same time establishing the importance of adaptability and remaining sensitive to the emotional vicissitudes of the death penalty debate. Campaign coordinators urged sections to prepare themselves for unexpected events and especially for the highly publicized crimes and trials that frequently inflame public opinion against abolition.[44] The global campaign plan also emphasized the utility of enlisting support from well-known public figures and even celebrities. Noting the success that AIUSA achieved with these techniques in its 1987 death penalty campaign, the International Secretariat reached out to artists, writers, singers, and other high-profile individuals whose lives had been affected by the death penalty or who simply wished to share their misgivings about capital punishment.[45] By enlisting icons from the cultural mainstream, AI hoped not only to cultivate a more youthful base of support, but also to dampen the effect of public opinion polls, which continued to show high levels of support for the death penalty in many of the retentionist countries.

Planning for the 1989 campaign also highlighted the issues of rendition and extradition, which have again found their way into the public discourse following the terrorist attacks of September 11, 2001.[46] AI reiterated its opposition to the practice of sending detainees and asylum seekers to countries where they might face the death penalty.[47] Moreover, AI used the campaign to launch a research project on the extent to which the death penalty had served as a barrier to extradition in Western Europe, where Article 11 of the European Convention on Extradition allowed for countries to refuse extradition requests on that basis. The campaign launch was set to coincide with the publication of a new death penalty report in April 1989, and the IS pressed national sections to use the occasion to generate additional publicity. A special "week of action" was planned for September 1989 to bring the campaign to a climax. Taking another page from the national campaign that AIUSA ran in 1987, the IS arranged to produce a short video outlining the group's case against the death penalty. The new campaign was to be not only multipronged, but also multimedia.

While the death penalty coordinators worked to capitalize on the rise of electronic media, print media remained at the heart of Amnesty's work. An updated and expanded death penalty report, *When the State Kills*, appeared in 1989 with a fresh format and a strident tone that reflected the lofty ambitions of the 1987 circular. The new report pointed to recent progress toward abolition, and it employed impassioned rhetoric that left little room for neutrality. In language aimed at a general audience, the report characterized the death penalty as an affront to human decency and as a crime to which all who did not actively seek its abolition were party. The report's introduction prodded citizens to confront their governments or accept responsibility for subsequent executions: "The death penalty, carried out in the name of a nation's entire population, involves everyone. Everyone should be aware of what the death penalty is, how it is used, how it affects them, and how it violates fundamental rights."[48] The report spared no one in its insistence that ordinary people, not faceless bureaucracies, bore ultimate responsibility for the continued exercise of capital punishment. While international treaties and covenants were important tools for the movement, the death penalty existed where citizens gave it license and ceased to where they did not. The 1989 report, thus, challenged its readers to take an active role in the death penalty debate and to energetically defend the universal rights that existed for their protection and benefit. The authors of the report surmised:

> The political will to abolish the death penalty comes ultimately from within a country. . . . The experience of countries which have abolished the death penalty gives ample evidence that the punishment is neither desirable nor necessary. But it is the people and the leaders of each country who must take the decision that a commitment to human rights and to finding genuine solutions to the problems of crime is furthered by an end to the death penalty.[49]

Somewhere between inspirational and cajoling, the tone of the report suggests that Amnesty saw the 1989 campaign as a critical moment for the abolition movement. Certainly, the organizers risked creating a rift in the human rights community by questioning the commitment of those who balked at their rallying cry. The report's militant language no doubt struck some as an indication of impatience (or desperation), but the internal documents outlining the strategy for the 1989 campaign suggest that Amnesty's

coordinators made a deliberate decision to take a more confrontational stance after seeing signs of a rising trend toward abolition. The early hints of democratization in east-central Europe also provided vital encouragement. Overall, the vigor of the 1989 campaign reflected a sense of growing optimism rather than frustration over lack of results, and subsequent developments showed that Amnesty's confidence was well founded.

A Global Movement Takes Hold, 1990–2007

The number of countries abolishing capital punishment has increased markedly in the two decades since Amnesty's 1989 campaign. Since the beginning of 1989, when fifty-two countries had abolished the death penalty, the number of abolitionist countries has more than doubled to 139.[50] Even as revamped initiatives faltered at the United Nations (e.g., the Eighth UN Congress on the Prevention of Crime and the Treatment of Offenders held in 1990 failed to adopt an Italian resolution proposing a moratorium on executions), there was progress at the regional and national levels. In 1990, one year after the publication of *When the State Kills*, eight countries, including five in Europe (Andorra, Croatia, Ireland, Czechoslovakia, and Hungary), abolished the death penalty for all crimes, while in Latin America, the American Convention on Human Rights adopted the Protocol to Abolish the Death Penalty.[51] By the end of the 1990s, another twenty-seven countries had abolished the death penalty either in law or in practice.[52] Though the sudden increase in the number of abolitionist countries was due in part to the creation of newly sovereign states at the end of the Cold War, the trend toward abolition in this period remains highly significant nevertheless.

One of the most important developments of the last decade is the large base of support and solidarity that Amnesty has kindled with other grassroots organizations working toward abolition. Whereas, in the 1950s, relatively few believed that the "right to life" described in the Universal Declaration of Human Rights could (or should) extend to a prohibition against the death penalty, today Amnesty pursues its death penalty work in the context of a worldwide abolition movement. In partnership with the Community of Sant'Egidio, a charitable and evangelical organization based in Rome, as well as two smaller organizations,[53] Amnesty collected three million signatures on a death penalty moratorium petition, which it presented to UN Secretary-General Kofi Annan in 2000.[54] In 2001, at the invitation of a French abolitionist group, Together Against the Death Penalty (*Ensemble contre la peine de mort*), Amnesty participated in a major international conference, the World Congress against the Death Penalty in Strasbourg, which has since convened twice more.[55] Participants in the first Congress drafted the Strasbourg Declaration, which, like earlier Amnesty documents, characterized capital punishment as a form of torture incompatible with human rights.[56] The 2001 declaration urged the Council of Europe to press specific countries (Russia, Armenia, and Turkey) for commitments on permanent abolition, which the council in fact received from two of the three by 2004.[57]

Capitalizing on the success of the first Congress, Amnesty teamed with more than thirty other organizations in 2002 to form the World Coalition Against the Death Penalty (WCADP). In addition to taking over the organization of the World Congress, the WCADP (now with ninety-nine members) also created the first World Day Against the Death Penalty in 2003. Held annually on October 10, this event brings local and regional abolition initiatives under a single, thematic banner. In 2005, the event featured more than 260 separate initiatives. The 2007 event,

which the WCADP publicized at five separate press conferences (in Puerto Rico, Morocco, Democratic Republic of Congo, Portugal, and the United States), ended with a new call to the United Nations to support an immediate moratorium on all executions.[58] The WCADP initiative received support from several high-profile political leaders, including Italian Prime Minister Romano Prodi, who pledged to put capital punishment back on the UN agenda after the details of Saddam Hussein's execution emerged in January 2007.[59] Never before had so much pressure for abolition been so tightly focused at the international level. Indeed, the UN General Assembly actually passed a resolution in December 2007 calling for a global moratorium on executions.[60] One hundred and four countries voted in favor of the nonbinding resolution; fifty-four countries voted against it; and twenty-nine abstained. With a majority of the General Assembly lining up behind them, should death penalty activists be optimistic about the prospects for universal abolition?

Looking Ahead:

The Prospects for Universal Abolition

Although the backing of international leaders and the emergence of a vigorous coalition of grassroots supporters both suggest that the abolition movement has attained a critical mass, prospects for universal abolition remain uncertain for the present. Despite passing the nonbinding resolution in favor of abolition in December 2007, the UN General Assembly remains divided over the question of capital punishment, and there is little to suggest that these differences will be overcome anytime soon. Even with 104 countries supporting the most recent abolition resolution, a sizeable faction within the General Assembly remains adamantly opposed to the measure, and many others are content to stand on the sidelines. The complex institutional architecture of the UN also represents an impediment to coordinated action. In April 2004, following the adoption of a resolution supporting abolition by the UN Commission on Human Rights, sixty-four delegations in the General Assembly submitted a joint statement dissociating themselves from the commission's findings. Still intent on framing the abolition movement as an example of cultural imperialism, the sixty-four signatories asserted that "no international consensus [exists] that capital punishment should be abolished." Citing the right of every sovereign state "to choose its political, economic, social, cultural, and legal systems, without interference in any form," the opponents of the 2004 resolution insisted, "It is inappropriate to make a universal decision on this question or to propose such action in the forum of an international forum." Without denying Amnesty's contention that capital punishment represents a violation of the right to life, opponents of the resolution simply countered that other rights must take precedence. According to the joint statement, the right of the convicted prisoner to life "must be weighed against the rights of victims [of crime] and the right of the community to live in peace and security."[61] Although two of the delegations that signed the statement of opposition in 2004 subsequently passed their own abolition measures (the Philippines and Rwanda), the long list of countries that remain opposed to universal abolition suggests that the Commission on Human Rights will not be able to push a mandate for abolition through the General Assembly. Although resistance to the abolition movement has diminished since the launch of Amnesty's 1989 campaign, their opponents, in most cases, show no signs of wavering. In fact, it could be that resistance will deepen as the advocates of abolition press their case more strenuously. When the

UN Commission on Human Rights adopted an even stronger resolution on the death penalty in 2005, it elicited another statement of dissociation from members of the General Assembly. Whereas the milder resolution in 2004 aroused sixty-four objections, the list of opponents in 2005 grew to include sixty-six countries. Is it reasonable to think that these holdouts will reverse themselves when and if the next resolution comes up for debate?

Amnesty's death penalty coordinators clearly believe that they can make additional headway. Reading the group's most recent literature, one certainly gets the impression (perhaps a false impression) that a victory for the abolitionists is just around the corner. In a report from January 2007, Amnesty noted that fifty-three executions were carried out in the United States in 2006, the lowest annual total for that country in more than a decade.[62] The numbers dropped again in both 2007 (forty-two) and 2008 (thirty-seven), as a result of a *de facto* moratorium on executions from October 2007 until May 2008 as the Supreme Court considered a new case challenging the legality of lethal injection.[63] Perhaps, then, Amnesty is correct in characterizing the use of the death penalty in the United States as a "dead-end experiment." Although the number of executions in the United States swelled slightly in 2009 (fifty-two) following the Court's ruling that lethal injection did not amount to cruel and unusual punishment, that total (excepting 2007 and 2008) is still the lowest since 1977 and less than half the number from 1996.[64] Because individuals who openly declare their opposition to the death penalty are almost always excluded from American jury pools in capital cases, the decline in the number of death sentences might indicate that support for the death penalty is dwindling even among so-called "death qualified" jurors. If that is so, then perhaps Amnesty makes a valid point when it states that:

An erosion of the public belief in the deterrence value of the death penalty, an increased awareness of the frequency of wrongful convictions in capital cases, and a greater confidence that public safety can be guaranteed by life in prison terms rather than death sentences have all contributed to the waning of enthusiasm for capital punishment [in the United States].[65]

Time has narrowed the gap between Amnesty's aspirations and the international norms regarding the death penalty. Retention of the death penalty is now a minority position in the United Nations General Assembly, and the countries that still sanction it are now being pressured from a variety of directions to fall in line with the majority. Activists seeking abolition like to point out that the vast majority of executions today (greater than ninety percent) are carried out in just five countries: China, Iran, Pakistan, Saudi Arabia, and the United States.[66] While this list of countries speaks volumes about the unlikelihood of getting a strict (i.e., binding) abolition mandate through the UN, the raw data certainly do give an impression that a handful of recalcitrant countries are insufficiently committed to the norms of twenty-first century liberal democracy and, therefore, standing in the way of history. Has Amnesty put itself on the cusp of victory?

Deciphering whether, or to what extent, the trend toward abolition can be attributed to the work of Amnesty is difficult. Clearly, there is a broader wave of democratization that needs to be accounted for. Pointing out the obvious: Amnesty's campaign coordinators did not topple the Berlin Wall; Mikhail Gorbachev launched his policy of *glasnost* without the help of the IS in London. Moreover, it is hardly believable if one suggests that Amnesty's reach was sufficient to single-handedly effect abolition in countries as diverse and as widely scattered as Kyrgyzstan (a

moratorium on the death penalty between 1989 and 2004; abolition thereafter), Mozambique (abolition for all crimes as of 1992), Guinea-Bissau (abolition for all crimes as of 1994), and Timor-Leste (abolition for all crimes as of 1999). Amnesty, of course, has never claimed to be the sole agent in the death penalty debate, but only to have staked a claim on the right side. Instead of asking whether Amnesty is responsible for the trend toward abolition, a better question is whether Amnesty has nourished the trend in some meaningful way. Having maintained essentially the same hard-line position against capital punishment since 1977, was it effective for Amnesty to work ahead of the curve?

Establishing causality here is tricky; however, there does appear to be a strong correlation between Amnesty's death penalty work and the sharp rise in the number of abolitionist countries after 1989. At the very least, one can say that the emergence of a stout human rights discourse played a critical role in the trend toward abolition and that Amnesty, as the most visible promoter of these discursive norms, has had a hand in the process. Without having made the death penalty an affront to human rights, would the abolitionist movement have generated the strength it now enjoys? Would eighty-one countries have quit the practice of capital punishment since 1989 if abolition had been framed only in terms of religious belief or economic practicality or psychological health? The answer almost certainly is "no." As Roger Hood has put it:

The new dynamic has seen many countries marching to abolition from retention in an unprecedented short period of time as they have come to embrace the view that capital punishment is not simply a weapon to be chosen by a state in response to its perceived and actual problems of crime, but a punishment which fundamentally involves, and cannot be administered without, a denial of the universal human right to be free of torturous, cruel and inhuman punishment.[67]

Whether or not one thinks that universal abolition is just around the corner, the human rights discourse has been and will continue to be an essential tool for the movement. The retentionist countries may wish to dig in their heels for the time being, but how long will they be able to afford that stance? Whether or not these countries will fully embrace the idealism that has fueled Amnesty over the years, they might end up dropping the death penalty sooner rather than later, if only to bolster their image and protect their bottom line in the global marketplace. In this case, old-fashioned pragmatism and *realpolitik* could be the decisive factors. But then what? Imagining for a moment that the UN *can* get a binding resolution against the death penalty passed, will the global community really have arrived at a universal agreement regarding the individual's right to life, or will human rights have become merely another bully stick?

Looking closely at the different paths that countries have followed to abolition, the either/or scenario depicted above seems inadequate. Where legislators and jurists have successfully opened the way to abolition, clearly they have not always done so out of deep personal conviction. Nor have political leaders typically supported abolition to attract votes or realize political gains on the domestic front. Instead, the regimes that have settled on abolition in the last twenty years have done so, in general, because there exists positive incentive in the international sphere to accommodate the demands of the human rights discourse. To be sure, such accommodation may vary in both degree and consistency, and countries that abolish the death penalty do not automatically establish pristine human rights credentials simply by doing so. But as to whether

states benefit by aligning themselves with the norms of the human rights discourse, there can be no doubt. While many states routinely flout human rights norms, none ever promotes itself as such. Even as the practice of torture today reveals that the UDHR guarantees very little where sovereign states imagine themselves governing in a state of exception, the human rights framework remains the only viable structure for international peace. The countries that circumvent the restraints of the UDHR cannot and do not propose to dismantle the human rights paradigm, but only to show how other rights might take precedence in exceptional circumstances. Progress toward universal death penalty abolition since 2001 (i.e., against the backdrop of the War on Terror) demonstrates that, while some countries play the human rights game only reluctantly, few can afford to ignore the rules altogether.[68] In this respect, human rights have played the decisive role in the increase of abolitionist countries. But if abolition stems more often from political calculation than from the wholehearted embrace of new ethical ideals, does it make sense to credit Amnesty, whose approach has been nothing if not exceedingly idealistic, with sparking the trend?

Amnesty has looked to the UN for support on abolition since 1971. The UN has responded unevenly for the most part. However, if one goes strictly by the numbers—the number of abolitionist states against the number of retentionist states—it is easy to see that a stunning reversal has already taken place there. Working out whether this wave of support for abolition is the result of newly internalized norms or merely a reflection of politics as usual is to some extent beside the point. The evidence shows that abolition is achievable and that states can follow a variety of different routes to abolition depending on circumstances and context. Amnesty's commitment to abolition and the work of its coordinators to frame capital punishment as a question of human rights has paid significant dividends. For some, Amnesty's descriptions of the death penalty resonate powerfully, and in these cases the injustices inherent to capital punishment make its continued use morally and ethically unbearable. For this set, abolition arises from a desire to live in accord with the absolute truth of human existence, and the death penalty debate is largely metaphysical. These true believers have no difficulty accepting with Amnesty that:

> The death penalty makes assumptions about a world that does not exist. It assumes the absolute perfection of the criminal justice system, and the absolute imperfection of the people it condemns to death. . . . It assumes that even if discrimination has not yet been eradicated in society, it can be overcome in the course of capital justice. And even if government is the focus of public distrust in a country founded on Revolution against a tyrannical monarchy, the state is still somehow assumed to be imbued with incorruptibility and infallibility when it turns its hand to executions.[69]

For others, the death penalty is primarily a political consideration. States either have the capability to resist the rise of human rights or they do not, and they make their decisions regarding the use of the death penalty on that basis. Currently, fewer and fewer states have the resources to opt out of the human rights regime. Where they do, states are subject to a barrage of criticism and in some instances (where interests and capabilities are aligned) to more forceful interventions. Tracing the history of Amnesty's work on the death penalty, it is appropriate that Amnesty receives credit for embedding the question of capital punishment into the human rights discourse. Perhaps in another ten or twenty years, Amnesty will have earned credit for even more than this.

Alexander Karn is Visiting Assistant Professor of Modern European History at Colgate University. He is the coeditor (with Elazar Barkan) of *Taking Wrongs Seriously: Apologies and Reconciliation* (Stanford University Press, 2006). His current work treats the role of historical commissions in conflict mediation.

Suggested Readings

Buchanan, Tom. "The Truth Will Set You Free: The Making of Amnesty International," *Journal of Contemporary History* 37, no. 4 (2002): 575–97.

Clark, Ann Marie. *Diplomacy of Conscience: Amnesty International and Changing Human Rights Norms.* Princeton: Princeton University Press, 2001.

Hood, Roger G. *The Death Penalty: A Worldwide Perspective.* 3rd ed. Oxford: Oxford University Press, 2002.

Hopgood, Stephen. *Keepers of the Flame: Understanding Amnesty International.* Ithaca: Cornell University Press, 2006.

Schabas, William A. *The Abolition of the Death Penalty in International Law.* 3rd ed. Cambridge: Cambridge University Press, 2002.

When the State Kills: The Death Penalty, A Human Rights Issue. New York: Amnesty International Publications, 1989.

Notes

1. Membership figures appear at: http://www.amnesty.org /en/who-we-are (accessed January 26, 2010).

2. Stephen Hopgood, *Keepers of the Flame: Understanding Amnesty International* (Ithaca: Cornell University Press, 2006), 111.

3. Tom Buchanan has traced the origins and foundations of AI in "The Truth Will Set You Free: The Making of Amnesty International," *Journal of Contemporary History* 37, no. 4 (2002): 575–97. Benenson launched the movement in 1961 with a letter to London's *Observer* in which he lamented the imprisonment of Portuguese students who reportedly had made a toast "to freedom" and called for the immediate release of these and all other "prisoners of conscience." Reprinted and circulated widely thereafter, Benenson's article began with a reference to the death penalty: "Open your newspaper

any day of the week and you will find a report from somewhere in the world of someone being imprisoned, tortured, or executed because his opinions or religion are unacceptable to his government."

4. For a complete list of members and background information on the coalition's history, see http://www.worldcoalition.org/modules/membres/ (accessed January 22, 2010).

5. This language appears widely throughout the AI web site. See, for example, "The Death Penalty: Questions and Answers" (AI Index: ACT 50/010/2007), which is available on-line at: http://www.amnesty.org/en/library/info/ACT50/010/2007/en (accessed January 25, 2010).

6. William Schabas indicates that some members of the drafting committee did support explicit language suggesting the goal of abolition, however this view failed to win a majority. See William A. Schabas, *The Abolition of the Death Penalty in International Law*, 3rd ed. (Cambridge: Cambridge University Press, 2002), 24.

7. Ann Marie Clark, *Diplomacy of Conscience: Amnesty International and Changing Human Rights Norms* (Princeton, NJ: Princeton University Press, 2001), 101.

8. Ibid. This was due, in part, to what some perceived as soft spots within the declaration. For example, Article 29 of the UDHR stated that the rights outlined therein were subject to limits, and while there was no language to determine the precise scope of those limits, the death penalty was frequently cited as a legitimate exception.

9. See Amnesty's external document, "Death Penalty Handbook. Part I: Amnesty International and the Death Penalty," published in 1982. AI Index: ACT 05/17/82.

10. Ibid.

11. The 1974 amendment is cited in an internal document from December 1987. See AI Index: ACT 51/01/87.

12. The "Declaration of Stockholm" appears in the *Report of the Amnesty International Conference on the Death Penalty*. Refer to AI Index: CDP 02/01/78.

13. Ibid.

14. Ibid. In the United States, Gallup polling shows that public support for the death penalty has varied widely over the past fifty years. While 65 percent of those polled in October 2009 responded that they supported the death penalty for persons convicted of murder (as opposed to 31 percent who opposed it), the level of support has been markedly lower at other times. For instance, the percentage of those who supported the death penalty never surpassed 54 percent in polling conducted between March 1956 and March 1972. In May 1966, Gallup polling showed that opposition to the death penalty (47 percent) actually exceeded support for its use (42 percent). In general, what the polling shows is a narrowing of opinion in 1953–1966, a widening divergence of opinion in 1966–1994, and another period of convergence in 1994–2000. The latest Gallup report on America's attitudes regarding the death penalty is available at: http://www.gallup.com/poll/123638/In-U.S.-Two-Thirds-Continue-Support-Death-Penalty.aspx (accessed January 27, 2010).

15. According to Amnesty, the death penalty helps to nurture and sustain a culture of brutality which extends to all of the individuals involved in its implementation, i.e., judges, jurors, lawyers, politicians with the power to grant clemency, prison staff where executions are performed, and to those who are condemned to die.

16. In 1995, James Liebman (Columbia University School of Law) published a study reviewing 5,760 capital sentences imposed in the United States between 1973 and 1995. According to his data, the rate of reversal for these cases was 68 percent, and Liebman cited inadequate representation as one of the primary reasons. The full study, titled "A Broken System: Error Rates in Capital Cases, 1973–1995," is available at http://www2.law.columbia.edu/instructionalservices/liebman/ (accessed January 27, 2010). The American Civil Liberties Union has also taken up the question of inadequate legal representation as part of its Capital Punishment Project. For more information on specific capital cases where legal representation was found wanting, refer to http://www.aclu.org/capital/unequal/10390pub20031008.html (accessed January 27, 2010).

17. Together with twenty-five other NGOs, Amnesty submitted a resolution seeking abolition of the death penalty to the Fifth United Nations Congress on the Prevention of Crime and the Treatment of Offenders in September 1975. Just over two years later (December 1977), and noting how little progress had been made on the issue, the United Nations General Assembly decided to return to the question of capital punishment in its thirty-fifth session, promising to consider the question of its use with "high priority." See UN General Assembly Resolution 32/61 of 8 December 1977 on Capital Punishment, Appendix G in the Amnesty Report cited in note 12.

18. Heading into 1977, the year of the Stockholm Conference, twenty-six countries had permanently abolished the death penalty, either for all crimes or for ordinary crimes (i.e., non-military, non-wartime). By 2006, that number had risen to 128, including thirty-one countries that had arrived at *de facto* abolition without having instituted legal prohibitions explicitly forbidding its practice. Figures taken from Amnesty's "List of Abolitionist and Retentionist Countries." See AI Index: ACT 50/001/2007.

19. The issue of cruelty has continued to arouse debate. The United States Supreme Court agreed in October 2007 to hear a case from Kentucky in which two death row inmates contended that the practice of lethal injection violated their constitutional rights under the Eighth Amendment. The Court, in a 7-2 vote, upheld Kentucky's method for execution. For details related to the

case, see Darryl Fears, "Lethal Injection to Get Supreme Test," *The Washington Post*, 23 November 2007.

20. The Court's ruling in *Furman v. Georgia* (408 U.S. 238) suspended the death penalty in 1972 on the basis that it resulted from arbitrary and capricious sentencing guidelines and, therefore, was to be considered a "cruel and unusual" measure and a violation of the Eighth Amendment prohibiting the same. The decision did not label capital punishment unconstitutional *per se*, but held that its implementation was open to abuse, leaving states free to rewrite the statutes under which the death penalty was employed.

21. Evans was tried and sentenced in Alabama in April 1977. His mother submitted an application for a stay of execution to the United States Supreme Court two years later after Evans refused to pursue any further appeals. See *Evans v. Bennett* (440 U.S. 1301).

22. Active in the southern states until the early 1990s, the coalition was formed in 1974 to "promote greater awareness of the problems of prisons and corrections, improve communication between the prison population and the outside world, and advocate for alternatives to the death penalty." Information on the coalition's work can be obtained through the National Death Penalty Archive at the University at Albany (SUNY-Albany). See: http://library.albany.edu/speccoll/ndpa.htm (accessed January 27, 2010).

23. Larry Cox, interview, July 18, 2007.

24. Ibid.

25. Ibid.

26. Both Gilmore and Evans asked to be executed.

27. For more on the episode with Governor Bob Graham and a profile on Cox, see: http://www.amnestyusa.org/Fall_2006/A_Committment_to_Change/page.do?id=1105195&n1=2&n2=19&n3=358 (accessed January 27, 2010).

28. Cox asserts that he discussed his tactics with then AIUSA chair, David Hinckley, and that both agreed his work in Florida would not be undertaken as an official representative of the organization.

29. According to Gallup polling, support for the death penalty never fell below 70 percent in the United States in the period between 1980 and 2000. See note 14 for more information on Gallup's death penalty data.

30. Quoted from a speech given by Larry Cox at the AIUSA annual meeting in Chicago on June 23, 1984. Typescript provided to author.

31. See section 4.3 in "Report on National Section Meeting on the Death Penalty." AI Index: CDP 01/07/78.

32. Those who are familiar with the United Nations know that the General Assembly is anything but monolithic. Taking any single resolution passed there, either in favor of death penalty abolition or against it, as an indication of unanimity, or even as evidence of strong majority support, is problematic and unwise. If one looks to

the UN for an overall trend on the death penalty during this period (1970s), one characterization would be lofty aspirations (i.e., repeated references to the "desirability" of abolition) and scant results (i.e., the inability to get universal abolition resolutions out of committee and passed in the General Assembly). For more on the politics of abolition at the UN, see "Looking Ahead: The Prospects for Abolition" at the end of this chapter.

33. According to the report: "The view that no world-wide, corporate effort to achieve abolition of the death penalty is possible has much support. To test it, Amnesty International convened an international conference, held in Stockholm in December 1977. The participants—among them theologians, lawyers, judges, politicians, psychologists, police officers, penologists and journalists—came from fifty countries. . . . It was abundantly clear from the Conference that there are people all over the world who believe that the death penalty should be totally abolished." See *Amnesty International Report: The Death Penalty* (London: Amnesty International, 1979), 17.

34. Refer to "Strategy for the Program Against the Death Penalty." AI Index: ACT 05/IEC01/79.

35. Ibid.

36. The Second Optional Protocol to the Covenant on Civil and Political Rights Aiming at the Abolition of the Death Penalty was adopted by the UN General Assembly in December 1989 and came into force on July 11, 1991. Cited in Schabas, *The Abolition of the Death Penalty in International Law*, 23.

37. See the discussion of strategy in Amnesty's "Report on the International Meeting on the Death Penalty." AI Index: ACT 51/04/81. National section representatives for Austria, Sweden, and the United Kingdom expressed their concern that the IEC's shift in emphasis signaled a retreat which would compromise their ability to work effectively at home.

38. Ibid.

39. This is consistent with the internal difficulties Larry Cox describes within AIUSA when the organization sought to actively address the death penalty after 1977. See note 23.

40. Of the eighty countries that had abolished the death penalty by 1988, fifty-three had done so on the basis of specific legislation while another twenty-seven had instituted *de facto* abolition. See AI Index: ACT 50/001/2007.

41. See "How Countries Come to Abolish the Death Penalty," AI Index: ACT 05/14/85.

42. Commissions of this kind have had an important impact on the death penalty debate in the United States during the past decade. After imposing a moratorium on executions in his state in 2000, Illinois governor George Ryan appointed a fourteen-member, bipartisan commission to review the death penalty and its application under

state law. In the commission's final report (April 2002), a majority of its members recommended that the death penalty should be abolished owing to moral concerns over its application and the impossibility of fully guarding against arbitrariness and discrimination. Despite this recommendation, the death penalty remains on the books in Illinois, and prosecutors continue to seek its implementation there. For a copy of the Illinois report, see: http://www.idoc.state.il.us/ccp/index.html (accessed January 27, 2010). Not Illinois, but rather New Jersey became the first state to abolish the death penalty since its reimplementation in 1976. Following a recommendation made by a state commission similar to that of Illinois in January 2007, Governor Jon Corzine signed the law to repeal the death penalty in December of the same year. See Jeremy W. Peters, "Death Penalty Repealed in New Jersey," *The New York Times*, 17 December 2007.

43. See "Campaign Against the Death Penalty, Circular No. 1: Campaign Plan." AI Index: ACT 51/01/87.

44. Ibid. Noting the effects that unexpected events can have on the shape of the death penalty debate, the first campaign circular states: "[A] highly publicized murder may temporarily enrage public opinion, making it hard to get the abolitionist message across, while revelations of a wrongful conviction can provide the atmosphere for emphasizing that the death penalty is irrevocable and can be inflicted on the innocent."

45. Among the first celebrities to take an active role in the global campaign were a handful of rock 'n' roll artists, including Bono, Eric Clapton, Peter Gabriel, Bruce Springsteen, and Sting.

46. The controversy over rendition heated up again in November 2007 after a Syrian-born Canadian, who was detained in New York's Kennedy Airport in 2002 and then sent to Syria, where he was detained and allegedly tortured for ten months, petitioned for and was granted a new hearing for a civil liberties case against the U.S. government. See Alan Feuer, "Federal Judge Calls Rendition 'Outsourcing,'" *The New York Times*, 10 November 2007.

47. These concerns originally emerged in 1985 in the context of Amnesty's work on behalf of political refugees. See AI Index: POL 33/02/85.

48. *When the State Kills* (New York: Amnesty International, 1989), 1.

49. Ibid., 72.

50. The first figure is taken from Roger Hood, "Developments on the Road to Abolition," which was presented in August 2007 at the Global Survey on Death Penalty Reform in Beijing, China. Manuscript provided to author. The second figure is taken from Amnesty's "List of Abolitionist and Retentionist Countries." See http://www.amnesty.org/en/death-penalty/abolitionist-and-retentionist-countries (accessed January 28, 2010).

51. While Article 4 of the American Convention on Human Rights already imposed strict limitations on the use of the death penalty, the Protocol to Abolish the Death Penalty, adopted June 8, 1990, formalized this commitment. Both documents can be retrieved at: http://www.cidh.oas.org/Basicos/English/Basic.TOC.htm (accessed January 27, 2010).

52. See note 50, "List of Abolitionist and Retentionist Countries."

53. The first of these groups, Hands Off Cain, is based in Rome and is affiliated with the Transnational Radical Party, a registered NGO with recognition from the United Nations. The second group, Moratorium 2000, operates in Louisiana under the auspices of the Moratorium Campaign, an organization founded by Sister Helen Prejean, who gained notoriety after the publication of her book, *Dead Man Walking: An Eyewitness Account of the Death Penalty in the United States* (New York: Random House, 1993). In 1995, Prejean's book was adapted for a Hollywood film production which earned both critical and popular acclaim. For more on these organizations, see http://www.handsoffcain.info and http://www.moratoriumcampaign.org (accessed January 27, 2010).

54. See http://www.amnesty.org/en/library/info/ACT53/001/2001/en (accessed January 27, 2010). The same petition was presented at the United Nations again in November 2007 with more than five million signatures collected in 154 countries. See: http://www.worldcoalition.org/modules/smartsection/item.php?itemid=236 (accessed January 27, 2010).

55. Montreal in 2004 and Paris in 2007. A Fourth World Congress is planned for Geneva, Switzerland, in February 2010. See http://www.abolition.fr/ecpm/english/congres.php?art=693&suj=208&topic=76 (accessed January 28, 2010).

56. The declaration can be accessed via the World Coalition Against the Death Penalty website: http://www.worldcoalition.org/modules/pages/indexphp?pagenum=8 (accessed January 27, 2010).

57. While Armenia and Turkey legally abolished the death penalty for all crimes in 2003 and 2004 respectively, Amnesty characterizes Russia as "abolitionist in practice," a designation given to countries "which retain the death penalty for ordinary crimes such as murder but can be considered abolitionist in practice in that they have not executed anyone during the past 10 years and are believed to have a policy or established practice of not carrying out executions."

58. The list of participants from 2007 reveals the event's global scope. At least one initiative was planned in each of the following countries: Austria, Belgium, Benin, Cameroon, Czech Republic, Democratic Republic of Congo, Denmark, Finland, France, Ghana, Iceland, India, Italy, Ivory Coast, Jamaica, Jordan, Germany,

Guinea, Lebanon, Luxembourg, Mali, Mexico, Mongolia, Morocco, Nepal, New Zealand, Nigeria, Palestine, Paraguay, Peru, Philippines, Portugal, Sierra Leone, South Korea, Spain, Switzerland, Taiwan, Togo, United States, and Yemen.

59. Prodi was among the first world leaders to condemn Saddam's hanging, which took place on December 30, 2006, after a leaked video revealed that the Iraqi dictator had been taunted on his way to the gallows and partially decapitated as a result of his hanging. See "Botched Executions in Iraq Prompt Renewed Calls to Abolish the Death Penalty Worldwide," *Associated Press*, 16 January 2007.

60. The resolution can be viewed on-line at: http://www. un.org/Docs/journal/asp/ws.asp?m=A/C.3/62/L.29 (accessed January 27, 2010).

61. The quotations here appear in UN document E/CN.4/2004/G/54, which is available on-line at: http://ap.ohchr.org/documents/alldocs.aspx?doc_id=9260 (accessed January 27, 2010).

62. See Amnesty's report from January 2007, "The Experiment that Failed: A Reflection on Thirty Years of Executions." AI Index: AMR 51/011/2007.

63. Following the Court's ruling and the resumption of executions, the number of executions in the United States swelled to fifty-two in 2009. Execution statistics for the United States (1976–present) can be accessed on-line at: http://www.deathpenaltyinfo.org/executions-united-states (January 27, 2010).

64. Ibid.

65. Ibid.

66. See http://www.amnesty.org/en/death-penalty/numbers for the most recent figures (accessed January 30, 2010).

67. Quotation from Hood, "Developments on the Road to Abolition: A Worldwide Perspective" (2007). Manuscript provided to author.

68. Since 2001, seventeen countries have enacted abolition measures.

69. AI Index: AMR 51/011/2007.

CHAPTER 8

The Celluloid Execution

HOLLYWOOD FILMS AND CAPITAL PUNISHMENT

Susanne Teepe Gaskins

IN THE darkened movie theater a sequence of familiar images appears on the screen: a murder, an investigation, an arrest, a trial, a conviction, a death sentence, and an execution. Hollywood filmmakers frequently use the device of crime and punishment to draw us into their cinematic storytelling. In fact, these images are often so familiar to moviegoers that audiences rarely stop to analyze the meaning behind the images and plotlines. From war movies to crime dramas, from thrillers to westerns, American cinema seems obsessed with issues of wrongdoing and justice. Countless American films, from the most profound to the most inane, explore the ever-present themes of revenge, retribution, justice, and punishment. How often does a movie villain die at the end of the film? Cinema's proverbial "bad guy" frequently meets his maker as a result of his own miscalculation and wrongdoing, sometimes accidentally, but often at the hands of an avenging hero. Whether through vigilante justice or the halls of justice, a reckoning is expected by American audiences and movies rarely fail to deliver.[1]

Take, for example, the film that made James Cagney a Hollywood star, *The Public Enemy* (1931).[2] Basically a gangster picture, it traces the steady descent of Tommy Powers (Cagney) into a life of crime. Becoming the enforcer for a Chicago bootlegging operation proves not only profitable, but allows him upward social mobility. When a gangland war breaks out, Tommy's partner is fatally shot and Tommy, following the law of the street, seeks retribution. While exacting his revenge, Tommy is wounded by gunfire and survives, only to be kidnapped by the rival gang and delivered to his mother's doorstep—dead. The moral of William Wellman's film suggests that criminal behavior will be punished one way or another, if not by the justice system then certainly by some other unforeseen means, be it street or divine justice.

Yet another genre of film takes crime and punishment as its main focus: the courtroom drama, or legal thriller. Here the operation of the American legal system and the goal of handing down and carrying out justice take center stage in a much more explicit way. In fact, legal dramas became so popular on the big screen in the last twenty years that images of courtrooms, lawyers, defendants, juries, and judges in film have become the topic of scholarly inquiry.[3] While legal professionals began to examine and analyze their Hollywood likenesses, the role of government's most severe penalty, capital punishment, and its cinematic portrayal, naturally, loomed in the discussion.[4]

Throughout its history, Hollywood has explored the death penalty in films like *Angels with Dirty Faces* (1938), *I Want to Live!* (1958), *Compulsion* (1959), and *In Cold Blood* (1967), but the 1990s saw a rash of movies wrestling with capital punishment.[5] The most critically acclaimed of the films was *Dead Man Walking* (1995), which was followed by *Murder in the First* (1995), *Last Dance* (1996), *The Chamber* (1996), *True Crime* (1999), and *The Green Mile* (1999). In more recent years filmmakers produced *Monster's Ball* (2001), *The Life of David Gale* (2003), and *Capote* (2005). Even when the death penalty is not the main theme of a film, it often rears up in the background as it does in *Monster* (2003),[6] the actual story of a Florida streetwalker who had been a childhood victim of sexual abuse. Aileen Wuornos, played by Charlize Theron in an Oscar-winning performance, killed seven of her "johns" while supporting and forging a romantic relationship with another young woman. During the last moments of the film she is convicted for the homicides and receives the death sentence.[7] Even when capital punishment fails to get a leading role in movies, frequently it plays a peripheral part.

Whether in a starring role or in a bit part, the death sentence garners attention from its opponents and supporters who hail or bemoan Hollywood's portrayal of capital punishment. One can never forget that Tinseltown creates movies to turn a profit and often story lines are simplified to a familiar dichotomy—good versus evil, crime versus punishment—in order to sell tickets.[8] But despite profits and simplified plots, films convey a message to audiences and movies that deal with capital punishment are no different. How audiences and individuals interpret the meaning behind death penalty movies has to do with the political views one holds about this highly charged issue. People who support

capital punishment view a film quite differently than those who commit themselves to fighting against state-sponsored executions. Those people who subscribe to the old abolitionist arguments will come away with another perspective on a film than those who find the new abolitionist position more persuasive. If religion is central in one's life a death penalty movie can elicit one type of response, while those who take a secular approach come to another conclusion. People who view individuals as ultimately responsible for their own actions make one interpretation of a film's message, and those who see society bearing some responsibility for criminal acts respond in a dissimilar manner. In conducting research and watching death penalty films for this article, it was striking to see how differently movie reviewers,[9] lawyers, scholars, and capital punishment opponents interpret these silver-screen releases.[10]

Discussions about Hollywood's depiction of capital punishment involve numerous conversations and perspectives.[11] Scholars examining the image of lawyers and the law in television and the movies weigh in with their judgments as do the opponents of capital punishment, both within the halls of justice and outside them. The voices of those who advocate capital punishment are present but seem decidedly more muted. Finally, filmmakers and the Hollywood community tend to make their views known through the movies they produce. Although Hollywood is no monolith and embraces various political positions, the makers of death penalty movies tend to be motivated to voice their opposition to state-sanctioned killing. Conducting a Google search using the search terms "Hollywood" and "capital punishment," the results reveal the tendency of some prominent Hollywood actors to oppose the death penalty vocally and actively. Hollywood's liberal inclinations seem to hold true when it comes to meting out the ultimate punishment the state inflicts for homicide. Most filmmakers who embark on creating a capital punishment film do so with the objective of at least getting audiences to question the practice, but are more often than not openly opposed to it.

From the very inception of movie-making, capital punishment emerged as a topic for nickelodeons and silent films. Some offered its viewers shocking details of hangings or electrocutions and were simply designed to titillate or appall its audience, but others took a stand against the death penalty. Silent films like *Thou Shalt Not Kill* (1913), *And the Law Says* (1916), and D. W. Griffith's *Intolerance* (1916) all took an anti-death-penalty stand, although in retrospect they may convey more about the pitfalls of the legal system than anything else. *Thou Shalt Not Kill*, made by Hal Reid of Vitagraph, placed an innocent, pregnant mother on death row for the shooting death of her husband. The governor orders her execution date delayed until her child is born and in the intervening months her innocence is proven and she is released. Other films took the race-to-save-the-innocent-man approach like *The City of Darkness* (1914). Here, a governor must dash to stop the execution of his brother who has been framed by the corrupt city boss, whose own son faced capital punishment when the now governor held the post of district attorney. In the governor's effort to stop his brother's wrongful execution he cuts power to the entire city, plunging the metropolis into darkness, before the brother is finally vindicated. Silent films also employed the device of putting the convicted to death only to discover, after the fact, that the person was guiltless of the crime for which he had been executed. Directed by Colin Campbell and produced by Selig Studios, *Who Shall Take My Life?* (1917) depicts a man facing execution based on flimsy evidence and only after his death do the authorities receive proof that his "victim" is alive.[12]

From the socially conscience films of the 1910s, which proudly trumpeted their opposition to capital punishment, the 1920s used the death penalty as a mere contrivance with which to conclude melodramas. In fact, silent-film historian Kevin Brownlow argues that "there were so many races to the rescue in the style of *Intolerance* that they became parodies of themselves."[13] The 1925 Clara Bow vehicle, *Capital Punishment*, stands as one of the few pictures of that decade to speak out against the death penalty more directly, but still turned out to be formulaic. *Capital Punishment* attempted to discredit the death penalty when two men make a substantial wager that they can have someone convicted and sentenced to death for a sham homicide. Their plan goes as expected and they frame a willing third party and send the murder "victim" on an ocean voyage. The vacationing man ends up being killed unintentionally by the other bettor, and he allows the blameless man on death row to take the rap. The film's only "twist" occurs when the truth is revealed, but the stay of execution comes too late to spare the life of the man who allowed himself to be set up.[14] While movies of the silent era established some of the formulas which future capital punishment films would continue to employ, a number of them telegraphed their intended message against state-sponsored executions. On the other hand, the 1930s films set a different and more ambivalent tone.

Angels with Dirty Faces, Director Michael Curtiz, Warner Bros. (1938)

Angels with Dirty Faces stands as one of the 1930s Hollywood productions that incorporated an execution scene and touched on the death penalty. A classic Warner Brothers gangster picture of the Depression era, two teenage boys grow up among the tenements of big-city America and both are drawn into the world of petty crime. But it is Rocky Sullivan, played by James Cagney, who ends up in the juvenile corrections system, while his friend Jerry Connelly, portrayed by Pat O'Brian, becomes a Catholic priest. While Rocky's path leads to escalating crimes of racketeering and violence, Father Jerry attempts to save the neighborhood boys from the lure and glamour of the gangsters' world. Upon Rocky's return to his old haunts, he becomes the object of hero worship among the neighborhood's juvenile delinquents.[15] At the same time he falls in with a corrupt lawyer named Jim Frazier, played by a still relatively little known Humphrey Bogart, and the gangster boss, Mac Keefer, depicted by George Bancroft.

When Father Connelly launches a reform movement against the crime and corruption of the city, Frazier and Keefer opt to have the priest killed, along with Rocky should he stand in their way. Having overheard their plan to murder his old childhood friend, Rocky shoots both men. The inevitable gangland shootout follows with Rocky holed up in a warehouse engaged in a battle with police, during which he guns down two police officers. With Father Jerry's intervention, Rocky surrenders himself to the authorities. Through a series of newspaper headlines the audience learns that Rocky Sullivan stood trial, was found guilty, and sentenced to death. During his last hours, Father Jerry visits Rocky and urges him to think of the neighborhood boys and their future by going to the electric chair "yellow." By meeting his death in a cowardly fashion, Jerry believes the teenagers will come to despise Rocky's memory rather than revere it. Clearly still in control of his emotions and not afraid to die, Rocky vehemently rejects his friend's proposal. Jerry offers Rocky a chance to redeem himself and reassures him that, although the world will remember him as a coward, the two old friends, and by implication God, will know the courage it took to put the welfare of the boys first.

The condemned Rocky Sullivan walks to his execution with confidence, defiance, and grim determination as exemplified in the last close-up of Cagney's face. In silhouette, as the guards take him by the arms to strap him into the electric chair, Rocky begins to scream for mercy, resisting the guards, clinging to a radiator, and shamelessly pleading for his life. The electrocution scene is represented by the throwing of a switch and the dimming of the lights behind the faces of the shocked witnesses which the camera focuses on before the scene fades to black. Sacrificing his pride for the sake of the neighborhood teens has the desired effect. The teenage gang members read the headlines concerning Rocky's cowardly death and their disappointment is evident. While they still harbor some doubts about the veracity of the newspaper accounts, Father Jerry, who they know was a witness to the execution, reassures them that all they have read is true. Their body language signals their deep disillusionment with their former gangland hero and they follow the priest up the stairs to say a prayer for "a boy that couldn't run as fast as I could," as Father Jerry puts it.

While *Angels with Dirty Faces* poses as a morality tale, the gangster genre films of the 1930s plainly glamorized the life of criminals, and audiences readily identified with the gangster character. It is Cagney's charismatic Rocky who has style, swagger, courage, defiance, and a disarming charm that audiences admire. The story of two boys who grow up to become men on opposite sides of the law provided the picture with its moral foundation. Unlike earlier gangster movies, *Angels with Dirty Faces* attempted to comment on the social factors that lead to a life of crime. The opening shots pan across the teeming immigrant neighborhoods of an urbanized America, where poverty-stricken people live in crowded, run-down tenements, where crimes large and small take place with regularity, and where juvenile delinquency is an ever-present problem. The film further suggests that Rocky's first stint in reform school and other, later incarcerations molded him into the felon he became. Moreover, not a single parental figure makes an appearance in the film. Neither Rocky nor Jerry seem to have a home or parents and the neighborhood delinquents seem equally homeless and parentless; in fact, Father Connolly provides the only adult guidance the neighborhood kids receive.

In addition, the Hollywood production codes of the 1930s demanded that lawbreakers receive their comeuppance, and in the end, Rocky is no exception.[16] He pays for his crimes with his life. What makes *Angels with Dirty Faces* somewhat different is that Rocky receives an opportunity not just to pay his debt to society with his death, but to redeem himself in the last moments of his life. The moral lesson is simple: criminal activity will end in the guilty being penalized. The film never raises any questions about the rectitude of the death penalty; it simply assumes the state's right to impose society's ultimate punishment on the guilty. In creating a highly symbolic execution scene, director Michael Curtiz's motion picture spares the audience from "witnessing" the cinematic recreation of Rocky's electrocution. Viewers never have an opportunity to grapple with whether sending someone to the electric chair constitutes cruel and unusual punishment. But it is the sounds of tough-guy Rocky Sullivan begging for his life and struggling with the prison guards that give the audience pause. Cagney stated in an interview that he deliberately tried to give his final scene an ambivalent feel, so audiences might question whether Rocky died in a blaze of redemptive glory or as a sniveling poltroon.[17] If movie viewers interpret Cagney's performance as that of a hardened thug suddenly reduced to a trembling, hysterical coward when confronted by his terrible fate, then they might question if anyone deserves to die by electrocution. However, if audiences see Cagney's actions as sacrificing his self-respect for the sake of others, as director

Curtiz most likely intended, then Rocky's status as a hero is confirmed and his ignoble death is merely a means of achieving his eleventh-hour atonement. Either way, capital punishment, pro or con, is hardly the main focus of the picture.

I Want to Live, Director Robert Wise, United Artists (1958)

On the other hand, 1958's *I Want to Live*, directed by Robert Wise, makes the death penalty its focal point. The film opens and closes with a statement that the story is based on facts and comes from documents collected and newspaper articles written by Edmund Montgomery, a Pulitzer Prize–winning reporter. Susan Hayward, who won an Academy Award for her portrayal, stars as condemned California murderer Barbara Graham in typical 1950s Hollywood biopic fashion. The film opens in a jazz club with patrons drinking, musicians smoking pot, and older men picking up younger women, all to the rhythms of improvised jazz music. Graham wakes up in a second-rate hotel room above the nightclub with a guy she clearly picked up for the night. When a vice cop shows up, he wants to arrest her male companion for violating the Mann Act, but she brashly tells the officer she is paying for the room and she gets arrested on a misdemeanor prostitution charge. "I've been there before," she flippantly announces. Like Cagney's Rocky Sullivan, Graham willingly takes the rap to spare another, in this case, her "john" from endangering his reputation and marriage. Moments before, moviegoers watched while she opened her client's wallet and confronted his family's photograph. Her parting words as she handed the open wallet to her companion were, "Don't lose this."[18] These early scenes show Graham as a prostitute and party girl, who is hard, brash, rebellious, but beautiful and prepared to protect love and family, even if they belong to someone else. Graham's character fails to conform to the typical 1950s image of women. In many respects, she is amoral, but she is nobody's victim and she lives on her own terms. She agrees to provide a false alibi for two criminal friends and ends up serving a year in jail for a perjury conviction. Upon her release, she quickly begins passing bad checks, acts as a shill at card games, and drives the getaway car when her buddies perpetrate a burglary. Although she has been married three times already, she weds again and has a baby boy, Bobby, with her drug-addicted husband, but the relationship soon falls apart.[19] Left destitute, Graham skips out on the landlord and parks the baby with her mother-in-law while she leaves town.

Newspaper headlines appear on screen that sixty-three-year-old Mabel Monahan, widowed and disabled, was beaten to death in her Burbank home during a robbery. Filmgoers never see the crime being carried out or even a picture of the victim. Rarely has a murder victim been quite so anonymous. The director also chooses not to supply a cinematic recreation of the crime, as so many Hollywood movies usually do. Despite the face-lessness of the victim, the perpetrators possess an identity and LAPD officers soon apprehend the suspects, Emmett Perkins and Jack Santos, in a warehouse. Graham, who was followed by police to their hideout, is taken into custody along with them. During her interrogation she is defiant, uncooperative, and belligerent. At times the film paints her in a rather unsympathetic light—she is, after all, a "bad girl"—but it suggests that she is innocent of the murder charge; at the very least it leaves the issue in doubt. Police question her without a lawyer present and without formally charging her, and Graham seems genuinely shocked to discover that she is being accused of murder. One of her codefendants, Bruce King, claims that Graham pistol-whipped the victim when she failed to reveal the stash of jewelry and cash thought to

be in the Monahan home. Graham realizes her chances of being found innocent remain quite slim because she cannot substantiate her alibi; she was at home with her junky husband and infant son at the time. Fearful of being convicted without a solid alibi, Graham agrees to allow a fellow prison inmate to arrange an alibi for her. For a price, Ben Miranda, a man Graham has never met, consents to testify that the two of them were together at the time of the crime.[20] He persistently fishes for an admission of guilt and, anxious that he might refuse to help her, Graham allows him to think what he likes. During her trial Graham comes off as insolent and desperate rather than sympathetic. Between King's testimony, her previous perjury conviction, and Ben Miranda turning out to be an undercover police officer, her fate is sealed. The jury finds her guilty, along with her criminal partners, Perkins and Santos; all are sentenced to death. Underlying her mistreatment by the police, precarious legal situation, and fatal punishment is a vaguely malevolent judicial system that discredits, ensnares, and finally executes its victims.[21]

When a new lawyer accepts her case he hires a psychologist and criminologist, Carl Palmberg, to examine Graham. Palmberg concludes she is completely amoral and a compulsive liar, but incapable of the violence the crime required. He also points out that Barbara is left-handed, but King testified that she used her right hand to bludgeon her victim. The criminologist theorizes that her codefendants framed her because they believed the justice system could not bring itself to execute a woman, and a mother no less. If the state refused to execute the actual perpetrator, it certainly could not put to death her male accomplices.[22] Graham also emphatically states that she is innocent, but in the end the courts deny her appeal and set her execution date. But Palmberg and her lawyer are not the only people who believe in Graham's innocence. Newspaper reporter Ed Montgomery, after first vilifying her in the press, comes to accept that there is no blood on her hands. *I Want to Live!* exposes the media's capacity to pillory or exonerate people with its coverage. With headlines referring to Barbara Graham as "Bloody Babs" and "the Tiger Lady" the point is driven home that crime, trials, and executions sell newspapers, whether Graham is guilty or not.[23]

Once the death sentence is handed down, the movie devotes its last 36 minutes (out of a total 120 minutes)[24] to Graham's stay on death row and the details leading up to her execution. As the cinematic execution date approaches, the film provides very long and detailed, almost languid, scenes of the preparation of the gas chamber: mixing chemicals, dispensing the cyanide pellets, and testing the gas chamber. With a sudden change in the film's pacing, the director created a terrible sense of suspense, an ominous waiting for the inevitable end. But Graham's demeanor hardly changes once she sits on San Quentin's death row; she alternately behaves with belligerence or defiance, hardly the image the public associates with a woman at the mercy of the courts. The nurse who attends her in her final hours musters compassion for Graham and sees her as a vulnerable human being who must face her eminent demise. But again Graham reverts to type, lying to the nurse about how good her marriage to Hank was and that she left him because she knew a girl like her would stand in the way of his big promotion to vice president of a well-known California bank. As Graham relates this story, doubt is written all over the nurse's face.

A Catholic priest comes to the death house, brings her a St. Jude[25] medallion, and hears her confession, although film spectators are not privy to what she says. Graham evidently holds religious beliefs, but there is no great show of remorse or a religious epiphany. She admits to Father Devers that she is prepared to face death

and that "it would be rather nice to come face to face with the one person in all the world who knows I am innocent."[26] When the priest indicates she means God, she replies that she meant her supposed victim, Mrs. Monahan. Newspaperman Montgomery waits all night to see the condemned Perkins, who he hopes will absolve Graham of guilt, but even as his own execution draws near Perkins refuses to see the reporter. Graham is granted several short stays of execution and one observes how torturous the delays are for the condemned woman. Each time the telephone rings the sudden, jarring sound further erodes her composure. Just prior to her last walk to the gas chamber, Graham requests an eye mask because she does not want to see the execution's witnesses, all middle-aged men, staring at her. The gas chamber scene is surprisingly long, but hardly gruesome. A guard straps the still-glamorous Graham into the chair and advises her to count to ten after she hears the cyanide pellets drop into the sulfuric acid and then take a deep breath. "It's easier that way," he confides. "How would you know?" she vehemently retorts.[27] As vapors begin to fill the chamber, the audience watches the blindfolded Graham's face grimace and she thrashes a bit in the chair, but basically her death appears to be fairly neat and "clean." As much attention as the film lavishes on Graham's demise, it wastes not a moment or a mention on the executions of Perkins and Santos.

Director Robert Wise and producer Walter Wanger clearly intended to create a film that depicted the death penalty in a negative light and showed the vagaries of the legal system and the horrors of someone caught up in it.[28] In many ways, it is typical of the "bad rap" approach, but Graham's guilt or innocence remains an issue for debate even today. There were those who came to believe she was innocent and wrongfully put to death and others equally convinced of her responsibility in the felony.[29] But while Wise's motion picture wants the audience to identify, and sympathize, with Graham, it ends up persuading viewers that Graham is inculpable in the murder of Mrs. Monahan. On the other hand, it portrays her as a liar, prostitute, and petty criminal. Compulsive lying gets her into trouble not once, but twice: her previous perjury indictment, and again in arranging a false alibi from her prison cell. But Graham claims on the witness stand that she realized she was facing the gas chamber and was desperate because she could not prove her alibi. "Have you ever been really desperate?" she cries. "Do you know what that feels like?" *I Want to Live!* implies that Graham faced conviction because of her unsavory reputation coupled with her inability to speak the truth.

Despite Graham coming across as the brazen nonconformist, the film seems to focus on whether *women* should receive the death sentence. The movie plays on Graham's gender, beauty, and her role as a mother. Graham, as portrayed by Hayward, shows great concern for her son and breaks down during her last visit with him. She even suggests that her death may be the best thing in the long run for her son, but she is clearly heartbroken at the thought of being separated from him by death. Would a film depicting a condemned man spend quite so much screen time focusing on fatherhood? Graham's death will make an orphan of her son, and a little boy losing his mother seems so much more tragic, cinematically, than a son losing his father. Beyond playing on the motherhood angle, some typical gender issues surface over the question of executing a woman; at the time, Graham was only the third woman put to death in California.[30] Obviously, the correctional officers are uncomfortable with the procedure of executing a woman. First, she must be transferred to San Quentin, a state penitentiary which only houses men, and isolated from the other prisoners, even from the male prisoners' view. Then because of her gender, the prison warden affords her privileges male inmates would never receive because they are seen as a greater threat to society, to prison guards, and to each other. For example, at the nurse's behest, the warden relents about having Graham undergo the strip search all new arrivals submit to at San Quentin; Graham, being a woman, minimizes the threat of her smuggling in a weapon or contraband. Apparently, the possibility of Graham committing suicide in her death cell failed to surface as well. The warden also permits her to wear her high heels to the execution when she should have gone barefooted. Would a prison warden be likely to make a concession over footwear to a male inmate? The guard who ushers her into the gas chamber takes pity on her and quietly gives her instructions to ease her way out of this world. Would he be as likely to do the same for a male prisoner facing his execution?

In fact, throughout the production Graham appears to be the best-dressed female criminal in the state. Even during her prison stays she remains the alluring young woman; prison never looked so good.[31] Making Graham look quite so young and glamorous further plays into gender stereotypes. Would a movie linger on the youth and good looks of a male convict? Even at the last, she remains deeply concerned about her appearance: her shoes, her earrings, and her suit, marred by a prison harness she must wear underneath it. Moreover, the filmmakers possessed a ready-made opportunity to condemn the death penalty wholesale by posing the executions of Graham's male codefendants in the same light as her state-sanctioned killing. *I Want to Live!* asks whether the state should be in the business of executing young, beautiful, if amoral and defiant, women who are mothers to boot. While the movie spends time raising questions about her guilt, it misses the opportunity to address whether the state should be authorized to execute anyone, male or female, innocent or guilty.

If Graham was innocent of the charges against her, then the film becomes a statement about a purportedly impartial judicial system gone wrong and the power of the press to condemn those doomed to be in its headlines. Here, Wise and Wanger may have anticipated the new abolitionist argument that the legal system is so essentially flawed that one can never be completely certain of a person's culpability. The very irreversibility of an execution and the surreal procedural details of carrying it out give the audience pause and opens the door to a deeper consideration of the issues involved. In light of the new abolitionist position, Wise's 1958 film may make a stronger across-the-board indictment of the death penalty today than even he originally intended. What rational person wants to see the guiltless sent to the gallows? The miscarriage of justice that ends in the death of the innocent is a travesty that both those for and against the death penalty can oppose. However, if Wise hoped to raise doubts whether the state possessed the moral right to put an end to the lives of actual murderers, he missed the mark.

Compulsion, Director Richard Fleischer, Twentieth Century Fox (1959)

Just a year after the release of the classic *I Want to Live!* another movie that confronted death penalty questions appeared in theaters, *Compulsion* (1959). The movie closely followed the famous 1924 Leopold-Loeb case. Two wealthy, brilliant young law students form a relationship built around the challenge of committing the perfect crime. Judd Steiner, portrayed by Dean Stockwell, the film version of Nathan Leopold, and Artie Straus (Bradford Dillman), a stand-in for Richard Loeb, plot to kidnap and murder a fourteen-year-old boy from their wealthy Chicago neighborhood. Thinking themselves far more intelligent

than those around them and their superior intellect somehow above the law (a la Friedrich Nietzsche), they lure the teenage boy into their car, knock him over the head several times, pour acid on the body to make identification difficult, and dispose of him in a remote culvert. Although their victim already lies dead, they send a ransom note to his parents, but the boy's body is discovered, along with a pair of glasses, before the ransom money can be paid. When Judd realizes his spectacles were those found near the victim's body, the killers coordinate and rehearse their alibi in the event that police should call them in for questioning. Artie Straus manipulates and belittles Judd Steiner at every turn, but Judd, in spite of his own fears and insecurities, remains fiercely loyal to and enamored of Artie.

Straus relishes his role in the crime and happily watches as the police chase one false lead after another, sometimes following his own misleading suggestions. The more press coverage the case gets and the more people discuss the senseless crime, the more Artie delights in it all. For his part, Steiner remains nervous and fearful, appalled when Artie discusses the murder case with police officers and newspaper reporters. When Artie discovers that Judd, a renowned local ornithologist, intends to take a female classmate (Ruth) bird watching, he maps out a plan by which Judd can rape her and orders him to do so. When Judd hedges, Artie confronts him, saying, "Now look, we agreed to explore all the possibilities of human experience, didn't we? Emotionally detached." During the bird-watching expedition Judd's comments about the murder begin to frighten Ruth. "Murder is nothing," he claims. "It's just a simple experience: murder, rape. Do you know what beauty there is in evil?" he emphatically states. Although Judd does attempt to assault Ruth, he cannot bring himself to go through with it because as he tries to instill fear in her and asks her if she is afraid of him, she cries, "I am afraid *for* you, Judd!" And well she should be afraid for him, as police investigators close in on Steiner and determine the eyeglasses belong to him. After hours of interrogating both Artie and Judd, authorities wrest a confession from first Artie and then Judd. Their well-to-do families hire the best trail lawyer in the country and a man strongly opposed to capital punishment, Jonathan Wilk.

Orson Welles takes the role of defense attorney Jonathan Wilk—Clarence Darrow defended the real Leopold and Loeb—who quickly realizes that the best he can do for the defendants is keep them from the gallows in a community united in its desire to see the accused hang. One reporter flatly argues, "They plotted a cold-blooded killing and went through with it like an experiment in chemistry." Wilk's legal strategy includes a guilty plea, which means a hearing before a judge rather than a jury trial; he hopes the judge will show more clemency than a jury. Psychiatrists testify to the mental states of Straus, a paranoid, and Steiner, a schizophrenic, both with the emotional maturity of seven year olds. Although neither of the accused show any signs of remorse and remain completely unrepentant, Wilk does his best to muster arguments that will sway the judge. He makes the case that their wealth turns out to be a disadvantage in this case, because their parents' wealth brings the case undue notoriety and harsher judgment than if the young men grew up in poverty. Orson Welles, channeling Darrow, makes an eloquent plea for the lives of the defendants, arguing that public opinion drives the call for blood. He draws a parallel between the premeditated planning of the murder and the "scheming" and plotting carried out by the court and community to hang the accused. Wilk proposes that cruelty only breeds more of the same and if the state cannot muster more mercy, compassion, and intelligence than the killers, then it is no better than they. Wilk passionately contends that "mercy is the highest attribute of men. Yes, I am pleading for the future; in this court of law I am pleading for love."

Knowing the outcome of the Leopold-Loeb case, it comes as no surprise that the judge does sentence each of them to life in prison, plus another ninety-nine years for the kidnapping. But for those not familiar with the famous 1924 case, Hollywood forgoing a chance to depict a gallows scene comes as quite the surprise. Although *Compulsion* makes much of the wealth and psychopathic brilliance of the killers, it only alludes to the homosexual relationship which seemed to feed the men's desire to perpetrate the crime. For early twenty-first-century audiences the movie obliquely makes reference to the sexual nature of the relationship between Strauss and Steiner, but to viewers of the late 1950s the coded illusions must have been more obvious. The fact that the defendants came from Jewish families also played a large role in the press and the minds of the public at the time, but warrants no mention in the film at all, almost as if anti-Semitism has disappeared in the United States by the late 1950s. While the performances of Stockwell and Dillman as the unaffected, coolly indifferent murderers prove to be riveting, it is Orson Welles who steals the show with his powerful and moving appeal against capital punishment. Much of the summation speech given by Welles came directly from the oration Clarence Darrow presented in the 1924 trial. Wilk relies on the traditional religion-based arguments of the old abolitionists to build his case for a life sentence, and his entreaty is so effective in part because these eighteen- and nineteen-year-old killers are not only guilty, but are utterly callous to the life they took and the pain they inflicted on their victim's family and their own. Mercy for the remorseful is easy; for the impenitent it is another matter. But clearly, *Compulsion* leaves the moviegoer with an unambiguous declaration against execution by the state, no matter how reprehensible the convict.

In Cold Blood, Director Richard Brooks, Columbia (1967)

Even as *I Want to Live!* and *Compulsion* faced the capital punishment debate head on and left its viewers in no doubt where the filmmakers stood, *In Cold Blood* (1967), based on Truman Capote's famous nonfiction work, leaves its audience with a much more ambivalent message. Scott Wilson takes on the role of Dick Hickock and Robert Blake recreates Perry Smith, two real Kansas ex-convicts who met in prison. In the opening scene Smith lounges at the back of a dark Greyhound bus, wearing a black leather jacket and playing the guitar. As he lights a cigarette, its glow illuminates his face and the viewer feels his menacing presence as the bus hurtles through the night. But Smith also possesses a vulnerable quality as he telephones a clergyman at his former prison for guidance, who urges him not to cross over into Kansas and violate his parole. Moviegoers also get a glimpse of the fantasies of fame and fortune that roll through Perry Smith's mind and provide him with a sense of humanity.

Perry travels into Kansas at the request of Hickock, who outlines an easy, foolproof score. As Perry and Dick shop at a hardware store to purchases the supplies they need to carry out their plan, the premeditated nature of the crime is evident. The Clutter family, the intended victims, go about their solidly middle-class, all-American lives. The film goes to some lengths to set up socioeconomic differences: the poverty of Hickock's family home; Smith's nomadic family life, riddled with violence and alcoholism; the relative wealth and comfort of the Clutter family; and the rumored safe filled with ten thousand dollars cash hidden somewhere in the farmhouse. To drive the point home, Dick reminds Perry that "no rich man ever fried in the electric chair." On the long car ride to the Clutter place in Holcomb, Kansas, Dick asks Perry, "Why'd you

kill that punk in Vegas?" "No special reason, just for the hell of it," he laconically brags.[32] But as the film establishes Smith's character as a killer with a conscience, Hickock comes off as an arrogant and callous, if charming, con man.[33] While Perry wants to move through the world without drawing attention to himself, Dick's bravado causes him to take stupid, unnecessary risks; he blithely acts as if he is invincible. As the two men drive up to the Clutter house and dim their headlights, Perry's sense of self-preservation kicks in and he urges Dick, "Let's pull out of here, now, before it's too late."

The film abruptly cuts to a scene of the Clutter farm the next morning. At this point movie viewers have not seen the crime committed on screen. Rather, the audience grasps the horrific nature of the events through the reactions of the police officers who come to investigate. Quickly, the crime unfolds through the eyes of the investigators: four people killed; the male victims, father and son, murdered in the basement; the women, mother and daughter, slain upstairs; all four tied up and mouths covered with electrical tape; the father's throat slit before being shot. The murders seem senselessly violent and without logic. After the slayings take place, the local townspeople feel vulnerable and one person in a diner remarks that "no one is safe anymore."

The action shifts back to Smith and Hickock's activities, revealing that Dick does not feel or show an ounce of remorse. Scoring only forty dollars during their murderous spree leaves them passing bad checks to purchase goods they can fence or pawn. Finally, they decide to head for Mexico and safety, but their money dries up and Dick opts to return to the United States with Perry in tow. The men drive aimlessly around the Southwest until they are apprehended in Las Vegas and charged with murder. While still in the desert, Smith, against the objections of Hickock, decides to pick up a seriously ill grandfather and his grandson and give them a ride. As Hickock grumbles, Smith feels compassion for the hitchhikers and shows them kindness. The young boy reveals that he and the old man survive by collecting glass bottles along the roadside and redeeming them for three cents each. What follows is both a pathetic and touching string of images of Perry and the boy as they retrieve bottles along the barren tracks of the highway and stow them in the back of the car while the ailing grandfather sleeps. In the end, the foursome net twelve dollars and sixty cents, a far cry from the ten thousand dollars the young men had hoped to steal from the Clutter safe.

Once in police custody and under interrogation, Dick eventually blames the killings on Perry, who ultimately acknowledges his role, claiming the momentum of the crime carried him along. Smith dreamily narrates that it was "like the whole crazy stunt had a life of its own and nothing could stop it." Not until the last forty minutes of the movie does the spectator witness the crime from Perry and Dick's perspective. Although the motive for the crime was burglary, from the first Dick hinted that he had no intention of leaving eyewitnesses who could testify against them. But Dick never planned to be the shooter; despite his ruthlessness, he is not capable of homicide. Instead he counted on Perry's hair-trigger temper to propel him to lash out at the victims. During the pair's assault on Mr. Clutter, Perry's acts of violence are interspersed with images of his own enraged father aiming a shotgun at him as a kid and firing, but the weapon was not loaded. This time the shotgun is loaded and Herb Clutter lies dead. In a statement obviously designed to describe himself and his father, Perry states, "I despise people who don't control themselves."

There is no doubt about their guilt since investigators obtained confessions, and their trial becomes a matter of determining the punishment to be doled out. Preying on the fears of the community, the prosecuting attorney informs the jury that a life sentence makes the killers eligible for parole in seven years. "They who had no pity, ask for yours; they who had no mercy, ask for yours," the prosecutor tells the jury earnestly. Not surprisingly, the jury takes only forty minutes to render a guilty verdict and the sentence handed down is death by hanging. Now the film employs the liberal reporter, Mr. Jensen, a moral stand-in for Truman Capote, to provide narration for the rest of the movie. Reporter Jensen verbally walks the viewer through the endless days of boredom on death row and the long process of legal appeals and stays of execution. He interviews Dick Hickock on death row and is surprised to find that the inmate supports capital punishment. Dick derisively relates that of all the men waiting to hang, "little Perry" is the only one "yapping" against the death penalty. "Hell, hangin's only getting revenge. What's wrong with revenge? I've been revenging myself all my life," Dick concedes blithely. But such sentiments, coming from the one person who so completely lacks a conscience, bring the audience up short.

Five years go by before the condemned face their executioner. In a dimly lit warehouse, accentuated by lighting, the gallows loom large as Hickock and Smith wait to die. A rookie reporter asks Jensen whether the hangman has a name. "We, the people," Jensen drolly retorts. The execution scenes roll by fairly quickly and rather unemotionally. Unlike *I Want to Live!* there is no lingering over every procedural detail of putting the condemned to death. As the remorseless Dick Hickock enters the room and sees the scaffold he looks around curiously, finding it all interesting, ostensibly unaware of what he is about to face. Still completely self-absorbed, Hickock tells the men around him that they are sending him to "a better world than this ever was" and his hanging takes place off screen. Perry Smith, however, is a different matter altogether and now the camera begins to linger. Perry comes across as all too human: nervous, vulnerable, desperate, and bewildered. He fears he will lose control of his bowels on the scaffold and asks to use the bathroom at the last minute. In a masterful piece of cinematography, Perry stands at a window on this his last, rainy, night. As the rain from the window reflects back on his face, tears appear to pour from his eyes as he recounts the story of building a hunting lodge in Alaska with his father, only to have the man turn his frustration and fury on the boy, taking aim at him with his shotgun and pulling the trigger. With the moment of miserable reflection over, barely controlled terror accompanies Perry to the hangman's noose. The seasoned reporter comments that the death toll now stands at six, four innocents and two guilty. The film closes with the sound of Perry's heart beating wildly before the trapdoors swing open, then the beating slowly winds down and finally stops.

Richard Brooks both wrote and directed *In Cold Blood* and created a work that focuses on the killers, a psychological study with a documentary feel. The movie asks its viewers to consider whether a sane man can commit a "crazy" act. It posits that neither Hickock nor Smith could have carried out the slaughter of four people alone. Some psychological dynamic generated between the two men gave birth to a third personality which overcame their individual aversion and drove them toward murder. From this perspective, the film might be seen as an apologia for the appalling homicides. Yet despite the flashbacks of Perry Smith's frightening and dismal childhood—and one assumes things were little better for Dick Hickock—the picture generates little sympathy for the two aimless drifters. Hickock appears as nothing more than a brutal, cold-blooded killer, although he was not the shooter, while Smith generates compassion despite being the actual gunman. Simply put, the world seems a better place without the likes of Dick Hickock and Perry Smith, even if viewers feel sympathetic toward Smith and comprehend some of the mitigating factors that underlie his murderous outburst.

An impression of senseless tragedy pervades the film: a burglary that produced no payoff, the slaughter of a respectable farm family; the lives of two damaged, undistinguished, rootless young men. Even Hickock and Smith's march to the gallows is tinged with a sense both futile and bleak. To reporter Jensen falls the duty of tacking on some meaning to the whole grim affair. Here, through Capote's proxy, *In Cold Blood* tries to make an unequivocal, if ham-fisted, anti-death-penalty statement. Director Brooks' preachy, rather artless message against capital punishment at the end of his film stands in opposition to the tone the rest of the movie presents. The strongest voice against execution comes from the one person audiences are least likely to identify with: Dick Hickock. If he, so lacking a moral and ethical code, so lacking in humanity, can favor letting the guilty swing, then are viewers not inclined to reject all he stands for, including his death penalty stance? While Truman Capote's book took a firm stand against capital punishment, the bleak and haunting film version of *In Cold Blood* leaves audiences with a more vague and contradictory message concerning ending the lives of society's worst transgressors.

Capote, Director Bennett Miller, Sony (2005)

Infamous, Director Douglas McGrath, Warner Independent Pictures (2006)

In Cold Blood has enjoyed a revival of sorts since the release of *Capote* in 2005 and *Infamous* in 2006. Both movies are biographical treatments of Truman Capote's life, but since his life, work, and literary reputation rested on *In Cold Blood*, both films deal extensively with the Holcomb, Kansas, murders and Capote's ingratiating himself into the community and with the killers to get his story. *Capote*, as depicted by Philip Seymour Hoffman, who earned a Best Actor Oscar for his role, comes across as too gay, too New York, and too odd with his high-pitched, squeaky voice and his effeminate manners for the people of rural Kansas. But with patience and the assistance of his childhood friend Harper Lee, he gains access to all the town's people touched by the crime. Particularly important, he fosters a relationship with the murderers themselves after their convictions and incarceration. Capote visits the prison regularly and offers to obtain the services of a quality defense lawyer who can file an appeal. Capote finds out from the prison warden that Perry Smith has refused to eat over the last month. The hardened warden expresses concern that Smith will have to be transferred to the infirmary soon to be force-fed because "it ain't his right to kill himself; it's the right of the people—the people of this state and that's who I work for." Both *Capote* and *Infamous*, with Toby Jones in the title role, draw distinct parallels between the traumas of Capote's childhood and that of Smith's upbringing and both films suggest that their shared childhood suffering forged a very strong bond between these two very different men.

Both films also stress Capote's desire to create an artistic masterpiece with this story of murder and his desire to present the killers very much as human beings, especially Perry. *Infamous* gives the relationship between writer and inmate a romantic intimacy which *Capote* lacks. In fact, the relationship between Dick and Perry in *Infamous* also carries sexual overtones and during the murder scene, it is Dick's goading Perry about his sexual feelings for their male victims that suddenly drives Perry into a murderous frenzy. Perry

played by Daniel Craig (*Infamous*) comes across as more hostile and harder to win over, but both depictions (Clifton Collins Jr. is Perry Smith in *Capote*) stress the character's lonely, vulnerable neediness; Clifton Collins gives Perry a more isolated, exposed, and artistic sensibility; at times, Perry seems almost childlike. While Capote did develop a close relationship with Perry Smith, he was not beyond manipulating and lying to him to get what he needed for his book, and the films reflect Capote's often calculating nature. Philip Seymour Hoffman's performance makes for a more selfish, self-absorbed, at times callous Capote, while Toby Jones softens the egocentrism. As both movies progress toward the execution of Smith and Hickock, Capote becomes ever more conflicted about his feelings. His book lacks an ending which the executions will provide, but he also realizes that the ultimate end for the criminals will mean the inevitable severing of his relationship with Smith. In *Capote*, as the executions draw near Truman feels wracked by guilt that he failed to do enough to help the condemned men get their death sentences commuted, but *Infamous* dwells more on the pain inflicted by the separation death will bring to the relationship between Perry and Truman.

It is in how each film handles death, whether the victims' or the perpetrators,' that they diverge. When Perry finally relates what happened during the crime, the two movies employ very different approaches. *Capote* takes its time in depicting the night of the murder and all that took place. Where the film's tone and color were rather grey and somber, the crime-scene colors become richer and more saturated. *Infamous*, on the other hand, keeps the portrayal of the murders fairly brief, although both show the brutality of the slayings and Perry being both tender and cold-blooded. Since the only courtroom depiction in *Infamous* involves sentencing, no trial recreation of the crime occurs. Even *Capote* uses the courtroom sessions to say more about the defendants than about the crime itself; Hickock appears apathetic while Smith's nervous doodling seems to take him into another world. But *Capote* forces a closer and longer look at hangings conducted by the state. Well before Dick and Perry confront their execution, another prisoner walks to the gallows across the prison baseball field. Perry watches the inmate proceed to the warehouse from his tiny cell window and listens intently as the execution progresses. Although the hanging takes place off screen, audiences catch a glimpse of a tractor carrying the corpulent body of the executed man out of the building. Both films spend some time on Capote's extreme reluctance to visit his condemned friends on their last day and to witness the executions, despite both inmates requesting he be present. Their awkward, painful farewell once Capote finally arrives at the prison with only minutes to spare receives attention in each movie; Truman seems more guilt-ridden in *Capote*, but the goodbye is more poignant in *Infamous* as Perry tenderly kisses Truman on the cheek and utters a simple, bittersweet, "Adios, amigo."

Dick Hickock's execution receives almost no attention at all in *Capote* but lingers on the details of Smith's demise, while *Infamous* dwells on the hanging of Hickock, but viewers do not witness Perry's death sentence being carried out because Capote bolts from the building at the last second. What strikes viewers in *Capote* is that Truman stands at a distance, almost in the shadows, as the camera zooms in on Perry's terrified face and one hears his labored breathing as a black fabric bag is drawn down over his head and the noose looped around his neck. The nearly thunderous noise of the trapdoors swinging open delivers an auditory shock and Capote (Hoffman) jumps in response. The camera cuts back to Perry's body falling, the jerk of the rope, and the body twisting and swaying from the scaffold. *Infamous* supplies much the same gallows scene for Hickock, but lingers on the dangling body; it took him an extraordinarily long time to breathe his last, nearly twenty-five minutes. The look of horror and revulsion on Capote's (Jones) face as the assembled witnesses see Dick being cut down turns to sheer panic as he realizes Perry is being lead in. As Perry stands on the gallows, the image is interspersed oddly by Perry singing and playing a Gene Autry song in his cell. The scene cuts back and forth from Perry on the scaffold, gasping for breath, to Perry calmly serenading Truman. Just after the guards put the blindfold and noose in place, Capote sprints from the warehouse into the pouring rain.

Although each of the films deals with Capote's life and his slow, steady decline after the publication of his masterwork, *Infamous* concentrates more on Capote's social circle in New York, offering a brighter, more vibrant picture of the man and his times. With Capote as the bereaved man who loses his intimate friend to the gibbet, he takes on the role of the person whose life is ruined by the execution of a loved one despite that death allowing him to finish a book that will bring him wealth and accolades. Because *Infamous* dwells less on the crime, sidelines the unsympathetic Hickock, and fashions a romantic relationship between Perry and Truman, it has an easier time generating compassion for Perry. Viewers see Perry through Capote's understanding and loving eyes, and the execution seems a rather extreme response to Perry's moment of blind rage during which he lashed out at the Clutter men. From an anti-capital punishment standpoint, *Infamous* makes a weaker statement because viewers feel the death of Perry more as Truman's deep personal loss, rather than a black mark on society's collective soul.

Each Capote biopic points out the double

meaning behind his now famous title; not only did Smith and Hickock kill "in cold blood," but they will be put to death by the State of Kansas in cold blood as well. But it is *Capote* that takes the implications of the title more seriously, because the subject of killing takes center stage. It is a darker, solemn, more brooding film which invests more time in the personalities of both killers and on the massacre of four members of the Kansas farm family. Early in the film, Capote sneaks into the funeral home where the Clutter bodies lie prepared and waiting in their closed coffins. He carefully lifts the lid of a casket to discover white gauze wrapped around the deceased's head, the shotgun blast causing too much damage to be repaired or disguised. The crime is never far from the audience's mind or from Capote's even though he makes an emotional connection with Perry. Hoffman's Capote seems always to maintain a certain distance, deeply conflicted over what is best for his book and what is best for his death row friend. Perry's aching humanity shines through when he shamefully confides, "He was just looking at me, lookin' into my eyes like he expected me to kill him—like he expected me to be the kind of person to kill him,"[34] and admitting he did not realize what he had done until it was over. He appears remorseful and even bewildered by his act of violence, almost like a lost child. Because the relationship between the men comes across as personal and affectionate, but less romantic and intimate than in *Infamous*, Perry's execution seems less a terrible private loss to Capote and more of an indictment of society's merciless punishment. His conscience plaguing him, Capote tells childhood friend Harper Lee, "There wasn't anything I could have done to save them." "Maybe not," Lee replies, "but the fact is you didn't want to." In the long run, something that happened during the researching and writing of *In Cold Blood* sent Truman Capote into a prolonged alcoholic, pill-popping tailspin.

My Cousin Vinny, Director Jonathan Lynn, Twentieth Century Fox (1992)

On a decidedly lighter note, *My Cousin Vinny* (1992) offers a comic approach to some very serious issues. While the film obliquely addresses the death penalty, like many other Hollywood films, it remains primarily in the background and only occasionally does it come into the spotlight. Sometimes capital punishment garners some gallows humor and other times it serves as a chilling reminder. The story recounts the road trip of two young men from Brooklyn on their way to college in the West. While in a convenience store in Alabama, Bill Gambini (Ralph Macchio) inadvertently steals a can of tuna, only to discover his mistake miles down the road. When police arrest Billy and his friend, Stan Rothenstein (Mitchell Whitfield), they think the whole affair concerns the pilfered canned fish and are prepared to cooperate and confess. They soon discover that they are being charged with the murder of the store clerk and the penalty, should they be found guilt, is death by electrocution. Witnesses mistake them for the men who ran out of the store and their 1964 metallic, mint green Buick Skylark is misidentified as the car that went careening out of the parking lot. As Billy and Stan have no money for a high-powered defense attorney, they get Billy's cousin Vinny Gambini, played by Joe Pesci, to travel to Alabama to defend them. Vinny, it turns out, is a newly minted personal injury lawyer, who has never been to court, never tried a case, and made six attempts at passing the New York State bar exam.

On one level, what follows is a classic "fish-out-of-water" story: Brooklyn urbanites, out of their element, flounder in rural Alabama. But the story goes deeper than this typical send-up as director Jonathan Lynne also tackles the prejudices and stereotypes that people from north and south of the Mason-Dixon Line hold about one another.

Lynne remarked that over and above the comical regional issues the movie addresses, it also tackles the subject of class differences; the clash between the moneyed establishment, represented by the courtly, but procedurally inflexible and hard-nosed, southern judge Chamberlain Haller (played by a show-stealing Fred Gwynne) and the district attorney, Jim Trotter III (Lane Smith), and the working-class, blue-collar set portrayed by Cousin Vinny and his fiancé, Mona Lisa Vito.[35] Vinny, clad all in black with the requisite leather jacket and gold chain, arrives in his great American land-yacht with his overdressed, shrewd, brassy, and sardonic girlfriend, hilariously performed by Marisa Tomei; she won a Best Actress Oscar for her role. Lynne also stated that he wanted the film to reflect just how easy it would be to convict two innocent, college-bound young men, not by corrupt, small-town Southerners out to frame the youths, but by hard-working, honorable, upstanding citizens of Beechum County, Alabama.

Yet for all the funny scenes and the laughs elicited by Vinny and Lisa's various problems and endless arguments in the movie, the specter of the death penalty hangs over the movie, even if it does not take center stage. Without any real malice, Sherriff Dean Farley (Bruce McGill) pointedly reminds Stan that if his friend Bill is found guilty, "we'll run enough electricity through him to light up Birmingham." Although the line is played for laughs, the potential threat for the young men remains very real. As Billy and Stan arrive at the prison gates, activists picket along the roadside, protesting the impending execution of a death row inmate. Each time Vinny emerges from yet another stint in lock-up after being found in contempt of court by Judge Haller, the demonstrators resolutely stand with their placards denouncing the death penalty. The message is subtle, but persistent. Later Stan and Billy discuss the wisdom of allowing the still inept and ineffective Vinny to represent them, even though he has never tried a single case in court much less a murder case. As the young men talk, Billy describes what it means to be a "quintessential Gambini," a person who does not shy away from confrontation, who thrives on argumentation and who lives to expose tricks and deceptions. Unexpectedly, the lights of their prison cell brown out and Stan quips that "there goes the quintessential Norton" [the prisoner being executed]. Again, jeopardy hangs over two innocent defendants and suddenly death seems very close and real.

While a guard walks the young men past the building that houses death row, he remarks that the electric chair "ain't workin' like it used to." He casually recounts the story of a recent electrocution gone wrong. The "guy we fried" required no less than three jolts of electricity to bring about his death, but during the procedure the man's head caught fire. He tells the young inmates there are no funds in the budget to get it repaired. However, he maintains that it is "cheaper to get it fixed than keep runnin' up those electric bills." Naturally, Billy and Stan glance horrified at the guard and then significantly at each other; this horrific end awaits us, the looks on their faces say. Of course, in the context of a college kid taking a can of tuna which he simply forgot to pay for, it all seems rather funny and far-fetched. But director Lynne reminds his audience the boys face real danger if they fail to build a good case in their own defense. In his director's commentary, Lynne revealed that the case of the botched electrocution and a man's head catching fire was an actual radio news story he heard while in Georgia shooting the motion picture.

During jury selection for the murder trial, prosecutor Jim Trotter asks potential jurors whether they "can participate in an endeavor in which the ultimate decision might be death by electrocution." A respectable, middle-class, gray-haired woman replies that she believes such matters should be decided by the murder victim's loved ones. As D.A. Trotter outlines the nature of the crime and proceeds to say that the alleged perpetrators "in a most cowardly fashion shot the clerk in the back," the sweet grandmotherly woman interrupts him, aggressively declaring, "Fry 'em." Just as Lynne conveys the regional and class differences of his film's characters, so, too, he attempts to show his quiet but insistent opposition to capital punishment. From the incongruity of a proper southern lady unsentimentally uttering, "Fry 'em," to the repulsive mental image of a person's head catching fire during a bungled execution, the movie suggests, often humorously, that there is something wrong with a system that puts people to death. With the local sheriff proposing to use enough voltage on the guilty to illuminate Birmingham, the movie plays on the ever-looming threat of the death sentence. The theme that the boys are genuinely in peril if they fail to find a competent lawyer who can mount a skillful defense suggests that innocent people can be found guilty even in a court that operates as it should, without any attempt at railroading the accused. And potentially that justice system can execute innocent people.

Similar cars equipped with identical tires and the testimony of three seemingly reliable eyewitnesses hold the fate of Bill and Stan in their hands. Viewers, of course, know that these college students hardly deserve the death penalty, but that is the fate that awaits them from good, southern folk who simply want to see justice done. Naturally, the witty courtroom, and bedroom, jousting between the characters becomes the comic focus; Judge Haller's unbending demands that Vinny conform to court procedure, the biting sarcasm and automotive expertise of the vaguely trashy, but insightful Mona Lisa, and Vinny's stubborn, streetwise approach to defending his clients, and his manhood, all make for the odd circumstances and amusing dialogue that keep audiences laughing. While there is no doubt that *My Cousin Vinny* goes for the laugh, out of the corner of the viewer's eye lies the ever-present threat of the electric chair.

Murder in the First, Director Marc Rocco, Warner Bros. (1995)

Where *My Cousin Vinny* took a droll approach, nothing humorous lies waiting for audiences of *Murder in the First*. The story focuses its attention on the life of Henri Young and his time in prison. During the mid-1920s, seventeen-year-old Henri Young (Kevin Bacon), out of sheer desperation, steals five dollars from a general store which also functions as a post office. After both his parents died he had made every effort to find work in order to care for and feed his younger sister, but to no avail. After his arrest and conviction on a federal charge he ultimately finds himself transferred to Alcatraz, a maximum-security federal penitentiary from which he makes a futile escape attempt in 1935, landing him in solitary confinement. According to the law the maximum stay in solitary confinement can be no longer than nineteen days, but Henri Young ends up in "the hole" for over three years. When the film begins, viewers see a figure lying naked, filthy, and shivering in a pitch-dark stone cell; Young seems more animal than human, barely hanging onto his sanity. What little interaction he has with other human beings usually constitutes a prison guard throwing food into his cell or severe beatings at the hands of the associate warden, Milton Glenn, portrayed with sinister and brutal bureaucratic efficiency by Gary Oldman. Young is finally released from his hellish nightmare in the dungeons of Alcatraz, but cannot cope with life in the general prison population. Warden Glenn continues to torment and physically abuse him. One day, goaded by another inmate, Young murders Rufus McCain, the prisoner who had tipped off the warden about his escape plan. Christian Slater stars as the inexperienced San Francisco public defender, James Stamphill, who draws this capital case—his first. Stamphill does not know what to make of Henri Young when he first enters his prison cell. Young sits huddled and unresponsive on a cot, seemingly out of touch with reality and the serious nature of his situation. The earnest Stamphill slowly draws Young out of his damaged shell and forges a bond with him, all the while trying to build his defense and save Henri from execution.

Stamphill's argument focuses on how Young entered the prison system a petty criminal and after three years of horrific treatment and punishment in solitary at the hands of the wardens of Alcatraz ended up a hardened murderer; the prison system and its inhumane treatment of inmates turned Young into the man who killed Rufus McCain. Of course, what appeared to be an open-and-shut case becomes an embarrassment to the federal authorities and behind the scenes those in political power want to bring the case to a quick close, including Stamphill's well-connected older brother who is supposed to keep his younger sibling in check. Under acute political pressure, the younger Stamphill resigns his position as public defender and embarks on a mission, not only to exonerate and save Young, but to indict the federal wardens and reform the prison system. During the trial Stamphill exposes Warden Glenn's sadistic predilections and it turns out that the man at the top, Warden Humson, supervises three federal penitentiaries in California and only visited Alcatraz two dozen times over a three-year period. Basically, Humson gave Glenn too free a hand in running Alcatraz with an iron fist and failed to keep a close eye on conditions at "the Rock." With the prosecutor (William H. Macy in a role that wastes his considerable talents) thundering on about Old Testament punishments of "an eye for an eye," and Stamphill railing

against prison brutality, Young sits haplessly by wearily watching the proceedings. The closer Stamphill gets to saving Henri from a death sentence the more uneasy he becomes, knowing he will likely return to Alcatraz and Warden Glenn's custody. Young admits to Stamphill that he would rather die than return to Alcatraz and the life he knew there. The crusading Stamphill wants to hear none of it and persuades Young to go along with implicating the prison system so that other prisoners will not have to endure the punishing conditions and cruelty meted out to him. In the end, Stamphill wins the case; the jury finds Henri Young guilty of involuntary manslaughter, and Young must return to "the Rock" for a few more years. As feared, Young again ends up in solitary confinement and at the mercy of Warden Glenn. As the movie wraps up, Stamphill's voiceover explains that Henri Young was found dead in his cell, but because of Young's suffering and his legal case, solitary confinement was later found inhumane and the practice ended; the voice reassures us that Warden Glenn was also brought up on charges and found guilty.

In some respects *Murder in the First* seems like a film about capital punishment. It does, after all, focus on a capital case and a trial in which a man's life hangings in the balance. But what appears to be death penalty movie is really about how prison life brings out the worst in people, making them violent, homicidal beasts, and a campaign to bring change to the merciless prison system. The naïve Stamphill tries to serve two masters and fails both. While he is supposed to save Young from execution, he ends up consigning his client to death at the hands of the state anyway. He places his burning desire to put an end to the absolute authority of sadistic prison wardens and the pitilessness of solitary confinement ahead of his client's best interests. Despite Young's admission that he feared going back to Alcatraz far more than he feared death, Stamphill still sacrificed Young's life in the name of prison reform. The movie intends to give Young's terrible suffering and death meaning by sacrificing his life on the altar of making prison life less barbaric. But Young being found dead in his cell makes his demise an unofficial death at the hands of the state rather than an official carrying out of the death penalty. There is little hint as to how Young died. Did a prison guard kill him? Did Warden Glenn finally go too far? Did another prisoner shank him? Did Young manage to bring his own life to an end? The message behind the film is that Young's death is acceptable as long as it serves a higher purpose; prison reform represents that higher purpose, while capital punishment does not, although advocates of the death penalty might argue that it does. In this particular case, the death penalty may have ended Young's suffering sooner and may have been the more merciful option; in the end, there are things worse than death. Of course, one wonders why Young needed to return to Alcatraz given that his treatment at the hands of Warden Glenn was now a matter of public record. Stamphill certainly could have asked the court to assign Young to a different federal facility to serve out his time. But logic and clear thinking do not always apply to the cinematic world.

Murder in the First also endeavors to build a relationship between the rookie lawyer and the abused prison inmate by indicating that they shared a number of things in common and might not have had such radically different lives if the theft of five dollars from a post office had not derailed the life of one man. Here the crusading and loyal attorney stands by his client and faithfully maintains his belief in Young's innocence. This typical Hollywood device might have worked much better had director Marc Rocco actually spent more time building a genuine relationship between the two men. But what the film does deal with in a more serious fashion is

society's responsibility in creating criminals. It asks why a desperate, orphaned teenager, trying to do the right thing in raising his sister, lands in federal prison for filching five dollars. It questions why such a minor crime would cause a man to be transferred to a place like Alcatraz and how it is that a prison warden possesses such abusive powers over the convicts. It inquires what responsibility society bears in allowing Young to grow so desperate that he resorted to stealing and what responsibility the penal system, and by implication society as a whole, shoulders in transforming a teenage petty thief into a homicidal adult. By extension, then, it also probes how someone convicted of a minor crime ends up on trial for a crime that carries the death sentence. While the film does raise some provocative and important questions, it makes prison brutality its focus rather than the death penalty. And oddly, *Murder in the First* undermines its rather mild abolitionist position by suggesting that Young's dying in his cell at Alcatraz served the greater purpose of making prisons more humane institutions. One way or another, prison for Henri Young meant death; whether he died officially at the hands of an executioner or unofficially at the hands of the bloodthirsty, vindictive Warden Glenn, his life expired within the walls of a prison.

Dead Man Walking, Director Tim Robbins, Polygram (1996)

If *Murder in the First* proved itself a rather minor film, *Dead Man Walking* (1996) became by far the most critically acclaimed death penalty movie and the one that stirred the most controversy. More than any other film that deals with capital punishment, *Dead Man Walking* places the death penalty and all that goes with it at its very center. In addition, religion becomes a major focus of the film as well. The story is based on the real experiences of a Louisiana nun, Sister Helen Prejean, as written in her book *Dead Man Walking: An Eyewitness Account of the Death Penalty in the United States* (Random House, 1993). Sister Helen (Susan Sarandon) ministers to a death row inmate, Matthew Poncelet (Sean Penn), convicted of the rape and murder of a teenage couple. Sister Helen gets drawn into visiting Poncelet in Louisiana's infamous Angola Prison after answering a letter he wrote. Despite warnings of caution from the prison chaplain[36] and her own misgivings about and initial aversion toward Poncelet, she agrees to assist him in filing an appeal. Viewers see Poncelet through the eyes of Sister Helen; he comes across as a vain, posturing racist, an unrepentant murderer, whose false bravado only makes him all the more repulsive. The audience witnesses Helen's own moral struggle to reconcile this man who elicits so little sympathy with her deep faith in Christian teachings. From the very beginning, audiences know this man's conviction is wholly justified, even if Sister Helen harbors some uncertainty. No doubt exists that this is the story of a man wrongly accused or falsely convicted; he is guilty as sin. Yet, despite the repugnance viewers may feel toward Poncelet, Sister Helen learns to see through his façade and forges a bond with him.

Viewers immediately sense that this movie is somehow different from any other, both for its willingness to place religion and capital punishment in the spotlight, but also because it concentrates some attention on the social issues that mold a killer. At the pardon board hearing, the lawyer Sister Helen procures for Poncelet, Hilton Barber (Robert Prosky), takes the time to paint Poncelet as a human being who grew up in poverty. Barber privately tells Helen, "It's easy to kill a monster; hard to kill a human being." The lawyer recounts the death of Matthew's father when the boy was only fourteen and the boy's use of drugs and alcohol. Later Matthew boastfully

recalls how his father took him as a twelve-year-old to a bar and got him drunk on Wild Turkey bourbon. Hilton Barber also points out Poncelet's poor legal representation during his trial; his state-appointed attorney specialized in tax law. Poncelet's accomplice hired a good defense lawyer and, although convicted, managed to escape the death penalty; Poncelet could have achieved the same outcome with a competent attorney, Barber implies. In addition, Barber provides the pardon board members, for the benefit of the moviegoers, with a verbal depiction of the supposed humaneness of lethal injection, but the verbal picture he paints is anything but humane. As one might expect, the prosecutor counters by asking for justice on behalf of the victims' families and when the board predictably denies Poncelet clemency, the reaction of his mother, who earlier was so emotionally overcome she could not testify on her son's behalf, is heart-rending. *Dead Man Walking* takes the time to show the effects the murders have on the family of the killer as well of those of his victims; the film articulates the grief, guilt, and shame of the perpetrator's loved ones.

But *Dead Man Walking* also grants attention to the families of the two young teenagers who died at the hands of Poncelet and his partner. After being confronted by the angry victims' parents, Sister Helen begins to see the devastating legacy of Poncelet's murderous actions. She visits the family of the dead teenage girl, Hope Percy, and her parents, thinking Sister Helen has altered her stance against the death penalty, exhibit their pain and anguish and provide some details of the crime. When it becomes apparent to the Percys that Sister Helen will continue to support Poncelet, they react badly. As Helen quietly emphasizes that "every person is worth more than their worst act," Clyde Percy furiously retorts, "This not a person, he's an animal. . . . Matthew Poncelet is God's mistake." Although moviegoers have seen indistinct black-and-white flashbacks of the murder, now the brutality of the crime becomes clearer as viewers experience the murder scene as Helen imagines it. She also calls on Earl Delacroix, the father of the murdered boy, who greets her visit with initial hostility but slowly softens toward her. He, too, feels devastated by the loss of his son, but also by his wife's divorcing him, his marriage another casualty of the crime. Helen's spirituality gives her the strength to look at the crime and all its varied consequences.

Her spirituality also allows her to see the humanity in the criminal. When Poncelet moves to the Death House he informs Sister Helen that ten guards watch over him to prevent his suicide. He admits, "I never had so many people carin' about what I was doin.'" Clearly, Sister Helen is one of those who cares about him and the fate that awaits him, and he seems to crave her attention. Yet, his ability to reciprocate that love is severely limited as demonstrated when Helen faints in the chaplain's office, delaying her ability to come to Poncelet's side. Matt remains concerned only that she wasn't there for him and cares little that she collapsed or about her well-being. But as Helen and Matt talk to each other through a Lucite window in his death cell, the scenes between them grow ever closer, almost intimate. She reminds him that he is a son of God, and realizing that his death is imminent, she pushes him to talk about the night of the murder and admit the part he played in the rape and killings of two innocent people. When he searches for a religious "loophole," she sets him straight; when he attempts to identify himself with the suffering Christ, she calls him on it. She sees beyond his crime to his humanity, but she stands firmly on the foundation of her Christian principles and will not be manipulated by them or dissuaded from them. Her goal of trying to get Poncelet to take moral responsibility is a spiritual/religious one, not a legal one. Being accountable for the crime he committed means he has the chance at some point to ask God's forgiveness, even if he cannot bring himself to do so yet. He need only be honest with himself before his death.

As his execution date arrives, the film covers the details of Poncelet's last day. His mother and brothers arrive for the family visit, their time together proving tense and awkward, with forced conversation or long, excruciating periods of silence as the hours tick by. As they awkwardly stand to say goodbye for the last time, the guards prevent Lucille Poncelet from touching or hugging her condemned son. Back in the death cell, guards weigh and measure Matthew and the film's spectators witness the preparations being made for Poncelet's execution by lethal injection. His last meal is brought and consumed as Sister Helen sits outside his cell. With death breathing down his neck and at her urging, he finally musters the courage to reveal his part in the rape and stabbing of Hope Percy and the shooting of Walter Delacroix. Again, the audience glimpses how the crime unfolded that night from Helen's perspective as Poncelet confesses to her what he did. Her sense of relief, gratitude, and love is palpable; he now can go to his death with some self-respect. She can see the criminal and the man who lies within; she can see his worth more than his worst act.

As the hour of his death draws closer, Helen doubts whether she possesses the strength to see Poncelet through his ordeal. She bolts for the privacy of the ladies' room, praying for the fortitude to see the task through. As she paces around the tiny confines of the restroom, she murmurs to herself, "It is such a terrifying place, so cold, so calculated with murder." But Helen has made a promise to Matthew and she intends to fulfill it: "I want the last face you see in this world to be the face of love, so you look at me when they do this thing. I'll be the face of love for you." The filmmakers went to great lengths to recreate the details of the death chamber accurately, researching the state execution processes of both Louisiana and Missouri.[37] Poncelet walks to the death chamber surrounded by guards, wearing a diaper under his clothing and a cheap pair of slippers on his feet, not the boots he had hoped to wear. When his knees give way, Sister Helen reaches for his shoulder and they touch for the first time. Helen waits in the witness room as the strap-down team lashes Poncelet to the surgical gurney and a nurse inserts the IV into his arm. With the gurney in a vertical position and Matthew in an eerie Christ-like pose[38] with arms outstretched, he utters his last words, "Killin' is wrong, no matter who does it: me, ya'all or the government." In close-ups of Poncelet lying on the gurney with his eyes locked on the compassionate Sister Helen, the intravenous tube running into his arm, the syringes of fatal medications lined up in their machine, the plungers gradually forcing the liquids out, Matthew slowly dies. As his life ebbs away, the movie intersperses full-color images of the crime as it took place, and for the first time the audience gets a complete picture of the vicious rape and murder Poncelet and his accomplice carried out. Viewers see that as Poncelet took the lives of Hope and Walter, so, too, is his life taken by the justice system.

Film critics generally, although not universally, praised *Dead Man Walking*'s even-handed approach and the outstanding performances of its principle actors. The film received numerous Academy Award nominations, for Best Director, Best Actor, and Best Actress, but only Susan Sarandon won, in the Best Actress category. The influential critic Roger Ebert gave the movie high praise: "It demonstrates how a movie can confront a grave and controversial issue in our society and see it fairly, from all sides, not take any shortcuts, and move the audience to a great emotional experience without unfair manipulation."[39] *The New York Times Guide to the Best 1000 Movies Ever Made*[40] (1999 Edition) named *Dead Man*

Walking as well as *In Cold Blood* and *I Want to Live!* to its list. But legal scholars, especially those opposed to capital punishment, formed a different opinion. Several legal professionals argued that while the film tried to make an anti-death-penalty statement, it actually reinforced the legitimacy of capital punishment.

Austin Sarat, Professor of Law and Political Science at Amherst College, and Carole Shapiro, Associate Professor of Legal Methods, Touro Law School (in Huntington, New York), suggest that while filmmakers may well have attempted to produce a movie against capital punishment, the message the viewing public leaves the theater with is exactly the opposite. Sarat believes this contradictory message stems from two main problems. One is that Hollywood productions tend to engage the audience by focusing on a single case and the relationship the death row inmate builds with a sympathetic outsider, be it a religious figure, as in *Dead Man Walking*, a humane guard, or a dedicated lawyer. This type of film encourages audience members to put themselves in the shoes of the sympathetic outsider and to perceive the convict with understanding and humanity. The problem, Sarat contends, is the stories' preoccupation with issues of individual responsibility and that they frequently hinge on an admission of guilt, a sign of remorse, a need to repent—all ultimately leading to taking personal responsibility for the crime committed. The convicted person accepting responsibility implies that crime is a function of individual choice and ignores the social issues that lead to violent criminal behavior. In the simple equation of crime and punishment, once responsibility is claimed, or assigned, then punishment not only can be but should be meted out. Factors such as poverty, racism, physical and/or sexual abuse, neglect, and addiction are set aside in favor of individual agency. In addition, the inherent flaws of the legal system, its racial and class prejudices, the political agenda behind the crime debate, and the very way in which society frames crime and punishment also get short shrift in Hollywood films. Simply assigning blame and responsibility to a particular person takes a highly complex problem, Sarat posits, and tries to provide a simple answer.[41]

While Sarat makes a good point that most films discount social and structural arguments in favor of personal responsibility, he treats *Dead Man Walking* too harshly. On the surface, *Dead Man Walking* seems to push the agenda of individual choice and responsibility, but it is Christianity that lies at the heart of this film. Sister Helen valiantly tries to help Matthew acknowledge his offense against God, and with that acknowledgment God's forgiveness becomes possible. She wants to send him to his ignoble death with the hope of God's love and forgiveness, as a child of God. Now, within hours of his execution and with the hope of clemency extinguished, it is his soul that matters to Sister Helen, not only his life. Sarat confuses Poncelet's accepting responsibility for his moral actions before God with legal accountability; he sees them as one and the same, whereas Tim Robbins would draw a distinction between ethical responsibility and legal guilt.[42]

On the other hand, legal scholar Carole Shapiro points out that Poncelet's contrition makes him more sympathetic to moviegoers, and the very fact that he is staring death in the face finally forces him to accept responsibility for his crime. Without Poncelet's admission of guilt, she insists, the movie would fail to work. He wins mercy and compassion from audiences because of his remorse. One wonders, in fact, how viewers would have reacted to Poncelet's execution had he not acknowledged his part in the homicides to Sister Helen. Conversely, one might argue that the genuine connection that develops between Sister Helen and Poncelet allows the audience to gain its picture of the vulnerability and humanity

of the man awaiting execution, even without his declaration of guilt. She suggests that Matthew hopes for redemption and his eleventh-hour confession to Sister Helen "buys" him that. In reality, she maintains that such confessions of guilt on the part of death row inmates are the exception rather than the rule. Her point here is well taken. While *Dead Man Walking* convincingly indicates that Poncelet's regret is genuine, his admission cannot help but be relentlessly driven out of him by his impending execution.[43]

However, Sarat concedes that a story about a specific person's behavior and/or misbehavior, and the narrative that can be built around it, proves much more compelling for an audience than examining social factors that give rise to crime.[44] But what Sarat misses is that those opposed to state-sponsored executions based on old abolitionist arguments, want people to see the convicted, not as monsters or animals, but as human beings. Their very individuality, their unique story and circumstances, compel us to see them as human, their lives as sacred, and as people worthy of mercy. Criminals tend to become one-dimensional and defined solely by the crime they committed: murderers, rapists, arsonists, drug dealers. But even the worst among us is not one-dimensional. In fact, putting a human face on the killer is what Hollywood death penalty movies do best and by Sarat's own admission the tactic defense lawyers employ prior to sentencing.[45]

Shapiro asserts that Robbins went too far in portraying Poncelet's abhorrent character, making him too much the ugly, hardened criminal and playing on the stereotypes the public holds concerning those on death row. She worries that making Poncelet guilty also contributes to audience expectations. Moviegoers can send him to his execution without having to worry that he is innocent.[46] No one wants to put an innocent person to death. As the new abolitionists so forcefully assert, that is the worst nightmare of capital punishment. But *Dead Man Walking* is not asking whether our society is willing to risk executing guiltless people within a defective justice system. Rather, it asks whether we are willing to put any person to death, even one as reprehensible as Poncelet, despite the glimmer of humanity we might see in him. In the end, his death seems as senseless as those of his victims because the audience has come to see Matthew Poncelet's human face, not just the face of a rapist and killer.

Moreover, Hollywood studios produce movies for the purpose of selling tickets and making money, not usually with the sole intent of promoting social change. Even when a film gets made that contains a serious social message, it does so in spite of its social conscience rather than because of it. *Dead Man Walking* takes its story from Sister Helen's book of the same title and it sets forth a more unequivocal statement against capital punishment, incorporating both the religious and political issues involved. Shapiro, too, sees Sister Helen's book as a stronger anti-death-penalty declaration than the film. Lamenting that *Dead Man Walking* failed to follow the same course as Sister Helen's book, she views the film as a missed opportunity. But Shapiro seems intent on comparing a book written by one person with a movie made by another. Although Sister Helen worked closely with Robbins on the film, the director remained free to produce the work he envisioned. Shapiro ends up critiquing the movie Robbins *did not* make rather than the one he did create. It might be easy to say he should have made a more nuanced exploration of the political issues involved, but he chose to create a capital punishment film focusing on religious issues.[47]

It is, however, difficult to argue with Sarat's point that movies often turn on the inmate coming to terms with his crime, something that rarely occurs in reality.[48] Hollywood gives brief attention to the political, economic, and social issues that contribute to violent crime and a capital conviction. If filmmakers tackle such concerns they do so more with a passing nod than bringing the issues into real focus: a remark about poverty, a mention of drug abuse, a reference to sexual abuse, an indication of a neglectful or abusive parent. Appearing tough on crime can reward political candidates at the polls; wealth means that the rich do not end up with a death sentence. Here *Dead Man Walking* proves instructive: Poncelet's poor, sharecropping father encouraging his son's drunkenness before he even reached his teens; his father's death when Poncelet was only fourteen; his mother's ramshackle house; his drugged and intoxicated state during the crime; his white supremacist stance. Poncelet also tosses off a comment about no rich man ending up on death row, and the film also hints at the political returns awaiting the elected official who stands firmly behind capital punishment. All these factors receive passing mention, but little focused attention as the roots of larger problems that give rise to criminal behavior. In addition, Sarat as well as other scholars and critics call attention to Hollywood's woeful failure to portray the large numbers, disproportionately so, of African Americans and Latinos on death row. Invariably, the condemned man or woman awaiting execution in a Hollywood production is Caucasian; *The Green Mile* (1999), *True Crime* (1999), and *Monster's Ball* (2001) are the few exceptions. And even here, the role racism plays in the arrest, conviction, and sentencing of murderers has yet to be addressed on film.

The second problem with death penalty films for Sarat is their very detailed cinematic representation of capital crimes and the process and mechanics of putting the condemned to death. The films leave audiences with the sense that they witnessed "what really happened" at the crime scene and can be certain of who is guilty. Numerous death penalty movies use the flashback technique to show snippets of the crime occurring. While early flashbacks are often indistinct, as the film progresses these scenes become clearer until the "truth" is revealed in the end. *Dead Man Walking* employs this storytelling device as does *In Cold Blood, Last Dance, The Green Mile,* and *The Chamber*. But *Dead Man Walking* goes a step further by intercutting Poncelet's execution scene with images of the crime he committed against Hope Percy and Walter Delacroix. Sarat argues that by reminding movie patrons of the terrible violence visited upon the teenage couple as Poncelet lies dying, the film supplies a formidable rationale *for* the death penalty or, at best, leaves the question open.[49]

Furthermore, viewers seem to gain a "full" understanding of the punishment, be it electrocution, hanging, poison gas, or lethal injection. Hollywood depictions of how the state carries out death sentences linger on the technology and procedure in obsessive detail; films concentrate compulsively on the paraphernalia of death. As Sarat and others have pointed out, this obsession stems from executions no longer being open, public affairs. Executions take place behind closed doors with a fairly small number of eyewitnesses, so the general public has very little idea what takes place inside death chambers within the confines of a penitentiary. Americans as a whole garner what they do know about the implementation of the death penalty through theatrical films and television movies. But despite attempting to present audience members with the "reality" of executions, they remain only a representation, something from which viewers can disassociate themselves because, after all, "it's only a movie." Sarat goes a bit further when he states,

the viewer of death penalty films sits at a safe remove, hidden from the condemned's gaze, "real or fictive." That gaze is, of course, the gaze of death itself; we escape it, and do not think

ourselves implicated in the fictive death that takes place before our eyes.[50]

Additionally, Sarat makes the case that because the camera affords the audience a more detailed, behind-the-scenes view of an execution, it separates us from the cinematic spectators in the prison's observation room. Sitting in a movie theater watching an execution's celluloid onlookers undermines the sense that we are really experiencing the end of a convict's life. As close as movie representations try to bring us, they underscore that we will likely never see the state implement capital punishment nor can we know death itself until it comes calling for us. Sarat makes a strong point that as movie "witnesses" viewers become inured to the images of the state putting people to death especially as those images become almost commonplace.

In contrast to Sarat's criticisms of *Dead Man Walking,* director Tim Robbins' commentary that accompanies the DVD version of the film makes it apparent that he endeavored to craft an anti-death-penalty movie.[51] "The movie decries violence of any kind," Robbins reveals, and he suggests that audiences possess enough humanity to feel Poncelet's pain and suffering *and* to behold the crime he committed and not feel differently about him. Despite being guilty of a pair of horrible murders, Matthew is still a human being who deserves society's clemency, not just God's mercy. Robbins thinks his audience intelligent enough to come to its own conclusions about the message of his film. Had he made a preachier, heavy-handed film he would have risked turning people away from the message that undergirds the movie and lost the chance to get viewers to think about where they stand on the issue and why. Robbins did what no other filmmaker to date accomplished by striving to take numerous perspectives into consideration: the criminal, the victims' families, the prison guards, the pro- and anti-death-penalty sides, and the family of the death row inmate. He sought not to romanticize the killer, but neither to forget about the victims. His commentary maintains that the final scene of the teenaged victims lying splayed in the field and the dead murderer spread-eagle on the gurney is a way of saying that "in the end, another person is dead." Robbins makes the statement that the movie is "not about who deserved to die, but who deserves to kill."[52]

Where Robbins left himself open to criticism was in adopting the older, religiously based abolitionist position. His film was not about the intrinsically flawed, arbitrary nature of the justice system which makes so many gaffs it cannot carry out death sentences with every assurance that the convicted are unequivocally guilty. His film harkens back to an older argument about Christian forgiveness, mercy, and the sanctity of human life. Furthermore, the new abolitionists want filmmakers to create movies with a clear, unambiguous anti-capital punishment message employing their secular position. When a film fails to do that, when it takes a more subtle approach or a religious tone, it triggers a discomfort in the new abolitionists. Unlike director Tim Robbins, abolitionists do not trust the public to come to their own conclusion. Would a stronger anti-death-penalty stand have really served the purpose? It seems getting audiences to question their position might be more important than preaching to the choir. What abolitionist critics lose sight of is that the old religious positions against capital punishment still hold sway for many Americans even if the current arguments against the death penalty have shifted to a secular stance.[53] In the end, what makes *Dead Man Walking* a great film is its willingness to allow its audience to examine the issues from multiple perspectives and to allow people to think for themselves. As one commenter succinctly noted, "it is a point of view that whispers rather than shouts."[54]

Last Dance, Director Bruce Beresford, Touchstone Pictures (1996)

Although *Last Dance* might be characterized as an above-average movie, having been released on the heels of *Dead Man Walking* invited comparisons which did the former film no favors. Even the star power of Sharon Stone could not add enough luster to prevent it from being overshadowed by the masterful production directed by Tim Robbins. Here, Rob Morrow plays a young lawyer, Rick Hayes, the brother of the governor's chief of staff in a nameless southern state, who wheedles a job on the state clemency board out of his successful older sibling. There he comes to know Cindy Liggett (Sharon Stone), a death row inmate convicted for beating two high school classmates to death during a burglary. In discussing her case with another government employee, Sam Burns (Randy Quaid), Hayes mentions that women do not usually commit such violent crimes, but Burns cynically urges him to just get the job done and not embark on some misguided crusade. Appeals are just a delaying tactic, he quips.

When Hayes finally meets Cindy Liggett, a twelve-year veteran of death row, she is a tough, foul-mouthed, indifferent woman facing execution in a mere thirty days. Life for Liggett in the women's prison appears sterile and bleak, the other female convicts depicted as brash and cynical. She claims that everyone knows the clemency board is a joke because the governor never grants stays of execution. But privately Cindy experiences deep remorse as she relives the horrors of her crime again and again. She had been up for two solid days high on crack cocaine before committing the homicides. As Rick Hayes looks into the case and interviews people about Liggett, the film reveals that her drug-addicted mother died when she was sixteen and it was Cindy's mother and boyfriend who had gotten her hooked on heroine as a young teenager. Subsequently, the mother's boyfriend raped her. Later Liggett admits to Hayes that the night of the murders lives inside her like a giant shadow. Envy and hatred motivated her; she hated everything she did not have. To escape her torturous thoughts and the oppressiveness of her prison surroundings, Cindy finds comfort in mail-order art and drawing lessons.

Against the advice of his coworker, Hayes, predictably, goes on a campaign to bolster Liggett's case for a reprieve; he visits Liggett's male accomplice in prison, who attacks Rick when he confronts him about the night of the homicide. Hayes finds himself promptly reassigned to another job in the governor's office. Hayes also calls on an African American death row inmate, John Henry Reese, portrayed by Charles S. Dutton, who earned a law degree and wrote a best-selling book from prison. Both Reese and Liggett will appear before the clemency board at approximately the same time, but the question remains who will be allowed to live, an accomplished African American man or an uneducated white woman and former junky. Here at least, a movie deals, if only briefly, with the large number of African Americans on death row but does so fairly superficially. Hayes becomes convinced Liggett has changed during her imprisonment and deserves mercy from the governor, but Burns warns Hayes again not to get sucked in by the prisoner and proceeds to tell yet another electrocution-gone-wrong horror story with all the attendant details: the condemned man's knees fused together; smoke poured off the body; and the smell of burning flesh appalled onlookers. Execution horror stories become a standard device of capital punishment films designed to shock and revolt audiences. Hayes goes to see the parents of Liggett's victims and each takes one side of the death penalty argument. The mother of her female victim quotes the biblical commandment, "Thou shalt

not kill," telegraphing her opposition to capital punishment despite her daughter's murder. The father of the male victim says Liggett must pay for her brutal crime. In the end the governor withdraws the execution order for John Henry Reese, but not for Liggett, suggesting that clemency for Reese is a political ploy to win the black vote in an upcoming election.

Slowly the viewer gets the sense that Hayes is falling for a softening, remorseful Liggett, an old Hollywood contrivance which seems badly misplaced here. It also comes to light that Liggett's first lawyer never introduced her highly intoxicated state during the crime and, in a new appeal, it could prove to be the mitigating factor that might spare her life.

At the urging of his older brother, Hayes attends the governor's party and his good sense is overcome by his passion to save Cindy from the gallows as he makes a vociferous and impassioned speech to the governor amid all the party guests, embarrassing everyone. As a result, he leaves his position in state government and loses his girlfriend. "Everyone gave up on her," he states, making it clear he will not abandon her. As the black sheep of his family he knows what it feels like to have people give up on him, including his successful and powerful brother, who forever undermines and belittles him in subtle ways.

As her execution date draws closer, prison authorities transfer Liggett to another penitentiary and a ridiculous situation takes place in which prison officials allow Rick Hayes, to whom Cindy has grown close, to stay in her death cell overnight; she sleeps on her bunk, and he in a chair. Rob Morrow's performance is rather wooden and passionless, especially in the scenes with deglamourized but still beautiful Sharon Stone. Liggett's younger brother, a man just reaching maturity but already headed down the wrong path, comes to see her as well. These scenes between brother and sister are quite touching, and in their last tender moments together she commands him to straighten up his life because she will be keeping an eye on him from the afterlife. In a sentimental and romantic gesture, Hayes purchases a dress for Cindy to wear at her execution and as she puts it on she becomes distraught. *Last Dance* provides the obligatory and detailed scenes of prison officials preparing for an execution. Director Bruce Beresford provides a cinematic representation of death through concentrated and close-up views of the paraphernalia associated with lethal injection. Audiences get a privileged tour of the machinery of death, a view that a real witness would never be privy to. Hayes proceeds to the witness room to be her support and focal point during the ordeal. Here *Last Dance* becomes somewhat reminiscent of *Dead Man Walking*—Rick Hayes becomes the "face of love" for Cindy Liggett.

With a dignity tinged with fear, Liggett walks to the death chamber and lies on the gurney to be strapped down. The curtain of the death chamber opens and Cindy and Rick gaze lovingly into each other's eyes. Just as the lethal drugs begin to be administered, the telephone rings and the execution team is ordered to "stand down." As the strap-down team releases her from the table, Liggett completely losses control of her emotions— she shrieks and cries, pummeling the men around her with her fists. The emotional strain of waiting and the rollercoaster of being ready to die only to be yanked back to earth are driven home in a way few other films manage; credit must be given here to Stone's genuine and unpretentious acting. Nevertheless, the eleventh-hour reprieve utilizes a plot construct that proves predictable and irritating. "I can't take any more," she sobs, and neither can the movie's patrons. Back in her cell with Rick by her side, she tells him it is time to let her go; he should stop working to save her life. Within a few hours word comes that a special panel of the federal court denied her last petition. The execution begins again. As she lies on the gurney they again look into each other eyes. The viewer sees the plungers pushing the deadly chemicals into her body; her eyelids flutter, and then close. Rick bows his head and her life is over. Later we see Rick looking at her drawing of the Taj Mahal; she had asked that he provide her with a photograph of it so she could sketch it. The last scene shows Rick Hayes in India strolling toward the famous building, a symbol of eternal love and devotion.

This type of heavy-handed, hokey symbolism combined with a contrived love story diverts audience attention away from the real issue the movie started out addressing, capital punishment. The attempt to saddle the film with a love story is badly out of place and frankly ridiculous and reduces the movie to the level of a melodrama with soap-opera tendencies. Having premiered only five months after *Dead Man Walking*, *Last Dance* suffers by comparison in almost every respect. It starts out as an earnest film with a strong and haunting performance by Sharon Stone, but in the end it is wasted. While clearly hoping to make an anti-death-penalty statement and placing the issue at the center of the film, *Last Dance* gets lost along the way. The motion picture focuses more on Hayes' struggles to navigate the capricious and arbitrary clemency process in order to save his client than on Liggett's personal journey, and plainly points to the political calculations that come into play when politicians decide who receives a commuted sentence. Hayes often seems to be chasing his own tail in steering through the court's pardon system, an institution replete with cynicism and obliquity. Like the 1999 film *True Crimes*, it concentrates more on Hayes trying to redeem himself than on proving the death penalty an unjustified practice. Sean O'Sullivan, an English sociologist and the coordinator of the Prison Film Project, contends that *Last Dance* does not so much put forth the idea that capital punishment is wrong overall, but wrong in this particular case.[55]

Director Bruce Beresford also missed several opportunities that might have allowed his film to hold its own. He overlooked a chance to deal more seriously with women imprisoned for violent crime and the dynamics and circumstances specific to murder committed by females.[56] To his credit, he did take some time to examine the relationships forged by female death row inmates and their show of solidarity when the execution date approaches for one of them. In crafting the first movie since *I Want to Live!* with a condemned female convict, Beresford had much to live up to. He also lost the occasion to explore more deeply the issue of the disproportionate number of African Americans on death row and the reasons behind it.[57] Unlike other filmmakers, however, credit must be give to Beresford for giving screen time to the topic of the high percentage of African American incarcerations, especially among those sitting with a death sentence over their heads.

Last Dance begins by absorbing the new abolitionists' structuralist approach that society bears some responsibility in molding people who commit wrongful acts. The film points to Liggett's neglectful and drug-addicted mother, the sexual assault she suffered at the hands of her mother's boyfriend, her own drug usage promoted by her parent, an apparently absent father, and her becoming an orphan at sixteen. In a world so fraught with danger and suffering, it is no wonder Liggett felt nothing but hatred and envy for those who had a better life, underscoring all that her life lacked. The film's emphasis on the highly politicized nature of seeking and being granted leniency also underlines the role social institutions play in whether someone lives or dies. Society writing off Cindy Liggett, and others like her, only served to dictate her path down the wrong road. Hayes goes so far as to suggest that those people who applaud and support government-sanctioned executions are no better than the murderers they profess to revile.

This design, Austin Sarat contends, is "what a structuralist response to crime would look like in popular culture."[58] But he argues that Beresford undermines the structuralist approach by putting so much emphasis on Liggett taking full responsibility for the murders from the outset. During her twelve-year stint in prison she has come to terms with her crime, her guilt, and her deep sense of regret. As Sarat points out, the film possesses a heavy emphasis on the criminal's individual responsibility, but that sense of personal responsibility also relieves society of its responsibility toward Liggett and others who commit acts of violence. To further salve the conscience of society, moviegoers "witness" the homicides through crime-scene photographs and through flashbacks as Liggett relives her killing spree in dreams. Because audiences get more information about the felony than any jury would, viewers get the feeling that they hold a clear, complete picture and can feel secure that the condemned is really guilty. The point is, however, rather unnecessary in *Last Dance* as no question exists about the guilt or innocence of Cindy Liggett; she fully admits to the killings. But Sarat rightfully worries that putting audience members, cinematically, in the position to judge and providing them with extensive information not available in the courtroom gives the false impression that jurors can be certain of a defendant's guilt or innocence. The notion that a jury can be absolutely certain of guilt only serves to bolster capital punishment in our society; it perpetuates the myth that the state only executes those it knows are to blame. Knowing Liggett stands before us culpable for her crime, *Last Dance* asks if she should be spared. The question the film should have posed, and *Dead Man Walking* did pose, is whether our society wants to save all those who stand guilty.

The Chamber, Director James Foley, Universal (1996)

Following the discussion and debate that *Dead Man Walking* and *Last Dance* generated in reviews and journals, Hollywood took yet another stab at producing a movie with capital punishment as its theme. Even with Gene Hackman in the title role, *The Chamber* (1996) possessed little chance of triggering the same dialogue spawned by Robbins's motion picture. In a small Mississippi town in 1967, a white supremacist blows up the offices of a Jewish civil rights attorney. The lawyer's young twin sons die in the blast and he suffers permanent injury; years later the maimed attorney takes his own life. Sam Cayhall (Gene Hackman) finds himself convicted of the crime and waits on death row in a story based on a John Grisham novel. Hoping to save Cayhall's life in the twenty-eight days remaining until his execution is a fervent young lawyer, Adam Hall (Chris O'Donnell), who happens to be the grandson of the condemned man. Even Cayhall's daughter (Faye Dunaway) seems to have little sympathy for her father and warns Hall about dredging up the past. "He'll destroy absolutely everyone who made the mistake of getting close to him," she asserts. Gene Hackman's character projects himself as anything but sympathetic; he is a virulent racist and anti-Semite, who remains wholly unrepentant and indifferent to everyone and everything. He proudly reports that he holds membership in the KKK and that every generation of Cayhalls have belonged to the Klan since Nathan Bedford Forrest founded the organization with a Cayhall by his side. As a child his daughter witnessed Cayhall shoot his African American handyman after their respective sons had a boyhood brawl, and as Sam claimed he acted in self-defense, he was never even arrested for the murder. But Cayhall's crime ends up having unintended consequences as his own son blames himself for the murder because the toy soldier the boys were fighting over was later found under his bed. Years later Adam's father, still overcome by guilt, commits suicide in his presence.

Cayhall expresses his reservations that Adam is capable of saving him from the gas chamber, saying, "Save me? You don't look like you can save a turkey from Thanksgiving." In an attempt to impress the seriousness of the situation on his grandson, Cayhall details the first gas chamber execution he "witnessed" while on death row and how it all went wrong; it took five minutes of agony before the inmate finally expired, a sobering description for the young lawyer and moviegoers. While discussing Adam's father, Cayhall launches into an ugly outburst about the suicide of his son, yelling that he had no right to take away the gift of life that his parents and God gave him. Later Cayhall's daughter shows Adam a photograph of a ten-year-old Sam at a lynching and mentions it was his third such event. The grandson begins to grasp that southern society and culture, with its unchecked racial hatreds, created the monster that his grandfather became. Rollie Wedge (Raymond J. Barry),[59] Cayhall's secret accomplice in the bombing and a Klan leader, visits Sam in prison and viewers learn that the twin boys were not supposed to be at the law office on the morning of the explosion. In addition, Wedge praises Cayhall's years of soldier-like loyalty to the Klan, but when Sam conveys regret about killing the children, Wedge embarks on a hate-filled diatribe that killing Jews, even accidentally, makes for a better world. Finally, the audience glimpses a conscience in Cayhall as he recoils from Rollie's venomous bigotry.

As Adam works feverishly to spare Cayhall's life, he realizes that powerful men in Mississippi government want certain files to remain sealed which might show Cayhall did not act alone and/or carried out the bombing under orders from someone higher up the political food chain. Since such files could prove politically embarrassing, the old-guard politicians close ranks to protect themselves, and the papers that could possibly mitigate Sam's situation remain inaccessible. Even the governor proves unwilling to intercede because the Cayhall conviction launched his political career and, despite wanting to follow his conscience, without new evidence in the case he cannot intervene without serious political fallout.

Only at the end of the film does Cayhall appear in a somewhat sympathetic light as he writes letters of apology to the widow of the Jewish lawyer and to the son of the murdered African American handyman. In his final hours, he and Adam sit together and Sam says,

> Of all the people and things I hated in my whole life, the one I hated most was me. . . . I never did anyone any good until you came down. See if I'm proud of you, I've got to be proud of your daddy [who took his own life]. He wasn't weak; he was strong—strong enough to get away, strong enough to give you whatever it is you got. If he was able to give that to you, I reckon, this old man passed on something good to him.

The tender moment between grandfather and grandson rings false when the bulk of the film paints Cayhall as a bitter, hardened racist and remorseless killer. Although *The Chamber* would like viewers to marshal some concern for Cayhall, his transformation comes across as phony and forced, and audiences find themselves as indifferent to Cayhall as he is to those around him.

Cayhall's execution in the gas chamber, to employ Austin Sarat's expression, is the typical fetishized treatment that Hollywood tends to present, more detailed and graphic than anything in *I Want to Live!* And yet, *The Chamber*'s handling of the execution scene seems gratuitous

and unnecessary because the film does not take the death penalty issue to heart. Gene Hackman's recounting the horrors of a gas chamber execution gone terribly wrong stands as the gravest moment in a production purporting to address the matter of capital punishment. The movie focuses more on the relationship between the generations, on destructive family dynamics, and on the way in which actions carried out by one generation visit themselves upon the next. The capital punishment question feels like mere window dressing, a device to provide the story with dramatic tension and a sense of urgency. In the end, *The Chamber*, badly misnamed, goes so far as to indicate that Rollie Wedge perpetrated the bombing and Cayhall acted as an accessory to the crime, implying that Adam's grandfather was wrongly executed. Where the film might have utilized the character of Adam Hall as an anti-death-penalty crusader, it makes him a wounded young man seeking to understand his father's suicide and his grandfather's racial violence. *The Chamber* tries to cobble together some of the old abolitionist arguments with a smattering of new abolitionist ideas without a commitment to either. At best, the film's death penalty message is noncommittal; at worst, it is, like Sam Cayhall, simply indifferent.

True Crime, Director Clint Eastwood, Warner Bros. (1999)

Director and producer Clint Eastwood created a typical race-to-save-an-innocent-man film in his 1999 send-up, *True Crime*. As Steve Everett, Eastwood is a crusty, cynical, but seasoned reporter who follows his instincts while writing for the *Oakland Tribune*. Newly sober, he makes a poor husband, a selfish, inattentive father, and an unapologetic adulterer. Once he wrote for a prestigious New York newspaper, but his penchant for bedding the wives and daughters of his bosses has landed him in the backwater of San Francisco's East Bay. Due to the unexpected death of a fellow reporter, he draws the assignment of interviewing a condemned African American man and subsequently covering his execution at San Quentin. His editors (played by Denis Leary and James Woods) warn him to avoid making this into a crusade like the "last time." Frank Beachum[60] (Isaiah Washington), sitting on death row for the shooting death of a pregnant convenience-store clerk, hardly fulfills the typical image of a prison inmate. Maintaining his innocence and angry at a system that has wrongly convicted him, he nevertheless remains calm and articulate with his beautiful, devoted wife (Lisa Gay Hamilton) and his lovely little girl at his side. The scenes of the family's last hours together possess heart and poignancy. Naturally, the parents attempt to hold themselves together for the sake of their young daughter, especially when she falls apart over a lost crayon, a reflection of the girl's terror and anguish over a situation she cannot quite comprehend but senses is dire.

While Beachum prepares himself for death, Everett gathers information about the man he will interview just hours before his execution. Although Beachum grew up with a druggie mother and committed some minor offenses in his youth, he cleaned up his act after marrying his Christian wife and turning to religion himself. The conference between Everett and Beachum goes predictably with the reporter asking his subject, point blank, whether he shot the expectant clerk. Beachum explains what occurred and the audience gets the cinematic representation. We observe Beachum entering the store and after an amiable conversation with the clerk asking to use the restroom. When he emerges he looks around for the woman and finds her lying behind the counter bleeding from a chest wound. He shouts for help and attempts to stop the flow of blood

but to no avail. When another patron walks in, Beachum abruptly rises from behind the counter covered in the victims' blood, but bolts from the store in sudden fear when he realizes that this white man thinks he is the killer. Later the witness identifies Beachum as the shooter, thinking he saw a gun in his hand. Of course, Everett embarks on the very crusade that his editors had feared. Convinced there must have been another person present during the homicide, Everett races through the city, breaks into the home of the recently deceased reporter to look for her notes, hunts down leads, interviews witnesses, and uncovers the identity of the real killer only to discover that he, an African American youth, was stabbed to death three years before. Everett's sudden epiphany that the locket that the killer's grandmother wears is the same one taken from the body of the murdered store clerk causes him to race to the governor's mansion with the hapless grandmother in tow.

In the meantime, the now-standard movie device of showing the preparations for an execution by lethal injection is paraded before the audience. San Quentin's old gas chamber, converted for lethal injection, serves as the room in which Beachum will die. The camera lingers on Beachum taking his walk to meet death, the details of his being strapped down, the intravenous needle puncturing his arm, and the chamber door being sealed. To heighten tensions even more, the scenes of Beachum being prepared for chemical death are intermingled with Everett dashing to beat the clock. Again the camera focuses on the waiting witnesses, the syringes, the buttons being depressed on the injection machine, the flow of fatal drugs through the tubing, the room spinning and Frank's eyes closing. Jarringly, the telephone rings and the execution halts. The warden and guards rush in, someone yanks the IV out of the innocent man's arm, while his panic-stricken wife stands at the death chamber window calling out his name and beating her clinched fist against the glass as the scene fades to black. The last scene finds Everett, with a book contract for the Beachum story and a possible Pulitzer Prize in the offing, in a toy store purchasing a gift for his daughter while he glibly propositions the attractive cashier. As he exits the store he notices the Beachum family happy and laughing, walking past the giant Christmas tree in the plaza. Frank acknowledges him with a small salute and Everett returns it.

True Crime makes a mockery of death penalty films that endeavor to take the issue seriously and promote the abolition of capital punishment. The website that accompanies the film includes a map of the United States indicating which states employ capital punishment and the method each uses, and links to other sites providing information about capital punishment.[61] But the story focuses more on Everett attempting to redeem his life and career, using Frank Beachum's life and death as a vehicle to accomplish that. As one of the few Hollywood films to place a main African American character on death row, one might think that racism would play a substantial role, but the opportunities are either missed or dismissed. True, the plot underlines some of the issues that divide whites and blacks in our society, in particular how easily the justice system is affected by racism. For example, the Caucasian witness instantly assumes Beachum is an armed killer when he pops up from behind the store counter, and Beachum, suddenly and acutely aware of his predicament, flees the crime scene in panic. At the same time, *True Crime* seems to undermine that message when Everett tells the grandmother that race has nothing to do with this homicide case. Is our leading man really so blind or is his cavalier statement intended to add another flaw to his badly tarnished character?

Information dealing with social issues of racism or drug addiction, like Frank's upbringing at the hands of a junkie mother, takes a backseat to Everett thumbing his nose at society's conventions. Scenes focus more on Everett as the incorrigible scoundrel and single-minded investigative reporter than on issues of injustice, racism, or capital punishment which shape the world of Beachum. The biting, sarcastic banter between Eastwood, Woods, and Leary prove more interesting than anything else in the movie. Good performances by Washington and Hamilton, as the couple soon to be parted by lethal injection, are wasted in a film that seems unable to take capital punishment or a justice system which condemns an innocent African American man to death seriously. To then concentrate so intensely and obsessively on the paraphernalia of execution is an insult to the issue; *True Crime* exploits state-sanctioned killing simply to shock and titillate its viewers. Moreover, the four-hour time span between Everett being handed the story and his having to appear at San Quentin for the interview are the longest in motion picture history. As one reviewer wrote, "The true crime is that the film refuses to decide how seriously to take its subjects—any of them."[62]

The Green Mile, Director Frank Darabont, Warner Bros. (1999)

The Green Mile premiered later the same year as *True Crime*, although it possesses an entirely different feel. If *True Crime* tasted a bit careless and arrogant, *The Green Mile* takes itself and its message seriously, perhaps too seriously. Despite its allegorical nature, capital punishment is central to the story and the film treats its subject earnestly, whether one finds its unique approach convincing or not. Tom Hanks portrays Paul Edgecomb, the reasonable, humane man in charge of the Green Mile, the name for death row, at the Cold Mountain Penitentiary in 1935 Louisiana. The other correctional officers follow Edgecomb's lead in their treatment of the prisoners with the exception of one man, Percy Wetmore (Doug Hutchison). This man—small in stature, shriveled of heart, and sadistic in nature—torments the inmates at every opportunity, much to the disapproval of the other guards. Wetmore represents the mean spirited pro-death-penalty position and sees the Green Mile as "a bucket of piss to drown rats in." Delivered to "the Mile" is John Coffey, an enormous, but timid and gentle African American depicted by Michael Clarke Duncan, found guilty of the rape and murder of two young sisters. His guilt seems in little doubt since he was found with his arms wrapped around the girls' bloody bodies crying out, "I tried to take it back, but it was too late." Of course, later we learn that Coffey attempted to breathe live back into the girls when he came upon their dead and forsaken bodies. When he arrives at the penitentiary the prison guards peg him as just another poor, uneducated black man whose size and race alone render him capable of terrible violence.

As death row environments go in Hollywood pictures, the Green Mile comes across as a less sinister place than most; the restraint room, a padded cell, has seen so little use that it houses extra furniture. But Edgecomb remains mindful of how much stress the prisoners contend with, as executions occur on a fairly regular basis. Audiences view three executions during the film with the first going through all the details of preparing for the procedure. Here again Hollywood displays its fetish with putting a person to death, this time in the electric chair. The first electrocution provides viewers with a picture of just how stomach-turning such a death can be and, postmortem, the face of the condemned man (Graham Greene) looks gruesome: the face bruised, the eyelids swollen, the scalp burned.

When the film begins Edgecomb suffers from a nearly debilitating urinary tract infection, but he refuses to see a doctor. While all around him watch Edgecomb endure the agonies of his illness, John Coffey unexpectedly provides the instant cure through his miraculous healing powers. Clearly, this inmate stands apart from the others and Edgecomb begins to look into the circumstances that brought him to death row. In a discussion with Coffey's indifferent and racist defense attorney (Gary Sinise), the southern lawyer took little effort with the case and simply assumed his taciturn African American client was guilty. But something about Coffey's case continues to nag at Edgecomb, especially later, when Coffey again demonstrates his phenomenal powers by resurrecting the beloved pet mouse of Eduard Delacroix (Michael Jeter), another condemned man, after the cruel Officer Wetmore purposely crushes the creature underfoot. When Delacroix sits in the electric chair, the merciless Percy Wetmore opts to conduct his own private experiment at Delacroix's expense without the knowledge of the other members of the strap-down team. He deliberately fails to wet a sponge placed between the scalp and the electrode, which normally increases the flow of electricity, killing the person faster. Moviegoers behold the ghastly suffering of Delacroix as his head catches fire during the execution and his body jerks and writhes violently despite being firmly cinched into the chair. Back in the cell block, John Coffey literally feels all the agony and pain that Delacroix just experienced, and in death "Del" lies completely burned and unrecognizable.

Convinced of Coffey's extraordinary ability, the death row guards concoct a plan to break him out of jail long enough to cure the warden's dying wife (Patricia Clarkson). The warden (James Cromwell), who runs the prison and oversees executions, finds himself unable to tell his adored wife that she has a malignant brain tumor. Coffey restores her health by drawing the disease into his own body, but he does not release it immediately as he did on previous occasions. The guards fear that he will choose to keep the disease inside, allowing it to kill him. Instead Coffey waits until the heartless Wetmore walks by his cell; he grabs him and transfers the "evil" to Percy, who then, trance-like, takes out his sidearm and kills Wild Bill, the actual rapist and killer of the two little girls. Wild Bill had ended up on death row for a different set murders committed during a robbery, but in flashback scenes, audiences see Wild Bill luring the young twins away from their home to be raped and murdered. Coffey comes to understand the deep-seated evil of Wetmore and the vicious, senseless crimes of Wild Bill through his power of touch and the knowledge that touching others brings him. "I punished them bad men," he tells Edgecomb simply. The now catatonic Wetmore is transferred to the local mental hospital to live out his days. But Edgecomb, faced with having to execute an innocent man and a person touched with the power of God, fears for his own soul and how he will answer for this sin. He cannot stop the execution, nor can he reconcile himself to killing one of God's "true miracles." Not knowing what to do, he turns to Coffey who gently tells Edgecomb:

> You tell God the Father it was a kindness you done . . . because I want it over and done. . . . I'm tired, boss. . . . Mostly I'm tired of people being ugly to each other. I'm tired of all the pain I feel and hear in the world every day. There's too much of it. It's like pieces of glass in my head all the time.

Edgecomb is doing Coffey a service by bringing his life and anguish to an end.

On the evening of his execution when the guards take him out of his cell and head for the electric chair, it is Coffey who consoles the distraught correctional officers. He tells them that although he is not afraid to die, he still fears the dark and refuses the death mask. The strain of carrying out this death sentence on the guards shows on their faces as they try to hold their emotions in check, but tears flow and their hearts are filled with regret. While Coffey's death is no horror show as Delacroix's was, it is clearly not a pleasant way to die. Coffey dies with dignity, at least, as much as an electrocution can afford. Many years later Edgecomb relates the story of John Coffey to a friend and he reveals that in reality he is 108 years old, Coffey having passed some of his life-giving powers, as well as the knowledge of Wild Bill's guilt, to Edgecomb. His longevity has proven more a curse than a blessing as he watches his friends and loved ones all die before him; he knows that each new person he befriends or loves, he will live to see them die as well. "It's my torment you see; it's my punishment, for letting John Coffey ride the lightning; for killing a miracle of God."

The allegorical nature of *The Green Mile* makes it harder to discuss and categorize than most of the films that embrace themes of capital punishment. At turns touching, controversial, profound, clichéd, and contradictory, analyzing *The Green Mile* proves frustrating and slippery. Sean O'Sullivan offered that the movie's multiple meanings render it essentially meaningless and it contributes nothing at all to the death penalty debate.[63] While he seems too quick to dismiss the film, movie reviewers of all stripes weighed in on the merits or flaws of the production and their perceptions of its central themes.[64] Some saw a religious allegory with Edgecomb as the Apostle Paul and John Coffey as Jesus Christ, ready to sacrifice himself for the sins of the human race, but others detected a more straightforward story of good and evil. Several commentators focused on its window into the past, history suffused with the supernatural and spiritual. A few commentators expressed their disgust with what they viewed as a highly racist film, while others applauded its depiction of the role racism played in railroading an innocent black man onto "the green mile" in the American South of the 1930s.

The Green Mile deals better with issues of how the judicial deck was, and still is, staked against African American defendants, and how inadequate or indifferent lawyers affect the outcome of a capital case, but it also portrays John Coffey in a surprisingly stereotypical manner. Initially, Coffey makes his appearance on screen as the hulking, deferential black man, a gentle giant, it seems, with the mind of a simpleton. Not only does he refrain from making trouble, but he soon displays his unique powers of healing. As one reviewer commented, Coffey proves useful to his white guards as long as he employs his curative gifts; he is their tool regardless of what the restorative process costs him physically and psychologically. Neither Edgecomb, after his initial interview with Coffey's defense attorney, nor the other prison guards make much effort to exonerate him, oppose his execution, or set him free. Despite knowing Coffey to be guiltless of the two murders for which he was convicted, the correctional officers still carry out his electrocution.[65] And this reading of the film is not without justification, but two things are missing from the racist assessment of the motion picture.

First, since the prison drama takes place during the Depression era, historical context matters. In 1935 Louisiana no African American man who hoped to live another day would behave much differently than Michael Clarke Duncan's portrayal of John Coffey, especially given his situation. When the posse conducting the search for the missing girls discovers Coffey embracing their dead bodies, it seems entirely historically plausible that he become the victim of a lynching. What seems unusual, and historically out of context, is that Coffey, even on death row, would be housed on the same cell block as white death row inmates. One would assume that African

American prisoners would be segregated from the white prison population, and more extraordinary still is that white correctional officers would treat Coffey with the respect and kindness shown him in the film. Would Edgecomb and his coworkers be likely to risk their jobs, reputations, and standing in the community to spare the life of a black man, despite their certainty of his innocence? Had they publicly come to his defense or raised the alarm about the terrible miscarriage of justice, southern society and institutions being what they were, their efforts almost certainly would have been in vain. A modern generation might point out that despite the racist climate of the day, not even trying to clear Coffey provides no excuse, and they would be right, but that is exactly what made racism so insidious. The roots of racism ran so deep and were so pervasive that even those who wanted to work against it knew their efforts would be fruitless.

The parallels between Coffey's character and Jesus Christ also help to explain his seemingly submissive stance. If Coffey represents a Christ-like figure, audiences would expect him, black or white, to behave much as he does. While one might initially take the view that the man is a simpleton, as the film progresses moviegoers develop a sense that Coffey possesses a quiet inner peace, a compassion and altruism absent in most men, a man not inarticulate, but careful and deliberate in his speech, a powerful, loving man who acutely feels the pain and suffering of this world. Like Jesus, John Coffey represents the ultimate outcast: black and poor in a white world; physically threatening; mentally disabled, or so it would seem; persecuted; a supposed rapist and murder, and of white girls no less; and endowed with powers no one comprehends. What could be more Christ-like than this self-contained man who appears meek, pure of heart, self-sacrificing, and blessed with supernatural abilities? Roman society called for Jesus's blood as southern society of the 1930s called for that of black men who killed whites. As heavy-handed as it might be, the symbolism also dictates that no escape from the electric chair can exist for Coffey, just as Jesus could not evade suffering and death by crucifixion.

The pain and suffering associated with death on the cross also has a cinematic parallel in the gruesomeness of death by electrocution. With the executions taking center stage, here *The Green Mile* attempts to make a potent anti-death-penalty statement. Of the three men who face being put to death, only Coffey's guilt raises any questions. The convictions of Arlen Bitterbuck and Eduard Delacroix elicit no doubts and neither man protests his innocence; they apparently accept responsibility for their misdeeds. Yet neither of the men comes across as inherently wicked or loathsome and, in fact, their humanity and dignity shine through despite their circumstances. Del Delacroix endears himself to almost everyone on the Mile and to audiences with the wonder and tenderness with which he regards his pet mouse, Mr. Jingles. Despite the screenplay reassuring us that Bitterbuck and Delacroix stand guilty of their crimes, we experience deep regret at their demise. As viewers take in each of the three filmed electrocutions, even those that go according to plan prove difficult to watch.[66] In the aftermath of the executions, audiences also get a picture of the deceased, their faces and heads swollen, burned, and bruised. The film drives home the notion that there is nothing humane about death by electrocution. As if to hammer the point, Delacroix's maliciously rigged experience in the electric chair stands out even more starkly for its grisliness and repugnance. But Coffey literally feels Delacroix's horrifically tortured death in every fiber of his being—his body violently twitches and shudders as if the electrical current is pouring through him as well as Delacroix—and the film implies we should feel it just as acutely. In carrying out Coffey's electrocution,

things seem to go along fairly routinely until the lights in the execution hall being to pop and explode sending sparks raining down. One other detail makes his death at the hands of the state unusual; he declines to wear the black hood because of his fear of the dark. As a result, moviegoers get a full view of his contorting face in the throes of being killed. His execution is all the more affecting because not only is he blameless but he has been touched by the grace of God. And yet, in this very moment *The Green Mile* undercuts it anti-death-penalty stand. The film cheats by positioning an innocent man in the electric chair and asking whether his death can be justified in either our hearts or minds.[67] And of course, the answer is resoundingly negative. No one in their right mind wishes to support the killing of the innocent, at the hands of either individuals or the state.

Also difficult to reconcile with an anti-death-penalty message is the shooting of the vile and murderous Wild Bill by the catatonic Percy Wetmore. Coffey, whose divine gift allowed him to extract disease from the warden's wife, transmitted the disease to the sadistic Officer Wetmore, causing him to remove his revolver from its holster and gun down Wild Bill in his cell. Evil preys on evil in the scene and audiences cannot help but believe that both men got their just deserts. But a sense of uneasiness remains when one realizes that Coffey facilitated the incident and it fails to square with his forgiving, peaceful Christian image.[68] Another troublesome point stems from asking audiences to swallow the idea that electrocution is a merciful release from life's sorrows and suffering, "an act of benevolence."[69] While death certainly can provide relief from worldly woes, one fails to imagine even the most determined to die lining up to undergo electrocution to bring their suffering to an end.

If one stands convinced that *The Green Mile* does project an anti-death-penalty argument, it does so more by employing old abolitionist positions rather than new. The film's sometimes burdensome religious overtones can lead us to the conclusion that although Coffey's gifts may be unusual, being "one of God's miracles," every person counts as one of God's wonders. If it is wrong to execute Coffey, is it not wrong to execute any person? The film also alludes to the heavy price paid by death row prison guards for "just doing their job" and the death of this innocent man finally causes them to confront the morality of their work. Edgecomb and his fellow guards all leave Cold Mountain Penitentiary shortly after the execution of Coffey for different jobs in the correctional system; Edgecomb ends up working with juvenile offenders and crime prevention. In the end, though, *The Green Mile* muddies any statement it hopes to make opposing capital punishment by undercutting its argument at several key points.[70]

Monster's Ball, Director Marc Forster, Lions Gate Films (2001)

Just two years after the release of *The Green Mile*, the extraordinary and controversial motion picture *Monster's Ball* (2001) appeared in theaters to mixed reviews. The film follows Hank Grotowski (Billy Bob Thornton), a corrections officer in rural Georgia who lives with his invalid and racist father, Buck (Peter Boyle), also a former prison guard, whose attitudes and hatred still rule the household with an iron grip, and his quiet, sensitive son, Sonny (Heath Ledger), who works with him at the penitentiary as well. Hank's racism, although clearly present, appears to be more out of habit than conviction, a legacy his father bestowed and he lacks the courage to shake off. Hank acts as the leader of the death row strap-down team and he and his fellow jailers practice for the electrocution of an African American inmate, Lawrence Musgrove (Sean "P. Diddy" Combs).

Musgrove's wife, Leticia (Halle Barry), and obese son Tyrell (Coronji Calhoun) join him on his last day. Although a warm relationship exists between father and son, Leticia appears to feel nothing but cool resentment toward her condemned husband. *Monster's Ball* makes no attempt to paint Musgrove as anything but guilty and he calmly, almost peacefully, expects to pay for his unnamed crime; audiences never know or witness Musgrove's crime, but with quiet dignity he acknowledges to his young son that he is "a bad man." Musgrove's poised resignation to his fate lends a worrisome note to the film; it feels like acquiescence, as if believing he deserves to die. Is it that quiet acceptance some people achieve when death comes calling, a self-destructive impulse, or a wish to see the end of the misery that only death row can bring? *Monster's Ball* supplies few hints beyond showing Lawrence taking responsibility for his misdeed and being prepared to meet his fate. Here, of course, Austin Sarat might offer that Musgrove's accepting responsibility plays to the culturally conservative construct of capital punishment. By Musgrove's own admission he stands accountable, so blame can be assigned and punishment meted out without regard to the social factors that contributed to his commission of a crime.

But the movie is more about the effects of an execution than about the offender and his execution, more about the lives of the people a condemned prisoner leaves behind and the long-term consequences for the strap-down team than about the individual being punished by the state. As Lawrence gathers his meager belongs, the men performing the execution pray. As the increasingly inebriated Leticia and her son wait at home for the final phone call, the warden decides that this last communication is a bad idea. Lawrence waits patiently in the death cell and draws the likenesses of Sonny, a rookie to executions, and Hank, the old hand, who both wait with him; Lawrence prefers portraits of people to photographs. He says, "It truly takes a human being to really see a human being," thus affirming his own humanity and that of Sonny and Hank. Sonny, attuned to Musgrove's distress, shows genuine concern toward the prisoner when in a moment of panic he cannot breathe. Ever cool and exacting, Hank intervenes with bureaucratic efficiency to restore the situation. The scenes of the guards preparing Musgrove for his execution take place, but this time with a quiet dignity not matched in other films. It is not Musgrove who falters on the "last mile," but Sonny who vomits during the final march, overcome by this odd, calculated ritual of death. Predictably, the camera takes its time with the electrocution—too long, frankly, as smoke rises from Musgrove's body.

On the heels of the execution, Hank physically and verbally attacks Sonny for ruining the last moments of Musgrove's life. The altercation between father and son continues at home the next morning when Hank rousts Sonny out of bed and Sonny, tired of being the victim of his father's abuse, pulls a gun on him. In the end, Sonny kills himself in front of his father and grandfather after Hank admits that he has always hated his son. The two elder Grotowskis appear indifferent at Sonny's burial, but shortly afterward Hank resigns from his post at the penitentiary and audiences learn that Hank's mother committed suicide as well. Buck launches into a vituperative harangue about his deceased wife; she was weak and worthless and she "quit on me," he bitterly announces, implying that Hank, too, like Sonny and his wife, is a weakling who quits when things get difficult.

In the interim, Leticia deals with her own problems. Her husband has been killed by the state, she faces eviction, her job is in jeopardy, she numbs her grief with alcohol, and, most painful of all, she stands helpless before her son Tyrell's pain and its very obvious physical manifestation, his out-of-control weight. For Tyrell, his only comfort in all the horror and chaos of his young life is a candy bar; he certainly cannot rely on his emotionally unavailable mother for the solace he so badly needs. On the night of the execution, while Leticia and Tyrell waited for the phone call which never came, she got drunk and in her anger and pain lashed out at the boy with both her cutting words and her pounding fists because of his obesity. One rainy night as Leticia and Tyrell leave the restaurant where she works and begin their long walk home, a car runs the boy down and he lies in the gutter with a hysterical Leticia kneeling next to him. Hank, the Good Samaritan, recognizes her from the restaurant and helps them to the hospital, but the boy dies and Hank finds himself escorting Leticia home.

When their paths cross again later, Hank confesses that his own son died recently, admitting that he was not a good father, feeling compelled to share some of his pain. Entering her home, Hank sees a drawing of the man he and Sonny recently executed; he put Leticia's husband to death. Wanting to give her some solace, they find comfort in each other's arms. Their raw sex, tinged with desperation, is motivated more by despair and sheer need than mutual attraction. A relationship develops between these two wounded adults until Leticia delivers a gift to Hank's home and encounters the racist, venom-spewing Buck. Appalled by his father, Hank packs Buck off to a nursing home in short order, cleans out the house of its old memories, and invites Leticia to move in. One night while Hank runs out to the store, Leticia discovers the drawings her husband made of Hank and Sonny on the night he was executed; now she, too, knows the role Hank played in the death of her husband. She joins Hank on the porch for a bowl of ice cream and she gazes over at the three gravestones in the Grotowski family burial plot: Hank's mother, wife, and son. Two more graves must loom in her mind, those of her own son and husband.

Most reviewers interpreted the film with an eye to interracial relations. The idea that mutual grief brought two people together comes into play, but is still overshadowed by race. The secondary characters, Sonny, the guard, and Lawrence, the condemned, both possess humanity and compassion while the main characters need to find theirs. *Monster's Ball* deals with the aftermath of capital punishment, for the family of the executed and for those who carry out the sentence. The person being punished is not the only one to pay a price for their crime. The men who dutifully follow protocol and procedure in an attempt to distance themselves from the task of carrying out a death sentence must count the cost as well. Despite the film's flaws, it is the only film that confronts the costs of capital punishment beyond the death of the convict. It also deals with race in an unexpected manner. In choosing to make Lawrence Musgrove an African American, the film does something few others even attempt—to reflect the actual makeup of death row inmates. But because the film chooses not to focus on the inmate himself and the crime he perpetrated, the racist nature of the justice system does not garner the attention. Rather, the racism of the wider society comes into focus. Buck's brand of southern, old-school racism leaves him free to utter the most vilely bigoted statements in a casual, off-handed manner to whoever is within earshot. His legacy of hatred infected his son whose tough exterior mimics his father's racist attitudes but without any real faith in their assumptions, but no less hurtful for their half-heartedness. Sonny, on the other hand, sees no point in treating others with anything but kindness and respect; he has witnessed hatred's effects at close range for too long to be sucked in by its destructive powers. Hank and Leticia turn to each other because there is no one else there, because no one else can understand the depth of

their pain from a series of violent deaths: her husband's execution, his son's suicide, her son's hit-and-run demise, his mother's death by her own hand. In the face of such devastating loss, their shared humanity becomes vastly more essential than any racial divide that might separate them. *Monster's Ball* probes the terrible costs of capital punishment and racism for two families and in doing so emphasizes the price our society pays when the government authorizes death as a punishment for murder.

The Life of David Gale, Director Alan Parker, Universal (2003)

Where *Monster's Ball* takes death penalty films into new territory and plums the depths of the effects it has on those it touches, *The Life of David Gale* seems to incorporate all the right ingredients but hits an entirely different note. Its approach encompasses the new abolitionist argument, but its plot turns left more than one reviewer outraged. The film begins with David Gale, played by Kevin Spacey, a former philosophy professor at the fictional University of Austin, who ends up being found guilty for the rape and murder of his female colleague and friend, Constance Harraway (Laura Linney). The ultimate irony is that both avidly worked for Death Watch, an organization dedicated to the abolition of capital punishment in Texas, and now he sits on death row. He invites a renowned New York magazine reporter, Bitsy Bloom (Kate Winslet), to interview him days prior to his scheduled execution, but the interviews come at a price, five hundred thousand dollars in cash. As their meetings begin, audience members slowly gain a picture of David Gale's story as he divulges it little by little to Bloom. He recounts how his marriage fell apart and he lost his job after a drunken sexual encounter with a student. The sex scene demonstrates that the young woman pursued him and the sex became increasingly aggressive at her request. She later accuses him of rape, then drops the charges and leaves town, but his marriage and career are left in tatters and he begins to drink heavily. Worst of all, Gale loses access to his young son with whom he is very close. No matter how he tries to pull his life together, the rape charge follows him everywhere. He wallows in self-pity until he learns that his close friend and former colleague, Constance Harraway, is fighting leukemia.

As Bitsy Bloom and her assistant do some digging of their own and ascertain that Gale's lawyer performed poorly in defending his client, a strange cowboy in a dilapidated pickup truck mysteriously tails them while Puccini's *Turandot* blares from his car stereo. The cowboy turns out to be Constance's boyfriend and fellow Death Watch member, Dusty Wright (Matt Craven). Upon returning to their motel room, the reporters find the place broken into and a videotape left for them. The video, taken by the killer who taped a plastic bag over Constance's head and allowed her to suffocate, documents her death and indicates that Gale was framed for the homicide. Viewers also learn that David and Constance, now terminally ill, had sex the night before she died; she wanted to feel alive and comforted by her long-time friend and he obliged her. Bloom comes to believe that Gale, an innocent man, is about to die and the film becomes another typical race-against-the-clock drama.

Bloom and her sidekick go to the murder scene, now a morbid museum, and reenact the crime. Bloom secures a plastic bag over her own head and asks her coworker not to rescue her before a certain time has elapsed. She concludes that Constance staged her own death with the help of her boyfriend, the mysterious cowboy, in order to frame an innocent man. Having Texas put a guiltless man to death proves that the justice system does kill innocent people; it is just what Death Watch needs to obtain a promised moratorium against executions from the governor, a very thinly veiled George W. Bush. Bloom believes that the cowboy, Dusty Wright, a zealous foe of capital punishment, will allow Gale to die for the cause. She breaks into Dusty's dumpy house and searches the place for the videotape she knows will exonerate Gale. Armed with the tape, but no cell phone and an unreliable rental car that breaks down, she races to save his life but is too late. Gale dies by lethal injection just minutes before her arrival at the prison. While Bloom engages in her frantic dash, audiences witness Gale's lawyer handing over the half-million-dollar interview fee to Dusty, who gets on a plane, despite a manhunt, and delivers the money to Gale's wife and son in Spain. Later, back in New York, Bloom receives yet another videotape revealing that Gale was in on the plot to discredit the justice system; he facilitated Constance's suicide, actively participated, and willingly became a martyr to the abolitionist cause.

The formulaic "race-to-save-the-innocent-man" gets a new and, frankly, unfortunate twist in *The Life of David Gale*. Three devoted death penalty opponents (Gale, Harraway, and Wright), together with Gale's corrupt lawyer, colluded to subvert the justice system and place an innocent person on death row; then they conspired to allow that man to die at the hands of the state, thereby furthering the very policy they so deride. Is the justice system not already flawed enough? Did four people really need to maneuver one of their own to the gallows to prove a point? Gale and his friends might argue that the ends justify the means if it puts a halt to state-sponsored executions in Texas. In fact, the motion picture's message suggests that the ends *do* justify the means. Four conspirators embraced the view that it was immoral and unethical for the State of Texas to take the life of another as a punishment, but then promoted and participated in two deaths with forethought and planning. That Constance Harraway wanted to face death on her own terms after being diagnosed with terminal leukemia is one thing, but to use her suicide to make a political point is another thing altogether. Wright, Gale, and Harraway hatched a plan to frame Gale at a time when Constance was terribly vulnerable and, possibly, not in the frame of mind to make rational decisions. Wouldn't a thorough autopsy have revealed that Harraway had a deadly form of leukemia which was likely to kill her soon? That three fervent supporters of Death Watch become involved in a murder that sent one man to death row, left one woman dead, and sent a second man on the run without raising suspicion with anyone in law enforcement seems ridiculous. Do Gale's friends and colleagues not see that he is obsessed with becoming a martyr? Adversaries of the death penalty come across, here, as a group of fanatics, whose lives are a mess and have no other purpose than to sacrifice themselves on the altar of capital punishment. Before deciding to forfeit his life to the hangman, David Gale might have benefited from a screening of *Monster's Ball* to make clear the costs his death would incur, a cost no half-million dollars could salve.

Moreover, the scenes of Harraway's suicide venture into the realm of snuff films. While one can applaud Laura Linney's very courageous and powerful performance,[71] the picture of her writhing naked on the floor with a plastic bag taped over her head and her hands cuffed behind her back while she asphyxiates is overly long and unnecessarily graphic. The videotape recording her suicide surfaces several times during the film and is played repeatedly for the edification of various characters. Of course, each time a character views the tape the audience is exposed to it again as well. Is it intended to drive home the heinousness of Gale's presumed crime or to shock audiences with Constance's sacrifice to the cause? One wonders what fascination the snuff footage

holds for director Alan Parker, especially, as one reviewer pointed out, when Bloom reenacts the murder/suicide and moviegoers view her thrashing, handcuffed on the floor with a bag covering her face.[72] In addition, the supposedly hard-nosed, driven Bitsy Bloom and her intern seem incapable of putting two clues together. Gale manipulates her from the outset and, famous and intelligent as she is, Bloom cannot see that Gale is using her for his own purposes, despite him dropping numerous hints. As a conscientious reporter Bloom would have searched out Gale's published works and likely seen in them a telegraphing of Constance's death and the outlines of the conspiracy. What took them so long to determine the identity of an enigmatic cowboy who listened to *Turandot* (a hint unto itself) in his pickup? And when yet another copy of the videotape, conveniently marked "off the record," turns up after Gale's execution, revealing that Gale was not framed after all but fully took part in the scheme to bring about his demise, Bloom cannot possibly remain silent and maintain any semblance of journalistic integrity.[73]

While *The Life of David Gale* spares audiences the usual march to the death chamber and multiple views inside it as the condemned man expires, it also spares viewers an intelligent plot. By his own admission, Parker stands firmly against capital punishment and hoped to provoke debate with his film[74] and he put together a first-class group of actors, who generally speaking gave good performances, but any serious attempt to address capital punishment is lost in a manipulative plot. Several reviews of the movie mentioned that it unintentionally offers more support to the pro-death-penalty advocates than it does to those who oppose it as it portrays dedicated activism being only for "crazed zealots."[75] One point the film does drive home: the flaws within the halls of justice know no limits if these emotionally troubled people can concoct and implement a plan, so obvious and deliberate in its intent, to subvert the system. The ease with which people can undermine and maneuver the justice system might be the more important and worthwhile point that lies below the surface of Parker's film, whether he intended that to be its mission or not. With a system so easily subverted by those who intend to discredit it, imagine the errors, oversights, negligence, and carelessness that take place without malice or deliberate exploitation. While acknowledging that the film placed the death penalty in its crosshairs and incorporates the new abolitionist approach, it is very tempting to suggest that *The Life of David Gale* does not consider its subject with any real gravity. Rather its desire to be a thriller, and a manipulative one at that, outweighs its need to treat capital punishment with the seriousness it deserves.

Conclusion

Over the last one hundred years, filmmakers have endeavored to create images for the screen that might inform and influence audiences about the role capital punishment plays in our society. Hollywood directors often genuinely try to construct an end product that deplores the death penalty, but sometimes their efforts fall short of their objectives. In failing to achieve their goal it does not necessarily follow, as Austin Sarat states, that they push a culturally conservative agenda and inadvertently bolster those who support capital punishment. Naturally, any film generates numerous opinions about its relative merits and flaws, both from the standpoint of the technical aspects of filmmaking, and its storyline and underlying themes. Opinions concerning a film can vary widely, from deplorable to sublime, and encompass a whole gamut of possible factors. Nowhere is this disparity more evident than among death penalty movies, likely because so much rides on

their persuasive power. Especially since the late 1970s, capital punishment in the United States has been a hotly debated, highly controversial topic and its depiction in American cinema falls under the same scrutiny as the punishment itself. Film critics, legal scholars, and film historians all weigh in with their varied opinions, but one thing becomes abundantly clear in the discussions about the mission and effectiveness of death penalty movies, a critic's viewpoint depends very much on his or her political ideology, social assumptions, religious beliefs, and cultural perspective. Where one stands in the capital punishment debate and which abolitionist arguments (old or new) most sway a person also determines one's perception of a movie purporting to oppose the death penalty.

With judgments abounding, and despite any individual strengths and weaknesses, Hollywood portrayals of capital punishment offer a decidedly mixed record. Early films of the silent era established some of the stock characters and plots which later films would continue to mimic, particularly the race-to-save-the-innocent-man storyline. If these films projected an early anti-death-penalty theme, the cinematic creations of the 1930s incorporated a different sensibility and premise. Depression-era movies took the state's power to put transgressors to death for granted and only in the most subtle terms can they be interpreted to oppose capital punishment. Films of the 1950s grappled with the issue head-on in *I Want to Live!* and *Compulsion.* The former exposed a legal system that convicts a person on insufficient evidence and tactics of entrapment—a conviction based more on who someone is than the commission of a wrongful act—and the power of the press to influence the outcome of a trial. The persuasive force of the media also rears its head in the latter film, but the impassioned humanist plea of the defense lawyer leaves no doubt about its abolitionist intentions. By the mid-1960s the attitudes of Hollywood productions toward capital punishment shifted again. *In Cold Blood* stands as the only film of the Vietnam War period to address the death penalty, and its position remains decidedly ambivalent.[76]

Another fifteen years would elapse before Hollywood ventured into the world of the execution chamber again and this time with a comedy.[77] Capital punishment in *My Cousin Vinny* lurks ever present in the background, menacing the lives of two youths who are guilty of no more than unintentionally pilfering a can of tuna. Director Jonathan Lynne underlines that the real threat lies in a legal system that, even when it works as it should, makes grievous errors and can potentially end the lives of innocent people. Other films of the 1990s seemed confused about their motives, contradicted their anti-death-penalty position or became distracted by other scenarios. While state sanctioned executions loomed in the settings of these films, directors often shied away from confronting the complex issues directly. Here, *Murder in the First, Last Dance, The Chamber, The Green Mile*, and *True Crime* prove instructive. But despite their flaws they do speak, if in muted and sometimes muddied tones, to some of the issues that bear on capital punishment. In the midst of this spat of films came *Dead Man Walking*, a serious, powerful, and thought-provoking film which examined the death penalty from numerous sides and posed the question whether we as a society are willing to show compassion even to those people guilty of the heinous crime of murder. Its strong religious component made the film provocative as well. While the other films awkwardly insist on a single capital punishment position, *Dead Man Walking*'s genius lies in its willingness to allow audiences come to their own conclusions, to provoke thought and discussion, not to dictate what viewers should think.

The parade of death penalty films continued its march in the early years of the 2000s, but *Monster's Ball* stood out with distinction because it adopted a very different focus: it highlighted the emotional costs of the death penalty for those who carry it out and for those left widowed and orphaned by it. Other films of the 2000s, specifically *The Life of David Gale*, proved to be manipulative and frustrating, leaving some spectators feeling betrayed and offended. Biographical films about Truman Capote's life also spawned a renewed interest in his masterpiece, *In Cold Blood*, and led to additional cinematic treatments of the hangings of Perry Smith and Dick Hickock. While the results proved mixed, *Capote* imbued its content with a stronger anti-death-penalty message than *Infamous*.

With Hollywood productions yielding such mixed results and offering sometimes contradictory messages, the medium does do some things quite well. In terms of telling individual stories of death row inmates viewers can identify with, films are at their best and, contrary to Austin Sarat's claim, not necessarily culturally conservative. As long as convicts remain nameless and faceless, society can continue to see them as monsters, as animals beyond our comprehension, beyond the reach of our compassion. Hollywood productions possess the capacity to individualize those incarcerated for a capital crime, to make them "real" people with serious problems, with haunting issues, who grew up in horrible circumstances that have landed them in prison with an axe hanging over their heads. Movies permit audience members to begin to identify with the "beast." Given the right set of conditions and circumstances, that animal could potentially be one of us. But, as Sarat asserts, these films also tend to hinge on accepting responsibility for misdeeds. Moviegoers can better identify with a repellant character like a Matthew Poncelet or a Sam Cayhall if the prisoner expresses contrition, accepting that they did something terribly wrong which caused others harm and pain. Sarat maintains that this act of repentance allows society to assign blame and, therefore, punishment with a clear conscience. In this respect, he makes a salient point. Nicole Rafter, a scholar of criminal justice and crime films, affirms that movies about crime can project a radical critique of the prison system, for example, while at the same time offering a more conservative perspective that reinforces institutions of social control.[78] This contradictory element is exactly what makes crime films so attractive to such a wide audience. But where Sarat acknowledges only the conservative reading of execution films, I see both the more radical implications of these films and their more subtly conventional position. Does holding someone responsible for their homicidal acts necessarily mean they must pay with their lives? Even if we do not execute murderers, we still hold them responsible and separate them from the rest of society. Sarat's more relevant point is that assigning blame to an individual relieves society of its role, and perhaps its guilt, in molding someone into a killer and fostering the circumstances that further criminal behavior.[79]

It would be interesting to see a silver-screen production in which the condemned communicates no remorse. How would movie spectators feel about such a person? Viewers could certainly get a sense of an inmate's humanity through the eyes of the devoted friend, such as Rick Hayes or Sister Helen. Learning about the life history of a criminal and the social factors that shaped him can illicit empathy as well. Can we remain indifferent to someone who suffered from parental neglect, experienced physical or sexual abuse, grew up in grinding poverty, became addicted to drugs, endured mental illness, or faced society's repeated rejection? Such mitigating factors surely call us to show mercy and compassion rather than impose the harshest punishment of the state.

On a lighter note, another trend seems likely to continue: actresses tapped to star in death penalty films will probably keep garnering Academy Award nominations for their roles and more than a few will carry home the coveted statuette. Halle Barry, Susan Sarandon, Marisa Tomei, Charlize Theron, and Susan Hayward all took home Oscars for their portrayals of women caught up with the death penalty. Among the male actors, only Philip Seymour Hoffman captured a Best Actor award for his depiction of Truman Capote, although Catherine Keener received a nomination for best supporting role in *Capote* as well. James Cagney and Sean Penn have been the only other men nominated for an Oscar in the Best Actor category, while Michael Clarke Duncan received a Best Supporting Actor nomination from the Academy of Motion Picture Arts and Sciences. Directors of capital punishment films have made the nomination cut as well—Michael Curtiz, Robert Wise, Richard Brooks, and Tim Robbins—but none have won. Among the Best Picture nods, only *The Green Mile* has earned a nomination but lost to *American Beauty*.

No matter the results at the box office, on Oscar night, or in the movie critics' columns, Hollywood filmmakers will continue to produce movies dealing with themes of capital punishment. With state executions hidden from the gaze of the general public, directors will persist in pointing their cameras into the death chambers which populate such films and satisfy our morbid curiosity, but therein lies a danger. Sarat makes a valid point in underscoring that cinematic depictions of the cool procedural process of putting the condemned to death may well "domesticate state killing." Becoming familiar with images of executions gives us the false impression that we can know and understand the costs involved, that we can assess the consequences of the death penalty.[80] It threatens to inure viewers to the horrors of so calculatedly taking a life while simultaneously allowing audiences to disassociate themselves from the image. Celluloid versions of hangings, gassings, or lethal injections may provide us with a glimpse into the shrouded world of state-sanctioned killing, but too many such frames remind us that no matter how realistic a portrayal, in the end, it is only a movie. We risk becoming indifferent to the image of an execution, to the price paid by the condemned, by his family, by his victim's loved ones, by guards who carry out these sentences, and by society as a whole.

All of these readings of films and the attempts to dissect their perspectives and meanings beg the question, what kind of death penalty movies should Hollywood be making? Here moviemakers need to be careful that the resultant film squares with the director's intentions. Many a filmmaker hopes to make some unequivocal statement against capital punishment but ends up with a final product that dilutes the message or sends a very different one. Often directors and writers seem to believe that audiences must always identify with someone innocent. Films are such a powerful medium that there should be ways to encourage audience identification with the guilty. Placing an innocent person on death row says that it is fundamentally wrong to kill *this* blameless person, but additionally suggests that there is nothing wrong with capital punishment otherwise. If it is wrong to kill, an act for which we imprison and execute people, is it not also wrong to give the government the power to kill in the name of society?[81]

The traditional dichotomy of crime and punishment needs to be reframed. It is in this very effort to reframe the two sides of the coin that Hollywood can inject the socioeconomic factors that contribute to violent crime and keep us from facing the ways in which our racial consciousness perpetuates prejudice and discrimination and the institutions that uphold them. To maintain any semblance of credibility in the future, Hollywood producers and directors must make their films reflect the racial and ethnic makeup of the current death row prison population. Without seriously addressing why an excessively large number of African Americans or Hispanics sit in prison waiting to die, filmmakers cannot possibly hope to make movies that have anything of substance to say about American justice. That *True Crime* and *The Green Mile*[82] are the only two execution movies with condemned African Americans as substantial characters marks movie producers as blind, insensitive, or fainthearted.

In addition, directors need to be clear about who they are trying to save from the gallows with their films, the innocent or the guilty. By presenting moviegoers with a person wrongly convicted, films make a fallacious argument because no one wishes to see the blameless sent to their demise. Even the pro-death-penalty camp hopes to avoid the execution of the innocent even as they acknowledge that killing the occasional guiltless person is the price of doing business. What movies about an innocent individual point out is how very vulnerable our justice system is to mistakes and discrimination, how capricious and random, how unreliable. In such a system how sure can we be that the wheels of justice treat people equally and fairly? How can we know with any degree of certainty that we are putting the guilty to the sword in a legal system so fraught with error and ambiguity? However, by gibbeting the blameworthy filmmakers probe a different but related subject: Do we want to endow our state and federal governments with the power of putting its citizens to death? It goes without saying that society wants to preserve the lives of the innocent. Are we equally willing to preserve the lives of the guilty in spite of their breaking society's most inviolable taboo? Films, while usually focusing on a specific case and whether the death penalty should apply, should be asking whether the government should be in the business of executing anyone at all, innocent or guilty. In short, more complex, more nuanced films need to be made, but whether they will draw audiences and bring in box office receipts remains to be seen.

In all these discussions concerning capital punishment films, the missing element is whether Hollywood movies have any real impact on the public's view of the death penalty. Although Sean O'Sullivan began to address that issue, assessing the impact of a film proves rather difficult.[83] Even tracking its popularity, the revenues it brings in, or the number of times a DVD goes out the door of a rental establishment does not get at how audience members interpret a film and whether it has an impact on their perception of a controversial issue. One cannot help but wonder if anyone other than movie reviewers and scholars of film, popular culture, and/or the law scrutinize the images they see on the screen in any significant depth. Does the average moviegoer feel inclined to probe and dissect a film's meaning, or are they likely to walk away with the message the director intended to convey?

While new abolitionist arguments against capital punishment may carry the day at some point in the future, older arguments about the sanctity of life, cruel and unusual punishment, or the right to life and the films about them need not be thrown out all together. Furthermore, opposition to capital punishment based on religious or humanist positions may not be foolproof, but in a land of predominately Christian believers the religious approach should not be dismissed out of hand by abolitionists or filmmakers. It is no accident that *Dead Man Walking*, with its religious themes, stirred so much discussion, garnered so much attention, and earned so much praise. Certainly conservative Old Testament arguments can be mustered to support the death penalty, but many individuals are still moved to contest the death penalty on religious grounds, as *Dead Man Walking* so eloquently attests. While plenty of disagreement exists surrounding the highly contentious subject, including Hollywood's depiction of it, one cannot help but embrace Austin Sarat's desire to move the debate away from the question of what the death penalty does *for* us as a society and move it toward what capital punishment does *to* us and our society.[84] Movies remain fruitful ground to explore all the questions related to the death penalty and its application in our society provided filmmakers tend their soil conscientiously, thoughtfully, and courageously.

Susanne Gaskins specializes in modern United States and European history with a special emphasis on the U.S. Home Front during World War II especially as it relates to women, industry, and the West. Her wide-ranging interests include research about nurses' roles in the U.S. military in the twentieth century and their fight for inclusion and equality within the military structure. Nearly a California native, she received her Ph.D. from the University of California, Riverside, and has spent more than twenty years teaching history as an adjunct at Southern California's various community colleges, private universities, and at California State University, Fullerton.

Suggested Readings

American Film Institute. "Robert Wise: American Filmmaker—I Want to Live, 1958"; accessed 23 Jan. 2008; available from www.afi.com/wise/films/i_want_to_live/iwant.html.

Anderson, Christopher P. *A Star, Is a Star, Is a Star: The Lives and Loves of Susan Hayward*. Garden City, N.Y.: Doubleday and Company, Inc., 1980.

Bingham, Dennis. "'I Do Want to Live!' Female Voices, Male

Discourse, and the Hollywood Biopic." *Cinema Journal* 38, no. 3 (Spring 1999): 3–26.

Brownlow, Kevin. *Behind the Mask of Innocence. Sex, Violence, Prejudice, Crime: Films of Social Conscience in the Silent Era.* Berkeley: University of California Press, 1992.

Byrge, Duane, and Gregg Kilday. "Wise Had 'a Special Gift.'" *Hollywood Reporter* 16 Sept. 2005 [online newspaper]; accessed 28 Jan. 2008; available from Factiva.

Canuel, Mark. *The Shadow of Death: Literature, Romanticism, and the Subject of Punishment.* Princeton: Princeton University Press, 2007.

Chase, Anthony. *Movies on Trial: The Legal System on the Silver Screen.* New York: The New Press, 2002.

Corcos, Christine A. "Capital Punishment in Popular Culture." Law and Humanities Website, Louisiana State University Law Center; accessed 1 Jan. 2008; available from http://faculty.law.lsu.edu/ccorcos/lawhum/CAPITALPUNISHMENT.htm.

Dow, David R. "Fictional Documentaries and Truthful Fictions: The Death Penalty in Recent American Films." *Constitutional Commentary* 17, no. 3 (Winter 2000): 511–54.

Ebert, Roger. Review of *Dead Man Walking* (PolyGram). *Chicago Sun-Times*, 12 Jan. 1996 [online newspaper]; accessed 31 Dec. 2007; available from http://rogerebert.suntimes.com/apps/pbcs.dll/article?AID=/19960112/REVIEWS/601120301/1023.

Foster, Teree E. "*I Want to Live!* Federal Judicial Values in Death Penalty Cases: Preservation of Rights of Punctuality of Execution?" *Oklahoma City University Law Review* 22, no. 1 (1997): 63–87 [article online]; (Law in Popular Culture Collection, Jamail Center for Legal Research, Tarlton Law Library, The University of Texas School of Law); accessed 2 Jan. 2008 available from http://tarlton.law.utexas.edu/lpop/etext/okla/foster22.htm.

Gillespie, Kay L. *Dancehall Ladies: Executed Women of the 20th Century.* Revised edition. Lanham, Md.: University Press of America, 2000.

Goldberg, Stephanie B. "Walking the Last Mile, on Film." *New York Times* 24 Dec. 1995, H6, H29.

Harding, Roberta M. "Celluloid Death: Cinematic Depictions of Capital Punishment." *University of San Francisco Law Review* 30, no. 4 (1996): 1167–79 [article online]; (Law in Popular Culture Collection, Jamail Center for Legal Research, Tarlton Law Library, The University of Texas School of Law); accessed 2 Jan. 2008; available from http://tarlton.law.utexas.edu/lpop/etext/usf/harding30.htm.

Hess, Peter E., and Maria F. Hess. "Law Reviews: Hollywood Capitalizes on Capital Punishment." *Delaware Lawyer* 21, no. 4 (Winter 2003/2004): 28, 26 [journal online]; accessed 3 February 2008; available from http://delawarebarfoundation.org/delawyer/Volume21_Number4_Winter2003-2004.pdf.

Johnson, Brian D. "Murderous States." *Maclean's* 109, no. 4 (22 Jan. 1996): 62.

Keough, Peter. "Death at the Box Office: Hollywood Makes Movie Capital out of the Ultimate Punishment." *The Boston Phoenix*, 8 December 1997 [online newspaper]; accessed 1 Jan. 2008; available from http://weeklywire.com/ww/12-08-97/boston_movies_1.html.

Kreisler, Harry. Conversations with History. "The Wise Touch: Conversation with Robert Wise." Part 6—Wise Films: *I Want to Live!* (Institute of International Studies at the University of California at Berkeley); 28 Feb. 1998; accessed 26 Jan. 2008; available from http://globetrotter.berkeley.edu/conversations/Wise/wise-con6.html.

Lesser, Wendy. *Pictures at an Execution.* Cambridge: Harvard University Press, 1993.

Levi, Ross D. *The Celluloid Courtroom: A History of Legal Cinema.* Westport, Conn.: Praeger Publishers, 2005.

Linet, Beverly. *Susan Hayward: Portrait of a Survivor.* New York: Atheneum, 1980.

Molloy, Patricia. "Face to Face with the Dead Man: Ethical Responsibility, State-Sanctioned Killing, and Empathetic Impossibility." *Alternatives* 22, no. 4 (Oct.–Dec. 1997): 467–92.

Lucia, Cynthia. *Framing Female Lawyers: Women on Trial in Film.* Austin: University of Texas Press, 2005.

Morris, Wesley. "Eastwood Does Oakland AH: He Plays East Bay Reporter in 'True Crime,' which Fails to Probe Justice Issues—or Anything Else—Seriously." Review of *True Crime* (Warner Bros. Pictures). *San Francisco Examiner*, 19 March 1999 [online newspaper] accessed 17 February 2008; available from http://www.sfgate.com/cgi-bin/article.cgi?f=/e/a/1999/03/19/WEEKEND3645.dtl.

O'Shea, Kathleen A. *Women and the Death Penalty in the United States.* Westport, Conn.: Praeger Publishers, 1999.

O'Sullivan, Sean. "Representing 'The Killing State': The Death Penalty in Nineties Hollywood Cinema." *The Howard Journal of Criminal Justice* 42, no. 5 (December 2003): 485–503.

Papke, David Ray. "Law, Cinema, and Ideology: Hollywood Legal Films of the 1950s." *UCLA Law Review* 48, no. 6 (2001): 1473–93 [article online]; (Law in Popular Culture Collection, Jamail Center for Legal Research, Tarlton Law Library, The University of Texas School of Law); accessed 2 Jan. 2008 available from http://tarlton.law.utexas.edu/lpop/etext/ucla/papke48.htm.

Rafter, Nicole. *Shots in the Mirror: Crime Films and Society.* 2nd ed. New York: Oxford University Press, 2006.

Randall, Kate. "Films Probe the Death Penalty: What Messages Do They Convey?" *The International Workers Bulletin*, 1 July 1995 [online newspaper]; accessed 31 Dec. 2007; available from http://www.wsws.org/public_html/prioriss/iwb7-1/film.htm.

Russell, Catherine. *Narrative Morality: Death, Closure, and New Wave Cinemas.* Minneapolis: University of Minnesota Press, 1995.

Sarat, Austin. "The Cultural Life of Capital Punishment: Responsibility and Representation in *Dead Man Walking* and *Last Dance*." *Yale Journal of Law and the Humanities* 11, no. 1 (Winter 1999): 153–90.

———. "Death Row, Aisle Seat." *The American Prospect*, 20 Nov. 2002 [magazine online]; accessed 31 Dec. 2007; available from http://www.prospect.org/cs/articles?article=death_row_aisle_seat.

———, ed. *The Killing State: Capital Punishment in Law, Politics, and Culture*. New York: Oxford University Press, 1999.

———. *When the State Kills: Capital Punishment and the American Condition*. Princeton, N.J.: Princeton University Press, 2001.

Sarat, Austin, and Christian Boulanger, eds. *The Cultural Lives of Capital Punishment: Comparative Perspectives*. Stanford: Stanford University Press, 2005.

Sarat, Austin, Lawrence Douglass, and Martha Merrill Umphrey, eds. *Law on the Screen*. Stanford: Stanford University Press, 2005.

Shapiro, Carole. "Do or Die: Does *Dead Man Walking* Run?" *University of San Francisco Law Review* 30, no. 4 (1996): 1143–66 [article online]; (Law in Popular Culture Collection, Jamail Center for Legal Research, Tarlton Law Library, The University of Texas School of Law); accessed 2 Jan. 2008; available from http://tarlton.law.utexas.edu/lpop/etext/usf/shapiro30.htm.

Shipman, Marlin. *"The Penalty Is Death": U.S. Newspaper Coverage of Women's Executions*. Columbia: University of Missouri Press, 2002.

Sklar, Robert. *Movie-Made America: A Cultural History of American Movies*. New York: Vintage Press, 1975.

Tonry, Michael. *Malign Neglect: Race, Crime and Punishment in America*. New York: Oxford University Press, 1995.

Tyler, Louise. "Crime and Punishment/Self Versus Other: The Cultural Life of Capital Punishment in European and American Film." In *The Cultural Lives of Capital Punishment: Comparative Perspectives*, ed. Austin Sarat and Christian Boulanger, 129–46. Stanford: Stanford University Press, 2005.

Walker, Samuel, Cassia Spohn, and Miriam DeLone. *The Color of Justice: Race, Ethnicity and Crime in America*. 3rd ed. Belmont, Calif.: Wadsworth-Thomson Learning, 2004.

Wilson, David, and Sean O'Sullivan. *Images of Incarceration: Representations of Prison in Film and Television Drama*. Winchester, UK: Waterside Press, 2004.

Notes

1. I have chosen to focus my discussion on Hollywood's big-screen productions rather than made-for-television movies and shows created for the television market. To even attempt the inclusion of television movies would demand a book-length work. Certainly their inclusion would be worthwhile in the future. In addition, future inquiries might focus on the differences between film and television productions in dealing with capital punishment and which medium proves more effective in getting its point across. Another fruitful avenue might be a comparison between European/international and American films.

   I opted to avoid certain film genres although the death penalty and executions are part of those types of movies. I decided against the inclusion of westerns, science fiction, or war films. I also excluded documentaries, foreign films, and historical dramas with the exception of *The Green Mile* (1999). My justification for these choices stems from an attempt to limit the size of the study and not confuse the discussion by mixing genres.

2. William Wellman, dir., *The Public Enemy*, with James Cagney, Jean Harlow, and Edward Woods, Warner Bros. (1931).

3. See especially the introductory chapter of Austin Sarat, Lawrence Douglass, and Martha Merrill Umphrey, eds., *Law on the Screen* (Stanford: Stanford University Press, 2005); Cynthia Lucia, *Framing Female Lawyers: Women on Trial in Film* (Austin: University of Texas Press, 2005) concentrates particularly on images of female lawyers in the Hollywood films of the 1980s and 1990s; Ross D. Levi, *The Celluloid Courtroom: A History of Legal Cinema* (Westport, Conn.: Praeger Publishers, 2005); Anthony Chase, *Movies on Trial: The Legal System on the Silver Screen* (New York: The New Press, 2002) attempts to expand the definition of the legal film beyond the courtroom drama and legal thriller to include the entire legal system; another rich source of information can be found in the Law in Popular Culture Collection of the Tarlton Law Library at the University of Texas at Austin School of Law, accessible online at http://tarlton.law.utexas.edu/lpop/index.html.

4. There are few items upon which scholars of death-penalty films can agree. One argument focuses on whether capital punishment movies constitute a sub-genre of the legal drama films and, second, whether within the subgenre there exist further categories. Austin

Sarat suggests one such category, the "injustice tale," concerning the innocent person on death row. At least the inmate's guilt remains questionable, and a terrible miscarriage of justice will occur if the authorities carry out the capital sentence. His other category, the "sentimental" tale, takes a more biographical approach and focuses on individual responsibility and repentance.

While no scholar has made a definitive case for a death penalty or execution film genre, I think a good case could be made that such a thing exists. I would argue that execution films make up a subgenre of crime films and possess certain stock characters (the condemned man or woman and a person outside the prison system trying to save the convict) and standard plots (racing to save the wrongfully condemned person or attempting to redeem the guilty) and plot devices (films almost never forgo an execution scene). While my speculation here is far from complete, it does hint at the likelihood that such a subgenre can be justified.

Austin Sarat, "Death Row, Aisle Seat," *The American Prospect*, 20 November 2002 [magazine online]; accessed 31 Dec. 2007; available from http://www.prospect.org/cs/articles?article=death_row_aisle_seat; Sarat refines these categories somewhat in his book, *When the State Kills: Capital Punishment and the American Condition* (Princeton, N.J.: Princeton University Press, 2001), n. 7, 305; for an opposing viewpoint see Sean O'Sullivan, "Representing 'The Killing State': The Death Penalty in Nineties Hollywood Cinema," *The Howard Journal of Criminal Justice* 42 (December 2003): 490–91. He sees the death penalty films less as a genre and more of a loose cycle of films. See also Nicole Rafter, *Shots in the Mirror: Crime Films and Society* (New York: Oxford University Press, 2006), 163–85.

5. Using the phrases "death penalty movies" or "capital punishment films" in a search engine will yield some lists of films widely considered to be death penalty works. I found a British website run by sociologist Sean O'Sullivan, the Prison Film Project (www.prisonfilmproject.com), quite helpful but since having begun this article the website has become defunct. Researchers can still refer to O'Sullivan's published works. Also the Pew Forum on Religion and Public Life supplies a listing of death penalty filmography with a brief synopsis of each at http://pewforum.org/deathpenalty/resources/filmography.php.

6. Patty Jenkins, dir., *Monster*, with Charlize Theron, Christina Ricci, and Bruce Dern (Media 8 Entertainment, 2003).

7. Aileen Wuornos has since been executed by lethal injection by the State of Florida in October 2002.

8. Moviegoers are not encouraged to identify with the criminal, but with the person who has stayed within the bounds of acceptable social behavior. In essence she says that American film is all about the dichotomy between good and evil, between the good self, which we as viewers identify with, and the bad other, which can only be dealt with through violence. The bad other gets what it deserves and society and the good self are safe once again. It is all about a cultural mythology that we all buy into and it desensitizes us to violence and makes us willing to accept the role of the state as executioner for the bad other. European films draw a less distinct line between self and other, between good and bad. Louise Tyler, "Crime and Punishment/Self Versus Other: The Cultural Life of Capital Punishment in European and American Film," in *The Cultural Lives of Capital Punishment: Comparative Perspectives*, ed. Austin Sarat and Christian Boulanger (Stanford: Stanford University Press, 2005), 142–43.

9. For basic movie reviews of nearly all the films under consideration, I have relied heavily on the invaluable Internet Movie Database (IMDb), accessible from http://www.imdb.com/. For each film in the database there exists an external link that takes you to an often long list of links to online reviews. In addition there is a link to newsgroup reviews (online). Reviews of the more modern films are so numerous that I have not listed each one I examined in the bibliography or footnotes unless I directly used material from it. I frequently explored the online reviews to get a feel for what critics were saying about a film when it was first released. In addition, IMDb provides nearly endless information about a film from its company credits to awards it was nominated for or won. It is a wonderful resource for exploring movies.

10. In one simple example, Roberta Harding suggests that the often bright lighting used in *Dead Man Walking* is a symbol of hope, while the director, Tim Robbins stated that he wanted to create a contrast between the bright, beautiful day outside and the ominous events impending inside the prison. Roberta M. Harding, "Celluloid Death: Cinematic Depictions of Capital Punishment," *University of San Francisco Law Review* 30 (1996): 1175, and n. 28; and Tim Robbins, dir., "Director's Commentary," *Dead Man Walking*, MGM Home Entertainment, DVD, 2000.

11. Often these discussions intertwine: lawyers opposed to the death penalty; filmmakers voicing their objections to capital punishment; film reviewers opposed to the death penalty; moviegoers critiquing Hollywood's capital punishment films.

12. Most of the silent films of the 1910s and 1920s are currently not available to the public. Many of them have either been lost altogether or are being rediscovered in archives and private collections. I have relied heavily on film historian Kevin Brownlow's interesting and detailed work about social thought films of the silent movie period. Kevin Brownlow, *Behind the Mask of Innocence. Sex, Violence, Prejudice, Crime: Films of*

Social Conscience in the Silent Era (Berkeley: University of California Press, 1992), 255–59.

13. Ibid., 259.

14. Ibid., 260–61.

15. The juvenile delinquents were played by the "Dead End Kids."

16. Sklar, Robert, *Movie-Made America: A Cultural History of American Movies* (New York: Vintage Press, 1975), 173–74.

17. Michael Curtiz, dir., "Special Feature, 'Whaddya hear? Whaddya say?'" *Angels with Dirty Faces*, Warner Home Video, DVD, 2005. The special feature discusses numerous aspects of the making of the film, including the careers of its stars and the director.

18. Dennis Bingham, "'I Do Want to Live!': Female Voices, Male Discourse, and the Hollywood Biopic," *Cinema Journal* 38 (Spring 1999): 18. See also Teree E. Foster, "*I Want to Live!* Federal Judicial Values in Death Penalty Cases: Preservation of Rights of Punctuality of Execution?" *Oklahoma City University Law Review* 22 (1997): 64, n. 3.

19. Wanger and Wise made Graham's character more palatable for audiences by reducing the number of children she had (three) and dispensing with her supposed drug use. Bingham, "'I Do Want to Live!'" 16.

20. The type of entrapment used by the police officer, ironically named Ben Miranda, to secure Graham's guilty verdict predates the Supreme Court's Miranda ruling of 1966 defining acceptable police procedure and spelling out the rights of the person in police custody. In particular, see Foster, "*I Want to Live!*" 69–74.

21. Bingham, "'I Do Want to Live!'" 9, 19.

22. On this point, see also Foster, "*I Want to Live!*" 66.

23. See also Bingham, "'I Do Want to Live!'" 6, 19.

24. American Film Institute, "Robert Wise: American Filmmaker—I Want to Live, 1958"; accessed 23 Jan. 2008; available from www.afi.com/wise/films/i_want_to_live/iwant.html.

25. St. Jude is the patron saint of lost causes.

26. Foster, "*I Want to Live!*" 67. Foster's article is less about the film than about the Graham case and how Supreme Court rulings, both under Chief Justice Earl Warren and more recent chief justices, would have affected her conviction.

27. Ibid., 68–69.

28. American Film Institute, "Robert Wise: American Filmmaker"; Harry Kreisler, Conversations with History, "The Wise Touch: Conversation with Robert Wise," Part 6—Wise Films: *I Want to Live!* (Institute of International Studies at the University of California at Berkeley); 28 Feb. 1998; accessed 26 Jan. 2008; available from http://globetrotter.berkeley.edu/conversations/Wise/wise-con6.html. The producer of *I Want to Live!*, Walter Wanger, felt quite strongly about making a film indicting prisons and capital punishment. In 1952 the producer spent nearly four months in jail for a crime of passion; he shot and wounded his wife's lover in a restaurant parking lot. He came away from his prison experience determined to expose the injustices of the judicial system and to resurrect his movie-making career. *I Want to Live!*, with its six Academy Award nominations, did the job nicely. Bingham, "'I Do Want to Live!'" 7–8.

29. According to Beverly Linet, after considerable research Hayward concluded that Graham was at the scene of the crime but did not bludgeon the victim, but that one of the other defendants did so. Christopher Anderson, another biographer of Hayward, writes that although the movie "was a searing indictment of capital punishment," Hayward did not become a convert to the abolitionist cause as a result of her work on the film. Beverly Linet, *Susan Hayward: Portrait of a Survivor* (New York, Atheneum, 1980), 222; Christopher P. Anderson, *A Star, Is a Star, Is a Star: The Lives and Loves of Susan Hayward* (Garden City, N.Y.: Doubleday and Company, Inc., 1980), 190–91.

The Los Angeles Police Department tried to persuade Wise to drop the film. The LAPD accused Wise of making a mockery of the case by portraying Graham as innocent. American Film Institute, "Robert Wise: American Filmmaker."

30. Kathleen A. O'Shea, *Women and the Death Penalty in the United States* (Westport, Conn.: Praeger Publishers, 1999), 70–71.

31. Bingham makes the point that the promotional materials for the film claimed that Graham cared deeply about her appearance and the movie accurately reflects Graham's fashions and makeup. True to life or not, Susan Hayward looks stunning as Graham in both grooming and style; modern audiences cannot help but wonder if Hollywood and/or Hayward did not add an extra layer of glamour to the role. Bingham, "'I Do Want to Live!'" 10–11.

32. Later Perry tells Dick that he killed the man in Las Vegas by beating him with a bicycle chain. Yet as Perry relates the Clutter crime to Agent Dewey, he reveals that he never killed anyone before the Clutter murders. It was just a boastful story he told Dick; Perry knew all along that should they get arrested Dick would spill his guts to the authorities.

33. The film reveals that Hickock has fathered children with two different women. As he plans the burglary and murder of the Clutter family, he feels no sense of responsibility to his children or their mothers.

34. Bennett Miller, dir., *Capote*, with Philip Seymour Hoffman, Catherine Keener, Chris Cooper and Clifton Collins, Jr., Sony Pictures (2005).

35. Jonathan Lynn, dir., "Director's Commentary," *My Cousin Vinny*, Twentieth Century Fox, DVD, (2000).

36. The prison chaplain is played by Scott Wilson, the

same actor who portrayed Dick Hickock in 1967's *In Cold Blood*.

37. Tim Robbins, dir., "Director's Commentary," *Dead Man Walking*, MGM Home Entertainment, DVD, 2000.

38. Director Tim Robbins goes out of his way to address the cruciform image in his director's commentary on the DVD. The gurney used in the film is a replica of that used in the penal systems of several states employing lethal injection. The image was not intended to draw any cinematic parallels to images of Jesus Christ on the cross. Robbins, "Director's Commentary."

39. Roger Ebert, Review of *Dead Man Walking* (PolyGram), *Chicago Sun-Times*, 12 Jan. 1996 [online newspaper]; accessed 31 Dec. 2007; available from http://rogerebert.suntimes.com/apps/pbcs.dll/article?AID=/19960112/REVIEWS/601120301/1023; Brian D. Johnson, "Murderous States," *Maclean's* 109, no. 4 (22 Jan. 1996): 62; Kate Randall, "Films Probe the Death Penalty: What Messages Do They Convey? *The International Workers Bulletin*, 1 July 1995; accessed 21/31/07 at http://www.wsws.org/public_html/prioriss/iwb7-1/film.htm.

40. Vincent Canby, Janet Maslin, and the Film Critics of the *New York Times*, Peter M. Nichols, ed., *The New York Times Guide to the Best 1000 Movies Ever Made* (New York: Random House, 1999).

41. Austin Sarat, *When the State Kills: Capital Punishment and the American Condition* (Princeton, N.J.: Princeton University Press, 2001), 211–13.

42. Robbins, "Director's Commentary."

43. Carole Shapiro. "Do or Die: Does *Dead Man Walking* Run?" *University of San Francisco Law Review* 30 (1996): 1152–53.

44. Sarat, *When the State Kills*, 214.

45. Ibid., n. 20, 306; Sean O'Sullivan, "Representing 'The Killing State': The Death Penalty in Nineties Hollywood Cinema," *The Howard Journal of Criminal Justice* 42 (December 2003): 489, 492.

46. Shapiro, "Do or Die," 1148–51.

47. Ibid., 1145, 1154.

48. Ibid., 1152–53.

49. Sarat, *When the State Kills*, 234; Shapiro, "Do or Die," 1163–65.

50. Sarat, *When the State Kills*, 234.

51. Robbins gives a long discourse about how sadistic we would consider a person who held someone against their will and told them they would be killed at sometime in the future, but delayed the murder repeatedly. We would consider that person an animal, but it seems perfectly acceptable within the prison system. Robbins, "Director's Commentary."

52. Ibid.

53. Wendy Lesser, author of *Pictures at an Execution*, found herself surprisingly unmoved by *Dead Man Walking* because, by her own admission, she is not religious. Lesser believes that the anti-death penalty approach of the film only resonates with those who hold religious beliefs. I agree that the movie would likely find a better reception among those with religious beliefs, but even those with a more secular outlook can find the film moving. Shapiro, "Do or Die," 1154; see Wendy Lesser, *Pictures at an Execution* (Cambridge: Harvard University Press, 1993), for a discussion about televising executions. Her work focuses on the public television station KQED's 1991 legal campaign to televise an execution at San Quentin State Penitentiary.

54. David R. Dow, "Fictional Documentaries and Truthful Fictions: The Death Penalty in Recent American Films," *Constitutional Commentary* 17 (Winter 2000): 550–51.

55. O'Sullivan, "Representing 'The Killing State,'" 495.

56. Nicole Rafter argues that *Last Dance* merely places a woman convict in a men's prison movie, albeit an execution film; Rafter, *Shots in the Mirror*, 175.

57. Michael Tonry, *Malign Neglect: Race, Crime and Punishment in America* (New York: Oxford University Press, 1995). See especially chapter 8 of Samuel Walker, Cassia Spohn, and Miriam DeLone, *The Color of Justice: Race, Ethnicity and Crime in America*, 3rd ed. (Belmont, Calif.: Wadsworth-Thomson Learning, 2004), which specifically deals with race and the death penalty.

58. Sarat, *When the State Kills*, 218.

59. Raymond J. Barry also played the father of Walter Delacroix in *Dead Man Walking*.

60. The character of Frank Beachum is spelled "Beachum" on the film's website (http://www.truecrimethemovie.com/), but on the Internet Movie Database's web site it is spelled "Beechum." (http://www.imdb.com/title/tto139668/fullcredits). I have opted to adhere to the spelling used on the Warner Brothers' *True Crime* web site.

61. See the *True Crime* website at http://www.truecrimethemovie.com/cmp/fr-links.html.

62. Wesley Morris, Review of *True Crime*, *San Francisco Examiner*, 19 March 1999 [online newspaper]; accessed 17 Feb. 2008 at http://www.sfgate.com/cgi-in/article.cgi?f=/e/a/1999/03/19/WEEKEND3645.dtl.

63. O'Sullivan, "Representing 'The Killing State,'" 493.

64. See the extensive list of external review links in The Internet Movie Database at http://www.imdb.com/title/tto120689/externalreviews.

65. Nick Davis, Review of *The Green Mile* (Warner Bros.), [online]; 10 Jan. 2003, accessed 1 June 2008 at http://www.nicksflickpicks.com/greenmil.html.

66. Here, again, Hollywood filmmakers cannot resist the temptation to commit to film their obsession with the procedures of state-sanctioned executions.

67. Dow, "Fictional Documentaries and Truthful Fictions," 553–54.

68. Sarat makes much the same point; Sarat, *When the State Kills*, 231.

69. Davis, Review of *The Green Mile*.

70. For another critique of the Christian symbolism of *The*

Green Mile, see Mark Canuel, *The Shadow of Death: Literature, Romanticism, and the Subject of Punishment* (Princeton: Princeton University Press, 2007), 171–73.

71. Parker revealed that Linney chose to perform the suicide sequence herself without using a body double. Alan Parker, "Director's Commentary," *The Life of David Gale*, Universal, DVD, 2003.

72. Dennis Lim, "Dead Man Gawking: Dull Heads among Windy Spaces," review of *The Life of David Gale* (Universal), 18 Feb. 2003, *The Village Voice* [online newspaper]; accessed 29 May 2008 at http://www.villagevoice.com/film/0308,1im,41971,20.html.

73. Roger Ebert, Review of *The Life of David Gale*, 21 Feb. 2003, *The Chicago Sun-Times* [online newspaper]; accessed 23 Jan. 2008 at http://rogerebert.suntimes.com/apps/pbcs.dll/article?AID=/20030221REVIEWS/302210304/1023.

74. Parker, "Director's Commentary."

75. Lim, "Dead Man Gawking"; Ebert, Review of *The Life of David Gale*.; Mick LaSalle, "Lack of Mystery Undermines 'David Gale': Muddled Treatise on Death Penalty," 21 Feb. 2003, *San Francisco Chronicle* [online newspaper]; accessed 29 May 2008 at http://www.sfgate.com/cgi-bin/article.cgi?f=/c/a/2003/02/21/DD97953.DTL; Michael Wilmington, "Movie Review, 'The Life of David Gale,'" 19 Feb. 2003, *The Chicago Tribune* [online newspaper]; accessed 29 May 2008 at http://chicago.metromix.com/movies/review/movie-review-the-life/158054/content.

76. The only other film to emerge is John Waters's campy *Female Trouble* in 1975, part of his self-styled "Trash Trilogy." Now cult favorites, his early films explored the limits of good taste and conventional propriety. Although he has moved to the edges of the mainstream, his films still are considered unorthodox.

77. William Friedkin's *Rampage* was finished in 1988 but not released until 1992 as it was caught up in the collapse of De Laurentiis Entertainment Group. It can be classified more as a serial killer film and, according to reviewers, projects a pro-death-penalty stance. The killer's attorney tries to defend him with an insanity plea, which does not carry the death penalty, while the prosecutor maintains the murderer was sane, which could mean his execution. Unfortunately, the film has not been released on home video or DVD. Roger Ebert, Review of *Rampage*, 30 Oct. 1992, *The Chicago Sun-Times* [online newspaper]; accessed 9 June 2008; available from http://rogerebert.suntimes.com/apps/pbcs.dll/article?AID=/19921030/REVIEWS/210300303/1023.

Another comedy that incorporates the death penalty premiered in 1992 and that was Robert Altman's *The Player*. Although the film has been available for a few years on DVD, I did not realize until it was too late that it might qualify for inclusion here.

78. Rafter, *Shots in the Mirror*, 13–14. See also Mark Canuel, *The Shadow of Death: Literature, Romanticism, and the Subject of Punishment* (Princeton: Princeton University Press, 2007), 173–74.

79. Sarat, *When the State Kills*, 232.

80. Ibid., 242.

81. Dow, "Fictional Documentaries and Truthful Fictions," 553–54.

82. Although Charles S. Dutton plays an African American death row inmate, his role is fairly minor in *Last Dance*. Sharon Stone's character, Cindy Liggett, remains the focus of the movie.

83. O'Sullivan, "Representing 'The Killing State,'" 497–99.

84. Sarat, *When the State Kills*, 14.

Part Two

Introduction II

REGIONAL ANALYSIS OF THE DEATH PENALTY

AMERICA DEVELOPED REGIONALLY and much of death penalty practices followed. Regions have histories and much of the literature of state law acknowledges the regional heritage. The essays that follow are regional in nature and develop the most significant themes of death penalty practice in that context.

Regional analysis drew heavy scholarly attention in the 1930s. Michael C. Steiner found that Americans needed a sense of place amid the intense and pervasive fear of rootlessness and disorder during the Great Depression.[1] Scholars of anthropology, geography, history, political science, and sociology turned their analytical pens to regional analysis.[2] Merrill Jensen's *Regionalism in America* (1951) brought regional studies out of depression concerns and to a national scholarly audience.[3] Region was a conceptual construct whether regarded as a geographic area or a cultural unity. It also was a community of people held together by functions and shared values. Most importantly, regional studies as a frame of reference for comparative study of society held the most promise for future scholarship. George B. Tindall writing in 1960 was not as optimistic as Jensen about the future of regionalism, but he found some utility in the enterprise. First, the sectionalism of America suggested by Frederick Jackson Turner held promise in the

study of politics and economics. Second, literary regionalism in American letters was clearly distinct. Finally, sociologists using regionalism as an integrated approach to the analysis of society and culture were on the right track. Those were the limits of utility by Tindall's lights.[4]

The 1970s moved regional studies out of the symposium mode and into the monographic analysis. Raymond D. Gastil's *Cultural Regions of the United States* (1975) identified thirteen major cultural regions in our borders. Specific cultural markers such as religion and voting behavior unified these regions. They also had common social indicators such as crime and educational levels.[5] Yi-Fu Tuan's *Space and Place* (1977) moved the conversation to collective memory in place and time. Tuan offered, "Place is an archive of fond memories and splendid achievements that inspire the present; place is permanent and hence reassuring to man, who sees frailty in himself and chance and flux everywhere."[6] Region was broadly defined and criminal law was part of the analytic matrix.

Scholars firmly founded in regionalism started to narrow the focus to particular regions and call for a "new regionalism." *Regionalism and the Pacific Northwest* (1983) was the product of another symposium and the pens of prominent historians. In particular, Richard Maxwell

Brown's call for a "new regionalism" was focused on personal and family identity telescoped into identity of a region. Brown's two most significant books focused on American crime and violence, *Strain of Violence: Historical Studies of American Violence and Vigilantism* (1975) and *No Duty to Retreat: Violence and Values in American History and Society* (1991). Robin Winks, author of numerous books including *Modus Operandi: An Excursion into Detective Fiction* (1982), argued that regionalism must be studied within a framework of culture, economics, geography, and history. Most importantly, Winks offered that interpretative judgments about cultural characteristics only have validity when compared with other representative regions.[7] Death penalty studies can gain a great deal when set in regional focus.

Tuan's thoughts about personal identity and place, like Richard Maxwell Brown's observation about identity and the identification of region, called for more personal, more cultural research. Barbara Allen and Thomas J. Schlereth's *Sense of Place: American Regional Cultures* (1990) moved in that direction. Its authors adopted folklore methodology to tease out meaning. Stories and memories test regional identity in search of a sense of distinctiveness.[8] Glen E. Lich's anthology, *Regional Studies: The Interplay of Land and People* (1992), focused on similar themes and included linguistics and religion as well as gender in the matrix.[9]

Politics and distinctiveness as a species of representation also is part of regionalism. Edward L. Ayers's *All Over the Map: Rethinking American Regions* (1996) makes clear that regional identities emerged from politics, particularly opposition to the federal government's intrusion into state jurisdiction.[10] Deborah A. Rosen's *American Indians and State Law: Sovereignty, Race, and Citizenship, 1790–1880* (2007) is in agreement. In fact, the states extend their criminal law and the death penalty over the tribes whether on reservations or on state land to 1880. Rosen uses regional analysis as well as state-specific case studies to interpret state action in both criminal and civil cases. Region is a powerful tool of analysis.

The most obvious regions to any student of American History are the North and the South derived from the tragedy of the American Civil War, 1861–1865. The cultures of each region as well as their economies were distinct. The South to 1861 was primarily agrarian and slavery characterized the plantation labor force. For many, slavery and Southern culture were intertwined with state's rights justifications for the "peculiar institution" of slavery. The North shed slavery in the eighteenth century and developed an industrial base tied to world trade. In the early nineteenth century Northern abolitionists organized to rid the country of African slavery. As the regions diverged in this and other significant ways, war resulted. Issues of race and death penalty practices diverged as well. In addition to African slavery, states both north and south extended their criminal jurisdiction over American Indians whether in Indian Country or within a state's boundary.

The Midwest was commonly thought of as the Old Northwest defined by the Northwest Ordinance of 1787. The states of Ohio, Indiana, Illinois, Michigan, and Wisconsin emerged from the Northwest Territory. Minnesota and Iowa, with similar lands and people, became identified with the region. Early emigrants to the region were hardly diverse. For example, Wisconsin until the mid-twentieth century was made up of Norwegians and Germans with Polish enclaves in Milwaukee and African Americans in north Milwaukee neighborhoods. As you read the chapter on the Midwest, note the similarities and differences among the states some of which was determined by the time of settlement and the regional heritage.

Moving on to the Great Plains, emigrants

experienced increased aridity as they moved west. The sea of grass that characterized the Illinois central plain and most of Iowa gave way to vast plains. The forests of Wisconsin and Minnesota gave way to treeless plains in the Dakota Territory. Settlement in villages that seldom developed into major urban centers characterized the Great Plains with a few obvious exceptions like Denver, Colorado. As emigrants looked further west, they saw the Rocky Mountains. In this context they developed law and death penalty practices. As Mark R. Ellis puts it in *Law and Order in Buffalo Bill's Country: Legal Culture and Community on the Great Plains, 1867–1910* (2007), "with a largely homogeneous population, a prosperous economy, and an efficient criminal justice system" the plains did not experience high levels of lethal violence witnessed in other regions.[11] When violence did occur, such as with Charles Starkweather, it was an exceptional event. The 1957–1958 murder rampage in Nebraska, Buffalo Bill's country, horrified a nation and inspired movies such as Terrence Malick's *Badlands* (1974), Quentin Tarantino and Tony Scott's *True Romance* (1993), and Oliver Stone's *Natural Born Killers* (1994). Starkweather went to the electric chair in Nebraska in 1959, and his accomplice, Caril Ann Fugate, was sentenced to life in prison and emerged from prison on parole in 1976. Beyond the movies, Liza Ward's novel *Outside Valentine* focuses on the pair and other couples caught up with "arrested adolescence and emotional paralysis."[12] Starkweather murdered Ward's grandparents. The horror lives on.

Film critic Charles Champlin thinks the horror is the Hollywood obsession. Writing in 1974 about Terrence Malick's film, Champlin offered that about the time the audience became "totally unclear whether the couple is very, very stupid or very, very sick," or started wondering whether the characters played by Martin Sheen and Sissy Spacek were "end-products of a sick society or as

role players acting out the distortions of pop culture," it was clear that the film could be "the object of its own scorn." In sum, the film created "an experience of violence in what is in fact the most frequent Hollywood tradition: violence separated from any real consideration of its consequences."[13] The horror was not just in the Midwest. The screen brought the violence nationwide without putting Starkweather in the electric chair.

The Pacific Northwest also developed from a particular culture of missionaries, small farms, timber industry, and two major ports, Portland and Seattle/Tacoma. Both Oregon and Washington also have lush coastal mountains and arid inland areas characteristic of the Rocky Mountain climate. They share much in historical experience.

Lynching is a topic outside the scope of this work, but part of the context for the death penalty, particularly in the South. Recent scholarship has focused increasingly on state and local cultural values and economics to explain the violence and racism of lynching. Some scholars of racial violence manifested in lynching have argued that lynchings were political acts intended to intimidate African Americans.[14] Other scholars locate the lynching culture within southern culture and in its legal system.[15] Most significantly, scholars have focused on local factors and cultural norms as they change over time to explain lynching and its demise.[16] One of the excuses for lynching in many areas was the ineffectiveness of law enforcement and the certainty of justice in local courts. Tolnay and Beck's study of ten southern states found this rationalization for lynching prevalent, but economic causes more significant. Poor whites feared competition from African Americans in the labor market and resorted to lynching to advance their interests.[17] Stephen J. Leonard's *Lynching in Colorado, 1859–1919* found a far more complex mix of causal factors including race (Italian and Chinese), economic competition, and the fact that lynchers assumed they would not be punished.[18]

California had a different trajectory. Criminals accompanied the gold rush to California. The formal legal system in 1849 was rudimentary and popular justice prevailed in many locations. San Francisco's vigilance committees of 1851 and 1856 are best known, but popular justice was part of the placer-mining boom of the early 1850s. Pioneer vigilantes took the administration of justice into their own hands, primarily for the purpose of establishing order and stability in newly settled areas.[19]

The California gold rush, by creating instant wealth and instant cities, provided lawmakers with the challenge of dealing with criminals in the streets and vigilance committees operating in lieu of legitimate authority.[20] As part of the legislative effort to stem popular justice and bring statutory law into accord with the culturally accepted penalties for certain crimes, the California legislature provided for the death penalty for grand larceny. George Tanner became the first to appeal his death sentence under this 1851 statute.

The 1851 statute amended the 1850 penal code by giving the jury discretion in robbery cases of setting prison sentences of one to ten years or death. Grand larceny received the same treatment. Petit larceny (i.e., stealing property worth less than fifty dollars) had the penalty of "imprisonment in the County jail for more than six months, or . . . fine not exceeding five hundred dollars, or . . . any number of lashes not exceeding fifty on the bare back, or . . . such fine or imprisonment and lashes in the discretion of the jury." Thus, the legislature put into formal law what the people had been putting into action in the rough-and-tumble environment of the gold fields.

The narrow legal issue in *People v. Tanner*, 2 Cal. 257 (1852), involved a juror's declaration against the death penalty. The California Supreme Court decided that a juror's declaration of conscientious scruples against the death penalty was sufficient under the current statute to exclude the person from a jury in a grand larceny case. The accused, George Tanner, had stolen 1,500 pounds of flour, six sacks of potatoes, five kegs of syrup, two and one-half barrels of meal, one keg of powder, and one-half barrel of mackerel, thereby running afoul of the 1850 California penal code, as amended. The court of sessions jury brought in a verdict of "guilty of grand larceny, punishable with Death." District Judge Gordon N. Mott upheld the verdict with the death penalty, and Tanner appealed to the California Supreme Court.

Chief Justice Hugh C. Murray delivered the opinion for a unanimous court. The statutory challenge of the district judge's order excluding the juror was rejected on statutory interpretation grounds. Legislators had provided that in cases where "the offence charged is punishable with death," a juror would "neither be permitted nor compelled to serve as a juror." Given the fact that the penal statute provided for the death penalty option, the challenge to the juror and the judge's order excluding the juror from service were sustained.

Beyond the narrow ruling on this important issue of criminal justice administration, the court commented on the penal statute and public policy. First, Murray wrote, "It was not [the court's] purpose to discuss the policy of the law." Then he went on to do so, criticizing the legislature's actions "in the face of the wisdom and experience of the present day" and to characterize the death penalty for crimes less than murder as "alike disgusting and abhorrent to the common sense of every enlightened people."

Regardless of its personal distaste for such a penalty, the court recognized that its role was limited. First, the court was to support legislatively define public policy. This was needed "to correct the administration of the law." Correct administration, would, in turn, "secure a due enforcement of the penalties ordained for its violation." Finally, the court was to implement the public policy declarations of the people through their duly elected representatives. "The law has ordained," Murray wrote, "that this offence shall be punished by death, and to allow jurors to sit upon a trial for larceny who declared that they would not impose this penalty, would defeat the intention of its framers, and practically work a repeal of its provisions." Such a result would be "a mockery of justice." It was the court's duty to prevent "the administration of justice from becoming a mockery." The judicial function was to be supportive of the statements of public policy in law regardless of personal philosophy.

Tanner contained several elements common to western criminal cases of the frontier period. The death penalty for property crimes, commonly associated with horse stealing, was broad and part of jury discretion. Tanner committed the crime on April 3, 1852, was brought to trial on April 14, lost his appeal in the district court on April 24, won a petition for rehearing before the supreme court on May 24, lost at the hearing on the petition on July 16, and was executed on July 23. Justice was swift in the frontier period.[21] California's legislature declared the crime wave over in 1857 and repealed that section of the code. Over a century later, the California Supreme Court stirred up a public clamor of a different stripe when it abolished the death penalty. The press got wind of the court's decision on February 18, 1972, when KNXT television reported that the justices had struck down the death penalty.[22] "No Death Penalty," shouted the headline when confirmed by "Justice Marshall F. McComb, the lone dissenter."[23] The decision set off a firestorm of comment. Mary Sirhan, the mother of Sirhan Sirhan, the assassin of Robert Kennedy approved. Governor Ronald Reagan was "deeply shocked by the decision." He declared, "In a time of increasing crime and increasing violence in types of crime,

capital punishment is needed, the death penalty is a deterrent to murder and I think the majority of people believe the same thing." Former governor and death penalty opponent Edmund G. "Pat" Brown thought the decision "correct" and that it would do more to "expedite criminal trials than anything in the last 100 years." Moreover, Brown offered that the death penalty had never been a deterrent and "in states where the death penalty is in force, there are more murders than in states which have abolished it."[24] The politics and public policy debates exploding in California were in the context of similar issues then before the United States Supreme Court.

In Washington, Anthony G. Amsterdam argued against the death penalty before the United States Supreme Court on behalf of Earnest James Aiken Jr. of California and William H. Furman of Georgia. Ronald M. George, deputy attorney general and later chief justice of the California Supreme Court, argued for the California death penalty on the ground of democracy: "[T]he people of the State of California through their elected representatives have the right to make the death penalty available." Dorothy T. Beasley, assistant attorney general of Georgia and later a judge on the Georgia Court of Appeals, argued that only a constitutional amendment could abolish the death penalty, not the court.[25] *Furman v. Georgia* (1972) would be far-reaching in the national death penalty debate.[26]

The debate in the press and politics in California was part of this greater national discourse. The *Los Angeles Times* quickly sided with the court. An editorial declared, "The Supreme Court of California, in a decision of persuasive clarity and wisdom, has found the death penalty unconstitutional under the state's won constitution." The grounds were multiple. Capital punishment was "impermissibly cruel." It "degrades and dehumanizes all who participate in its procedures." The 1849 California Constitution's provision prohibiting "cruel or unusual" punishment provided the justices with focused inquiry into cruelty in the enlightened times of 1972. The "standards of another age," including "whipping, branding, pillorying, severing and nailing ears and boring of the tongue," were not the standards of 1972. Rather, capital punishment was "lingering death" causing mental anguish and "brutalizing psychological effect" as the condemned waited for death. The court maintained, and the *Los Angeles Times* agreed, that the decision was "not grounded in sympathy for those who would commit crimes of violence but in concern for the society that diminishes itself whenever it takes the life of one of its members." The editorial concluded, "The quality of society is the heart of the matter. The court has contributed to that quality once again."[27]

Alan M. Dershowitz, a Harvard law professor, editorialized in the *New York Times*, "The decision, of course, could be 'overruled' by a state constitutional amendment. But any such amendment would operate prospectively only." All of the people on death row in California had been saved by the decision, including Sirhan Sirhan and Charles Manson. Further, "fundamental constitutional provisions—such as the one prohibiting 'cruel or unusual punishments'—are not lightly repealed." Professor Amsterdam had saved 107 on death row, but when asked, he offered, "I'm more worried about the 579 people still left on Death Rows."[28]

Richard Howard Wels disagreed in a letter to the editor of the *New York Times*. Wels was a Harvard Law School graduate and influential in the reform of New York State's divorce laws. In 1937–1938, he was Special District Attorney in Manhattan. In 1941–1942, he was special assistant to the Attorney General of the United States and to the United States Attorney for the Eastern District of New York. He voiced another constitutional position noting that in 1947 the United States Supreme Court sent Willie Francis back to the Louisiana

electric chair after the first electrocution was unsuccessful. He repeated the Court's language, "The cruelty against which the Constitution protects a convicted man is cruelty inherent in the method of punishment, not the necessary suffering involved in any method employed to extinguish life humanely." This was not the cruelty the California Supreme Court focused upon in *People v. Anderson* striking down the death penalty. Wels declared that arguments against the death penalty were the province of the legislature and courts should not take "the law into their own hands" and legislate for the state.[29]

Governor Ronald Reagan started the campaign to reverse the ruling on February 29, 1972, with a news conference declaring, "There's cruelty when you execute a chicken to have a Sunday afternoon dinner."[30] George Deukmejian carried Reagan's amendment through the California Senate Judiciary Committee on an 8–3 vote. Attorney General Evelle J. Younger and Senate Democratic leader George R. Moscone (assassinated in 1978 by Dan White who was convicted of manslaughter creating the "Twinkie defense") debated the issue in committee. Moscone relied on American constitutional history in his testimony, but the deterrent argument prevailed.[31]

With the amendment moving through the legislature, the press continued to enjoy the debate. Roy L. Herndon, a justice of the California Court of Appeals, joined the chorus of voices opposing the *Anderson* decision. Justice Herndon thought, "The decision represents an about-face by the high court. It contradicts a long line of decisions of the highest state and federal courts. Furthermore, it seems to me that the death penalty is a matter for the determination of the people of the State of California, acting either directly or through their representatives in the Legislature." Herndon defended McComb who pointed out that in the *Anderson* case of 1966, authored by McComb, the court was unanimous upholding the death penalty. Again in 1968, the court in *Anderson* rejected "every argument of counsel for Anderson had advanced against the death penalty." Herndon concluded that the death penalty was a deterrent.[32]

When the United States Supreme Court issued *Furman v. Georgia* (1972), it sent legislators scrambling to rewrite state death penalty statutes. Further, it called into question the California death penalty initiative then on the November ballot.[33] The ballot measure and the debate pushed "the level of public opinion in California in favor of the death penalty for serious crimes—66% to 24%—[to] the highest point since the California Poll began its measurement on this issue 16 years ago," the *Los Angeles Times* announced.[34]

The debate, particularly the attack on the court's authority to decide such questions, caused Chief Justice Donald R. Wright to retort in the *California Law Review*. Seldom the stuff of journalism, the law review article was page-three fodder for the *Los Angeles Times*. Wright defended judicial review on basic constitutional separation of powers and historic judicial authority grounds.[35] What was almost surprising about the Wright article was that it was written at all, but given the debate's intensity, a law review was the only appropriate venue in its time.

The people of California approved Proposition 17 reinstating the death penalty and President Richard M. Nixon was soon on the bandwagon calling for a new federal death penalty to thwart "soft-headed judges."[36] Governor Reagan signed the bill fleshing out Proposition 17 and creating a mandatory death sentence for eleven categories of crime in conformance with *Furman v. Georgia* (1972). The death penalty abolitionists would continue the appellate court strategy, fixing focus on the cruelty aspect of execution.

Today, California legal experts cannot agree on how to fix the system. Justice was swift in the 1850s, but now "California has the biggest backlog of death penalty cases, and the time between conviction and execution is double the national average, legal experts say. The current wait averages more than 17 years."[37] One reason for the delay is lethal injections. In February 2007 a federal judge ordered a moratorium on California executions.[38] In August, federal appellate justice Arthur L. Alarcon criticized the California state system calling "for a radical overhaul of what he described as systemic problems, including a critical shortage of defense lawyers to represent death row inmates on appeal and an inefficient use of judicial resources." Alarcon argued for "a major infusion of cash to attract lawyers to the difficult cases. He also proposed shifting automatic judicial review of death penalty cases to the state's appeals courts."[39] The debate continued in and out of court. In 2009 the *Los Angeles Times* noted the case of Thomas Francis Edwards who died of natural causes on death row. The newspaper editorial declared it, "Death Row Futility."[40] With 680 death row inmates, Governor Arnold Schwarzenegger and his legal team moved the debate over lethal injection to public review and out of the judicial system in an effort to resume executions at San Quentin.[41] In March 2009, the *Times* noted the fact that many states were looking at the cost of the death penalty. In particular, New Mexico's legislature had voted to abolish it on March 13, 2009.[42] On March 19 the paper reported that Governor Bill Richardson had signed the abolition bill into law in New Mexico.[43] California, like so many other states, has its history to account for its death penalty record, and the inmates on death row in San Quentin await their fate as public policy evolves.

Gordon Morris Bakken
Fullerton, California

Notes

1. Michael C. Steiner, "Regionalism in the Great Depression," *Geographic Review* 73, no. 4 (Oct. 1983), 444. Also see Wayne Franklin and Michael Steiner, *Mapping American Culture* (Iowa City: University of Iowa Press, 1992). David M. Wrobel and Michael Steiner, *Many Wests: Place, Culture, and Regional Identity* (Lawrence: University Press of Kansas, 1997).

2. See Constance Rourke, "The Significance of Sections," *New Republic*, 76 (1933), 147–51. Donald Davidson, *The Attack on Leviathan* (Chapel Hill: University of North Carolina Press, 1938). John Gould Fletcher, "Regionalism and Folk Art," *Southwest Review*, 14 (1934), 429–34. Howard W. Odum and Harry Estill Moore, *American Regionalism: A Cultural/Historical Approach to National Integration* (New York: Henry Holt, 1938).

3. Merrill Jensen, ed., *Regionalism in America* (Madison: The University of Wisconsin Press, 1951). The book had an introduction by Felix Frankfurter, a justice of the United States Supreme Court.

4. George B. Tindall, "Introduction to the Status and Future of Regionalism—a Symposium," *The Journal of Southern History*, 26, no. 1 (Feb. 1960): 22–24.

5. Raymond D. Gastil, *Cultural Regions of the United States* (Seattle: University of Washington Press, 1975).

6. Yi-Fu Tuan, *Space and Place* (Minneapolis: University of Minnesota Press, 1977), 154.

7. William G. Robbins, Robert Frank, and Richard E. Ross, eds., *Regionalism and the Pacific Northwest* (Corvallis: Oregon State University Press, 1983).

8. Barbara Allen and Thomas J. Schlereth, eds., *Sense of Place: American Regional Cultures* (Lexington: University Press of Kentucky, 1990).

9. Glen E. Lich, ed., *Regional Studies: The Interplay of Land and People* (College Station: Texas A & M University Press, 1992).

10. Edward L. Ayers, ed., *All Over the Map: Rethinking American Regions* (Baltimore: Johns Hopkins University Press, 1996).

11. Mark R. Ellis, *Law and Order in Buffalo Bill's Country: Legal Culture and Community on the Great Plains, 1867–1901* (Lincoln: University of Nebraska Press, 2007), 214–15.

12. Elissa Schappell, "He Looked Like James Dean: A novel based on the Charles Starkweather–Caril Ann Fugate murders of 1958 and their haunted survivors," *New York Times*, September 26, 2004, A12.

13. Charles Champlin, "'Badlands' Traces a Murder Spree," *Los Angeles Times*, March 29, 1974, C1.

14. W. Fitzhugh Brundage, *Lynchings in the New South: Georgia and Virginia, 1880–1930* (Urbana: University of Illinois Press, 1993). Stewart E. Tolnay and E. M. Beck, *Festival of Violence: An Analysis of Southern Lynchings, 1882–1930* (Urbana: University of Illinois Press, 1995). Also see W. Fitzbugh Brundage, *Under Sentence of Death: Lynching in the South* (Chapel Hill: University of North Carolina Press, 1997).

15. Margaret Vandiver, *Lethal Punishment: Lynchings and Legal Executions in the South* (New Brunswick, N.J.: Rutgers University Press, 2006). Christopher Waldrep, *Roots of Disorder: Race and Criminal Justice in the American South, 1817–1880* (Urbana: University of Illinois Press, 1998).

16. William D. Carrigan, *The Making of a Lynching Culture: Violence and Vigilantism in Central Texas, 1836–1917* (Urbana: University of Illinois Press, 2004). Christopher Waldrep and Donald G. Nieman, *Local Matters: Race, Crime, and Justice in the Nineteenth-Century South* (Athens: University of Georgia Press, 2001).

17. Tolnay and Beck, *Festival of Violence*, 239–58.

18. Stephen J. Leonard, *Lynching in Colorado, 1859–1919* (Boulder: The Press of the University of Colorado, 2002), 156–57.

19. Gordon Morris Bakken, *Practicing Law in Frontier California* (Lincoln: University of Nebraska Press, 1991), 100.

20. The following is taken in whole or in part from Gordon Morris Bakken, "Death for Grand Larceny," in John W. Johnson, ed., *Historic U.S. Court Cases, 1690–1990* (New York: Garland Publishing, 1992), 34–35.

21. Also see R. M. Senkewicz, *Vigilantes in Gold Rush San Francisco* (Stanford: Stanford University Press, 1985).

22. "Death Penalty Held Void, Report Says," *Los Angeles Times*, February 18, 1972.

23. Gene Blake, "No Death Penalty: Cal. Court Voids It: Appeal Likely," *Los Angeles Times*, February 18, 1972.

24. Ed Meagher, "Court Setting Itself Above the People, Governor Charges," *Los Angeles Times*, February 19, 1972.

25. Richard Halloran, "Death Penalties Argued in Court," *New York Times*, January 18, 1972.

26. David R. Dow and Mark Dow, eds., *Machinery of Death* (New York: Routledge, 2002), 46–48.

27. "The Death Penalty Overruled," *Los Angeles Times*, February 21, 1972. Also see Earl Caldwell, "California Court, in 6–1 Vote, Bars Death Sentences," *New York Times*, February 19, 1972.

28. Alan M. Dershowitz, "A Decision that May Reach Far Beyond California," *New York Times*, February 20, 1972.

29. Richard H. Wels, "California Ruling on Capital Punishment," *New York Times*, February 27, 1972.

30. "Reagan Calls on California to Reinstate Death Penalty," *New York Times*, March 1, 1972.

31. "Drive to Restore Death Penalty Wins 1st Round," *Los Angeles Times*, April 12, 1972.

32. Roy L. Herndon, "The Death Penalty—a Matter for the

People, Not the Courts, to Decide," *Los Angeles Times*, April 27, 1972.

33. "Death Penalty Ruling," *Los Angeles Times*, June 30, 1972. "Death Penalty Measure Vital Now, Busch Says," *Los Angeles Times*, July 1, 1972.

34. Mervin D. Field, "Support for Death Penalty Up, Poll Finds," *Los Angeles Times*, September 7, 1972.

35. Philip Hager, "Justice Defends Court's Ban on Death Penalty," *Los Angeles Times*, September 21, 1972.

36. Robert Rawitch, "Death Penalty OK'd but Its Use Could Be Years in Future," *Los Angeles Times*, November 9, 1972. Ronald J. Ostrow, "Bring Back Death Penalty, Nixon Says," *Los Angeles Times*, March 11, 1973.

37. Eric Bailey, "Legal Experts Agree Death Penalty Needs Reforms but Disagree on How," *Los Angeles Times*, January 11, 2008.

38. Henry Weinstein, "Executions Unlikely for the Rest of the Year: October Hearings Are Set for Legal Challenges to California's Lethal Injection Procedure," *Los Angeles Times*, June 2, 2007. Also see Timothy V. Kaufman-Osborn, *From Noose to Needle: Capital Punishment and the Late Liberal State* (Ann Arbor: University of Michigan Press, 2002). Theodore Hamm, *Rebel and a Cause: Caryl Chessman and the Politics of the Death Penalty in Postwar California, 1948–1974* (Berkeley: University of California Press, 2001).

39. Henry Weinstein, "Changes to death row are urged: A federal judge calls for a radical overhaul, saying California's backlog shows the system is broken," *Los Angeles Times*, August 30, 2007.

40. "Death Row Futility," *Los Angeles Times*, February 23, 2009.

41. Carol J. Williams and Maura Dolan, "A New Strategy on the Death Penalty," *Los Angeles Times*, February 24, 2009.

42. Steve Mills, "States Weigh Cost of Capital Punishment," *Los Angeles Times*, March 14, 2009.

43. "N.M. Repeals Death Penalty," *Los Angeles Times*, March 19, 2009.

CHAPTER 9

The Death Penalty in the South[1]

Michael A. Powell

CAPITAL PUNISHMENT has been incorporated into southern legal systems since the first surviving English settlement at Jamestown in 1607. Just as the settlers brought their language, customs, and culture to North America, so, too, they sought to transplant their legal code and punishments. While the enforcement and applicability of the death penalty might vary or be modified over time, the punishment itself would remain. And two characteristics of the death penalty in the South have remained constant until recently: its resistance to reform and its overwhelming application and enforcement toward blacks. Yet today, the emphasis of racial disparity with respect to the death penalty has changed its focus from the race of the defendant to that of the victim, and capital punishment is firmly embedded as a sentencing option among southerners.

The dubious distinction of being the first recorded southerner put to death by the government goes to George Kendall, a councilor at Jamestown. Kendall had already served a prior prison sentence for creating discord between the Council and the president. In 1608, he was accused of spying for the Spanish and, based upon the testimony of only one witness (rather than the usual two), was found guilty by a jury and was shot to death. While the colony would ultimately execute other Virginians, both white and black, Kendall's execution is the only recorded instance of capital punishment during the first fifteen years of the Virginia settlement.[2]

Virginia, with its tobacco-based economy relying heavily upon indentured servants and later slaves, was one of the most violent societies among the seventeenth-century English North American colonies. With a disproportionate male/female ratio, exceedingly high death rate, low birth rate, and fiercely competitive economic environment, human life was at a premium. The result was that, despite the number of crimes committed with capital punishments, executions tended to be rare.[3] In 1611, the governor of Virginia, Sir Thomas Dale, trying to instill the discipline necessary for the colony's survival, enacted the "Lawes Divine, Morall, and Martial," known as Dale's Code. In force until 1618, these laws mandated the death penalty not only for blaspheming the Holy Trinity and murder, but also for convictions of perjury, trading or bartering with the Indians, stealing from a garden or vineyard, and even stealing an ear of corn. Capital punishment for these offenses, though harsh to modern sensibilities, was consistent within the English legal tradition from which the laws were derived. Despite the potential severity of punishments under Dale's Code, however, there was not a single instance of the imposition of the death penalty.[4] Yet after the Crown assumed possession of the colony in 1624, the death penalty was conformed to be consistent with capital crimes in England: treason, murder, arson, rape, burglary, robbery, larceny, horse stealing, witchcraft, and assault and battery. Those convicted of capital offenses in the colonies were hanged, but spared the disemboweling and quartering still employed in England.[5]

In the years following the American Revolution and up to the Civil War, states north of the Mason-Dixon Line experienced a reduction in the number of capital crimes applicable to whites, while the southern states generally retained the death penalty as a punishment for a multitude of crimes. In the North, white defendants could be sentenced to death, in most instances, only for convictions of murder, although white burglars, robbers, and horse thieves were reportedly hanged in scattered instances. There is no record of white rapists facing the death penalty. In the 1790s, Virginia and Kentucky followed Pennsylvania's lead by dividing murder into first and second degree, with capital punishment reserved solely for those whites convicted of the former.[6] With the creation of the penitentiaries in the decades before the Civil War, many southern states also reduced the number of crimes for which the death penalty was applied to whites, but white southerners could be sentenced to death for more than the conviction of murder. Although Tennessee also limited the death penalty to first-degree murder, Alabama imposed the death penalty for convictions of treason and involvement in a slave revolt, as well as first-degree murder. Many states in the South retained the death penalty for whites in cases of rape (Florida, Louisiana, North Carolina, and South Carolina), burglary (Louisiana, North Carolina, and South Carolina), and arson (Florida, Louisiana, Mississippi, North Carolina, South Carolina, and Virginia). In isolated instances, capital punishment was enforced for the crimes of aiding fugitive slaves, forgery, and sodomy.[7]

An overwhelming majority of whites who were executed in the South between 1800 and 1860 had committed the crime of murder. In Alabama, twenty-three of the twenty-eight whites executed received the death penalty for murder, and one each for counterfeiting, robbery, and aiding a runaway slave. Of the twenty whites who were executed in Louisiana, twelve were convicted of murder, one of attempted murder, two of piracy, and one of aiding in a slave revolt.[8]

Although the offenses for which capital punishment applied to whites diminished in the South, the same was not true for blacks; the list of crimes for which they could be punished by death became more extensive rather than less. In an 1856 treatise that examined laws pertaining to slaves in the southern states, George Stroud found sixty-six capital crimes for slaves in Virginia and only one for whites. Slaves were subject to the death penalty for committing any offense for which the punishment would be three years or more if committed by a white person. Attempted rape, for example, was a capital offense for blacks in Florida, Louisiana, Mississippi, South Carolina, Tennessee, and Virginia.[9]

And just as the number of capital punishment crimes was higher for blacks than whites, so, too, were the number of blacks executed. Between 1800 and 1860, Louisiana executed 108 blacks for murder, attempted murder, robbery, aiding in a slave revolt, poisoning, burglary, and arson, whereas only twenty whites were executed.[10] From 1785 to 1865, slaves in Virginia were hanged by a twelve-to-one margin when compared to whites and Native Americans. The figures are comparable as well for South Carolina.[11]

In the antebellum period, slaves confronted not only the statutory capital punishment, but a criminal justice system that supported white dominance over the slave. In Virginia, Kentucky, and Georgia, penitentiaries were meant for both punishment and reformation of the prisoner. However, state statutes expressly limited incarceration in the first two states to whites, while Georgia's statute implied they were built solely for whites. In addition, the criminal proceedings also prejudiced slaves. If a slave was charged with a capital crime in Mississippi, the grand jury proceeding was eliminated. North Carolina, South Carolina, Virginia, and Louisiana limited trial by jury only to whites charged with capital crimes. And in Tennessee, the sheriff would select the judge and jury if a black was charged with a capital crime.[12]

The South's resistance to reforms with respect to capital punishment was consistent with its resistance to the reform movements sweeping the North in the antebellum era as well as its acceptance of a culture of violence. While the movement to abolish capital punishment in the North was among the many reforms embraced by the "benevolent empire," the spirit of reform that infused the North was inhibited in the South by the economic and social importance of slavery. The commitment to the institution of slavery precluded involvement in many of the reform causes, including capital punishment, lest they lead to the most politically charged reform of all: abolition of slavery. In addition, southern culture's sense of honor encouraged a level of violence which had become unacceptable in the North by the antebellum era. A Connecticut Yankee observed, "As in the colonial and antebellum period, all classes [in the South] seemed touched with violence: 'It permeates all society; it has infected all individualities. The meekest man by nature, the man who at the North would no more fight than he would jump out of a second story window, may at the South resent an insult by a blow, or perhaps a stab or pistol shot.'"[13] Not only did this violence exist between whites, but particularly by whites against blacks as a means of maintaining white

superiority. These factors, combined with the South's continued acceptance of the public hanging as spectacle, contributed to the maintenance of the death penalty as an important means of punishment in the antebellum South.

While there was vocal and organized opposition to the death penalty in the North, no such organization existed in the South. Only rare and isolated voices were heard against capital punishment throughout the southern states in the antebellum years. In 1779, Thomas Jefferson of Virginia proposed abolishing the death penalty except for treason and murder. As punishment for those convicted of rape and sodomy, Jefferson advocated castrating men and drilling at least a half-inch hole in the nose cartilage of women. These proposals died in the legislature.[14] Edward Livingston of Louisiana, an attorney appointed by the state legislature in 1821 to draft a new criminal code, proposed one based upon rehabilitation rather than retribution, including the elimination of the death penalty. Hailed throughout Western Europe for its humane and far-sighted principles, Livingston's Code was never approved by Louisiana's legislature. Nor was his subsequent proposal, offered as a senator from Louisiana, to abolish capital punishment for federal crimes adopted by the federal government.[15] In the same vein, Governor John Sevier of Tennessee and Thomas Smith Grimké of South Carolina were two of the very few southerners who pressed for the abolition of the death penalty, while Francis Lieber urged the governor of South Carolina to abolish the death penalty except for convictions of murder. But these were solitary voices, and their pleas went unheeded.[16]

The four years of the Civil War witnessed expansion of the death penalty to war-related offenses. Due to the nature and circumstances of war, the exact number of executions was undoubtedly underreported, but available evidence suggests hangings for spying dominated the early years of the war, whereas the death penalty for desertions prevailed during the war's final years. Georgia executed eight individuals in 1862 and 1863 for espionage, while Virginia executed one in 1862.[17] A *cause célèbre* involved the hanging, not of a Confederate turncoat, but of a Confederate spy in Tennessee: twenty-one-year-old Sam Davis. Davis was captured carrying Union battle plans and refused to inform federal authorities where he procured the documents. The Union soldiers about to witness Davis's hanging in November 1863 implored the convicted spy to cooperate, but he allegedly responded: "I would rather die a thousand deaths than betray a friend." After his death, the boy hero of the South was celebrated throughout the Confederacy for his loyalty to the then-withering nation.

Desertion from the Confederate army reached epidemic proportions toward the end of the war, which necessitated military and civil action to both punish the offenders and deter potential deserters. Confederate military records report the courts martial and executions for desertion; however the states, most notably North Carolina, also executed those fleeing their military obligations. The Tar Heel State hanged twenty-two deserters over a seventeen-day period in April 1864, sending a clear message to other soldiers that desertion would not be tolerated.[18]

Only two individuals, both Kentuckians, are recorded to have been executed in the South for guerrilla activity during the war.[19] This figure is misleading, however. By 1864 and 1865, when the two were executed, the Union army was in complete control of the state and executed Southern sympathizers. In addition, those engaged in guerrilla activities may have been charged with other offenses, such as destruction of property or homicide. Of the reported hangings in the South during the Civil War, those based upon conviction of guerrilla activity are probably among the most misrepresented.

In the years following the Civil War, while capital punishment remained entrenched as a punishment throughout the South, the method and location of executions underwent a transformation. During the eighteenth and the first half of the nineteenth centuries, executions were public spectacles. Men, women, and children of all ages and classes, frequently numbering in the thousands, would attend the affair designed not only as retributive justice, but as a reminder to all of the consequences of committing such acts. At least one minister, and sometimes more, provided a sermon on the spiritual consequences of the condemned's criminal sins and the power of forgiveness. The condemned then was expected to speak, usually on the errors of his ways, and to admonish the spectators to lead a life of virtue. Typical in many ways was the case of the Reverend Preston Turley. Convicted of killing his wife in January 1858, Turley was executed on September 17 of that year in Charleston, Virginia. As reported in the *New York Times*, the atmosphere was somber and unusually sad because of Turley's position in the community as a minister. Before the execution, hymns were sung, and a local minister led the spectators, and the condemned, in prayers. Turley then addressed the crowd for approximately forty-five minutes, blaming his situation in large part on whiskey, confessing that he was a sinner, and asking for God's forgiveness. He was then hanged.[20]

Yet there is evidence that the public's attitudes toward public executions were evolving. As a sense of refinement became more widespread among the increasing numbers of middle class, they became more attuned both to a specific code of public behavior as well as to the violence that attends the act of hanging. By the mid-nineteenth century, Mississippi and Alabama had joined several northern states in removing public execution to the privacy of the jail yard. Georgia joined them in 1859. Virginia, Louisiana, Missouri, Kentucky,

South Carolina, and Tennessee also abolished public hangings by 1900, although as late as 1920 Kentucky still permitted public hangings for rape and attempted rape, at the local authorities' discretion. While Georgia and Mississippi also reinstated public executions briefly at the turn of the century, the introduction of the electric chair, by its very means of death, forced executions indoors.[21]

The last public execution in the United States occurred in Owensboro, Kentucky, on August 14, 1936. Rainey Bethea, a twenty-two-year-old black man, was convicted of raping seventy-year-old Lischia Edwards, who was white. Estimates were that up to twenty thousand people were in attendance at the execution, a number of whom had attended "hanging parties" the night before. Although evidence as to the crowd's behavior is in dispute, newspapers covering the event reported that it was a "jolly holiday," with vendors selling hot dogs, popcorn, and soft drinks. There were reports that after Bethea was declared dead at 5:44 a.m., the crowd surged toward the gallows, tearing at the hood covering the deceased's face for a souvenir.[22] Public outrage at the coarse behavior of the crowd and the circus atmosphere resounded throughout the country. The Kentucky legislature banned public executions two years later, and the day of the public execution had come to an end.

Throughout the nineteenth century, critics of hanging assailed the gruesome barbarity of the act and the pain inflicted upon the condemned. If the prisoner's neck did not snap immediately upon the drop, he could struggle for as much as ten minutes, while slowly and agonizingly suffocating to death. Although the condemned's faces would be covered, they could become engorged and turn blue, the tongue could protrude from the mouth, capillaries on the face and eyes would burst, and urine and feces would be eliminated. On occasion, blood would seep through the nose

and mouth, staining the hood, or the condemned might become nearly decapitated by the process.

With the increasingly widespread application of electricity in the late nineteenth century, critics of hanging found a more "humane" way of execution: electrocution. Virginia (1908), North Carolina (1909), Kentucky (1910), and South Carolina (1912) were among the first states to replace hanging with the electric chair. Arkansas and Tennessee quickly followed suit in 1913. By 1950, the electric chair had also been selected by the remaining southern states of Alabama, Florida, Georgia, Louisiana, and Mississippi. In adopting the electric chair as a reform measure, the South did not lag behind the rest of the country; in fact, the region switched far more quickly than the West.[23]

Attempting to minimize pain for the condemned, states adopted regulations for the administration of voltage. For example, at the execution of James E. Messer Jr. in Jackson, Georgia, in 1988, two electrodes were connected to Messer's head and right ankle. A leather hood was then placed over his head. Three volunteers each pushed a button, the first of which sent 2,000 volts into the condemned. After four seconds, the voltage was decreased to 1,200 volts. After eight more seconds, it was decreased again to 220 volts, which lasted for two minutes. An automatic cut-off terminated the electricity at that point. After a cool-down period, doctors checked Messer's heartbeat and pronounced him dead.[24]

The relative speed with which the southern states switched to electrocution and the lack of controversy over its adoption was facilitated by the United States Supreme Court. William Kemmler (aka John Hort) was sentenced to death by electrocution for a murder committed in New York in 1889. Kemmler challenged the constitutionality of death by electrocution under both the Eighth Amendment (cruel and unusual punishment) and the Fourteenth Amendment (due process clause) of the United States Constitution. The Supreme Court agreed with the decision of the New York Court of Appeals that "[t]he determination of the legislature that the use of electricity as an agency for producing death constituted a more humane method of executing the judgment of the court in capital cases was held conclusive."[25]

Around the same time that electrocution was introduced, experimentation with gas was undertaken. Critical was a determination of the most efficient and painless mixture of gases to administer. Construction of the chamber required it to be airtight, with necessary fans to blow gas both into the chamber for the execution and out of the chamber upon completion. Once perfected, death by gas was adopted by North Carolina (1935), Missouri (1937), and Mississippi (1954). However, a number of particularly gruesome deaths heightened sensitivity to this form of death. Jimmy Lee Gray was sentenced to death in Mississippi for murdering and sodomizing a three-year-old girl. In an execution gone awry, prison officials were forced to remove witnesses eight minutes after the 1983 execution began as Gray went into convulsions, was gasping for air, and slammed his head repeatedly into a steel pole in the chamber.[26] As a result of these types of deaths and the efficacy of lethal injection, North Carolina eliminated the use of gas in 1998 and mandated lethal injection. Mississippi, too, removed the option of death by gas in the same year and prescribed lethal injection as the only manner of execution. Only Missouri has retained death by gas as an alternate manner of death.

Regardless of the method of capital punishment, blacks in the South during the first three-quarters of the twentieth century were more likely to be sentenced to death than whites. While the Civil War and the post–Civil War amendments provided constitutional freedom and liberty for blacks, the post–Civil War landscape in the South, with respect to capital punishment for blacks, resembled the antebellum period. In 1954, rape by blacks was punishable by death in all of the southern states. Robbery by blacks was a capital crime in Alabama, Georgia, Kentucky, Mississippi, Missouri, and Virginia. With respect to arson committed by blacks, Alabama, Arkansas, Georgia, North Carolina, and Virginia retained the death penalty. Four southern states—Alabama, Kentucky, North Carolina, and Virginia—allowed for the death penalty upon the conviction of blacks for burglary.[27]

A number of southern cases reflected the growing disparity in perception between the North and South over capital punishment, and especially its racial application. Perhaps the most notorious case relating to race during this period occurred in 1931 in Scottsboro, Alabama, when nine black teenagers were charged with raping two white women. Although one of the women later recanted her testimony, all of the "Scottsboro Boys" were found guilty and all but the thirteen-year-old were sentenced to death. As the case wound its way through the state and federal courts, it was perceived by many around the nation and the world as a travesty of justice and illustrated the extent to which racial prejudice permeated the southern legal system. Two important Supreme Court decisions resulted from this matter: *Powell v. Alabama*, which held that "in a capital case, where the defendant is unable to employ counsel, and is incapable adequately of making his own defense because of ignorance, feeblemindedness, illiteracy, or the like, it is the duty of the court, whether requested or not, to assign counsel for him as a necessary requisite of due process of law,"[28] and *Norris v. Alabama*, which overturned the defendants' convictions by holding that there had been racial discrimination in the selection of the jury, which included no blacks.[29]

Statistics also demonstrate that blacks have

been subjected to the death penalty in greater proportion than whites. Between 1870 and 1950, 701 out of 771 individuals executed for rape were black. The disparity was similar for robbery (31 of 35 executed were black) and burglary (18 of 21). During the same time period in Mississippi, of the 277 executions where the race of the condemned is known, 226 were black. All but one of the 48 whites were convicted of either murder or murder/robbery; the one was convicted of rape. Blacks were convicted of murder, murder/robbery, murder/burglary, and rape. In the upper South, a marked disparity was also notable. In Virginia, of 356 executions between 1870 and 1950 in which the race of the condemned is known, 296 were black and 60 were white. All of the whites executed were convicted of either murder or murder/robbery. Blacks were convicted of murder, murder/robbery, rape, rape/murder, rape/robbery, attempted rape, or arson. Of those executed for rape, attempted rape, rape/murder, or rape/robbery, 78 were black, and only one was white (for the crime of rape/murder).[30] Given the number of blacks executed in comparison to whites, and the nature of the crimes for which the condemned were convicted, the death penalty appears to have been used as a means of social control and maintaining white dominance over blacks in the South.

Recently, criticism again has been directed at the racial disparity in death penalty punishments. In a 1990 study to determine "if the race of either the victim or the defendant influences the likelihood that defendants will be sentenced to death," the United States Government Accounting Office conducted an evaluation of existing studies on the topic and concluded that "[i]n 82 percent of the studies, race of victim was found to influence the likelihood of being charged with capital murder or receiving the death penalty, i.e., those who murdered whites were found to be more likely to be sentenced to death than those

who murdered blacks."[31] The study did not find as clear an influence relative to the race of offender.

While the Government Accounting Office findings were national in scope, a study conducted by Professors Isaac Unah and John Charles Boger confirmed, with respect to capital punishment for those convicted of homicide within North Carolina, the race of the victim "played a real, substantial, and statistically significant role in determining who received death sentences in North Carolina during the 1993–1997 period. The odds of receiving a death sentence rose by 3.5 times or more among those defendants (of whatever race) who murdered white persons."[32] Likewise, an American Bar Association examination of the administration of the death sentence in eight sample states (including Tennessee, Florida, Alabama, and Georgia) found "significant racial disparities in imposing the death penalty, particularly associated with the race of the victim."[33] The focus over the past twenty years, therefore, has shifted from the race of the defendant to the race of the victim. The studies have all reached the identical conclusions with respect to the death penalty: those defendants who have committed homicides against whites are at a higher risk of being sentenced to death than if the victim was black.

In a major, and unexpected, development, the Supreme Court in 1972 declared the death penalty unconstitutional as a violation of the Eighth Amendment's prohibition of cruel and unusual punishment. With a decline across the North and West in the number of executions, and public opinion, both in the United States and internationally, moving toward abolishing capital punishment, the Court was responding to the changing public perceptions of the death penalty. Also facing society was the ongoing discrimination of blacks, which had not been cured by the Civil Rights Act of 1964, and the inequitable application of the death penalty toward blacks. The opportunity for the Court to insert itself in these issues presented itself in *Furman v. Georgia*.[34] William Furman, caught burglarizing a home when the owner returned, was attempting to escape when he fell and the gun he was carrying accidentally discharged, killing the owner. After his conviction and subsequent death sentence, Furman ultimately appealed to the Supreme Court, where his case was consolidated with two others. All three cases originated in the South, all three defendants were black, and all were sentenced to death for their convictions. The common issue presented to the Supreme Court was the imposition of the death penalty by the juries without any guidelines or limits to their discretion. In an extremely divided opinion, the two justices opposed, *per se*, to the death penalty combined with three who found the randomness with which defendants received the death penalty to declare that the arbitrariness of imposition of the death penalty constituted cruel and unusual punishment. The Court, therefore, ordered a moratorium on all executions. In effect, as Stuart Banner has observed, the Court's use of the word "randomness" was essentially a mask for the Court's addressing the racial discrimination prevalent in capital sentencing.[35]

States with the death penalty, including those in the South, responded by establishing new capital punishment statutes. Some states, like North Carolina and Georgia, mandated the death penalty for specific crimes, such as first-degree murder and aggravated rape. Other states followed the Model Penal Code's example by creating a separate sentencing proceeding once a defendant had been found guilty of a capital crime. The code identified eight "aggravating circumstances," or factors, that the sentencing jury could consider. At least one of these circumstances must be present for the imposition of the death penalty. Likewise, the code listed eight "mitigating circumstances," or factors, that would make a death sentence inappropriate. Many states, including Florida and Georgia, adopted the Model Penal Code approach. The Court, in *Gregg v. Georgia*, upheld those states with guidelines that conformed to the Model Penal Code.[36] In a case decided the same day, *Woodson v. North Carolina*, the Supreme Court invalidated North Carolina's mandatory death penalty for first-degree murder (and, by extension, for any other crime). The Court's opinion emphasized that statutes requiring mandatory sentences did not treat defendants as individuals but as part of a faceless mass and hence violated the Eighth Amendment.[37]

The net effect of *Gregg* and *Woodson* has done little to reduce the regional disparity in executions and death sentences. Between 1977 and 1999, the states with the most executions in the nation were from the South: Virginia (73), Florida (44), Missouri (41), Louisiana (25), South Carolina (24), Georgia (23), Arkansas (21), Alabama (19), and North Carolina (15). The non-southern state with the highest number of executions during the same time period is Arizona (19). The trend has continued through 2007. From 1976 through April 17, 2009, eight of the ten states with the highest number of executions per capita were from the South.[38]

What accounts for this regional difference? Southern states certainly have the opportunity to impose the death sentence more often, since the murder rate in the South is higher than any other region in the country. Studies indicate a high correlation exists between the number of murders and the number of death sentences in the states. In addition, the South's longstanding tradition of violence would seem to make southerners more willing to accept the death penalty.

A new method of execution could also be a factor, one allegedly so painless and efficient that it could assuage any pangs of guilt. By the end of the twentieth century, the dominance of electrocution and the gas chamber as the methods of carrying out death sentences had given way to lethal injection. No other type of execution in the United States was adopted so quickly and with so little controversy. Three drugs are injected into the condemned: an anesthetic (sodium thiopental) is first released into the body, followed by a paralytic (pancuronium bromide), and lastly a drug that causes cardiac arrest (potassium chloride). The difficulties encountered with this procedure have been few but significant: lack of training by prison officials, difficulty in locating a useable vein on the condemned (particularly if a habitual drug user), and allergic reactions to the chemicals.[39]

By 2007, Louisiana, Mississippi, and North Carolina exclusively employed lethal injection in the administration of death sentences. Alabama, Arkansas, Kentucky, and Tennessee have established that lethal injection would be administered after a date specified by the legislature but would allow the death row inmate to choose lethal injection or the electric chair if the crime were committed before that date. Florida, South Carolina, and Virginia allow the condemned to select either lethal injection or electrocution, while Missouri allows either lethal injection or gas. In 2001, the Georgia Supreme Court declared that death by the electric chair violated the state's constitutional prohibition against cruel and unusual punishment. The court noted that electrocution as a means of capital punishment "inflicts purposeless physical violence and needless mutilation that makes no measurable contribution to accepted goals of punishment."[40] The legislature, in anticipation of the court's decision, had passed a bill the year before declaring that lethal injection would replace electrocution should either the state or federal courts declare electrocution unconstitutional. In addition, the law mandated that lethal injection would be applied to those sentenced to death after May 1, 2000.

Tennessee passed legislation in 1998 and 2000

that lethal injection would be the preferred method of execution, unless the condemned specifically requested death by electrocution. In addition, for any crime committed after January 1, 1999, lethal injection alone would be administered. A federal district court in 2007 ruled that the state's lethal injection amounted to cruel and unusual punishment, thus violating the Eighth Amendment of the Constitution. In November 2007, the state's attorney general, Robert E. Copper, opined that "electrocution may be substituted as a method of execution for an inmate who has not chosen it only in the event that lethal injection is declared unconstitutional by the United States Supreme Court, Tennessee Supreme Court, or other appellate court specified in Tenn. Code Ann. § 40–23–114(d)." Since only the condemned could choose electrocution and the lower federal court had declared lethal injection unconstitutional, the three pending death sentences scheduled for December 2007 and January 2008 could not be carried out.[41]

On September 25, 2007, the Supreme Court granted a writ of certiorari to determine whether the three-drug mixture employed in lethal injections violated the Eighth Amendment's cruel and unusual punishment, thus placing in abeyance imposition of the death penalty across the country. Ralph Braze and Thomas Bowling, two death row inmates from Kentucky, claimed that the mixture, used by all states (including those in the South), could cause unnecessary pain. During the execution, if the anesthetic were administered improperly and proved ineffective, the condemned would be conscious and feel the pain of a heart attack while paralyzed, but awake. The Court, in a plurality opinion dated April 16, 2008, noted that "(s) imply because an execution method may result in pain, either by accident or as an inescapable consequence of death, [sic] does not establish the sort of 'objectively intolerable risk of harm' that qualifies as cruel and unusual."[42] The thirty-eight states that employ lethal injection have adopted identical procedures to Kentucky, and any alternative procedures "must be feasible, readily implemented, and in fact significantly reduce a substantial risk of severe pain."[43] The Court, in its plurality, concurring, and dissenting opinions, clearly stated that the *Baze* opinion did not address the constitutionality of the death penalty itself, but questioned only the procedure. As a result of the Court's decision, the seven-month hiatus on capital punishment ended with the May 6, 2008, execution of William Lynd in Georgia.

The Court also had the opportunity in the spring of 2008 to review the constitutionality of applying the death penalty to defendants convicted of raping a child. Patrick Kennedy so brutally raped his eight-year-old stepdaughter in Louisiana in 1998 that she required surgery. Six states (including the southern states of Louisiana, Georgia, and South Carolina) had enacted legislation since 1977 authorizing the death penalty as a punishment for rape of a child. Recognizing the changing societal "standards of decency," the Court, in a five-to-four decision, found that "a death sentence for one who raped but did not kill a child, and who did not intend to assist another in killing the child, is unconstitutional under the Eighth and Fourteenth Amendments."[44] The Court continued, "We do not address, for example, crimes defining and punishing treason, espionage, terrorism, and drug kingpin activity, which are offenses against the State. As it relates to crimes against individuals, though, the death penalty should not be expanded to instances where the victim's life was not taken."[45] The dissent assailed the Court for identifying a national consensus regarding this issue where none exists, and for exercising its "independent judgment" in concluding that the Louisiana law authorizing the death penalty in convictions of child rapists violated this purported national consensus.

While neither of the Court's recent decisions in *Baze* and *Kennedy* appears to undermine the constitutionality of capital punishment, debate in the South over the death penalty continues. Despite the region's high number of executions, death penalty reformers in the southern states tenaciously persist in their call for the abolition of this punishment. At the execution of Linwood Briley in Virginia in October 1984, two groups stood outside of the prison on the day he was electrocuted: one group was chanting "Burn, baby, burn," and the other was singing "What a Friend We Have in Jesus."[46] While the debate over the morality and constitutionality of the death penalty may endure, capital punishment has support among southerners. A 2006 Gallup Poll revealed that 62 percent of southerners did not believe that capital punishment serves as a deterrent, yet a 2004 Gallup Poll revealed that 64 percent of southerners believed that the death penalty was fairly applied. And an overwhelming 72 percent of southerners believed in 2006 that the death penalty was an appropriate punishment for a murder conviction.[47] It appears that, barring a Supreme Court ruling, capital punishment continues to have the support of southerners and will endure as a viable and available sentence.

Michael Powell is a professor of history at Frederick Community College. He has coedited two books, *Mid-Maryland: A Crossroads of History* and *Mid-Maryland: Conflict, Growth, and Change*. In addition, he has also published book chapters and encyclopedic entries in constitutional and political history.

Sources

American Bar Association. "Death Penalty Moratorium Implementation Project," State Death Penalty Assessments Key Findings, http://www.abanet.org/moratorium/home.html.

Ayers, Edward. *Vengeance and Justice: Crime and Punishment in the 19th Century American South*. New York: Oxford University Press, 1984.

Banner, Stuart. *The Death Penalty: An American History*. Cambridge, MA: Harvard University Press, 2002.

Bessler, John D. *Death in the Dark: Midnight Executions in America*. Boston: Northeastern University Press, 1997.

Cabana, Donald. *Death at Midnight: The Confessions of an Executioner*. Boston: Northeastern University Press, 1996.

Death Penalty Information Center. Available from http://www.deathpenaltyinfo.org/ (2008).

"Executions in the U.S. 1608–2002: The Espy File." Available from http://www.deathpenaltyinfo.org/article.php?scid=8&did=269.

Friedman, Lawrence M. *American Law in the 20th Century*. New Haven, CT: Yale University Press, 2004.

——. *Crime and Punishment in American History*. New York: Basic Books, 1993.

Greenberg, Douglas. "Crime, Law Enforcement, and Social Control in Colonial America." *The American Journal of Legal History* 26 (October 1982): 293–325.

Hartung, Frank E. "Trends in the Use of Capital Punishment." *Annals of the America Academy of Political and Social Science* 284 (November 1952): 8–19.

Hindus, Michael S. *Prison and Plantation: Crime, Justice, and Authority in Massachusetts and South Carolina, 1767–1878*. Chapel Hill: University of North Carolina Press, 1980.

Husband, Eliza. "A Geographical Perspective on United States Capital Punishment, 1801–1960." Ph.D. dissertation, Louisiana State University, 1990.

K.M.M.: A.J.S. Note, "Capital Punishment in Virginia." *Virginia Law Review* 58 (January 1972): 97–142.

Konig, David Thomas. "'Dale's Laws' and the Non-Common Law Origins of Criminal Justice in Virginia." *The American Journal of Legal History* 26 (October 1982): 354–375.

Latzer, Barry. *Death Penalty Cases: Leading U.S. Supreme Court Cases on Capital Punishment*. Boston: Butterworth-Heinemann, 1988.

Mackey, Philip English. "Edward Livingstone and the Origins of the Movement to Abolish Capital Punishment in America." *Louisiana History* 16 (1976): 145–166.

Morris, Thomas D. *Southern Slavery and the Law, 1619–1860*. Chapel Hill: University of North Carolina Press, 1996.

Preyer, Kathryn. "Penal Measures in the American Colonies: An Overview." *The American Journal of Legal History* 26 (October 1982): 326–353.

Schwarz, Philip J. *Twice Condemned: Slaves and the Criminal Laws of Virginia, 1705–1865*. Baton Rouge: Louisiana State University Press, 1988.

——. *Slave Laws in Virginia*, Athens, GA: University of Georgia Press, 1996.

Spindel, Donna J., and Stuart W. Thomas, Jr. "Crime and Society in North Carolina, 1663–1740." *The Journal of Southern History* 49 (May 1983): 223–244.

Stroud, George M. *A Sketch of the Laws Relating to Slavery in the Several States of the United States of America*. Philadelphia: Kimber and Sharpless, 1827.

——. *A Sketch of the Laws Relating to Slavery in the Several States of the United States of America*. Philadelphia: Henry Longstreth, 1856.

Tushnet, Mark. *The Death Penalty*. New York: Facts on File, 1994.

United States Department of Justice. *Sourcebook of Criminal Justice Statistics*, 31st ed. Available from http://www.albany.edu/sourcebook/.

United States Government Accounting Office. *Report to the Senate and House Committees on the Judiciary: Death Penalty Sentencing*, GGD-90-5, February 26, 1990.

Unah, Isaac, and John Charles Boger. "Race and the Death Penalty in North Carolina: An Empirical Analysis: 1993–1997," April 16, 2001, http://www.common-sense.org/pdfs/NCDeathPenaltyReport2001.pdf.

Wyatt-Brown, Bertram. *Southern Honor: Ethics & Behavior in the Old South*. New York: Oxford University Press, 1982.

Notes

1. For the purposes of this essay, the South will include the states of the former Confederacy, with the exception of Texas. In addition, this essay addresses only *de jure* capital punishment and does not include extralegal forms such as lynching.

2. David Thomas Konig, "'Dale's Laws' and the Non-Common Law Origins of Criminal Justice in Virginia." *The American Journal of Legal History* 26 (October 1982): 364. Also see "Executions in the U.S. 1608–2002: The Espy File," http://www.deathpenaltyinfo.org/article.php?scid=8&did=269.

3. Douglas Greenberg, "Crime, Law Enforcement, and Social Control in Colonial America," *The American Journal of Legal History* 26 (October 1982): 302–304.

4. "Executions in the U.S. 1608–2002: The Espy File."

5. Kathryn Preyer, "Penal Measures in the American Colonies: An Overview," *The American Journal of Legal History* 26 (October 1982): 329–330.

6. Stuart Banner, *The Death Penalty: An American History* (Cambridge, MA: Harvard University Press, 2002), 98–99.

7. Banner, *The Death Penalty: An American History*, 139.

8. The disparity between the total number of whites executed and the various crimes is a result of convictions based upon crimes not known in the Espy file. "Executions in the U.S. 1608–2002: The Espy File."

9. George M. Stroud, *A Sketch of the Laws Relating to Slavery in the Several States of the United States of America*, 2nd ed. (Philadelphia, PA: Henry Longstreth, 1856), 75–87.

10. "Executions in the U.S. 1608–2002: The Espy File."

11. Philip Schwarz, *Slaves Laws in Virginia* (Athens: University of Georgia Press, 1996), 64.

12. George M. Stroud, *A Sketch of the Laws Relating to Slavery in the Several States of the United States of America* (Philadelphia, PA: Kimber and Sharpless, 1827), 120.

13. John W. DeForest, *A Union Officer in the Reconstruction*, James H. Croushore and David Potter, eds. (New Haven, CT: Yale University Press, 1948), 178–179, as quoted in Edward L. Ayers, *Vengeance and Justice: Crime and Punishment in the 19th-Century American South* (New York: Oxford University Press, 1984), 10.

14. Lawrence M. Friedman, *Crime and Punishment in American History* (New York: BasicBooks, 1993), 73.

15. Philip English Mackey, "Edward Livingstone and the Origins of the Movement to Abolish Capital Punishment in America," *Louisiana History* 16 (1976): 145–166.

16. Banner, *The Death Penalty: An American History*, 138–139.

17. "Executions in the U.S. 1608–2002: The Espy File."

18. Ibid.

19. Ibid.

20. *New York Times*, October 2, 1858.

21. Banner, *The Death Penalty: An American History*, 154–155.

22. John D. Bessler, *Death in the Dark: Midnight Executions in America* (Boston, MA: Northeastern University Press, 1997), 32–33.

23. Banner, *The Death Penalty: An American History*, 189.

24. *Atlanta Journal*, July 29, 1988.

25. *In Re Kemmler*, 136 U.S. 436, 443 (1890).

26. *New York Times*, September 2, 1983. Also see Donald Cabana, *Death at Midnight: The Confessions of an Executioner* (Boston, MA: Northeastern University Press, 1996), 7–8.

27. Banner, *The Death Penalty: An American History*, 228–229.

28. *Powell v. Alabama*, 287 U.S. 45, 71 (1932).

29. *Norris v. Alabama*, 294 U.S. 587 (1935). See also Dan Carter, *Scottsboro: A Tragedy of the American South* (Baton Rouge: Louisiana State University Press, 1969, 1979).

30. "Executions in the U.S. 1608–2002: The Espy File."

31. United States Government Accounting Office, *Report to the Senate and House Committees on the Judiciary: Death Penalty Sentencing*, GGD-90-5, February 26, 1990, 5.

32. Isaac Unah, Ph.D., and John Charles Boger, J.D., "Race and the Death Penalty in North Carolina: An Empirical Analysis: 1993–1997," April 16, 2001, http://www.common-sense.org/pdfs/NCDeathPenaltyReport2001.pdf.

33. American Bar Association, "Death Penalty Moratorium Implementation Project," State Death Penalty Assessments Key Findings, http://www.abanet.org/moratorium/home.html.

34. 408 U.S. 238 (1972).

35. Banner, *The Death Penalty: An American History*, 265.

36. 428 U.S. 153 (1976).

37. *Woodson v. North Carolina*, 428 U.S. 280 (1976).

38. Death Penalty Information Center, Executions by State, http://www.deathpenaltyinfo.org/ (2008).

39. Banner, *The Death Penalty: An American History*, 297–298.

40. *Moore v. State of Georgia*, 274 GA 229, 243 (2001).

41. Op. Att'y Gen., No. 07–151 (November 13, 2007).

42. *Baze et al. v. Rees et al.*, 553 U.S. 35 (2008), No. 07–5439 at 11 (2008).

43. Ibid., No. 07–5439 at 13 (2008).

44. *Kennedy v. Louisiana*, 554 U.S. 129 S.Ct. 1 (2008).

45. Ibid., No. 07–343 at 26–27.

46. *Times-Dispatch* (Richmond, VA), October 13, 1984.

47. United States Department of Justice, *Sourcebook of Criminal Justice Statistics*, 31st ed. http://www.albany.edu/sourcebook/, Section 2 (Public attitudes toward crime and criminal justice-related topics).

CHAPTER 10

The Death Penalty in the North

Dino E. Buenviaje

THE NORTH'S experience with the death penalty evolved from an unquestioning faith during colonial times that capital punishment was divinely sanctioned, to outright abolition in the twentieth century. Its origins were intertwined with English common law which changed in the years after independence. During the early nineteenth century, Americans in the northern states debated among themselves regarding the utility and morality of capital punishment, and each state would address the death penalty in its own way during the twentieth century.

The Colonial Experience

The death penalty in the United States has its origins that fall back as early as 1608, when English colonists transplanted English common law to their settlements. Before the creation of the prison system, capital punishment was seen as the only way to deter serious crime, such as murder. Capital punishment fulfilled three objectives in colonial society. The first was deterrence, to prevent crimes from being committed. The second was retribution, the just compensation to society for the damage caused by crime. The third was penitence, by allowing the prisoner to confess his or her crimes, and thus take the final opportunity for eternal salvation. These three motives justified the need for capital punishment.[1]

The criminal codes of the northern colonies during the early seventeenth century created three categories of crimes: crimes against property, such as theft and arson; crimes against persons, such as murder and rape; and crimes against "morality," such as blasphemy or sodomy. During the early years of the northern colonies, the punishment for crimes against property was lighter than that in the mother country. For example, in Connecticut, Massachusetts, Plymouth, and Pennsylvania, burglary and robbery were not considered capital crimes. In New York, New Hampshire, and New Haven, they became capital only after the third offense. In the colonies of New York, Massachusetts, Connecticut, and Pennsylvania, arson was not considered a capital crime.[2] Each colony had it own trajectory.

In the category of crimes against persons, the northern colonies were consistent with England, though still lenient in some aspects. Murder was a capital punishment in all of the colonies, yet manslaughter was not capital in Pennsylvania and western New Jersey. Rape was not capital in the early codes of Massachusetts, New York, and Pennsylvania. Thus, the mid-Atlantic colonies gained the reputation of having the most lenient legal systems in the English-speaking world.

While the northern colonies were lenient in the categories of crimes against property and the crimes against persons, they were harsher in the category of crimes against morality. Early northern colonies such as Massachusetts Bay were established along religious lines, as the Puritans expressed their goal of building "a city on a hill." It was a beacon to the world of what a Godly commonwealth should constitute. Connecticut, Massachusetts, New Hampshire, and New York deemed idolatry a capital offense. New York, Connecticut, and Massachusetts made adultery a capital offense. Sodomy and bestiality were also capital offense in all of the northern colonies. While these offenses were in the law books, they were rarely enforced. During the mid-seventeenth century, the only case of execution for religious beliefs was when four Quakers in Massachusetts were executed, but that was only after they returned after having been banished. The only example of executions for adultery happened in 1643 when James Britton and Mary Latham were hung in Massachusetts. Hangings for other crimes, such as sodomy or bestiality, however, were more regularly witnessed.[3]

By the late seventeenth and early eighteenth centuries, Parliament extended the offenses eligible for capital punishment. These covered mainly crimes against property, such as poaching deer, and pickpocketing. By the second half of the eighteenth century, the English criminal code included two hundred criminal offenses that were eligible for the death penalty, making England's criminal code the harshest in Europe.[4] The colonies followed suit, though in an inconsistent manner. Crimes against property became capital by the eighteenth century. In Massachusetts, robbery became a capital crime after a third conviction in 1642; by 1711 after a second; and after a first in 1761. New Hampshire followed suit in 1682 by reducing the offenses from three to two, and by 1718, to one. Arson became a capital

crime in Connecticut and Massachusetts during the second half of the seventeenth century. Of the northern colonies, Pennsylvania held out the longest, with murder as the only capital offense, due to its origins as a Quaker colony. However, by 1718, after much pressure from London, Pennsylvania added a host of capital offenses, such as manslaughter, rape, highway robbery, maiming, burglary, arson, witchcraft, and sodomy, to be followed by counterfeiting, squatting on Indian land, and prison-breaking later in the century.[5] New York added piracy, counterfeiting, and perjury. Yet, despite the additions of new capital offenses to the law books, their enforcement was haphazard. In Pennsylvania, it took another eighteen years for the colony to hang its first burglar, and thereafter, executions became more frequent. As slavery became more an integral part of the colonial economy, the harshest penalties were reserved for slaves. New York was the first colony that instituted capital punishment for slaves who committed attempted murder and attempted rape. Colonies whose economies heavily depended on slave labor added to the list of capital offenses, including destruction of property, conspiring to rebel, raping a white woman, and even preparing and administering poison. These laws sent the message that the whites were clearly in power and had the ability to destroy any slave who would dare rise against them, as well as any white citizen.[6] The fact that African slaves made up to one-quarter of the labor in New York propelled lawmakers into this harsh criminal regimen.

To twenty-first-century sensibilities, the list of capital offenses during the colonial period must appear draconian. However, it is important to look at capital punishment through the eyes of the colonists of the seventeenth and eighteenth centuries. To colonial Americans, the reasoning behind capital punishment would be what criminologists would call deterrence.[7] By exercising capital punishment frequently, and in public, the authorities send the message that the punishment for severe crime is death, and that the act of the execution, itself, would burn its image into the minds of the viewers who watched it and perhaps dissuade any potential offenders from any life of crime. A contemporary, Nathan Strong, reasoned more bluntly, "Death should be publicly inflicted on the wicked that others may see and fear." Public executions were common fodder for newspapers and sermons in colonial America. Most Americans of the seventeenth and eighteenth centuries saw executions as a fact of life and a direct consequence of wrongdoing.[8]

Religion played an intricate role in capital punishment, particularly since colonies like Massachusetts were founded with a religious mission. Colonial jurists, such as Cotton Mather, cited frequently from the Old Testament, which clearly sanctioned the justification for the death penalty. By the reasoning of the Old Testament, "the land that has been defiled by bloodshed cannot be cleansed unless with the blood of him who shed it."[9] The sixth commandment, "Thou shalt not kill," was also seen as a justification for capital punishment. In other words, this was the principle of *lex talionis*, the law of retaliation, which is articulated in Leviticus: "And he that killeth a beast, he shall restore it: and he that killeth a man, he shall be put to death." Colonial Americans did not consider the criminal's environment as a breeding ground for crime. Rather, their explanation for the causes of crime or any other social ill was Original Sin, which lay within every man and woman since the fall of Adam and Eve in the Garden of Eden. Thus, the individual had the primary responsibility of checking his sinful tendencies, and the blame was his alone, and not society's.[10]

After the sentence of death was handed down, the condemned on average had a week to prepare for execution. During this time, the clergy visited the condemned exhorting them to repent for the sake of their immortal souls. By repenting of their sins, the prisoner had assurance of salvation in the afterlife, despite their wrongdoings on earth. Prisoners had the privilege of going to church on the Sunday before their execution. However, the sermon revolved around the prisoners in question, and sometimes the prisoners had the opportunity to select the biblical passage for the sermon. For example, in 1717 Jeremiah Fenwick earned capital punishment for chopping up his neighbor with an ax. The text he chose for Cotton Mather's sermon was taken from Matthew 10:28, which reads, "Fear not them which kill the body, but are not able to kill the soul; but rather him which is able to destroy both the soul and body in hell."[11]

Some prisoners made use of these clerical visits to their own advantage. Many times, prisoners would repent and find conversion at the end of their visits. Prisoners suddenly discovered the evil of their ways and gave witness to their religious experience. In doing so, there was the chance that the colonial authorities could grant clemency. However, there was little probability of redemption. Many last-minute conversions were borne out of desperation, rather than sincerity, and over time, both the clergy and the authorities grew skeptical.[12] At times, visits became debates between prisoners and clergy over views on religion. To the clergy, a rejection of spiritual consolation was perplexing because the prisoner was turning his or her back on the only sure course to salvation.[13]

Even before the execution, the news of an impending hanging was enough to stir public interest. In addition to visits by clergy, ordinary townspeople visited the condemned. Some came out of genuine Christian charity, to give comfort and to pray with them, following the words of Christ, when he said in the New Testament, "I was a prisoner, and you visited me." Many, however, came for more mundane motives. The most common reason was curiosity, of watching a human being in the last moments of life. Many people came to give their own stern sermons, while others saw the occasion as another opportunity to socialize and gossip with friends. Thus, momentum gathered until the day of the execution.[14]

Public executions involved planning and a great deal of ceremony. Long before modern forms of entertainment, such as movies and television, public executions attracted citizens of all ages and ranks in large numbers. The condemned was escorted in a procession from the jail to the gallows, which was usually located in the center of town in order to gain the largest audience.[15] After a few pronouncements by the authorities, followed by a statement from the condemned, the hangman executed his office. Though considered macabre today, children were especially invited to such events because executions were educational tools to show them the consequences of wrongdoing. To criminals of lesser offenses, executions were meant to deter them from repeating their crimes, the principle known to criminologists today as "incapacitation." Whatever the reason, executions were a sober reminder to colonial society that the state had the right and the power to execute its laws and its citizens who would break its laws.[16]

There were times, however, when capital punishment did not necessarily mean an execution. Rather, the *symbol* of capital punishment was deemed more important than the penalty of death, itself. Such cases were the result of clemency handed down by the colonial governor. According to colonial jurisprudence, the death penalty was the harshest punishment.[17] The colonial governor could use his discretion in granting clemency to the condemned. Usually, these were instances when connections mattered most. A gentleman or a slave owner was most likely receive a pardon from the governor, either for himself or one of his slaves, rather than someone from the lower classes. Clemency could also be obtained as a result of errors committed during the trial. These instances, again, were most likely if the defendant had access to legal counsel. Other circumstances might include youth or inexperience, and the "character" of the defendant, whether he or she would be less likely to commit a second offense. Sometimes, clemency included less-charitable motives, other than to implicate other suspects in a given crime. The act of clemency showed the state's powers at its disposal in establishing law and order.[18]

In addition to clemency, the colonial authorities had other methods to exercise their power short of execution. One such method, "benefit of clergy," was commonly employed by colonial authorities as far back as 1608.[19] All a defendant needed to do was prove that he could read, and he was immune from execution as clergy. Instead of an execution, the defendant was branded on his thumb to show proof of immunity. The literacy test was eventually abolished in 1707, as more people outside the clergy were literate, and it evolved into another instrument of leniency for first-time offenders. The concept of benefit of clergy was also applied in the American colonies, though modified by limiting its application to certain crimes and by the maximum punishment of burning the hand. Benefit of clergy remained in the criminal codes of the colonies through the eighteenth and early nineteenth centuries.[20]

The authorities frequently applied symbolic hanging as a means of deterrence, short of execution. This method of capital punishment first appeared in Massachusetts in 1693 for the crimes of burglary and robbery. For the second offense, the condemned would be required to sit on the gallows for an hour with a rope around his or her neck, followed by a whipping.[21] The third offense would be an outright execution. Symbolic hangings took the place of executions by the end of the seventeenth century, as offenses such as adultery, incest, and blasphemy were no longer punishable by death. In 1695, when adultery was no longer punishable by death, the punishment was sitting upon the gallows with a rope around the neck, followed by whipping and wearing the letter A. Nathaniel Hawthorne's novel *The Scarlet Letter* was inspired by these symbolic executions in Massachusetts. Dueling was also punishable by symbolic hanging in 1729, but only when no one died from the duel.[22]

By the eighteenth century, symbolic hangings became prevalent throughout New England and continued into the early decades of the nineteenth century. The condemned prisoners were always deliberately made unaware of the sentence. As far as they were concerned, they were spending their last moments on earth and were expected to settle their final affairs.[23] On the day of the presumed execution, the prisoners felt genuine fear of being hanged at the gallows, until the final moment when the executioner read the pardon to the prisoner. Timing was of the essence in symbolic hangings because the goal was to keep the prisoner in mortal dread of his or her execution. By offering a last-minute pardon, the prisoner was overwhelmed by gratitude to the point of repenting and promising to live a virtuous life thereafter. Whereas, if the prisoner were to learn of the reprieve, as occasionally happened, the entire exercise was in vain because the prisoner could not have elicited the desired effect. Symbolic hangings fulfilled the requirement of a "capital punishment," while showing the state's capacity for mercy.[24]

The state could also be capable of great cruelty. There were occasions when a hanging could not suffice. Indeed, colonial governments exacted harsher methods of executions to send a message to the community about the heinousness of the crime.[25] Thus, it was not enough to kill the body. Some punishments were designed specifically,

either to give the condemned a lingering death, or to desecrate the human body. Dismemberment was one such punishment. Reserved for the crime of treason, dismemberment began with the disembowelment of the prisoner, who was then hung while still alive. After death, the body was cut into four parts, known as "quartering."[26]

The most prominent example of extreme capital punishment was to be burned at the stake. Punishment by immolation had long been in practice in Europe for witchcraft and heresy. However, burning was not used as a punishment for witchcraft or other religious offenses in the North American colonies. The punishment for witchcraft at the Salem witch trials was death by hanging.[27] Burning at the stake then was the punishment reserved for slaves who had murdered their masters or who were plotting a revolt, or for women who had murdered their husbands. The message was that the state was not only responsible for enforcing the law, but also for maintaining the social order. By linking the state with the family, the authorities sent the message that anyone who attempted to disrupt the racial or gender order was to suffer the most public, painful, and lingering death available. However, because being burned alive was so painful and frightening, it was not performed often. On the few occasions that it was, the prisoners were sometimes hanged first before being burned, as a last-minute gesture of mercy.[28]

While burning alive was the severest punishment the state could inflict upon a living person, the state also had methods of punishment that were inflicted upon the body of the condemned prisoner. Thus, the body would be covered with tallow or pitch to delay decomposition, and placed inside an iron cage called a "gibbet" and be "hung in chains." The gibbet was reserved for piracy and for slaves who had committed crimes such as rape. One particularly notorious pirate, known as Joseph Andrews, was hung in chains in full view of the people of New York on an island in New York Bay, known as Pest Island, known today as Liberty Island.[29] On other occasions, the body of the criminal was handed over for dissection in medical schools so that medical students could learn about anatomy. Dissection was reserved for mutiny and other forms of revolt, and was considered a most dishonorable death. Yet, that did not deter the condemned criminals, themselves, from making a profit by selling their bodies to surgeons and medical schools, since the proceeds would go to the families of the prisoners. The disgraceful showing of the body after death was considered to be a deterrent for crime in a society that believed in a bodily resurrection on Judgment Day. In colonial society before the advent of the prison system, death was a standard from which to determine the punishment of the convicted criminals.[30]

The Early Republic

In the years after independence, the states became secularized. Thus states like Massachusetts decriminalized offenses such as blasphemy and adultery. Unlike during the colonial period, there was a movement by state governments to restrict the use of capital punishment. Instead, the ideas of the Enlightenment strongly influenced Americans of the early republic.[31] For example, in Massachusetts there were twelve crimes punishable by death in the mid-seventeenth century. After the Revolutionary War, there were only eight. At the same time, in England, there were 223 capital crimes as late as 1819.[32] Also, in the years after the Revolution, the states followed a trend of distinguishing various degrees of murder, as there had been degrees of death during the colonial period. Under traditional English law, all murder was considered a capital offense, which merited death. Juries became increasingly uncomfortable

applying the death penalty to all cases of murder and precipitated what would then be called "jury nullification." A Philadelphia physician and signer of the Declaration of Independence, Benjamin Rush, wrote an essay entitled *Considerations on the Injustice and Impolity of Punishing Murder by Death* in 1792, which drew upon the work of Italian jurist Cesare di Beccaria, *On Crime and Punishment*. Rush's work gained the support of Benjamin Franklin, and they both lobbied to reform the criminal statutes of Pennsylvania.[33] In 1794, Pennsylvania was the first state to introduce degrees of murder, with first-degree murder, defined as a premeditated and deliberate killing, being a capital offense. This allowed juries discretion in assigning punishment for various types of murder. Later, first-degree murder included murder committed in the act of arson, rape, robbery, or burglary. By the end of the nineteenth century, executions were no longer public. By 1900, most states followed Pennsylvania's lead in providing at least two degrees of murder, restricting capital punishment for murder in the first degree. As a result, capital punishment became less frequent.[34]

The Northern Debate over Capital Punishment

Starting in the 1780s and 1790s, the northern states entered into debate over whether capital punishment should be abolished, and groups formed to explore this issue. The Massachusetts Society for the Abolition of Capital Punishment, founded in Boston, organized regular debates on the issue of abolition, which included prominent figures such as Wendell Phillips and William Lloyd Garrison. Foreign observers, such as Alexis de Tocqueville and Harriet Martineau marveled at the desire to eliminate capital punishment in the North. The debate around capital punishment in the North centered on three issues: the effectiveness of capital punishment as a deterrent to crime; its legitimate use by the government for retribution; and the possibility of using prison to reform prisoners.[35]

Northern reformers during the nineteenth century argued that capital punishment was an ineffective deterrent to crime. Northern periodicals such as the *American Jurist* cited statistics from Belgium in 1838 concluding that reducing hangings would lead to a reduction in crime.[36] However, statistics were rarely employed in the debate over capital punishment, and advocates of both sides relied more on rhetoric and abstractions. Abolitionists argued that criminals were more likely to be deterred by life imprisonment in which they would be denied everything but death, while death penalty advocates, or "retentionists," argued that death was an effective deterrent for criminals. The Bible was central in debates between abolitionists and retentionists.[37] Abolitionists emphasized the message of love and forgiveness from the New Testament, while retentionists emphasized the Old Testament's message of retribution and the law of "an eye for an eye." For instance, Abolitionists often quoted from the Sermon on the Mount where Jesus said, "Ye have heard that it hath been said, an eye for an eye, and a tooth for a tooth: But I say unto you, that ye resist not evil: but whosoever shall smite thee on thy right cheek, turn to him the other also."[38] Abolitionists earned criticism for their overly optimistic belief in the march of progress, without taking into account real world conditions. Retentionists concluded that abolitionists of capital punishment were too faint-hearted and had "womanly" sensibilities in executing justice.[39]

However, public sensibilities toward executions were beginning to change in the middle of the nineteenth century. During the colonial period and the years after independence, executions were carried out under local authorities. By the end of the nineteenth century, executions became the sole jurisdiction of the state governments. Vermont was the first state to centralize executions in 1864. By the 1920s, most state governments, except in the South, carried out executions rather than local governments.[40]

During the colonial period, public executions were educational tools to teach the public about the "wages of sin" and of the state's prerogative to take life in order to maintain order in society. People of all ages and classes during the seventeenth and eighteenth centuries witnessed public executions, not solely for edification, but also for some entertainment value. However, by the early 1800s, the elite were growing less inclined to attend public executions, which they saw as "unrefined" and fit only for "the masses." In 1824, Pennsylvania's legislature initiated the first bill to abolish public executions. The reason was that the people who derived the most benefit from the lessons of capital punishment were not likely to attend, and instead, public executions became another excuse for less-respectable people to drink, carouse, and cause a public disorder. The bill failed, but eventually public executions were abolished in Pennsylvania.[41]

Gender roles also influenced the change in attitudes toward public punishment. In the Victorian era, men and women occupied separate spheres, with men dominating public life and women relegated to the home. Critics of capital punishment complained that public executions were not suitable material for women to see because of their status as the "gentler sex."[42] Public perceptions of death, itself, began to change during the nineteenth century. Traditionally, families were intimately connected with disease and death, which were ever present in the home. Because of advances in medicine during the nineteenth century, disease and death were moved to the hospitals, and people grew less exposed to the nature of dying. Victorian middle-class sensibilities no longer tolerated being in the presence of death, having moved cemeteries away from the cities. This, obviously, extended to capital punishment, since abolitionist reformers came from the same ranks of the middle class.[43] In 1830, Connecticut was the first state to abolish public executions. By 1836, this trend was followed by other northern states, such as Massachusetts, New Hampshire, New Jersey, New York, Pennsylvania, and Rhode Island. The South continued public executions for several decades, the last public execution being held in Kentucky in 1936.[44]

With the abolition of public executions, capital punishment was then carried out within prison walls. Ironically, the same genteel society that bristled at public executions took front-row seating to witness executions. This elite crowd consisted of journalists, politicians, doctors, and lawyers, in addition to the police officials. States such as New York established guidelines limiting the number of spectators to twelve. In this crowd, women were totally absent because men would have greater access to executions by virtue of their positions.[45] The same rituals remained, but in an abridged form. The clergy were still allowed to visit the condemned and offer their prayers. There was still a procession from the jail cell to the gallows, though much shorter, and the prisoner was still given the opportunity to make a statement.[46]

On the day of the execution, mobs would still gather outside the prison walls hoping for a glimpse of the condemned. There, the carnival atmosphere of the old public executions remained, with vendors hawking their wares to the public. For those who were not able to attend executions, mass communications through newspapers allowed people to experience some of the emotions of a public hanging through the details provided by journalists of the "penny presses." Mass media kept audiences hooked, from the trial to the hanging itself.[47] However, once executions were no longer public, capital punishment

ceased to be a deterrent. Having lost its power to frighten the public into obeying the law, the end of public executions gave ammunition to the those who sought to abolish the death penalty.[48]

The Role of Technology

Another turning point in the history of capital punishment was the role of technology. The invention of anesthesia in the nineteenth century meant that it was possible to escape pain, not only during surgery, but also in other aspects of life. Thus, society had become more sensitive to pain and began to debate over the most painless means of execution. Hanging had been the preferred method of execution because it was considered to be the most "humane."[49] The prisoner had a noose tied around his neck. The executioner released the trapdoor, and the prisoner fell. Ideally, a short jerk severed the spinal cord, resulting in instant death. However, the application fell short of the ideal because of the many factors involved, such as the elasticity of the rope, the physical dimensions of the condemned prisoner, and the skills of the hangman.[50]

To eliminate these variables, officials began to consider alternatives beyond the traditional gallows. In 1831, New York instituted the "upright jerker" as a more humane alternative to the gallows. Instead of dropping the condemned through the trapdoor, the prisoner is yanked upward to induce instant and painless death, through the use of weights that would propel the prisoner upward and sever the spinal cord. The upright jerker was the standard gallows for New York City by 1845, and was also adopted by other New York counties as well as Chicago, and Plymouth, Massachusetts. However, the upright jerker failed to meet its potential. Instead of instantaneous death, the upright jerker inflicted lingering pain on the prisoners, sometimes taking as long as fifteen minutes, and resulted in scathing reviews by the press. Cases of mismanaged executions prompted state authorities to consider other methods besides hanging.[51]

In the 1880s, New York pioneered the use of electricity for executions. In 1886, the New York legislature created a commission to investigate the most humane and practical executions. Thomas Edison proposed death by using electricity, despite his opposition to capital punishment, because it would be the fastest and least painful way to induce death.[52] The commission received more than two hundred responses from judges, sheriffs, lawyers, and physicians, of which eighty-seven preferred electricity, followed by eighty votes for hanging, eight for poison, and five for the guillotine.[53] The New York Society of Medical Jurisprudence debated the merits of both electrocution and the guillotine, but ultimately decided in favor of electrocution as being more humane than the guillotine, which conjured images of the French Revolution.[54] Unlike hanging, which does not always kill the prisoner, who can thus be revived, electrocution stops the heart completely. Even though the guillotine was equally as swift, the effusion of blood that followed was objectionable. Electrocution was also considered to be cost effective at about one thousand dollars because all that was required was a chair, a foot- and headrest, and an electrode, which could be connected from the same power source as the prisons. Adopting electricity was seen as a step forward to progress because just as electricity provided cleaner lives, electricity was a cleaner alternative for death.[55]

The first execution by electric chair took place on August 6, 1890, when a man from Buffalo, New York, named William Kemmler was electrocuted for murdering his girlfriend. His execution was delayed by a legal challenge mounted by his attorney on the basis that death by electric chair was cruel and unusual punishment and violated New York's constitution. The Supreme Court ruled that death by electric chair did not infringe on any of the defendant's rights.[56] On the day Kemmler was to be executed, twenty-five witnesses were invited, which included doctors, state officials, and the press. It took seventeen seconds for 1,700 volts of current to run through his body. When the warden began to disconnect the electrodes from the body, it appeared that Kemmler was still alive. The current was run through again to make sure that the prisoner was dead. The electric chair was run for one minute, and the smell of burning flesh revolted the spectators.[57] After the execution, the coroner concluded that the first electrocution had indeed killed Kemmler. What appeared to be breathing was merely muscle spasms. Despite the gruesome effects of the first execution, the state of New York continued to use the electric chair for executions. One year after Kemmler's execution, there were four more executions performed in one day with smooth efficiency. The electric chair was steadily adopted by other states by the beginning of the twentieth century, throughout the North, the South, and the Midwest. By 1937, the federal government abolished hanging for federal crimes, and instead adopted the execution method of the state where the death sentence was imposed.[58]

In the quest for ever more humane methods of execution, gas was considered as another alternative to hanging. The first experiments using gas date back to the 1890s when it was used to euthanize dogs. Between 1896 and 1897, the Medical Society of Allegheny County, Pennsylvania, recommended the use of gas as an alternative to electricity because the prisoner would not experience pain, and would not have to undergo a ceremony that would lead to his own death. Maryland was the only state in the North to adopt the gas chamber in 1955, having switched from the electric chair. The gas chamber was more readily adopted by the western states, which perceived it to be more modern and humane than the electric chair.[59]

The consequences of the adoption of the electric chair and the gas chamber were that they made capital punishment even more remote from the public. Because of the complexity of the machinery involved, executions were not only moved within prison walls. They had to be relocated deep within the bowels of the prison itself. The audience remained limited to a small group of state and medical officials. As a result, with capital punishment removed from the public's everyday experience, it became possible for abolitionists to launch their attacks.[60]

Abolition

Between the 1820s and 1850s, the movement to abolish capital punishment in the northern states accelerated. Felonies such as arson, burglary, rape, and robbery were no longer capital offenses. Maine had decapitalized rape in 1829, as did Massachusetts in 1852. By 1860, murder and treason became the only capital offenses in the northern states, which followed Pennsylvania's example of establishing degrees for murder. The New York legislature debated seriously on whether capital punishment should be abolished.[61] John O'Sullivan, a lawyer and editor of the periodical *United States Magazine*, chaired a committee that produced a 165-page report recommending the abolition of the death penalty. The bill abolishing capital punishment lost by a narrow margin. Other state legislatures followed suit. In Massachusetts, Robert Rantoul sponsored the abolition of the death penalty in 1835, 1836, and 1837, and failed. Abolitionists headed petitions for the end of capital punishment in Pennsylvania, Connecticut, and New Jersey, without much success.[62]

Abolitionists scored a major victory in 1837 when the state legislature of Maine passed a law that delayed execution for one year since the conviction. The governor had to take a public stand by signing a warrant of the execution at the end of that year. The purpose of the law was to wait for emotions to cool with the passage of time. As a result, Maine had abolished capital punishment *de facto*, as not a single execution took place between 1837 and 1863. The "Maine laws" were soon adopted by Vermont, New Hampshire, Massachusetts, and New York. After Michigan in 1846 became the first state in the union to abolish capital punishment for murder, Rhode Island followed suit in 1852, and then by Wisconsin in 1853.[63] However, the movement to abolish capital punishment lost steam during the 1850s for two reasons. First, the sectionalist controversies surrounding slavery became the main concern facing the country. Second, the reformers themselves were too involved in other movements, such as the temperance movement and women's suffrage, and did not remain focused on the abolition of the death penalty. By the 1860s, the carnage of the Civil War made the abolition of the death penalty a low priority in American society, and it was not resurrected until well into the twentieth century.[64]

By the beginning of the twentieth century, as capital punishment became less of a communal event and more of an exclusive event attended only by state and other elected officials, its purpose as a deterrent and as a teaching tool became less evident. Through medical and technological advances, the public was less willing to withstand exhibitions of pain. These societal and cultural changes fueled the abolitionist movement. Maine and Rhode Island had abolished capital punishment by the last quarter of the nineteenth century.[65] At the turn of the twentieth century, the legislatures of New Jersey, New York, Connecticut, and Massachusetts debated on whether to amend their constitutions by abolishing capital punishment. However, the First World War suspended further discussion of abolition as the nation switched its attention to the war in Europe. During the postwar years, the spike in crime caused by Prohibition and sensational cases such as the Lindbergh kidnapping created a wave of support for capital punishment.[66]

At the same time, however, public certainty for the necessity and the morality of capital punishment began to waver by the 1930s. The Sacco and Vanzetti case in 1927 led many people to believe that the government was unfairly prosecuting those two men for their political beliefs. The Scottsboro case of the 1930s, involving the teenage boys in Alabama accused of rape, raised questions on the racial inequality associated with capital punishment. Starting in the 1930s, the rate of executions experienced a marked decline in the North. For the entire Northeast alone, the number of executions between 1930 and 1934 was 155, at a rate of 1.97 executions per 100 homicides. By the years 1960 to 1964, the number of executions in the Northeast had decreased to 17, at a rate of 0.28 executions per 100 homicides. Broken down by state, New Jersey, for example, averaged at 4.0 executions per year between 1931 and 1935 and had decreased to 2.0 per year from 1936 to 1940 to 1.6 from 1941 to 1945. In the years between 1930 and 1945, the average rate of executions in Pennsylvania dropped from 8.2 to 3.6; in New York, from 15.3 to 11.4; and in Massachusetts from 1.8 to 0.9. Juries became more reluctant to impose the death penalty. In 1935, juries issued 158 death sentences. By 1950, the number had been sharply reduced to 79. In contrast, rates of execution in southern states did not begin to decline until the 1940s, and would still continue to carry out the most executions in the country. Such changes in the public's willingness, particularly in the North, left open to abolitionists the opportunity to challenge capital punishment in the Supreme Court.[67]

The most significant challenge to capital punishment in the United States was *Furman v. Georgia* in 1972, which challenged its constitu-

tionality. The question behind *Furman v. Georgia* was whether capital punishment was considered "cruel and unusual punishment" under the Eighth Amendment and whether it violated the equal protection clause of the Fourteenth Amendment. The Supreme Court ruled that capital punishment under arbitrary state laws violated the Eighth Amendment.[68] Four years later, in response to another Supreme Court case, *Gregg v. Georgia*, the Court upheld the use of capital punishment, but rape and other offenses were no longer considered capital crimes. In the wake of the *Furman* decision, the Supreme Court imposed a moratorium on capital punishment to allow states to conform to the rulings in the *Furman* case. While many states have since reinstated capital punishment, many northern states such as Maine, Massachusetts, or West Virginia did not. These cases marked the current status of capital punishment in the United States. Currently, of the thirteen states that have abolished capital punishment, six of them are in the northeast: Maine, New Jersey, New York, Pennsylvania, Vermont, and West Virginia.[69]

Dino E. Buenviaje is a Ph.D. Candidate at the University of California, Riverside, where he is specializing in early-twentieth-century American cultural history. His dissertation will analyze the role of American and British elites in the entrance of the United States to the First World War. He received his MA in history at California State University, Fullerton, where he completed his thesis titled *Correspondence and Community: Elite Friendships in the Anglo-American Rapprochement, 1895–1910*. He received his Bachelor's degrees in history and political science at University of California, Irvine. He is a current recipient of the California State University's Chancellor's Doctoral Incentive Program. He is the author of numerous articles on American history, military, and intelligence.

Suggested Readings

Acker, James, Robert M. Bohm, and Charles S. Lanier. *America's Experiment with Capital Punishment: Reflections on the Past, Present, and Future of the Ultimate Penal Sanction*. Durham, N.C.: Carolina Academic Press, 2003.

Banner, Stuart. *The Death Penalty: An American History*. Cambridge, Mass.: Harvard University Press, 2002.

Bedau, ed. *The Death Penalty in America: Current Controversies*. New York: Oxford University Press, 1997.

Bowers, William J. *Legal Homicide: Death as Punishment in America, 1864–1982*. Boston: Northeastern University Press, 1974.

———. *Executions in America*. Lexington, Mass.: D. C. Heath, 1974.

Galliher, John F., et al. *America without the Death Penalty: States Leading the Way*. Boston: Northeastern University Press, 2002.

Paternoster, Raymond. *Capital Punishment in America*. New York: Lexington Books, 1991.

Vila, Brian, and Cynthia Morris, eds. *Capital Punishment in the United States: A Documentary History*. Westport, Conn.: Greenwood Press, 1997.

Notes

1. Stuart Banner, *The Death Penalty: An American History* (Cambridge, Mass.: Harvard University Press, 2002), 6.
2. Ibid.
3. Ibid., 7.
4. Ibid.
5. Ibid., 8.
6. Ibid., 9.
7. William J. Bowers, *Legal Homicide: Death as Punishment in America, 1864–1982* (Boston: Northeastern University Press, 1974), 5.
8. Banner, 10–11.
9. *Capital Punishment in the United States: A Documentary History*, Bryan Vila and Cynthia Morris, eds. (Westport, Conn.: Greenwood Press, 1997), 6.
10. Banner, 12–14.
11. Ibid., 20–21.
12. Ibid., 25.
13. Ibid., 20.
14. Ibid.
15. Raymond Paternoster, *Capital Punishment in America* (New York: Lexington Books, 1991), 6.
16. Banner, 28.
17. Ibid., 54–55.
18. Ibid., 55.
19. Ibid., 62.
20. Ibid., 63.
21. Ibid., 64.
22. Ibid., 65.
23. Ibid., 68.
24. Ibid., 69–70.
25. Ibid., 70.
26. Ibid., 75.
27. Ibid., 71.
28. Ibid., 72.
29. Ibid., 73.
30. Ibid., 79–80.
31. Bowers, *Legal Homicide*, 6.
32. Paternoster, 6.
33. Bowers, *Legal Homicide*, 7.
34. Ibid., 8.
35. Banner, 113.
36. Ibid., 116.
37. Vila and Moris, 35.
38. Ibid., 7.
39. Banner, 126–27.
40. Paternoster, 7.
41. James Bowers, *Executions in America* (Lexington, Mass.: D. C. Heath, 1974), 5.
42. Banner, 152.
43. Ibid., 153.
44. Ibid., 154–56.
45. Ibid., 157.
46. Ibid., 159.
47. Ibid., 163–65.
48. Ibid., 168.
49. Ibid., 170.
50. Ibid., 171.
51. Ibid., 172.
52. Ibid., 178.
53. Ibid., 179.
54. Ibid., 180.
55. Ibid.
56. Ibid., 184.
57. Ibid., 185–86.
58. Ibid., 189.
59. Ibid., 196–99.
60. Ibid., 206–7.
61. Paternoster, 8–9.
62. Banner, 132–33.
63. Ibid., 134.
64. Ibid., 135–37.
65. Ibid., 220.
66. Ibid., 225.
67. Ibid., 226–27.
68. Bowers, *Legal Homicide*, 174.
69. Ibid., 176.

CHAPTER 11

The Death Penalty in the Midwest

Melody M. Miyamoto and Charles W. Showalter

THE HISTORY of the Midwest contains fewer stories of violence than those of other regions. Racial lynching, vigilante justice, and capital punishment are seldom associated with states like Illinois, Indiana, Iowa, Michigan, Minnesota, Ohio, and Wisconsin. Yet, these states have not been without executions and the controversy that surrounds them. In the United States, only twelve states currently have no death penalty statutes. Of those twelve states, four are in the Midwest. Of the three Midwest states with death penalty statutes, one, Illinois, has issued a moratorium on executions and another, Wisconsin, recently placed an initiative to abolish the death penalty in front of voters. Given these figures, it might be easy to conclude that the Midwest has a lower incidence of capital punishment than the rest of the nation. However, another Midwest state, Ohio, has the fifth-highest death row population in the nation, and ranks in the top 25 percent of states for number of executions in the last thirty years. Like the death penalty in the rest of America, capital punishment in the Midwest appears to follow few set patterns and there are few explanations for the divergent death penalty stances of the various midwestern states. However, there are some trends among the states in the Midwest. For example, several have seen abolitionist movements crop up as a response to

botched executions, overturned convictions, or as part of a larger, nationwide abolitionist movement. Similarly, some states have either reinstated or considered reinstating the death penalty in response to highly publicized murders. The Midwest's relationship with the death penalty has produced dozens of famous executions, a landmark United States Supreme Court decision, and a number of current controversies over present death penalty statutes.

Illinois

Prior to 1976 (when the Supreme Court ruled, in *Gregg v. Georgia*, that the death penalty is not cruel and unusual, and can be implemented), the state of Illinois executed 348 inmates. The state legally reenacted the death penalty in 1974, and since then has put to death twelve people. Crimes punishable by death include first-degree murder with one of twenty-one aggravating circumstances, including killing a police officer or fireman, an employee or prisoner in a prison or jail, an emergency medical worker while on duty, a community policing volunteer, or a teacher or other school employee near a school. The death penalty can also be used when a person is convicted of killing multiple people with separate intent or by separate acts, or when hired or by hiring another person. The death penalty can also be implemented for intentionally killing someone in the course of an intentionally violent felony, in a "cold, calculated and premeditated manner," or in a way that involves torture. Also, murder as a way to prevent or retaliate against the victim for aiding in persecution, or murder of someone under order of protection from the murderer, may also result in the death penalty. Persons convicted of murdering a disabled person, killing someone over sixty or younger than twelve, a murder involving torture, drive-by shootings, gang or drug conspiracies, or an act of terrorism are all eligible for the death penalty. As of 2006, there were eleven people on death row, none of whom were women. In the state of Illinois, life without parole is an option and the jury determines the sentence. The mild end of the punishment spectrum for such a crime is twenty to sixty years imprisonment, but persons found guilty of a felony can be put to death even though he or she was not responsible for the murder. The state has freed eighteen people from death row and has granted 127 clemency requests. Male prisoners are given a lethal injection at Pontiac Correctional Center in Pontiac, Illinois, while women face their deaths at Dwight Correctional Center in Dwight, Illinois. The governor can grant clemency with the nonbinding advice of the Board of Pardons and Paroles. The murder rate per ten thousand people is six.

Since the reinstatement of the death penalty in 1974, Illinois has allowed the punishment for first-degree murder, at the request of the prosecutor, and it may be imposed by a jury or a judge. The judge can choose the death penalty without consulting the jury, and the judge may also override the jury's sentence of death and may opt for life imprisonment instead. The first execution since reinstatement came in 1990 when fifty-year-old Charles Walker, a white man, was put to death by lethal injection on September 12 for killing two white victims.

However, later in that decade, the trend toward executions stopped. In 1996 Governor Jim Edgar, who ran on a strong pro-death-penalty platform, commuted the death sentence of Guinevere Garcia. Garcia had previously served ten years in jail for smothering her baby. Then, in 1991, she, the victim of alcohol abuse and sexual molestation, tried to rob her husband, but ultimately shot him while the two argued. Although Garcia had accepted her fate of death, Governor Edgar decided that her crime compared to others committed by persons who had not been sentenced to death, and he commuted her sentence.[1] Then, in November 1998, the Illinois Supreme Court stopped the execution of Willie Enoch as more DNA tests were being done. Enoch had been convicted of murdering Amanda "Kay" Burns in 1983. Enoch had four prior convictions for rape, and was also charged with kidnapping and attempted rape, in addition to the murder of Burns. The defense asked for independent, not state labs to test DNA findings.[2] However, Enoch died while on death row in June of 2000, the same year that Illinois Governor Ryan halted the death penalty.

Illinois presents a unique case regarding the death penalty because in 2000, then Governor George Ryan, who campaigned as a strong supporter of the death penalty, called for a moratorium on executions. This followed a 1998 conference at Northwestern University, called the National Convention on Wrongful Convictions and the Death Penalty. There, thirty wrongfully convicted inmates, who had been released because of volunteer efforts and new technology, brought further attention to the faults in the justice system. As a result, Governor Ryan imposed a moratorium on the death penalty, suspending all lethal injections. He said, "There is a flaw in the system, without question, and it needs to be studied," as he noted that there had been more people exonerated than put to death since Illinois reinstated the death penalty. The governor claimed to support the death penalty, but believed the state must ensure that "the person who is put to death is absolutely guilty." The moratorium made Illinois the first state to stop all executions while it reviewed the death penalty process.[3] The governor instituted a commission to review the capital punishment system, and the commission made over eighty suggestions, including reducing the number of death eligibility factors, prohibiting capital punishment for convictions based on only one eyewitness, controlling the use of testimony by jailhouse informants, and using the Illinois Supreme Court to ensure that the punishment was appropriate and proportionate to similar cases.[4] In January 2000, the state had released thirteen wrongfully convicted inmates in the same time that it had executed twelve prisoners.

By 2006, Ryan, then the former governor, had become an abolitionist. "All my life I believed in the death penalty and I thought it was the right system and it was done by people who knew what they were doing . . . and I was wrong. Now I'm an abolitionist. The death penalty is arbitrary, capricious, unjust, racist, and unfair to the poor. We need to have a national and international moratorium on the death penalty," he stated. Ryan's stance on the death penalty came even prior to his viewing of *Race to Execution*, a documentary that exposes the racial inequalities of the death penalty. Madison Hobley, a black Chicago man, was the subject of the film. A jury made up of eleven whites convicted Hobley of starting a fire that killed his wife and child, and Ryan had pardoned Hobley. Ryan, who had recently been convicted of corruption, claimed that he commuted the death sentences of everyone on Illinois's death row because "legislators didn't have the political courage to pass the reforms of the state's criminal justice system recommended by

his commission of experts."[5] Then governor of Illinois Rod Blagojevich said, in 2003, that he would not repeal the moratorium.

Although there is a moratorium on the death penalty in Illinois, it continues to be a sentencing for which prosecutors can strive. Thus, the Illinois Capital Litigation Fund is in place to help pay for defendants' trial costs. This taxpayer-funded system has helped to offset the high costs of capital punishment trials since 2000, when it was implemented to equalize the system for those who could not afford proper representation. The fund currently sits at $4.5 million, up $1 million since its original budget. From that, $3 million is reserved for counsel's expenses, $1 million for state's attorneys, and $500,000 for public defenders. This fund began in conjunction with Governor Ryan's concern for the fairness of the death penalty.[6]

Indiana

Indiana legalized the death penalty in 1973 and resumed executions in 1981 under Governor James R. Thompson. Prior to 1976, the state executed 131 people and has killed seventeen since. The current population of death row is twenty-four. Murder with any of sixteen aggravating circumstances is punishable by death. As in Illinois, the jury may decide on the death sentence, even for those responsible for a felony but not the murder. Inmates are put to death by lethal injection. Two innocent people have been freed from death row, and three clemencies have been granted. The governor may grant clemency with the nonbinding advice of the Board of Pardons and Paroles. Indianapolis houses death row for women, and men are held in Michigan City. Life without parole is an option. The murder rate per 100,000 people is 5.7.

According to the information maintained by

the Office of Code Revision, Indiana Legislative Services Agency, "The state may seek either a death sentence or a sentence of life imprisonment without parole for murder by alleging . . . the existence of at least one of the aggravating circumstances" listed below. After a guilty conviction, the state must then prove, beyond a reasonable doubt, the existence of at least one of the alleged aggravating circumstances.

In the state of Indiana, the defendant can be put to death when the aggravating circumstances outweigh the mitigating circumstances beyond a reasonable doubt. The murderer may face the death penalty for killing a victim while committing or attempting to commit arson, burglary, kidnapping, rape, robbery or carjacking. Also included in that list is child molestation, criminal deviant conduct, criminal gang activity, and dealing a narcotic drug or cocaine. Convicted murderers who use the unlawful detonation of an explosive with the intent to injure a person or damage property may also qualify for the death penalty, as would people who commit the murder by lying in wait, by hiring another person to kill, or by being hired to kill. Defendants may also face the death penalty if the victim of the murder is a corrections employee, probation officer, parole officer, community corrections worker, home detention officer, firefighter, judge, or law enforcement officer, and either the victim was acting in the course of duty or the victim's actions while in the course of duty motivated the murder. Other circumstances that could lead to capital punishment are if the defendant had already been convicted of another murder, or committed another murder, regardless of conviction. The state of Indiana also implements the option of the death penalty for convicted prisoners if the defendant was under the custody of the county sheriff or the department of corrections, on probation after receiving a sentence for committing a felony, or on parole during the time when the

murder was committed. The defendant may also face the death penalty if he dismembers the victim, burns, mutilates, or tortures the victim while he is still alive, or murders someone under the age of twelve. Furthermore, if the victim was also a victim of battery as a Class C or D offense, kidnapping, criminal confinement, or a sex crime, for which the defendant was convicted, then she could also be put to death. Murders committed to prevent a witness from testifying are punishable by death, as are those committed when firing into a dwelling or from a vehicle. Defendants who intentionally kill pregnant women and viable fetuses may also be put to death.

The state of Indiana has mitigating circumstances when it comes to sentencing convicted felons with the death penalty. Defendants who have no record of prior criminal conduct, were under extreme mental or emotional disturbance when committing the murder, or were under eighteen years of age at the time of the murder may qualify. Also eligible are defendants who did not commit the murder but rather were accomplices with minor roles, or were under the "substantial domination" of another person. Other circumstances include impaired judgment due to mental disease or intoxication. And finally, the state includes the clause "any other circumstances appropriate for consideration."

Sentencing can be done by the jury or the court. The jury and the court can consider evidence throughout the trial as well as new evidence at the sentencing hearing. For a decision of either the death penalty or life without parole, the jury must find at least one aggravating circumstance beyond a reasonable doubt. If the jury cannot come to that conclusion, then the court can make the decision. Once the defendant is sentenced to death, the execution is to take place one year and one day after the defendant's conviction. Only the state supreme court can stay the execution of the death sentence, and if it does so, it sets a new date for the execution. The convicted person can file a petition for post-conviction relief and the court is to set a date for a hearing to consider that petition within ninety days. The state supreme court automatically reviews a death sentence, and the convicted person can also file a written petition to present new evidence.

Iowa

Iowa had the death penalty when it entered statehood in 1846 and has executed a total of forty-five people. Iowa had an abolitionist movement in the second half of the nineteenth century before abolishing the death penalty in 1872. Like many other states, Iowa's move to abolition was only a quick experiment; in 1878 Iowa reestablished the death penalty. In 1872, Iowa's murder rate was 1 in 800,000 people. During the next six years, at which time Iowa did not execute prisoners or impose death sentences, Iowa's murder rate decreased to 1 in 1,200,000 people.[7] However, Iowans reinstated the death penalty in 1878 in response to a highly publicized murder by outlaw Jesse James. Jesse James and his brother Frank James robbed a Rock Island road train near Adair, Iowa, in 1873. The robbery resulted in the death of an engineer. The outlaw gang's exploits received great publicity and consequently caused speculation among the Iowa public. An Iowa newspaper in 1878 wrote, "No longer will murderers lure their victims from Missouri to Iowa hoping thus to escape hanging. The good people of the state will breathe easier and fewer of them will have their skulls split open this year than were last."[8] This event undoubtedly brought capital punishment to the forefront of public debate. Yet, Iowa is only one of three states that abolished the death penalty between the end of the Civil War and 1900.[9] Nationwide abolition movements, which had been strong from the 1830s to 1850s, were pushed away from the forefront of public discourse as the nation moved closer to war.

Although Iowa reinstated the death penalty in 1878, it historically has not executed a large number of prisoners. In fact, between 1930 and 1965, Iowa executed eighteen inmates; only five states executed fewer people during that same period. One of Iowa's few prisoners to be executed was convicted murderer Ira Pavey. In 1922, Pavey became the first person in twelve years to be executed by the state of Iowa. Pavey gained attention with his pre-execution behavior. Fort Madison prison officials were appalled by Pavey's nonchalant attitude as he smoked a cigarette while walking to the gallows. Onlookers noted that Pavey kept a smile on his face until the hood was pulled over his head.[10] Another notable Iowa execution happened in 1962. Charles Kelley, a convicted murderer, did not receive great press or public attention at the time of his hanging in September of that year. He does, however, stand out because he is the last Iowa state prisoner to be executed.[11] In 1965 Iowa abolished the death penalty for a second time. Unlike the 1872 abolition, Iowa's 1965 abolition of the death penalty was part of a larger national movement. Many proponents of these national abolition movements cited the death penalty's inability to deter crime as the main reason for halting executions. In the years leading up to Iowa's 1965 abolition, state legislators heard a variety of arguments for and against the death penalty, ranging from Biblical to scientific. In 1963, sixteen members of the Senate judiciary committee heard testimony from eighteen people. Eight clergy members testified, five for and three against the death penalty. The state penal director, Benjamin Bauer, and the state penitentiary warden, John Bennett, provided the strongest criticisms of the death penalty; these two men had overseen Kelley's execution just months before their testimony. All prison officials who testified cited the death penalty's inability to deter crime as the best reason for abolishing it. However, noteworthy law enforcement officials spoke out in favor of the death penalty. The Linn and Blackhawk County sheriffs, as well as the Iowa City police chief, all argued that the death penalty was a much-needed deterrent to crime. One law enforcement official said that although he had never been the executioner for a death row inmate, he would not have any problem performing an execution if it were his duty.[12] This 1963 special hearing highlighted the spirited debate among Iowans in the years preceding abolition of the death penalty. Less than two years later, after more vigorous legislative debate, Iowa abolished the death penalty.

Although Iowa's 1965 decision still stands, it has been challenged numerous times in the last four decades. Most recently, the Iowa legislature has passed bills through House committees, only to have them die later in the legislative process. The Iowa legislature considered imposing the death penalty as part of the state's 2005 movement to strengthen sex abuse laws, a result of a highly publicized kidnapping and killing of ten-year-old Jetseta Gage. Iowa's proposed death penalty law made death a possible sentence for those who kidnap, sexually assault, and kill a child. Proponents of the bill argued that it proscribed death to only society's worst criminals. Those opposed argued that Iowa's current life-without-parole sentence is equivalent to a death sentence because convicted offenders will never live outside prison walls again.[13] Ultimately, the proposed bill did not muster the needed support and did not become law. As a result, Iowa has been without the death penalty for over forty years.

Michigan

Michigan does not impose the death penalty on offenders, and since the national legalization of the death penalty in 1976, no one has been put to death. Before then, the number stood at thirteen. Life without parole is an option in Michigan, and the murder rate per 100,000 is 6.1. Michigan became a state in 1837, and even before then, the settlers reinforced "New England's progressive influence [and] included an active and reformist approach to social issues of the time . . . in particular, the abolition of capital punishment, a cause in which Michigan led the nation."[14] Michigan's last execution occurred in 1830, when Stephen Gifford Simmons was hanged in front of the Wayne County Jail. Prior to that, Michigan territory had hanged one man in 1821, and the federal government had executed only two men there since 1796. Few people opposed Simmons's punishment, and two thousand people reportedly watched the hanging. Yet, Michigan did have a history of opposition to hangings. Mackinac Island was the scene of the first abolitionist protests. In 1827, the federal government executed White Thunder, an indigenous person, for killing a white fur trapper. Though protest did no good, there were stirrings of discontent.

In the nineteenth century, Michigan saw several executions. One of the earliest was that of Patrick Fitzpatrick, a Detroit man who lived in what is now known as Windsor, Canada. Canadian officials arrested Fitzpatrick for the rape and murder of his landlord's daughter. Despite the circumstantial evidence, the Canadian government found Fitzpatrick guilty and hanged him in 1828. Seven years later, Fitzpatrick's roommate admitted to the rape and murder. The next execution occurred in 1830. Stephen Simmons had beaten and eventually killed his wife and their unborn child. Simmons was charged with murder and sentenced to death. The sheriff, however, did not believe that Simmons meant to kill his wife, and claimed that Simmons was too drunk to know what he was doing. The sheriff then resigned, rather than carry out the death sentence. His successor, Sheriff Ben Woodworth, stepped into the limelight. He turned the execution into a spectacle, complete with invitations, bleachers, and people vying for the best seats. The atmosphere also included a brass band and local officials selling souvenirs. Simmons was then paraded on an indirect route so more onlookers could see him. When asked for his last words, Simmons sang out for forgiveness. The onlookers stood stunned and ashamed, one even going so far as to call the execution "cruel and vindictive."

That same year, Reverend William Ferry and residents of Mackinac Island petitioned President Andrew Jackson to rescind the death sentence for a soldier. The movement increased in the following decades and the 1835 meeting to draft a state constitution for Michigan considered abolishing the death penalty. That was to no avail, but the newly formed Michigan Senate differentiated between first- and second-degree murder, the first punishable by death and the second by imprisonment, and it also banned public executions, as well as ones for the insane or pregnant. The press was instrumental in publicizing the controversy, detailing execution scenes, and giving coverage to the abolition bill of 1843, sponsored by Democrat Flavius Littlejohn. The Michigan House of Representatives became the first to abolish capital punishment, but the bill died in the Senate that year. By 1846, the bill was revised to condemn first-degree murderers to life in prison with hard labor, and on March 1, 1847, Michigan became the first English-speaking jurisdiction in the world to ban capital punishment for first-degree murder.[15] Today, the punishment is mandatory life in prison, without the possibility of parole. Only the governor can commute the sentence.[16]

Minnesota

Minnesota does not utilize the death penalty; instead, it offers life without parole as an option.

Prior to 1976, the state executed sixty-six people. The murder rate per 100,000 people is 2.2. Minnesota abolished the death penalty in 1911. Recently, on December 2, 2003, Governor Tim Pawlenty revealed that he believed Minnesota should reinstate the death penalty and the issue of a constitutional amendment went before the state legislature in the spring of 2004.

John D. Bessler, one of the leading scholars on the death penalty, wrote the primary work on the death penalty in Minnesota. *Legacy of Violence: Lynch Mobs and Executions in Minnesota* provides a comprehensive look at the topic.[17] Minnesotans used both executions and lynching to promote their ideals of justice. The death penalty in Minnesota originated in 1849, when Minnesota became a territory, and Congress declared that people who were convicted of premeditated murder would automatically receive the death penalty and solitary confinement. By 1851, convicts faced isolation for one year, and in 1853 that was lowered to one to six months. The first man given the death penalty was a Dakota Indian named U-ha-zy, who murdered a German woman in 1852. The jury found U-ha-zy guilty, and the imposed isolation period gave his supporters time to file appeals on grounds that the defendant was intoxicated and that he was a "savage" who could not comprehend the value whites placed on human life. Despite the appeals, U-ha-zy was hanged on December 29, 1854, in St. Paul. His hanging became a public spectacle with reactions ranging from glee to disgust.

Throughout Minnesota's history, there have been several incidents of execution that deserve mention here. One occurred with the assistance of President Abraham Lincoln and involved Dakota Indians. In 1851, the Dakota ceded much of their land, leaving them with little land, lots of starvation, and an exposure to the sale of whiskey. The Homestead Law of 1862 put them at a further disadvantage as even larger populations of whites continued to settle. The changes led to an alteration of the Dakota lifestyle, and, as Bessler explains, farming Indians who dressed as whites were seen as traitors and were harassed by those who clung to traditions. Tensions mounted as the two groups contended with broken promises, and the violence escalated when the Dakota faced starvation as they waited for paltry annuity payments. Then on August 17, 1862, four Dakota killed five white settlers while returning home from a failed hunting trip. Fearing the backlash, several Dakota leaders met to discuss their options, but to no avail as other Dakota warriors attacked. Thirteen people were killed in the original attack, and the final death count of whites stood at nearly fifty in one county alone. The indiscriminate killing spread, and families were slaughtered throughout twenty-three counties. Minnesota's governor, Henry Sibley, raised 1,400 men to suppress the uprising, and pursued the warring Indians. By the end of September, the many deaths demoralized the Indians and Sibley promised protection to innocent Indians and war upon the guilty. Nearly 2,000 Indians surrendered, and eyewitness testimony was used to sentence the participants, who had no lawyers or criminal trial rights, to death. The military trials went quickly and by November, 392 prisoners had been tried and 303 faced death. Episcopal bishop Henry Whipple and Commissioner of Indian Affairs William Dole hesitated over the high number of hangings, and President Abraham Lincoln waited to approve the executions. Lincoln, a veteran of the Black Hawk War, and whose grandfather had been killed by Indians in Kentucky, was kept abreast of Indian affairs but was preoccupied by the country's struggles with the Civil War and his own son's death. Lincoln hesitated to carry out the military sentencing, and was warned that his failure to do so would lead to the mass killing of all Indians by Minnesotans. Lincoln acknowledged the failure of the federal government's Indian policies

as he addressed the murder of over 800 whites in Minnesota's Indian Wars. Finally, on December 8, after much thought and the threat of mob rule in Minnesota, Lincoln ordered the execution of thirty-nine of the offenders on December 19. The others, he insisted, would be held until further evidence could be determined. The execution date was too soon. It did not allow Sibley enough time to ensure the protection of the other inmates or to preserve the peace. Also, there was no proper rope in Mankato so the execution was rescheduled for December 26. Then, the Indians were bound, sang death songs, and prayed with a Catholic priest. At 10:15 A.M., the scaffold platform dropped and thirty-eight men (one man had gotten a last-minute reprieve) hanged. The men were buried in a mass grave, and then their bodies were dug up for use as medical cadavers. Sibley later discovered that one of the hanged men had been executed in place of another who had a similar name. Despite the high number of deaths, the conflict between the Dakota and the whites in Minnesota did not end, and the battling continued until the 1890 slaughter at Wounded Knee.

Another highly publicized execution was that of Ann Bilansky in 1860. Ann moved to Minnesota in 1858 and later married Stanislaus Bilansky, a poor, drunken, abusive man who took ill in 1859. According to the coroner, he died of "natural causes." After Bilansky's body was buried, witnesses claimed that Ann Bilansky had purchased arsenic, had an extramarital affair with her nephew, and, essentially, murdered her husband. A second coroner then found that Mr. Bilansky had died of arsenic poisoning, and a grand jury convicted Ann in fewer than six hours. The Minnesota Supreme Court heard Ann Bilansky's appeal, and confirmed that she was indeed guilty of first-degree murder. Her sentence was solitary confinement, followed by hanging. Members of the Minnesota State Legislature pushed to abolish the death penalty and save her life. But this was to no avail, and Governor Alexander Ramsey set her execution date for March 23. The legislature next tried to pass a law preventing women from being executed, others wrote letters asking for clemency, and even the prosecutor admitted that he had doubts about her guilt. On March 23, 1860, hundreds of people gathered near the gallows, despite the state's attempts to carry out a private hanging. Ann Bilansky became the first and only woman ever executed in Minnesota.

Ann Bilansky's execution prompted an abolition movement in Minnesota. On March 5, 1868, Governor William R. Marshall signed a bill into law requiring jurors to vote for the death penalty, and thus, life sentences became more commonplace. This was effected too late, however, to spare the life of Andreas Roesch, a convicted killer whose own son's testimony helped to convict him. Roesch had been sentenced before the 1868 law passed, and was hanged the day after the law passed. In 1883, the state passed a new law that proclaimed that first-degree murder was punishable by death, unless "exceptional circumstances" called for life imprisonment instead. Two years later, John Waisenen, a Finnish immigrant, was convicted of killing his employer. He hanged in front of a mob in August of 1885. Next, Nels Olson Holong was convicted of killing and mutilating a fifteen-year-old girl, and then feeding parts of her body to hogs. Although Holong had been kicked in the head as a teenager, his insanity plea did not work. He was hanged in front of the press and other spectators on April 13, 1888. The next year saw more executions as John Lee and Martin Moe were sentenced to death for murder and counseling to commit a murder, respectively, and Timothy and Peter Barrett were convicted of murdering a streetcar driver. Lee's and Moe's hangings were to be viewed only by law enforcement officials, physicians, ministers, newspaper reporters, and those holding admission tickets. Lee was hanged, but Moe was granted a reprieve

at the last minute and his sentence was changed to life in prison. Conversely, the sheriff in charge of the Barretts' hangings sent invitations, with 150 people viewing and near 5,000 waiting outside the jailhouse. The Barretts were hanged on March 22, 1889. These public murders were seen as lessons for the people.

The publicity that the Barretts' executions received again spurred the abolitionists. Representative John Day Smith pushed for outlawing public executions. With the passage of the eponymous law on April 24, 1889, all executions in Minnesota would henceforth be done "before the hour of sunrise" and either within the walls of the jail or in an enclosure built higher than the gallows. The law also limited the people who could see the inmate while in solitary confinement and prohibited the press from covering the execution. This "midnight assassination law" was put into effect in time for the July 19, 1889, hanging of Albert Bulow, a horse thief and murderer. He hanged at 1:47 A.M. and no reporters or ticket holders saw the execution. Newspapers argued for and against Smith's law, claiming that it was of "moral importance" that the public be informed of the execution, while others said details "cultivated in the young a taste for sensational blood-and-thunder literature." The next few years saw more hangings under the midnight assassination law, including Thomas Brown (1889) for murdering a police officer, William Brooker (1890) for killing a couple whom he believed drove his wife away from him and then provided her with shelter, and William Rose (1891) who supposedly killed a neighboring farmer after the farmer's daughter rejected Rose as a suitor. Rose fell at 4:56 A.M., but the rope broke. His unconscious body was then carried back up to the scaffold and a second noose wrapped around his neck. Four minutes after the first attempt, the door sprang again and he hanged. Next, Adelbert Gohen was executed in 1891 for murdering Rosa Bray, a love interest. Later, Clifton Holden, who was convicted of shooting a man in the head and sentenced to death in 1890, challenged the complexities that the Smith Law presented. The state supreme court ruled against him, and upheld the Smith Law (but to his great fortune, the governor commuted his punishment to life in prison). The next hanging occurred in 1894 when Charles Ermisch and Otto Wonigkeit were executed for killing a bartender. Their 5:00 A.M. hanging was viewed by reporters and friends of the sheriff, while thousands of others viewed the gallows. Despite the Smith Law, many officials ignored it, and thus people like the sheriff allowed friends, reporters, and thousands of others to witness the execution.

In 1894, a bizarre murder case occurred that would once again add conflict to the death penalty. Harry Hayward paid, bribed, and threatened a man named Claus Blixt to murder Catherine Ging, whose life insurance policy benefited Hayward. Hayward's plan was easily discovered, and he received the punishment of hanging while Blixt, who actually committed the murder, received a life sentence. Hayward's execution was the first to be scheduled midweek, and with clemency denied, Hayward requested that the gallows be painted red. The sheriff received many requests to view the hanging and some were even willing to pay admission. The jail became swamped with crowds waiting to visit, and Hayward even sold sample hangman nooses as souvenirs. Ultimately, women were turned away from viewing the hanging, and the red gallows went to a museum.

The executions continued, and in 1903, Minnesota legally put to death Charles Henderson, the first and only black man executed by the state, who had been convicted of stabbing his mistress seventeen times. Each of these additional executions was done in quasi-private, with men who wanted to view the execution often being deputized to gain entrance to the spectacle.

Perhaps the most famous execution case in Minnesota's history is that of William Williams. Williams was accused of killing his friend and love interest, Johnny Keller, and Keller's mother in 1905. He was found guilty and sentenced to hang on February 13, 1906. The sheriff made attempts to keep the hanging private, and it did not go as scheduled. When the trap door sprung, Williams fell to the floor—the rope stretched and was too long. The deputies, then, had to pull the rope up and Williams died fourteen and a half minutes later. Publishing details of the debacle landed Minnesota newspapers in court, contending with accusations of violating the Smith law, and defending their coverage of the execution. The Minnesota Supreme Court ruled that the spirit of the Smith law should be upheld, that executions should be done with secrecy, and that they should take place before dawn, within an enclosure. The results of the ruling, in the end, made little difference, as Williams was the last person to be executed in Minnesota.

Minnesota abolished the death penalty in 1911. The push began in earnest in 1891 when Representative Hans Bjorge proposed life imprisonment instead. He argued that innocent people were hanged, and guilty ones were freed for fear of necessitating the death penalty. The bill failed to pass, as did other attempts in 1895 and the early 1900s. Then, in 1911, Minnesota governor Adolph Eberhart confronted the legislature, claiming that more convictions would be made if capital punishment was abolished or if imposed only in extreme cases with the order of the court or the unanimous recommendation of the jury. He also called executions an "antiquated practice." That same year, Representative George MacKenzie promoted an abolition bill which passed the House, then the Senate, and was signed into law by Governor Eberhart on April 22, 1911. Since the passage of the bill, both the House and the Senate have seen bills to reinstate the death penalty, but none have come close to passing.[18]

Minnesota has banned the death penalty for nearly one hundred years now, but in 2004 the issue of reinstating capital punishment came up for discussion. State representative Tom Hackbarth (a Republican) introduced a measure that would make the death penalty a choice for juries in "particularly heinous or brutal murders in the first degree." Hackbarth believed that such a punishment would "send a strong message to those who killed in cold blood that those who violently take human life have given up their own." Relatives of murder victims supported the idea claiming it would give them closure and would send a strong message to would-be murderers. Senator Mady Reiter (R) introduced the bill that went to the Crime Prevention and Safety Committee. She claimed that "morally bankrupt" people commit crimes, despite knowing the differences between right and wrong. According to her, the bill would be a way to bring justice, not revenge, to the victims and their families. She also stated that the death penalty is a deterrent, as inmates said that they did not want to live in a death penalty state. She argued that the death penalty would be applied fairly, not targeting any racial or social group. Opposition to the bill came from the public and from politicians and included the notion that the state could be tough on crime without imposing the death penalty. The bill did not make it out of committee, and was voted down by a two-to-eight roll-call vote.[19]

Ohio

From its inception as a state in 1803 until 1885, Ohio allowed individual counties to handle all executions. Since then, Ohio has executed 369 convicted murderers. The state of Ohio executed its first inmate in 1885, and about thirty more prisoners died at the gallows before adoption of the electric chair in 1897. Between 1885 and 1963, Ohio executed 172 prisoners. With the 1972 *Furman* decision by the United States Supreme Court, which declared the death penalty unconstitutional, 103 Ohio death row inmates had death sentences reduced to sentences of life in prison. In response to *Furman*, the Ohio State Legislature revised its death penalty statutes. The Ohio Assembly's 1974 attempt to meet the United States Supreme Court's standards did not pass the high court's test.

The Supreme Court struck down Ohio's revamped 1974 death penalty legislation in the 1978 landmark case, *Lockett v. Ohio*. The Supreme Court's decision in *Lockett* is significant because it reformed death penalty sentencing statutes across the country and its precedent still stands today. The *Lockett* case drew national attention to Ohio state law and the role of mitigating factors in the sentencing phase of a trial. Sandra Lockett, a twenty-one-year-old woman, encouraged and drove the getaway car for a robbery that resulted in the murder of a pawnshop owner. State prosecutors charged and convicted Lockett of aggravated murder—a capital offense. At the sentencing phase of trial, Ohio law allowed Lockett to present mitigating factors concerning her background, character, and the nature of her crime. For example, Lockett argued that her young age and good character made her a prime candidate for rehabilitation in the penal system. Lockett also presented evidence concerning her low IQ and her relatively clean criminal record. She also argued that she played a "minor role in the robbery and did not participate in the actual killing, and that the killing itself was unintentional."[20] Ohio law allowed the judge to consider any mitigating circumstances concerning victim inducement, offender "duress, coercion or provocation," and "psychosis or mental deficiency."[21] Thus, although Lockett presented considerable evidence of mitigating factors, the judge could not consider them because they did not fall under the three categories defined by Ohio law. Lockett's sentencing judge said that he had "'no alternative, whether he liked the law or not,' but to impose the death penalty."[22]

Lockett appealed her death sentence to the United States Supreme Court. The Court held that the Eighth and Fourteenth Amendments required the consideration of more mitigating factors than defined by Ohio law. For example, the Supreme Court said a sentencing judge can consider a defendant's character and history, as well as any circumstances of her offense. The Court found that Ohio's death penalty law unconstitutionally restricted a defendant's right to consideration of pertinent factors. This United States Supreme Court decision broadened a 1976 ruling that gave consideration to mitigating circumstances; however, Lockett is significant because it required sentencing judges to give all mitigating factors independent weight. As a result of the Supreme Court's decision in Lockett, Ohio and the rest of the death penalty states had to ensure their laws permitted consideration of mitigating circumstances. The Lockett decision effectively made execution permissible because after meeting the standards set by the Supreme Court, state laws ensure a sentencer can make a "reliable moral decision."[23]

After Lockett, the Ohio State Legislature rewrote laws to comply with the Supreme Court's new standards; these laws took effect in 1981. However, another execution did not take place until 1999, when Wilford Berry, a thirty-eight-year-old man convicted of aggravated murder, armed robbery, and aggravated burglary, died by lethal injection. Berry is known as Ohio's "volunteer" for execution because he waived his right to appeal his death sentence. Since 1999, Ohio has executed twenty-six prisoners, all by lethal injection.[24] Prior to 2001, Ohio prisoners could choose either lethal injection or electrocution as their method of execution. However, in late

2001, Ohio lawmakers made lethal injection the only permissible means of execution. This change came in response to a controversy surrounding the planned execution of John W. Byrd, a thirty-eight-year-old convicted murderer. Aside from claiming innocence, Byrd drew attention to his plight by demanding he be electrocuted because he said it would reveal the cruelty of capital punishment.[25] State officials resisted Byrd's demands because they argued that an electrocution was more likely to go awry, causing stress for prison personnel and trauma for witnesses and the victim's family. Ultimately, a state issued postponement of Byrd's execution, pushed the date back, and, in the meantime, Ohio legislators passed a law outlawing electrocution.

In 2006, Ohio still dealt with controversy and concern over executing prisoners (by which time, twenty-two prisoners had been executed since 1999). One of the issues regarding the lethal injections in Ohio happened in May 2006, when the executioners could not find a suitable vein in the arm of prisoner Joseph Clark, an African American man found guilty of murdering a white victim. The delay of ninety minutes led to new guidelines, requiring officials to find two suitable injection sites and using a low-pressure saline drip to test those sites. Prior to Clark's botched execution, examiners only needed to do a visual check and a review of the prisoners' medical files.[26]

Despite current controversies surrounding Ohio's death penalty statutes, including an urging from the state bar association to outlaw capital punishment, the state continues to impose death sentences. Currently, Ohio has one woman on death row in Marysville, and Mansfield holds the 185 men who are also waiting on death row.[27] Life without parole is an option and the state has freed five innocent people. Ohio's governor has granted clemency (with the nonbinding advice of the Board of Pardons and Parole) to nine people. Like other midwestern states, defendants can be put to death for felonies in which they were not responsible for the murder. Aggravated murder with at least one of ten aggravating circumstances is the offense punishable by death. The aggravating circumstances for Ohio include: if the offense was committed for hire, to escape the law, while the offender was under detention, if the victim of the offense was a law enforcement officer or a potential trial witness, if the offense was committed while the offender was trying to commit terrorism, or if the offense was the assassination of the president.

Wisconsin

In 1853, Wisconsin outlawed the death penalty. That year, Representative Christopher Sholes and Senator Marvin Bovee organized to outlaw capital punishment. These state representatives helped to pass the Death Penalty Repeal Act on March 9, 1853, through the House. The Senate also passed the bill and it was signed into law by Governor Leonard Farewell on July 10, 1853. In the following years, lynch mobs murdered defendants which led to a renewed interest in the death penalty. By 1857, a bill to repeal the prohibition of the death penalty was introduced but did not pass, as has been the case ever since.[28] The 2007 murder rate per 100,000 people was 3.5, and life without parole is a possibility for offenders.

There are sixteen reported executions in Wisconsin's history. These men primarily were associated with either Native American nations or the military. In 1815, a British firing squad executed the nephew of a Sioux chief for murdering two traders. The next was in 1821 when Ketawtah, an Ojibwe, was executed for murdering a military surgeon named William S. Madison. On that same day, Kewabushkim, a Menominee, was executed for stabbing a French settler. On August 17, 1829, Sgt. John Renaka was hanged for shooting

a fellow officer. The next year, another soldier, Daniel Hempstead was hanged for murdering a boat builder. Matthew Beckwith, another soldier, was hanged for shooting an officer in 1832. That same year, a solider named Patrick Doyle murdered a superior officer and was later hanged. The next execution in Wisconsin took place in 1838, when Edward Oliver was hanged in Lancaster for shooting another man named John Russell. Tribal law took precedence in the 1840 execution of Isaac Littleman, a Stockbridge Indian, when he was hanged for murdering another member of the Stockbridge Nation. It also was effective in the case of Peter Green, an Oneida Indian who was hanged for murdering his three children in 1842. That same year, William Caffee was hanged for shooting Samuel Southwick. The next execution came on May 16, 1846, when Robert Brewer was hanged for shooting Francis DeLasseaulx the month before. In June of 1848, white settlers executed an Ojibwe Indian named Little Sauk for murdering two fur traders. Then, in 1851, John McCaffary was hanged for drowning his wife. Although McCaffary's execution paved the way for ending the death penalty in Wisconsin, 1868 saw the execution of Jacob Fowles. However, this was done on tribal lands and under the tribal laws for the Oneida Indians.

John McCaffary was the last person executed under Wisconsin state law. He was found guilty of drowning his wife and was sentenced to death by hanging. Two thousand spectators gathered to watch as the man was left hanging for eight minutes before a doctor checked his status. Since he was still alive, he was left to hang for ten more minutes. Among the spectators was Senator Christopher Latham Sholes, and after that, Sholes pushed for ending the death penalty in Wisconsin. Sholes, the editor of the *Kenosha Telegraph*, used his position to publicize his opposition to the death penalty, and when he was elected to the House in 1852, he and Senator Marvin Bovee joined together in their fight to end capital punishment. At the same time, Waupun, the first penitentiary in Wisconsin neared completion and life imprisonment became a possibility.[29]

The state of Wisconsin abolished the death penalty in 1853, but the issue was reintroduced to voters as recently as 2006. Voters got to voice their opinions on whether defendants found guilty of first-degree, intentional homicide supported by DNA evidence should face the death penalty.[30] The current penalty is life in prison, with no possibility of being released. This referendum served as an advisory only; the yes or no vote would not change the law. A yes vote would recommend to legislators that the voter wanted them to change the penalty for homicide from life in prison to death.

This was the first time that the question of the death penalty had ever been brought directly to the people.[31] Republicans who supported the bill claimed that it was simply a way to gauge the reactions of the people. Democrats who opposed the bill claimed that it would encourage bringing back a policy that could "execute wrongly convicted people."[32] The American Civil Liberties Union of Wisconsin testified against the resolution, stating that the death penalty risks the killing of innocent people, that DNA evidence can be contaminated or misinterpreted, that support for the death penalty has declined when life without parole is an option, and that it is not a deterrent for crime. The testimony also included an argument that the death penalty was unfair. Race, economic and social class, as well as education level all affect whether a person is sentenced to death. Further, the attitudes of the prosecutor, where the defendant lives, and the prejudices of the judge and jury also affect the jury's decisions. Finally, the ACLU of Wisconsin promoted the notion that the death penalty costs more than life without parole. The care that goes into a death penalty case includes costs for expert witnesses and extensive investigations. Appeals add to the costs, but no one who promotes the death penalty would be willing to risk a cheaper trial at the risk of convicting an innocent person. The ACLU representative also claimed several specific faults with the Wisconsin resolution, including ambiguous terminology and the fact that requiring DNA evidence misleads the public into believing that the evidence is error free, when that is not always the case.[33] The November vote resulted in 1,163,163 yes votes and 932,286 no votes, with a 55.5 percent to 44.5 percent majority in favor of the advisory referendum. However, since November of 2006, the death penalty issue has lost momentum in Wisconsin.

Summary

In summary, by 2007 only three states in the Midwest practice legalized executions and enforce the death penalty. Michigan abolished the death penalty in 1847, Wisconsin in 1853, Minnesota in 1911, and Iowa in 1965. Illinois currently has a moratorium on the death penalty, but like Indiana and Ohio, legalized lethal injections to put convicted murderers to death. In the 1930s, Ohio executed eighty-two prisoners, Illinois executed sixty-one, Indiana thirty-one, and Iowa eight. The numbers decreased in the 1940s. Ohio executed fifty-one people, Illinois eighteen, Indiana and Iowa seven. The pattern of decrease continued in the 1960s, with Ohio at seven, Illinois and Iowa at two, and Indiana at one. After *Gregg v. Georgia* (1976) overturned the national prohibition of the death penalty decision in *Furman v. Georgia* (1972), the numbers slowly rose. Indiana executed two people in the 1980s, and the other states executed none. But in the 1990s, the number of executions increased, with twelve executions in Illinois, five in Indiana, and one in Ohio. By then, Iowa outlawed the death penalty. In the first decade of the twenty-first century, Illinois implemented a moratorium on the death penalty but executions continued in Indiana and Ohio. Indiana executed ten people between 2000 and 2006, and Ohio executed twenty-three during those years. In 2007, Illinois, Indiana, and Ohio each had prisoners sentenced to death. Although examination of the death penalty in the Midwest does not produce any steadfast patterns or rules, it does provide an excellent cross-section of the differing stances on capital punishment in America. Midwestern states have abolished capital punishment for a variety of reasons, and those currently considering abolition or reinstatement are listening to the best arguments from both sides of the issue. Unlike some areas of the nation that have historically been either inclined to or away from the death penalty, the midwestern states have divergent stances on the death penalty for a variety of reasons. The death penalty in the Midwest is representative of the great debates surrounding capital punishment in America. The history of the death penalty in the Midwest offers examples of reasons why states have or have not chosen to impose the death penalty.

Melody M. Miyamoto is a professor of history at Collin College. She attended the University of Hawaii where she received her B. Ed., and she earned her M.A. and Ph.D. in history from Arizona State University. Her main area of study includes the nineteenth-century American West. She is particularly interested in vigilante justice and how that affected white identity and society.

Charles W. Showalter is attending the University of Iowa College of Law. He graduated from Coe College in May 2008 with a B.A. in history and political science.

Notes

1. "Woman Thanks God as Execution Commuted," 16 January 1996, in *CNN Interactive*, at http://www.cnn.com/US/9601/garcia_execution/index.html, accessed 17 October 2007.

2. Andy Thayer, "Justice Denied for Enoch," *The New Abolitionist: Newspaper of the Campaign to End the Death Penalty* 2, no. 3 (May 1998), at http://www.nodeathpenalty.org/newab007/willieEnoch.html, accessed 17 October 2007.

3. CNN, "Illinois Suspends Death Penalty: Governor Calls for Review of 'Flawed' System," 31 January 2000, at http://archives.cnn.com/2000/US/01/31/illinois.executions.02, accessed 17 October 2007.

4. Illinois Government News Network, "Governor Ryan Introduces Death Penalty Reform Legislation: Calls on General Assembly to Hold Hearings with Key Parties," 13 May 2002, at http://www.illinois.gov/PressReleases/ShowPressRelease.cfm?SubjectID=3&RecNum=1773, accessed 17 October 2007.

5. Abdon M. Pallasch, "Ryan Urges End to Death Penalty," in *Sun Times*, 19 November 2006.

6. Death Penalty Information Center, "COSTS: Counties Use Illinois Capital Litigation Fund to Cover High Costs of the Death Penalty," 13 August 2007, in *The News-Gazette*, at http://www.deathpenaltyinfo.org/article.php?did=2424&scid=64, accessed 17 October 2007.

7. Newton M. Curtis, "Capital Punishment Not a Deterrent of Crime," in *New York Times*, 21 January 1900, 23.

8. Celience Nold Bruce, "Jesse James Revived Gallows in Iowa," in *The Cedar Rapids Gazette*, 1 April 1969, A-4.

9. John D. Bessler, *Kiss of Death: America's Love Affair with the Death Penalty* (Boston: Northeastern University Press, 2003), 54.

10. "Man Is Hanged in Iowa," in *New York Times*, 9 September 1922, 7.

11. Harrison Weber, "Note Rise in Iowa Murders," in *The Cedar Rapids Gazette*, 2 October 1967, A-4.

12. Donald R. Finley, "Death Penalty Conflict," in *The Cedar Rapids Gazette*, 29 March 1963, 10.

13. O. Kay Henderson, "Death Penalty Bill Appears Doomed in Senate," in *Radio Iowa*, 23 February 2006, at http://www.radioiowa.com/gestalt/go.cfm?objectid=D0EEA

A1A-B638-4263-8968766398896A65, accessed 5 October 2007.

14. David G. Charavoyne, "The Northwest Ordinance and Michigan's Territorial Heritage," *The History of Michigan Law*, Paul Finkelman and Martin J. Hershock, eds. (Athens: Ohio University Press, 2006), 28.

15. Ibid., 13–36.

16. Marietta Jaeger-Lane, "Michigan's Death Penalty History," in *Citizens United for Alternatives to the Death Penalty*, at http://www.cuadp.org/michhist.pdf, accessed 17 October 2007.

17. The information for this section on Minnesota comes from John D. Bessler, *Legacy of Violence: Lynch Mobs and Executions in Minnesota* (Minneapolis: University of Minnesota Press, 2003). The quotations and details from this section can also be found in his study.

18. Minnesota House Public Information Office, *Session Weekly*, 1992.

19. "Death Penalty Denied," in *Senate e-Briefly*, 26 March 2004, at http://www.senate.leg.state.mn.us/briefly/2004/brief0326.htm, accessed 17 October 2007.

20. Randy Hertz and Robert Weisberg, "In Mitigation of the Penalty of Death: *Lockett v. Ohio* and the Capital Defendant's Right to Consideration of Mitigating Circumstances," *California Law Review* 69, no. 2 (1981): 324.

21. *Lockett v. Ohio*, 438 U.S. at 593–594.

22. Ibid., at 594.

23. Louis D. Bilionis, "Moral Appropriateness, Capital Punishment, and the 'Lockett' Doctrine," *The Journal of Criminal Law and Criminology* 82, no. 2 (1991): 286.

24. "Death Row Inmates," in *Ohio Department of Rehabilitation and Correction*, at http://www.drc.state.oh.us/Public/deathrow.htm, accessed 5 October 2007.

25. Francis X. Clines, "Inmate's Chosen Means of Execution Starts New Debate," in *New York Times*, 20 August 2001, A-14.

26. "Ohio Set to Execute Man Using New Injection Guidelines," WBNS-10TV, 12 July 2006, at http://www.10tv.com/?sec=search&story=10tv/content/pool/200607/1338987220.html, accessed 5 October 2007.

27. "Death Row Inmates," *Ohio Department of Rehabilitation and Correction*, at http://www.drc.state.oh.us/Public/deathrow.htm, accessed 5 October 2007.

28. Alexander T. Pendleton and Blaine R. Renfert, "Brief History of Wisconsin's Death Penalty," at http://www.wisconsinhistory.org/dictionary/index.asp?action=view&term_id=11148, accessed 17 October 2007.

29. John O. Holzhueter, "Executions Stained Area's History," in *Wisconsin Then and Now* (June 1979) at http://wisconsinhistory.org/dictionary/index.asp?action=view&term_id=13881&keyword=Death+Penalty, accessed 17 October 2007.

30. "Constitutional Amendment and Advisory Referendum to Be Considered by Wisconsin Voters November 7, 2006," 4 October 2006, in *Wisconsin Briefs: From the Legislative Reference Bureau* at http://www.legis.state.wi.us/lrb/pubs/wb/06wb12.pdf, accessed 17 October 2007.

31. Bob Ziegelbauer, "'Death Penalty': November 7, 2006 *Advisory* Referendum," 4 October 2006, in *2005–06 Issue Summary #9* at http://www.legis.state.wi.us/assembly/asm25/news/Death_Penalty.pdf, accessed 17 October 2007.

32. Associated Press, "Death Penalty on Wisconsin's Ballot," 6 May 2006, in *Lacrosse Tribune* at http://www.lacrossetribune.com/articles/2006/05/17/news/001ead.txt, accessed 17 October 2007.

33. American Civil Liberties Union of Wisconsin, "ACLU of Wisconsin Testimony before the WI State Legislature against the Proposed Death Penalty Resolution SRJ 5," April 2006, at http://www.aclu-wi.org/wisconsin/death_penalty/200604deathpenaltytestimony.shtml, accessed 17 October 2007.

CHAPTER 12

The Death Penalty in the Great Plains

John Gregory Jacobsen

T HE TEN states of the Great Plains run along a regional fault line where North, South, and West intersect. The historical pattern of capital punishment in this vast and open area follows wider regional trends, and therefore divides almost predictably along these invisible geographic boundaries. Although the generally higher execution numbers along the western side of the Plains stand in relative contrast to the smaller totals of the upper eastern, or "midwestern" side of the region, both areas are dwarfed by the voluminous statistics of the southern Plains states. The pattern also holds steady for gender, with all nine women executed in the history of the Great Plains dying in the region's southernmost states. This study traces the history of capital punishment in the Great Plains, taking a state-by-state approach up the region's western arch and back down the eastern side to the southernmost Plains states, examining the historical patterns, laws, and people of this core region of the United States.

New Mexico

Convicted murderer Marcus Butler died on the gallows in New Mexico in February 1851—the first recorded legal execution in New Mexico Territory under U.S. jurisdiction. Since that day, at least seventy-three additional executions have taken place, including twenty-eight since New Mexico statehood in 1912 and one in the post-1976 modern era of capital punishment. With executions conducted at the county level through the 1920s, early records are scant, pushing the likely number of executions well beyond the forty-seven recorded in the territorial period.

Fully accurate or not, records list the overwhelming racial majority of those executed in New Mexico Territory as Hispanic, a group representing twenty-five of the forty-seven executions, or 53 percent of the total. Fourteen whites make up only 30 percent of those executed in the territorial period, although the record also lists eight racially "unknown" individuals. Three African Americans make up 6 percent of the total. When including the statehood period, the racial gap only widens with forty-seven of the seventy-four persons executed listed as Hispanic. Whites represent 26 percent, African Americans 6 percent, and racially unknown 11 percent of those executed in both the territorial and statehood periods. No legal recorded execution of an American Indian has occurred in New Mexico, a state with the nation's fourth-largest Indian population. Indeed, in the modern era of capital punishment, only one of the sixty death sentences handed down to American Indians in the United States, and none of the eight executions, has occurred in New Mexico. Notably, the lone death sentence of an American Indian in New Mexico during the modern era has since been overturned or commuted.[1] The only execution of a woman in New Mexico occurred in the territorial period when Paula Angel, age unknown and of Hispanic origin, was hanged for murder on April 26, 1861.

New Mexico presents one of the more unusual execution histories of the Great Plains states, including its unfortunate place as the setting for Pancho Villa's march, the 1916 cross-border raid on the town of Columbus, and the six death sentences carried out in its wake. Of the seven Villa men captured and condemned, the first two, Francisco Alvarez and Juan Sanchez, died in Deming, New Mexico, in June 1916. Amazingly, Sanchez resumed breathing after being cut down. Hanged for only ten minutes, the unconscious Sanchez was returned to the scaffold and again hanged, this time successfully. An additional four of the condemned Villa men, Taurino Garcia, Eusiero Renteria, Juan Castillo, and Jose Rangel, died in Deming later that month, all hanged, this time for twenty minutes. The seventh of the condemned men, Jose Rodriguez, had his sentence commuted to life imprisonment. New Mexico's capital history for 1916 included an additional noteworthy, if gruesome irregularity in November of that year when Lucius Hightower lost his head while being hanged for killing his wife. Hightower's was the first—and last—accidental decapitation in New Mexico since Thomas Ketchum experienced the same ghastly fate there in 1901.

Three years prior to the events surrounding the infamous Villa invasion, the first legal executions of the statehood period occurred when Ivory Frazer, convicted of murdering a deputy sheriff and another man in a jailbreak, and Francisco Granado, guilty of a murderous robbery, died on the gallows together in Socorro, New Mexico, on April 25, 1913. As the *Santa Fe New Mexican* reported, "Avenging Rope Sends Frazer and Granado to Great Beyond."[2]

In April 1923, ten years after the new state conducted its first execution, convicted murderer Francisco Vaisa became the last person to die on the gallows in New Mexico. Not only would there be no death sentences carried out for another decade, but in 1929 the New Mexico legislature mandated use of the electric chair as the sole means of execution. Henceforth, all executions would take place at the State Penitentiary in Santa Fe rather than in the county of the crime. Pretested with the execution of a goat, two men, Thomas Johnson and Santiago Garduno, died in the chair just thirty-four minutes apart in the early hours of July 21, 1933. Convicted of multiple murders, the two men received electricity for seven and eight minutes, respectively. With an audience of approximately seventy men in observance, the prison warden afterward noted the scientific efficiency of the new method of execution, although the voltage on Johnson had to be lowered when smoke rose from one of his legs during his time in the chair.

A total of seven people died in New Mexico's electric chair between 1933 and 1956, when New Mexico adopted the gas chamber as its new method of execution. Unlike most of the eleven southern and western states adopting lethal gas as a mode of execution from the 1920s to the 1950s, New Mexico used the electric chair prior to the switch. Most of these states, all western or southern, moved straight from hanging to what was believed to be painless execution by gas, although lingering memories of gas warfare during the first World War slowed public acceptance of the new technology.[3] On August 11, 1960, just one day after prison officials used a pig to test the new gas chamber, David Cooper Nelson spent eight minutes inside to become the only person to die by lethal gas in New Mexico's history. Despite Nelson's gasps, the prison warden found the new execution process efficient. Nelson's was the last execution in New Mexico prior to the United States Supreme Court's halt to capital punishment in the 1972 case of *Furman v. Georgia* and subsequent reversal of the ban in *Gregg v. Georgia* (1976).[4] Lethal gas remained the manner of execution when, in 1979, New Mexico again adopted the death penalty, although the state executed no prisoners before switching to lethal injection in 1980.

Despite placing twenty-eight men under sentence of death, with the large majority of these convictions or sentences eventually overturned or commuted, New Mexico's post-*Gregg* record includes only a single execution.[5] The modern period, however, has not been without controversy. In 1986, New Mexico's anti-death-penalty governor Toney Anaya, in one of his last official acts, reduced the sentences of the state's five death row inmates to life imprisonment. While the outspoken politician's controversial move sent shockwaves across the state, one convicted murderer missed the call—and paid with his life. Hoping to avoid a long legal process and share in Governor Anaya's pardoning sweep, Terry Clark pleaded guilty to the kidnapping and murder of nine-year-old Dena Lynn Gore, who had been bound, raped, and shot in the head three times. At the time of the murder, Clark was out on bond while appealing a conviction for raping a six-year-old girl. Clark's plan failed when his sentencing was suspended until after Anaya left office. Sentenced to die in 1987, Clark began a long series of on-again, off-again appeals. In 1995, his lawyers managed to get his sentence thrown out on a technicality, but a new sentence soon returned him to death row. In March 2001, Clark dropped

all further appeals and on November 6 became the first and, to date, the only person executed in New Mexico during the modern era of capital punishment. New Mexico never fully developed its execution process for lethal injection, and as a result brought in prison officials from Huntsville, Texas, to carry out Clark's execution.

Under current New Mexico law, convicted murderers are eligible for a death sentence with the existence of one of seven aggravating circumstances.[6] In addition, New Mexico law allows nine mitigating circumstances to be considered in avoiding a death sentence.[7] New Mexico law prohibits the execution of retarded persons or anyone under eighteen years of age, and grants to the governor sole power to suspend a capital sentence.[8]

In recent years attempts have been made to both eliminate and expand capital punishment in the state. Most recently, in March 2007, a bill to replace the death penalty with life imprisonment without the possibility of parole died in a senate committee.[9] With determined voices on both sides of the issue, however, and with two men currently sitting on New Mexico's death row, debate will continue.

Colorado

Colorado's death penalty history contains several unique features, including the alleged one-time use of a gallows triggered by the condemned prisoner himself.[10] Courthouse hangings ruled the day throughout Colorado's territorial period and first decade and a half of statehood, a time that may consist of as many illegal executions as it does legal, documented or otherwise. Records show twenty-four executions for this period. Five of the eleven executions documented prior to Colorado statehood in 1876 occurred under the brief and unrecognized Jefferson Territorial jurisdiction of 1859–1861. All of the condemned men executed during this brief period were white or of unknown race. The early courtyard executions could be unruly affairs, particularly during the tumultuous 1860s, a period of minimal U.S. troop presence and of violent conflict between white militias, often made up of local miners, and the various Indian tribes of the area. Incredibly, no record exists of the legal execution of an American Indian in Colorado history. Lack of documentation does not mean executions did not occur, but rather that such incidents were never recorded. In 1889, in a largely unsuccessful effort to counter graphic execution reporting, Colorado became one of six states banning journalistic accounts of legal executions, which after 1890 were carried out in the state penitentiary at Canon City.[11]

Lynching proved to be a chronic problem for the young state. One study claimed that sixty-three lynchings occurred in Colorado between 1882 and 1902. Nearly all of the victims were white, leaving the actual number of undocumented lynchings involving African Americans, Hispanics, and Indians lost to history. Indeed, it is vigilante justice that led to both the 1890 requirement that executions be conducted at a centralized location and the state's abolishing of capital punishment altogether in 1897. Continued lynchings reversed this decision within four years, however, making Colorado the only state in U.S. history to reenact the death penalty as a deterrent to lynching.

In total, 63 white, 14 Hispanic, 7 black, and 18 racially unknown men have been legally executed in the territory and state of Colorado. Of the 101 executions conducted prior to the modern post-*Furman* era, 69 men died on the gallows between the years 1859 and 1933, and 32 in the gas chamber after 1934. Colorado is one of eleven southern and western states to move directly from hanging to gas as a method of execution, skipping an electrocution technology slow to reach the western parts of the country.[12]

The fact that the U.S. Supreme Court in the 1972 *Furman* decision temporarily halting executions did what Coloradans refused—eliminate the death penalty—does not mean some state lawmakers did not try. Besides the four-year ban on capital punishment imposed between 1897 and 1901, the state senate voted to end the death penalty in 1933, just prior to making the switch from hanging to gas, but the effort failed to muster sufficient support in the house. In 1955 and 1957, legislators again introduced but failed to pass bills ending capital punishment. Finally, in 1966, the legislature offered Coloradans a ballot referendum abolishing capital punishment, which voters rejected two to one. Despite the people's overwhelming sentiment, Louis Monge's death by lethal gas in Canon City on June 2, 1967, proved to be the last pre-*Furman* execution conducted in both Colorado and the United States, marking the beginning of a ten-year national hiatus on executions.

Following the narrow five-four *Furman* ruling, Colorado revised its death penalty statute and submitted the issue to voters, who again affirmed their support for capital punishment by a two-to-one margin. The new law went into effect on January 1, 1975, but now included only three death-penalty-eligible offenses: first-degree murder, kidnapping resulting in the death of the victim, and felony murder. Persons convicted of one of these three capital offenses are eligible for a death sentence with the existence of one of seventeen aggravating factors.[13] In addition, Colorado law allows consideration of twelve mitigating factors, which may outweigh any established aggravating factors in avoiding a death sentence, including any nonenumerated evidence that in the court's opinion touches the question of mitigation.[14]

Execution of retarded persons or of persons under the age of eighteen is prohibited. The sentence is determined by the trial jury, and the method is lethal injection. Execution dates are set by the trial judge and carried out at the penitentiary at Canon City at an undisclosed time during the week named on the warrant. The Colorado governor alone may grant clemency. The state carried out its sole execution of the modern era on October 13, 1997, when Gary Lee Davis died by lethal injection for the kidnapping and murder of Virginia May. The race of both murderer and victim was white.

Colorado's death row houses only a single prisoner since the April 2007 vacating of the capital sentence but not the murder conviction of Edward Montour Jr. In pleading guilty to the bludgeoning death of a prison kitchen employee, according to a taped confession, for the purpose of elevating his status with the inmate population, Montour automatically waived his right to have his sentence determined by a jury under the state's death penalty law.[15] As per the state supreme court ruling, however, linking the waiver of a defendant's right to a sentence by jury to a guilty plea is unconstitutional. A jury will resentence Montour, at this writing.[16]

Attempts to end capital punishment in Colorado continue to be introduced—and defeated. The most recent repeal measure, introduced in January 2007, included a component for funding state bureau of investigation forensic and cold case units with the money to be saved from fighting death penalty appeals.[17] Facing certain defeat in committee, the bill's sponsor, Representative Paul Weissmann, an annual anti-capital-punishment legislative sponsor, then offered an amendment accepting capital punishment while cutting the state's death penalty prosecution team in half, from four to two prosecutors. Opponents aptly labeled the amendment a not-so-covert attempt to repeal Colorado's death penalty by defunding capital prosecutions. The measure died in the house on April 18, 2007.[18]

Despite inevitable legislative attempts to the contrary, Colorado's death row likely will remain open for the foreseeable future.

Wyoming

Prior to achieving territorial status in its own right in 1868, Wyoming had been a part of no less than five separate jurisdictions beginning with the Oregon Territory in 1848, Washington Territory in 1853, Dakota Territory in 1861, Idaho Territory in 1863, and Montana Territory in 1864 before again becoming part of Dakota Territory that same year. Wyoming's first recorded execution occurred in 1884, however, leaving the actual number of death sentences carried out during the previous thirty-six years, if any, legal or otherwise, unknowable.

Compared with most of the other Great Plains states, Wyoming's record of twenty-three total executions appears scant. Only four executions were recorded during the territorial period, the last just six months before statehood in 1890. Of the remaining nineteen death sentences carried out in the state of Wyoming, the bulk conducted during the 1910s and 1930s, only one occurred after World War II, in 1965, while the lone execution of the post-*Furman* modern era took place in 1992. In all, seventeen of the death sentences were carried out by hanging between 1884 and 1933, five by lethal gas (adopted in 1935) from 1937 to 1965, and one by lethal injection in 1992. Like several other western states, Wyoming bypassed the electric chair by moving directly from hanging to gas.[19] Racially, the majority of the executed were white, although two condemned men were listed as racially unknown. Of the others, all men, two were African American, executed in 1916 and 1944; two Asian/Pacific Islanders, executed in 1912 and 1922; one American Indian, executed in 1930; and one Hispanic—the last man to be executed in Wyoming before the *Furman* decision's temporary halt to all executions in 1972.

Wyoming readopted the death penalty on February 28, 1977, and withstood its constitutional challenge six years later.[20] The method of execution is lethal injection and lethal gas only if injection is held unconstitutional. Male prisoners are executed at the state penitentiary at Rawlins and females at the women's facility at Lusk, Wyoming, although no women occupy death row. Under present Wyoming law, persons committing murder "purposely and with premeditated malice, or in the perpetration of, or attempt to perpetrate, any sexual assault, sexual abuse of a minor, arson, robbery, burglary, escape, resisting arrest, kidnapping or abuse of a child under the age of sixteen years . . . [are] guilty of murder in the first degree" and eligible for a sentence of death. A 2004 amendment raised the minimum age for execution from sixteen to eighteen years, while a 2007 amendment added "sexual abuse of a minor" to the special circumstances making murder a capital offense.[21] Thus, the death sentence is available in both premeditated and felony murder cases, the latter as a deterrent to individuals "committing negligent or accidental killings during the perpetration of an underlying felony."[22]

All death sentences are imposed by a jury and automatically reviewed by the Wyoming Supreme Court, which among other things must determine if the sentence was imposed under the influence of passion, prejudice, or any other arbitrary factor.[23] Before imposing a death sentence, a jury will determine whether any of twelve aggravating circumstances exist beyond a reasonable doubt.[24] A jury, however, may not consider nonstatutory aggravating evidence as aggravating circumstances.[25] Likewise, Wyoming law allows consideration of eight mitigating factors, which may outweigh any established aggravating factors in avoiding a death sentence, including any fact or circumstance of the defendant's character or prior

record or matter surrounding his offense which serves to mitigate his culpability.[26] While the governor possesses sole right to grant clemency, death sentences commuted to life without parole are by law ineligible for further commutation.[27]

Wyoming conducted its only execution of the modern era of capital punishment on January 22, 1992. On that date, Mark Hopkinson, a white male, was put to death by lethal injection for ordering both the 1977 arson murder of Vincent, Beverly, and John Vehar, and the related 1979 mutilation killing of Jeffery Green. Although committing none of the four murders directly, Hopkinson is Wyoming's first execution since Andrew Pixley died for the rape and murder of a twelve-year-old girl twenty-seven years earlier.

As bizarre and full of twists and turns as the Hopkinson case is, Wyoming's most recognized murder case in recent history ended with no death sentences at all. In 1999, Russell Henderson and Aaron McKinney each received two life sentences for the 1998 kidnapping and murder of a homosexual college student, Matthew Shepard. The case drew national attention and talk of the death penalty became routine. Ultimately, Henderson arranged for a guilty plea and two life sentences while McKinney's jury refused to bring a first-degree murder conviction, convicting him instead for felony murder, for which he was still eligible for a death sentence. Shepard's family called for life imprisonment as a show of "tolerance," to which the prosecution reluctantly agreed.[28]

Currently two men, both white, occupy Wyoming's death row at Rawlins.

Montana

As with many other western areas of the country, Montana's early history involved multiple territorial associations. Prior to achieving territorial status in 1864, no less than seven different U.S.

jurisdictions claimed parts of Montana beginning with Louisiana, followed by Missouri, Oregon, Washington, Nebraska, Dakota, and, finally, for one year, Idaho. Montana's lone execution came at the tail end of this period with the hanging of Peter Horan on August 25, 1863. The next recorded execution occurred twelve years later, in 1875, more than a decade after the creation of Montana Territory. In all, sixteen men went to the gallows during the territorial period, which ended with statehood in 1889.

Of Montana's seventy-four total executions, fifty-five occurred in statehood prior to the 1972 *Furman* decision. Transcending national trends on methods of execution, and even the western state trend toward skipping the electric chair and moving straight to lethal gas, Montana avoided both of the newer technologies by staying with hanging throughout the pre-*Furman* era, although the last execution came in 1943. Lethal injection is Montana's method in the modern era.

Racially, fifty-seven of the seventy-four persons executed in Montana were white, representing fully 77 percent of the total. Nine African Americans have been executed, including William Spears in the territorial period and Philip Coleman Jr. in 1943, the last man to hang in the state. Of the five American Indians executed in Montana, four died on the same day, and in fact at the same time, in Missoula on December 19, 1890. The four men, Antley, La La See, Pascale, and Pierre Pane, were hanged after being captured by Bill H. Houston, Missoula County's first sheriff under statehood, and charged with the murder of over fifty white men in the "mountain wilds" of the state. According to a letter signed by witness F. J. Arkins, the men "were hanged and in 24 minutes from the time of the drop, the last one was placed in his coffin." The same source proclaimed that "no hanging in the state ever attracted more attention than that of the four Indians."[29] Two Asian/Pacific Islanders died on the gallows in 1883 and 1906,

and one Hispanic man, John Cuellae, in 1918.

Montana reinstituted the death penalty on March 1, 1974, less than two years after the Supreme Court's temporary halt to executions in the United States. Under the present law, the possibility of a death sentence is triggered for persons convicted of deliberate homicide.[30] Persons convicted of deliberate homicide are eligible for a death sentence with the existence of one of seven aggravating circumstances.[31] In addition, Montana law allows seven mitigating circumstances to be considered in avoiding a death sentence. Notably, the court may consider other existing facts in mitigation of the penalty.[32] Under Montana's current death penalty statute, capital sentences are automatically reviewed by the state supreme court.[33] Executions for males are conducted at the state penitentiary at Deer Lodge, and if necessary, for women at Warm Springs. The governor has sole authority to grant clemency, but with the advice of the Board of Pardons and Paroles.

Montana has executed three men during the modern era, most recently David Dawson for the 1986 kidnapping and murder of a young family he had kidnapped in their Billings motel room. Dawson had bound and gagged his victims before strangling three of them with a telephone cord over two days' time. The dead included both parents and their eleven-year-old son. A fifteen-year-old daughter was rescued largely unhurt. Dawson spent the last two years of his twenty-year incarceration, nineteen under a sentence of death, resisting all legal efforts to delay or avert his own execution. He met with success on August 11, 2006.[34]

In recent years, Montana legislators have attempted but failed to subvert the wishes of the state's pro-death-penalty majority through biennial legislative efforts to abolish the death penalty, including when a house bill failed to make it out of committee in March 2007. With two current occupants on Montana's death row, the debate is certain to continue.

North Dakota

As a state without capital punishment since 1915, and with just eight executions on the record, North Dakota stands as an anomaly on the Great Plains. Of its meager total, two executions occurred prior to North Dakota's 1889 statehood, the first in the northern half of Dakota Territory in 1885 and the latter after the 1887 split of the territory into northern and southern jurisdictions. Of the six men executed under statehood, two died on the same day, September 14, 1900, and the last in 1905. In all, seven of the men executed in North Dakota were white and one racially unidentified but with an anglicized name. All died by hanging.

Among the eight capital cases in North Dakota's history is the state's first multiple murder, committed on July 7, 1893, near the community of Cando. Romantically spurned by Anna Kreider, the teen-aged daughter of Daniel Kreider, twenty-two-year-old Albert F. Bomberger killed her parents and four of their eight children before raping Anna, who survived the ordeal. The other children fled. Bomberger, who had worked on the farm for five years, was captured in Manitoba, brought to Grand Forks, North Dakota, and promptly tried and hanged.

On September 14, 1900, North Dakotans viewed the eventful ends of both Hans Thorpe and Ira Jenkins, the former at Minot, the latter at Bismarck. The only dual executions in North Dakota history, the cases were nevertheless completely disconnected. Convicted of shooting his wife to death in a jealous and drunken rage just before botching his own suicide, Thorpe died preoccupied with reporters and had to be distracted by authorities before being dropped through the floor. Even more unusual was Jenkins's angry demise. Convicted of robbing and killing a fellow worker in his father's mine, Jenkins cursed violently in the hours before his death. Although leaving a note admitting guilt, Jenkins remained defiantly bitter, if flamboyant, proclaiming his innocence as he went to the gallows smoking a cigar.

North Dakota's final execution lacked the drama surrounding the deaths of Thorpe and Jenkins. It occurred on October 17, 1905, when John Rooney went to the gallows without incident. The head of a roving gang of bandits, Rooney was convicted of murdering Harold Sweet in a botched robbery attempt near Fargo. He denied being the triggerman, however, and through the services of a pair of capable attorneys, managed to get his execution delayed several times before finally meeting his fate. Because of a 1903 law mandating that all executions be conducted at a central location, Rooney was also the first and only North Dakota prisoner to be executed at the state penitentiary in Bismarck, all previous executions being conducted in the counties. Ten years later, North Dakota abolished the death penalty altogether.

The legislature's 1915 rejection of capital punishment spared three prisoners under sentence of death, two of them for brutally killing a pair of transients with stones. Although conducting no executions after 1915, North Dakota retained the option of a death penalty for prisoners convicted of murdering a prison guard while serving a life sentence until disallowed by a new criminal code effective on July 1, 1975.[35]

While North Dakota has carried out a minimal number of executions, the state has a comparable record of unofficial executions. Three of these killings occurred in the territorial period and six under statehood, including a triple lynching in 1897, prompted, perhaps, by the conviction of one the three men being vacated by the state supreme court. The most recent lynching took place on January 29, 1931, when a lynch mob seized twenty-two-year-old Charles Bannon from a Schafer, North Dakota, jail and hanged him off a bridge. Accused of murdering a family of six persons, Bannon had been taken from the same jail holding James Bannon, his father and accused accomplice.[36]

In 1979 and again in 1995, the North Dakota legislature considered readopting the death penalty, but failed to do so. The state, however, has not been void of capital punishment news. Despite lacking a death penalty statute, North Dakota may soon have its first execution in over a century. Alfonso Rodriguez Jr. was convicted in 2006 for raping and killing Dru Sjodin, a student at the University of North Dakota in 2003. Rodriguez had dumped the body in Minnesota, a state that, like North Dakota, has no death penalty. Crossing state lines in the commission of his crime, however, made Rodriguez eligible for federal prosecution, prompting prosecutors to drop state charges against him and move his case to federal court where he became eligible for the death penalty.[37] Polls showed a majority of North Dakotans favoring a death sentence for Rodriguez, which is exactly what he received on September 22, 2006.[38]

North Dakota marks the western end of an arch of nine states without death penalty statutes stretching from New England across the upper Midwest. Although neighbored by other non-death-penalty states such as Minnesota and Iowa, North Dakota remains an anomaly among the Great Plains states. But with a majority of North Dakota's residents shocked by a brutal sex murder and in favor of a death sentence for its perpetrator, since realized at the federal level, it remains to be seen if that legal distinction continues.

South Dakota

South Dakota's execution of Elijah Page on July 11, 2007, was just the second death sentence carried out in the state since 1913 and the first since the 1940s. There have only been sixteen executions overall in South Dakota, and four of those occurred prior to statehood in 1889, including three in 1882. Aside from the lethal injection method used in 2007, and the electric chair in 1947, the other fourteen men executed, between 1877 and 1913, died by hanging. Notably, South Dakota abolished the death penalty in 1915 and continued without capital punishment for nearly twenty-five years before renewing it in 1939. Thereafter, executions would be conducted at the state penitentiary in Sioux Falls with electrocution as the new method. Following the Supreme Court's 1972 halt to all executions in the United States, South Dakota readopted the death penalty on January 1, 1979. Electrocution remained the execution method until changed to lethal injection in 1984. Racially, eight of the sixteen condemned men were white, including Elijah Page. Five American Indians have been executed, one in the territorial period, another in 1894, and three on separate dates in the fall of 1902. Two African Americans went to the gallows in 1897 and 1913, and one racially unidentified man in 1882.

In 1877, Jack McCall made history by killing Wild Bill Hickok in the Black Hills community of Deadwood, and shortly thereafter as the first man legally executed in South Dakota. Of the other three men executed in the territorial period, all in 1882, Thomas Egan may have died an innocent man, or at least not alone in guilt, as his stepdaughter later made a deathbed confession to the crime. That same year witnessed the first execution of an American Indian in South Dakota when Brave Bear was hanged at Yankton for killing a homesteader. Another American Indian, Chief Two Sticks, though not committing the murder himself, was hanged at Deadwood in 1894 for conspiracy to kill four cowboys. Of the three other American Indians executed in South Dakota, all in 1902, Ernest Loveswar died at Sturgis for killing settlers, Allen Walking Shield was hanged at Sioux Falls for killing an Indian woman,

Ghost-Faced Bear, and convicted murderer George Bear also walked the gallows at Sioux Falls in December of that year. South Dakota's last execution of the twentieth century occurred in 1947, when George Sitts became the only man to die in the state's electric chair. Sitts had been convicted for murdering a store clerk in Minnesota but escaped before beginning his prison sentence. He fled to Spearfish, South Dakota, where he killed state crime agent Thomas Matthews and Sheriff Dave Malcolm.[39]

Under current South Dakota law, juries must weigh the possibility of imposing a death sentence for persons convicted of first-degree murder, kidnapping resulting in gross permanent physical injury, or felony murder, and in doing so will consider any mitigating circumstances, not enumerated in the South Dakota code, and must find at least one of ten aggravating circumstances.[40] South Dakota law prohibits the execution of retarded persons and for crimes committed while under the age of eighteen.[41] The South Dakota Supreme Court automatically reviews all death sentences.[42] The governor has sole authority to grant clemency with nonbinding advice from a parole and pardons board. In 2006, Governor Mike Rounds exercised this prerogative in part when granting a twelve-month stay to Elijah Page over a potential conflict regarding the drug protocol used in executions. Although an execution must be carried out during a week designated on the execution warrant, the warden sets the time and date, which remain a secret until the final forty-eight hours.[43]

On July 11, 2007, twenty-five-year-old Elijah Page was executed by lethal injection at the state penitentiary in Sioux Falls. South Dakota's most recent capital case is unusual for the relatively short lapse of time between the crime and the execution. The first execution in South Dakota in sixty years followed one of the most horrific torture murders on record. Page, with two accomplices, tortured nineteen-year-old Chester Poage for over three hours before killing him in March 2000. Poage, who had befriended the trio, was robbed and taken to a remote creek in freezing and snowy conditions, and there made to strip off most of his clothing, lie down in frigid waters, and endure several hours of near drowning, kicks to the head, beatings with large rocks, and finally stabbings to the head. His body was left in the creek where it was discovered over a month later.[44] Page's request for death and refusal to seek appeals explains the relatively short duration of time between his crime and execution. One of his accomplices, Briley Piper, currently sits on South Dakota's death row where he is just beginning a lengthy appeals process. One death row inmate committed suicide in 2003, leaving Piper and two other inmates the sole occupants of South Dakota's death row.

Nebraska

On a winter day in 1879, Samuel Richards walked the gallows in front of an anxious crowd to become the first person executed in the state of Nebraska.[45] Since that date, thirty-six other men have paid the ultimate penalty for their crimes, including three in the post-*Furman* modern era. Notably, no executions occurred during the territorial period or the first twelve years after Nebraska's 1867 statehood. Of those executed, twenty-two men died by hanging from 1879 to 1913 and fifteen by electrocution from 1920 to 1997. Racially, twenty-six of the condemned men were white, including one of the three prisoners executed in the modern era. Six African Americans have faced execution, four between 1907 and 1922, and two in the modern era. Timothy Iron Bear died in the electric chair in 1948, the only American Indian executed in Nebraska history, although two others had their death sentences commuted in 1987 and 2001.

Four racially unknown men died on the gallows in the 1890s.

Although initially carried out in the counties, since 1903 all executions have taken place at the state penitentiary in Lincoln. In 2002, Nebraska moved death row to the Tecumseh State Correctional Institution while keeping the electric chair in the state penitentiary at Lincoln. A week prior to their scheduled execution dates, condemned male prisoners are transferred to the state penitentiary and placed on deathwatch. Although unoccupied, Nebraska's death row for women is located in the women's correctional facility at York. Nebraska has employed just two execution methods, hanging and electrocution, the latter adopted in 1913 and retained to the present.[46] Nebraska, however, may be the only state ever to combine the two technologies in a single execution, and that is exactly what happened on January 17, 1908, when Frank Barker used a self-invented electrical device strapped to his leg to spring the trap door at his own hanging.[47] Nebraska is currently the only state offering no alternative to the electric chair.

Several cases stand out in Nebraska's history of capital punishment. Albert Price was the last man to die on the gallows in Nebraska, hanged in 1913 for killing a deputy sheriff in the prison chapel the previous year. Two years after Price's demise, Emil Muzik received a death sentence but spent the next forty-five years in prison after having his sentence commuted to life just four months after it was received. Muzik died in 1960 and is the last convict to be buried in the Nebraska prison cemetery. On December 20, 1920, Allen Grammer and Allison Cole, in that order, made history as the first people to die in Nebraska's electric chair and as participants in the state's only dual execution. Perhaps the most well known of Nebraska's capital cases involved the then nineteen-year-old Charles Starkweather, who in 1958 left ten victims in his wake as he and a fourteen-year-old female

accomplice crossed the state in a murderous robbery spree. His 1959 death in the electric chair was the last of the pre-*Furman* era.

Just one year after the *Furman* case halted all executions in the United States, Nebraska reinstituted the death penalty, on April 20, 1973. Under current law, persons become eligible for a death sentence if convicted of committing first-degree murder purposely and with deliberate and premeditated malice, or in the perpetration of or attempt to perpetrate any sexual assault in the first degree, arson, robbery, kidnapping, hijacking of any public or private means of transportation, or burglary, or by administering poison or causing the same to be done; or if by perjury or subornation purposely procures the conviction and execution of any innocent person.[48] Before a death sentence may be imposed, however, a jury must find the existence of one of nine aggravating circumstances.[49] The State must prove one or more of the statutory aggravators beyond a reasonable doubt.[50] In addition, Nebraska law allows seven mitigating circumstances to be considered in avoiding a death sentence.[51]

Under Nebraska's current statute, capital sentences are automatically reviewed by the state supreme court, which, aside from examining any aggravating and mitigating circumstances, must determine whether the sentence is excessive or disproportionate to the penalty imposed in similar cases.[52] A three-member executive panel, which includes the governor, holds authority to grant clemency. The execution of retarded persons or of persons under the age of eighteen is prohibited.[53]

Three inmates have gone to Nebraska's electric chair in the modern era, all within a three-year span from 1994 to 1997. Following years of legal appeals and a televised clemency hearing in 1991, Harold Otey became the first man executed in Nebraska's electric chair since Starkweather in 1959. Convicted in 1978 for the brutal rape and murder of Jane McManus, a crime he first admitted and later denied, Otey's case captured national attention and was the subject of a 1992 CBS television documentary.[54] Convicted child killer John Joubert, who in the early 1980s frightened Omaha metropolitan area residents in the months prior to his capture, died by electrocution in 1996. Nebraska's most recent execution occurred the following year, when Robert Williams went to the electric chair for the murder of three women in 1977.

One of the most legally astounding moments in Nebraska's death penalty history occurred in 2001 when condemned prisoner Jeremy Sheets became possibly the only person in modern U.S. history to be freed directly from death row. Sheets had been convicted for the 1992 rape and murder of Kenyatta Bush on testimony from an alleged accomplice, who committed suicide prior to Sheet's trial. The Nebraska Supreme Court overturned Sheet's conviction because he had been unable to confront his accuser in court.[55]

A 1993 national headlines-grabbing triple murder case in a Humboldt, Nebraska, farmhouse again made news in September 2007 when Tom Nissen, whose unsubstantiated testimony placed blame for the killings on his former friend and codefendant, John Lotter, admitted to being the trigger man after all. Already serving three life sentences for his role in the killings, Nissen admitted giving false testimony in an effort to avoid a death sentence. The killings, which involved the murder of a twenty-one-year-old woman who had posed as a man before being exposed, raped, and killed by Nissen and Lotter, fascinated the nation and inspired a book, television documentary, and ultimately a movie. James Elworth, lead prosecutor in the case, has noted the irrelevance of Nissen's recent truthfulness, which many people have doubted since his 1995 conviction. Elworth's sentiment is echoed by State Attorney General Jon Bruning, who considers the two men equally guilty in the killings even while conceding the possibility of Lotter's eventual removal from death row.[56] Besides Lotter, nine men currently occupy Nebraska's death row.

Kansas

Of the fifty-nine men executed in Kansas history, all but one—the first—died under statehood. Likewise, all but one, again the first, died by hanging. In fact, the first individual to be executed in Kansas was John Coon Jr., an American Indian who died by firing squad on a murder charge in January 1853. The execution occurred one year before the Kansas-Nebraska Act opened the territory to settlement. Despite the territory's popular label as "bloody Kansas," no other executions are recorded for the years prior to statehood in 1861, although twelve legal hangings occurred before 1870. With the exception of three hangings in 1887 and 1888, two on the same day, no additional executions occurred before 1907 when Kansas eliminated the death penalty altogether. With this move, Kansas led the way for eight other states abolishing capital punishment in the years before World War I. All but two of these states, Minnesota and North Dakota, eventually reinstituted the death penalty, including Kansas in 1935.[57]

Racially, thirty-nine of those executed in Kansas were white. Additionally, six African Americans have gone to the gallows, the first two together on November 21, 1888. The others died in the 1940s and 1950s, and the most recent in 1959. Besides Coon in the territorial period, two other American Indians have been executed in Kansas, both in 1866.

Fourteen of Kansas's fifty-nine executions occurred on three days in 1945 at the United States Disciplinary Barracks at Leavenworth, site of the last mass execution in the United States.

There, on July 10 and 14 and August 25, fourteen German prisoners of war were hanged for the mock court-ordered executions of three fellow prisoners suspected of collaborating with American authorities.[58] The condemned men are buried at the Fort Leavenworth Military Prison Cemetery.[59] Notably, the last two persons executed in Kansas were American soldiers, absent without leave, hanged for murder on June 22, 1965. Kansas's most famous execution, also a dual affair, occurred on April 14, 1965, when Perry Smith and Richard Hickock walked the gallows for murdering a farm family in a botched robbery attempt. The murder and executions is the subject of Truman Capote's well-known book, *In Cold Blood*.[60]

Not until April 22, 1994, twenty-two years after the *Furman* decision temporarily halted all executions in the United States, and nearly thirty years after the last execution in the state, did Kansas readopt the death penalty for capital murder.[61] Under Kansas's current death penalty statute, persons convicted of capital murder are eligible for a death sentence with the existence of one or more of eight aggravating circumstances.[62] In addition, Kansas law allows nine mitigating circumstances to be considered in avoiding a death sentence.[63] The law also prohibits the execution of retarded persons and of persons under the age of eighteen.[64] Death row for men is located at the penitentiary at El Dorado and for women at Topeka, but executions are carried out at the corrections facility at Lansing. The method is lethal injection. Although capital sentences are automatically reviewed by the state supreme court, the governor alone may grant clemency.[65]

As in other states, Kansans continue to debate capital punishment, as evidenced by the January and February 2007 introduction of legislative bills for its abolition. The bills, Senate Bill 222 and House Bill 2510, had yet to reach committee level.[66] The proposed legislation, however, comes on the heels of a major victory for death penalty advocates, in which the United States Supreme Court upheld a challenged section of the state's capital punishment statute, and did so by overturning a ruling of the Kansas Supreme Court.[67] At issue was the law's allowance for a possible death sentence even when the jury finds that aggravating and mitigating circumstances are equally balanced. For the majority, Justice Clarence Thomas stressed a state's "range of discretion in imposing the death penalty, including the manner in which aggravating and mitigating circumstances are weighed."[68] The decision left Michael Lee Marsh II under sentence of death for the brutal 1996 murder of Marry Ane Pusch and her nineteen-month-old daughter, Marry Elizabeth. After illegally entering his victim's home and waiting for her return, Marsh shot and stabbed Marry multiple times and cut her throat before setting the house on fire, burning her young child to death.[69] Besides Marsh, eight men currently occupy the Kansas death row.

Oklahoma

Of the two hundred and fourteen persons executed in Oklahoma's history, eighteen died in what was, from 1834 to 1890, the Indian Nation. And with the exception of Daniel Luckey, an African American hanged for murder in 1882, all of those executed during this period were American Indians. Thirteen of the eighteen men were shot rather than hanged, although one—the first—died by an unknown method in 1841. Indeed, prior to the state's change to electrocution in 1913, as many condemned men faced a firing squad as walked the gallows. Notably, a lengthy hiatus followed the initial executions of the 1840s, with no additional death sentences being carried out until the early 1880s. Twenty-four executions occurred during the territorial period between 1890 and 1907, including eleven by firing squad.

The last man in Oklahoma to face execution by that method died in 1899.

Ninety death sentences were carried out in the period between Oklahoma statehood in 1907 and the last pre-*Furman* execution in 1966. With the exception of a federal prisoner hanged in 1936 on a kidnapping charge, eighty-two of the ninety condemned persons died in the electric chair, beginning with Henry Bookman in 1915. In the modern era, which for Oklahoma did not begin until 1990, eighty-two persons, including thirty-one since 2003, have died by lethal injection, the most recent on August 21, 2007.[70]

Oklahoma's early death penalty history reveals a striking pattern of racially concentrated periods of executions. As noted, American Indians dominate the earliest period, representing nearly eighty percent of all executions conducted in Oklahoma before 1900. Next, African Americans fill the execution roster between 1903 and 1918. Indeed, with the exception of three racially unknown persons, all persons executed during that same period, fourteen of seventeen or eighty-two percent of the total, were black, including the first woman executed in the state. Two Hispanics and two Asian/Pacific Islanders have been put to death, both in the modern era. One hundred and five whites have been executed in Oklahoma, none before 1899, and with no regularity until the period after World War I when notable racial patterns disappeared. Whites represent 63 percent of those executed in Oklahoma since 1915, while blacks represent 30 percent for the same period, and American Indians less than 4 percent.[71]

Of the three women executed in Oklahoma's history, the first, Dora Wright, was hanged in 1903. The others died by lethal injection in 2001: Wanda Allen, a forty-one-year-old African American woman, on January 11, and forty-year-old Marilyn Plantz for conspiracy to murder, on May 11.[72] Plantz, who was white, died for hiring two teenagers to kill her husband, James Plantz, in a life insurance scam. After beating their victim senseless with baseball bats taken from the Plantz children's bedroom, killers Clinton McKimble and William Bryson followed Marilyn's orders and burned her still-living husband in his truck in order to make the death appear accidental. Plantz and Bryson, who was Marilyn's boyfriend at the time of the murder, were tried together and sentenced to death in March 1989. McKimble received life in prison in exchange for his testimony. Of the condemned, Bryson died first, on June 15, 2000.[73]

Under current Oklahoma law, persons become eligible for a death sentence if convicted of murder with planned malice, murder related to forcible rape, robbery with a dangerous weapon, kidnapping, escape from legal custody, first-degree burglary, and arson, and murder of a child injured, tortured, or maimed.[74] Before imposing a death sentence, a jury must consider any mitigating circumstances, not enumerated in the Oklahoma code, and find at least one of eight aggravating circumstances.[75] Oklahoma law prohibits the execution of persons who were mentally retarded prior to age eighteen. In addition, the Oklahoma Supreme Court automatically reviews all death sentences. The governor has authority to grant clemency with the consent of the Board of Pardons and Paroles.[76]

Oklahoma's execution history is exceptional among the states of the Great Plains for its early heavy use of the firing squad and, especially, for its striking pattern of racial concentration visible in the period before World War I. Overshadowed only by its large and active southern neighbor, Oklahoma is also unusual among the Great Plains states for its high volume of executions conducted since readopting capital punishment in 1990. No stranger to controversy, the state has only accelerated the pace since 2003 and, as of 2007, is credited with the third-highest number of modern-era executions in the United

States.[77] Although surviving previous state and federal court challenges to its present execution protocol, on October 3, 2007, legal challenges elsewhere led Oklahoma attorney general Drew Edmondson to ask the state Court of Criminal Appeals to schedule no executions until hearing from the U.S. Supreme Court on the constitutionality of the lethal injection method. Should injection become legally problematic or banned altogether, Oklahoma law allows for the alternative methods of electrocution and firing squad in that order.[78]

Texas

Like the Lone Star State itself, Texas death penalty history looms large over the states of the Great Plains, dwarfing its neighbors in time and circumstance, but especially in execution volume. Stretching back across 160 years of statehood, four years as a member of the Southern Confederacy, nine years as an independent republic, and fifteen years as a part of Mexico—seventeen years for those counting an 1819 execution for piracy under the tottering Spanish Empire—the Texas execution roster includes 1,160 names, nearly double the number of executions for all of the other Great Plains states combined.

Texas's execution history began slowly, with just two death sentences carried out prior to Texan independence in 1836. Six men were executed under the flag of the Texas Republic, including two on the same day in 1838. During the long period between Texas statehood in 1845 and the adoption of electrocution and a centralized death row in 1923, a total of 394 persons faced execution, nearly all in the counties under local authority. The total includes two African American women and one Hispanic woman put to death between 1854 and 1863. During the American Civil War, five men were hanged for

treason and three shot for desertion. Racially, all of those executed for treason or desertion were white. One black man also faced a firing squad for attempted rape in 1863. Indeed, under slavery, blacks could hang in Texas for a host of crimes, including the attempted robbery or rape of whites. The phenomenon of lynching aside, justice for blacks could be swift. In 1906, one African American suspect ran the entire gamut of indictment, conviction, and gallows in the short span of four hours.[79] Of all persons executed between 1845 and 1923 in Texas, 228, or 58 percent of the total, were African American, while 100 were white, 47 Hispanic, and 17 racially unknown. Two American Indians were hanged in 1878 and 1879.

Over a forty-year span beginning in 1924, Texas made active use of its electrocution technology. Time, however, had brought little change to some aspects of Texas law. By the 1950s, robbery and rape were still capital crimes.[80] A total of 361 men died in Texas's electric chair before mounting legal challenges produced an effective statewide hold on executions. Notably, no fewer than 97 of these prisoners died for robbery or rape without an accompanying murder charge. Racially, 108 men, or 30 percent of those executed during this period, were white. Twenty-three Hispanics and one racially unidentified person also died in the electric chair. By contrast, 229 African Americans, representing an enormous 63 percent of the total, faced electrocution during the same period, including Joseph Johnson Jr., who on July 30, 1964, became the last person to die in Texas's electric chair.[81] Eighteen years passed before the next Texas execution.

Texas's death penalty history includes several notable features. For instance, five men occupied the state's electric chair on its first day of operation, February 8, 1924. The following year, Texas executed the first of six pairs of brothers to be put to death in the state. Eight of the twelve brothers died in pairs in 1924, 1925, 1936, and 1938. Curtis and Danny Harris entered the Texas death chamber within a month of each other in 1993, while five years separated the 1994 execution of Jessie Gutierrez from his brother Jose's own lethal injection in 1999. Arguably, the most infamous prisoner executed in Texas history was "Bonnie and Clyde" gang member Raymond Hamilton, who managed to escape from death row before being recaptured and executed on May 10, 1935.[82]

Following the Supreme Court's *Furman* decision halting all executions in the United States, Texas governor Preston Smith commuted the sentences of all fifty-two occupants of death row to life imprisonment. Texas, however, reinstituted capital punishment on January 1, 1974, and within two months the first condemned prisoner had arrived on death row.[83] Under the present law, the possibility of a death sentence is triggered for persons convicted of capital murder, defined as murder involving one of nine circumstances.[84] At the sentence proceeding for capital cases, both the state and defendant present arguments for or against a sentence of death. As a result of a 1989 U.S. Supreme Court decision requiring jury consideration of mitigating evidence when weighing a possible death sentence, Texas law employs a four-step approach requiring juries to consider the offense, the defendant's character and background, and the personal moral responsibility of the defendant before deciding if sufficient mitigating circumstances exist to warrant a sentence of life imprisonment without parole rather than death.[85]

Under current Texas law, capital sentences are subject to automatic review by the state Court of Criminal Appeals. Appeals can continue to the Texas Supreme Court, the U.S. Circuit Court of Appeals, and ultimately to the United States Supreme Court.[86] Execution of prisoners for an offense committed while the person was younger than eighteen years is prohibited.[87] Death row is located at the Texas Department of Criminal Justice's Polunsky unit in Livingston. Condemned women are kept at the Mountain View unit in Gatesville. Executions, however, are conducted at the Huntsville unit, which is located about forty-five minutes from Livingston. Prisoners are transferred the day before their scheduled executions. The governor may grant clemency with the recommendation and advice of a majority of the Board of Pardons and Paroles.[88]

In the modern era, Texas has executed 405 prisoners, a higher number than any other state in the country for the same period. Yet the first years of the modern era, which for Texas did not begin until 1982, offered few clues to the eventual rapid execution pace. Indeed, ten years after the state's first use of lethal injection the execution total stood at a relatively scant 49. Yet, aided by a concurrent appeals system and, after a 1998 multiple escape attempt, a new facility with improved security, this initial decade would be followed by an intensely active period of 359 executions.[89]

Racially, this group included 196 whites, 144 African Americans, 63 Hispanics, and 2 Asian/Pacific Islanders. Two of the executed persons were women, both of whom were white. One, Karla Faye Tucker, drew national attention. Convicted and sentenced to death for her part in the brutal pickaxe murder of two persons in 1983, Tucker became a born-again Christian in prison and by all accounts underwent a dramatic personal transformation. Despite nationwide pleas for her life, on February 3, 1998, she became the first woman executed in Texas in 135 years. On February 24, 2000, sixty-two-year-old Betty Lou Beets also died by lethal injection, becoming only the fifth woman to be executed in Texas history. Currently, ten women, five white and five black, occupy the women's death row at Gatesville, Texas.

With nearly four hundred condemned persons on Texas's death row, the accelerated execution pace does not look to change any time soon, although legal challenges to lethal injection based on the Eighth Amendment's cruel and unusual punishment provision may eventually slow or even suspend executions in the state, as they have in neighboring Oklahoma.[90] Texas's death row itself, which isolates prisoners in a sixty-square-foot cell with one hour of outdoor exercise per day, may also raise legal challenges to the state's death penalty law. Complaints and lawsuits have attacked the Spartan environment of the Polunsky unit at Livingston where, in 2006 and 2007, several inmates employed hunger strikes in a desperate attempt to attract national attention to prison conditions. Death row inmate Roy Lee Pippin launched one such strike on February 19, 2007, and within a month's time was twenty pounds lighter and subject to daily medical evaluation.[91] Pippin's strike, however, ended abruptly with his execution on March 29, 2007.

Conclusion

In law and practice, each region of the country presents its own unique set of dynamics, and so, too, within the regions themselves. With capital punishment, the Great Plains offers a microcosm of the larger United States, most notably in the southern Plains states where, due to enormous execution numbers, Texas is sometimes considered a distinct regional category exclusive of either the West or the South, the nation's busiest death penalty region with which it is often associated.[92]

The pattern is even more striking when isolating the modern era of capital punishment that followed the Supreme Court's 1972 landmark decision halting all executions in the United States.[93] During this period, no Plains state outside of Oklahoma and Texas has executed more than three prisoners; most have executed just one, and Kansas and North Dakota, none. During this same period, Oklahoma and Texas together have conducted nearly five hundred executions, and have done so at a progressively rapid pace. Death row populations tell the same story. In stark contrast to the 481 condemned persons occupying death row in Oklahoma and Texas, stands the other Plains states' combined death row population of 28, with two-thirds of these condemned men residing in Kansas and Nebraska. Such disparities may reflect the Bible belt values especially prevalent in Texas, Oklahoma, and much of the American South. In this view, government's God-given role is to maintain order and provide security for citizens under the law. Rather than a contradiction, opposition to practices such as abortion and euthanasia harmonize with support for capital punishment since the execution of those taking innocent life affirms the very sanctity of life.

Finally, despite a similar pattern evident through much of the region, it is little surprise that of the Plains states only North Dakota is without a death penalty statute. Indeed, North Dakota lies at the western end of a string of New England and upper midwestern states without capital punishment and, on this issue at least, may have more in common with the neighboring states of Minnesota, Wisconsin, Iowa, and Michigan than fellow Plains states of Oklahoma and Texas. Such is the varied history of capital punishment in that vast northern, southern, and western meeting ground that is the Great Plains.

John Gregory Jacobsen is Assistant Professor of History at Williams Baptist College in Walnut Ridge, Arkansas. With a constitutional/legal specialization and a broad interest in American history, he has published book reviews on legal texts and an article on local Arkansas history. Currently, Professor Jacobsen is serving his country as a chaplain in Iraq.

Table of Cases

United States
Furman v. Georgia 408 U.S. 238 (1972).
Gregg v. Georgia 428 U.S. 153 (1976).
Kansas v. Marsh 548 U.S. 163 (2006).
Penry v. Lynaugh 492 U.S. 302 (1989).
Ring v. Arizona 536 U.S. 584 (2002).
United States of America v. Alfonso Rodriguez, Jr. United States District Court for the District of North Dakota, Northeastern Division, C2–04–55, 162, September 25, 2005.

Colorado
No. 02SA365, Colorado Supreme Court, *The People of the State of Colorado v. Edward Montour, Jr.*, April 23, 2007.

Kansas
278 Kansas 520, 534–535,102 P. 3d 445, 458 (2004).

Nebraska
State v. Gales, 265 Neb. 598, 658 N.W.2d 604 (2003).
State v. Reeves, 216 Neb. 206, 344 N.W.2d 433 (1984).
State v. Sheets, 618 N.W.2d 117 (Neb. 2000).

Wyoming
Harris v. State, 933 P.2d 1114, 1997 Wyo. LEXIS 48 (Wyo. 1997).
Hopkinson v. State, 664 P.2d 43, 1983 Wyo. LEXIS 325 (Wyo. 1983).
Olsen v. State, 2003 WY 46, 67 P.3d 536, 2003 Wyo. LEXIS 57 (Wyo. 2003).

Statutes

United States
18 United States Code, § 1201.

Colorado
Colorado Statutes, 18–1.3–1201 subsection (4).
Colorado Statutes, 18–1.3–1201 subsection (5).
House Bill 07–1094, Introduced.

Kansas
Kansas Statutes Annotated, 21–3439.
Kansas Statutes Annotated, 21–4622.
Kansas Statutes Annotated, 21–4623.
Kansas Statutes Annotated, 21–4625.
Kansas Statutes Annotated, 21–4627.
Senate Bill 222, Introduced.
House Bill 2510, Introduced.

Montana
Montana Code Annotated, 45–5-102.
Montana Code Annotated, 46–18-303.
Montana Code Annotated, 46–18–304.
Montana Code Annotated, 46–18–307.

Nebraska
Nebraska Revised Statutes, 28–303.
Nebraska Revised Statutes, 29–2519.
Nebraska Revised Statutes, 29–2522.
Nebraska Revised Statutes, 29–2523.

New Mexico
New Mexico Statutes, 31–20A-5.
New Mexico Statutes, 31–20A-6.
New Mexico Statutes, 31–18–14.
New Mexico Statutes, 31–20A-2.1.

Oklahoma
Oklahoma Statutes, 21–701.7.
Oklahoma Statutes, 21–701.10.
Oklahoma Statutes, 21–701.11.
Oklahoma Statutes, 21–701.12.
Oklahoma Statutes, 21–701.13.
Oklahoma Statutes, 57–332.2.

South Dakota
South Dakota Code, 23A-27A-1.
South Dakota Code, 23A-27A-42.
South Dakota Code, 23A-27A-26.1.
South Dakota Code, 23A-27A-9.
South Dakota Code, 23A-27A-15.
South Dakota Code, 23A-27A-17.

Texas
Texas Penal Code, 3.12.31 (a).
Texas Penal Code, 5.19.01.
Texas Penal Code, 5.19.03.
Texas Penal Code, 8.07 (c).
Texas Code of Criminal Procedure, 37.071.2 (a)(1).
Texas Code of Criminal Procedure, 37.071.2 (e)(1).
Texas Code of Criminal Procedure, 37.071.2 (h).
Texas Code of Criminal Procedure, 48.01.

Wyoming
Wyoming Statutes, 6–2-101.
Wyoming Statutes, 6–2-102 subsection (h).
Wyoming Statutes, 6–2-102 subsection (j).
Wyoming Statutes, 6–2-103.
Wyoming Statutes, 7–13–807.

Suggested Readings

Allan, Mark. "Capital Punishment or Compassion: Executions in the State of New Mexico: The Death Penalty since Territorial Days." www.angelo.edu/services/library/librarians/mallan/capital-punishment-nm.htm, 2001.

Banner, Stuart. *The Death Penalty: An American History.* Cambridge: Harvard University Press, 2002.

"Bill to Halve Death Penalty Team Rejected." *Rocky Mountain News.com*, April 19, 2007.

"Bruning: Lotter Still Guilty of Murder." *Lincoln Journal Star.* September 20, 2007.

"Capital Cases Hard to Defend." *Casper StarTribune.net*, March 20, 2004.

Capote, Truman. *In Cold Blood*, Vintage Publication, 1965.

Benson, Kit, and Morgan Benson. "Corp Johannes Kunze." July 28, 2004. www.findagrave.com/cgi-bin/fg.cgi?page=gr&GSsr=41&GScid=98461&GRid=9194867&.

Carson, David. *Txexecutions.org.* www.txexecutions.org/default.asp.

"Current Events." The Kansas Coalition against the Death Penalty. www.kscadp.org/Events.htm.

"Dawson Put to Death Six Minutes Past Midnight," *Independent Record, HelenaIR.com*, August 11, 2006.

"Death Row Information." Texas Department of Criminal Justice, 2007. www.tdcj.state.tx.us/stat/deathrow.htm.

"Death Sentence for Student's Slaying," *Washingtonpost.com*, September 22, 2006. www.washingtonpost.com/wp-dyn/content/article/2006/09/22/AR2006092200584.html.

Edwards, Darby Lea. "Fort Leavenworth Military Prison Cemetery," November 07, 2003. www.interment.net/data/us/ks/leavenworth/ftleav_prison/index.htm.

"Execution in South Dakota, Delayed a Year by Debate on Method, Is First in 6 Decades." *The New York Times*, July 13, 2007. www.nytimes.com/2007/07/13/us/13execute.html?_=1&adxnnl=1&oref=slogin&adxnnlx=1191385079-SGOWNgMMJZ2/MimNZESwJw.

"Facts about the Death Penalty." Death Penalty Information Center, October 23, 2007, 3. www.deathpenaltyinfo.org/FactSheet.pdf.

"High Court Drops Killer's Death Penalty." *denverpost.com*, April 24, 2007.

"I'm Truly Sorry." *ABCNEWS.com*, Nov. 4, 1999.

"Inmate Fighting to 'Bitter End,' Refuses Food," *Houston Chronicle*, March, 20 2007. www.ncadp.org/news.cfm?articleID=57.

Jennings, Carol A. "State Historical Society Researches Capital Punishment in South Dakota." South Dakota State Historical Society, March 10, 2006. www.sdhistory.org/soc/news/2006/po6March09.htm.

"Marilyn Kay Plantz." ClarkProsecutor.org, 2001. www.clarkprosecutor.org/html/death/US/plantz711.htm.

Mentor, Kenneth W. "The Death Penalty Returns to New Mexico." http://kenmentor.com/papers/nm_deathpen.htm, 2002.

Nebraska Department of Correctional Services. *Policies: Capital Punishment.* www.corrections.state.ne.us/policies/capital_punishment.html.

"Nissen: 'I Am the Person Who Shot and Stabbed Teena Brandon.'" *Lincoln Journal Star.* September 20, 2007.

"Number of Executions by State and Region since 1976." Death Penalty Information Center. www.deathpenaltyinfo.org/article.php?scid=8&did=186.

"Oklahoma Attorney General Asks Hold on Executions." October 3, 2007. www.reuters.com/article/topNews/idUSN0326969320071003?sp=true.

Oklahoma Department of Corrections: Death Row. Execution Statistics, 2007. www.doc.state.ok.us/offenders/deathrow.htm.

Perry, Steven W. A BJS Statistical Profile, 1992–2002: *American Indians and Crime.* Bureau of Justice Statistics, 2004.

"Pols Kill Death Penalty Bill." *Las Cruces Sun News.* March 8, 2007.

"Quadruple Indian Hanging, Missoula, Montana Dec. 19th 1890." Heritage Auction Galleries. www.americana.ha.com/common/view_item.php?SaleNo=679&LotIdNo=13395&txtSearch=&hdnSearch=true.

Reha, Bob. "North Dakota's First Capital Punishment Case in 100 Years Set to Begin in Fargo." Minnesota Public Radio. June 26, 2006. minnesota.publicradio.org/display/web/2006/06/13/nddeathpenalty.

Sandstrom, Dale V. "Four Capital Murder Trials since the Last Execution in 1905." North Dakota Supreme Court News, 2006. www.ndcourts.gov/_court/news/fourcapitalmurdertrials.htm.

Smith, Leigh. "One German POW's Story." www.epcc.edu/ftp/Homes/monicaw/borderlands/12_one_german_pow's_story.htm.

Snell, Tracy L. *Capital Punishment, 2005,* NCJ 215083. Bureau of Justice Statistics, 2006.

South Dakota Department of Corrections. Frequently Asked Questions: Capital Punishment. www.state.sd.us/CORRECTIONS/FAQ_Capital_Punishment.htm.

"Supreme Court Upholds Kansas Death Penalty." About.com: Crime and Punishment. June 27, 2006. crime.about.com/b/a/257012.htm.

"Television Review: Battling Over the Life of a Convicted Killer." *The New York Times*, December 14, 1994.

"The Last Mass Execution." History.com. www.history.com/classroom/admin/study_guide/archives/thc_guide.0632.html.

Vyzralek, Frank. "Capital crimes and criminals executed in northern Dakota Territory and North Dakota, 1885–1905." Bismarck: North Dakota Supreme Court News, 2000. www.ndcourts.gov/_court/news/executend.htm.

Notes

1. Perry, *American Indians and Crime*, 3, 25.
2. Allan, "Capital Punishment or Compassion."
3. Banner, *The Death Penalty*, 199.
4. *Furman v. Georgia* 408 U.S. 238 (1972); *Gregg v. Georgia* 428 U.S. 153 (1976).
5. Snell, *Capital Punishment, 2005,* 16.
6. 31–20A-5 NMSA.
7. 31–20A-6 NMSA.
8. 31–20A-2.1; 31–18–14; 31–14–3 NMSA.
9. *Las Cruces Sun News*, March 8, 2007.
10. *New York Times*, January 24, 1982, 16:5; cited in Banner, *The Death Penalty*, 174.
11. Banner, *The Death Penalty*, 163.
12. Ibid., 199.
13. 18–1.3–1201 (5) CRS.
14. 18–1.3–1201 (4) CRS.
15. *denverpost.com*, April 24, 2007.
16. No. 02SA365, Colorado Supreme Court, *The People of the State of Colorado v. Edward Montour, Jr.*, April 23, 2007.
17. House Bill 07–1094.
18. *Rocky Mountain News.com*, April 19, 2007.
19. Banner, *The Death Penalty*, 199.
20. *Hopkinson v. State*, 1983.
21. W.S. 6–2–101.
22. *Harris v. State*, 1997.
23. W.S. 6–2–103.
24. W.S. 6–2–102 (h).
25. *Olsen v. State*, 2003.
26. W.S. 6–2–102 (j).
27. W.S. 7–13–807.
28. *ABCNEWS.com*, Nov. 4, 1999.
29. Heritage Auction Galleries, americana.ha.com.
30. M.S. 45–5–102.
31. M.S. 46–18–303.
32. M.S. 46–18–304.
33. M.S. 46–18–307.
34. *Independent Record, HelenaIR.com*, August 11, 2006.
35. Frank Vyzralek, "Capital Crimes and Criminals."
36. Dale V. Sandstrom, "Four Capital Murder Trials."
37. 18 U.S.C. § 1201; *U.S. v. Rodriguez* (2005).
38. Bob Reha, "North Dakota's First Capital Punishment Case in 100 Years," *Washingtonpost.com*, September 22, 2006.
39. South Dakota Department of Corrections, Capital Punishment; Carol A. Jennings, "State Historical Society Researches Capital Punishment."
40. SDCL 23A-27A-1.
41. SDCL 23A-27A-42; SDCL 23A-27A-26.1.
42. SDCL 23A-27A-9.
43. SDCL 23A-27A-15; SDCL 23A-27A-17.
44. *The New York Times*, July 13, 2007.
45. Banner, *The Death Penalty*, 161.
46. Nebraska Department of Correctional Services, *Policies*.
47. Banner, *The Death Penalty*, 174.
48. NRS 28–303; NRS 29–2519.
49. NRS 29–2523 (1); NRS 29–2522.
50. *State v. Gales*, 265 Neb. 598, 658 N.W.2d 604 (2003).
51. NRS 29–2523 (2); NRS 29–2522.
52. *State v. Reeves*, 216 Neb. 206, 344 N.W.2d 433 (1984); NRS 29–2521.03.
53. NRS 28–105.01.
54. *The New York Times*, December 14, 1994.
55. *State v. Sheets*, 618 N.W.2d 117 (Neb. 2000).
56. *Lincoln Journal Star*. September 20, 2007.
57. Banner, 221–222.
58. Benson, "Corp Johannes Kunze," 2004; Smith, "One German POW's Story"; "The Last Mass Execution," History.com.
59. Edwards, Darby Lea. "Fort Leavenworth Military Prison Cemetery," November 07, 2003.
60. Capote, *In Cold Blood*, 1965.
61. K.S.A. 21–3439.
62. K.S.A. 21–4625.
63. K.S.A. 21–4626.
64. K.S.A. 21–4622; K.S.A. 21–4623.
65. K.S.A. 21–4627.
66. "Current Events." The Kansas Coalition against the Death Penalty.
67. K.S.A. 21–4624(e); *Kansas v. Marsh*, U.S. Cert, 04–1170 (2006); 278 Kan. 520, 534–535,102 P. 3d 445, 458 (2004).
68. *Kansas v. Marsh* (2006).
69. Ibid; "Supreme Court Upholds Kansas Death Penalty," About.com: Crime and Punishment, 2006.
70. Oklahoma Department of Corrections: Death Row, Execution Statistics, 2007.
71. Ibid.
72. Ibid.
73. "Marilyn Kay Plantz," ClarkProsecutor.org, 2001.
74. O.S. 21–701.7.
75. O.S. 21-701.10c; O.S. 21-701.11; O.S. 21–701.12.
76. O.S. 21-701.10b; O.S. 21-701.13; O.S. 57 332.2.
77. "Number of Executions by State and Region since 1976," DPIC.
78. "Oklahoma Attorney General Asks Hold on Executions," Reuters.com, October 3, 2007.
79. Banner, 141, 229.
80. Ibid., 228.
81. Texas Department of Criminal Justice, 2007.
82. Ibid.
83. Carson, *Txexecutions.org*.
84. TPC 12.31(a); TPC 5.19.01; TPC 5.19.03.
85. *Penry v. Lynaugh*, 1989; TCCP 37.071.2(a)(1); 37.071.2 (e)(1).
86. TCCP 37.071.2(h).
87. TPC 8.07(c).

88. TCCP 48.01.

89. Carson.

90. "Oklahoma Attorney General Asks Hold on Executions," October 3, 2007.

91. "Inmate Fighting to 'Bitter End,' Refuses Food," March 20, 2007.

92. "Facts about the Death Penalty," DPIC, 2007, 3.

93. *Furman v. Georgia*, 408 U.S. 238 (1972).

CHAPTER 13

The Death Penalty in the Pacific Northwest

Joseph Laythe

Introduction

THE PACIFIC NORTHWEST—Oregon and Washington—has historically been a safe place for its white residents. The region was abundant in resources that could be easily tapped by the whites who sought to settle there. The region afforded its citizens, according to historian Gordon Dodds, a "pleasant, undemanding life."

That ease of life, however, had two important implications for the region. First, it meant that those individuals enjoying the region's plentiful offerings would, on occasion, have to defend their territory, their prosperity, and their power from perceived outside threats. There were many tools and techniques used to accomplish that defense, among them the use of capital punishment. The death penalty was used in the Pacific Northwest in the 1850s, 1860s, and 1870s as a means of pacifying the region's original inhabitants. By the end of the nineteenth century, Native Americans were effectively removed as "obstacles to progress" and threats to social order, and so the use of the death penalty diminished. Washington and Oregon renewed their use of the death penalty when new perceived threats to social order emerged. This occurred in the 1880s and 1890s with the growing presence of Chinese and the economic setbacks of those eras, in the 1910s and 1920s with the threat of radical labor, and in the 1970s, 1980s, and 1990s because of a changing population and culture.

In periods of peace and prosperity, however, northwesterners spent their lives in blissful isolation. The isolation, prosperity, and absence of socioeconomic and cultural conflict allowed the citizens of the region to engage in "careful civic and economic experimentation." That experimentation included the right to public initiative and legislative referendum. In short, Oregon and Washington citizens empowered their state legislatures with the right to refer important issues to a direct public vote. Likewise, they gave themselves the power to introduce legislation. This initiative and referendum system made the controversy of capital punishment a public issue. And, as a result, nowhere in the United States has the public voted more times on the subject than in the Pacific Northwest. The civic experimentation of the Pacific Northwest can thus be seen in the periodic abolition of the death penalty in the 1910s and again in the 1960s.

The Oregon Country and the Institution of Laws

Over the course of the first half of the nineteenth century, much of the Pacific Northwest was called the "Oregon Country." This area encompassed what is now modern-day Oregon, Washington, British Columbia, Idaho, and part of Montana. Between 1818 and 1846, the area was contested terrain between Britain and the United States. In the 1830s and 1840s, the tide of overlanders into the area, spurred on by "Oregon Fever," enabled the United States to secure sole ownership of the region. That influx of settlers, however, did not come without costs. The new settlers wanted reassurance of a stable society and, as a result, sought the establishment of new laws for their region. They did not have to reinvent their laws, however. Instead, they simply transplanted the laws from their home states to the new territory. On July 5, 1843, for example, the Legislative Committee of the Provisional Government accepted a motion to adopt the laws of the Iowa Territory. In the years following, lawmakers and jurists in Oregon tweaked those laws to accommodate the unique circumstances that the region afforded and adjusted the laws to insure the constitutionality of their criminal procedures. In 1850, the transplantation phenomenon was furthered when Oregon adopted the Pennsylvania-style statute of dividing murder into first-degree and second-degree charges.[1] By this point in time, the region had adopted the practice of capital punishment.

Between 1850 and 1859, when Oregon achieved statehood, the territory's federal courts were impaired by "erratic attendance and failure to act in a responsible manner."[2] Two decades of settlement and legal establishment had done little to stabilize the region and provide a blanket of equal justice to the people of the Pacific Northwest. The arbitrary justice applied in the Oregon Country can best be seen in the Cayuse Trial of 1850.

In November 1847, at a place called Waillatpu, not far from modern-day Walla Walla, Washington, Cayuse Indians attacked and massacred the inhabitants of the Whitman Mission, including Marcus and Narcissa Whitman. Over the course of the next two years, an army of whites from the Willamette Valley hunted down the Cayuse. In 1850, however, in an effort to stave off further persecution, the Cayuse sacrificed five members of their tribe to the American justice system. In the case of *U.S. v. Telokite et al.* (1850), grand jury indictments were handed down against Tiloukait, Tomahas, Klokomas, Isaiachalakis, and Kiasumkin. Defense attorneys were provided by both the territory and the U.S. Army. The defense attorneys immediately argued that the site of the incident, known as Cayuse Country, was not subject to U.S. jurisdiction or laws because the U.S. had not formally acquired the territory at the time of the incident. This appeal was denied and the judge instructed them to place their indictment pleas. The Telokite defendants pled not guilty and their attorneys requested a change of venue on the grounds that the jury would be prejudiced in this highly publicized case. Their appeal was denied. Nearly twenty peremptory challenges were made during the trial's jury selection in an effort to prevent prejudice. Judge Orville Pratt, however, continued to rule overwhelmingly in the prosecution's favor. Moreover, Pratt aided the prosecution's charge by instructing the jury that the Cayuse nation's surrender of the defendants was, in effect, an admission of their guilt. The defense attorneys also made motions for a new trial on the grounds that Pratt was the only judge in the territory, there was no jail sufficient to house the defendants, and that without that jail the defendants might be lynched at the whim of a mob. The Cayuse Trial is reflective of the justice system in early Oregon history. The institutions and laws were in place, but were tainted by the frontier circumstances of a sparse number of jurists, fear of Indian depredations, and vigilante mentality. The Cayuse were, in the words of Caroline Stoel and Carolyn Buan, "pre-doomed to die." On June 2, 1850, in the small Willamette Valley town of Oregon City, the five Cayuse Indians were hanged. They were the first official executions in Oregon history.[3] In short, "Oregon Fever" killed.

A Provincial Society

The State of Oregon and Territory of Washington, 1853–1889

In 1853, U.S. Congress created the Territory of Washington. Isaac Stevens was named the territory's first governor. It has been argued that because the new territory was so large and with such a small population, the authorities in the region were given greater autonomy and responsibility. Those same frontier features may have also sparked fear in Governor Stevens's mind that the new territory would be a lawless place where crime ran rampant and vigilantes were the last bastion of justice. In his address to the Territorial Legislative Assembly in December 1854, Governor Stevens stated, "In every political society, the mere fact of the existence of laws for the prevention of crimes and misdemeanors, presupposes their occasional violation. It is a remark no less common than true, that nothing tends more to prevent the commission of crime, than the certainty of punishment." He later added that an "unwelcome visitor—crime—has made its appearance among us."[4] Stevens, it appeared, was going to provide swift and certain punishment for those who violated the territory's laws. To his

south, in the Oregon Territory, lawmakers were not as enthusiastic about that blanket of authority and justice. They were principally interested in pursuing only those laws that directly benefited them. As Oregon's population grew, its attitudes about crime and punishment also shifted.

In 1859, because of that population growth, Oregon was granted statehood. By 1864, the new state codified the death penalty for all first-degree murders. Between that date and 1903, the authority to perform executions was granted to the county sheriffs. Around that time, in 1866, Oregon also began its construction of the Oregon State Penitentiary in Salem. Both the acceptance of capital punishment and the creation of the Oregon State Penitentiary reflect the growing power of the state and the perceived need to address social disorder. It should be further noted that officials at the Oregon State Penitentiary, between the 1860s and 1920s, consistently used corporal punishment as a means to establish order, prevent anarchy, and instill values into the inmates.[5] The development of a prison system also occurred in Washington Territory. That prison, first at Seatco and then at Walla Walla, was regarded as the most effective means "of stopping at once and forever the atrocious murders, robberies and plunderings" that were being committed in the territory.[6]

Between 1870 and the 1890s, both Oregon and Washington experienced profound change. Oregon's population, for example, grew from 52,465 in 1860 to 90,923 in 1870. By 1880, the population had again almost doubled to 174,768. Washington also grew during this time period. The territory began the 1860s with a population of only 11,594, doubled it to 23,955 by 1870, and more than tripled to 75,116 in 1880.[7] The population growth for both Oregon and Washington meant profound social change for the two places. For much of the first half of the century, for example, some

Oregon communities tolerated certain criminal behaviors because they were seen as central to their economies. Pendleton, Oregon, for instance, gave shoulder-shrugging tolerance to its rowdy cowboys, miners, and sheepherders because they contributed so much to that town's economy by depositing their funds in the city's banks, shopping at their stores, and drinking at their saloons. Portland, Oregon, tolerated the criminal practice of "crimping"—or forced service on a sailing ship—because the shipping trade was vital to that city's economy.[8] But, as the region grew in population and grew more economically stable, it became increasingly imperative to address certain crimes in a much more rigorous manner. In the face of that population change, Oregon and Washington residents increasingly turned to law enforcement as a means of coping with that change and restoring order to their provincial communities.

Oregon and Washington had a high turnover rate among its justices. Judicial positions were often regarded as political and financial "tools."[9] Given the lack of career motivations for judges during this early period and the absence of uniform training or appointment criteria, it is perhaps not surprising to find that these judges' court decisions were often tainted with racism. Roscoe Pound noted that "jury prejudice and jury lawlessness were the weapons of the plaintiff's lawyer."[10] Brad Asher further stated that, at least in Washington, the courts "stressed a race-differentiated system, in which due process was the preserve of whites and Indians were subject to exercises of private discipline."[11] This was not to say that justice was always denied people of other races and ethnicities within these native-born Protestant-dominated areas. Native Americans were acquitted of charges on several occasions. In 1883, Washington territorial governor William Newell postponed the execution of Erminio Gionini on the grounds that he believed the defendant was insane and that a medical commission should investigate.[12] Judicial officials gave lip service to the fairness of their courts. Washington justice John Wyche, for example, once said,

> The Constitution of the United States is co-extensive with the vast empire that has grown up under it, and its provisions securing certain rights to the accused in criminal cases, are as living and potent on the shores of the Pacific as the city of its birth. In the matter of these rights it knows no race. It is the rich inheritance of all, and under its provisions in the Courts of the country, on a trial for life, the savage of the forest is the peer of the President.[13]

But the population growth between 1860 and the 1880s in both Washington and Oregon meant greater potential for conflict between the races. East of the Cascade Range, for example, the growing number of white settlers touched off the Yakima and Nez Perce Wars. Native Americans were overwhelmingly blamed for the conflict. When it came time for the application of justice, it was unevenly delivered. In Jefferson County, Washington, for example, Native Americans who killed whites were more likely to be hanged than when white defendants murdered whites. Of twelve Native Americans convicted for murder in that county, five (or 42 percent) were hanged. Of the fifteen whites convicted of murder in the same county, only four (or 27 percent) were hanged.[14] Between 1850 and 1889, 42 percent of Oregon's executions were against Native Americans. In Washington Territory that figure was over 46 percent. By the end of the 1870s, the Native Americans of the Pacific Northwest were pacified.[15]

But just as quickly as one perceived threat to social order disappeared, another arose. A "Chinese Must Go" mania swept the region in the 1880s and 1890s. As had been the case with Native Americans, the Chinese population in the

Pacific Northwest rarely appeared in the courts unless they themselves were the defendants. In both Oregon and Washington, the discrimination against the Chinese was endorsed by both Republican and Democrat officials alike. In 1885, in communities throughout the region, anti-Chinese riots and violence erupted. The administration of Governor Sylvester Pennoyer in Oregon was particularly opposed to the presence of Chinese. His bias against Chinese defendants is most evident in the case against Chee Gong. In November 1887, a Chinese man, Lee Yick, was murdered in a Chinese theatre in Portland. Despite conflicting reports from within the Chinese community, Chee Gong was identified as the sole killer, was arrested, and convicted. Gov. Pennoyer refused to commute the sentence despite the larger doubts of guilt. Chee Gong, who was by all evidence innocent of the crime, was hanged on August 10, 1889.[16]

In the face of population growth and increased diversity within that population, the people of the Pacific Northwest sought alternative measures to address what they perceived as "social disorder." They believed in the tried-and-tested use of capital punishment. Harvey Scott, owner and editor of the *Oregonian*, the state's largest and most powerful newspaper, once wrote, "Prompt trial and swift execution of the death penalty is the sharpest and best medicine to cure a cutthroat: the grave is a prison more frightful to the ordinary assassin than ever the living death of life imprisonment, whose cell is never so dark but is lighted by that ray of hope we call executive pardon."[17] The citizens of the State of Oregon and the Territory of Washington clung to the use of the death penalty. They recognized, however, that public execution itself also held great potential for social disorder. While they endorsed the practice, they believed the "public spectacle" associated with it was a sign of barbarism. In the early 1870s, as a result, Oregon required all executions to occur on the secured grounds of the county courthouses and within an enclosed jail or jail yard.[18]

Between 1853 and 1889, Oregon executed thirty-one men. Almost 30 percent of those executions were against Native Americans with only one Asian and one African American being executed. Whites comprised almost 65 percent of all Oregon executions. Washington, in contrast, only executed thirteen individuals—six Native Americans (46 percent), two Asians (13 percent), and five whites (38 percent).

Power of the People and an End to Capital Punishment, 1889–1914

In 1889, the Territory of Washington was granted statehood. With that Congressional Act came the establishment of separate federal district and circuit courts. Washington's new state constitution was pieced together from other constitutions, but most notably borrowing from the Oregon Constitution.[19] Between that date and the end of World War I in 1919, the Pacific Northwest experienced tremendous growth. Oregon's population swelled from 174,768 in 1880 to 317,704 in 1890, and by 1910 had more than doubled to 672,765. Washington grew from 75,116 in 1880 to 357,232 in 1890 to 1,141,990 in 1910. Seattle, Washington, surpassed Portland, Oregon, as the premier city in the Pacific Northwest. In 1890, for example, Seattle trailed Portland in population by nearly 4,000 people. By 1910, in contrast, Seattle had over 30,000 more residents than its neighbor to the south. Seattle's remarkable growth can, in large part, be attributed to the Klondike Gold Rush in the late 1890s. In 1897 the first cargo of gold entered into Seattle from the Klondike region to the north. This infusion of wealth, the growth of a working population, and the massive purchase of consumer goods gave the "Emerald City" a period of marked prosperity.[20]

The growth of these cities and their concomitant vice communities helped spawn the development of a Populist and Progressive movement in Oregon and Washington. William S. U'Ren's "Oregon System," a populist ideology that called for greater power in the hands of average citizens, included among its platforms the initiative and referendum, recall, direct election of senators, and a voter's guide. While Populism had died with the election of 1896, many of the basic tenets were adopted by a growing number of Progressives in the region. Progressivism was an urban reform movement designed to curb the growing problems in American society—poverty, crime, drunkenness, and vice. Because of Seattle and Portland's rapid growth, it's not surprising that this political and social reform movement took root there as well. But also tucked among the Progressives' goal was an overhaul or reform of the existing legal and judicial system. Progressives, for example, had been successful in the creation of separate juvenile courts to address the growing problems among that population and to offer greater hope to them. Many progressives in Oregon and Washington also advocated the abolition of the death penalty.[21]

Oregon governor George Chamberlain expressed distaste for the practice of capital punishment. In his 1903 inaugural address to the state legislature, he included an explicit reference to the Wade-Dalton executions. Two years earlier, in November 1901, John Wade and William Dalton murdered James Morrow. The two men were sentenced to hang in the courtyard of the Multnomah County Courthouse in downtown Portland. A twenty-foot privacy wooden wall was built to surround the makeshift gallows. On the morning of January 31, 1902, over four hundred special guests arrived to witness the affair. They had been issued tickets. Many more observed the hanging from afar—atop adjacent buildings, hanging out of nearby windows, and scaling poles. It was

"part carnival and part martyrdom." When it was all over, George Chamberlain referred to those onlookers as "morbidly curious" and regarded their behavior as uncivilized and a blemish upon the region's character.[22] Always eager to prove themselves equal to their eastern state counterparts, Washington and Oregon state officials consistently sought to assert their civilized character. Shortly after the turn of the century, Oregon, for example, ordered that executions would no longer occur within the counties of jurisdiction, but were to occur solely and safely behind the walls of the Oregon State Penitentiary. As a result, on January 29, 1904, Harry D. Egbert became the first individual lawfully executed at OSP in Salem. Egbert had been convicted and sentenced to die for his role in the murder of two law enforcement officers in Harney County. The act of removing executions from the counties served a dual purpose. It signaled an end to the barbarous practice of executions as "public spectacle." More importantly, perhaps, it demonstrated the growing power of the state and the role of the state as a civilizing force.[23]

Over the course of the next decade progressive reformers in both states campaigned to end the use of the death penalty altogether. Leading the charge in Oregon was Governor Oswald West, who succeeded Chamberlain. West was a pure progressive who would, in the course of his career, campaign for tougher banking regulations, reform the railroad commission, modernize the state's budgeting policies, establish a minimum wage and workmen's compensation, and advocate the development of public highways.[24] In 1911, Governor West opened his campaign to abolish the death penalty. In his inaugural address he noted, "Capital punishment should be abolished . . . in this state. The system of paying for a life with a life is, in my belief, merely a relic of that ancient and barbarous doctrine of an eye for an eye and a tooth for a tooth."[25] He further questioned the reliability of circumstantial evidence that had been so often used in the conviction of murderers. Until he could convince the state legislature to abolish capital punishment, West promised to stop the practice through executive orders. In November 1911, for example, he commuted the death sentence of Jans M. Hassing, stating, "There will be no hanging in Oregon as long as I am governor of the state." He added, "The belief that bloodshed must be expiated by the shedding of blood is . . . a relic of barbarism and not in consonance . . . with the spirit of the twentieth century."[26]

By November 1912, West was successful in getting a ballot measure to abolish the death penalty before Oregon voters. Unfortunately for West, the ballot measure was defeated by a vote of 64,578 in favor of the continued practice of capital punishment and only 41,951 against the death penalty. The defeat of West's ballot measure was attributed to poor campaign organization and a series of high-profile crimes. West was forced to reassess his political position, despite his personal conviction against capital punishment. Public pressure also began to play upon West. On December 13, 1912, four men from four different murder cases across the state of Oregon were taken to the gallows at the Oregon State Penitentiary. Over one hundred protesters attended the executions demanding that West maintain his inaugural pledge and commute their death sentences. He did neither. All four were hanged.

Over the course of 1913 and 1914, however, West continued to campaign. Joined by the Anti-Capital Punishment League, West and his supporters drew up a second initiative petition calling for the end of the death penalty in Oregon. In the meantime, on March 22, 1913, the State of Washington abolished the death penalty. Washington's more diverse and cosmopolitan population was more inclined toward liberal policies. In Oregon, however, it appeared that the abolition measure was simply too radical for the state's more homogeneous, conservative, and provincial population. When the 1914 vote was taken, however, West and his allies had scored a surprising victory. The measure passed with 50.04 percent of the vote. Oregon abolished the death penalty by only 157 votes—100,552 to 100,395. William Long, in his work *A Tortured History*, suggests that Oregon's recent passage of women's suffrage was enough to tip the balance in favor of abolition. In 1915, Governor West proudly declared "the old barbarous system of capital punishment has been abolished." In the first two decades of the twentieth century, up to 1917, seven other states abolished the death penalty: Kansas (1907), Minnesota (1911), South Dakota (1915), North Dakota (1915), Tennessee (1915), Arizona (1916), and Missouri (1917). It is safe to argue that neither Oregon nor Washington were pioneers in the abolition of the death penalty. Oswald West had simply led the charge in Oregon as part of a much larger national phenomenon. West's dream, however, was short-lived. As Hugo Adam Bedau later noted, "West's legacy was not the constitutional abolition of the death penalty, as he had hoped it would be, but the very reverse, the inspiration for his successors to enshrine it in the state constitution." In short, West's close victory galvanized his opponents.[27]

Despite the changing attitudes toward capital punishment over the course of the late nineteenth and early twentieth century, both Oregon and Washington experienced a substantive increase in the number of executions. Oregon oversaw the execution of forty-five men between 1889 and the abolition of the death penalty in 1914. Ninety-one percent of those men who were executed were white. There were only four individuals who were not identified as white that were executed—two Asians, one Hispanic, and one African American. It should be also noted that nine of those Oregon executions occurred during the governorship of Oswald West. In Washington the figures varied only slightly. Of that state's thirty-two executions, between 1889 and the abolition of capital punishment in 1913, 84 percent were committed against whites. Of the five nonwhites executed during this time period, four were Asian and one was African American.

Fear of the Changing World, 1915–1950

In 1913 and 1914, during the governorship of Oswald West, unemployment in the state of Oregon increased. The economic uncertainty of the era gave further support to the burgeoning labor movement and "rumblings" from the Industrial Workers of the World (IWW). For many in Oregon, the rise of radicalism seemed to be linked to the recent abolition of the death penalty. An editorial in the *Oregonian* at the time claimed that because of the end of capital punishment, "those treasonably disposed may carry on their favorite amusements unhindered." As World War I began winding down, "reactionary politics" in the Pacific Northwest increased.[28]

The 1917 murder of a prominent business leader in Washington prompted some to call for a restoration of the death penalty in that state. The murderer in that case had apparently boasted that he would be able to live the rest of his life in prison being tended to by his guards. Washington citizens may have had legitimate concern about the spate of crimes hitting their region. John R. Cranson, warden at the Washington State Penitentiary in Walla Walla, noted that "records available . . . indicate there was an increase in the number of capital crimes during that period." More importantly, labor strife at the end of the decade seemed to legitimize their fears about a changing world. In February 1919, over sixty thousand workers went on strike in Seattle. Seattle's mayor, Ole Hanson, warned that the general strike in his

city was part of an impending Bolshevik revolution. Many Washingtonians shared his fears. On March 14, 1919, Washington reinstated the death penalty. It had been almost six years to the day since it had been abolished.[29]

Washington's restoration of the death penalty did little to stop labor discontent. In November 1919, an incident occurred in Centralia, Washington (about halfway between Seattle and Portland) that pitted American Legionnaires, some of whom had just returned from war, against members of the IWW. Violence ensued and several legionnaires were shot. In the end, one Wobbly, Wesley Everest, was lynched. The murder of two prominent Oregonians on the heels of that crisis, in combination with the chaos of the growing Red Scare, prompted Portland mayor George Baker to call for a reinstatement of Oregon's death penalty.[30]

Oregon governor James Withycombe was equally alarmed. He noted that without the death penalty the state of Oregon had no punishment for treason. In the face of the Red Scare, the growth of the IWW, and the strikes that plagued Boston and Seattle, reinstatement, he believed, was necessary. Withycombe died, however, before re-election and he was replaced by Secretary of State Ben Olcott. Despite being a good friend and brother-in-law of Oswald West, Olcott also believed reinstatement was necessary. "Since the adjournment of the regular session in 1919," he said, "a wave of crime has swept over the country. Oregon has suffered from this criminal blight, and during the past few months the commission of a number of cold-blooded and fiendish homicides has aroused our people to demand for greater and more certain protection." Olcott called a special emergency session of the Oregon legislature in 1920 and began campaigning for the restoration of the death penalty. As a result, in 1920, Oregon voters revisited the death penalty in the form of a public referendum.[31]

Both states' reassessment of the death penalty was part of a larger move toward conservative politics in the region in the 1920s. State senator B. L. Eddy, in separate comments made to the *Oregonian*, suggested that the Bolshevik movement was "a deadly ferret clutching at the throat of the American eagle . . . the worst menace that has ever faced civilization." Oregon's death penalty debate was increasingly wrapped up with patriotism and the Red Scare.[32] When the voting was completed, 81,756 Oregonians voted in favor of reinstating capital punishment with only 64,589 opposed. In two short years, Washington and Oregon had both reinstated the death penalty.[33]

In Washington, the Red Scare gave great publicity to William David Askren. Askren served as Pierce County prosecutor and led the prosecution against thirty-six members of the IWW under criminal syndicalism laws. In 1925, Askren was elected to the Washington State Supreme Court where his conservative opinions helped shape law for the next four years. Serving on the court with Askren in the late 1920s was Justice Kenneth Mackintosh. Mackintosh had applauded the citizens of Centralia, Washington, for their fight against the Wobblies. Mackintosh had a history of being tough on crime. He also apparently supported the use of capital punishment. In one case involving a twelve-year-old boy convicted of murder, Mackintosh reportedly suggested that the boy be hanged.[34]

Between 1920, when it reinstated the death penalty, and 1963, the State of Oregon executed thirty-four individuals. Almost 90 percent of those individuals were white while only 9 percent were African American. In Washington State the figures were close to the same. Ninety percent of the fifty-eight executed in Washington were white and 7 percent were African American. Interesting patterns emerge when one examines the two states' executions by decade. Of Oregon's thirty-four executions in this time period, almost 45 percent occurred in the conservative 1920s, only two executions total in the 1930s, and 35 percent in the 1940s. In Washington, however, the numbers were almost exactly reversed. Only 19 percent of that state's fifty-eight executions were done in the 1920s, 40 percent in the 1930s, and back down to 28 percent in the 1940s.

These fluctuations and differences may be attributed to the shifts in economies for the two states and the population growth both experienced. In 1920, Oregon had a population of a little under 783,389 with Portland as its largest city at 258,288 (almost one-third of the state's entire population). By 1940, the state had grown to over 1,089,684 people with Portland at 305,394. Washington, in contrast, started the 1920s out with a population of 1,356,621 with Seattle at 315,312 (or one-fourth of the state's total). By 1940, Washington State topped at 1,736,191 people with Seattle having 368,302 residents. Oregon and Washington's growing populations and growing economies served to attract a much more diverse population than ever before. Large numbers of African Americans moved into the Pacific Northwest, and a sizeable number of Hispanic migrant workers also began to trickle into the region's farmlands. This shift in the composition of the population in the Pacific Northwest alarmed many of the region's racist residents. These racial fears, combined with the anxiety of the Great Depression, World War II, and the subsequent Cold War, may have only legitimized their commitment to death penalty.[35]

The Movement against Capital Punishment, 1950–1964

In 1949, Morris Leland was convicted for the murder of a Multnomah County teenage girl and was sentenced to die. There was question, however, as to whether or not Leland was sane at the time of the incident. Over the course of the following years, however, Leland's appeals fell on deaf ears and the Oregon Supreme Court ultimately affirmed his sentence. Three years later, in 1952, the United States Supreme Court heard oral arguments addressing the need for standards and definitions for proof of "insanity." Oregon law required that any charge of "insanity" be proven "beyond a reasonable doubt." Oregon was one of the last states to maintain that strict definition. In the end, the United States Supreme Court upheld Oregon's standard of "insanity" despite the "thunderous dissent" from Justices Hugo Black and Felix Frankfurter. Leland was executed in January 1953. The Leland case, on the surface, appears to have been a defeat for those opposed to capital punishment in the Pacific Northwest. The case had, however, generated enough attention and scrutiny that Oregon lawmakers instituted an automatic appeal to all death sentence cases. This automatic appeal went into effect in 1955 and serves as an indicator of the region's doubt about sentencing procedures and decisions.[36]

The region's position on capital punishment seemed to be slowly shifting away from its commitment to swift and certain retribution. In 1956, Robert Holmes, a Democrat, assumed the office of the Governor of Oregon. He took that office in fulfillment of his predecessor's term. In 1958, however, Holmes ran for re-election against Republican Secretary of State (and future U.S. senator) Mark Hatfield. Holmes had been vehemently opposed to capital punishment. William Long, Oregon's foremost death penalty scholar, suggests that where Oswald West had opposed capital punishment on pragmatic and utilitarian grounds, Holmes opposed the death penalty for purely moral purposes.[37]

In the months preceding that gubernatorial election, Oregon Democrats introduced House Joint Resolution 11 which called for a constitutional amendment to add a provision fixing the punishment for first-degree murder at life imprisonment. By doing this, they believed, they prevented capital punishment. By fall, however, as the election came closer, the anti-death-penalty referendum had gained attention. Although Governor Holmes was in a position of authority and was well known for his adamant opposition to capital punishment, he may have done more harm than good to the campaign. Two years earlier, in April 1956, Billy Junior Nunn sexually assaulted and murdered fourteen-year-old Alvin Eacret. Governor Holmes's practice of commuting death sentences prompted the Eacret family to file suit against the governor in the Jackson County Circuit Court. They sought to prevent the governor from commuting the sentence of the man who had killed their son. Holmes's position on the death penalty was increasingly cast as a personal opinion that ran in contrast with the opinion of the larger public and a decision that betrayed the trust of the victim's family. A Jackson County judge subsequently issued a restraining order against Holmes. In December 1958, the Oregon Supreme Court heard the case and on Christmas Eve rejected the family's plea. Holmes was given a free hand to continue his practice and in January 1959 commuted Nunn's death sentence. Unlike Governor Oswald West, Governor Holmes was able to fulfill his promise of no executions. When the anti-death-penalty referendum went before the Oregon voters, however, they overwhelmingly opposed it. Thirty-five of the state's thirty-six counties voted against it. Among those counties in opposition to the referendum was Jackson County. In 1912, that county had been among the leaders in favor of abolishing capital punishment. In 1914, that same county had the second largest margin of victory in opposition to the practice of capital punishment. But, with the memory of the Eacret case so fresh in their minds, Jackson County rejected the anti-death-penalty referendum with 54 percent of the votes. But, those examining the election results were quick to realize that the referendum lost by only 8,000 votes in Multnomah County, the state's most populous county, and that one-third of all votes cast on that issue came from that one county. This was enough to further galvanize the anti-death-penalty movement in the state.[38]

As Oregon entered the 1960s, a new leader in the anti-death-penalty movement in the Pacific Northwest emerged—Hugo Adam Bedau. Bedau received his Ph.D. from Harvard in 1961 and soon thereafter joined the faculty at Reed College in his hometown of Portland. Bedau was opposed to capital punishment. He believed that a systematic examination of capital punishment would reveal its failures. The utilitarianism of Oswald West and the moralism of Robert Holmes were simply not enough to stop the practice of capital punishment. Instead, Bedau argued, those elements needed to be buttressed with facts and evidence that demonstrated its failure to provide social order. Bedau, as a result, sifted through volumes of academic literature to provide an objective lesson on the practice of capital punishment.[39] He later wrote:

> During earlier centuries, the death penalty played a plausible, even justifiable, role in society's efforts to control crime and mete out just deserts to convicted offenders. After all, the alternative of imprisonment—the modern form of banishment—had yet to be systematically developed.[40]

He noted that the death penalty was a product of historical circumstances and that those conditions, in Oregon and elsewhere in the United States, had changed to such an extent that capital punishment was no longer necessary. Bedau wrote:

> The death penalty, today as in the past, symbolizes the ultimate power of the state, and of government of society, over the individual citizen. . . . This is precisely why, in the end, we should oppose the death penalty in principle and without exception. As long as capital punishment is available under law for any crime, it is a temptation to excess.[41]

By making that argument, Bedau was not only appealing to moralists in the state, but to those who feared the power of the government. This appeal fit within the state's tradition of Populism and the ability for Oregonians to make policy decisions for themselves.

In January 1963, two bills were introduced in the Oregon state senate by Senator Don S. Willner. Willner had received his law degree from Harvard in 1951, served as a state representative between 1957 and 1959, and had only recently taken his new position as senator in 1963. The first of Willner's bills, Senate Joint Resolution No. 3, proposed a constitutional amendment referring the issue of capital punishment back to the voters of Oregon in the 1964 general election. His second bill, Senate Bill No. 10, valid only if SJR 3 passed, called for a minimum of ten years to life for the crime of murder. This second bill was designed to remedy the absence of punishment guidelines were capital punishment to be removed. The Oregon Senate Judiciary Committee forwarded the bills in April 1963 and they were passed by the state legislature the following month. Willner's bill had supporters that included Myron Katz, an economist with the Bonneville Power Administration; Keith Burns, an attorney and clerk for the U.S. District Court; and Janet McLennan, a local citizen active in liberal politics. More importantly, however, these supporters of the referendum (opponents of the death penalty) in combination with Bedau had assembled a strong coalition and a strategy for victory to accompany Willner's bills.[42]

The Oregon Coalition Against the Death Penalty (OCADP) developed a strategy to organize a statewide force, mobilize support from allied organizations such as churches, design a mass-media campaign with particular focus on the metropolitan Portland area, and raise a minimum of ten thousand dollars to fund the larger campaign. As research director for OCADP, Bedau lent scholarly credibility to the campaign. Moreover, the publication of his book *The Death Penalty in America* in 1964 brought further publicity to the campaign. It was clear to Bedau and his colleagues in OCADP that the Oregon public simply needed to be better informed on the subject. To accomplish that task, OCADP arranged for radio and television announcements, prepared research papers for both the press and their own campaign speakers, encouraged their allied clergy to deliver sermons on the issue, and held a national conference on the death penalty at Lewis and Clark College in Portland.[43]

As the campaign got underway, Janet McLennan handled the logistics of waging the crusade against capital punishment. She organized the distribution of leaflets and saw to it that a booth at the state fair was staffed with representatives from OCADP who could articulate their argument. OCADP also took great care to write a detailed and informative description of their position for the Oregon *Voter's Pamphlet*. In mid-October, the conference at Lewis and Clark College was held featuring Donal E. J. MacNamara, president of the American League to Abolish Capital Punishment, and Clinton Duffy, a former warden at San Quentin. OCADP also purchased large billboards throughout the city of Portland that were emblazoned in black, white, and "lurid orange" with the words "You are the Executioner! End the Death Penalty! Vote Yes on No. 1." The intense campaign ultimately forced Governor Mark Hatfield to state his position of the issue. Hatfield "cautiously" supported the bill, but

wisely reassured the voters that in all decisions, he would follow the strict order of law. Hatfield's lukewarm endorsement was followed by slightly more enthusiastic support from Multnomah County sheriff Donald Clark and Multnomah County district attorney George Van Hoomissen. For whatever reason, no sustained opposition to the 1964 referendum ever materialized. It almost appeared ordained.[44]

When the votes had all been tabulated, the 1964 anti-death-penalty referendum won with 455,654 votes to only 302,105 in opposition. The vote, unlike its 1958 predecessor, carried thirty-two of the state's thirty-six counties, including Jackson County. Multnomah County, as had been expected, helped turn the tide. In just that one county, the referendum won by nearly 69,000 votes. Bedau later suggested that the growing number of young voters in that election may have helped secure that victory. Thus, on November 4, 1964, one day after the election, Governor Hatfield proclaimed that capital punishment had been abolished in the state of Oregon. It has been argued that Oregon's 1964 vote "set in motion a wave of legislation repealing the death penalty" across the United States. Oregon's abolition of the death penalty in 1964 was quickly followed by Iowa, West Virginia, Vermont, New York, and New Mexico.[45]

A Region under Pressure, 1960s–Present

Beginning in the 1960s, the culture and economy of the Pacific Northwest began to change. In 1968, for example, Boeing employed about 100,000 individuals in Seattle. Commercial airplane sales dropped between 1968 and 1971, however, and two-thirds of those workers (roughly 65,000) were laid off. By 1971, Seattle's unemployment rate was at 13 percent, one of the highest in the United States. The long, prosperous timber industry in both states also suffered a series of serious setbacks. The timber industry woes were further complicated by a growing number of northwesterners who regarded that industrial loss with indifference. "New urban refugees" moved into Washington and Oregon in greater numbers. They sought lower taxes and the luxury of small-town life that the region afforded. Places like Bend, Oregon, along the eastern edge of the Cascades, North Bend, Oregon, along the coast, and Hoquiam, Washington, near Puget Sound grew rapidly because of this influx. This invasion ultimately helped drive up property values. More importantly, however, these new urbanites did not share the same cultural values as the native-born residents. The division between these "invaders" and the native-born northwesterners was seen in the development of a series of bumper stickers that identified the owner of the vehicle to which it was attached as a "Native Oregonian." The sensitivity to this outside invasion can be further seen in Oregon governor Tom McCall's 1971 comments about tourism in the region. "We want you to visit our State of Excitement often," McCall said. "Come again and again. But, for heaven's sake don't move here."[46]

But while the Pacific Northwest was increasingly divided between native and nonnative residents, a more important schism developed between the region's urban and rural residents. Between 1950 and 1990, the state of Oregon grew from 1.52 million residents to 2.84 million residents. Washington's growth was even more remarkable. That state grew from nearly 2.4 million residents in 1950 to almost 5 million in 1990. The new demographic patterns in the Pacific Northwest also meant new political patterns. Throughout the region, as was the case nationwide, the urban areas overwhelmingly voted Democratic while the rural areas supported the Republican Party. The division between the

region's urban liberals and rural conservatives was evident in a series of high-profile issues that included debate over immigration, the environment (and Spotted Owl), homosexuality, and physician-assisted suicide.[47]

The economic setbacks, growing division between northwesterners, and the change in population composition ultimately manifested itself in a renewed debate about the death penalty. In 1972, the U.S. Supreme Court's review of a death penalty case, *Furman v. Georgia*, allowed that renewed discussion in the Pacific Northwest to explode in a series of profound changes for the region's death penalty policy. In *Furman v. Georgia*, the U.S. Supreme Court ruled that existing death penalty statutes in the United States were unconstitutional where there was unlimited jury discretion to determine the death penalty and where there was no meaningful basis to distinguish the cases where it was imposed from those cases where it was not. In short, the U.S. Supreme Court called into question the consistency of the states' application of the death penalty. Between 1972 and 1976, in a series of Supreme Court decisions born out of the *Furman v. Georgia* case, several states amended their statutes to accommodate that decision.[48]

In 1975, the Washington state legislature abolished capital punishment. But, on November 4, 1975, the citizens of Washington, through a state referendum, rejected that abolition and reestablished the death penalty. In keeping with other Supreme Court rulings, the death penalty in Washington was not officially reinstated until 1977. That reinstatement instituted the death penalty as the mandatory sentence for first-degree aggravated murder.[49] The opinion of Washington citizens on the issue of the death penalty may not have been too far removed from those of the courts in Washington State. In King County, Judge Carolyn Reaber Dimmick, who would later serve on the state's supreme court, was lenient with first offenders, but addressed repeat offenders and violent criminals "more severely." At the supreme court level in the 1970s, Justice Charles Wright openly endorsed capital punishment. "I think a man might think twice before he shot a policeman," Wright said, "if he knew he might hang for it."[50] Oregon, however, was "spared" the work of rewriting its death penalty statutes because it had already abolished the death penalty. That changed in 1978.

Beginning in the mid-1970s, the state of Oregon started revisiting the idea of reinstituting the death penalty. Oregon governor Robert Straub, who was personally opposed to the death penalty, was convinced that a "steady parade" of murders and grisly crimes had affected public opinion in favor of capital punishment. As early as 1974, with Carl Cletus Bowles's murder of a couple in Washington, new discussions about capital punishment began developing. Richard Marquette's murder of a Scio, Oregon, woman in 1975 after having been recently paroled for a similar crime further called into question the efficacy of the state's prison system and generated even more feverish debate about the death penalty. In 1977, the Oregon Legislature crafted House Bill 2321 to restore the death penalty. In 1978, in what was the state's fifth historic election on capital punishment, Oregon residents reinstated the death penalty with 64 percent of the vote. This reinstatement, through Ballot Measure 8, was not a constitutional amendment, but simply a revision of statutes.[51]

In Washington, efforts were consistently underway in the 1970s to reinstate the death penalty through state initiative. In 1979, in *State v. Green*, the Washington Supreme Court struck down a death penalty initiative on the grounds that it violated the cruel and unusual punishment provisions of the Bill of Rights.[52]

The reinstatement of the death penalty in Oregon was quickly challenged on the grounds that it violated the defendant's right to jury determination. The new death penalty statute had delegated the power of death penalty sentencing to the judge. In 1981, as a result, in the case of *State v. Quinn*, 290 Or. 383, the Oregon Supreme Court ruled that the new statute was, in fact, unconstitutional.[53]

The debate over capital punishment, however, was far from over. In 1982, death penalty advocates tried to restore capital punishment through the initiative process, but had an insufficient number of votes to get it onto the ballot. In 1984, again using the power of public initiative, those death penalty advocates were able to get it onto the ballot and the state of Oregon passed two initiatives. The first initiative amended the state constitution such that the death penalty was exempt from constitutional provisions against cruel and unusual punishment. The second initiative re-established the death penalty. Oregon death penalty scholar William Long suggests that Oregon voters, because of the lack of clarity in Ballot Measures 6 and 7, did not necessarily understand the issues upon which they were voting.[54] The restoration of the death penalty in Oregon passed with 893,818 votes (75 percent) to 295,988 votes against (25 percent). It was the largest margin of victory in Oregon's history of voting on the issue.

The new Oregon death penalty statute was explicitly based on a Texas model, despite the gross differences between the two states and their respective cultures. The Texas model was in sharp contrast to the standard Model Penal Code that most states used. The Model Penal Code encouraged juries to examine the mitigating factors of each case before committing themselves to the death sentence decision. The Texas Model, in contrast, required the jury to weigh the "future dangerousness" of the offender in their decision. Oregon was the only state in the 1980s to accept the Texas model. The adoption of a Texas-style statute suggests that Oregon was increasingly distressed by the grim realities of crime within the region. Faced with the profound change of a burgeoning population and skyrocketing drug problem, Oregonians chose to get "tough on crime." Their 1984 endorsement of the death penalty was, in the words of William Long, fueled by "a spate of ghoulish murders" and the growing victims' rights movement.[55]

New challenges to the restored death penalty soon arose. On June 26, 1985, Jeff Wagner killed Linn County resident Jeri Koenig. Koenig had been scheduled to testify against Wagner in another trial. Wagner was arrested for aggravated murder. As the trial approached in 1986, Wagner asked that he be given the opportunity to defend himself. The court approved. On the date of the trial, however, Wagner changed his plea from "not guilty" to "guilty" and, in doing so, placed himself at risk of receiving the death penalty. At his sentencing, Wagner offered no defense of his actions and the jury sentenced Wagner to death. Wagner's case went automatically into appeal in accordance with Oregon laws. In this case, the Oregon Supreme Court had to wrestle with two important questions. First, was it legal or ethical to give the death penalty to an individual who asked to provide their own defense, but then offered none in the course of the trial? Second, is it ethical that the state cooperate with the commission of what may, in fact, be a "death wish"? The Oregon Supreme Court ruled that the Texas Model upon which the Oregon death penalty statute was based was still "good law" and that Oregon's statute was, as a result, also constitutional. This decision was what William Long called "scholastic syllogism." This first Wagner case, known as *Wagner I*, was made without any examination of the mitigating factors in the case. This ran in contrast to the national trends and maintained the Texas Model without any understanding of the significant differences between the two states.[56]

In 1988, however, Oregon's adoption of the Texas Model came back to hurt them. In October 1979, a retarded John Paul Penry killed a woman in Livingston, Texas. When his case went to trial, it reopened the constitutionality question of Texas' death sentencing procedures. And, because the U.S. Supreme Court was reexamining the Texas Model, Oregon's system was also in peril. The "Penry problem," as William Long notes, was "costly in Oregon." In 1988, the U.S. Supreme Court ruled that the Texas death sentence statute was unconstitutional because it violated the Eighth Amendment as "cruel and unusual punishment." The Penry decision, as a result, required new trials or new sentencing phase trials for all of Oregon's death row inmates. Of the nearly two dozen individuals on Oregon's death row in 1989, only eleven of them returned there after the Penry case and the state's reconciliation with that decision.[57]

Over the course of the 1980s, in keeping with national trends, Washington's supreme court remained firmly conservative in its approach to criminal law and sentencing patterns. Justice William Henry Williams, for example, was so well known for his firm sentencing practices that he was called "Walla Walla Williams" by the inmate population at the state penitentiary. William Goodloe, another supreme court justice, said during the same time period, "The trend of the supreme court in protecting the criminal defendant's rights as opposed to the victim's rights has been extremely out of balance."[58]

In 1990, because the U.S. Supreme Court remanded the case of *State v. Wagner II*, 390 Or. 5, the Oregon Supreme Court was required to review the case again. In the end, the Oregon Supreme Court invalidated the death penalty statute. That same court, however, suggested that the statutory defect described in *Wagner* could be easily resolved by amending the statute to include an instruction where the jury was to be "expressly informed" of its obligation to review all mitigating evidence and its responsibility to determine whether or not the defendant deserved the death penalty. The Oregon legislature amended the statute as recommended.

Oregon's struggle with stricter laws and its campaign of getting tough on crime had serious consequences for the state. Washington, likewise, struggled with its changing social order. In 1993, for example, through a ballot initiative, the state of Washington enacted the nation's first "Three Strikes and You're Out" law. This new law required life imprisonment for an individual's third felony conviction. But while the state was cracking down on drug crimes and other offenses, its courts came to an understanding of the power of mitigating factors in those crimes. In 1993, the state abolished the juvenile death penalty. In the following year, the state also ended its long-standing use of hanging for capital punishment. On May 27, 1994, Charles Rodman Campbell, a triple murderer, was the last man hanged in Washington State.[59]

In 1996, after much legal debate, Douglas Franklin Wright was executed in Oregon for his 1991 murder of five homeless men on the Warm Springs Indian Reservation. He was the first individual to be executed in the state since Leeroy Sanford McGahuey's execution in 1962. Oregon citizens took one more step toward tougher and stricter crime sentencing laws. In November of that year, Oregon voters supported the passage of Ballot Measure 40, a victims' rights initiative that called for the lengthening of sentences for serious crimes. The initiative, however, was so poorly worded that it was unclear how the new laws would affect those cases pending in Oregon courts. Moreover, it was later ruled, the initiative had purported to be a single constitutional amendment, but was, in fact, multiple amendments wrapped up in one. It was therefore ruled unconstitutional. In December 1996, as the state

supreme court wrestled with its implications, all death penalty cases were placed "in abeyance" until it could be fully resolved.[60]

Washington State was also faced with the challenges associated with the "hypertrophy of procedure." In effect, the complexity of the American legal system, the protections afforded defendants and offenders, and the rights of victims and their families made all legal maneuvers complicated, costly, and time consuming. On March 2, 1994, for example, U.S. District Judge Robert Bryan overturned the 1985 conviction of Benjamin Harris for the 1984 murder of Jimmy Turner. Bryan overturned the conviction, and as a result Harris's death sentence, on the grounds of incompetence on the part of Harris's defense counsel. Harris's attorney at the time of the case had only interviewed three of the thirty-two available witnesses and had only met with Harris himself some two hours before the trial commenced. Harris, after having served twelve years on death row in Walla Walla, was released and taken to the Western State Hospital in Lakewood, Washington. Former Washington state senator and Tacoma lawyer Neil Huff said Harris was "in essence . . . still in prison for a crime he never committed." In all, Washington had nineteen death sentence reversals in the 1990s and 2000s. Of those reversals, two were based on constitutional error, nine because of judicial error, two for prosecutorial misconduct, one for jury misconduct, and five for ineffective defense counsel.[61]

The "hypertrophy of procedure," constitutional wrangling, and stricter criminal sentencing laws came at a significant cost to the taxpayers of the Pacific Northwest. The Indigent Defense Fund in Oregon, for example, spent over $4 million to address its twenty-five death penalty cases and almost $9 million total. Moreover, the estimated costs associated with death penalty cases were nearly ten times that for the housing of an inmate in Oregon for life. In Washington, the cost of death penalty trials cost about $300,000 to $500,000 more than non-death-penalty trials for aggravated murder.[62] Since Douglas Franklin Wright's execution in 1996, only one other individual in the state of Oregon has been executed. In Washington State, four have been executed—Charles Campbell, Wesley Dodd, Jeremy Sagastegui, and James Elledge. Seventeen cases in Washington were reversed. The combined cost and complexity of the death penalty in the Pacific Northwest promises that the divisions already existent in the region will continue to widen and that the debate over the issue is long from over.

If the Pacific Northwest was once offered a "pleasant, undemanding" life, then those days are long gone. The region's politics are increasingly divisive and polarized. The economy of abundance has yielded to developers, exploiters, and new settlers from California, the rest of the United States, and beyond. The blissful isolation of the Pacific Northwest has been broken. To what degree the death penalty will play a role in the shaping of the new Pacific Northwest is unknown. In Oregon and Washington, whatever may happen, it will be by an act of the people.

Joseph Laythe is a professor of history at Edinboro University of Pennsylvania. He received his B.A. from Carroll College of Montana, his M.A. from Portland State University, and his Ph.D. from the University of Oregon. His research interests include crime and punishment in the Pacific Northwest, northwestern Pennsylvania, and western New York. He teaches courses in American Violence, U.S. Police History, and American Urban Development. He is the author of *Crime and Punishment in Oregon, 1875–1915: A Study of Four Communities* (2008).

Notes

1. Gordon Morris Bakken, ed., *Law in the Western United States* (Norman: University of Oklahoma Press, 2000), p. 43; William R. Long, *A Tortured History: The Story of Capital Punishment in Oregon* (Eugene: The Oregon Criminal Defense Lawyers Association, 2001), pp. 22–23; and John R. Wunder, *Inferior Courts, Superior Justice: A History of Justices of the Peace on the Northwest Frontier, 1853–1889* (Westport, CT: Greenwood Press, 1979), pp. 3–9.

2. Caroline P. Stoel and Carolyn M. Buan, "Oregon's First Federal Courts, 1849–1859," in Carolyn M. Buan and Caroline P. Stoel, *The First Duty: A History of the U.S. District Court for Oregon* (Portland: U.S. District Court of Oregon Historical Society, 1993), p. 13.

3. Ibid., pp. 36–43.

4. Charles M. Gates, ed., *Messages of the Governors of the Territory of Washington to the Legislative Assembly, 1854–1889* (Seattle: University of Washington Press, 1940), p. 14.

5. Joseph Laythe, "A Cycle of Crisis and Violence: The Oregon State Penitentiary, 1866–1968," M.A. Thesis, Portland State University, 1992.

6. Gates, p. 108.

7. Susan B. Carter, et al., eds. *Historical Statistics of the United States: Earliest Times to the Present*, vol. 1 (New York: Cambridge University Press, 2006), pp. 324, 365.

8. Joseph Laythe, "Bandits and Badges: Crime and Punishment in Oregon, 1875–1915," Ph.D. Dissertation, University of Oregon, 1996. See also Joseph Laythe, "Crime and Punishment in a Mining Town: Jacksonville, Oregon, 1875–1915," *The Mining History Journal* (2002): 28–41, and Joseph Laythe, "'Trouble on the Outside, Trouble on the Inside': Growing Pains, Social Change, and Small Town Policing—The Eugene Police Department, 1862–1932," *Police Quarterly* 5, no. 2 (March 2002): 96–112.

9. Laythe, "Bandits and Badges," pp. 47–48; Charles Carey, *General History of Oregon* (Portland: Binfords and Mort, 1935), pp. 806–807; and Wunder, pp. 47, 50.

10. Roscoe Pound in review of *Handbook of the Law of Code Pleading* by Charles E. Clark, in *The Yale Law Journal* 38, no. 1 (November 1928):127.

11. Brad Asher, "Coming Under the Law: Indian/White Relations and Legal Change in Washington Territory, 1853–1889," Ph.D. Dissertation, University of Chicago, 1996, as quoted in David Peterson Del Mar, *Beaten*

Down: A History of Interpersonal Violence in the West (Seattle: University of Washington Press, 2002), p. 29.

12. Gates, p. 245.

13. Asher, *Beyond the Reservation*, p. 131.

14. Ibid., p. 137, and "Executions in the United States, 1608–1987: The Espy File," (http://users.bestweb.net/~rg/execution/OREGON.htm).

15. Carlos Schwantes, *The Pacific Northwest: An Interpretive History* (Lincoln: University of Nebraska Press, 1989), p. 119; Louis J. Palmer Jr., ed. *Encyclopedia of Capital Punishment in the United States* (Jefferson, NC: McFarland Company, Inc., 2001), p. 302; and Long, p. 24. In the 1870s, four Modocs were executed for the murder of Gen. Edw. Canby during their escape from their reservation.

16. William Robbins, *Oregon: This Storied Land* (Portland: Oregon Historical Society Press, 2005), p. 71; Wunder, p. 159; Laythe, "Bandits and Badges," pp. 65–67; and Avery, pp. 197–198. See also *State of Oregon v. Chee Gong et al.* No. 4061, File No. 02163, Journal Entry Vol. 9, p. 726, May 7, 1889, Oregon Supreme Court Appeals File, Oregon State Archives, Salem.

17. Long, p. 40, and Charles Sheldon, *The Washington High Bench: A Biographical History of the State Supreme Court, 1889–1991* (Pullman: Washington State University Press, 1992), p. 5.

18. Sheldon, p. 24.

19. Avery, p. 460, and Schwantes, pp. 212–214.

20. Carter et al., pp. 324, 365; Peterson Del Mar, *Beaten Down*, p. 97; Avery, p. 202–204; and Gordon Dodds, *The American Northwest: A History of Oregon and Washington* (Arlington Heights, IL: The Forum Press, Inc., 1986), p. 134.

21. Schwantes, pp. 268–269; Peterson Del Mar, *Oregon's Promise*, pp. 131–132.

22. Long, pp. 24–27; Goeres-Gardner, p. 245; and Robert H. Dann, "Abolition and Restoration of the Death Penalty in Oregon," in Hugo Adam Bedau, ed., *The Death Penalty in America* (Chicago: Aldine Publishing Co., 1964): 344.

23. Oregon Department of Corrections, "History of Capital Punishment in Oregon," http://www.oregon.gov/DOC/PUBAFF/cap-punishment/history.shtml, accessed 2/19/2007. See also Van Tiffin, *Prison Tours and Poems: A Sketch of the Oregon State Penitentiary* (Salem: 1904). Tiffin was an inmate at OSP.

24. Robbins, pp. 90–91.

25. Long, p. 28.

26. Ibid., p. 29.

27. Dann, p. 344; Long, p. 30; and Hugo Adam Bedau, "The 1964 Death Penalty Referendum in Oregon: Some Notes from a Participant-Observer," *Crime and Delinquency* 26, no. 4 (1980): 528–536. It should be further noted that while Governor West opposed the barbaric tradition of the death penalty, he also supported the eugenics

movement in Oregon spearheaded by Dr. Bethenia Owens-Adair. Eugenics called for the forced sterilization of certain individuals for the sake of social control. The Oregon Board of Eugenics was established in 1917.

28. Arthur H. Bone, ed., *Oregon Cattlemen/Governor, Congressman: Memoirs and Times of Walter M. Pierce* (Portland: Oregon Historical Society, 1981), p. 130; Long, p. 33; and Robbins, p. 110.

29. Bedau, *Death Penalty in America*, p. 334; Long, pp. 33–34; Richard Gerstein, "A Prosecutor Looks at Capital Punishment," *Journal of Criminal Law, Criminology, and Police Science* 51 (July–August 1960): 254; and Robbins, p. 107.

30. Long, p. 34.

31. Dann, pp. 344–345, and Bone, p. 138.

32. Dann, pp. 346–347, and Bone, pp. 120–139.

33. Dann, p. 344, and Michael Reggio, "History of the Death Penalty" (pp. 1–11) and David J. W. Vanderhoof (pp. 201–210), in Laura E. Randa, ed., *Society's Final Solution: A History and Discussion of the Death Penalty* (New York: University Press of America, 1997).

34. Sheldon, pp. 77, 236.

35. Oregon Department of Corrections death penalty file; Peterson Del Mar, *Beaten Down*, p. 157.

36. Long, p. 85. See *Leland v. Oregon*, 343 U.S. 790 (1952).

37. Bedau, "The 1964 Death Penalty Referendum in Oregon," pp. 529–530.

38. Long, pp. 46–47; Bedau, "The 1964 Death Penalty Referendum in Oregon," p. 530; and Bedau, *The Death Penalty in America*, p. 233.

39. Bryan Vila and Cynthia Morris, eds. *Capital Punishment in the United States: A Documentary History*, (Westport, CT: Greenwood Press, 1997), p. 224, and Long, p. 52.

40. Hugo Adam Bedau, *Death is Different: Studies in the Morality, Law, and Politics of Capital Punishment* (Boston: Northeastern University Press, 1987), pp. 246–247, as quoted in Vila and Morris, eds. *Capital Punishment in the United States*, p. 224.

41. Ibid.

42. Long, pp. 49–51; Buan and Stoel, *The First Duty*, p. 320; and Bedau, "The 1964 Death Penalty Referendum in Oregon," pp. 530–531.

43. Bedau, "The 1964 Death Penalty Referendum in Oregon," pp. 528–534, and Long, p. 52. Bedau would further publish *Capital Punishment in the United States* (1976), *The Courts, the Constitution, and Capital Punishment* (1977), *Death is Different* (1987), and *In Spite of Innocence* (1992). In 1966, Bedau left Oregon to serve as chairman of the Philosophy Department at Tufts University in Medford, Massachusetts.

44. Bedau, "The 1964 Death Penalty Referendum in Oregon," pp. 528–534.

45. Ibid., pp. 534–536.

46. Robbins, p. 181, and Schwantes, pp. 317–319, 321.

47. Carter et al., pp. 111, 324, 365; Robbins, pp. 182–197,

204; and William Dietrich, *The Final Forest: The Battle for the Last Great Trees of the Pacific Northwest* (New York: Penguin Books, 1992).

48. Long, p. 57–58.

49. Palmer, p. 562. The death penalty statute in Washington was revised several times including changes in 1981 and 1998.

50. Sheldon, pp. 115, 357.

51. Long, pp. viii, 59, 70, and Bedau, "The 1964 Death Penalty Referendum in Oregon," p. 529.

52. Sheldon, p. 192.

53. Long, pp. vii, 37, 64.

54. Ibid., p. 64.

55. Ibid., pp. 1, 60–63.

56. Ibid., pp. 139–140.

57. Ibid., pp. 3, 150–154, 163, and Michael Reggio, "History of the Death Penalty," in Randa, *Society's Final Solution*, p. 11. See also *Penry v. Lynaugh*, 492 U.S. 302, 316 (1988).

58. Sheldon, pp. 162–164, 352.

59. Judith Greene, "Getting Tougher on Crime: The History and Political Context of Sentencing Reform Developments Leading to the Passage of the 1994 Crime Act," *Sentencing and Society: International Perspectives* (2002): 21; and Adam Caine Ortiz, "Juvenile Death Penalty: Is It 'Cruel and Unusual' in Light of Contemporary Standards?" *American Bar Association Criminal Justice Magazine* 17, no. 4 (Winter 2003): 1. See also *State v. Furman* 858 P. 2d 1092 (Wash. 1993).

60. Long, pp. 4–5.

61. Maureen O'Hagan, "Exonerated but Never Set Free," *Seattle Times*, 31 March 2003, and Washington Coalition to Abolish the Death Penalty, "Death Penalty Reversals in Washington State," (http://www.abolishdeathpenalty. org/Reversals.htm), accessed 3/23/2007.

62. Long, pp. 9–10; Mark Larranaga and Donna Mustard, "Washington's Death Penalty System: A Review of the Costs, Length, and Results of Capital Cases in Washington State"; and *Seattle Post-Intelligencer* 19 February 2007.

CHAPTER 14

To Do No Harm

MEDICINE AND THE DEATH PENALTY IN ENGLAND AND TEXAS

Norwood Andrews

THE "MEDICALIZATION" of the death penalty, by the 1990s and early 2000s, was both a well-developed part of ongoing practice and a leading theme of the perennial debate surrounding the practice. Spurred by legislative debates and continuing litigation over the use of legal injection, advocates of abolition brought greater publicity to the extent of physician participation in the carrying out of executions and the acquiescence in this degree of involvement by the medical profession more generally.[1] Physicians and medical ethicists contributed their own reflections on this issue, sometimes noting the failure of the profession as a whole to constrain effectively its individual members.[2] State medical associations and the AMA all proscribed the involvement of doctors in putting condemned prisoners to death, but in almost all cases the rules were intended mainly to protect the associations themselves from being linked to the practice, rather than to ensure that no doctors were involved.[3]

Critics of medicalized execution protocols implied that the development compromised medical ethics in disturbing new ways, linking it to a broader narrative of professional decline. In fact, the history of the death penalty in modern Western civilization was always connected to the history of medicine in various ways, and the fate of capital punishment in the twentieth century was no exception to the rule. While contemporary medical techniques for determining criminal responsibility and executing condemned criminals might be new in their particular details, in a larger sense they are neither unprecedented nor unanticipated within the medical, legal, and political realms. The same kinds of advances in professional knowledge, and the same kinds of professional organizations, could serve to promote capital punishment in one historical context and help abolish it in another.

While the identification of Texas as the death penalty capital of America usually rests on its disproportionately large share of executions carried out, the claim also has a strong historical basis. The state was the first to perform a lethal injection, and it developed methods and protocols which others would also employ (including the use of the hospital gurney and other mimicry of medical procedures). Less heavily publicized (although still notorious, and perhaps equally important) was the state's pioneering use of psychiatric testimony in sentencing convicted defendants to the gurney. In part because the controversies and news coverage surrounding these practices are so familiar—part of the background noise of life in Texas, even for the vast uninvolved majority of the public—a comparative historical perspective may prove helpful in gauging their significance. In the case of England, many of the same developments that characterized capital punishment in Texas were at least anticipated and discussed, but ultimately history took a very different path. I argue that the comparison bears out the critical role of medicalization in determining the fate of capital punishment—and that the historical divergence between the cases studied reflects a divergence between medical professions in their social and political contexts.

I.

In Albion, known for its fatal tree and "Bloody Code," the abolition of capital punishment was the work of many generations. The rise of commerce and industry, agricultural enclosure, and related social unrest coincided with a chaotic proliferation of capital-offense statutes—and a rising crimson tide of dispatched offenders. Then, as middle-class reformers gained parliamentary influence, capital crimes were pared back and the ritual of hangings in public was ended (although whether the accompanying cultural shift was toward humanitarianism or sentimental hypocrisy remains in dispute).[4] But by blunting the momentum for abolition, these limitations helped sustain the practice.[5] After the 1860s, death by hanging remained the prescribed penalty for murder for very nearly a full century.

At a distance, with the passing of decades since the last legal executions were carried out, and with the death penalty now banned by the European Convention of Human Rights, abolition in twentieth-century Britain may now be half-remembered as a necessary response to social transformation and shifting values. But any closer look at the political battles over abolition shows otherwise—that the outcome was anything but inevitable. "It is quite possible," in the view of one magazine writer, "that, had there not been a resurgence of abolitionism following the Second World War, Britain would have gone down the same path as the United States," with capital punishment perpetuated once again by being modified and brought up to date.[6]

The critical moment, in this view, came in the wake of a parliamentary initiative that ended in defeat for the abolitionist cause—and threatened to bring the reinforcement, rather than the abolition, of capital punishment in Britain. In 1948, with Clement Attlee's Labour government committed to passage of a comprehensive criminal-justice reform bill, party backbenchers unexpectedly succeeded in attaching an abolition amendment—only to have the amended bill resoundingly rejected by the House of Lords, with the apparent support of the general public. Ultimately all the insurgents had to show for their efforts was the creation of a royal commission to study possible reforms in sentencing and procedures (not to include abolition itself). Instead of confirming the obsolescence of the Bloody Code's remnants, this outcome demonstrated what one historian calls "the enduring political, judicial, and public resistance to the reforming ethos."[7] What finally undermined this resistance was a trio of dubious capital cases—occurring, almost unbelievably, in rapid succession—which sapped the credibility of the justice system and highlighted the irreversible consequences of its failings.[8]

Compared with these controversies and with the acts of legislation that followed them, the work of the Royal Commission on Capital Punishment of 1949–1953 has often been viewed as having played a secondary role (at most) in promoting change. With the terms of its appointment ruling out consideration of abolition as a policy alternative, it had no opportunity to register any direct support for the cause, and ultimately few of its necessarily limited recommendations were ever adopted. What such assessments overlook is the potential significance of the commission as a force for perpetuating the death penalty, instead of the opposite. Along with their mandate, the commissioners were given the opportunity to propose the kinds of modernizing changes that might well have sent Britain down the American path in following years. In fact, the commissioners' refusal to endorse such changes was itself a historic defeat for the death penalty in Britain—and a crucial victory for the cause of abolition, made all the more significant by the commission's lack of positive identification with the cause.

The royal commission's conclusions were not preordained. They depended heavily on the recommendations and testimony provided by a host of witnesses over two years of hearings. On the key practical questions relating to the reform and modernization of the death penalty—how to reconcile the definition of criminal responsibility with the views of modern psychology and psychiatry, and how to reconcile the method of execution with modern standards of humane treatment—those representing the medical profession had a critical role to play. I argue that the leaders of the profession—most importantly the representatives of the British Medical Association—acted so as to foreclose the possibility that a modernized, medically sanctioned death penalty would emerge from the commission's work. The BMA never endorsed the abolitionists' cause—and, as with the commission itself, avoiding being identified with the cause was necessary for the maintenance of its standing and influence. But it maintained longstanding objections to the existing legal definition of responsibility (insisting instead on a definition which, while accommodating the views of experts on mental disease and deficiency, posed insoluble political dilemmas of

its own). And it steadfastly refused to endorse or facilitate execution by lethal injection, leaving the commission without an alternative to hanging that it could recommend. The leading medical men in Britain had no interest in allowing their profession to be seen as agitating against capital punishment—but neither would they tacitly support the practice, at a time when it required this support. Ultimately Britain followed the European path of abolition, rather than the American path of modernized capital punishment, for reasons large and small. The large ones included the position of the British medical establishment and the influence that it wielded.

The objections of British medical men to the common law's test of criminal responsibility were part of a longstanding critique of the prevailing legal standard of mental guilt (or *mens rea*)—a critique that accompanied the gradual development of psychiatry as a medical discipline and followed from its core assumptions. The standard came from the controversy that followed the acquittal, on grounds of insanity, of political assassin Daniel M'Naghten in 1843. Replying to questions from the House of Lords, a panel of judges concluded that juries, when necessary, should be instructed

> that, to establish a defense on the ground of insanity, it must be clearly proved that, at the time of the committing of the act, the party accused was labouring under such a defect of reason, from disease of the mind, as not to know the nature and quality of the act he was doing, or, if he did know it, that he did not know he was doing what was wrong.

The fateful adoption of the M'Naghten Rules by both English and almost all American state courts reflected jurists' insistence on narrow formal limits on jurors' discretion. Psychiatrists and psychologists were dissatisfied from the beginning. Their objection, in essence, was that the reference exclusively to cognitive failures meant that the rules applied strictly only to some mentally diseased defendants and excluded others who were equally unable to control their actions.[9] The definition of responsibility solely in terms of knowledge, leaving out all other mental conditions affecting the ability to act (or not act), ran counter to the very construction of mental malfunction in medical terms—as a form of disease affecting the mind as a whole.[10] Strict application of the M'Naghten Rules meant that expert medical witnesses found their testimony limited to the state of a defendant's knowledge, regardless of their overall diagnosis of the defendant's mental state. Judges viewed the limitation of the scope of psychiatric testimony as necessary to keep medical men from dominating trial outcomes—and to keep the loophole of "irresistible impulse" from obviating the traditional principle of criminal responsibility. The medical men saw the rules as a rejection of the value of their professional expertise—all the more so as the state of their art developed over time while the rules stood unchanged.

The British Medical Association's longstanding sponsorship of the psychiatric critique of *M'Naghten* was both a bid for influence over criminal justice, on behalf of the medical profession, and a typical assertion of the BMA's own status as representative of the profession at large. The BMA's leaders normally exercised a certain prerogative to speak on behalf of the profession and "medical practitioners" generally. In fact, a class divide separated the emerging mass of general practitioners, whose own organization grew into the BMA itself, from elite specialists and consultants, who retained their affiliations with traditional orders (the ancient and prestigious Royal Colleges). But the GPs' growing numbers and success in organizing their own ranks enabled them, beginning in the middle of the nineteenth century, to win substantial control over the whole profession and the course of its development. The

long war over extending national health insurance, culminating in the Labour government's introduction of the National Health Service, illustrated the BMA's sense of its own prerogatives and the limits of its actual influence. Like its American counterpart—but with less success—the BMA fiercely opposed publicly funded provision of health care, and mobilized doctors to join in defense of the "doctor-patient relationship" and other purported values of the profession. In 1947–1948, its efforts failed, in large part because Health Minister Aneurin Bevan broke down the opposition by exploiting the old intraprofessional divide. But even in defeat, the BMA retained both a formal role and considerable influence as the GPs' representative in advising and bargaining with the Ministry of Health, inspiring later commentary on a health service functioning less for its patients than for its professionals.[11]

As with the campaigns against national health insurance, the BMA's longstanding opposition to *M'Naghten* invoked the values of medicine while asserting its professional prerogative. The association first took this stand before a study panel (the Committee on Insanity and Crime, chaired by Lord Atkin) appointed in 1922, in the wake of a legal controversy over a murder conviction followed by a medical reprieve. Both the BMA and the psychiatrists' own group (the Medico-Psychological Association) came before the committee to criticize the M'Naghten Rules and propose alternatives. The BMA's memorandum recommended that the rules should also exclude actions in which mental disease or deficiency kept a person "from controlling his own conduct." The existing formula as amended, according to the BMA Council, "might be accepted by the Medical Profession as a fair definition of responsibility for crime."[12] (Rather than trying to amend the rules, the Medico-Psychological Association concluded that they should simply be abrogated, and "the responsibility of a prisoner should be left as a question of fact to be determined by the jury on the merits of the particular case.")[13] Ultimately the Atkin Committee basically adopted the BMA's position—recommending that defendants not be held responsible "when the act is committed under an impulse which the prisoner was by mental disease in substance deprived of any power to resist."[14]

The BMA's contributions to the Atkin Committee's work forged a fateful connection with the debate over capital punishment itself—although the BMA avoided being drawn directly into this larger debate. Despite the Atkin Committee's work, or perhaps because its conclusions were unexpected, its report was set aside by the government upon its submission. But abolitionists took note of the medical-legal divide over the insanity defense. In 1929, Labour Party leaders under pressure from their abolitionist members appointed a House of Commons Select Committee on Capital Punishment. Reflecting the closely balanced forces in the Labour-led chamber, the committee narrowly approved a report that mainly addressed the question of abolition and recommended a five-year moratorium on executions. But it also identified conditions for any further use of the death penalty—one of which was "bringing the M'Naghten Rules up to date, so as to give the fullest scope to general medical considerations and to extend in some way the area of criminal irresponsibility."[15] The select committee did not call medical men to testify, but instead invoked the gist of the BMA's recommendations to the Atkin Committee—as well as the accompanying implication that rejection of the law's rules of criminal responsibility was intrinsic to modern medicine.

The BMA remained similarly detached from the battle in Parliament over abolition in 1948. The "Medical Profession," like other established institutions—including the leadership of the Labour Party itself—had no interest in being identified with abolitionists or spending its political capital on their cause. Surveys indicated that the death penalty retained longstanding majority support among the British public, and advocates of abolition had traditionally acted as dissenters from an established consensus, among society at large or within their own institutions. Supporters of abolition included a few contrarian nobles and bishops, a subgroup of middle-class reformers who specialized in criminal justice, and a more substantial number of Labour politicians and constituents who expressed class grievances, sympathy with reform views, or both. By the late 1940s there were two respected but small organizations that advocated for the cause: the Howard League for Penal Reform (which, through its research and lobbying, served as the standard-bearer of progressivism in criminal justice, while maintaining close ties with the Home Office) and the National Council for the Abolition of the Death Penalty (which existed more as a one-person operation than as an actual council, and ultimately folded itself into the Howard League).[16] Staunch opponents included the leaders of the Conservative Party, the entire judicial establishment, and the Church of England.[17] The questions debated among these forces in Parliament—whether capital punishment was morally acceptable, whether it affirmed or denied the sanctity of human life, whether it served to deter murder—were mostly outside of medicine's realm.

The issues of dispute changed with the appointment of the Royal Commission on Capital Punishment. As approved by Attlee and the rest of the cabinet, the commission's assigned topics included "whether liability under the criminal law in Great Britain to suffer capital punishment for murder should be limited or modified, and if so, to what extent and by what means." The question of abolition itself had actually been included in the commission's terms of reference as first proposed to the cabinet, but had been removed at the cabinet's insistence.[18] What remained in the terms of reference was generally understood as a reference to the idea of creating degrees of murder, which had never existed in English law. But in a broader sense, taking abolition off the table necessarily implied that the commission was to serve an anti-abolitionist function—finding ways of adjusting and improving existing practices so that the death penalty itself could be made most widely acceptable.[19] In keeping with this broad purpose, Attlee later asked the panel to consider "methods of execution" as well.[20] Attlee and his fellow cabinet members also obviously wanted a thorough inquiry that would be sure to continue until after the next general election. The members of the panel, chaired by veteran civil servant Sir Ernest Gowers, represented varied specialties and were apparently chosen for their lack of known commitment to either side of the abolition debate.[21] As it turned out, the commission held hearings for two years, followed by research travel, and did not release its report until 1953.

The terms of reference directed the commission back to the old unsettled argument over criminal responsibility—as well as the broader question of how the medical profession could help serve the commission's task of proposing a new, improved death penalty. Shortly after its appointment, the commission formally invited the BMA to submit evidence. During the months leading up to the BMA's appearance before the commission, the association's council found itself having to consider not only its longstanding position on *M'Naghten* but also how it would field other likely questions.

At the council's formal meeting on January 18, 1950, it became clear what exactly that meant:

The chairman of the Committee [on Capital Punishment] stated that possibly the Royal Commission might contemplate recommending intravenous injection as a method of execution if it were assured that the medical profession would not object to the prison medical officer being required to give a preliminary injection of a narcotic drug for the purpose of facilitating the lethal injection by a non-medical examiner.

The committee chairman went on to report that the committee "had considered this possibility" and concluded that while the prison medical officer's actions "must remain a matter for his professional discretion," nevertheless "in no circumstances could the profession approve of the medical officer being under instructions to carry out an injection as a preliminary to the execution procedure."[22]

The council endorsed this position, while also voting its approval of the memorandum drafted by the capital punishment committee and the list of witnesses to testify before the commission. One other piece of information reported to the council by the committee reflects the association's continuing concern over its representation of the profession as a whole. The psychiatrists' organization (now, with its crown charter, titled the Royal Medico-Psychological Association) had also been asked to address the commission and, like the BMA, was expected to discuss the M'Naghten Rules in light of its past statements to the Atkin Committee. A representative of the RMPA had explained the psychiatrists' views to the BMA committee, much to the committee members' dismay:

The Committee had hoped that the BMA and the RMPA, which have given conflicting evidence in the past on the revision of the M'Naghten Rules, would be able to speak with one voice on the present occasion. It regrets to report that the views expressed in its memorandum cannot be reconciled with those of the RMPA.[23]

Before the medical men appeared, the Royal Committee held thirteen full days of hearings over five months, starting with the Home Office and continuing through the organizations representing law enforcement, the prison services, and the judiciary—all emphatic supporters of the death penalty, all tending to echo the positions which had prevailed in the recent parliamentary debate. Especially with eminent legal witnesses, the commissioners devoted much attention to the question of degrees, the "constructive malice" doctrine, and other issues and possible modifications in the law of murder. But the panel also drew out witnesses' views on the M'Naghten Rules and the question of alternative execution methods. Virtually none of the early witnesses acknowledged any misgivings about hangings. But on the law of criminal responsibility, things were slightly more complicated. Only a few were now willing to insist that the M'Naghten Rules precisely identified an appropriate strict standard of responsibility. But most still supported the rules as they stood, arguing that a loose interpretation of them was now customary and that judges and juries exercised their discretion to stretch them when appropriate. In large part, the defense of the status quo had pivoted away from the rules themselves and now rested on how they were applied. "Most of these witnesses," according to the final report, "recognized the imperfections of the Rules, but argued that the formula worked well enough in practice and that it was impossible to devise a better one which a jury would be able to understand and apply—or at least that no one had ever succeeded yet in doing so."[24]

The BMA submitted its memorandum in January 1950 and gave evidence before the Royal Commission on February 3. The memorandum offered a reworked statement of the BMA's position on M'Naghten and tried to relate it to the new state of the debate and the kinds of arguments the commission had been hearing. According to the

memorandum, the BMA acknowledged the necessary difference between insanity, as defined by medicine, and irresponsibility, as defined by law. Thus, "instead of criticizing the M'Naghten Rules as embodying a conception of insanity which is obsolete, it prefers to criticize them as embodying a conception of irresponsibility which, in the light of modern psychological knowledge, must be regarded as incomplete."[25]

The memorandum cited two arguments being used to defend the M'Naghten Rules in practice—that judges had leeway to apply them loosely, and that another safeguard existed in the form of the post-verdict review that the Home Secretary was required by statute to conduct. In the first case, the memorandum noted the likelihood of starkly conflicting conclusions by different judges on similar cases. As for relying on the Home Secretary, the memorandum suggested that it reduced the solemn trial to "a grim farce" and transferred to the executive "a grave responsibility that properly rests with the court." Neither argument amounted to a vindication of the rules themselves:

In the first case, the inexactness of the Rules is acknowledged, the claim being that, by reason of their inexactness, the Judge can extend their application at his discretion to meet the circumstances of the individual case. The second argument frankly admits the imperfections of the Rules and claims merely that the resulting errors are subsequently rectified outside the court.

Either way, the BMA insisted that the defense of the rules in practice ultimately served to show their insufficiency on their own terms—as a statement of the conditions of legal irresponsibility.[26]

The BMA's own recommendations followed from its own restated analysis of the essential flaw in the M'Naghten Rules—that their definition of irresponsibility was "incomplete." To show how incomplete they were, the memorandum cited an appeals court ruling that a defendant's awareness of the illegality of an action made it impossible to claim that he "did not know he was doing what was wrong," as the rules required—which would mean assigning responsibility even to "an insane person who clearly knew that his act was punishable by law, but believed that he was called upon by the Deity to commit the act."[27] But even if a judge avoided this kind of conclusion by fudging the rules—or interpreting them "loosely"—the basic problem of irresistible impulse (or inclination) would remain. Acknowledging that the rules did not amount solely to a test of cognitive faculty—that they accounted for emotional states that interfered with cognition—the BMA nevertheless reiterated its long-held view that "awareness of the nature and wrongfulness of the act may co-exist with a state of emotional disorder, resulting from mental disease, of such a nature that the person so afflicted does not possess sufficient power to prevent himself from committing the act." The M'Naghten Rules "cannot cover such cases unless the meaning of the words is stretched beyond any reasonable interpretation."[28] As in its statements to the Atkin Committee, the BMA again proposed language to enable the M'Naghten Rules to cover such cases. This time the formulation referred to "a disorder of emotion such that, while appreciating the nature and quality of the act, he did not possess sufficient power to prevent himself from committing it."[29]

At the same time that it proposed expanding the definition of irresponsibility, the BMA found it necessary also to endorse the idea of degrees of responsibility, or "diminished responsibility," which existed in Scottish but not in English law. According to the memorandum, "there are mentally abnormal persons charged with murder who cannot be absolved from all responsibility but whose responsibility should be held to be so reduced . . . as to make it undesirable that

they should suffer the extreme penalty."[30] In their appearance before the commission, the BMA witnesses noted that "diminished responsibility" was no substitute for expanding the M'Naghten Rules—it could not cover cases of full irresponsibility due to insanity—but it was necessary to include it "if we are to be in line with scientific developments."[31] It must have also seemed prudent to offer reassurances that a medically sanctioned expansion of full irresponsibility would not open the door too wide.

The memorandum devoted a separate section to alternative execution methods, which made clear the BMA's apprehension about the prospect of being pressured to sanction lethal injection. "No medical practitioner should be asked to take part in bringing about the death of a convicted murderer," the document stated. "The Association would be most strongly opposed to any proposal to introduce, in place of judicial hanging, a method of execution which would require the services of a medical practitioner, either in carrying out the actual process of killing or in instructing others in the technique of the process."[32] Based on its study of previous testimony before the commission, and its own discussion with a prison medical officer, "the Association considers that hanging is probably as speedy and certain as any other method that could be adopted."[33] Intravenous injection of a narcotic drug would be "a speedy and merciful procedure"—except that "the practical difficulties encountered in many cases when injection into a vein is attempted are such as to render the method quite unsuitable for the purpose of execution."[34] Other injection methods (subcutaneous or intramuscular) "would not bring about sudden death or instantaneous loss of consciousness."[35] The memorandum went so far as to suggest gas as perhaps "the best alternative to the present procedure," albeit "one which has highly unpleasant historical associations."[36]

The memorandum included a brief passage indicating the position reached by the BMA Council on possible requirements placed on prison medical officers. It stated merely that the association had considered the question "of the administration of sedatives to condemned persons before execution" and had concluded "that this is a matter which is best left to the discretion and the humanity of the prison medical officer."[37] Exploration of this question in detail was clearly not a discussion the medical men looked forward to having.

As carefully developed in the memorandum, the BMA's position sought to affirm the profession's authority within its realm of expertise, without extending its claims beyond this realm. The same task belonged to the BMA's chosen representatives before the Royal Commission, which typically approached expert witnesses as a politely skeptical lay audience. Much of the hearing, as with the BMA's examination of other witnesses, amounted to elaboration of the professionals' views and the presentation of supporting evidence. The commission members did little to challenge the doctors' descriptions of mental disorders that affected the ability to act, or not act, regardless of knowledge of the significance of the action, and the lack of provision for such cases under the M'Naghten Rules.[38] The BMA's suggested amendment of the rules also elicited little debate (perhaps because the witnesses made it clear that the BMA did not consider that its role was to insist on any particular language). "Diminished responsibility" actually proved more troublesome, because the concept cut more than one way—if it kept partially irresponsible defendants from being fully shielded by an expanded definition of irresponsibility, then it would also be used to try to defend those who deserved to be held fully responsible. Chairman Gowers told the medical witnesses that he considered the doctrine "dangerous," because it might be "interpreted too

leniently by emotional members of the jury" and with too great variations among judges.[39]

Methods of execution also brought a brief but revealing confrontation between the claims of the BMA witnesses and the apparent inclinations of the commissioners. Gowers asked the witnesses to explain the "practical difficulties" of lethal injection. Was it "merely a technical difficulty of skill"? Dr. R. G. Gordon (who had chaired the BMA's capital punishment committee) replied:

Yes. Of course it is easy enough to give an intravenous injection if the patient is expecting it and willing to co-operate because he knows it is going to do him good and save him pain; but it would be a very different matter with a criminal who knew that this was the end, and who probably would not submit to it in the same way as a patient in hospital would. We feel that if there is not complete cooperation on the part of the subject it is a matter that would be very difficult to carry out with any certitude, that is to say, the slightest struggling would mean that the needle would either slip out of the vein, so that he would not get the injection, or go through the vein and the injection go into the tissue.[40]

But why not make the "patient" unconscious first? This was equally unacceptable, according to Dr. Gordon: "We feel very strongly that it is most undesirable that a doctor should act under any rule or instruction or regulation whereby he is, so to speak, forced to give any kind of medication. That is our objection to that on principle." Prison medical officers might offer sedatives based on their own judgment, or as an act of compassion, but not as a responsibility under execution procedures.[41] The BMA's position had clearly been crafted so as to keep physicians out of actual participation in executions.

The medical men would not be drawn into the

process—and neither were they willing to delegate their role in the process to others. Gowers asked whether a doctor was necessary for a lethal injection. Dr. T. Rowland Hill (one of the other BMA representatives) answered:

> An intravenous injection is a highly skilled procedure that would really have to be done by a doctor. In practice in the hospitals one meets occasionally with an experienced hospital sister who does intravenous injections, but that is very exceptional. It must be borne in mind that, although with some people an intravenous injection would be quite easy, there are quite a number of people with whom it is technically extremely difficult, and sometimes it is quite impossible.[42]

One of the commissioners, Dr. Eliot Slater (an eminent psychiatrist, and the only physician appointed), tried to compare the current procedure for hanging—obviously requiring great skill, but no medical qualifications—with what the BMA was insisting on. If doctors would not perform lethal injections, why not train others to do so? Dr. Gordon's reply was brief but conclusive: "The Committee felt that that training, having the object that it has, should not be given by medical men. That was the opinion of the Committee."[43] The profession would neither sanction participation by its own members nor facilitate the participation of others.

As they took their stand before the Royal Commission, the leaders of the BMA knew that the medical profession actually was not united in support of their position. The evidence given by the Royal Medico-Psychological Association showed the commission what the BMA Council had already learned—that the gap between the BMA and some of the leading psychiatrists was deep and wide. At the time of the Atkin Committee the RMPA had basically shared the BMA's

criticisms of the M'Naghten Rules, but had suggested abolishing rather than amending them. But now, somehow, even as the RMPA had grown more dismissive of the rules themselves, its position on criminal responsibility had swung toward that of the judicial establishment. The RMPA's representatives told the commission that the courts in recent years had stretched the rules to the point of abandonment—and that "justice is better served as the result."[44] It was best to leave in place rules which, because of their known obsolescence and inapplicability, effectively left judges free to issue jury instructions based on their own best judgments. "If you did get a better substitute," one of the RMPA witnesses argued, "you might have it very rigidly interpreted and get a worse position than at present."[45] The existing flexibility, in the RMPA's view, actually allowed for the consideration of "diminished responsibility" and made the BMA's proposed degrees of guilt unnecessary as well. Pressed by the commissioners to explain the evolution of their views, the RMPA witnesses suggested that, as frequent expert witnesses, they preferred not to challenge the judges' preference for established rules—especially when they had little to gain from the fight, in terms of their ability to express their own judgments. "One has certain embarrassments in being cross-examined, because one never knows what the Judge is going to let one say," said one of the witnesses. "But in my experience they let you have pretty wide rope."[46]

Given the conflicting evidence and views on criminal responsibility that had been offered, the Royal Commission members shared perhaps a surprising degree of consensus—but still they faced divisions of their own. The commissioners generally agreed that the M'Naghten Rules "could not be considered a theoretically successful criterion of criminal responsibility" and—despite all the evidence given by judges, other officials, and the RMPA—they also agreed that the rules "did not in practice exempt from responsibility all those who ought in principle to be exempted."[47] The fault line was between those who believed the M'Naghten Rules should be disposed of entirely and those who insisted that they should be retained in some form. Several of the commissioners (including Dr. Slater and the veteran Home Office civil servant, Sir Alexander Maxwell) believed that the tendency of judges and juries to work around the existing rules weighed against any effort to impose specific rules—so therefore the juries should be given a broader question (such as whether the defendant's mental illness caused a given action) which would fully contain the actual issue at hand. On the far end of the opposite divide, Leon Radzinowicz (then still rising toward his later eminence as a criminologist and historian of criminal justice) believed abolition of the rules would do little to simplify dilemmas for medical witnesses that were rooted in the "complexities of human personality." Even trying to amend the rules, he argued, would run into certain facts of political life:

> The great difficulty about *extending* the Rules was that the medical witnesses who had appeared before the Commission had not been unanimous in desiring that this should be done; this difference of opinion within the medical profession showed how difficult the problem was. Any facile solution must therefore be treated with suspicion, and since any change would certainly meet very strong opposition, it ought to be supported by overwhelming arguments.[48]

Ultimately no position was fully satisfactory—and this may have raised the importance of pragmatic political considerations. Chairman Gowers himself supported abolition, but he agreed with Radzinowicz that, especially if the commission itself proved divided and even if it achieved unanimity, "it was unlikely that such a recommendation would be accepted and it was doubtful whether such a radical change was consonant with the normal process of development of English law."[49] He proposed, as a compromise, that the report should say that while the majority of the commission believed the M'Naghten Rules should be abolished, "practical considerations had led them unanimously to recommend a less fundamental change." The report language eventually followed a similar formulation.

Despite the compromise that Gowers devised, the commissioners continued to spar with each other over their disagreements over many months that followed. Maxwell, Slater, and others continued to assert that the rules should be abolished and that the commission should recommend doing so. At one point the commissioners voted to approve this recommendation. But Radzinowicz kept raising possible practical difficulties following from the abolition of rules—and the political impracticality of the recommendation. In June 1952, citing a recent appeals court ruling, he said it showed once again "that the judges would strongly oppose any attempt to abolish the M'Naghten Rules. Whatever the merits of the case for abolition, the attitude of the judges, in view of their practical experience, would carry great weight with public opinion and with Parliament."[50] With several alternative formulations on the table—and the assumption that any of them might be disregarded just as the existing M'Naghten Rules apparently were—Gowers again intervened to try to split the differences. The existing draft chapter, he suggested, should be revised to say "that, if it was thought essential to have some rules, such and such a proposal appeared least open to objection, but that all (or most) Members of the commission considered that it would be better to dispense with rules altogether."[51] The final text followed directly from this suggestion.

On the question of criminal responsibility,

the BMA—as the leading voice insisting that the flaws in the rules made it necessary to change the rules and practices—had succeeded (perhaps better than its leaders expected) in setting the bounds of the debate within the commission. The fact that most of the commissioners actually wanted to go beyond what the BMA was willing to recommend (abolishing the M'Naghten Rules rather than amending them) inevitably begs the question of whether the BMA itself might have gone farther. The cautious tone and substance of its recommendations suggests a preoccupation with forging a moderate consensus, both within its own ranks and among other groups of medical professionals (such as the Institute of Psycho-Analysis and the Institute for the Scientific Treatment of Delinquency, both of which seconded the BMA's arguments and recommendations). Still, with the RMPA breaking ranks, the BMA's limited ability to offer realistic proposals for drastic change must have been obvious. And, in fact, Radzinowicz proved correct in anticipating the fate even of the recommendations that the Royal Commission tailored so carefully before putting forward. Given the resistance to change within the judicial establishment, the BMA had little real hope of sweeping aside the formal rules that determined whether convicted murderers lived or died. What it could do—and did—was to help delegitimize them.

The more serious challenge to the BMA's agenda—and the more serious possibility of modernizing the death penalty—came from the commission members' skeptical response to the association's position on lethal injection. The members clearly recognized the position as a calculated effort to head off the development of the procedure by ruling out physician involvement. Sitting in with the commission in July 1951, Sir Frank Newsam (the top-ranking civil servant at the Home Office, and lead-off witness at the first

formal hearing) told the commission members that he hoped to see a recommended alternative to hanging, "which he personally regarded as barbarous."[52] One commissioner (Florence Hancock) supported lethal injection "after the condemned man had been rendered unconscious." Dr. Slater then said "that the difficulties of this course had been exaggerated; it would require little training to inject a drug into an unconscious man." The commission agreed to seek further guidance on this subject from an "experienced anaesthetist" and agreed to ask the BMA for a reference.[53]

The direction of the commission's further inquiry could not have been reassuring to the BMA leaders. A private meeting that October with Dr. Geoffrey Organe (a prominent anaesthetist) reinforced the commissioners' sense that there were perfectly feasible ways to introduce lethal injection—at least as an option. Dr. Slater said that Dr. Organe's evidence "showed that intravenous injection would be a painless, humane, and practicable method of execution, which would give rise to no administrative or psychological difficulties provided that the injection were made an alternative to, and not simply a substitute for, hanging."[54]

A clearer understanding of what was actually being offered to the commission came when Organe and several other anaesthetists (speaking for themselves, not for their specialists' organization) came to give evidence in public two months later. In a memorandum to the commission, the anaesthetists offered a vision of lethal injection as an ordinary alternative within a system of capital punishment—but an optional one, available only under certain conditions. Dr. Organe and his fellow witnesses discussed alternative drugs with comparative effects (ultimately endorsing a single dose of "a short-acting barbiturate," either hexobarbitone or thiopentone). But whichever drugs were chosen, intravenous injection requires a fair degree of skill which can be maintained only by constant practice. Workers in veterinary surgery and in animal laboratories have the necessary skill. The executioner should have no connection or association with the medical profession. Intravenous injection is not possible in all cases.

Intravenous injection would be more difficult in a struggling subject and the idea is repellent. It should be offered as an alternative, pleasanter method of executions and should be used only when it has been willingly accepted.[55]

The commission developed each of these claims at length in the hearing. While the commission had expected the anaesthetists to show how much more feasible lethal injection was than the BMA had claimed, the more telling point surely involved the limits of what anaesthetists themselves would actually do. What made lethal injection perfectly feasible, they said, was the level of skill at "venepuncture" attained by laboratory technicians. Neither the anaesthetists present nor any members of their specialty organization would perform the procedure on condemned prisoners. Perhaps technicians might also be unwilling but, as Dr. Organe put it, "You cannot tell until you have tried recruiting them."[56]

Moreover, the fact that lethal injection was unsuited for various cases meant that it would never serve to replace the gallows entirely. At the commission's insistence, the anaesthetists offered a lengthy, gruesome set of explanations of the techniques of venepucture and the difficulties posed by physiology, in some cases, or by uncooperative patients. "Certain arms," observed Dr. Alexander Low (president of the Association of Anaesthetists), "have no visible veins. In other words, you get the rather plump individuals who have veins, naturally, but they also have a layer of

maybe an eighth of an inch or more of fat over the top of the veins, which makes it quite impossible to see them."[57] In other cases, veins would shrink, due to cold or anxiety, and anyone looking for a vein would have to bathe the arm in warm water. Any movement on the part of the patient would make it impossible to catch the vein with the needle (and not pierce the other side of the vein). This actually even ruled out the possibility of rendering subjects unconscious first, because reflex movements would still occur. By the end of the hearing, it was clear to the commissioners that even doctors who refused to endorse the BMA's position were not inclined to offer up lethal injection as an easy option or smooth over the practical obstacles.

This evidence did not dictate the committee's conclusions, but its impact was decisive nevertheless. Like its skepticism about the BMA's position, the commission's discussions immediately after the anaesthetists' hearing clearly reflected its own clear determination to recommend lethal injection—if it had been given a way to do so. Commissioner Hancock "said that she had been ready to support an alternative to hanging, but she had been very much discouraged" by the anaesthetists. Another commissioner, Sir Edward Jones, went so far as to say that "personally, he would prefer to be hanged and he could not bring himself to support any recommendation in favor of an injection." Still others (such as Gowers, and Newsam, once again sitting in) still hoped for some alternative to recommend because hanging, they believed, was "barbarous" and must be ended. But the wind had shifted. The commission secretary, Francis Graham-Harrison, even began coming up with further likely problems, beyond what the anaesthetists had cited: "It appeared that intravenous injections were difficult if the patient flinched, and impossible if he struggled. Was he not more likely to flinch from a lethal injection than from an injection for ordinary medical purposes?" Yet another concern: "Lethal injection would also differ from all other methods of execution in one important respect: the executioner would be required to cause the prisoner's death by an operation involving direct contact with his body, not indirectly by the mechanical operation of a switch or lever. This would be most distasteful to many qualified persons." Gowers finally interrupted Graham-Harrison and told him to draft a report chapter on execution methods without stating any conclusions.[58] Ultimately the commission decided to list the pros and cons of lethal injection, while stating that it had been unable to agree on substituting this method for hanging at the present time. It recommended reconsidering the practicality of the option as techniques evolved further.[59]

When the full report of the Royal Commission finally was published in 1953—well after the Labour government that appointed the commission had passed from the scene—its painstakingly documented chapters and nuanced, ambivalent conclusions ended up serving functions far different from what had originally been intended. Its various (mostly small-bore) positive recommendations to Parliament were first ignored, then dismissed by the Conservative leadership. Instead, the report became more a symbol of the loosening grip of capital punishment on "respectable" opinion among governing-class circles. Given its narrow original terms of reference and the distance separating its members from the likes of the Howard League, what was crucial was the very fact that the commission did not perform as expected—that it did not find, in the advanced realms of law, science, and medicine, the solutions to the death penalty's problems.

One of the concluding notes struck in the commission report elicited wide comment, as an example of testing the boundary of the commission's mandate. On the question of degrees of murder, the commission had ultimately failed to find criteria for degrees and instead recommended expanding jury discretion over sentencing, as a way of allowing for mitigating circumstances. The commission acknowledged that many others were bound to advance a contrary view:

> If this view were to prevail, the conclusion would seem to be inescapable that in this country a stage has been reached where little more can be done effectively to limit the liability to suffer the death penalty, and that the issue is now whether capital punishment should be retained or abolished.[60]

The implicit necessity of abolishing a practice that one would prefer to be able to improve (but could not) was the commission's parting message to its official and public audiences. Even such a message—perhaps the most powerful support for abolition that a royal commission could offer, amplified by the high standing and political detachment of its source—could not move Britain much closer to abolition; other circumstances would be required and further parliamentary struggles would ensue. But a teleological standard of assessment fails to account for the real likelihood that the commission could have reached other conclusions, and spent its prestige on reaffirming the legal foundations of capital punishment and modernizing its procedures. This outcome was averted by the leaders of the medical profession—not because they were abolitionists, but because they would not acquiesce in existing practices or proposed procedures that violated their professional values. When called upon by the commission to speak on their profession's behalf, the leaders of the BMA affirmed these values, despite the divisions among doctors that actually existed. The outcome reflects both the particular choices made by key actors in the leadership of the profession (such as Dr. Gordon) and the structural conditions (the physiology, in a sense) of a political system that made the muffled voice of medicine speak decisively in the debate.

II.

In a newspaper profile from 1988, Dr. James P. Grigson, perhaps the most famous (or notorious) physician in Dallas, reflected with some frustration on the nickname—Dr. Death—by which he was best known to the rest of the world. "Stop for one second and think," he said, "of how many children, men and women are walking around today alive because we incarcerated or terminated individuals who could be identified as people who are going to continue to kill." So, he claimed, "it would be more appropriate, if you were going to put a tag on me, to put Dr. Life." The reporter followed the doctor to the courtroom, where he offered a typical display of his arguably death-dealing—or life-saving—work as a witness. The description contained in the story was fairly typical of contemporary efforts to capture the doctor at work:

His tone is always modulated, precise, direct. The word that comes to mind watching him is "patrician."

Yet he's like a favorite uncle, the one who took you fishing when you were supposedly sick and had to stay home from school. He's a good ol' boy from Texarkana, oldest son of the man who ran the Rock of Ages tombstone business and the woman who worked for the phone company.

His combination of homespun virtues and unshakable opinions has long carried great weight with juries in Dallas County and other parts of Texas. His demeanor on the stand is legendary, his testimony devastating in its withering straightforwardness.

The classic scene: Turning to face the jury,

his back straight and head still, Grigson says, "(Such and such) is the most severe type of sociopath and would commit future crimes if returned to society." It is appropriate for defense attorneys to blanch at this time.[61]

With his well-honed performances, Dr. Grigson created a leading role in the revival of the death penalty in Texas which began in the 1970s and grew into one of the world's most prolific systems of judicially mandated killing. The new system represented a new phase in the state's history of capital punishment, which to this day retains part of the stigma of a vicious past (as did the practice in England, albeit in a different way). Starting after the Civil War, whites in Texas communities (as in other southern states) used both legal hangings and extralegal rituals of violence to overwhelm Reconstruction governments, enforce a precarious social order, and vent communal fury against transgressors. Both vigilantism and its (often barely distinguishable) legal counterpart, as enforced within localities, targeted black men and asserted racial privilege. Ultimately state leaders felt compelled to try to temper the violence and preempt the worst outrages. In 1923, a new Texas statute took condemned inmates out of the hands of county sheriffs and made state prison officials responsible for administering death by electrocution. Over the next four decades, while the goal of substituting orderly state killing for lynch law may have been achieved in some degree, the accumulated statistical record ultimately left the state exposed to a range of possible challenges on grounds of discrimination, among other constitutional challenges. In 1964, Texas joined other southern states and the rest of the nation in a moratorium on executions. The hiatus ended up lasting for eighteen years, during which the legal landscape of capital punishment was transformed yet again.[62]

What emerged by the 1980s was a new set of

trial practices, sentencing criteria, and execution protocols that included the testimony of expert witnesses like Grigson, as well as other uses of medical expertise and medical symbolism. Grigson and his followers and imitators ultimately made up a cohort of "killer shrinks" who served a specialized function—diagnosing the "future dangerousness" of capital murder convicts—that followed from developments in Texas law and the peculiar drafting of the new capital murder code. Especially during the early years of the revived death penalty regime, the killer shrinks and their vociferous critics struggled with each other, before trial juries and appeals court judges, over how far the use of medicine to facilitate capital punishment could be taken.

The parties to the struggle included local prosecutors, frustrated defense attorneys, representatives of organized medical professionals at the national level, and various individual scholars of law and criminal justice. What was completely missing, all through the period up to the present, was any meaningful participation by the organizations representing the Texas medical profession. Keeping a fixed focus on higher priorities, the Texas Medical Association and its affiliated specialty societies attempted no policing of their own ranks, avoided passing judgment on the use of medical professionals in various roles, and essentially offered no resistance to the medicalization of capital punishment. As a result, Texas prosecutors and legislators were able to use white coats and needles where necessary to legitimize their initiatives and fend off legal challenges. Instead of giving pause, psychiatric evaluation and lethal injection gave capital punishment in Texas the go-ahead.

The relationship between medicine and criminal justice followed largely from the orientation of medicine itself at the state level. In Texas, as much as anywhere, mid-twentieth-century medicine was a sovereign profession. Celebrating the 1953 centennial of the Texas Medical Association, chronicler Pat Ireland Nixon proclaimed that the organization "stands out as a towering beacon. From small and uncertain beginnings, it 'has come to be one of the sturdiest of state associations.'"[63] Dr. Nixon's was no empty boast. With its record of success in legislative enactments and its feverish commitment to the war against national health insurance, the TMA exemplified the American medical profession's exercise of political influence in support of guild interests.[64]

Coinciding with the ascendancy of the sturdy state association in medical politics was the birth and spectacular growth of Texas medical institutions—military and veterans' hospitals, aerospace biomedical research installations, new medical schools, and specialized care facilities contained in high-rise hospitals in sprawling medical center complexes—which reflected the postwar boom in federally supported research and development and the growing funding ability of the state.[65] Also at the same time, however, official neglect, underfunded public services, and rudimentary health care still prevailed across much of what remained a poor state. As in the rest of the shadow-crossed Sunbelt—only perhaps most dramatically in Texas—cutting-edge medicine developed amid unsolved problems of public health and basic health care provision, reflecting both the longstanding budgeting practices of the state and the particular priorities of its medical establishment.

In its own way, mental health care followed the general pattern, but its scale, scope, and pervasiveness gradually forced philanthropic and professional elites to engage with questions of broad social policy and provision of care. By 1931 the doctors had managed to secure state funding for a psychopathic hospital on the medical school campus in Galveston, and after the war a psychiatric research facility was created among the other specialized hospitals and clinics in the Texas

Medical Center. Meanwhile, for decades, the insane asylums and "state hospitals" were overcrowded warehouses, with their limited funding being used almost exclusively for custodial functions. (A "psychopathic hospital" was also set up on the lower floors of the prison hospital at Huntsville, consisting basically of holding areas and cells with restraints.) Newspaper exposes, and reports by outside agencies such as the U.S. Public Health Service, occasionally reminded the Texas public of the conditions inside the institutions. Eventually organizations such as the Hogg Foundation for Mental Health, which began its activities by advocating for "mental hygiene" among the public at large, began emphasizing the public's responsibility for the institutionalized population.[66] During the 1950s, intermittent legislative efforts brought modest results, given the prohibitive expense of actual treatment provision for a massive institutionalized population. Comprehensive reform during the 1960s required both the availability of federal funds and a broad programmatic shift toward deinstitutionalization and outpatient care.[67]

As the progressive turn in Texas mental health care slowly proceeded, one focus of reform was in the legal realm. New court procedures transferred new powers to psychiatrists and gave greater weight to medical expertise—perhaps more even than the reformers intended. A survey of the institutions by the business-funded Texas Research League yielded recommendations for changes in the legal structure of the hospital system, and the state board responsible for the hospitals put up no resistance.[68] Supported by a Hogg Foundation grant, a team of University of Texas law professors drafted a pair of bills—a new Mental Health Code and a set of procedures for commitment of the criminally insane—which were enacted in 1957. Both reforms sought to bring standard legal proceedings into accord with up-to-date ideas about mental illness (as opposed to

the traditions and stigmas surrounding "lunacy") and to force the state to begin providing treatment instead of mere confinement. In both involuntary civil commitment hearings and criminal cases, the statutes included new requirements for medical examination and diagnosis (a written certificate in civil cases, plus testimony by two physicians in hearings for indefinite commitment, and a requirement of "competent medical or psychological testimony" for commitment of criminal defendants found insane).

Advocates for the new mental health code assumed that to protect the rights of individuals found to be insane—in both civil and criminal cases—it was necessary to keep the court from excluding relevant medical diagnosis and judgments. New procedures were supposed to force courts to make use of medical expertise in rendering their judgments. But what happened in practice was that when physicians were given a role, they largely took over the decision making. Emergency procedures allowed judges to approve a civil commitment for up to ninety days without even having to hold a hearing, as long as the medical forms were signed and cosigned. To be committed indefinitely, patients had to have been already held for the temporary period. This was intended to raise the bar for indefinite commitment, but the effect was to give unchallengeable authority to the institutional physicians who had been observing the patient in question for up to ninety days. At the Austin State Hospital in 1966, a dismayed observer found that indefinite-commitment hearings amounted to quick rubber-stampings of the hospital psychiatrists' uncontested decisions.[69]

The redefinition of criminal responsibility in Texas reflected the same currents of gradual reform, with advocates and representatives of leading professional groups perceiving a responsibility to replace obsolete relics of old-time Texas with modern rules informed by national standards and up-to-date scholarship. The M'Naghten Rules, in Texas as in England, defined criminal responsibility in terms of the cognition of the wrongness of an act. During the 1960s the State Bar of Texas took on two Herculean projects in succession, first proposing a reworking of the code of criminal procedure and then embarking on a complete redrafting of the penal code. The new code of criminal procedure adjusted the rules for insanity pleas at various phases of court proceedings, but left the M'Naghten Rules in place. The penal code effort, pursued by a committee chaired by Dean Page Keeton and staffed by the University of Texas law school, undertook a deeper inquiry into the principles of criminal responsibility and confronted the question of substantive change.

Dean Keeton's committee engaged the same debate over the scientific obsolescence and practical utility of the M'Naghten Rules which had preoccupied the Royal Commission on Capital Punishment and had long resounded in American courts, law reviews, and state legislatures. For over a century M'Naghten defined the standard of criminal responsibility in most U.S. jurisdictions, over the objections of generations of neurologists, alienists, and their successors in psychiatry and clinical psychology.[70] But unlike the English system, the decentralized American judiciary had allowed several variations on the rules. In the 1950s, the release of the Royal Commission's final report had nearly coincided with the landmark D.C. Circuit Court ruling by Judge David Bazelon in *Durham v. United States*, which held a defendant not responsible "if his unlawful act was the product of mental disease or mental defect."[71] Legal observers in Texas, as elsewhere, took note of the alternatives to M'Naghten raised by the Royal Commission and the *Durham* court. But the failings in practice of Judge Bazelon's carefully crafted test—psychiatrists offering diagnoses and theories of illness as conclusive claims

about irresponsibility, judges and juries deferring to these claims—kept alive the debate over whether the M'Naghten test remained preferable to any up-to-date alternative.[72] The American Law Institute's influential Model Penal Code tried to supersede M'Naghten while identifying the key issues more precisely: a defendant would not be held responsible for his conduct "if at the time of such conduct as a result of mental disease or defect he lacks substantial capacity either to appreciate the criminality (wrongfulness) of his conduct or to conform his conduct to the requirements of the law."[73]

Keeton ensured a full hearing before the committee of the case for replacing M'Naghten by assigning the matter to Fred Cohen, one of the young professors whose presence on the law school faculty was undoubtedly viewed by others as an example of the dean's weakness for liberal firebrands. Cohen had stated his strong support for the American Law Institute's effort: "An authoritatively and clearly stated rule that identifies major impairments of cognition, volition, and emotion has the advantages of placing controls on prosecutorial and judicial arbitrariness, bringing criminal responsibility into line with respected psychiatric authority, and providing the jury or judge with sensible guidelines."[74]

The stage was set for a showdown—at least within the committee—over whether the M'Naghten Rules should remain in Texas law. Cohen drafted a new penal code chapter on criminal responsibility that included the Model Penal Code's formula, as well as procedures for insanity pleas, claims of mental incompetence to be tried, and psychiatric examinations and commitments to be ordered by the court. On March 15, 1968, the full committee met to consider the draft, section by section, starting with the new formula. Carol Vance, the Harris County (Houston) district attorney, spoke up for most of his fellow prosecutors and law-enforcement officials, according to the meeting minutes: "Most people who committed crimes had some kind of mental defect, and at the same time this was no reason they should be excused." The law, Vance argued, "should encourage people to be responsible." Also, Vance voiced a continuing suspicion of psychiatric experts and their excuse-making diagnoses: "In his interpretation of this definition, a person that was just 'down right mean' could show a history of a violent temper and might come under this definition." The one psychiatrist sitting in as a guest, Dr. Robert Glen, took particular exception to Vance's last argument, and complained about the archaic constraints that M'Naghten placed on expert testimony. Cohen politely acknowledged that Vance had raised the key issue (perhaps anticipating the outcome). In the end the committee members (not including Glen) voted, eight to four, to approve the formula in Cohen's draft. The new penal code itself, with its multiple chapters and various separately controversial provisions, went before the legislature in 1971 and was finally enacted—with several modifications but with Cohen's chapter on criminal responsibility left intact—in 1973.[75]

Like the mental health code, the redefinition of criminal responsibility in Texas was an achievement for medicine—both a victory for the principles of diagnosis and treatment over prior traditions that predated medical advances, and an extension of psychiatric influence over court case outcomes—for which medicine itself could claim little credit. Change came due to the efforts of leaders of the legal profession, along with various individual advocates (and sympathetic sources of grant funding). Aside from individual participants such as Dr. Glen, the professional organizations of Texas medicine—unlike the BMA, and the RMPA—had no stated position on the M'Naghten Rules or how medicine should inform the determination of criminal responsibility. The TMA did not completely ignore changes in criminal law that affected its members and patients—its monthly publication, *Texas Medicine*, periodically ran articles tracking and explaining legal developments—but it never included these changes among its legislative priorities.[76] It was leaders of other professions (and a few individual doctors) who identified progressive reform with medical standards of diagnosis and treatment, and sought to require authoritative guidance from doctors in reaching difficult but necessary judgments in criminal justice—all while the medical profession itself tended separately to its own interests.

Uninvolved as it was in reforms that were intended to use medical expertise to protect defendants, organized medicine maintained the same distance as the legislature fulfilled the last precondition—together with the rise of medical influence over criminal trials—for the use of "killer shrinks" in capital cases. This was the death penalty law itself—which was passed in the same regular session of the 69th Texas Legislature (in 1973) as the new penal code. Unlike the years-long efforts to modernize legal codes overseen by the State Bar, the death penalty revival effort ran on a legislative fast track from the beginning, reflecting the nationwide political backlash against the invalidation of all state death penalty laws by the U.S. Supreme Court's 1972 ruling in *Furman v. Georgia*.[77] (Outgoing governor Preston Smith even summoned a special session of the Texas Legislature in late 1972, which passed a bill in the Senate but not the House.) In Texas, as in other states, bill drafters studied the confusing array of separate concurring and dissenting opinions in *Furman*, and many persuaded themselves that since two majority justices were mainly concerned with the irregular application of the penalty, a mandatory death penalty with fewer possible exceptions would be upheld. The original bill passed by the Texas House of Representatives was deliberately crafted as a mandatory scheme, with much debate over the types of murders to be included but no proposals to allow juries to consider mitigating factors in individual cases.[78] The Senate, which debated the House bill, narrowly preferred a scheme with aggravating and mitigating factors based on the Model Penal Code.[79] Even in the Senate, the debate was dominated by questions of constitutionality rather than actual policy.

What was actually enacted, reflecting the haste and chaos all too typical of the end of a general session in Austin, lacked even the questionably serious scrutiny given to the original bills passed separately in the two chambers. The final compromise reached by the conference committee was a death penalty scheme unique to Texas: a set of three "issues," or questions which, if all answered affirmatively by the sentencing jury, would require the death penalty. The crucial one of the three special issues was—and is—"whether there is a probability that the defendant would commit criminal acts of violence that would constitute a continuing threat to society."[80] The language was worked out by conferees meeting behind closed doors, in the small hours of the night before the closing day of the session, and was hurriedly passed in both chambers with minimal floor debate. Thus, for a law that would determine life or death, no public record of discussion existed to shed any light on the precise meanings of the terms newly introduced and suddenly enacted (such as "probability"). Essentially the legislators got the main thing they needed—a bill passed and signed— and left their own due diligence in the hands of the courts. This would take years to resolve but, nevertheless, for those whose priority genuinely was to see the death penalty upheld and resumed, it was ultimately a very successful outcome.

The enactment of the "future dangerousness" test made prior developments in mental health law, and the authority accorded to psychiatric testimony, part of the legal context of the Texas death penalty. While the farcical final days and hours of the legislative session made the new standard legal, the weight already given to expert medical predictions of future behavior would see it through the court challenges of the coming years. What made the future even more dangerous for all Texas capital defendants was the curious combination of power and weakness that now characterized medical expertise itself. Medical authority in criminal trials was not a priority for leaders of the medical profession. This authority was augmented not because doctors and psychiatrists organized to seek and win it, but mainly because others had fought the battle to confer it upon them. Consequently, there was no previously worked-out set of ideas prevailing among psychiatrist-witnesses, or among doctors generally, about how their augmented powers should be exercised, and no professional structures in place that were prepared to enforce any such standards. The way was open for individual practitioners, carrying the weight accorded to the medical profession but unconstrained by professional standards or discipline, to provide *de facto* certification of "future dangerousness" and effectively make Texas death penalties a matter of prosecutorial discretion.

Dr. James Grigson, together with the Dallas County district attorney's office, took up the task. Formerly a psychiatry professor at Southwestern Medical School, Grigson and his students had been drawn into the handling of mental health cases in the Dallas courts by participating in a federally funded research program. Unlike his academic colleagues and most of his fellow practitioners, Grigson liked dealing with criminal defendants and sought out more courthouse work. Eventually he made a full-time job of it, examining defendants and testifying at hearings on their competence and sanity (under the rules of the Mental Health Code and the Code of Criminal Procedure). As judges increasingly responded to encouragement from higher courts to verify the competence of defendants as a matter of course, Grigson became more and more familiar with the routines of examination and testimony. He was at the right place at the right time in 1973, as the new death penalty law went into effect. According to one local reporter, the DA's office hatched the idea of establishing a defendant's future dangerousness by using testimony from the same psychiatrist who had already examined the defendant for competence.[81] Henry Wade, the longtime Dallas County district attorney and the dominant figure in local criminal justice, was notorious for pitting his assistant DAs against each other and advancing them according to their conviction rates. These prosecutors needed new ways of winning under the new sentencing rules. As fate would have it, the doctor already at work in the courthouse offered a perfect combination of experience, skills as a courtroom witness, speed and volume of diagnostic judgments—and commitment to the prosecutors' own objectives.

As Wade's chief prosecutor Doug Mulder and other assistant DAs started using their new weapon repeatedly in capital cases, their questions and Grigson's answers took on the routine quality of the courtroom terms and procedures applied by experienced practitioners. In these exchanges, however, the doctor was making the exact same deliberately crafted claims about the individual nature and certain future actions of one convicted defendant after another. Ernest Smith's case brought this *modus operandi* before federal appeals courts and a broader audience.[82] Smith and an accomplice had together robbed a grocery store and killed the cashier. After Smith was arrested and indicted but before his trial convened, the trial judge, R. T. Scales, asked Grigson to conduct the usual competence exam. On February 18, 1974, Grigson met with Smith and (as he later testified) spent some ninety minutes carrying out a "complete psychiatric evaluation." He

sent a letter back to Judge Scales affirming that Smith was "aware of the difference between right and wrong and is able to aid an attorney in his defense." Smith was then tried and quickly convicted of capital murder.

Smith now faced the penalty phase of the trial, in which the jury would hear evidence and decide on the three special issues, including his future dangerousness. Ernest Smith was a twenty-six-year-old black man who had served three years in the army and fought in Vietnam, but had been unable for some years to keep a steady job. To John Simmons, Smith's defense attorney, the convicted defendant stood a reasonable chance in the penalty phase: his accomplice had actually fired the fatal shot, and—more importantly—he lacked a record as a violent criminal (having been convicted only once, for marijuana possession). Mulder began by resting the prosecution's case, "subject to reopening," and Simmons called three witnesses: Smith's stepmother, his aunt, and the dealer who sold him his gun (which was defective and had misfired).

Mulder then reopened his case and summoned a single witness—Dr. Grigson. The doctor's name had not been included on a list of prosecution witnesses that had been given to the court, and Simmons was unprepared for his appearance. Judge Scales overruled the defense counsel's objections, and Grigson began his testimony by citing his professional credentials and his past examinations of between seven and eight thousand criminal defendants. Affirming that he had carried out the pretrial competence exam, he outlined his standard procedure. Based on this exam, Mulder asked, what was the doctor's diagnosis? Grigson explained that Smith had "a sociopathic personality disorder":

It is not an illness or a sickness, it's simply a descriptive term. . . . Primarily [sociopaths] are individuals that do not have a conscience that most of us develop at an early age. They have no type—say guilt feelings, remorse feelings. When they, say, do wrong, they are very much aware of the difference between right and wrong. . . . Also, they have a tendency to be able to manipulate people. Since they don't operate on the same type value system [*sic*] with regard to, say, a conscience, they are able to very freely manipulate people without, say, considering, "Well, I shouldn't do that." It's "I can do that and get away with it."

As the testimony proceeded, Mulder led Grigson through a sequence of questions and answers designed to leave the jury only one option. Were sociopaths truth tellers? "Oh, no, sir," Grigson replied. "Only if it serves their purpose. They will tell the truth if it serves their purpose. If it's harmful, whatever distortion of the truth is necessary is what they will use." After the doctor stated that there were varying degrees of sociopathic disorder, Mulder asked what kind of sociopath Smith was. "Well, he would have to be way down to the severe end—at the very end." What was the doctor's prognosis for Smith? "Oh, he will continue his previous behavior—that which he has done in the past. He will again do it in the future." Could Smith ever break the pattern? "No. This is not what you would consider a stage. This is a way of life. . . . It's only something he will continue."

Having identified Smith as a "sociopath," Grigson drew upon his own definition of the alleged condition to assert the specific, lethal circumstances that the sentencing scheme required. "Mr. Smith does not have any regard for another human being's life, regardless of who it may be. This is what makes him such a very severe sociopath. He has complete disregard for another human being's life." Mulder asked the doctor what could be done for someone with this condition. "We don't have anything in medicine or psychiatry that in any way modifies or changes this

behavior. We don't have it. There is no treatment, no medicine. Nothing that's going to change this behavior." So, the prosecutor asked, what was Grigson's opinion about the possibility of Smith's future dangerousness? "Certainly Mr. Smith is going to go ahead and commit other similar or same criminal acts if given the opportunity to do so."

Carefully calculated as his direct testimony was, Grigson's improvised responses to cross-examination could reinforce his claims even more effectively—although, in the Smith case, being a surprise witness obviously helped. Not having had the chance to investigate Grigson, Simmons nevertheless tried to expose the doctor as a "hatchet man" making baseless, exaggerated claims—but, bleak as things were for his client, Simmons actually made them worse. Exactly what, he asked, had made Grigson so perfectly certain that Smith was a sociopath, in the course of a ninety-minute examination? Grigson had an answer. In describing his crime to the doctor, Smith had recalled that after his accomplice fired the fatal shot, he himself had "walked around over this man who had been shot—didn't look to see if he had a pistol in his belt or in his coat. . . ." Simmons tried to interrupt, but Judge Scales let Grigson finish his answer:

> Didn't check to see if he had a gun nor did he check to see if the man was alive or dead. Didn't call an ambulance, but simply found the gun further up underneath the counter and took the gun and the money. This is a very—sort of cold-blooded disregard for another human being's life. I think that his telling me this story and not saying, you know, "Man, I would do anything to have that man back alive. I wish I hadn't just stepped over the body." Or, you know, "I wish I had checked to see if he was all right" would indicate a concern, guilt or remorse. But I didn't get any of this.

The jury deliberated for a few hours over the special issues and answered yes to all three questions. Smith was sentenced to die in the Texas electric chair.

In the course of the appeals process, the record of Grigson's testimony made the Smith case into a *cause célèbre* within the legal profession and shaped the debate over Texas capital sentencing within the courtroom and beyond. The overall effect of the testimony was polarizing: from the perspective of defense attorneys and some critically minded journalists, it exposed a pattern of obviously manipulative tactics and clear abuse of professional medical authority, but at the same time it was apparent that what outraged the defense bar was all but lost on jurors themselves (and those segments of the public that Dallas County jurors represented). The spectacle of quackery carrying the day in the courtroom did ultimately provoke a response by mental health professionals, but the ensuing battle made plain the disunity of the medical profession and the limited influence of mental health specialists over legal opinions on a matter of their own expertise. Just as Grigson used his mantle of professional expertise and authority to ensure that convicted murderers got death sentences, so did his critics base their counterattack on the actual state of the art in psychiatric diagnosis and the credibility of those representing the psychiatric profession as a whole. The key argument (made as much by legal advocates as by mental health practitioners) was that claims of certain prediction of future dangerousness had no grounding in medical knowledge. As it made its way to the U.S. Supreme Court, the Smith case became a vehicle for the confrontation between Grigson's critics and his supporters. What worked to the advantage, in a sense, of the latter was that the very egregiousness of Mulder's handling of the Smith case created several alternative grounds for reversal on appeal. Discreditable as the prosecution's actions were, this did

not ensure that Grigson's predictions themselves or the predictability of "future dangerousness" would be discredited.

The automatic review of the Smith case by the Texas Court of Criminal Appeals actually did raise specific criticisms of Grigson's predictions, but these criticisms were withdrawn from the court record under curious circumstances.[83] In *Smith v. State*, Simmons raised a dozen various points of appeal, including the use of Grigson as a surprise witness. The majority of the three appeals court judges quickly dismissed each point, treating the contentions about Grigson as no more serious than the others. The majority opinion treated Grigson's claims not as arguments by a prosecution witness but as findings by the court's own expert: "His [Smith's] entire conduct was calculated and remorseless, and the jury was justified in finding that this appellant will always constitute a continuing threat to society." Even the way in which the prosecution introduced Grigson as a witness was perfectly fine because, the judges claimed, the doctor was being summoned in rebuttal (since Mulder had initially rested, then reopened his case). "Since Dr. Grigson had examined appellant prior to trial, his appearance as a witness in rebuttal did not surprise appellant."[84]

One of the three judges, John Wendell Odom, saw it differently. In his dissenting opinion, Odom specifically challenged both the majority's unquestioning reliance on Grigson's testimony and the testimony itself. He drew attention to the way in which Grigson's damning characterization of Smith followed from the doctor's own definition of sociopathy instead of anything Smith himself had actually said: "Never once did he [Grigson] give any basis other than this: that appellant had no sense of guilt or remorse with respect to the commission of the offense for which he was on trial. . . . The expert testimony went far afield of any demonstrated logical connection to the results of appellant's examination by the psychiatrist." This by itself undermined Grigson's insistence on Smith's future dangerousness, but Odom went on to indicate that his main objection was to the use of psychiatric testimony itself to establish the certainty of future behavior. In one of his key passages, he indicated that Grigson himself was not really at issue: "Dr. Grigson's qualifications as a psychiatrist may be fine, but I find no testimony which qualifies him as an expert in predicting the future." The problem was that "such future-telling testimony" was by itself "admissible under no theory of law and prejudicial beyond belief." Thus, Odom concluded, "I am unable to find that much of the testimony offered was from this side of the twilight zone. The introduction of such highly prejudicial psychiatric speculations deprived appellant of a fair trial at the punishment stage."[85]

Even Odom's dissent would soon disappear from the record, as the U.S. Supreme Court made clear its prevailing view of the role of psychiatric testimony, with specific reference to the Smith case. After the state appeals court ruled but before its ruling was published, the high court issued a landmark set of rulings and opinions on the new capital-sentencing procedures enacted in several states after *Furman*. One was the case of Jerry Lane Jurek, whose conviction and sentencing in February 1974 were the first under the new Texas death penalty statute (and, as of then, the only other death sentence yet upheld by the Texas appeals courts). In *Jurek v. Texas*, the defense had pressed different Eighth Amendment claims against the Texas statute, arguing that the special issues failed to resolve the "arbitrary and capricious" aspects of death sentencing which three members of the *Furman* majority had cited.[86] The prosecution's case for Jurek's future dangerousness had not included any psychiatric testimony, but the defense nevertheless criticized the dangerousness standard (as well as the other special-issue questions) as an insufficient

safeguard against "capriciousness and discrimination."[87] This opened the way for the Supreme Court majority, in upholding the Texas statute, to affirm the dangerousness standard as well. "It is, of course, not easy to predict future behavior," wrote the authors of the majority opinion. "The fact that such a determination is difficult, however, does not mean that it cannot be made." The opinion cited examples of routine decisions about future dangerousness by judges setting bail, sentencing authorities in general, and parole boards. The task facing juries weighing a death sentence was "thus basically no different from the task performed countless times each day throughout the American system of criminal justice."[88]

The affirmation of "future dangerousness" was by itself significant, but the *Jurek* majority actually went further. For the majority justices, the critical issue in *Jurek* and in cases involving other states was whether new post-*Furman* procedures would "allow the sentencing authority to consider mitigating circumstances"—and, in the case of Texas, whether the special-issue questions "allow consideration of particularized mitigating factors."[89] With no other examples yet available of how the Texas statute was applied, in practice, all the way through the state courts, the justices examined the Smith case as described in the Texas appeals court's ruling. In a passage which in retrospect seems almost like a cruel joke, the justices took at face value the Texas court majority's representations about Smith that followed directly from Grigson's testimony—and then went on to assert that the appeals court's citation of Grigson's claims ("the conclusion of a psychiatrist that [Smith] had a sociopathic personality and that his patterns of conduct would be the same in the future") actually served to demonstrate that the court *accommodated* potentially mitigating factors rather than excluding them. Thus the constitutionality of the Texas death penalty statute rested, in significant part, on the notion that taking Grigson's testimony into account amounted to a safeguard for the defense. Odom's objections to Grigson's conclusions—and to his fellow judges' unquestioning citation of them—went completely unacknowledged. Judge Odom got the message. Twelve days after the *Jurek* ruling, as the Texas Court of Criminal Appeals dealt with Smith's motion for rehearing, he withdrew his dissenting opinion.

The *Jurek* decision not only upheld the Texas death penalty but implied the willingness of a majority of the Supreme Court to accept psychiatric predictions of future dangerousness like Grigson's. Others remained determined to force judges—and ultimately the high court—to confront the reality of Grigson's methods and actions. After the withdrawal of Odom's dissent in *Smith v. State*, the most heated response in the ensuing commentary came from George E. Dix, a professor at the University of Texas law school. Stating the obvious after recounting Grigson's testimony at Smith's trial, Dix noted that the doctor's testimony "was—consciously or otherwise—influenced by a strongly-held view as to how the penalty issue should be resolved."[90] For Dix, whose scholarship at the time focused largely on both the death penalty and the role of psychiatry in civil and criminal cases, the Smith case displayed "a total and unobscured abdication by both state and federal courts of the responsibility for assuring that imposition of the death penalty based upon predictive testimony by mental health professionals bear some relationship to accuracy, reliability, or rationality."[91]

Dix's law review article on the Smith case was important not merely for its condemnation of Grigson and the courts' endorsement of Grigson's testimony, but also because it confronted a crucial factor—the absence of constraints on a rogue practitioner representing himself in court cases as the voice of psychiatric expertise. The resolution of the case amounted to a failure of professionalism—an inability or unwillingness to uphold actual standards, even as professional authority was being invoked:

> Mental health professionals who testify in Texas death penalty proceedings do so under circumstances in which there can be no reliance upon the legal profession or the courts to assure adequate scrutiny of the testimony. There is no assurance that defense counsel will point out the lack of support for propositions advanced by prosecution witnesses or contrary positions held by other mental health professionals. If the jury accepts the expert testimony, the state appellate court will give the matter nothing resembling adequate scrutiny. And the United States Supreme Court appears to be totally unreceptive to indications that the assumptions upon which the constitutionality of the entire procedure rests are simply inaccurate.[92]

One arguable implication of Dix's argument was that the failure of the courts to perform a gatekeeping function reflected the psychiatric profession's own failure to assert its standards effectively, even as its practitioners gathered ever more influence over legal outcomes. As the background history of the evolution of mental health law demonstrates, the failure was not just that of mental health professionals themselves, but also of legal advocates and others who actually drove the extension of medical and psychiatric authority over the legal realm because they viewed it as a progressive reform. Since psychiatrists had not organized themselves to demand this grant of authority so as to carry out any particular set of practices, the effect—in Dallas County, and increasingly elsewhere in Texas—was to empower not the profession itself but individual practitioners and opportunistic prosecutors.[93]

In discussing *Smith*, Dix chose to emphasize

the past failure of courts and the legal profession, rather than the psychiatric profession itself, to impose standards for court testimony. But in any event, he went on to argue that the psychiatric profession should take on the burden. Mental health providers themselves should, "in recognition of the apparent fact that any limitations upon such testimony must be self-imposed, formulate their own standards for professionally-acceptable testimony as to the dangerousness of a person."[94] Dix proposed a set of procedures to force courts and witnesses to place greater weight on mainstream arguments within the discipline about what kinds of judgments could be ventured. To qualify as an expert witness, Dix argued, "a mental health professional should demonstrate reasonable acquaintance with the developing literature on prediction and behavior."[95] Witness testimony would be constrained by guidelines governing the examination and diagnosis of a defendant (such as "an exhaustive history" and "a complete and consistent diagnostic framework, with broad professional support"), and assertions about dangerousness should avoid drawing conclusions about matters of law and should be framed as comparisons with rates of probability among members of particular groups (rather than estimates of an individual's percentage likelihood to commit violent acts). Essentially Dix was using the Smith case as a vehicle to try to extend the influence of then-recent work by the American Psychiatric Association's Task Force on Clinical Aspects of the Violent Individual, which had drafted a report in 1974 summing up the state of the art within the discipline and emphasizing the limits of predictive knowledge.

As the Smith case proceeded through the federal appeals courts, it became a test case whose outcome was understood as critical to the future of the Texas death penalty. Dix's article fed a debate over psychiatric testimony—and Grigson's practices—between the contending parties in the ongoing case and, to a degree, before the broader public as well.[96] But while the ultimate resolution addressed some of the injustices done to Smith himself by the prosecutors at his trial, its broader significance for psychiatric testimony in capital cases was fairly modest. Despite Dix's framing of the significance of the case, the appeals process never yielded a decision about the legitimacy of Grigson's judgments about Smith. Instead, with Smith's defense team fulfilling its obligation to put forward all potentially mitigating arguments, the courts overturned Smith's conviction because of the use of the competency exam to elicit what was in effect self-condemning testimony by Smith and the use of Grigson as a surprise witness.

The federal district court's handling of Smith's appeal ensured that the case would remain focused on the circumstances surrounding Grigson's testimony rather than the substance of the testimony itself. Four days before Smith's scheduled execution, in April 1977, U.S. district court judge Robert W. Porter issued a stay and agreed to consider Smith's petition for a writ of habeas corpus. Petitioning the judge to dismiss Smith's petition, the Texas attorney general's office referred to Grigson as "an eminently qualified psychiatrist," described Grigson's work as "merely a physician's examination of the health of the defendant," and argued that testimony presented at the punishment phase could not, technically, be self-incriminating: "It is difficult to perceive a violation of Fifth Amendment rights when such testimony is only to the evaluation of mental condition and is admitted only after a finding of guilt."[97] In refusing to acknowledge the way in which Mulder had played fast and loose with the introduction of Grigson's testimony, the state appears to have encouraged Judge Porter to examine the defense's claims more closely. Porter requested and obtained affidavits from Simmons, Smith's other trial counsel, and Judge Scales which effectively established that Grigson was in fact a surprise witness—the prosecution never listed Grigson as a potential witness, and the trial judge had never formally notified the defense of Grigson's examination of their client, even after the fact. Porter's ruling was essentially based on this finding. "I do not believe," he wrote, "that psychiatric testimony should be excluded per se from the guilt/innocence trial and/or circumscribed in the punishment stage as some legal scholars have suggested." Instead he held "only that when the state introduces psychiatric testimony on dangerousness at the punishment phase of a capital trial, the defense must have a fair opportunity to cross examine that testimony and rebut it with expert testimony on behalf of the defendant."[98]

Propelled in part by Dix's arguments, the American Psychiatric Association involved itself in the case as it continued through the appeals courts, arguing for a broader ruling against the use of psychiatric testimony but also affirming the more limited grounds on which the district court had overturned Smith's sentence. Smith's appellate lawyers and supporters together succeeded in keeping the district court's decision from being overturned, but they failed to win the broader ruling. For the Fifth Circuit, whose ruling in September 1979 affirmed Judge Porter's conclusions, the prosecution's "irresponsible conduct" actually had the ironic effect of protecting Grigson's testimony itself from being the object of an appellate court ruling, because it was possible to conclude that the prosecution's conduct had preempted an effective cross-examination at the original trial.[99] The APA, which had appeared as *amicus curiae* before the Fifth Circuit, did so as well before the Supreme Court and offered a much-reworked version of the argument against the admissibility of Grigson's testimony *per se*. By this stage of the case, the argument had been refined so as to target not psychiatric predictions of dangerousness generally but specifically long-term ones: "In Texas, the inquiry focuses

on the defendant's lifetime, not on a discrete time period where psychiatric expertise might be more relevant."[100] The Supreme Court did not bite. The high court's ruling acknowledged that "some in the psychiatric community" held the view about long-term predictions contained in the APA brief, but went on to affirm the earlier rulings on the previously cited Fifth and Sixth Amendment grounds.[101]

The high court, it turned out, would never defer to the American Psychiatric Association as the authoritative voice of psychiatric expertise, or concede that an individual practitioner's prediction of future dangerousness should be kept out of court. With *Smith* having yielded new *Miranda*-like rules for psychiatric examination of murder defendants, the test case on the core issue became that of Thomas Barefoot, who was convicted in November 1978 of murdering a police officer in Bell County (north of Austin) and sentenced to death after Grigson and one other psychiatrist testified that he was a sociopath. In addition to the familiar psychiatric diagnosis, there was a new procedure for reaching it. Prosecutors had adapted to the appeals of the Smith verdict and the surrounding controversy by avoiding direct examination entirely; instead, Grigson now drew his damning conclusions on the basis of detailed hypothetical questions posed by prosecutors which included the facts of the case established in the guilt-or-innocence phase of the trial. For Grigson and the prosecutors, this proved to be the solution to the legal problem. The federal district and appeals courts rejected Barefoot's appeals, but the defense managed to obtain a stay and brought the case before the Supreme Court. The APA's *amicus* brief essentially repeated its argument in the *Smith* case about long-term predictions of dangerousness, stating that their unreliability "is now an established fact within the profession."[102] Adapting the argument to the developing literature on the subject, the brief cited a prominent new study by John Monahan (a psychologist and legal scholar) which concluded that psychologists' long-term predictions were borne out in roughly one of every three cases. Supporting the fallback argument presented by Barefoot's defense, the APA brief went on to argue that the Court "at a minimum" should recognize the absurdity of drawing certain diagnostic conclusions about Barefoot on the basis of a hypothetical question, and should require diagnostic testimony to be based on an actual examination.

The majority of justices would have none of this. Writing for himself and five others, Justice Byron White not only defended the use of predictive testimony but explicitly attacked the APA's claim to speak for its profession. "The *amicus* does not suggest that there are not other views held by members of the Association or of the profession generally," White pointed out. "Indeed, as this case and others indicate, there are those doctors who are quite willing to testify at the sentencing hearing, who think, and will say, that they know what they are talking about, and who expressly disagree with the Association's point of view." Having implicitly accorded Grigson and the APA the same degree of credibility, White argued that whether either of them deserved greater weight was for the jury to decide:

> Neither petitioner nor the Association suggests that psychiatrists are always wrong with respect to future dangerousness, only most of the time. Yet the submission is that this category of testimony should be excised entirely from all trials. We are unconvinced, however, at least as of now, that the adversary process cannot be trusted to sort out the reliable from the unreliable evidence and opinion about future dangerousness, particularly when the convicted felon has the opportunity to present his side of the case.[103]

After the administration of lethal injection to Charlie Brooks in December 1982, the execution of Texas capital murder convicts identified as dangerous was resumed at a gradually increasing rate. The *Barefoot* decision did not by itself loosen the floodgates, but it did clear the way for the execution of those whose dangerousness had been established by psychiatric testimony. Both Dallas County prosecutors and DAs in rural counties continued using Grigson to testify in cases where convicts lacked lengthy criminal records. Grigson himself continued to ply his trade as an expert witness, issuing his predictable but well-crafted diagnoses, well into the 1990s. Dangerousness claims made by psychiatrists have remained a feature of the landscape of Texas capital case law, up to the present day.[104]

Ultimately, Dix's article served as a historical artifact documenting the failures and weakness of organized psychiatry at a crucial early stage in the history of its relationship with courts and the criminal sentencing process. And while the national organization of psychiatrists at least acted, belatedly, the medical profession as a whole remained silent. Far from being drawn into the controversy over the role of medical authority in ensuing death sentences, the Texas Medical Association kept its distance from the fray, as always. In parrying the lunging efforts of defense attorneys to establish his disrepute within the medical profession, Grigson confidently portrayed the APA not only as less credible than himself, given his own vast experience, but as culturally alien to the jurors—"a bunch of liberals who think queers are normal."[105] In the absence of censure by the TMA, or any similarly familiar group of peers, Grigson represented professional authority itself, posing before juries as the profession's one truly accessible representative. Deprived of an effective appeal to responsible professional authority, defense attorneys and experts appalled by Grigson's methods were forced to construct their own body of knowledge, over time, showing the low incidence of reoffense among convicts who had been labeled conclusively as dangerous, and establishing the lack of factual support for assertions that arguably should have been dismissed as farfetched to begin with.[106] For the medical profession in Texas, the failure to counter or constrain Dr. Death was an act of omission as significant as it was silent.

A similar act of omission was the Texas medical profession's response—or nonresponse—to the pioneering of execution by lethal injection, and to the official rearrangement of the act of killing into a set of pseudomedical and medically monitored procedures. In quietly refusing to act preemptively, the TMA differed little from other state medical organizations, which generally followed the lead of the American Medical Association in staying distant and dissociated while nevertheless allowing state authorities to draw upon the legitimacy of some of the profession's own symbols and rituals. When the Texas Legislature considered changing the method of execution to lethal injection in 1977, committee hearings included no witnesses representing the medical profession. After the legislation passed, the TMA's Board of Councilors adopted the formal opinion that "a physician may be present at a chemical execution for the sole purpose of pronouncing legal death." This formulation sought to confirm that the doctor's role would be the same as it had been in executions in years past.[107] In 1980, when the AMA House of Delegates passed a resolution that a physician "should not be a participant in a legally authorized execution," the TMA councilors responded by forwarding their 1977 opinion to the TMA House of Delegates, which approved it at its November meeting. This was as far as the Texas medical profession would go. When Charlie Brooks was executed with a physician in attendance, an activist group brought the matter back before the TMA Board of Councilors, which responded by proposing that the House of Delegates formally substitute the AMA's stated policy for the board's own 1977 opinion. At their May 1983 meeting, the TMA delegates declined even to take this half-step. The reference committee that received the councilors' proposal reported that it "heard considerable discussion on this item, but concluded that the Texas Medical Association's current policy statement serves its purpose well and requires no revision."[108]

III.

The contrasting roles of the medical professions in England and Texas—and the drastically different outcomes that they promoted, in the case of capital punishment—contribute to an explanation for which more conspicuous cultural differences cannot fully suffice. Vigilante violence as a race-based community prerogative, as depicted in Franklin Zimring's most recent work on capital punishment, largely distinguishes the American South from England, as well as from other U.S. regions. Doctors considering capital punishment in their role as citizens, rather than simply as professionals, undoubtedly acted on these views, differently in different places, as individuals and collectively. But the example of England shows that for doctors to act effectively against the future administration of the death penalty, it is not necessary for them even to oppose the death penalty in principle. The question was whether they would take (or acquiesce in) specific actions upon which the future of the death penalty had come to depend.

One clear difference between the political contexts in which the two medical organizations (the BMA and the TMA) operated is the existence of a Royal Commission, with its command of time, expertise, and resources exceeding anything available to a mere standing committee of a state legislature. No such institution compelled the TMA to put forward views on criminal justice questions that lay outside its own institutional interests. Yet, in giving evidence the BMA visibly reflected not the reluctance of a witness under subpoena, but the determination of a group with a role to play and broad interests to uphold. The inaction of the TMA, in its own different way, may reflect the same thing.

The existing literature on the BMA as a political actor focuses on the relationship between it and the Health Ministry—two entities each of which comprises the other's main concern. A somewhat archaic but still prominent interpretive theme in discussion of British politics is the twentieth-century emergence of a corporatist governing regime, in which Parliament as representative of the public is marginalized by continuous, mutually self-serving relationships between organized pressure groups and state administrative agencies.[109] Historians have applied this paradigm mainly to industrial relations from World War I through the 1970s, but the politics of nationalized health care are portrayed even to this day as a leading example of the corporatist tendency.[110] It seems that doctors, in the British context, have at least had the opportunity to establish a certain standing, as custodians of a recognized social order, such that they command legitimacy by virtue of established social placement rather than simply their healing work or their financial resources. Within recognized limits, the BMA exercised a prerogative to make its views known, not simply as a representative of its members' individual views but as an institution entitled to a degree of deference within its sphere. The rare, famous exceptions—most of all the imposition of national health-care schemes over the fierce objections of many doctors—suggest the limits of the rule but not its invalidity.

In the Texan context, the differences arguably extend to the very definition of a profession. To a greater degree even than in neighboring southern states, the changes in the political climate of Texas after World War II—with the rise, fall, and eventual diversification of an energy economy; with the abrupt impact of industrialization, immigration, and metropolitan area growth; with modern developments grafted uneasily onto persistent social conditions and traditional hierarchies—promoted the narrow concentration of political power more effectively than its broad distribution. The most influential historical narrative of mid-twentieth-century Texas politics describes a near-monopoly of power maintained at the statewide level by "the Establishment"—"a loosely knit plutocracy comprised mostly of Anglo businessmen, oilmen, bankers, and lawyers."[111] The machinery of plutocratic rule did ultimately break down, by the 1970s, but by the end of the century, the intensive targeting and harvesting of white conservative voters had allowed for the reestablishment of one-party dominance and a political order that empowered the best-funded corporate interests and kept potential challengers (unions, consumer groups, trial lawyers) relatively marginalized. Professional groups have developed within an environment in which the presence of an "Establishment" has been nearly constant.

In this context, the notion of professional autonomy—of an independent standing accorded to members of a professional group, or the expectation of deference—seems like a categorical mistake to be corrected by a more clear-eyed analyst. Leading histories of Texas professional institutions suggest that professional power almost inevitably has derived from patronage, service, and proximity to the center where power has been concentrated. Thus Kenneth Lipartito and Joseph Pratt's authorized history of the Houston law firm of Baker & Botts portrays the influence of the powerful corporate law firm over the developing institutions of the Texas legal profession—and the firm's deep identification with the technical needs and broader interests of its corporate clients.[112] Lipartito has subsequently crafted a broad, synthetic account of American professions during the twentieth century which portrays subordination as the norm. "The years between 1950 and 1970 were the exceptional ones," he argues. "In those stable decades, professional practitioners could pretend to be above the competitive fray and free from the taint of commerce."[113] TMA commands political power, by virtue of its own deep pockets and carefully tended relationships with corporate and other allies—but it cannot expect to command deference for an unpopular position, by virtue of its own standing. If the gap between the respective fates of capital punishment in England and in Texas is explained in part by the responses of the separate medical professions to medico-legal problems, then the gap between these particular features of the political landscapes of England and Texas may serve to explain these responses.

Norwood Andrews is a researcher in the Center for the History of Medicine at the University of Warwick (U.K.) and the Summerlee Fellow for the Study of Texas History, William R. Clements Center for Southwest Studies, Southern Methodist University, in 2009–2010. He is currently writing a manuscript on penal reform, professional expertise, and social class formation in Texas and in England.

Notes

1. See American College of Physicians et al., *Breach of Trust: Physician Participation in Executions in the United States* (published March 1994); Robert G. Truog and Troyen N. Brennan, "Participation of Physicians in Capital Punishment," *New England Journal of Medicine* 329, no. 18 (Oct. 28, 1993): 1346–1350; Amnesty International, *Lethal Injection: The Medical Technology of Execution* (published Jan. 1998); and Human Rights Watch, *So Long As They Die: Lethal Injections in the United States* 18, no. 1(G) (April 2006).

2. Key recent examples include Atul Gawande, "When Law and Ethics Collide—Why Physicians Participate in Executions," *New England Journal of Medicine* 354, no. 12 (3/23/06): 1221–1229; and Peter A. Clark, "Physician Participation in Executions: Care Giver or Executioner?" *Journal of Law, Medicine, and Ethics* (spring 2006): 95–104. The debate within medicine, which had continued to brew since the introduction of lethal injection, was stimulated further by newly raised questions regarding the specific procedures employed. See Leonidas G. Koniaris et al., "Inadequate anaesthesia in lethal injection for execution," *The Lancet*, vol. 365 (4/16/05): 1412–1414, and the related editorial in the same issue, "Medical collusion in the death penalty: an American atrocity" (1361).

3. Some years after lethal executions had been initiated, a new round of state and national medical-professional resolutions and legal cases were provoked by new laws in several states, including Illinois and California, which sought to ensure the precise carrying out of execution procedures by mandating doctor inclusion. See *So Long As They Die*, pp. 39–42.

4. See V. A. Gatrell's argument in *The Hanging Tree: Execution and the English People, 1770–1868* (New York: Oxford Univ. Press, 1994).

5. See the discussion of the Royal Commission report of 1866 in Leon Radzinowicz and Roger G. Hood, *The Emergence of Penal Policy in Victorian and Edwardian England* (New York: Oxford Univ. Press, 1986), chapter 20, especially pp. 661–671 and 685–688.

6. See Tom Phillips, "The Abolition of Capital Punishment in Britain: The End of the Rope, Part 1," *Contemporary Review* 272, no. 1585 (1998): 57–63. Phillips's one observation about the Royal Commission on Capital Punishment that reported in 1953 was that it "concluded hanging was no deterrent but failed to recommend abolition" (p. 62), which seems a fair example of the abolitionist perspective on the commission's work.

7. Victor Bailey, "The Shadow of the Gallows: The Death Penalty and the British Labour Government, 1945–51," *Law and History Review* 18, no. 2 (2000): 349.

8. A convenient summary of the successive Bentley-Craig, Evans-Christie, and Ruth Ellis cases and their

impact on public discussion of capital punishment is provided by Brian P. Block and John Hostettler, *Hanging in the Balance: A History of the Abolition of Capital Punishment in Britain* (Winchester: Waterside, 1997), chapters 17–19.

9. The Royal Commission report itself provided a scholarly historical survey of the origins of the M'Naghten Rules and the long-standing objections of medical men. See Royal Commission on Capital Punishment (1949–1953), *Report* (London: H.M. Stationery Office, 1953) (hereafter Royal Commission report), specifically Appendix 8(d) (pp. 397–406).

10. The Royal Commission report cites the eminent Victorian legal scholar Sir James Fitzjames Stephen as the leading exponent among jurists of the view of *M'Naghten* which the report attributes generally to medical men. See Royal Commission report, p. 80, and Appendix 8(d), pp. 399–401.

11. Key secondary sources on the BMA and its role in the politics of health care include Peter W. J. Bartrip, *Themselves Writ Large: The British Medical Association, 1832–1966* (London: BMJ, 1996), especially chapter 10 (pp. 248–266), and Harry Eckstein, *Pressure Group Politics: The Case of the British Medical Association* (Stanford Univ. Press, 1960), which contrasts the BMA's seemingly high-profile failures with "a much more impressive record of not-so-public successes, greatest of all on minor matters, points of 'detail,' but impressive also in the case of 'principles'" (p. 96). In *Health, Happiness, and Security: The Creation of the National Health Service*, Frank Honigsbaum also offers a revisionist argument about the institutional politics of national health legislation but reaffirms the basic understanding of the undermining of the BMA's position by Bevan's collaboration with Lord Moran, then president of the Royal College of Physicians, at pp. 148–150. Asa Briggs reviews Lord Moran's role in *A History of the Royal College of Physicians of London, Volume 4* (New York: Oxford Univ. Press, 2005), pp. 1296–1310.

12. The Report of the Committee on Insanity and Crime of 1923 is quoted in Royal Commission report, Appendix 8(d), para. 16, p. 404.

13. Royal Commission report, para. 16, p. 404.

14. Ibid., p. 405.

15. The Report of the Committee on Insanity and Crime of 1923 is quoted in Royal Commission on Capital Punishment (1949–1953), *Minutes of Evidence* (London: H.M. Stationery Office, 1949–1951) (hereafter Royal Commission minutes), 8/4/49, para. 94, p. 13.

16. Gordon Rose describes the work and illustrates the perspective of the Howard League in *The Struggle for Penal Reform* (Chicago: Quadrangle Books, 1961).

17. See Harry Potter, *Hanging in Judgment: Religion and the Death Penalty in England from the Bloody Code*

to Abolition (London: SCM Press, 1993), especially pp. 142–166 (including chapter 14, "Godly Butchery," on the Church of England's longstanding reliance on the symbolic power of the execution ritual).

18. Bailey states this finding from primary sources in "The Shadow of the Gallows," at p. 345.

19. Characterizations of the unenthusiastic response of abolition supporters (who were not aware of the commission's appointment until the public announcement) implies that they merely expected the commission to be unhelpful to their cause. I maintain that the commission actually had the opportunity to do far-reaching harm to the cause, which may be more apparent in retrospect (and in comparison with the United States). Bailey interprets the terms of reference to imply "some new method of classifying murders by degrees, which the Lords had ridiculed, the Opposition in the Commons had opposed, and the abolitionists disliked." See "The Shadow of the Gallows," p. 345.

20. See the beginning of Chapter 13, "Methods of Execution," at Royal Commission report, para. 700, p. 246.

21. James B. Christoph, *Capital Punishment and British Politics* (Chicago: Univ. of Chicago Press, 1962), p. 79.

22. Minutes of the BMA Council, 1949–1950, p. 6, in British Medical Association Collection (SA/BMA), Box 268, Wellcome Library, London (hereafter BMA Collection).

23. Minutes of the BMA Council, 1949–1950, Appendix I, p. 14, in BMA Collection, Box 268.

24. Royal Commission report, para. 244, p. 86.

25. "Memorandum Submitted by the Council of the British Medical Association," para. 9, in Royal Commission minutes, 2/3/50 (hereafter BMA memorandum).

26. BMA memorandum, section II, paras. 7–14, Royal Commission minutes, 2/3/50.

27. BMA memorandum, section II, para. 20, Royal Commission minutes, 2/3/50.

28. BMA memorandum, section II, para. 21, Royal Commission minutes, 2/3/50.

29. BMA memorandum, section II, para. 25, Royal Commission minutes, 2/3/50.

30. BMA memorandum, section II, para. 23, Royal Commission minutes, 2/3/50.

31. Examination of Witnesses, para. 4008, Royal Commission minutes, 2/3/50.

32. BMA memorandum, section II, para. 27, Royal Commission minutes, 2/3/50.

33. BMA memorandum, section II, para. 28, Royal Commission minutes, 2/3/50.

34. BMA memorandum, section II, para. 29, Royal Commission minutes, 2/3/50.

35. BMA memorandum, section II, para. 29, Royal Commission minutes, 2/3/50.

36. BMA memorandum, section II, para. 31, Royal Commission minutes, 2/3/50.

37. BMA memorandum, section II, para. 32, Royal Commission minutes, 2/3/50.

38. Examination of Witnesses, paras. 3945–3953, Royal Commission minutes, 2/3/50.

39. Examination of Witnesses, para. 3934, Royal Commission minutes, 2/3/50.

40. Examination of Witnesses, para. 4039, Royal Commission minutes, 2/3/50.

41. Examination of Witnesses, para. 4040, Royal Commission minutes, 2/3/50. Also see para. 4046.

42. Examination of Witnesses, para. 4042, Royal Commission minutes, 2/3/50.

43. Examination of Witnesses, para. 4048, Royal Commission minutes, 2/3/50.

44. "Memorandum Submitted by the Council of the Royal Medico-Psychological Association," part III ("The M'Naghten Rules and 'Guilty but Insane'"), para. 11, in Royal Commission minutes, 5/4/50. Also see Examination of Witnesses, paras. 6638, 6639, 6656, 6666, and 6667.

45. Examination of Witnesses, para. 6638, Royal Commission minutes, 5/4/50.

46. Ibid.

47. "Minutes of the Seventeenth Meeting," January 4–5, 1951, pp. 4–5, in Royal Commission on Capital Punishment: Evidence and Papers, Box HO-301/2, The National Archives, Kew. (Hereafter the minutes of the Commission's closed meetings—as distinct from the "Minutes of Evidence" from its public hearings—are cited as Minutes, Royal Commission.)

48. Minutes, Royal Commission, 1/4–5/51, p. 6.

49. Ibid.

50. Minutes, Royal Commission, 6/5/52, p. 1.

51. Ibid., pp. 2–3.

52. Minutes, Royal Commission, 7/5–6/51, p. 8.

53. Ibid.

54. Minutes, Royal Commission, 10/4/51, p. 1.

55. "Statement of the Views of Consulting Anaesthetists: Alternative Methods of Execution," para. 5, in Royal Commission minutes (Minutes of Evidence), 12/6/51.

56. Examination of Witnesses, para. 9025, Royal Commission minutes, 12/6/51.

57. Examination of Witnesses, para. 8955, Royal Commission minutes, 12/6/51.

58. For all quotations and paraphrases in this paragraph, see Minutes, Royal Commission, 12/6–7/51, pp. 3–4.

59. See Minutes, Royal Commission, 2/7/52, p. 2 (specifically comments by Slater and Sir Alexander Maxwell), and Royal Commission report, Chapter 13, specifically para. 749 (p. 261).

60. Commission report, para. 611, p. 214.

61. Steve Levin, "The Life of Dr. Death," Dallas Morning News, 9/19/88.

62. The standard analytical treatment of the historical background summarized here is provided in James W. Marquart, Sheldon Ekland-Olson, and Jonathan R. Sorensen, The Rope, the Chair, and the Needle: Capital Punishment in Texas, 1923–1990 (Austin: University of Texas Press, 1994), chapters 1–4.

63. See introductory remarks in Pat Ireland Nixon, A History of the Texas Medical Association, 1853–1953 (Austin: University of Texas Press, 1953).

64. See Florita Indira Sheppard, "The Texas Medical Association: History, Organization, and Influence," master's thesis, Lyndon B. Johnson School of Public Affairs, The University of Texas at Austin, 1980.

65. See Chester R. Burns, "The Health Sciences," in Leo Klosterman, Loyd S. Swenson, and Sylvia Rose, eds., 100 Years of Science and Technology in Texas (Houston: Rice Univ. Press, 1986), and Burns, "Medicine in Texas: The Historical Literature," Texas Medicine, Vol. 82 (January 1986).

66. See The Hogg Foundation for Mental Health: The First Three Decades, 1940–1970 (Austin: University of Texas Press, 1970), pp. 11–22.

67. See K. D. Gaver, "Mental Illness and Mental Retardation: The History of State Care in Texas," Impact [bimonthly publication of the Texas Department of Mental Health and Mental Retardation], vol. 5, July–August 1975, and also Joel Warren Barna, "State Mental Health Services: Change Under Pressure," in House Study Group Special Legislative Report (Austin: Texas House of Representatives, 1984), p. 4. Gerald Grob chronicles the broad programmatic shift and the significance of federal funding in From Asylum to Community: Mental Health Policy in Modern America (Princeton Univ. Press, 1991).

68. See Texas Research League, "Legal Structure for the Texas State Hospital System" (Report no. 13 in a survey of the Board for Texas Hospitals and Special Schools), and Millard H. Ruud, Interpretation of the Mental Health Code, 1st ed. (Austin: Hogg Foundation for Mental Health, 1957).

69. Fred Cohen, "The Function of the Attorney and the Commitment of the Mentally Ill," Texas Law Review, vol. 44 (1965): 427–431. Cohen points out that anyone eligible for indefinite civil commitment had to have been previously subjected to temporary commitment—which effectively placed them at the mercy of the institutional physicians during the later hearing.

70. A voluminous legal scholarly literature now records the prevalence of the M'Naghten test and the existing variations among states, including those few which sought to incorporate an "irresistible impulse" test. One particularly helpful and well-crafted historical case study is Charles E. Rosenberg, The Trial of the Assassin Guiteau: Psychiatry and Law in the Gilded Age (Chicago: Univ. of Chicago Press, 1968).

71. 214 F.2d 862 (1954).

72. For a sympathetic discussion of Bazelon's thinking see William Wayne Justice, "Is the Law's Treatment of the

Insane Sane?" (Louis Faillace Lecture Series, Univ. of Texas at Houston Medical School, 2002).

73. Section 4.01 (1), *Model Penal Code* (Philadelphia: American Law Institute, 1985 reprint).

74. Fred Cohen, "Reflections on the Revision of the Texas Penal Code," *Texas Law Review* 45 (1967) 429 (footnote 56).

75. For the Feb. 9, 1968, meeting, see Stare Bar of Texas, Committee on Revision of the Penal Code, "Summary of Minutes" [concerning Chapter 4, Responsibility] (March 15, 1968), Tarlton Law Library, University of Texas at Austin.

76. See T. C. McCormick, M.D., "Insanity as a defense and the Texas Penal Code of 1974," *Texas Medicine*, vol. 71 (Sept. 1975): 64–65, and Harold K. Dudley, M.D., et al., "The mentally ill defendant in Texas: a new perspective," *Texas Medicine*, vol. 72 (Dec. 1976): 68–76.

77. For discussion of the post-*Furman* backlash see Stuart Banner, *The Death Penalty: An American History* (Cambridge, Mass.: Harvard Univ. Press, 2002), chapter 10, and Herbert Haines, *Against Capital Punishment: The Anti-Death Penalty Movement in America, 1972–1994* (New York: Oxford Univ. Press, 1996), especially pp. 45–47.

78. Eric F. Citron, "Sudden Death: The Legislative History of Future Dangerousness and the Texas Death Penalty," *Yale Law and Policy Review* 25, no. 3 (2006), p. 165.

79. Ibid., p. 167.

80. The other two original "issues"—whether the defendant's actions that caused the victim's death were "committed deliberately and with the reasonable expectation that the death of the deceased or another would result," and whether these actions were "unreasonable in response to the provocation, if any, by the deceased"—were in practice answered affirmatively in virtually all cases, meaning that only the issue of future dangerousness distinguished the Texas scheme from a *de facto* mandatory penalty. See James W. Marquart, Sheldon Ekland-Olson, and Jonathan R. Sorenson, "Gazing Into the Crystal Ball: Can Jurors Accurately Predict Dangerousness in Capital Cases?" *Law and Society Review* 23, no. 3 (1989), pp. 449–468.

81. See Jim Atkinson, "Witness for the Prosecution," *D Magazine*, June 1980.

82. My reconstruction of the handling of the Ernest Smith case and his trial draws upon the court record as reconstructed and summarized in the defense and *amici curiae* briefs in *Estelle v. Smith*, 451 U.S. 454 (1981); Atkinson, "Witness for the Prosecution"; and George E. Dix, "The Death Penalty, 'Dangerousness,' Psychiatric Testimony, and Professional Ethics," *American Journal of Criminal Law* 5, no. 2 (May 1977): 151–214.

83. *Smith v. State*, 540 S.W. 2d 693 (1976).

84. In his scathing commentary, Dix drew attention to the majority's use of Grigson's assertions as information rather than advocacy. The characterization of Smith as "remorseless" showed that the judges "clearly relied upon" the doctor's testimony. "There was no suggestion in the majority opinion that Dr. Grigson's testimony was subject to doubt, that any other mental health professional might have arrived at other conclusions, or that the testimony may have left the jury with anything other than a complete and accurate picture of the present state of the diagnostic and predictive art." See "The Death Penalty," p. 162.

85. For the quoted excerpts from the text of Judge Odom's dissent (which was withdrawn before the final publication of the court ruling in the *Southwestern Reporter*) see Dix, "The Death Penalty," pp. 161–166.

86. *Jurek v. Texas*, U.S.S.C. No. 75–5394, Consolidated Reply Brief for Petitioners.

87. *Jurek v. Texas*, reply brief, p. 51.

88. *Jurek v. Texas*, 428 U.S. 262 (1976) at 274–275.

89. Ibid., 271–272.

90. Dix, "The Death Penalty," p. 172.

91. Ibid., p. 167.

92. Ibid., pp. 168–169.

93. See John Bloom, "Killers and Shrinks," *Texas Monthly* (July 1978): 64, 66, 68.

94. Dix, "The Death Penalty," p. 169.

95. Ibid., p. 175.

96. See Bloom, "Killers and Shrinks."

97. See *Smith v. Estelle* (445 F.Supp. 647), Defendant's Motion to Dismiss and Answer.

98. *Smith v. Estelle*, 445 F.Supp. 647, at 657.

99. *Smith v. Estelle*, 602 F.2d 694 (1979).

100. *Estelle v. Smith* (451 U.S. 454), *Amici* Brief of the American Psychiatric Association.

101. *Estelle v. Smith*, 451 U.S. 454 (1981).

102. *Barefoot v. Estelle* (463 U.S. 880), *Amici* Brief of the American Psychiatric Association.

103. *Barefoot v. Estelle*, 463 U.S. 880, at 900–901.

104. See *Deadly Speculation: Misleading Texas Juries with False Predictions of Future Dangerousness* (Houston: Texas Defender Service, 2003).

105. Trial transcript, *Fuller v. State* (CCA No. 71,046), cited in *A State of Denial: Texas Justice and the Death Penalty* (Houston: Texas Defender Service, 2000), p. 30.

106. See Marquart, Ekland-Olsen, and Sorenson, "Gazing into the Crystal Ball," and *Deadly Speculation*, chapter 3, pp. 21–35.

107. See Report of Subcommittee on Medical Discipline, in Minutes, Board of Councilors, Texas Medical Association, May 11, 1977, p. 2.

108. Report of Reference Committee on Public Health and Scientific Affairs, Texas Medical Association, May 1983, pp. 3–4.

109. See Samuel H. Beer, "Pressure Groups and Parties in Britain," *American Political Science Review*, vol. 50 (1956): 1–23, and more recent commentary by Wyn

Grant in *Pressure Groups and British Politics* (New York: St. Martin's Press, 2000), pp. 51–53. Eckstein's discussion of medical politics emphasizes corporatist ties; see *Pressure Group Politics*, chapters 2 and 3, pp. 40–91.

110. See Keith Middlemas's argument in *Politics in Industrial Society: The Experience of the British System Since 1911* (London: Andre Deutsch, 1979), and the influential discussion by Harold Perkin in *The Rise of Professional Society: England Since 1880* (New York: Routledge, 1989), chapter 7, pp. 286–358.

111. George Norris Green, *The Establishment in Texas Politics: The Primitive Years, 1938–1957* (Norman: Univ. of Oklahoma Press, 1979), p. 17.

112. See *Baker & Botts in the Development of Modern Houston* (Austin: Univ. of Texas Press, 1991).

113. Kenneth J. Lipartito and Paul J. Miranti Jr., "The Professions," in Stanley I. Kutler, ed., *Encyclopedia of the United States in the Twentieth Century* (New York: Charles Scribner's Sons, 1996), vol. 3, p. 1428. Also see Lipartito and Miranti, "Professions and Organizations in Twentieth-Century America," *Social Science Quarterly* 79, no. 2 (June 1998): 301–320.

CHAPTER 15

Means of Death

METHODS OF EXECUTION IN CALIFORNIA, 1937–2007

Thomas Bojorquez

THE STATE of California has continuously used the death penalty as a method of punishment for those lawfully convicted of certain criminal acts. From the day the United States annexed California as a territory in 1846 up until 1937, hanging was the sole officially sanctioned method of execution for condemned prisoners convicted in state courts. On May 7, 1937, Governor Frank Merriam signed into law a legislative act that abolished hanging as the state's method of execution and instituted the gas chamber as the new means of death. On February 18, 1972, the California Supreme Court issued a decision banning the death penalty in California; the state's last execution in the gas chamber was in 1967.

The United States Supreme Court's ruling a few months later on June 29, 1972, declared all state death penalty statutes unconstitutional. In 1977 the United States Supreme Court reinstated capital punishment for certain crimes, giving the California legislature the opportunity to draft a new death penalty law that complied with the new standards, but the state did not carry out a death sentence until 1992, twenty-five years after the last execution. The gas chamber remained California's sole method of execution until January 1,

1993, when Governor Pete Wilson signed into law a bill allowing the condemned inmate to choose lethal injection or the gas chamber.

Less than two years later, on October 4, 1994, a federal judge, Marilyn Hall Patel, ruled that the state's use of the gas chamber as a means of death constituted cruel and unusual punishment and therefore violated the Eighth Amendment of the United States Constitution, leaving lethal injection as the sole method of execution. On December 15, 2006, federal judge Jeremy Fogel suspended the state's use of lethal injection, citing evidence that the state's procedure for administering the lethal injection also violated the condemned prisoner's Eighth Amendment rights. Fogel's ruling did not abolish the death penalty in California, but required the state to change its procedures for administering the lethal injection to a more humane method that would not violate the condemned's rights under the Eighth Amendment.

The various changes to California's means of death for condemned prisoners reflected the political philosophies and social trends in effect at the time of each change. In the early twentieth century, correctional institutions in California absorbed the spirit and philosophy of the progressive reform movement and adopted a professional approach to their responsibilities, incorporating education, technology, and innovation into the corrections system in an effort to improve conditions and modernize their policies, procedures, and methods. Accordingly, most of the attempts at reforming the state's use of the death penalty during the 1920s and 1930s came from within the corrections profession. With the assistance of the legislature and governor, the state prison bureaucracy voluntarily, albeit with some internal dissent, implemented these reforms as a part of their efforts to improve their system.

By the middle and late part of the twentieth century, the calls for death penalty reform came from outside the corrections profession and anti-death-penalty advocates used the legal system as a catalyst to force the state and the prison bureaucracy to adopt changes to the system with the eventual goal of revoking the death penalty. These reformers consisted of nongovernmental organizations including the American Civil Liberties Union (ACLU), political and social activists, as well as some members of the federal and state judiciary, and state, local, and federal appointed and elected officials. Nonetheless, the California public has continuously and strongly supported the death penalty.

While the earlier reformers were correctional professionals who instituted reforms as a part of ongoing bureaucratic procedure and worked with the judiciary, legislature, and governor when necessary, the new death penalty reformers sought, and are seeking, to completely abolish the death penalty through judicial decisions. Despite numerous, lengthy, and costly efforts to abolish it, the public's incredibly strong desire to maintain capital punishment has continued to guarantee its survival, although a small segment of the citizenry has continuously voiced its opposition. This has forced the new reformers to circumvent the bureaucracy and legislative process and go straight to the courts in their efforts to restrict and eventually abolish the death penalty in California and in the United States.

Until 1891, California executions were local affairs. While the courts sent prisoners convicted of felonies to the state prisons located at San Quentin and Folsom, county sheriffs maintained custody of condemned prisoners in county facilities and carried out the death sentences on those premises "within the walls or yard of a jail, or some convenient private place in the county," between thirty and sixty days after the conviction.[1] The state did not carry out any executions; for example, the sheriff of San Rafael County was responsible for the execution of any prisoners sentenced to death after their conviction of a capital crime committed while incarcerated at San Quentin.[2]

This requirement placed a distasteful and expensive burden on the counties, and local officials sought relief from this task from the legislature, arguing that the prisoners and their executions were the responsibility of the state. On March 31, 1891, Governor Henry Markham signed into law a bill passed in the state legislature mandating that "all executions must thereafter take place in the prison at San Quentin, under the jurisdiction of the warden."[3] At San Quentin, Warden W. E. Hale directed prison staff to erect an interior gallows on the top floor of the sash- and blind-manufacturing building, complete with a "death watch" cell made of wood slats and equipped with a gas jet for lighting the area at night, and designated a row of cells in a nearby barracks as "murderers' row."[4] Hale did not want the gallows built in the yard because he did not want the executions to become a public spectacle, which could create a riot, or, at the very least, cast a dark shadow over prison life and cause unnecessary stress and strain inside the walls.[5]

The new law generated press coverage, controversy, and litigation reminiscent of contemporary debates and legal maneuvering on capital punishment. Longshoreman John McNulty, convicted of murdering fellow dockworker John Collins on Second Street in San Francisco in 1888, was one of the first condemned prisoners the state scheduled for execution at the San Quentin gallows. The court initially sentenced McNulty to die at the hand of the San Francisco County sheriff on November 30, 1888.[6] McNulty delayed his execution date following a lengthy and involved appeal of his sentence to the California State Supreme Court.

By the time the California Supreme Court denied his appeal and ordered the death sentence carried out, county sheriffs no longer handled executions and the state now wanted McNulty executed at San Quentin under the new law. McNulty argued that the state could no longer punish him because the law governing executions had changed and no longer applied to his case. The California Supreme Court carefully considered the argument but finally decided, in Justice Thomas McFarland's majority opinion, that while the new law was unconstitutional with regard to convictions reached prior to its enactment, it "is clearly constitutional as to future crimes, while it leaves past offenses to be punished under the law as it was when the offenses were committed." The United States Supreme Court heard McNulty's appeal and issued a ruling on May 15, 1893, affirming the California Supreme Court's opinion.[7] The state remanded McNulty to San Francisco County Sheriff Charles Laumeister for execution of the trial court's sentence.[8]

After avoiding the death penalty six different times (including an instance where a superior court judge almost jailed Sheriff Laumeister for contempt when he refused to carry out the sentence because the order for McNulty's death sentence had expired and the court had not issued a new one) and receiving a commutation of his sentence to life in prison in 1894, Governor Henry Gage pardoned McNulty on January 9, 1903, and he walked out of San Quentin a free man.[9]

Executions at San Quentin from the 1890s through the 1930s took on a dramatic and almost medieval flair and generated much public attention, especially when famous murderers went to the gallows. When McNulty escaped death at San Quentin, Jose Gabriel, better known as "Indian Joe," convicted in San Diego for the murders of Mr. and Mrs. John Geyser,[10] became the first prisoner executed on the San Quentin gallows on March 3, 1893.[11] Indian Joe requested that the warden execute him during daylight hours.[12] Warden Hale presided over the first white prisoner's execution the following year. On the same day, newly hired prison guard William Duffy, the father of future San Quentin warden Clinton Duffy, started work; the ancestry of one of the executed men led him to remark, "'Tis a fine welcome I'm getting, they're hiring one Irishman, then hanging another to make it even."[13]

The staff stretched the hanging rope for as long as two years to take the "bounce" out of it. On the night before the execution, guards moved the condemned man from murderers' row to the death watch cell next to the gallows in the sash-and-blind building and gave him his last supper. The following morning, known as "Black Friday," the prisoner had breakfast and could receive visitors. The prison shut down all activities and staff confined prisoners to their cells. When the execution time (usually 10:00 A.M.) neared, the witnesses (often as many as 120, with no females allowed) gathered around the gallows. The guards then led the condemned man out of the death watch cell. The warden of San Quentin led the procession to the gallows; the condemned followed behind, often accompanied by a chaplain. Guards followed the condemned man as their captain and the hangman brought up the rear.

The warden and captain remained below as

the others continued up onto the scaffold of the gallows. There, the hangman adjusted the noose around the neck of the condemned man and placed a black shroud on his head. When the noose was tight, the hangman signaled to the warden below. When all was ready, the warden raised his hand, giving the signal to three guards in a nearby sentry box to sever three ropes, releasing the trap door under the prisoner. Sometimes the prisoner died instantly; others hung for twenty minutes or longer before prison officials were satisfied that the sentence was complete. In 1898 entrepreneurs got hold of the rope allegedly used to hang Theodore Durrant, the notorious murderer of Blanche Lamont, and sold it in San Francisco on street corners for one dollar per inch.[14]

Although most Californians of the late 1800s and early 1900s supported the death penalty, some openly opposed it and criticized the procedure while often sympathizing with the condemned. Some supporters of capital punishment had reservations about the death penalty and questioned the use of hanging as the state's official means of death, fearing that it was medieval and primitive. Following the execution of Jose Gabriel, or "Indian Joe," a *San Francisco Chronicle* editorial opined that "'the only point conclusively proved by Gabriel's execution is that the California law concerning capital punishment is swift and sure in the case of a murderer who has no friends or money.'"[15] More in line with public opinion, the *Los Angeles Times* noted, perhaps sarcastically, that "[t]he California Legislature failed to pass any eulogy upon the Indian Gabriel, who was hanged last week, nor did it adjourn for the day. What an oversight!"[16] Many of the perspectives and opinions expressed in the late 1800s and early 1900s regarding executions and the means of death bear a distinct similarity to views expressed decades later, both pro and con.

Especially revealing was a letter from a "J. Grey" to the editors of the *Los Angeles Times* dated December 20, 1893, and published in the *Times* on December 24, 1893. Grey was obviously upset after reading a *Times* story describing John McNulty's fifth stay of execution and that "McNulty's neck will yet be saved through the efforts of the Daughters of the Good Shepard of this city [San Francisco]," who helped to circulate a petition calling for Governor Markham to commute McNulty's death sentence to life imprisonment. The article reported that eight thousand citizens, including "United States Senators White and Perkins, Archbishop Riordan . . . and eight of the jurors who convicted the prisoner," had signed the petition.[17]

Grey wrote, "The reason that there are so many murders in the United States is that not one murderer in thirty-five is hanged" and downplayed the value of such petitions: "Women go around with such petitions, and they are so persistent that a business man will sign to get rid of them. Then they get school children to sign, and the loafer on the corner." Grey went on to interpret the thought process of a murderer weighing in on his chances of getting away with his crime in the light of such a permissive and forgiving society as found in the 1890s:

"If I should be arrested and tried for the killing, the chances are twenty to one that I can get off on a plea of insanity, or some technicality, or some fool juryman will stand out for me and save me. If I should be found guilty and sentenced to hang, all I have to do is join some church and pretend to be pious, and immediately all the soft-headed old maids in the community will get up a petition to the Governor, and he will commute my sentence to imprisonment for life, and in a year or two the same Governor will let me out . . . and I can then go out and marry one of the women who got up my petition; and I can kill her afterwards if she does not suit me."[18]

Grey criticized those who sympathized with condemned murderers because they ignored the killers' victims and their survivors:

> If the women who circulate these petitions would spend one-half time and energy in obtaining subscriptions for the family bereft of support by the red hand of the murderer, they could raise a fund that would put these sufferers beyond want. But they have no interest in the ruined family. They can starve. All flowers and prayers and delicacies are for the man whose hands are red with the blood of his innocent victim.[19]

In 1901, Samuel E. Dutton, one of the jurors who sentenced Durrant to death in 1895, received a jury summons for another San Francisco murder trial, this one featuring a Chinese immigrant, Soo Hoo Mon, as the accused. An assistant district attorney recognized Dutton and told the prosecutor that he should pick Dutton as a juror: "Get that man; he'll give you a verdict, sure. That's Dutton, who was one of the Durrant jurors." When the prosecutor questioned him, Dutton replied that he opposed capital punishment, shocking everyone in the courtroom, including ex-superior court judge Murphy, who presided over the Durrant trial and now represented Soo Hoo Mon as a defense attorney. Dutton replied, "[S]ince the Durrant trial, I could never sit again as a juror in a murder case where the death penalty might be pronounced. I could not do it." Dutton had been the only juror present at San Quentin to witness Durrant's execution.[20]

During the early 1900s, the "progressive" reform movement gained influence in California, especially following the 1911 election of Progressive Republican Hiram Johnson to the governor's office. Reform-minded citizens sought to limit political corruption and influence peddling, and improve political, social, and economic conditions while wrestling power and influence from "Tammany Hall"–style politicians and economic juggernauts like the Southern Pacific Railroad. The adoption of a "professional" approach to improve government's efficiency, service, and integrity was a crucial part of California's progressive reform movement.

Progressives saw the prison system as corrupt, brutal, and mired in the past. Part of the change in attitude stemmed from the fact that as progressives clamped down on political corruption, more and more wealthy, influential, and articulate white-collar criminals entered the prison system and viewed for themselves the problems within. During the 1920s, San Quentin inmates included the former Alameda County sheriff, a former member of the Los Angeles County Board of Supervisors, Sidney T. Graves, and at least seven millionaires.[21] Asa Keyes, the former Los Angeles County district attorney, was also an inmate.

Keyes, who entered San Quentin in 1929 following a bribery conviction, had, according to Warden James B. Holohan, "sent up nearly a third of all the men in San Quentin at the time he arrived to begin his term," including several dozen under the sentence of death. After his parole in 1931, Keyes wrote, "Prison doesn't help any man. . . . It's a poison, degrading all but the strongest individuals. I don't know what to substitute for penitentiaries, but if I were District Attorney again, I would hesitate about sending many men to prison. It's far more terrible than many people realize."[22] These influential perspectives made the public more aware of prison life and garnered sympathy for conditions behind the walls.

Progressives believed that technology and the application of scientific and rational academic principles could make prisons more humane. Newly developed academic disciplines, including sociology, psychology, public administration, and police science, brought sophisticated and innovative ideas and solutions to the correctional bureaucracy, including professional management, a reliance upon technology, and the concept of incarceration not only as punishment but as a rehabilitative tool. By the late 1920s, almost three thousand San Quentin inmates were taking vocational instruction in nearly two hundred fields, correspondence lessons, University of California extension courses, and in-house classes, many taught by inmate instructors, including several who had engineering degrees from the University of Chicago and Johns Hopkins University.[23]

The new philosophies also suggested to reformers that some of those who committed crimes often did so because their unfortunate social and economic circumstances left them no choice. To reformers, this meant that the penal system could correct bad behavior and through humane treatment, psychological counseling, and job training, transform some convicts into law-abiding, productive citizens. San Quentin warden Holohan observed that "A small percentage of convicts are inherently criminal, crooks or killers by nature. But most of them are the products of poor environments: undisciplined, they come from broken homes, poor, weak, spineless mortals, to a certain extent, yet with possibilities of being made useful citizens."[24]

This commitment to reform and improvement also caused many in the correctional field to reconsider the application of the death penalty and its effect upon the rights and humanity of condemned prisoners. The public's perception of capital punishment as an unpalatable and repulsive but necessary evil remained; however, they became more amenable to reforming the process. For perhaps the first time in California's history, correctional professionals began to seek more humane and publically acceptable methods of execution.

The steps leading to the first major death penalty reform in California began when Governor C. C. Young appointed Holohan, a former United

States marshal, as warden of San Quentin on September 1, 1927. The governor usually appointed one of the two state prison wardens from his own party and the other from the opposing party. "Generally, the party in power usually took over the pleasant marine vistas of San Quentin, while the opposition was banished to the sweltering stone barrens of Folsom, a hundred miles from the fleshpots of San Francisco."[25] The Republican governor appointed Holohan, a Democrat, to the San Quentin post in a spirit of Progressive Republican nonpartisanship. Holohan, in turn, openly cooperated with the Progressives and conscientiously sought to institute reform and improvement along progressive lines.

The Great Depression and other pressing issues interfered with the reform movement. San Quentin, built for a population of around twenty-five hundred inmates, had exploded to over six thousand when United States Attorney General Homer Cummings visited in August 1934. The severe overcrowding led him to remark, "It was one of the saddest sights I ever saw."[26] Holohan lamented that the overcrowding left San Quentin "unable to do its full job of reclaiming men."[27] Eager to implement reforms in areas that he could control, Holohan focused upon the means of death used to carry out the state's death penalty.

California was not alone in the quest to make capital punishment more humane. Nevada was the first state to adopt lethal gas as a means of death in 1921. According to author George Bishop, many residents of Nevada, including Governor Emmet Boyle, wanted to abolish or modernize capital punishment to improve Nevada's "Wild West" reputation. "Clearly, one way to bring Nevada's newly civilized status to the attention of the country was to stop shooting and hanging people, either illegally or legally."[28] The Nevada State Legislature considered abolishing capital punishment when they had trouble selecting a "modern" method, but eventually chose lethal gas as the state's means of death. The procedure provided that the state would gas the prisoner in his cell as he slept, a logistically difficult proposition. Governor Boyle signed the act into law, "feeling that he had, in effect, outlawed capital punishment by the simple method of rendering its implementation impossible."[29]

Gee Jon, convicted of murdering a rival tong member in Mineral County, Nevada, in 1921, was the first prisoner sentenced to death by lethal gas. Nevada State Prison officials were unable to carry out the sentence in Jon's cell and he appealed, claiming that lethal gas was cruel and unusual and therefore violated the constitutions of both the United States and Nevada. In January 1923, the Nevada State Supreme Court held that the death sentence was legal and directed the state to carry out the order.

> Our [death penalty] statute inflicts no new punishment; it is the same old punishment, inflicted in a different manner, and we think it safe to say that in whatever way the death penalty is inflicted it must of necessity be more or less cruel. But we are not prepared to say that the infliction of the death penalty by the administration of lethal gas would in and of itself subject the victim to either pain or torture. . . . We must presume that the officials entrusted with the infliction of the death penalty by the use of gas will administer a gas which will produce no such results, and will carefully avoid inflicting cruel punishment.[30]

The Nevada ruling addressed the major legal challenges to the implementation of lethal gas as a means of death and opened the door for California to adopt the gas chamber.

Nevada had to construct a gas chamber to carry out the court's order and executed Gee Jon on February 8, 1924, in a procedure that the attending physicians claimed was swift and painless.

"Several of them said they considered it the most merciful form yet devised, less gruesome than hanging, entailing less suffering than shooting or beheading, or any of the other traditional ways of execution."[31] Soon, Colorado, Arizona, Wyoming, and North Carolina adopted the gas chamber as their means of death, and California began to consider this "state of the art" method.

In 1932, both houses of the California State Legislature considered the passage of a bill adopting the gas chamber as California's means of death. Governor James Rolph Jr. detailed Warden Holohan to go to Nevada to observe a lethal gas execution. Holohan believed that capital punishment was a necessary evil. Later in his career, he wrote, "An execution is an ugly thing. I went through a mental hell on each of the fifty-seven times I had to officiate at the killing of a fellow human. But I firmly believe that the death penalty should be retained."[32]

On November 28, 1932, Warden Holohan and Warden Court Smith of Folsom Prison traveled to the Nevada State Prison at Carson City to observe a lethal gas execution. "After viewing this execution . . . I believe that the lethal gas method is the simplest and most humane way to dispose of such a case. There was no evidence of suffering."[33] Holohan also feared that problems during a hanging (the accidental beheading of a prisoner or a broken rope) could cause the public to reject the death penalty. "While not one hanging has ever gone wrong in California, there is always that fear. The tension among prison guards is terrific. Such a mishap, should it occur, might give impetus to a movement to abolish capital punishment."[34]

Warden Smith, on the other hand, was horrified and criticized the procedure. Both houses passed the bill, but at the end of the legislative session Governor Rolph vetoed it as a reckless experiment. The experience made a lasting impression on Warden Holohan, who in 1936 resigned as warden during a scandal started when the San Francisco office of the United States Secret Service uncovered a major prisoner-run currency counterfeiting ring operating out of San Quentin's print shop. Santa Cruz area voters soon elected Holohan to the state senate; he immediately coauthored Senate Bill 338 to establish lethal gas as the official means of death for California. Holohan's timing was perfect.

By the mid 1930s, years of suffering under the Great Depression and the resulting cultural and social transformation elicited significant public support for new correctional methods. President Franklin Roosevelt's New Deal programs provided new ideas and, more importantly, new federal funding for prison reform programs, both technological and rehabilitative. This gave the struggling prison reform movement new life and brought major changes in the treatment of prisoners, especially the condemned. The perspectives expressed were the same as those of the reformers of the early 1900s, but this time, they had plenty of money on their side.

Contemporary prison bureaucrats echoed the progressive and experimental philosophy driving the reform movement. Kate Richards O'Hare, the former assistant to the state director of penology, told a joint legislative fact-finding committee discussing the state's construction of a new prison at Chino, "It would not be an institution on which we depended on steel and iron, but an institution on which we depended on men. . . . [M]y contention was that there should not have been more than twelve cells at Chino and if [a prisoner's assignment to] Chino was made as a reward for good behavior and good conduct and generally for rehabilitation you wouldn't need cells."[35]

SB 338 was a significant part of this late 1930s prison reform movement. Technology was an important part of the reforms; for example, legislators and corrections bureaucrats called for new, electrically operated cell doors for the new Chino prison to enhance the safety of both prisoners

and guards.[36] With the reform movement in full swing and with plenty of money available to make it a reality, the gas chamber bill sailed through both houses and Governor Merriam signed the measure into law on May 7, 1937. While the state originally planned to build a second gas chamber at Folsom, officials decided to maintain the state's sole death row at San Quentin.[37]

Even elements of the press supported the concept of the gas chamber as a modern and humane form of execution. One Southern California journalist described an encounter with the mixture of potassium cyanide, water, and sulfuric acid, known as hydrocyanic acid, or HCN, used in the gas chamber.

"Southern California's citrus growers . . . use it to fumigate their orange and lemon trees against pesky scale insects. . . . The question has been raised whether or not suffocation by hydrocyanic acid gas is as painless as it is generally supposed to be. . . . [T]his writer once had a brush with HCN that may help form an opinion. While earning money for college in the summer of 1931, I worked with a fumigating gang near Corona. . . . You could smell the heavy, bittersweet odor of the gas—[it smelled] like peach pits.

My knees sagged under me and the first thing I knew somebody was sloshing cold water in my face. I had passed out cold. But there was no feeling of pain and no warning of what was happening. It was just a sudden loss of consciousness. Criminals who die in San Quentin's new gas chamber will probably meet death in the same way. There will be no physical torture."[38]

The same writer also observed, "Execution by gas is said to be the most painless and humane method of capital punishment ever devised.

. . . California's adoption of the gas chamber is a progressive step toward enlightened criminal methods."[39]

In a reprisal of the McNulty case, Roy Leon Righthouse, who pled guilty on May 15, 1937, to a murder committed in Fresno that Justice J. Edmond of the California State Supreme Court found "too gruesome to detail," appealed the legality of his death sentence under the new method. In his automatic appeal, Righthouse claimed that the state had no legal basis to execute him. He asserted that because the legislature had repealed hanging on May 7, and the new means of death would not become effective until August 27 of that year, there was no death penalty effective in California when he committed the murder on May 11.

The State Supreme Court rejected the appeal, stating that the legislature clearly intended that hanging would remain the lawful means of death for crimes committed until August 27: "So where the legislature passes an act to amend a statute then existing, the latter remains in full force during the time between the passage of the amendatory act and the time when it becomes effective."[40] Ironically, right after the murder and before turning himself in to police, Righthouse had tried to commit suicide using gas.[41] The warden of San Quentin, House Smith, carried out Righthouse's sentence of death by hanging on February 18, 1938.[42]

In total, the state hanged 217 condemned prisoners on the San Quentin gallows. The state selected a Denver, Colorado, exterminator named D. B. Castle to build the new gas chamber for five thousand dollars. Castle, who had also built Nevada's gas chamber, delivered the steel, octagon-shaped chamber (eight feet across and seven feet high, with two chairs inside) to San Quentin in March 1938.[43] California's chamber was simple: once guards tied down the condemned in one of the chairs, they sealed the chamber.

The executioner then pulled a lever, dropping a container filled with potassium cyanide pellets into a two-gallon jar filled with distilled water and sulfuric acid already placed under the prisoner's chair. The resulting fumes then caused the condemned to suffocate. Chamber designer Earl Liston claimed that "[o]ur calculations show that this new chamber should snuff out life in about fifteen seconds."[44] During a test run on March 19, a pig took thirty-five minutes to die in the chamber in a process that disturbed some reporters.[45]

On December 2, 1938, California used the gas chamber for the first time, executing two prisoners convicted of kidnapping and murdering Warden Clarence Larkin of Folsom Prison and a prison guard during a wild and bloody escape attempt on September 19, 1937. The new means of death immediately generated controversy. "Prison attendants, used to watching men die, said the exhibition sickened them." The chaplain of San Quentin, Father George O'Meara, commented, "That was the most terrible thing I've ever seen. . . . I've witnessed fifty-two hangings. I could find nothing humane about it and I never want to watch anything like it again." San Francisco attorney Melvin Belli also threatened to challenge the new law in court (but never did). Witnesses said that what made this execution worse was the fact that death took a little longer than hanging (up to fifteen minutes as opposed to ten) and that the faces of the condemned were not covered with hoods, as in the case of hanging.[46]

Despite these concerns, the gas chamber was in California to stay. The progressive reformers believed that they had achieved a balance between humanizing capital punishment and the inherent brutality of an execution by any means. Science and engineering, they believed, overcame negative aspects of capital punishment. During the second gas chamber execution, on December 9, 1938, prison officials implemented lessons learned from the first execution and bled off excess air from the gas chamber to allow the gas to fill the space more quickly, speeding up the time it took to suffocate the two condemned prisoners.[47]

Long-time (1913–1951) San Quentin physician Doctor L. Leonidas Stanley, who was well known for his earlier medical experiments where he implanted testicular material from the unclaimed bodies of executed prisoners into elderly convicts to see if they became healthier and stronger,[48] "said that the changes were made to make the death more humane, but that he still is opposed to gas deaths."[49] The press also came out in support of the gas chamber as the most civilized means of delivering the stern message that progressives hoped the death penalty would send to society:

We do not, and should not torture even torturers. Remembering, on the other hand, that the supreme penalty is not revenge but deterrent punishment, we need not be in too great haste to rob it of all its grimly exemplary qualities. It is not an argument for unnecessary brutality to say that if other potential murderers can be imbued with a wholesome fear of the gas chamber, society will be the safer for it.[50]

With the start of the Second World War and on through the Korean War, the death penalty debate and any controversy regarding the gas chamber took on a secondary role in California. By the 1950s, society had stabilized enough to allow death penalty opponents an opportunity to reconsider the issue, although public opinion was against them. Despite this sentiment, a few elected state officials, including California Attorney General and later Governor Edmund G. "Pat" Brown, advocated the eventual abolition of the death penalty. The debate over capital punishment ebbed and flowed as interest groups raised the issue on a regular basis, periodically stimulating discussions over the death penalty's role and future. In 1957, an assembly interim committee

under Democratic Los Angeles assemblyman Lester McMillan introduced bills outlawing capital punishment or imposing a five-year moratorium, but the assembly Judiciary Committee defeated them.[51]

Calls to abolish capital punishment failed in California then for the same reason that similar measures failed in other eras: the public strongly supported the death penalty, despite the efforts of activists and some elected officials, including Governor Brown, to end or amend the procedure.

The abolishment of the death penalty is regularly attempted and never succeeds, although one of the favorite arguments against it is that the people of California have had enough of executions. This is pretty hard to show by the record of the people's representatives and by the juries of ordinary citizens who not only find certain defendants guilty but decide whether they shall die or be imprisoned for their crimes. In short, there is no evidence that the majority of the people of California desire that capital punishment be abolished.[52]

Because of this popularity, the state legislature and the prison bureaucracy refused to support any restriction on the death penalty in California, leaving abolitionists without an easily accessible avenue of support.

The gas chamber execution of Caryl Chessman on May 2, 1960, gave new life to the abolition movement. With public opinion strongly in favor of capital punishment, activists found a new route to seek restrictions to death penalty procedures. "Another strategy, however, was beginning to gain the attention of abolitionists. This method of abolition could sidestep the enduring problem of the popularity of the death sentence. It was, simply stated, to have the courts declare capital punishment unconstitutional."[53] This method marked a major change in the methodology reformers used to make changes to the death penalty. Past reforms, like centralizing executions at San Quentin, or replacing hanging with the gas chamber, came from within the system via the legislature with the concurrence of the correctional bureaucracy. Now, interests from outside the system attempted to use the courts to impose changes with or without the support of the public, their elected officials, or the correctional profession.

Death penalty abolitionist-sponsored legal challenges were highly successful during the 1960s, both in directly stopping the procedure or creating a climate of self-restriction. The Vietnam War and serious social challenges to traditional society distracted many Americans from supporting capital punishment issues. Public opinion mattered little inside a courtroom, and in the face of strong legal challenges, the state virtually stopped carrying out executions in response to legal orders halting execution proceedings or to minimize litigation.

In 1961, the year California executed Chessman, there were forty-two executions in the United States. In 1967, that number had fallen to only two. There were no executions in California from 1968 until February 18, 1972, when the California State Supreme Court ruled in *People v. Anderson* (*Anderson II*) that capital punishment violated the California Constitution's prohibition on "cruel or unusual punishment."[54] The court also justified its ruling through its assertion that capital punishment offended contemporary standards of decency, showing its reliance upon 1958's United States Supreme Court ruling, *Trop v. Dulles*.[55] *Anderson II* automatically commuted the death sentences of California's 108 condemned prisoners to life imprisonment. On June 29, 1972, the United States Supreme Court ruled in *Furman v. Georgia* that all death penalty statutes in the United States violated the United States Constitution because they allowed juries to arbitrarily

apply the death penalty without legislative guidelines or consideration of the circumstances of the crime or the defendant's situation. This ruling suspended all executions in the United States until state legislatures could rewrite their laws to comply with *Furman's* provisions.

The *Anderson II* ruling immediately sparked a pro-death-penalty backlash in California. Los Angeles's chief of police, Edward M. Davis, issued a statement asserting that "[t]he decision of the 'San Francisco Court' is bound to result in the slaughter of many California citizens by an army of murderers who have been waiting for years in Death Row for such an unrealistic judicial judgement."[56] California Attorney General Evelle Younger led the movement to overturn *Anderson II*, claiming that "[t]he court has enacted its personal views into law over the will of a protesting public."[57] Younger believed that "the court was substituting its judgement on matters which were purely legislative decisions." The court's decision demonstrated how the role of the judiciary had changed. In *Nevada v. Gee Jon*, the Nevada Supreme Court had opined:

We think it fair to assume that our legislature, in enacting the law in question, sought to provide a method of inflicting the death penalty in the most humane manner known to modern science . . . the legislature has determined that the infliction of the death penalty by the administration of lethal gas is humane and it would indeed be not only presumptuous, but boldness on our part, to substitute our judgement for theirs, even if we thought differently upon the matter.[58]

Both the California and United States Supreme Courts declined to hear Younger's petition to reconsider *Anderson II*. When a state constitutional amendment to reinstate capital punishment stalled in the legislature, death penalty proponents gathered more than a half-million signatures in two months and qualified the amendment for the November 7, 1972, election. The voters, terrified and sickened that mass murderers like Charles Manson were no longer sentenced to death and would soon be eligible for parole, passed the proposition with 66 percent of the vote.[59] Attorney General Younger summarized the public's mood: "Maybe our state Supreme Court will have some second thoughts and consider the vote of the people as significant . . . and realize they overreached. . . . Well, the people of California spoke on the question of contemporary standards of decency and the Supreme Court of California was just plain wrong."[60]

In 1973, the legislature enacted a death penalty law, but the California Supreme Court struck it down because it did not allow for mitigating circumstances. In *Gregg v. Georgia* (428 U.S. 153, 1976), the United States Supreme Court upheld a Georgia death penalty statute that properly addressed the requirements of *Furman*. In 1977, state senator and future California governor George Deukmejian sponsored SB 155, a death penalty law that complied with the legal requirements established in *Furman*, *Gregg*, and other decisions. Governor Edmund "Jerry" Brown, elected in 1975 (like his father, former Governor Edmund "Pat" Brown, an opponent of the death penalty), vetoed the bill. Both houses of the state legislature overrode the veto and reactivated capital punishment in California on August 11, 1977. "After a decade of unemployment, while the courts struck down death penalty statutes and the Legislature re-enacted the law, the gas chamber in San Quentin will resume its function, not on a regular basis but on a piecework contract."[61]

The abolitionists' long-term strategy of using the courts to circumvent the legislative process and the expressed will of the majority to implement what they saw as a greater good had failed and they were right back where they were in 1967:

the death penalty as a legal, but rare, form of punishment. The opponents of the death penalty had succeeded in pushing capital punishment to the forefront of public policy in the hope of eliminating it, but their attempts to eliminate a popular and valued system of punishment, combined with a perception of judicial overreach, alarmed the public so much that many were motivated to stop what they regarded as an assault on the sovereignty of the people, and the courts soon followed with favorable decisions. "Thus, those who strove to end capital punishment in California were defeated by a United States Supreme Court which found the death penalty valid in certain circumstances and by a State Constitutional Amendment which tied the hands of the California Supreme Court."[62]

Complicated abolitionist legal arguments frustrated even the normally Byzantine bureaucracy of the American legal system, creating judicial confusion with numerous challenges in state and federal courts. In their *Lockett* decision, the United States Supreme Court recognized this and observed,

> In the last decade, many of the States have been obliged to revise their death penalty statutes in response to the various opinions supporting the judgements in *Furman* and *Gregg* and its companion cases. The signals from this court have not, however, always been easy to decipher. The states now deserve the clearest guidance that the court can provide; we have an obligation to reconcile previously differing views in order to provide that guidance.[63]

The public had demonstrated its desire to maintain capital punishment, and the legislature, governor, and California Supreme Court followed suit. In 1986, voters removed Chief Justice Rose Bird and Justices Cruz Reynoso and Joseph Grodin from the California Supreme Court because the public believed that they were overturning all the death penalty appeals that came before them because of their personal opposition to capital punishment. Governor Deukmejian, the author of the 1977 death penalty bill, replaced them with justices who did not seem to arbitrarily oppose capital punishment.

The judges of the appointed federal judiciary were immune to a public referendum and were therefore more open to arguments from abolitionists. However, there were no executions in California until 1992; this placed the issue "on the back burner" because the abolitionist strategy of litigation over legislation meant that they had to wait for the next execution to challenge capital punishment in court. With no real sympathy from any branch of the state government, death penalty opponents would now focus their efforts in federal court and challenge gas chamber executions as a form of cruel and unusual punishment.

As in the 1890s and 1930s, supporters of capital punishment within the legislature reformed the state's means of death to make the procedure more humane and to eliminate controversy. In April 1992, the state executed double murderer Robert Alton Harris in the San Quentin gas chamber. The ACLU had filed suit in Ninth Circuit to stop the gas chamber execution as cruel and unusual punishment, but continued the suit after Harris's death on behalf of other condemned prisoners (*Fierro, Harris, and Ruiz v. Gomez, et al.*). Within hours of the first execution at San Quentin since 1967, Republican assemblyman Tom McClintock introduced a bill allowing the condemned prisoner the choice of lethal injection as an alternative to the gas chamber, the most significant change to the state's means of death since adopting the gas chamber in 1937. The state continued to use the gas chamber as the execution site, placing a cot inside the cell.

Under the lethal injection procedure, staff housed the condemned in the holding cell until thirty minutes before the execution. Staff members then tied the condemned prisoner to the cot and inserted two intravenous (IV) catheters into the inmate (one as a backup in case of failure), usually in the arm, and connected them to tubes leading outside the chamber. The executioners then sealed the condemned inside the chamber and, once the warden gave the approving signal, introduced sodium pentothal into the IV, rendering the inmate unconscious. Staff then added pancuronium bromide to paralyze the diaphragm, causing the inmate to stop breathing. They then injected potassium chloride into the condemned, stopping the inmate's heart.[64]

Death penalty opponents were not satisfied with the new option. A death penalty abolition group member said, "It is intended to put a humane face on killing, when reality is that the death penalty, capital punishment, is a barbaric practice that has no place in a civilized society. . . . We object strenuously to efforts to make the death penalty more palatable to the public."[65] Lethal injection, however, was very popular with the public. The legislature quickly passed the bill and Governor Pete Wilson signed it into law to take effect on January 1, 1993. "Wilson made it clear that his purpose was to stop last-minute appeals by condemned prisoners who might argue that lethal gas is cruel and unusual punishment."[66]

The ACLU continued its suit to ban the gas chamber option and received support from Jewish survivors of German World War II concentration camps through affidavits and in newspaper editorials comparing the state's gas chamber to the ones used in the German death camps.[67] Many of the abolitionists went to illegal extremes in their efforts to ban capital punishment. A private investigator working for Morales on his legal challenge fabricated statements from jury members of Morales's original trial and submitted the forgeries to the court in support of Morales's death sentence appeal. The private investigator pled guilty to forgery, perjury, and filing false documents, stating, "I believe the death penalty is illegal. It's barbaric and it's an atrocity. . . . Any acts I committed are done out of a firm belief against the state killing these people."[68]

In a 1995 academic study, researchers found that a sizeable number of California residents preferred lethal injection as the state's method of execution. Seventy-seven percent of the respondents had a favorable impression of lethal injection, while only 15 percent wanted it abolished. Forty-six percent favored retaining the gas chamber, while 42 percent wanted it abolished, with 11 percent undecided.[69] The majority of those polled thought that lethal injection was the least painful and mildest method of execution.[70]

On October 4, 1994, the ACLU won its suit to stop the state's use of the gas chamber as a means of death. United States District Judge Marilyn Hall Patel ruled that

[t]he evidence presented concerning California's method of execution by administration of lethal gas strongly suggests that the pain experienced by those executed is unconstitutionally cruel and unusual. This evidence, when coupled with the overwhelming evidence of societal rejection of this method of execution, is sufficient to render California's method of execution by lethal gas unconstitutional under the eight amendment.[71]

According to the ACLU, this was the first time that a court had declared a specific means of death unconstitutional.[72] This was also the first time a court had imposed a procedural change upon the corrections bureaucracy; previous changes came from within the system.

Death penalty opponents now focused upon challenging lethal injection's constitutionality. Obviously, if they could have courts declare all existing means of death unconstitutional, abolitionists could effectively end capital punishment without banning it outright. The ACLU filed suit on behalf of condemned murderer Michael Morales (*Morales v. Hickman, et al.*, 415 F. Supp. 2d. 1037), asserting that "California's procedures for executing prisoners by lethal injection fall short of standards set by the veterinary profession for animal euthanasia and were formulated with less care than methods in China, the world leader in capital punishment."[73]

The ACLU lawyers claimed that the state correctional personnel did not properly administer the lethal injections to inmates, causing them undue pain and unnecessary suffering that violated the Eighth Amendment. The suit alleged that prison personnel were not trained to handle the procedure and that the execution site, inside the old gas chamber, was deficient. On December 16, 2006, Judge Fogel agreed and issued a ruling that halted California's administration of lethal injection until the Department of Corrections and Rehabilitation could fix the identified problems to the court's satisfaction.[74] As of May 2, 2007, there were 662 condemned prisoners on California's death row as Governor Arnold Schwarzenegger authorized construction, pending legislative approval, of a new, seven-hundred-thousand-dollar execution chamber at San Quentin to replace the seventy-year-old gas chamber.[75]

California has always sought to retain but improve the death penalty, even when faced with challenges to the existence of capital punishment. When applying the death penalty, California has continued to seek the most humane and efficient methods possible using the latest technology and new philosophies to reform the system. The state used hanging as a means of death until that method seemed too cruel. Reformers in the legislature then looked to technological advances to find a more scientific and humane method: the gas chamber. When the gas chamber was no longer the most advanced and humane method available, the legislature added lethal injection as an option.

Initially, the legislature and the corrections bureaucracy led the death penalty reform process, making improvements as part of an effort to professionalize and streamline the system. The courts maintained a narrow focus regarding the actual means of death, reviewing in many cases only the legality of a petitioner's particular circumstances and avoiding comment on the death penalty in general terms. After World War II, activist groups attempted to use the legislature to address capital punishment's abolition, without success. Following the United States Supreme Court's 1958 *Trop v. Dulles* decision, activists switched their focus to the court system and attempted to have the judicial system declare capital punishment cruel and unusual.

The abolitionists achieved success in the 1960s, reducing the number of executions in California from forty-two in 1961 to none in 1968. In 1972, both the California and United States Supreme Courts placed moratoriums on the death penalty, but the California public quickly reinstated capital punishment via a state constitutional amendment later that year. Following several favorable legal decisions, the legislature rewrote the capital punishment statutes and the state reactivated the death penalty in 1977. In 1992, the legislature added lethal injection as an additional means of death. Later legal challenges ended the state's use of the gas chamber in 1994, and, in late 2006, a federal judge temporarily halted the state's use of lethal injection until officials reform the process.

Abolitionists faced a dilemma: they opposed a popular form of punishment and therefore had to side-step traditional democratic processes to achieve their goals via litigation. Despite numerous legal challenges, the people of California have demonstrated that they are committed to the maintenance of the death penalty and consider it a distasteful but necessary crime deterrent, and, as proprietors of California's government, have indicated over the decades that they will ensure that capital punishment remains a viable sentencing option for first-degree murder and selected other crimes.

Thomas A. Bojorquez is a Sergeant of Police, Los Angeles Police Department, assigned to a patrol division. Bojorquez earned a B.A. in history from Tulane University and an M.A. in history from California State University, Fullerton.

References

Bishop, George. *The Legal Ways of Death*. Los Angeles: Sherbourne Press, Inc., 1965.

Catania, Sara. "Will Schwarzenegger's New Death Chamber Actually Help Inmates?" <http://www.salon.com> (May 2, 2007).

Duffy, Clinton T. *The San Quentin Story*. Garden City, N.Y.: Doubleday and Co., 1951.

Fierro, Harris, and Ruiz v. Gomez, et al., 865 F. Supp. 1387 (1994).

Lamott, Kenneth. *Chronicles of San Quentin: The Biography of a Prison*. New York: David McKay Company, Inc., 1961.

Lockett v. Ohio, 438 U.S. 586 (1978).

The Los Angeles Times.

McKanna, Clare V., Jr. *Race and Homicide in Nineteenth Century California*. Reno: University of Nevada Press, 2002, 22–27.

McNulty v. California, 149 U.S. 645 (1893).

Mendyuk, Dara Bashakevitz. *Dying on Death Row in America—Public Perceptions Regarding Methods of Execution in the United States*. Master's Thesis, California State University, Fullerton, 1995.

Morales v. Hickman, et al., 415 F. Supp. 2d. 1037 (2006).

Nevada v. Gee Jon, 46 Nev. 418 (1923).

People v. Anderson, 6 Cal. 3d 628 (1972).

People v. Righthouse, 10 Cal. 2d 86 (1937).

Report of Joint Legislative Fact-Finding Committee on the Southern California Prison at Chino, March 5, 1941, James H. Phillips, Chairman. Sacramento: California State Printing Office, George H. Moore, State Printer.

The San Francisco Chronicle.

Switzer, Walter E. "Capital Punishment." *The Pacific Historian* 23, no. 4 (Winter 1979): 45–80.

Tropp v. Dulles, 356 U.S. 86 (1958).

Notes

1. *McNulty v. California*, 149 U.S. 645, at 645.
2. Lamott, Kenneth, *Chronicles of San Quentin: The Biography of a Prison* (New York: David McKay Company, Inc., 1961), p. 151.
3. "M'Nulty Must Hang," *Los Angeles Times (LAT)*, February 23, 1892, p. 3.
4. Lamott, p. 157.
5. Ibid., p. 156.
6. "Writs Granted," *LAT*, October 12, 1888, p. 5.
7. *McNulty v. California*, at 648.
8. "M'Nulty," *LAT*, February 23, 1882, p. 3.
9. "14 Convicts Pardoned by Gage," *LAT*, January 10, 1903, p. 3; "The Sheriff Sustained," *LAT*, September 17, 1892, p. 2.
10. See Clare V. McKanna Jr., *Race and Homicide in Nineteenth Century California* (University of Nevada Press, 2002), pp. 22–27.
11. Lamott, p. 156.
12. "Indian Joe: The Otay Murderer to Die at San Quentin," *LAT*, December 17, 1892, p. 2.
13. Clinton T. Duffy, *The San Quentin Story* (Garden City, N.Y.: Doubleday and Company, 1951), p. 17.
14. Lamott, pp. 159–160.
15. Ibid., p. 156.
16. "Amusements Tonight," *LAT*, March 8, 1893, p. 4.
17. "Five Times Reprieved," *LAT*, December 20, 1893, p. 2.
18. J. Grey, "For Hanging," *LAT*, p. 2.
19. Ibid.
20. "Durant Case Did Him: Ex-Juror against Hanging," *LAT*, April 17, 1901, p. 4.
21. James B. Holohan, "My San Quentin Years, Installment XIII," *LAT*, May 8, 1936, p. 7.
22. Holohan, "My San Quentin Years, Installment XII," *LAT*, May 7, 1936, p. 10.
23. Holohan, "My San Quentin Years, Installment XIII," *LAT*, May 13, 1936, p. 7.
24. Holohan, "My San Quentin Years, Installment XXII," *LAT*, May 17, 1936, p. A16.
25. Lamott, p. 161.
26. Holohan, "My San Quentin Years, Installment XXII," *LAT*, May 17, 1936, p. A16.
27. Ibid.
28. Bishop, George, *The Legal Means of Death* (Los Angeles: Sherbourne Press, Inc., 1965), p. 162.
29. Ibid.
30. *Nevada vs. Gee Jon*, 46 Nev. 418, at 437.
31. "Gas Execution Is Inaugurated," *LAT*, February 9, 1924, p. 3.
32. Holohan, "My San Quentin Years, Installment X," *LAT*, May 5, 1936, p. 15.
33. "Murderer Dies in Gas Chamber," *LAT*, November 29, 1932, p. 7.
34. Andy Hamilton, "New Design for Death," *LAT*, August 22, 1937, p. 17.
35. *Report of the Joint Legislative Fact-Finding Committee on the Southern California Prison at Chino, March 5, 1941, Assemblyman James H. Phillips, Chairman* (Sacramento: California State Printing Office, George H. Moore, State Printer), pp. 82–83.
36. Ibid., p. 83.
37. Lamott, pp. 227–28.
38. Hamilton, "New Design for Death," *LAT*, August 22, 1937, p. 17.
39. Hamilton, "The Hangman Kills Himself," *LAT*, March 27, 1937, p. 17.
40. *People vs. Righthouse*, 10 Cal. 2d 86, at 88.
41. "Man Spirited to Prison As He Admits Killing Nurse," *LAT*, May 13, 1937, p. 15.
42. "Two Slayers Die Together," *LAT*, February 19, 1937, p. 19.
43. Lamott, p. 227.
44. Hamilton, "The Hangman Kills Himself," *LAT*, March 27, 1937, p. 17.
45. "Execution Test Made with Pig," *LAT*, March 20, 1938, p. 8.
46. "Spectators Sickened As Two Die in Gas Cell," *LAT*, December 3, 1938, p. 1.
47. "Folsom Pair Executed in Gas Chamber," *LAT*, December 10, 1938, p. 1.
48. Lamott, p. 212.
49. "Folsom Pair Executed in Gas Chamber," *LAT*, December 10, 1938, p. 1.
50. "Those Gas Chamber 'Horrors,'" *LAT*, December 5, 1938, p. A4.
51. "Bill to Abolish Cal. Death Penalty Beaten," *LAT*, April 2, 1957, p. 1.
52. "The Call on Capital Punishment," *LAT*, February 26, 1960, p. B4.
53. Walter E. Switzer, "Capital Punishment," *The Pacific Historian* 23, no. 4 (Winter 1977): 47.

54. *People v. Anderson*, 6 Cal. 3d 628, p. 654.

55. *Trop v. Dulles*, 356 U.S. 86 (1958). This ruling held that the definition of the Eighth Amendment's "cruel and unusual" clause was based upon society's evolving standards.

56. Ed Meagher, "LA Death Penalty Ban Assailed by Reagan," *LAT*, February 19, 1972, p. A1.

57. "Younger Asks U.S. High Court to Nullify Ban on Death Penalty," *LAT*, April 1, 1972, p. 1.

58. *Nevada v. Gee Jon*, at 437.

59. William Endicott, "Death Penalty Approved," *LAT*, November 8, 1972, p. A1.

60. Robert Rawich, "Death Penalty OK'd but Its Use Could Be Years in the Future," *LAT*, November 9, 1972, p. A20.

61. "Our Second Defilement," *LAT*, August 14, 1977, p. D4.

62. Switzer, p. 69.

63. *Lockett v. Ohio*, 438 U.S. 586 (1978).

64. "Ruling Halts Execution," *LAT*, December 16, 2006, p. A1.

65. Ibid.

66. Paul Jacobs, "Execution by Lethal Injection OK'd," *LAT*, August 29, 1992, p. 17.

67. Vivian Berger, "Column Left," *LAT*, August 23, 1992, p. 5.

68. Mark Martin, "5 Year Term for Investigator in Forgery Case," *The San Francisco Chronicle*, May 1, 2007, p. B1.

69. Dara Bashakevitz Mendyuk, *Dying on Death Row in America—Public Perceptions Regarding Methods of Executions in the United States*, Master's Thesis, California State University, Fullerton, 1995, p. 73.

70. Ibid., p. 76.

71. *Fierro, Harris, and Ruiz v. Gomez, et al*, 865 F. Supp. 1387 (1994), p. 1415.

72. Mendyuk, p. 37.

73. "San Quentin's Execution Team Is Called Incompetent," *LAT*, November 29, 2006, p. B.2.

74. "Ruling Halts State Method of Execution," *LAT*, December 16, 2006, p. A1.

75. Sara Catania, "Will Schwarzenegger's New Death Chamber Actually Help Inmates?" http://www.salon.com (May 2, 2007).

CHAPTER 16

Capital Punishment and Executions in Montana

Ellen Baumler

ONTANA HAS had a death penalty since the first miners trickled into its newly discovered gold fields in the early 1860s. Despite a long history of capital punishment, comprehensive criminological studies have been lacking. Even the compilation of a list of executions in the state, not attempted until 1968, is problematic. The boundaries of Montana Territory's original nine counties have been carved and recarved into today's fifty-six counties. County seats also changed as boundaries and demographics shifted. State law long mandated that counties carry out the state's executions. By 1960, in fact, Montana was the only state that still allowed its executions in local venues. Because criminal cases in these counties were not indexed by type of crime, and early sheriffs did not always keep records, a comprehensive list of executions carried out in Montana can never be absolute.[1]

The state's capital punishment history must necessarily begin with a discussion of the early period of settlement, the chaotic events that precipitated many extralegal hangings, and the difficulties lawmakers faced in the turbulent formative years from the first gold rush in 1862 to statehood in 1889. Montana laws evolved slowly from a disorganized political quagmire and were not codified until 1870 and 1871, well beyond the creation of Montana Territory in 1864. Even after

the territorial laws were on the books, justice was haphazard. Montana's first settlements were wild and remote with a burgeoning population that demanded protection. This need fueled and even justified extralegal executions. It was only as the new territory matured that the legal system began to take control of capital punishment.

The summer of 1862 brought the first waves of miners to what would later become Montana Territory. The vast area was at that time part of Washington Territory. The first gold rush to Grasshopper Creek gave birth to the boom town of Bannack where four hundred to five hundred people had settled by the fall of 1862. Other smaller mining camps began to dot the countryside. As in other places across the West where there were no law enforcement personnel, miners elected officials and established "miner's courts" in these early settlements. Miners, however, established their courts, based on the California model, to decide mining-related issues and were ill-equipped to deal with the violence that characterized Montana's camps. At Gold Creek on August 26, 1862, the miner's court sentenced C. W. Spillman to death for horse stealing and quickly administered the punishment. Spillman was the first man hanged in Montana and the first of eleven men sentenced to death by a miner's court between 1862 and 1871. Spillman did not protest his sentence, and details of his hanging are not extant. But Granville Stuart, who was present, wrote:

> Justice was swift and sure in those days. There was no moving for a new trial or any of the thousand other clogs upon the wheels of justice. . . . Punishment was severe beyond all proportion to the crime, but it must be remembered that there was no recognized court in the country and the nearest jail was at Walla Walla. . . . The communities were too small and too poor to indulge in costly criminal prosecutions and hence it was advisable to inflict punishment as would strike terror to the minds of the evildoers. . . . I now think that [Spillman] was so stunned by the fearful calamity that had overtaken him that despair seized him and he thought it was useless to try to escape death. As to the letter he wrote [to his father for forgiveness] I have an indistinct impression that Brother James destroyed it for, of course, we would not send such a letter to anyone's father.[2]

Idaho Territory, created in March of 1863, encompassed western Montana's remote gold camps, but the seat of government at Lewiston across the Continental Divide was too far removed. As the rush to Alder Gulch in late spring of 1863 brought another great population wave, the miner's courts dealt with difficult problems and the unsavory element that preyed upon others' hard-earned gold dust. The miner's court sentenced a second man to hang nearly a year to the day after Spillman. Some consider the hanging of Peter Heron (or Horan) on August 25, 1863, the first "legal" hanging because it was conducted in an orderly manner with a physician present to pronounce the victim dead. Heron, who killed his mining partner, was hanged on the first gallows constructed in Montana. Bannack's Sheriff Henry Plummer constructed this hoist-type gallows of two sturdy ten-foot beams sunk into the ground with a third beam across the top. The rope was thrown over the beam and the victim dropped from a wagon.

Montana's third miner's court execution, that of George Ives on December 21, 1863, was a cornerstone event and one of the most dramatic incidents of the early settlement period. Several thousand witnessed the miner's court trial held in the main street of Nevada City in Alder Gulch. Ives, a suspected member of a dangerous gang of road agents, stood trial for the brutal murder of young Nicholas Thiebalt (Tiebolt). There were many supporters both for and against the guilty verdict, and the volatile crowd came dangerously close to exploding into violence. The prosecuting attorney, Wilbur Fisk Sanders, built a stellar career upon this case. His oratory skills and legal expertise many years later sent him to Washington, D.C., as one of Montana's first U.S. senators.

The Ives trial played out in an extraordinary manner. The miner's court judge, Dr. Don Byam, sat on a wagon. Another wagon served as a makeshift jury box. A large bonfire in the center kept the chill of the December air somewhat at bay. The jury found Ives guilty, and within the hour, willing workers converted a building frame into a makeshift gallows with a rope thrown over a beam. Spectators crowded on rooftops and thronged in the street as the executioner kicked a dry goods box out from under Ives. The conviction and immediate hanging of Ives was the catalyst that led to the forming of the original vigilantes a few days later. Miner's court hangings continued sporadically after creation of the territory until the last one in Granite County on October 31, 1871.

After the Ives hanging, the vigilantes—acting outside the law—signed an oath of secrecy and began to round up the road agents, including Sheriff Henry Plummer who they believed was the leader of the operation. The road agents terrorized the countryside with murders and robberies in Beaverhead and Madison counties. On January 10, 1864, less than a year after Sheriff Plummer built the gallows on which he hanged Peter Heron, Plummer himself swung from the same gallows along with his two deputies, Buck Stinson and Ned Ray. Several vigilantes held the rope taut as Plummer sat on the shoulders of several others who dropped him. The men hoisted up Stinson and Ray. Ray continued to struggle, his hand in the noose against his neck. He finally strangled to death when vigilantes pulled his hand away from his throat. There are still heated debates among some Montana historians regarding Plummer's guilt or innocence. The contemporary accounts from a wide variety of people who were not involved with the vigilantes provide good reasons to believe that Plummer was guilty. R. C. Rawley was the fifth and last victim of this gallows, hanged on October 30, 1864, for threatening to expose the identities of the vigilantes.

The most spectacular of these extralegal vigilante hangings, however, was a quintuple hanging on the roof beam of an unfinished building in Virginia City. On January 14, 1864, George Lane, Jack Gallagher, Frank Parrish, Haze Lyons, and Boone Helm died together in a small commercial building that still stands on Wallace Street. None of these men stood accused of murder, but rather each was found guilty of crimes associated with the robberies and other activities of the road agents. The five men were buried in the town cemetery, but because of the stigma surrounding them, the town established a second cemetery and most had their loved ones' remains removed from "Boot Hill."

The creation of Montana Territory on May 26, 1864, and the federal presence Virginia City's designation as territorial capital in 1865 brought to Alder Gulch, eventually ended the work of the original vigilantes. Their last hanging was that of

Charles Wilson on September 25, 1867, on the outskirts of town for informing road agents about the cargo and schedules of Wells Fargo's stagecoaches. The original vigilantes of Beaverhead and Madison counties hanged at least thirty-one men.

Other vigilante groups, however, continued to operate elsewhere. These extralegal groups targeted victims in many counties across the state. Some of their victims committed murder, but others were executed for offenses not outlined in the statutes. Helena in Lewis and Clark County, born of Montana's third great gold rush in 1864, saw a number of these vigilante hangings. A large Ponderosa pine, the only tree left standing after the miners denuded the countryside, served as gallows for the execution of at least a dozen men. A few of these were executed by order of the miner's court, but most were victims of a local vigilante group. The last hanging on this tree was the spectacular double execution of Arthur Compton and Joseph Wilson in 1870. A group of twelve self-proclaimed vigilantes conducted the trial in a warehouse, steps away from the legal seat of government at the Lewis and Clark County courthouse. A twenty-man jury found Compton and Wilson guilty of highway robbery and assault with the intent to commit the murder of a local rancher. Over the protests of District Attorney John Shober and District Court Judge George Symes, the jury opened the question of punishment to a throng gathered around. The crowd voted to hang the two men. The next morning, Compton and Wilson were positioned beneath the infamous tree in a Murphy wagon, the executioner placed the ropes around their necks, covered their faces with white handkerchiefs, and with a whip to the horse, the wagon lurched forward. Compton died immediately, but it took eight minutes for Wilson to strangle to death.

Hometown vigilante groups across Montana eliminated men who were certainly guilty and some who were probably innocent. The last organized vigilante hanging was that of William Rigney in Miles City, Custer County, in 1883. Accused of the attempted assault of the two daughters of a prominent Miles City resident, a newly constructed Northern Pacific train trestle at the end of the town's main street served as the gallows. By the mid-1880s, vigilante groups had mostly dispersed, but their activities remain controversial and the actions of these groups represent a painful, yet significant, period in Montana's history.

The stock-growing industry in Montana Territory became big business by the early 1880s. Vast tracts of open-range grazing land across the hills and prairies made the territory a prime target for illegal activities. Horse stealing and cattle rustling grew to epidemic proportions in 1884, prompting stockmen to take the law into their own hands. "Cowboy stranglers" executed an unofficial count of forty-seven men during this year. After 1884, no more executions have been attributed to these cowboys, but mob lynchings continued in both urban and rural settings until the last illegal execution, that of L. C. Collins at Mondak in Sheridan County in 1913. Collins, a thirty-four-year-old African American, was hanged from a telephone pole for the murders of the local sheriff and his undersheriff.

While the new territory struggled to adopt and enforce its own code of laws in the mid-1860s, officials operated under the statutes of Idaho Territory, of which Montana had most recently been part. During this disorganized period, before Montana's laws were codified in 1870 and 1871, and even after, vigilantes and miner's courts haphazardly tried and executed many men for crimes ranging from disturbing the peace to cold-blooded murder. Official records of these proceedings are lacking, but eyewitness accounts, written descriptions, newspaper coverage, and oral traditions combine to present fairly detailed

documentation of many of these events, including those outlined above. A recent comprehensive study records 174 hangings between 1862 and statehood in 1889.[3] The territorial courts carried out only 16 of these executions.

The territorial legislature passed the first laws governing the death penalty when it convened in Bannack on December 12, 1864. The first legislators defined murder under Criminal Practice Acts, "An act concerning crimes and punishment," Chap. IV, Section 15, as "the unlawful killing of a human being with malice aforethought." These first laws further state that "every person convicted of murder of the first degree shall suffer death." Sec. 23 further states that, in order to charge murder or manslaughter, "the party must die within a year and a day after the stroke was received." Chap. V, Sec. 55 defined first-degree arson as the malicious burning of a dwelling "in the night-time," where someone is known to be inside, and also carried a mandatory death penalty. Capital punishment, further defined in Chap. VIII, Sec. 90, required the death penalty in the case of the willful perjury of an individual resulting in the conviction and execution of an innocent person. "An act to regulate the proceedings in criminal cases in the courts of justice in the Territory of Montana," Chap. I, Sec. 219, required that punishment be carried out in the county where the crime occurred and specified "hanging by the neck" as the method of death. Sec. 222 further mandated that the execution take place in a private enclosure as near the jail as possible in the presence of the sheriff, the judge, the prosecuting attorney, the clerk of the court, two physicians, and twelve invited citizens.[4]

Because Montana's territorial statutes specified that county sheriffs carry out the death penalty in the county where the crime was committed, it was the practice of one county to borrow another county's gallows. From Montana's first legal hanging in 1875 to its last hanging in

1943, lawmen constructed a total of twenty-two gallows. Of these, six gallows—or their essential mechanisms—served at hangings in more than one county, earning the epithet "galloping gallows." Three of the six were of the trap type and three were of the jerk type. These galloping gallows altogether served as the death instruments in forty-seven legal executions during the territorial period and after statehood; some of them served the purpose in both.[5]

Galloping gallows number one was a trap-type gallows. The case involved the murder of an Austrian-born charcoal burner on his property ten miles west of Helena in Lewis and Clark County. He was known to keep cash on the premises. Discovery of the mutilated corpse of Franz Warl, hands tied behind him and the cord wrapped around his neck, led to the arrest of William Wheatley. While in the Lewis and Clark County jail, Wheatley gave evidence implicating Fred Shaffer and William Sterres and testified in court against Sterres. Shaffer escaped the authorities but Sterres, who received a second trial, was later hanged for the crime. When the jury rendered its guilty verdict in the Wheatley case, because of Wheatley's willing testimony against the other two men, the jury recommended life in prison. But according to territorial law, the judge had no authority to order clemency. Chief Justice Decius Wade presiding on the bench had no choice but to pronounce the mandatory death sentence. He could only pass the jury's recommendation to the governor who could commute the sentence. Governor Benjamin Potts, however, chose not to do so.

Legendary lawman Sheriff Seth Bullock was the arresting officer and the official upon whom it fell to conduct Wheatley's hanging. The gallows he built for Wheatley was a simple trap-type gallows, with two posts about fifteen feet high, a platform, and a crossbeam some seven feet from the platform. A rope secured the hinged trapdoor mechanism directly beneath the hangman's noose. Cutting the rope allowed the floor to give way, dropping the victim. This type of scaffold gallows was common across the West. Wheatley's hanging, pointedly scheduled in August on Friday the thirteenth, presented some logistical problems. The scaffold was quite high, and Sheriff Bullock realized he could not carry out the letter of the law that prohibited uninvited citizens from witnessing hangings. He built a tall fence around the scaffold, but buildings crowded around courthouse square and it was impossible to enforce privacy. So Sheriff Bullock changed the time specified in the death warrant from midday to midnight. At the stroke of 12:00 A.M., the death warrant was read and Father Lawrence Palladino, a Catholic priest, led Wheatley to the courtyard. At 12:20, the anonymous executioner secured the noose and placed the black hood over Wheatley's head. Even with the change in time, a thousand spectators crowded on the surrounding rooftops to witness the hanging by the light of the moon. Subsequent preparations for Montana hangings included the construction of a fence around the scaffold to prevent, or at least demonstrate an attempt to prevent, public viewing of the execution.

William Sterres, whose trial preceded Wheatley's, received a second trial on a technicality. When the jury pronounced him guilty in the first trial, the verdict simply read that he was guilty, but failed to specify of what crime: first- or second-degree murder or manslaughter. Chief Justice Wade rendered the Supreme Court decision that Sterres was entitled to a new trial. There was some speculation that Justice Wade made this decision because he thought more evidence might come out in a new trial and aid in the capture of Fred Shaffer, the third accomplice. The second trial took a very short time, and the jury came back with a first-degree murder verdict in less than ten minutes. As in William Wheatley's hanging, Sheriff

Bullock feared too many witnesses, so he conducted the business at midnight on October 28, 1875. Sterres was hanged on the same gallows as Wheatley, but his body convulsed violently and it took him eight minutes to die of strangulation.

Madison County officials borrowed the trap mechanism from Lewis and Clark County's galloping gallows number one for the execution of François Joseph Robert at Virginia City on October 31, 1878; this was the county's first legal hanging and the first example of one county borrowing another's gallows. The circumstances were unusual because Robert, a prospector who murdered his partner, committed the crime on the Crow Indian Reservation. The trial was at Virginia City in the Madison County courthouse and conducted by the United States government. The jury found Robert guilty and he was the only man executed in Montana Territory by federal order. Madison County borrowed only the trapdoor mechanism and fitted it to a scaffold built at the rear of the courthouse. Officials returned the mechanism where it served twice more in Lewis and Clark County for the hangings of Peter Pelkey in 1881 and Henry Furhmann in 1883.

The simple hoist-type gallows used at Bannack gave way to the more sophisticated trapdoor type gallows and the more economical jerk type. Both continued in use into the twentieth century. The first use of the jerk-type gallows was for the hanging of John Douglas at Virginia City in 1881. This type of gallows utilized a heavy weight. The release of the weight jerked the victim into the air, breaking his neck either in the initial jerk or in the resulting fall. Douglas committed one of the most horrendous crimes the territory had seen to date, shooting Mrs. Celestia Alice Earp as she rode atop the stage from Red Bluff to Virginia City. Mrs. Earp had spurned Douglas's advances and was fleeing the territory when he caught up with the stage and emptied his Winchester into her. On the morning of May 27, 1881, officials led Douglas to the small enclosure constructed around the scaffold in the courtyard of the Madison County courthouse. The rituals of placing the noose and hood completed, the sheriff gave the signal and the weight fell, jerking Douglas into the air. Four minutes later his pulse had ceased.

Galloping gallows number two, a jerk type constructed in 1887 for the execution of Thomas Harding, was the second use of this method in Montana. A 290-pound box of sheet tin originally served as the weight. Harding received the death penalty for the murder of a stage driver during the attempted robbery of a stage carrying six passengers and silver bullion. The execution was the first legal hanging in Beaverhead County where nine vigilante, miner's court, and mob hangings had previously occurred. Harding's execution illustrates the lax extension of the law regarding witnesses. It was standard practice to send invitations to all the county sheriffs in Montana, but there were many more witnesses than the twelve prescribed by law. Some one hundred sheriffs from Montana and Idaho territories were present at this execution.

After several failed attempts at statehood, lawmakers of Montana Territory began to prepare for the final and successful bid that came when Congress passed the Organic Act in 1889. Compilation of the statutes in 1888 was part of this preparation. At that time, the compilation of the statues pertaining to capital punishment reiterated the definition of murder in the first degree and death by hanging as the punishment. The statutes further specified the county where the crime took place or the county attached for judicial purposes as the place of execution. The law placed no temporal limit on prosecution for murder or manslaughter, allowing it to commence at any time after commission of the crime.[6]

The case of George Bryson serves as an interesting example of one of the last hangings before statehood. Bryson stood accused of murdering his mistress, Anna Lundstrom, in Lewis and Clark County on August 21, 1888. He bashed her head in, dragged the body with a leather strap, and threw it into a prospector's hole. Her suspicious disappearance prompted authorities to arrest Bryson. He was about to be released for lack of evidence when a miner, determined to earn the three-hundred-dollar reward Helena's mayor offered for the discovery of the body, found Anna's corpse. This was such a heinous crime rumors of a lynching flew around Helena. S. A. Baillet was Bryson's attorney at the time of arraignment, but several weeks later, voters elected Baillet county attorney. He could not prosecute someone he had once represented, so the county had to hire special prosecutor William Wallace Jr. Granted a change of venue, the jury convicted Bryson in Boulder. Since the trial took place in Jefferson County, the hanging took place there. Bryson became the first man hanged in Jefferson County on August 9, 1889. The jerk-type galloping gallows number three upon which Bryson died had been used twice before, first at Dillon and then at Helena.

Two weeks after Bryson's execution, the hanging of W. H. Roberts took place at Butte on August 23, 1889, for the murder of J. W. "Long Tex" Crawford. Galloping gallows number four, a jerk type employed for Roberts's execution, had been used the previous year at Deer Lodge for the hanging of Martin Luther Scott on February 17, 1888. Roberts's was the last hanging before statehood, achieved on November 8, 1889. Thereafter Montana's territorial laws regarding capital punishment continued to suffice unchanged for decades. Hangings continued as prescribed under territorial law as the only method of execution allowed, with the execution held in the county where the crime was committed or where judicial action occurred.

The same jerk-type galloping gallows number three that dispatched George Bryson was one of Montana's most famous. It went on to serve seven times more at Boulder, Fort Benton, Helena, and Choteau before its retirement in 1900. On April 6, 1896, William Biggerstaff was its seventh victim. The forty-two-year-old black man murdered a popular professional boxer in a dispute over a white woman. The case brought Helena's black community to the forefront as many advocated clemency. The victim's mother and her family even visited Biggerstaff in his jail cell. Sheriff Henry Jurgens issued invitations to the double hanging of Biggerstaff and William Gay, convicted of an unrelated crime around the same time. Gay's execution on the same gallows, however, was delayed until June 8. A double invitation served for both and was unique. Along with pictures of both men was a somber, poetic verse composed by the sheriff himself.

The most famous of Montana's traveling death machines, galloping gallows number four with its 350-pound weight, served at thirteen executions, more than any other Montana gallows. Miles Fuller was one of its later victims. His execution on May 18, 1906, for the grisly murder of Henry Gallahan received much publicity. The two old-time prospectors had long been sworn enemies. Fuller claimed that Gallahan had laced his flour with powdered glass and his sugar with strychnine, but witnesses testified that it was the other way around. Gallahan had been shot in the head and his throat slashed from ear to ear. Fuller never admitted guilt.

Officials assembled the already veteran galloping gallows number four in Butte's jail yard in view of Fuller's cell. A member of the sheriff's force prepared the regulation hangman's rope, ordered from Chicago, and tied the noose with the required nine wraps and proper knot. Despite the fear some had for Fuller, he was a pitiful figure, elderly and frightened. He went to the gallows wearing his old, tattered hat, while a large crowd, some having scaled walls and climbed rooftops, tried to get a view. Only those with invitations, as the law prescribed, were inside the yard. Fuller's death took only two minutes from the jailhouse door to the end.

The career of the famous galloping gallows number four was not yet over. It was the instrument in the two unusual and famous hangings in 1908 and 1909 of George Rock and W. A. Hayes, inmates at the Montana State Prison at Deer Lodge who staged an escape. In their bid for freedom, they fatally slit Deputy James Robinson's throat with a pocketknife and severely slashed Warden Frank Conley before officials subdued them. Conley's wounds required more than one hundred stitches. Both Rock and Hayes suffered gunshot wounds, but Conley carefully nursed them back to health so that they could take their punishment and serve as examples to the other prisoners.

Both men faced first-degree murder charges. Rock pled guilty and asked the judge to sentence him to death and get it over as quickly as possible. Thus Rock received his death sentence without a jury trial and was the first of the two to hang. Hayes, also sentenced to death, appealed to the Montana Supreme Court. The higher court upheld his sentence, but because of the delays his hanging took place nearly a year after Rock's. The two men had to face the gallows at Deer Lodge in Powell County where they committed the crime. Rather than hang at the Powell County jail, however, Rock and Hayes kept their appointments with the hangman in the yard of the prison. The prison wall provided the enclosure as the law prescribed. Invitations went out to all county sheriffs twice: once for the hanging of George Rock on June 16, 1908, and again for the hanging of W. A. Hayes on April 2, 1909. These were the only two hangings carried out at the Montana State Prison. According to prison lore, when Conley pulled the trap to launch Rock into eternity, the warden hissed, "Vengeance is mine!"

The noose malfunctioned and failed to tighten

around Rock's neck. The initial jerk when the weight dropped rendered him unconscious, but his neck did not break and he slowly strangled. Hayes's death was even worse. Again, the jerk failed to break his neck. Witnesses saw Hayes clench and unclench his fists several times and twice he drew up his knees, his chest heaving as he struggled for air. Although the executions took place inside the prison walls, the only witnesses were officials and invited guests. No prisoners witnessed either hanging. In each case, after doctors pronounced death, inmates brought the coffin from the prison carpenter shop and helped place the body in it. This same gallows went long unused until 1922 when officials at Missoula brought its weight, trap, and pulleys out of retirement to serve for the execution of Joseph Vuckovich. He was the thirteenth, and last, person executed on galloping gallows number four.

The largest gallows constructed in Montana was the death instrument for four men hanged simultaneously at Missoula on December 12, 1890. The four Indians executed at this hanging were the most men to die together in a legal execution in Montana. Sheriff William Houston of Missoula County obtained plans for the gallows from Cook County, Illinois, authorities who conducted a quadruple hanging in 1887. The Cook County sheriff also gave Sheriff Houston the Cook County hangman's four previously used ropes. All four men, convicted of murdering six white men, died on the huge trap-type gallows. Pierre Paul, Lala See, Antley, and Pascale admitted guilt in the three separate incidents, but they viewed their crimes as retaliation for whites killing Indians. White man's whiskey also played a role in some of their crimes. The trials and executions form a chapter darker than most in the state's history of capital punishment. Pomp and circumstance befitting a great civic event accompanied these legal executions. After the hangings, the headline in the *Missoulian*, December 19, 1890, read:

DEATH'S DECREE
THE MURDERED WHITES AVENGED
THE DEVIL HAS HIS DUE
Pierre Paul, Lala See, Pascale, and Antley are
good Indians now.
They were hanged this morning.

The headline set the tone for eight pages of the most minute details of each of the four hangings and other aspects of the event. The gallows, rebuilt to a smaller scale, served for one more hanging, that of John Burns at Missoula, exactly two years later on December 16, 1892.

On October 6, 1916, a gang of seven black railroad workers boarded a freight train at Nihill. As the train pulled away and gathered speed, all seven pulled out weapons and confronted three white men who were riding in the car. During the ensuing robbery, the men shot all three victims; one of them died. Authorities arrested all seven gang members. Three of them—Henry Hall, Leslie Fahley, and Harrison Gibson—received the death penalty for the murder of Michael Freeman. The case caused discussions about capital punishment because the three black men were uneducated and ignorant. Some advocated executive clemency, but Governor Sam Stewart, who was a strong proponent of capital punishment, refused to commute the sentences. He carefully reviewed the cases and concluded that although the three white victims were not specific targets, the men had armed themselves with the intent to commit robbery. While some believed race played a role in the sentencing, the governor concluded the trial was fair and that the crime recalled the days when gangs of road agents preyed upon travelers. The similar circumstances demanded like punishment.

The triple hanging took place at White Sulphur Springs in Meagher County on February 16, 1917. There had been no legal hanging in Montana since 1909, and so there was no working gallows

available. County officials brought an unused 1884 scaffold out of storage. Using its trap mechanism, they constructed a gallows inside a cavernous county-owned barn. There was further public outcry because the barn sat a hundred yards from the public school, and the hangings were to take place during the morning when school was in session. However, the three simultaneous executions took place as scheduled. Among the forty witnesses was one of the three robbery victims. In 1975, the barn with its gallows intact was removed to Nevada City, Montana, where it is on display.

In the first decades of the twentieth century, several counties built new jail facilities incorporating gallows into their designs. When Gallatin County, for example, built a new jail at Bozeman in 1911, it included a built-in gallows. Located in a small room with a high ceiling, the platform was at the head of a concrete staircase with railing around it and a steel trap in the floor. The new gallows stood idle until the hanging of Seth Danner on July 18, 1924. According to tradition, the executioner was anonymous. But to insure anonymity, two sets of ropes led from the gallows but only one was actually attached to the trap. At the signal, both men cut their ropes, but neither knew which one had actually sprung the trap and the identity of the real executioner was unknown even to the executioners themselves. This former jail now houses a museum and the gallows remains intact.

Butte in Silver Bow County is credited with more legal hangings than any other county. The tenth and last, the execution of Anthony Vettere on October 1, 1926, was the most spectacular. Vettere received the death penalty for a shooting rampage in Butte that left three men dead and eighteen children fatherless. Prior to the crimes, Vettere had lived with the Joseph Ciccarelli family. Ciccarelli took Vettere to court for taking liberties with one of his young daughters, and the judge ordered Vettere to post bond or leave Butte.

On November 22, 1925, Vettere returned to Butte and ambushed Ciccarelli and his friend Antone Favaro. In his haste to flee the scene, Vettere encountered John Deranja, a night watchman on his way home from work, and shot him dead, too, likely mistaking him for a policeman. Vettere was eventually convicted only of the Favaro murder because the dying man named him as his killer.

On the day of the execution, Vettere went berserk in the jail as officers tried to take him from his cell to the scaffold. Screeching like a fiend, he attacked deputies with a pipe ripped from the shower room and a knife made from a spoon. In an effort to subdue him, deputies filled the entire cellblock full of tear gas, subjecting themselves and the other prisoners to its effects. Deputies finally overwhelmed Vettere, strapped his arms and legs, and dragged him into the jail yard where the scaffold awaited. As Vettere struggled, he swore venomous oaths, promising to return for vengeance even as deputies put the noose in place. His was Montana's only legal execution that required restraining the condemned.

The trap-type galloping gallows number five, assembled for the hanging of Anthony Vettere, previously served for the triple hanging of Sherman Powell, Frank Fisher, and John O'Neill in Butte on January 14, 1918. Butte building contractor Michael D. O'Connell built this state-of-the-art gallows so that it could be disassembled in seconds and stored or shipped. It stood above a concrete pit ten feet deep and sixteen feet square. The condemned stood on the crack where two hinged doors joined. At the touch of a lever, the doors opened and the men fell, theoretically breaking their necks so they would not strangle. Powell fainted before the executioner pulled the lever, and the other two had to wait several minutes while deputies revived him. Next to die on the new gallows were Monte Harris and William Harris. These men, not related to each other, murdered a hotel desk clerk during a robbery.

They died together on this gallows in 1923. Galloping gallows number five traveled out of Silver Bow County to serve at two hangings, that of Roy Walsh at Boulder in 1925 and at the hanging of its last victim, George Hoffman, at Choteau in 1933.

The hanging of W. Lee Simpson at Rygate on December 30, 1939, was the next to last in Montana. Sentenced to death for the murder of Undersheriff Arthur "Buzz" Burford on April 14, 1938, Simpson was the seventh victim to die on this trap-type scaffold, galloping gallows number six. It had already traveled in the eastern part of the state for use at Forsythe, twice in Hysham, twice at Miles City, and once at Columbus. It was set up inside the Golden Valley County jail for Simpson's execution and was the state's last galloping gallows.

The last execution by hanging in Montana occurred on September 10, 1943, when Philip J. Coleman Jr. was put to death at Missoula on the last gallows constructed in the state. Coleman bludgeoned Carl Pearson to death and fatally stabbed his wife with a butcher knife during an early morning robbery at the couple's home in Lothrop at the western edge of Missoula County. The Pearsons' seven-year-old son discovered the bodies. Judge Albert Besancon sentenced Coleman to death for the first-degree murder of Mrs. Pearson without a jury trial. His execution took place only forty-eight days after sentencing. This was the shortest amount of time between sentencing and hanging in the state. While incarcerated awaiting the execution, the twenty-five-year-old black man claimed to have killed twenty-three other persons in other states since he was fourteen, and named eight of his victims. The hanging took place inside the Missoula County jail on September 19, 1943. The trap-type gallows is today stored at the Fort Missoula Historical Museum.

In 1921, legislators amended the law concerning capital punishment for the first time since the creation of Montana Territory. Where death by hanging had previously been the only punishment allowed for murder in the first degree, Chap. 16 Sec. 10957 RCM (1921) added life in prison as an option. A life sentence could be imposed if it were left up to the court or at the discretion of the jury. The laws, recodified in 1947, reiterated hanging as the means and the county where the trial took place as the location. Chap. 23 Sec. 95-2303 RCM (1947) provided the death penalty for first-degree murder, kidnapping, and treason.

The Forty-eighth Legislature amended Section 46-19-103 MCA (1983) to allow hanging or lethal injection at the election of the defendant and to eliminate county executions, redefining the location of the fulfillment of the death penalty as within the confines of the Montana State Prison. The law further charged the warden to find a suitable place within the confines of the prison and to take care of the details. These changes, in effect, reflect an overhaul of Montana's death penalty.

These several significant changes in Montana's death penalty laws took place after the state's last hanging in 1943, but the new legislation was untried until the execution of Duncan Peder McKenzie Jr. on May 10, 1995. McKenzie was put to death twenty years after his 1975 sentencing for the aggravated kidnapping, torture, and homicide of Conrad-area teacher Lana Harding. The Montana Supreme Court upheld McKenzie's conviction and rejected his appeals (*State Ex Rel McKenzie v. District Court* 12797). McKenzie claimed an error during his court trial. Twice the United States Supreme Court referred petitions for certiorari to the Montana Supreme Court. Upon the fourth review on appeal in 1980, the Montana Supreme Court ruled that the error was harmless beyond a reasonable doubt (*McKenzie v. Osborne* 81-110). McKenzie then unsuccessfully attempted three federal habeas petitions; the last was dismissed on the eve of his execution (*State v. McKenzie* 95-161).

Montana's Governor Marc Racicot carefully considered McKenzie's petition for clemency, waded through piles of legal documents, and sought extensive counsel from every conceivable secular and spiritual entity. Governor Racicot, a devout Catholic, concluded that religious dogma does allow for the death penalty in delineated circumstances. McKenzie's refusal to admit guilt led the governor to question the man's sincerity in asking for clemency. A converted house trailer parked at the Montana State Prison at Deer Lodge became Montana's death chamber. The trailer allowed mobility should there be a future need to convey it to the Montana women's prison in Billings.

Wearing orange prison overalls, McKenzie had no last words. As he lay on a gurney, McKenzie became the first in Montana to die of lethal injection on May 10, 1995.

When the 1997 legislature further amended 46-19-103 MCA to eliminate hanging as a form of execution in Montana, Terry Allen Langford had already been on "death row"—a symbolic term as there has never been a formally designated "death row" in the Montana State Prison—for nine years. He received the death penalty in Powell County for the kidnapping and brutal slayings of Edward "Ned" and Celene Blackwood at their ranch near Ovando in 1988. The Montana Supreme Court reviewed and affirmed these convictions (*State v. Langford* 89-255).

After two unsuccessful petitions for post-conviction relief, the district court set Langford's execution for January 17, 1992. Langford chose hanging as the method of death, but then moved for the district court to declare hanging cruel and unusual punishment and a violation of the Eighth Amendment to the U.S. Constitution. The court declared the position moot since Langford himself elected the method. The Supreme Court agreed (*State v. Langford* 92-098). Langford persisted, however, petitioning the United States

District Court, District of Montana, for a writ of habeas corpus that eventually went to the United States Supreme Court (*State v. Langford* 92-098 and 93-368). During these proceedings, the legislature removed hanging as an option. The Eighth Amendment angle became moot and Langford withdrew it from his petition for writ of certiorari to the Supreme Court. The court denied Langford's petition on October 6, 1997.

With the signature of the governor on March 19, 1997, the amended 46-19-103(3) MCA provides lethal injection as the only means of execution and hanging thereby passed into the annals of the state's history. Langford argued that the amending of the law deprived him of death by hanging and the final opportunity to avoid the death penalty. If the Supreme Court had agreed that hanging was cruel and unusual punishment, the law would not have allowed his execution. Langford, also convicted of the murder of an inmate during a riot at the Montana State Prison in 1991, lost this argument and became the second person in Montana to die by lethal injection in the converted house trailer on February 24, 1998.

The cruel and unusual punishment argument again surfaced in Montana in 2006 with the impending execution of David Thomas Dawson. Dawson kidnapped and killed Monica and David Rodstein, along with their eleven-year-old-son, Andrew, in a Billings motel room in 1986; police rescued their fifteen-year-old daughter, Amy, who survived the attack. Dawson fought his conviction for years, but gave up the fight in 2004 to become a willing participant in carrying out his death sentence (*State v. Dawson* 03-577).

A month before Dawson's scheduled execution, the American Civil Liberties Union of Montana led a coalition arguing that the state's method of administering lethal injection was cruel and unusual punishment. The law, 46-19-103(6) MCA (2007), stipulates that the executioner need not be a physician, registered nurse, or licensed practical nurse but only someone selected by the warden and trained to administer a lethal dose. The dissenting groups claimed that the lethal substance, if improperly administered, could cause excruciating pain and thus violate the U.S. and Montana Constitutions. The Montana attorney general decided, however, that there was no indication that lethal injection had caused pain and that the groups had nothing personally at stake. They thus had no reason to be involved. Dawson wanted the execution to go forward and not to do so would infringe upon his constitutional rights. The courts had no right to infringe on Dawson's rights in the attempt to uphold the concerns of others. Dawson was executed by lethal injection on August 11, 2006.

Montana has legally executed seventy-five individuals since Montana Territory carried out its first hanging in 1875. Of those executed, 23 percent have been minorities. As of January 2007, there are two men on Montana's symbolic "death row." The Montana legislature considered abolishment of the death penalty in 2007, with the passage of a repeal bill, SB 306 in the Montana Senate, but the legislation died in State House committee by a single vote.

Remnants of Montana's violent past are scattered about the state in the form of gallows on display in small museums. The most dramatic example sits in the Old Prison Museum at Deer Lodge in the burned-out W. A. Clark Theatre. The Ryegate gallows used in the hanging in 1939 of W. Lee Simpson is on public display. Its symbolic thirteen steps to the platform and the crossbeam with its dangling noose are chilling examples of western justice and a reminder of how it was done during most of Montana's history.

Ellen Baumler is interpretive historian at the Montana Historical Society and author of *Dark Spaces: Montana's Historic Penitentiary at Deer Lodge* (University of New Mexico Press, 2008) and *Spirit Tailings: Ghost Tales from Virginia City, Butte, and Helena* (2002); *Beyond Spirit Tailings: Montana's Mysteries, Ghosts, and Haunted Places* (2005); and *Girl from the Gulches: The Story of* *Mary Ronan* (2003), published by the Montana Historical Society Press; and dozens of articles on various topics including violence and prostitution in the American West.

For Further Reading

Allen, Frederick. *A Decent and Orderly Lynching: The Montana Vigilantes*. Norman: University of Oklahoma Press, 2004.

"Death Row Inmate Duncan McKenzie Jr. Executed." *Helena Independent Record*, May 10, 1995.

Donovan, Tom. *Hanging Around the Big Sky: The Unofficial Guide to Lynching, Strangling and Legal Hangings*. Great Falls, Montana: Portage Meadows Publishing, 2007.

http://www.clarkprosecutor.org/html/death/US/dawson 1039.htm, accessed 10/13/07.

McKee, Jennifer. "Judge to Rule Today on Dawson Execution Appeal." *Helena Independent Record*, August 10, 2006.

Raffety, Robert O. *The History and Theory of Capital Punishment in Montana*. Unpublished Thesis, University of Montana, 1968.

Notes

1. Robert O. Raffety, *The History and Theory of Capital Punishment in Montana*, unpublished master's thesis, University of Montana, 1968, pp. 4–7, discusses the difficulties in analyzing and compiling these statistics. He notes that cases are filed in their respective counties only by their titles, The State of Montana v. The Defendant. The list of hangings he compiled for this study was the first of its kind in Montana.

2. Granville Stuart, *Forty Years on the Frontier* (Cleveland: Arthur H. Clark Co., 1925), p. 221.

3. Tom Donovan, *Hanging Around the Big Sky: The Unofficial Guide to Lynching, Strangling and Legal Hangings* (Great Falls, Montana: Portage Meadows Publishing, 2007), pp. 597–99.

4. *Acts, Resolutions and Memorials, of the Territory of Montana, Passed by the First Legislative Assembly* (Virginia City, Montana Territory: D.W. Tilton & Co., 1866), pp. 178–180, 187, 250.

5. Donovan, 540.

6. *Compiled Statutes of Montana* (Helena, Montana: Journal Publishing Company, 1888), pp. 409–410, 438, 504, 505.

CHAPTER 17

The Death Penalty in Arizona and New Mexico

Daniel Stackhouse

Introduction

T HE UNITED States purchased much of its modern southwest as a part of the Treaty of Guadalupe Hidalgo (1848), which officially ended the Mexican War. Two of the territories carved from this Mexican cession were Arizona and New Mexico. For the remainder of the nineteenth century, both territories served as home to much of what became associated with the Old West. The Southwest's desert geography and weather, cattle ranches and cattle drives, and lawmen and lawbreakers were all staples of the image of the American West that were passed down to the present in novels, movies, and tourist attractions.

However, the Old West in general and Arizona and New Mexico in particular were also the scene of many developments in American law. The rapid expansion of the United States after the Civil War concluded in 1865 often left settlers and towns years ahead of the arrival of traditional institutions of law and order such as legislatures, courts, and jails.[1] This fostered an environment where ingenuity, creativity, and spontaneity in dealing with crime and punishment were inevitable and even necessary. A region that offered land, gold and silver, and freedom, the West proved welcoming to the law-minded and otherwise. When confronted with lawlessness, the essentially law-abiding majority of farmers, ranchers, miners, and other settlers of the Old West attempted to re-create the legal system of the East.

One aspect of this system was the death penalty. Although prosecutors had often sought capital punishment during the years of Mexican rule (1821–1846), the Mexican government never executed anyone for murder in New Mexico[2] (which included Arizona at that time). Between 1821 when Mexico won its independence from Spain and 1846 when the United States took control of the territory, the only executions were for an insurrection in 1837.[3] At least sixty-two legal executions took place under U.S. territorial rule.[4] Americans would not hesitate to use the death penalty to help bring law and order to a dangerous land.

Arizona

The Territorial Period, 1846–1912

General Stephen Watts Kearny entered Santa Fe in the fall of 1846 during the Mexican War. He then set up a provisional government, and annexed the Mexican province of New Mexico for the United States. This included what is today Arizona. The war ended in 1848 and the U.S. established a territorial government for New Mexico in 1850. Arizona was merely an unknown and sparsely populated part of western New Mexico until the federal government built Fort Yuma, Fort Buchanan, Fort Breckinridge, Fort Defiance, and Fort Mohave to protect travelers from Indian attacks.[5]

With the reopening of silver mines at Tubac, the region's population began to climb. In 1860 citizens of Tubac, Tucson, and Mesilla established the provisional Territory of Arizona due to their belief that they were not being properly represented at Santa Fe, New Mexico's territorial capital. The following year the territory joined the Confederacy during the American Civil War. However, mining interests pushed for a bill creating the Territory of Arizona which President Lincoln signed on February 24, 1863. Prescott became the capital and the legislature adopted the Howell Code, a body of laws combining Mexican, Californian, and New York laws, and named after the Chief Justice of Arizona.[6]

According to the territorial laws of Arizona, the county sheriff was responsible for carrying out a death sentence. *The Compiled Laws of the Territory of Arizona* (1871) stated that after a judge had decided upon the death penalty for a convict, he would sign a death warrant attested to by the clerk of the district court, and have it delivered to the sheriff. The sentence had to be carried out between thirty and sixty days afterward. The law also stipulated that the prisoner should be hanged "by the neck until he be dead." The sheriff's fee for his service ranged from fifteen dollars in 1846 to one hundred in 1890.[7]

The sheriff was also responsible for the preparations leading up to the execution. This included maintaining an Old West Era "death row" to house and feed the prisoner before carrying out the sentence. The sheriff assigned a guard to watch the

condemned man in a cell separate from other prisoners. He also found carpenters to construct the scaffold and gallows.[8]

For the hangings, Arizona sometimes utilized one of the newer techniques called the "jerk plan" instead of the more traditional trapdoor in the floor. The method of gallows construction featured two upright beams with one cross beam. A noose hung from the center of the crossbeam by a pulley, and the noose's rope was run along the beam and fed through another pulley. From there the rope was attached to a four-hundred-pound weight. A second rope held the weight approximately six feet in the air before being cut. This would cause the weight to drop, pulling the rope through the two pulleys, jerking the prisoner in the air and usually breaking his neck, but occasionally strangling him to death.[9]

One of the first known legal hangings in the Arizona Territory took place on May 3, 1873, when Manuel Fernandez was executed in Yuma County.[10] When Fernandez was sentenced he boasted to Sheriff Francis H. Goodwin: "What an idea! Just imagine for a moment me being suspended by the neck! What a beautiful picture I'd make!"[11] However, Fernandez lost his bravado as his judgment day neared. When the sheriff placed a black cap over his head, the condemned prisoner simply uttered, "Ah! What a disgrace this is."[12]

Sheriffs sometimes tried to make a prisoner's stay on death row more pleasant. This included providing inmates with food, drink, playing cards, and musical instruments. In 1884 Sheriff Jerome Ward gave four prisoners sentenced to death in Bisbee "oysters and other delicacies," as well as allowed them to approach the scaffold without being shackled or handcuffed.[13] Sheriffs often found the "deathwatch" unpleasant and revealed a remarkable amount of sympathy for their condemned charges. Efforts at easing a doomed convict's time on death row included attempting to meet the last requests of condemned men as often as possible, and on at least one occasion even providing for some "female companionship."[14]

The unpleasantness of deathwatch duty actually led some sheriffs to avoid performing executions. According to Arizona territorial law, if the sheriff received the consent of the district judge, he could gather citizens to form a jury to determine a death row prisoner's sanity. If the jury decided the inmate was mentally ill, the sheriff would suspend the sentence. Pima County Sheriff Frank Murphy believed that Teodoro Elias, who was convicted of murdering a Tucson policeman, was deranged. Acting Governor W. F. Nichols assembled several doctors who told District Judge George R. Davis and the sheriff that Elias was indeed out of his mind. The governor then commuted his sentence to life in prison. The public apparently did not share the sheriff's concern and compassion for Elias as they failed to reelect Murphy.[15]

Despite its reputation for being violent and brutal, the Old West maintained the principle held in the rest of the country that women should not be executed. Although women were often convicted of murder by district courts, governors nearly just as often commuted the sentences. Another way women could escape the gallows was if they were judged insane. In addition, pregnancy could save a condemned woman's life. The sheriff was authorized by statute to have a doctor examine a woman if he thought she was expecting.[16]

When a judge sentenced Dolores Moore to death in 1869 for murdering her husband, it set off a debate in Arizona between the Tucson *Arizonan* and the Prescott *Weekly Arizona Miner*. The editor of the Tucson paper believed Moore deserved the ultimate penalty, while his counterpart in Prescott thought that executing a woman was disgraceful. Meanwhile, the condemned Mrs. Moore sat in the Tucson jail under the watchful eye of Sheriff Peter Brady. Eventually the governor commuted her sentence to life.[17]

At least in the early territorial period, executions were often open to the public. While most had a more distant view, a fortunate few received special invitation cards from the sheriff to get an up-and-close look at a prisoner's last moments and final punishment. Sheriffs had a lot of discretion in deciding upon a place of execution. Arizona state law only mandated that the hangings had to be "within the walls or yard of a jail, or some convenient private place in the county."[18]

Although the sheriff could attempt to regulate the size of the audience, sometimes people came up with ingenious ideas to catch a glimpse of an execution. Approximately a thousand spectators were present at an 1884 Tombstone execution of four condemned murderers from Bisbee.[19] However, the sheriff had to restrict many more from the courtyard. Those left out then attempted to view the event from a nearby lot where some entrepreneurs had built a grandstand and sold spots to folks wanting to have a look. Seeing this as an unseemly attempt to make a profit, outraged citizens tore the stands down.[20]

Even in the Old West, the death penalty could be controversial. Some desired revenge for crimes and were also curious to see a just punishment meted out. Others were concerned that the public executions supported by some members of the public and even some sheriffs would negatively affect how the rest of the country viewed the territories, especially when it came time to seek official statehood. Many journalists as well as sheriffs were disgusted and tired of public curiosity. Gradually, sheriffs such as Maricopa County's Carl F. Hayden and Cochise County's Jack F. White garnered support for moving executions away from the county seats and to the territorial prison at Florence. With the prospect of statehood, public support for the spectacles also gradually waned.[21]

However, the controversy surrounding the death penalty was not about its morality as a means of punishing crime and restoring justice. At issue was the way the executions were conducted. The American West was often very dangerous due to Indian attacks against fragile settlements on the frontier. Perhaps even more of a danger was the criminal element often fleeing to the West to escape punishment or in search of easy takings from mostly law-abiding settlers. The use of the death penalty and even public attendance at such events could make a community feel both secure and unified.[22]

As Arizona grew, so did its criminal justice system. Construction of the state's first territorial prison began in 1875. The Yuma Territorial Prison opened the following year and housed inmates until 1909. For the next thirty-three years over 3,000 prisoners were held at Yuma, 111 of whom died. Many of those were buried in the prison graveyard. Tuberculosis caused one third of the deaths, but typhus, scarlet fever, and smallpox were also responsible for prisoner fatalities.[23]

The Yuma prison became notorious for its terrible conditions and severe discipline. One of the worst punishments was the Dark Cell or "snake den," a ten-foot-by-ten-foot room dug into a hillside and containing an iron cage with only a small ventilation shaft for light and air. Prison overcrowding was also a problem, eventually causing the prison to close in 1909. It is now a state historical park and the Arizona Department of Corrections asserts that its cruel reputation is totally unwarranted.[24]

In 1908 another prison opened at Florence, replacing the Yuma facility.[25] One of the features of the new prison was a scaffold with a trap door through which hanged prisoners fell. The first execution at Florence was in 1910 when Jose Lopez was hanged.[26]

According to very incomplete records, at least forty-nine prisoners were legally hanged in the territory of Arizona. This total included executions by the ten Arizona counties, by the Arizona

Penitentiary at Florence, and by the military at Fort Grant. Often state records reported that a death warrant was issued by the governor, but lacked confirmation of the actual execution. Cochise County had the most hangings with eight and Navajo County had the fewest with one. Many more were executed by vigilantes.[27] Hanging remained the mode of execution in Arizona until 1933.

Statehood, 1912 to Present

Arizona gained statehood status in 1912. Eight more executions followed until a 1916 initiative ended the death penalty for those convicted of first-degree murder. After the death penalty's restoration in 1918, nineteen hangings occurred between 1920 and 1931.[28]

In 1931 Arizona governor Thomas E. Campbell[29] reported murder conviction figures to the British Select Committee on Capital Punishment. From 1914 to 1916 there were forty-one murder convictions in the state. From 1916 to 1918 when there was no death penalty in Arizona, there were forty-six convictions for murder. The following two years, forty-five prisoners were convicted of the same crime.[30] These numbers suggest that the state's two-year experiment with abolishing capital punishment did not result in a rise in murder. However, the two-year period of abolition may not have been a sufficient amount of time to register any noticeable increase in homicides.

During Arizona's territorial history and early years of statehood, hanging remained the means of execution. However, in 1933 the state began using gas to execute its condemned on death row.[31] The following year brothers Manuel and Fred Hernandez were the first prisoners executed in this manner. In 1962 Manuel E. Silvas received the same punishment. However, Silvas was the last convict executed in Arizona for the next thirty years.[32]

Arizona made consistent use of the death penalty during the middle years of the twentieth century. Whether or not this was due to a high level of violence is difficult to determine, but there is some evidence that the state was more violent than its much larger and more populous neighbor, California. From 1925 to 1929 Arizona had a mean annual murder rate per 100,000 people of 14.0 compared to California's 7.2. From 1930 to 1934 Arizona's rate of 12.8 exceeded California's 7.3, and from 1935 to 1939 Arizona led 10.7 to 5.9. The gap eventually narrowed, but nevertheless, Arizona maintained a higher murder rate for much of the century.[33] Although California executed a much larger number of convicts due to its larger population, Arizona did perform sixty-three executions from 1910 to 1963. Only one of those executed during those years was female.[34] This continued a tradition dating back to Arizona's territorial days in the 1800s, when women were almost always excluded from the death penalty.

During the twentieth century, Arizona maintained several crimes on its law books that could earn the death penalty. Among them were murder, kidnapping for ransom if the victim was harmed, treason, perjury in a capital case if it resulted in an innocent person being executed, armed assault by a prisoner sentenced to life, and robbing a train.[35] Sometimes prisoners had their sentences commuted from death to life in prison. Later, if the Board of Paroles and Pardons recommended such an action, the governor could then grant parole. The board also had the right to end or revoke parole.[36] Despite its reputation, in general the western region of the United States (Montana, Idaho, Wyoming, Colorado, New Mexico, Arizona, Utah, Nevada, Washington, Oregon, California, Alaska, and Hawaii) maintained a level of executions similar to other regions, with the exception of the South, which far surpassed the rest of the country during the period 1930 to 1970.[37]

Beginning in the 1960s, the United States Supreme Court issued numerous decisions protecting and expanding the rights of the accused. Although criminal matters had been the purview of local officials since the Colonial Era, the Court "nationalized"[38] or applied the protections provided in the Bill of Rights against the federal government to the state governments. The Fifth Amendment stated that citizens were entitled to "due process" in dealing with the federal government. "Due process" referred to such rights as trial by jury, the right to confront your accusers, the right to counsel, and the right to no cruel or unusual punishment. The Fourteenth Amendment said citizens should also be given "due process" in their dealings with the state governments. Therefore, the Court reasoned, the rest of the protections in the Bill of Rights collectively known as "due process" also protected citizens against the states.

Cases such as *Mapp v. Ohio* (1961—illegally obtained evidence), *Gideon v. Wainwright* (1963—right to an attorney), *Escobedo v. Illinois* (1964—right to an attorney and protection against self-incrimination) and *Miranda v. Arizona* (1966—police guidelines when arresting suspects) compelled state governments to grant more rights to the criminally accused.[39] In *Furman v. Georgia* (1972), the Court effectively told all fifty states that they could no longer carry out the death penalty because it violated the Eighth Amendment's protection against cruel and unusual punishment. Although the federal and state governments had practiced the death penalty throughout American history, the Court now argued that without appropriate guidelines, the ultimate punishment was being issued in an "arbitrary and capricious" manner.[40]

As with many states, Arizona's homicide rate increased in the years after *Furman*. From 1967 to 1971 Arizona had 7.3 murders per 100,000 people. The rate rose to 9.9 from 1972 to 1975. The willful homicide rate also rose, surging from 6.8 to 8.4.[41] The rise suggested that unlike Arizona's previous attempt from 1916 to 1918 to rid itself of capital punishment, this time the absence of the death penalty could have resulted in more homicides. However, again the period of time may have been too brief to make an accurate assessment.

As a result of *Furman*, Arizona and many other states began creating formal rules for determining what crimes and under what circumstances would merit the death penalty. In 1973 the Arizona legislature passed a statute that provided for a separate hearing after a murder trial to determine punishments. The law also described six factors that could mandate capital punishment.[42] These included: a previous conviction that merited a death sentence; past serious offenses involving the threat or use of violence; serious risk of loss of life to others; paying or promising to pay for a murder; committing murder for profit; and a murder committed with particular cruelty and depravity. Over the next twenty years, the Arizona legislature added four more special circumstances: committing murder while being held in the criminal justice system; committing more than one murder; murdering a victim under age fifteen or over age seventy; and killing a police officer.[43] Under the 1973 statute and its later amendments, the government had to prove beyond a reasonable doubt that at least one of the special or aggravating circumstances was present during the commission of the crime.

If the prosecution was successful, the defense then had the opportunity to present one or more mitigating circumstances whereby the defendant could avoid the ultimate punishment. Possible mitigating factors were: an inability to tell right from wrong; being under exceptional duress; having a minor role in the crime; an inability to reasonably predict that an action would result in death to another; and the defendant's age. The court would then determine if any of the

aggravating circumstances or mitigating factors was present, and then decide if the death penalty was warranted. The statute's procedure was upheld by the Arizona Supreme Court in *State v. Richmond* (1976).[44]

Two years later the Arizona Supreme Court stopped executions in the state. In *State v. Bishop* (1978), the court decided that the list of circumstances in the 1973 statute that could mitigate against a convict receiving the death penalty was too limited. The court clarified matters the same year when it ruled in *State v. Watson* that the portion of the death penalty law that was improper could be separated from the rest of the statute, and the defendant could then be allowed to demonstrate a reason why he should not be executed. Subsequently, all prisoners on Arizona's death row were given new hearings to present any evidence that would argue against execution. The following year Arizona updated its death penalty procedures[45] to allow the defense or prosecution to present evidence that would show a sentence lighter than death should be given.[46]

However, the United States Court of Appeals for the Ninth Circuit invalidated the Arizona death penalty statute in *Adamson v. Ricketts* (1988). The court claimed that the defendant had a right to be sentenced by a jury, the "especially heinous, cruel or depraved" aggravating circumstance was too arbitrary, the list of mitigating circumstances was insufficient, and the law had a presumption of death.[47] The U.S. Supreme Court declined to review the case.

However, it did review *Walton v. Arizona* two years later. In this case the Court upheld the Arizona statute and stated that aggravating circumstances could be determined by a judge and not a jury, and that the "especially heinous, cruel or depraved" condition did not violate Eighth and Fourteenth Amendment protections.[48]

Under the statute, when a defendant did receive the death penalty, the sentence was reviewed by the Arizona Supreme Court. If the court found that capital punishment was not appropriate to the case, it would reduce the sentence to life. If the court approved the death penalty, it would begin a post-conviction relief proceeding. The defendant could use this process to question whether: his trial counsel was adequate; there was any new evidence that if presented at the original trial would have altered the verdict or sentence; or there had been a statute change that could have been applied retroactively and therefore changed the outcome of the trial or sentence. The decision of the trial court during the post-conviction relief phase could be appealed to the Arizona Supreme Court by either side and then submitted to the U.S. Supreme Court as well.[49]

A state prisoner could also have recourse to the federal court system. If the defendant first claimed a violation of his constitutional rights in state court, he could then bring the question to a federal court. During a habeas corpus procedure, the federal court would determine whether or not a state court ruled in conflict to a U.S. Supreme Court controlling authority. If the defendant did not first present his claim of a rights violation in state court, he could still seek relief from the federal system if he could show "cause and prejudice" to explain why he did not first present the issue at the state level. Also, a case could be made in a federal court if the defendant could show that not considering his claim would cause a "fundamental miscarriage of justice," meaning the convicted was innocent or the crime was not worthy of a death sentence. The decision of the U.S. District Court could then be appealed by either side to the Ninth Circuit and, finally, the U.S. Supreme Court.[50]

Even after the appeals procedures in state and federal court, an Arizona convict could only be executed under certain conditions. If mentally incompetent or pregnant, a prisoner would not be executed. Also, he must have been able to comprehend that he was being punished for murder and that his punishment would be death. If he was found mentally unable to understand his situation, the Department of Corrections would send the convict to a mental health specialist for competency restoration treatment. The sentence was suspended during treatment.[51]

The Arizona Board of Executive Clemency was the last hope for a prisoner facing capital punishment. The governor appointed the five-member panel and the state senate approved it. At a hearing where the defendant, his attorneys, the state's attorneys, and the victim could all participate, the board reviewed all death sentences and could recommend a reprieve, commutation, pardon, or make no recommendation to the governor. The governor could then take action, but only if the board recommended it.[52]

When Arizona put Donald E. Harding to death by lethal gas in 1992, he became the first prisoner executed by the state in thirty years. Later the same year, state voters decided that Arizona's death row prisoners should receive lethal injection when being executed. Prisoners convicted of crimes that occurred before November 23, 1992, could choose which method of execution they would receive—gas or injection. In 1999 Walter B. LaGrand was the last inmate executed by lethal gas in the state of Arizona.[53] All Arizona prisoners sentenced to death since November 15, 1992, are executed by lethal injection.[54]

Up until 2002, Arizona was one of nine death penalty states that allowed judges to determine if any "aggravating factors" were present in a crime, thereby warranting death for the perpetrator. However, the U.S. Supreme Court again intervened in *Ring v. Arizona*. At the time there were 128 people on death row in the state. Timothy Ring had been convicted in 1994 of murdering an armored truck driver while committing a robbery. The trial judge sentenced him to death after finding two aggravating factors including committing a crime for profit and doing so in a particularly brutal way.[55] Although the trial judge found Ring's limited criminal record as a mitigating factor, he did not believe it warranted a lighter sentence. Ring appealed by arguing that Arizona's death penalty law violated his Sixth Amendment right to a jury trial because a judge had been the finder of fact in determining a sentence.[56] Two years before, the Court ruled in *Apprendi v. New Jersey* that any fact which could potentially increase a sentence beyond the maximum allowed under the law had to be decided by a jury. However, the opinion in *Apprendi* stated that it would not invalidate state death penalty laws such as Arizona's.[57] The Ring case served to clarify this contradiction. After *Ring*, a jury would decide if a crime included aggravating factors which merited a death sentence. Twenty-seven Arizona convictions were sent to county prosecutors to carry out the Court's new ruling.[58]

Shortly after the Supreme Court ruled Arizona's death penalty statute was unconstitutional, the state legislature went to work to pass a new capital punishment law. However, in the interim two accused murderers took advantage of the short window of time where there was no death penalty to plead guilty. Nicholas S. Sizemore and Scott B. Brian had already been incarcerated for murder when they killed fellow inmate Carlos R. Ceniceros. By pleading guilty on July 24, 2002, Sizemore and Brian sought to avoid a death sentence; Brian, who was already serving life, would effectively avoid any punishment at all. Prosecutor Joseph Duarte conceded that, at that moment, there was no death penalty in the state of Arizona. The following week Arizona passed a new death penalty statute. Duarte then decided to pursue the death penalty for Sizemore and Brian and said they could withdraw their guilty pleas.[59]

Some argued that the new death penalty statute was necessary to ensure fairness. Death penalty opponents reasoned that judges, who could be removed from office by voters, were more likely to sentence a convict to death due to popular political pressure. Judges also saw many criminals in their line of work and were more likely to be jaded and have less empathy for a prisoner. However, if a defendant were sentenced by a jury, the twelve would bring a variety of experiences and be much less likely to come to an agreement on a sentence of death.[60]

The *Ring* case elicited calls for Arizona to not just revise its death penalty statute, but end capital punishment altogether. Although it was true that the unconstitutionality of the Arizona statute could be rectified by providing for hearings where juries would determine a convict's fate, this would only suffice until the next Supreme Court decision. Some argued that the best thing to do in light of DNA evidence, which had found that 101 people given a death sentence since 1970 were innocent, was for Arizona to simply abolish the practice. In fact, number 100 of the 101 prisoners found innocent in recent previous decades had been an Arizonan, Ray Krone, who had spent ten years in various Arizona prisons, including three years on death row.[61]

In 2002 Arizona attorney general Janet Napolitano's office published a Capital Case Commission Final Report, which included a list of twenty-one recommendations for improving how the death penalty was implemented in Arizona. Several of the suggestions were put into effect. A 2001 law provided for a pretrial procedure to determine if a prisoner accused of a capital offense was mentally retarded. The legislation also protected those suffering from mental retardation from capital punishment. In 2002 the Arizona Supreme Court agreed to the commission's recommendation to amend the Arizona Rules of Criminal Procedure to allow sixty days after arraignment to file a notice of intent to seek the death penalty, in hope that this would lead to more careful deliberation when considering capital punishment. The court also adopted the commission's proposal to provide investigators and expert witnesses in addition to legal counsel for those unable to afford such services. In addition, the court agreed with the commission's suggestion that both crime victims and defendants had a right to have a more prompt resolution to their cases, and that this should be considered when courts rule on allowing extensions.[62]

Several other commission recommendations have been rejected thus far. In 2001 and 2002 legislation to create a statewide office to defend those accused of capital offenses at the trial level and in rural counties failed. In 2002, legislation to establish a minimum age for those eligible for the death penalty also failed to pass. The attorney general's Law Enforcement Advisory Board has not yet agreed to make the murder of an off-duty police officer an aggravating factor which could merit the death penalty, even if the officer's status was a motivation for the crime. The board did not reject, but questioned how to provide resources for, a proposal to preserve DNA obtained from unsolved murders until a potential defendant could request evidence. Also in 2002, legislation to commute death sentences if the defendant was found incompetent to be executed after the sentence was announced did not receive enough votes to become law.[63]

The U.S. Supreme Court accepted another Arizona death penalty case in 2006. Convicted of murder in Oklahoma, Jeffrey Landrigan escaped from prison in 1989. The next month in Arizona, he murdered Charles Dyer, was convicted, and sentenced to die. The Ninth U.S. Circuit Court of Appeals ruled that a lower court should review whether or not Landrigan had poor legal counsel because his lawyer did not present evidence that could have saved him from a death sentence. Landrigan's father had died while he was on death row in Arkansas. This was part of the basis for a claim that the convicted murderer was predisposed to violence. Landrigan also argued that he

suffered from brain damage and was unable to comprehend what he was doing. The Supreme Court accepted Arizona's appeal to review the Ninth Circuit's decision.[64]

New Mexico

The Territorial Period, 1846–1912

A dispute over the exact location of the southern Texas border brought the United States and Mexico to war in 1846. While General Winfield Scott invaded Mexico en route to capturing Mexico City, General Stephen Watts Kearny entered Santa Fe to seize the northern Mexican provinces known as New Mexico. The general put a legal framework called the Kearny Code into effect, establishing a military rule that lasted until 1851. The United States then created a traditional territorial government. New Mexico's southern boundary was formalized with the Gadsden Purchase in 1853, a strip of land crucial to completing a southern railroad to California. During the Civil War, the Confederacy attempted a takeover of New Mexico, but was ultimately as unsuccessful there as they were in Arizona.[65]

In the early years of the postwar period, most New Mexicans saw the Apache and Navajo Indians as the gravest dangers. The Indians of the region were pacified by 1870, most notably by Kit Carson, who imprisoned Mescalero Apaches and Navajos at the Bosque Redondo reservation at Fort Sumner. Geronimo and his Apaches were finally brought to heel in 1886 when they surrendered to General Nelson A. Miles.[66]

New Mexico's Lincoln County War of 1878–1881 was one of the most deadly and memorable conflicts in the Old West. The most widely recognized figure from that conflict was William H. Bonney, later known as Billy the Kid, who eventually found himself as one of the earliest residents of New Mexico's death row. Bonney became an employee and close friend of an Englishman named John Tunstall, a New Mexico rancher. When Tunstall was murdered in February 1878 by hired guns of a rival rancher named L. G. Murphy, the Kid swore vengeance: "I'll shoot down like a dog every man who had a hand in this murder."[67] Ironically, although Bonney would one day be the subject of a massive manhunt by the U.S. Marshals Service, he initially rode with that service as part of a posse to apprehend Tunstall's killers.[68] However, he proceeded to wage a campaign to personally execute as many of Murphy's men as possible.[69] Attention on the Kid intensified when he murdered Murphy's hand-picked sheriff of Lincoln County, William Brady,[70] on April 1. Brady had refused to arrest Murphy's men who killed Tunstall.[71]

The ranchers' fight turned into a territory-wide war as the Murphy side retaliated for Brady's killing by murdering Alexander McSween, a friend of both Tunstall's and the Kid's. New Mexican ranchers then asked President Rutherford B. Hayes to intervene. Hayes appointed a new territorial governor, Lew Wallace (who also authored the great biblical-era historical novel, *Ben Hur*). Wallace promised the Kid immunity if he would meet him in Lincoln to talk. Billy agreed, but when the governor asked him to give up his guns or leave New Mexico, the Kid refused.[72] Billy spent the next couple of years cattle rustling and counterfeiting.[73]

It was left to a Texas buffalo hunter named Patrick F. Garrett to end the Kid's rampage.[74] Garrett became a Lincoln County deputy sheriff in November 1880 and later sheriff. He established a posse and captured the Kid in December at Stinking Springs.[75] It was not the last time Garrett would have to apprehend Billy.

Billy the Kid's trial for the first-degree murder of Lincoln Country Sheriff Matthew Brady was held in Mesilla,[76] New Mexico. State law mandated a punishment of death.[77] Therefore when the jury reached a guilty verdict, the judge was left with no option. On April 13, 1881 Judge Warren Bristol[78] supposedly pronounced to the Kid: "You are sentenced to be hanged by the neck until you are dead, dead, dead[!]" The Kid reportedly responded, "And you can go to hell, hell, hell[!]"[79] According to the sentence, Billy was to die on May 13 between 9 A.M. and 3 P.M. The Kid expressed hope that the governor would pardon him, but Wallace told a Las Vegas, New Mexico, reporter, "I can't see how a fellow like him should expect any clemency from me." Although at least fifty men had been indicted for various crimes committed during the three-year Lincoln County War, only Billy was convicted. His conviction and sentencing were due at least in part to the specific notoriety he had earned, and the governor's refusal to offer a pardon reflected political pressure from powerful ranchers and others who wanted order on their frontier lands.[80]

Security around the death-row-bound prisoner was tight. The Kid was escorted by a deputy U.S. marshal, a deputy sheriff, and five others deputized specifically for the journey. The seven-man guard took their prisoner in secret to avoid a potential rescue or lynch mob. At Fort Stanton, they met Garrett who took official possession of the prisoner.[81] When the cadre reached Lincoln, the Kid was held at Murphy's old store, which had been turned into a courthouse.[82] Garrett described his makeshift death row:

Lincoln county has never had a jail, until the last few weeks, that would hold a cripple. The county had just purchased the large two-story building, formerly the mercantile house of Murphy & Dolan, for the use of the county as a public building, but no jail had been constructed; hence I was obliged to place a guard over The Kid. I selected Deputy Sheriff J.W. Bell and Deputy Marshal Robert Olinger, for this duty, and assigned them a guard room in the second story of the building, separate and apart from the other prisoners. This room was at the north-east corner of the building, and one had to pass from a hall, through another large room to gain the only door to it. There were two windows—one on the north, opening to the street, and the other on the east, opening into a large yard, . . . a small hall and broad staircase . . . was the only . . . means of access to the second story of the building.[83]

Despite Garrett's precautions, the Kid avoided execution, at least temporarily. One account is that the prisoner convinced Bell to take him to the outhouse. Upon returning, Billy reached the top of the inside stairwell before his guard and momentarily turned into the hallway out of view. He then slipped one of his small hands free, and swung the cuff at Bell. The guard was knocked over, and Billy then attacked him, grabbing his gun. When Bell tried to escape, the Kid shot him. Bell fell down the stairs and then stumbled out the back door before falling dead outside the courthouse.[84] According to another account, the Kid convinced Bell to play cards with him. When Billy pretended to drop a card, he reached down to pick it up, but grabbed his guard's gun and shot him.[85] A third story says after Bell took Billy to the outhouse, the Kid grabbed a gun secretly stored there by a friend and used it to escape.[86] Whatever his method of dispatching with Bell, Billy proceeded to Garrett's office, grabbed the shotgun of his other guard, Olinger, and waited. When he saw Olinger returning with several prisoners he had taken for dinner, Billy shot him from the northeast corner of the second story. Although he regretted having killed Bell who had treated him well, the Kid delighted in shooting Olinger who

had taunted Billy mercilessly.[87] The two guards were his twentieth and twenty-first victims. He completed one of the most daring and dramatic escapes in the history of the Old West by forcing a jail cook to loosen his leg chains and then stealing a horse from the county clerk.[88]

The entire state of New Mexico as well as much of the country was both enthralled and horrified at the incredible escape of Billy the Kid. Americans in the East had long been fascinated by tales of the Wild West, and the Kid's escape undoubtedly was just the kind of story they loved. Governor Wallace was not as pleased. He offered his second reward of five hundred dollars for Billy's capture. Over the next few months his presence in and around Fort Sumner was reported in several papers including the Las Vegas *Gazette* and the *New Mexican*. However, Billy had many friends, particularly in Fort Sumner, who both had sympathy for him and saw him as a modern-day Robin Hood. When Lincoln County Deputy Sheriff John W. Poe got a report confirming the Kid's presence in Fort Sumner, he relayed the information to Garrett. In July 1881 the sheriff tracked Billy down at Pete Maxwell's house and shot Billy slightly above his heart, instantly killing him.[89] He was twenty-one years old.

Although the Lincoln County War and the exploits of Billy the Kid were over, New Mexico continued to develop from a territory into a state. Under American free-trade policies, New Mexico blossomed economically, which helped bring the Santa Fe, Southwestern Pacific, and Denver and Rio Grande railroads to the territory. Subsequently, both the sheep-raising and cattle-ranching industries experienced dramatic growth. The prospect of cattle fortunes lured many Texas entrepreneurs including John Chisum.[90] These were followed by job-seeking cowboys who added to the volatility of frontier New Mexico.

New Mexico's frontier sheriffs were some of

the government officials most likely to come into contact with lawbreakers drawn from the ranks of cowboys and elsewhere. As in Arizona, New Mexico sheriffs' duties included presiding over those sentenced to die. New Mexico law also provided a means by which sheriffs could avoid what many considered an unenviable task. Grant County Sheriff Harvey Whitehill had to hang William "Parson" Young in February 1881. The sheriff considered Young insane, and had four doctors examine the condemned man. If the physicians had agreed, Young would have escaped the gallows. However, they found Young sane and Whitehill was ordered by the governor to carry out the execution.[91]

Public executions could draw large crowds. New Mexico law tried to limit attendance to by invitation only. The sheriff could invite a doctor, the district attorney, and at least a dozen "reputable citizens," while the prisoner was allowed two ministers and five friends and family members if he wished. Sheriffs also could invite law enforcement officers.[92]

Toward the end of the nineteenth century, New Mexico ended public executions. Journalists and then the legislature at Santa Fe became convinced that the spectacles were distasteful and hurt the territory's image with the rest of the country. A state law directed sheriffs to enclose the scaffold, but this did not always keep out the curious.[93]

In 1909, New Mexico governor George Curry publicly announced his support for abolishing the death penalty and recommended that the state assembly enact legislation to that effect. Curry had been a sheriff and said that most murderers had no friends and no money to raise a defense. He concluded that "[t]he deliberate murderer has no fear of death," and so capital punishment was no deterrent. Curry added that many murderers looked at execution as a chance to demonstrate toughness and fearlessness. The lawmakers did not act on his suggestion. Three years later New

Mexico became a state. Overall, at least forty-six people were legally executed in territorial New Mexico from 1846 to 1912.[94]

Statehood, 1912 to present

During the early years of statehood, New Mexico maintained hanging as its means of execution. From 1912 to 1933, nineteen men were sent to the gallows. The hangings generally took place in the county where the crime had been committed. Beginning in 1929, the state carried out all executions at the state penitentiary at Santa Fe.[95] The state adopted a new death penalty statute in 1933,[96] perhaps spurred on by a 13.5-per-100,000 homicide rate.[97] Electrocution replaced hanging.[98] In 1939 New Mexico became the last state before the Second World War to change from mandatory capital punishment to the discretionary variety. Although a sentence of death would no longer be automatic, but up to a jury's discretion, homicide rates fell in New Mexico from 1935 to 1943 (as they did in the rest of the country). New Mexico's murder rate fell even more than its neighbor, Arizona, despite the latter's maintaining of mandatory death sentences for homicide.[99] If the change from mandatory to discretional capital punishment weakened the death penalty's deterrent effect, New Mexico's murder rate should have increased relative to Arizona's.[100]

A death sentence was not necessarily definite. The governor could commute a sentence from death to life. Subsequently, the penitentiary warden could parole a prisoner serving life who was not a four-time offender, had not attempted to escape, and had not previously violated parole. A prisoner's parole could then only end due to a violation, which would result in the warden ordering the parolee's return to custody. The former death row inmate was only required to report for a year. Thereafter he was placed on lifetime probation, but with no requirement to report or be supervised.[101]

A 1959 New Mexico case involving the diminished capacity defense had ramifications across the country. In *State v. Padilla*, the defendant's attorney asked the judge to inform the jury that they could consider a charge of second-degree murder instead of murder in the first, if they found Padilla had a "disease or defect of the mind," but was not actually diagnosed as insane. Padilla was convicted without any such notice by the judge to the jury. The state supreme court overturned the verdict. New Mexico law stipulated that a person could be so intoxicated that he could not actually be said to have premeditated a murder. The court then reasoned that this protection could be extended to those with mental disorders, and many other courts agreed. The decision was in spite of the utter cruelty of Padilla's crime, which included kidnap, rape, and murder of a five-year-old little girl after he spent the day drinking beer and smoking marijuana.[102]

New Mexico ended its use of the electric chair in 1956 and replaced it with lethal injection. Four years later the state performed its only execution using this new method.[103] Although the U.S. Supreme Court temporarily halted executions in the United States with its 1972 *Furman* decision, New Mexico had not put anyone to death since 1960 anyway.[104] Prior to this temporary hiatus, New Mexico gave death sentences as punishments for a variety of crimes such as murder, kidnapping when the victim was physically harmed, killing a guard when breaking into a jail, assault on a train in order to commit a felony, using force to free a capital offender, and train-wrecking.[105] From 1930 to 1960 only eight executions were carried out in New Mexico.[106] In 1962, New Mexico's murder rate was 6.1 per 100,000, compared to 5.7 for Arizona and 3.9 for California.[107]

While New Mexico had not executed anyone for nearly a decade, in 1969 the state officially abolished capital punishment for many crimes. New Mexico did retain the death penalty for offenses that were considered particularly destructive to the administration of the criminal justice system or in some cases involving premeditation. Anyone accused of killing a police officer or prison or jail guard who was on duty was eligible for capital punishment, as well as "in cases where the jury recommends the death penalty and the defendant commits a second capital felony after time for due deliberation following commission of the first capital felony."[108]

There is some evidence that New Mexico's reduction of the number of crimes which could earn a death sentence may have led to increased murder rates. From 1967 to 1971, New Mexico had a homicide rate of 7.8 per 100,000. It increased to 12.0 in 1972 to 1975. The willful homicide rate increased from 8.0 to 11.8 during the same two periods.[109] The U.S. Supreme Court's 1972 *Furman* decision, which temporarily ended the death penalty across the nation, could also have been a contributing factor.

New Mexico responded to the Supreme Court's description of the death penalty's implementation as "arbitrary and capricious." The state passed a new death penalty statute making execution the mandatory sentence for anyone convicted of first-degree murder. However, the Supreme Court also invalidated that law and decreed that mandatory death sentences violated the Eighth Amendment protection against cruel and unusual punishment. Nevertheless, in 1976 the Supreme Court reversed itself in *Gregg v. Georgia*, when it ruled that the death penalty was constitutional if it was not arbitrary or discriminatory in its application.[110]

In response, the New Mexico legislature passed a new death penalty statute in 1978. The legislation changed the execution method from lethal gas to lethal injection. The warden of the state penitentiary would supervise executions.[111]

For much of the eighties and nineties the statute

was not implemented. In 1986 Governor Toney Anaya commuted five death sentences. In 1992 the Office of the Secretary for the New Mexico Department of Corrections claimed that the state did not have any execution procedures as no one had been put to death there in over thirty years. Although Governor Gary Johnson was elected in 1994 after taking a strong stance in favor of the death penalty, all of the bills he submitted to limit death penalty appeals failed.[112]

It was not until 2001 that New Mexico resumed executions.[113] Fifteen years earlier Terry Clark pled guilty to murdering Dena Lynn Gore. Although he hoped to receive the clemency that Governor Anaya gave to other death row prisoners, Clark's judge delayed sentencing until after the governor left office. Clark was killed on November 6, 2001, ending a period of forty-one years without an execution in New Mexico.[114]

Even before executions resumed in New Mexico there were also efforts to abolish the death penalty in the state.[115] In a complete reversal of policy, Governor Johnson placed repeal of capital punishment on the legislative agenda in 2002, but no new statute was forthcoming. In 2005 state representative Gail Beam (D-Albuquerque) introduced a new bill that would replace the death penalty with life without parole. Although it passed in the House, 38 to 31, the bill did not survive in the Senate, at least in part to Governor Bill Richardson's lack of support.[116]

New Mexico law strictly regulates under what conditions a convict can be sentenced to death. Only first-degree murder with one or more aggravating circumstance merits execution. As with Arizona post-*Ring*, a jury determines whether or not a convicted murderer will be killed by the state. The jury is also charged with determining whether any of the following aggravating factors were present during the crime: the victim was an on-duty law enforcement officer; the murder included an attempt to commit kidnapping

or criminal sexual contact of a minor or criminal sexual penetration; murder with intent while escaping from criminal custody; murder inside a penal institution; murder for profit; murder of a witness or potential witness to a crime or as retaliation for witness testimony.[117]

Even if convicted and sentenced to death, a defendant will have an automatic appeal to the New Mexico Supreme Court. The court will then determine if one of the state legislature's conditions for disallowing a death sentence is present: no aggravating circumstance; mitigating factors outweigh aggravating circumstances; the death sentence was imposed in an arbitrary way; or a death sentence is a disproportionate punishment for the crime committed.[118]

Even if the sentence passes the New Mexico Supreme Court's test, the case is still returned to the district court for a post-conviction review. According to a 2004 report of the New Mexico State Bar, this step is essential to ensuring that the defendant had a qualified defense and all of his rights protected. Previously the federal courts had served this function; however, their role has been greatly reduced by the 1996 Antiterrorism and Effective Death Penalty Act, which limits both the time to file a petition for a federal review and the breadth of that review.[119]

New Mexico death row inmates tend to have a long stay. Terry Clark's 2001 execution remains the only one in forty-seven years in the state. Clark waited fourteen years between the time he was sentenced in 1987 and when his execution was actually carried out. Timothy Allen, who was convicted for attempted rape, kidnapping, and murder of a seventeen-year-old girl, has been on death row for twelve years as of 2007. Robert Ray Fry has waited five years since his conviction for rape and murder, despite also being convicted of three previous murders.[120] The length of time spent on death row reveals more than simply an elaborate system of appeals in capital cases. It is also suggestive that while New Mexico allows for capital punishment, it nevertheless has trepidation about taking a human life. Some have even argued that were it not for its geographic proximity to Texas, which utilizes the death penalty much more frequently, New Mexico would have abolished capital punishment long ago.[121]

New Mexico's struggle with capital punishment continued into 2007. In February, the New Mexico House of Representatives again passed a bill to abolish the death penalty in the state (this time HB 190, which passed 41–28). In June, State District Judge Tim Garcia ruled that capital punishment was unconstitutional based upon the National Science Foundation's Capital Jury Project data which concluded that juror biases can never be removed. This was in spite of two other district judges previously rejecting the same argument. The foundation studied juries in fourteen states, and concluded that biases like racism made the death penalty arbitrary, and therefore, unconstitutional. Judge Garcia was especially concerned about jurors making up their minds about sentencing before hearing the facts of the case or being instructed on the law.[122]

The judge's decision came from the case of Jesus Aviles-Dominguez and Daniel Good, two inmates in the Santa Fe jail. Aviles-Dominguez and Good were charged with beating to death Dickie Ortega, another inmate at Santa Fe.[123] The defendants based their appeal on the Capital Jury Project, the testimony of Dr. Wanda Foglia and Dr. William J. Bowers, and other studies. The state challenged the defense's claims but did not present any witnesses or evidence of its own.[124]

The Capital Jury Project was a detailed and wide-ranging study of juror behavior. The study lasted several years and examined surveys of more than 1,200 jurors from 354 death penalty cases after they had reached a decision. The fourteen states that were studied were holding about 76 percent of all death row inmates as of

June 2002, and had executed about 79 percent of all prisoners killed between 1977 and September 2002. Although New Mexico was not one of the states surveyed, Dr. Foglia and Dr. Bowers stated that New Mexico's capital punishment process was similar to those states studied.[125]

The Capital Jury Project featured a long list of flaws in the way states reached a decision on issuing a death sentence:

a. Premature death penalty decision making by the jury;

b. Failure of the jury selection process to remove a large number of death-biased jurors;

c. Failure by jurors to comprehend and/or follow death penalty instructions;

d. Erroneous beliefs amongst jurors that the death sentence is required;

e. Evasion of responsibility for the decision imposing the death penalty; and

f. Racism in the determination and imposition of the death penalty.[126]

The expert testimony was also based upon the project. The witnesses described significant statistical problems associated with capital-sentencing schemes in many states:

a. Approximately 50 percent of all jurors absolutely thought they knew what punishment should be given during the evidentiary (guilt) phase of trial and prior to the start of the sentencing phase (30 percent absolute for imposing the death penalty and 20 percent absolute for not imposing the death penalty). These jurors do not waiver from these decisions which were made prior to the start of the sentencing phase.

b. 60 percent of jurors with a pro-death-penalty position did not change their premature death penalty position and 97 percent of all pro-death-penalty jurors felt strongly about their pro-death-penalty position during the evidentiary phase of trial.

c. 30 percent of jurors fail to understand the instruction that aggravation must be proven by a standard of beyond a reasonable doubt.

d. 30 to 44 percent of jurors fail to understand the instruction, legal standard, and legal considerations regarding mitigating evidence.

e. 24 to 71 percent of jurors believed that the death penalty was the only acceptable punishment for six specific types of murder.

f. 37 to 44 percent of jurors understood that the death penalty would be required if the defendant would be dangerous in the future or the defendant's conduct is heinous, vile, or depraved.

g. Only 15 percent of jurors believe that individual jurors or the jury as a whole is/are responsible for the defendant's punishment (imposition of the death penalty).

h. Jurors in all fourteen states underestimated (by statistical median averaging) the sentence the defendant would receive if the death penalty was not imposed.

i. At sentencing, jurors who estimated the non-death-penalty sentence to be twenty years or longer are 11.8 percent less likely to impose the death penalty over jurors who estimated the non-death-penalty sentence to be from zero to nine years.[127]

The project also analyzed issues of race. It found concerns in those cases "where black/white racial dynamics occur within the jury or where the accused is a black defendant." However, New Mexico's population featured large percentages of Hispanics and Native Americans, and so the court did not consider those parts of the project dealing with race. Both defendants were Hispanic or Anglo-Hispanic, but the project did not examine issues of ethnicity.[128]

Judge Garcia recommended a possible solution to the problem of juror bias. In New Mexico a jury first heard evidence while deciding guilt and then during a second hearing to determine punishment. Garcia implied that leaving the decision to a jury may not be enough to ensure fairness in sentencing if jurors had already decided on the issue of capital punishment. Consequently, the judge suggested two juries be selected, one for the trial and one to determine a sentence. The judge reasoned that a second jury that had not been saturated with evidence and testimony would be fairer when considering a final punishment:[129]

The only way to properly and adequately protect the sentencing phase from being tainted by a premature jury determination during the evidentiary phase of trial is to impanel a separate jury for the sentencing phase of trial. Such a requirement is contrary to the statutory scheme established by the New Mexico Capital Felony Sentencing Act. . . . All portions of the New Mexico Capital Felony Sentencing Act inconsistent with the impanelment of a separate jury for the death penalty sentencing phase of this trial are determined to violate the United States Constitution and the New Mexico Constitution.[130]

In light of the judge's idea, it is clear that he viewed the death penalty as unconstitutional, but only because of the way it was determined. His offering of a solution suggested he did not see capital punishment in general as a violation of the Eight Amendment's protection against "cruel and unusual punishment."

According to State Representative Gail Chasey (D-Albuquerque, formerly Gail Beam), who sponsored HB 190, besides being unjust, the death penalty needlessly costs the state of New Mexico millions of dollars. Fourteen prisoners faced the death penalty after a Santa Fe prison riot in the early 1980s, but none were executed.

Subsequently, thirteen more prisoners were charged with the first-degree murder of prison guard Ralph Garcia during another prison riot at Santa Rosa in 1999. Although ten of the defendants eventually pled guilty to lesser charges, three more could still potentially be executed. Approximately $4 million was spent on the Santa Rosa prosecutions.[131]

Due to the complexity and finality of capital cases, they are frequently long and expensive. Costs include lawyers' fees, the trial, appeals, and professional experts. In addition, death penalty cases are actually two trials: a guilt phase and a sentencing phase.[132]

Representative Chasey added that the two phases of a capital case contribute to another negative side-effect. The time spent on these cases causes a backlog that can result in other cases being postponed. If a case is postponed long enough, either witnesses or evidence may not be available when the court date finally arrives. In many instances, a case dismissal can be the result.[133]

Chasey also argued that the state received little or nothing for its investment. From 1979 when capital punishment was reintroduced in New Mexico through 2007, the state sought the death penalty 208 times. She pointed out that Terry Clark's execution in 2001 remained the only one,

and that Clark had asked his attorneys to end the appeals process and let him be executed. If the state would abandon capital punishment for a maximum penalty of life without parole, the state would save money and time that could be devoted to other cases.[134]

However, Chasey neglected to mention that the cost of capital cases is due in part to the same people who criticize capital punishment for its expense. The sentencing trial, appeals process, and post-conviction review are all safeguards instituted at the insistence of those opposed to the death penalty. A streamlined process limiting the number and length of appeals could solve problems such as excessive cost and clogged court dockets complained of by capital punishment's foes.

Daniel S. Stackhouse Jr. earned his bachelor's and master's degrees in history from California State University, Fullerton, and is currently studying for his doctoral degree in history from Claremont Graduate University. He has taught at Fullerton and Cypress colleges in Orange County, California, for the last ten years. He is the author of entries on the Arapaho, Crow, and Gros Ventre Indians in the *Encyclopedia of Immigration and Migration in the American West* (2006), published by Sage Publications.

Suggested Readings

Arizona Department of Corrections. "Arizona Death Penalty History." http://www.azcorrections.gov.adc/history/deathpenalty.asp.

Arizona Department of Corrections. "Early ADC History." http://www.azcorrections.gov/adc/history/index.asp.

Ball, Larry D. *Desert Lawmen—The High Sheriffs of New Mexico and Arizona, 1846–1912.* Albuquerque: University of New Mexico Press, 1992.

Brown, Dee. *The American West.* New York: Touchstone, 1994.

Garrett, Pat F. *The Authentic Life of Billy, The Kid—An Annotated Edition with Notes and Commentary by Frederick Nolan.* Norman: University of Oklahoma Press, 2000.

The League of Women Voters of New Mexico. "Death Penalty Study Guide." www.lwvnm.org/deathpenalty.html.

Sellin, Thorsten. *The Penalty of Death.* Beverly Hills: Sage Publications, 1980.

State of New Mexico, County of Santa Fe, First Judicial District Court. *State of New Mexico v. Jesus Aviles*

Dominguez and State of New Mexico v. Daniel Good. 8 June 2007.

Turk, David S. "Billy the Kid and the U.S. Marshals Service." *Wild West* (February 2007): 34–39.

Utley, Robert M. *Billy the Kid: A Short and Violent Life.* Lincoln: University of Nebraska Press, 1989.

Notes

1. John Phillip Reid, *Law for the Elephant—Property and Social Behavior on the Overland Trail* (San Marino, Calif.: The Huntington Library, 1980), 4.
2. Jill Mocho, *Murder & Justice in Frontier New Mexico, 1821–1846* (Albuquerque: University of New Mexico Press, 1997), 18.
3. Ibid.
4. Ibid., 178.
5. Howard R. Lamar, ed., *The New Encyclopedia of the American West* (New Haven, Conn.: Yale University Press, 1998), s.v. "Arizona," by Harwood P. Hinton, 45.
6. Ibid.
7. Larry D. Ball, *Desert Lawmen—The High Sheriffs of New Mexico and Arizona, 1846–1912* (Albuquerque: University of New Mexico Press, 1992), 148.
8. Ibid.
9. Ibid., 149.
10. Ibid., 375–377.
11. Ibid., 150.
12. Ibid.
13. Ibid.
14. Ibid., 151.
15. Ibid., 153.
16. Ibid., 158.
17. Ibid.
18. Ibid., 159.
19. Ibid., 159–160.
20. Ibid., 160.
21. Ibid., 161–162.
22. Ibid., 163.
23. Arizona Department of Corrections, "Early ADC History," http://www.azcorrections.gov/adc/history/index.asp.
24. Ibid.
25. Ibid.
26. Arizona Department of Corrections, "Arizona Death Penalty History," http://www.azcorrections.gov/adc/history/deathpenalty.asp.
27. Ball, 164, 375–377.
28. Arizona Department of Corrections, "Arizona Death Penalty History."
29. Thorsten Sellin, *The Penalty of Death*, Sage Library of Social Research, vol. 102 (Beverly Hills: Sage Publications, 1980), 169.
30. Thorsten Sellin, "Experiments with Abolition," in *Capital Punishment*, ed. Thorsten Sellin (New York: Harper & Row, 1967), 123.
31. Arizona Department of Corrections, "Early ADC History."
32. Arizona Department of Corrections, "Arizona Death Penalty History."
33. Sellin, *The Penalty of Death*, 170.
34. Ibid., 67.
35. Hugo A. Bedau, "Offenses Punishable by Death," in *The Death Penalty in America*, ed. Hugo Adam Bedau (Chicago: Aldine Publishing Company, 1964), 48.
36. G. I. Giardini and R. G. Farrow, "The Paroling of Capital Offenders," in *Capital Punishment*, ed. Thorsten Sellin (New York: Harper & Row, 1967), 169.
37. Raymond Paternoster, *Capital Punishment in America* (New York: Lexington Books, 1991), 14, 15.
38. Kermit L. Hall, William M. Wiecek, and Paul Finkelman, *American Legal History—Cases and Materials* (New York: Oxford University Press, 1991), 541.
39. Ibid.
40. Arizona Department of Corrections, "Arizona Death Penalty History."
41. Sellin, *The Penalty of Death*, 136.
42. Arizona Department of Corrections, "Arizona Death Penalty History."
43. Office of the Attorney General of the State of Arizona, *Capital Case Commission Final Report*, 12/31/02, http://www.azag.gov/ccc/FinalReport.html.
44. Ibid.
45. Arizona Department of Corrections, "Arizona Death Penalty History."
46. Office of the Attorney General of the State of Arizona.
47. Ibid.
48. Ibid.
49. Ibid.
50. Ibid.
51. Ibid.
52. Ibid.
53. Arizona Department of Corrections, "Arizona Death Penalty History."
54. Arizona Department of Corrections, "Early ADC History."

55. Linda Greenhouse, "Major Death Penalty Appeal Accepted," *The New York Times*, 12 January 2002, http://www.deathpenaltyinfo.org/article/php?scid=17&did=323.

56. Cornell University Law School, Supreme Court Collection, *Ring v. Arizona (01–488) 536 U.S. 584 (2002)*, http://supct.law.cornell.edu/supct/html/01–488.ZS.html.

57. Charles Lane, "Justices to Consider Whether Judge Alone May Decide on Capital Punishment," *The Washington Post*, 12 January 2002, http://www.deathpenaltyinfo.org/article.php?scid=17&did=317.

58. Arizona Department of Corrections, "Arizona Death Penalty History."

59. Adam Liptak, "A Supreme Court Ruling Roils Death Penalty Cases," *The New York Times*, 16 September 2002, http://www.deathpenaltyinfo.org/article.php?scid=17&did=304.

60. Gregory J. Kuykendall, "The Politics of Death in Arizona—Supreme Court Considers Arizona Case that Affects Colorado," Coloradans against the Death Penalty, http://www.coadp.org/thepublications/pub-2002-2-AZ_OpEd.html.

61. "Arizona Should End Death Penalty," *Arizona Republic*, 28 July 2002, http://www.deathpenaltyinfo.org/article.php?scid=17&did=295.

62. Office of the Attorney General of the State of Arizona.

63. Ibid.

64. The Associated Press, "Supreme Court Accepts Arizona Death Penalty Case," 27 September 2006, http://www.law.com/jsp/law/LawArticleFriendly.jsp?id=1159261522138.

65. Howard R. Lamar, ed., *The New Encyclopedia of the American West* (New Haven: Yale University Press, 1998), s.v. "New Mexico," by Maria E. Montoya, 786–787.

66. Ibid.

67. Dee Brown, *The American West* (New York: Touchstone, 1994), 304.

68. David S. Turk, "Billy the Kid and the U.S. Marshals Service," *Wild West* (February 2007): 36.

69. Brown, 304–305.

70. Ibid., 305.

71. Turk, 37.

72. Ibid. Brown, 306–307.

73. Turk, 37.

74. Brown, 307.

75. Turk, 38.

76. Ibid., 39.

77. Robert M. Utley, *Billy the Kid: A Short and Violent Life* (Lincoln: University of Nebraska Press, 1989), 173.

78. Turk, 39.

79. Brown, 308.

80. Ibid., 174–175.

81. Ibid., 176, 178.

82. Brown, 308.

83. Pat F. Garrett, *The Authentic Life of Billy, The Kid* (Norman: University of Oklahoma Press, 2000), 159–160.

84. Utley, 180, 181.

85. Brown, 308.

86. Frederick Nolan, ed., *Pat F. Garrett's* The Authentic Life of Billy, The Kid (Norman: University of Oklahoma Press, 2000), 166, note 2.

87. Utley, 181–182.

88. Brown, 308.

89. Utley, 188–191, 194.

90. Lamar, 787.

91. Ibid., Ball, 153–154.

92. Ibid., 160–161.

93. Ibid., 163.

94. Ibid., 163–164.

95. The League of Women Voters of New Mexico, "Death Penalty Study Guide," 2005–2006, 2. www.lwvnm.org/deathpenalty.html.

96. William J. Bowers, *Executions in America* (Lexington, Mass.: D.C. Heath and Company, 1974), 38.

97. Sellin, *Penalty of Death*, 170.

98. Bowers, 10.

99. William J. Bowers, *Legal Homicide—Death as Punishment in America, 1864–1982* (Boston: Northeastern University Press, 1984), 120.

100. Bowers, *Executions in America*, 153. Also see Robert J. Torrez, *Myth of the Hanging Tree: Stories of Crime and Punishment in Territorial New Mexico* (Albuquerque: University of New Mexico Press, 2008).

101. Giardini and Farrow, 174.

102. Lawrence M. Friedman, *Crime and Punishment in American History* (New York: Basic Books, 1993), 402–403, 406.

103. Bowers, *Executions in America*, 11.

104. The American College of Physicians, Human Rights Watch, National Coalition to Abolish the Death Penalty, and Physicians for Human Rights, *Breach of Trust—Physician Participation in Executions in the United States* (Philadelphia: The American College of Physicians, 1994), 63.

105. Bedau, "Offenses Punishable by Death," 50.

106. U.S. Department of Justice, "Executions 1962," in *The Death Penalty in America*, ed. Hugo Adam Bedau (Chicago: Aldine Publishing Company, 1964), 115.

107. Hugo A. Bedau, "Volume and Rate of Capital Crimes," 68.

108. Bowers, *Executions in America*, 6.

109. Sellin, *The Penalty of Death*, 136.

110. The League of Women Voters of New Mexico, 2.

111. The American College of Physicians, 63.

112. The League of Women Voters of New Mexico, 2; also, The American College of Physicians, 63.

113. Death Penalty Information Center, "New Mexico," http://www.deathpenaltyinfo.org/article.php?did=513&scid=.

114. The League of Women Voters of New Mexico, 2.

115. Deborah Baker, "New Mexico Votes to Abolish Death Penalty," Associated Press, 28 February 2005, http://www.freenewmexican.com/story_print.php?storyid=11081.

116. The League of Women Voters of New Mexico, 2; see also Baker.

117. Ibid., 2–3.

118. Ibid.

119. Ibid.

120. Kevin Wilson, "Death Penalty Process Lengthy," cnjonline.com, 20 June 2007, http://www.cnjonline.com/news/death_21951_article.html/penalty_years.html.

121. Amnesty International USA, "New Mexico Judge Rules Death Penalty Unconstitutional," 21 June 2007, http://blogs.amnestyusa.org/death-penalty/archive/2007/06/21.

122. Ibid. Caitlin Price, "New Mexico House Passes Death Penalty Repeal Bill," *Jurist Legal News & Research*, University of Pittsburgh School of Law, 12 February 2007, http://jurist.law.pitt.edu/paperchase/2007/02. See also Amnesty International USA.

123. Ibid.

124. State of New Mexico, County of Santa Fe, First Judicial District Court, *State of New Mexico v. Jesus Aviles Dominguez and State of New Mexico v. Daniel Good*, 8 June 2007.

125. Ibid.

126. Ibid.

127. Ibid.

128. Ibid.

129. Amnesty International USA.

130. State of New Mexico, County of Santa Fe, First Judicial District Court.

131. Gail Chasey, "Death Penalty Costs New Mexico Millions, Justice," ABQJournal.com, 4 November 2007, http://www.abqjournal.com/opinion/guest_columns/607917opinion11-04-07.htm.

132. Ibid.

133. Ibid.

134. Ibid.

CHAPTER 18

Arkansas and Missouri

THE DEATH PENALTY

Timothy R. Finch

CHANGING ATTITUDES and changing standards have been the hallmarks of the death penalty in the United States. Stuart Banner's *The Death Penalty: An American History* (2003) exemplified the national debate concerning capital punishment. Mirroring aspects of the dialogue concerning the deterrent and the retribution bases typically given for keeping this ultimate punishment, while many of the other countries of the world are doing away with state-sponsored executions, Banner walked the reader through a history of the death penalty in the United States. The most compelling direction of this work, though not addressed in his introduction, and not present until the book's midpoint, was a geographic and cultural comparative of the death penalty in the North and the South.

Starting with English law in the colonies, which incorporated such methods as drawing and quartering, lashing, the gallows, burning, and displaying the corpses on gibbets as a warning to future criminals, Banner used mainly archival newspaper accounts and correspondence for his primary source material. He bookended his volume with an execution for the early nineteenth-century capital crime of setting fire to a barn at night, and a Missouri man who was given a death sentence without having what Banner called proper representation, which was in the guise of a state-paid public defender. The professor of law at the University of California at Los Angeles pointed out that "many aspects of capital punishment today appear paradoxical without an appreciation of its history."[1]

Death penalty's history, naturally, did not begin with England's American colonial laws and Banner enlightened us with its background. Steeped in a western tradition of the Bible's Leviticus, the Magna Carta, and many of the Enlightenment era's writers, eighteenth-century writer Cesare Beccaria subtly questioned the reasoning behind "an eye for an eye" and "the crime should fit the punishment." Banner questioned the very nature of the death penalty in the United States. "It could take so long to review the propriety of a death sentence only in a culture that had grown uncertain about the death sentence."[2] Are this comment and the introductory capital sentence, along with the epilogue death penalty, revelatory of Banner's position, or a Socratic method put to the reader?

The author brought to mind another question involving his predominant theme in over half the book, of the death penalty's interpretation in northern and southern states. Does the author base his statistically driven conclusion that the southern states, in the past and the present, approach lawbreakers' consequences more aggressively than the northern states, on a cultural or geographical basis? The nineteen states Banner considered southern (listed in endnote 42 on page 358) included Arkansas and the other ten former Confederate states. Possibly for cultural reasons, he added a Union state, Kansas, four of the five Civil War border states—Delaware, Kentucky, Maryland, and Missouri, with West Virginia left out—in addition to Civil War–era territories Arizona, New Mexico, and Oklahoma. The additional states increase the south's execution numbers when compared with northern states, but not significantly enough to disprove Banner's assertions about the differences in death penalty interpretation that exist in the northern and southern regions.

The regional differences in death penalty interpretation can be measured statistically. Results from the Clark County, Indiana, Prosecutor's Office death penalty website showed the addition of non-Confederate-era states to Banner's list of southern states increased that region's portion of the top fifteen execution states from 1976 to 2006. All but two states, Ohio and Indiana, are part of Banner's South, with the added border states of Oklahoma and Missouri at numbers three and four, with eighty-one and sixty-six executions, respectively. Arizona, which is neither a former Confederate nor a border state, is number twelve with twenty-two executions (behind Arkansas's twenty-seven), and border state Delaware is at number fifteen with fourteen executions; the addition of these two states gives the southern region an even more disproportionate ratio of the top twenty death penalty states in the United States.[3]

The South's capital punishment numbers are not so one-sided compared to the North in a study of the years 1608 to 1976. According to the nonprofit Death Penalty Information Center, New York, Pennsylvania, and California are in the top ten states, with 1,130, 1,040, and 709 executions, respectively. Arkansas is eleventh in the country and Missouri is twenty-first out of the fifty states researched, plus Washington, D.C.[4] Not only should there be consideration for the records kept in the years before the Revolutionary War, where many of today's states were territories or their existence was not even known, but this period predates many of the twelve states that have a capital punishment moratorium.

Moratoriums have been part of the death penalty's changing standards and attitudes. Missouri and eight other states abolished the death penalty between 1907 and 1917. It was reinstated in Missouri in 1919 after some well-publicized murders, and in other states at other times for much the same reason. "In Arkansas the electric chair would be unplugged and used for giving haircuts." California constitutionally banned the death penalty, but that state's citizens voted in favor of reinstatement by a two-to-one margin in November 1972. The change in the national consensus, if considered a main reason, was quite different from only ten years before, the beginning of the moratorium for many states, where, for example, "in New Hampshire the execution chamber would be used to store vegetables."[5]

An article in the October 18, 2007, *New York Times* posed the question, "Is there a moratorium in place in New York?" Linda Greenhouse reported that "the Supreme Court has granted two stays of execution and refused to vacate a third in the three weeks since it agreed to hear a challenge to Kentucky's use of lethal injection." The case involved New York's last death row inmate. She connected that event with news that "the top criminal court in Texas, a state that accounts for 405 of the 1,099 executions carried out in this country since 1976 has indicated that it will permit no more executions until the Supreme Court rules." According to the article, other states' cases were also affected, including Nevada, Alabama,

Virginia, and Georgia. However, an Arkansas case that "raised the lethal injection issue nine years" after the final ruling was denied another judgment.[6]

Arkansas and Missouri newspapers reported crime that resulted in prosecutor offices that asked for the ultimate punishment. Under the headline "Bluntforce, Strangulation Listed as Causes of Death," Arkansas's *Ashley County Ledger* reported the preliminary autopsy report on thirty-one-year-old Jennifer Carpenter. After listing the location of the deceased's body with the date and time of discovery, the *Ledger* also reported Carpenter's husband was being held in the county jail, the arraignment time, the judge's name, and that the prosecutor was asking for the death penalty. The September 22, 2007, article also stated "the capital murder was committed in an especially cruel and depraved manner" and the husband had "previously committed another felony." The newspaper reported the husband as the only suspect in the second-grade teacher's death.[7] Arkansas had thirty-seven inmates on death row as of January 2007, according to Death-PenaltyInfo.com, the nineteenth-highest state in the nation.

Twenty-four hours before the *Ashley County Ledger* article, the west Missouri community of Farmington's *Daily Journal* contained the headline "Prosecutor to Seek Death Penalty in Haynes Murder." The paper reported that St. Francois County prosecuting attorney Wendy Wexler Horn announced her intention to seek the death penalty against a twenty-two-year-old male, of Park Hills, and another in the death of Ricky Haynes. "They are both charged with first-degree murder and two counts of stealing," and had two previous charges including assault and stealing. The men admitted they beat the victim and then returned to finish him off, which meant they "got his car out of the deal."[8] Missouri had fifty-one death row inmates as of January 2007, as reported by DeathPenaltyInfo.com and Clarkprosecutor.org websites, respectively, which showed Missouri with the sixteenth largest capital punishment population in the United States.

In comparison, the Department of Justice 2005 year-end report listed the states with the top three most populous death rows as California with 646, Texas with 411, and Florida with 372 awaiting execution.[9] An updated DeathPenaltyInfo.org page showed, for January 2007, California's death row population at 660, Texas at 393, and Florida at 397, an increase for California and Florida and a decrease for Texas in just over one year's time. The highest numbers, which change intermittently, for state death row populations and executions were also mostly southern states, with eleven of the top fifteen at latest report.

The changes in death row numbers are more clearly seen when contrasted with totals from over a decade before. Among the thirty-eight death penalty states, the Justice Department's 1993 report showed a different ranking in both executions and "number of prisoners under sentence of death." Out of thirty-eight executions nationwide for the year, Missouri was third with four, behind Virginia with five and Texas with seventeen. And the total number of death row inmates nationwide in 1993 was 2,716, compared to 3,350 in January 2007, again according to the Department of Justice's year-end 1993 report and DeathPenaltyInfo.org, respectively.

A comparison of methods of execution in 1993 and 2006 also showed changes. "Lethal injection was the predominant method of execution (25 states): 12 states authorized electrocution, 8 states lethal gas, 3 states hanging, and 2 states a firing squad," according to the 1993 Justice Department report on the thirty-nine execution methods.[10] The Clark County Prosecutor's Office website listed lethal injection as the method of execution in all but one case for both 2006 and 2007, the remaining execution in each of those years being by the electric chair. The total executions in 2006 were fifty-three, an increase over the 1993 total of thirty-eight.[11]

The means of execution in Arkansas in every case from 1820 to 1913 was hanging, except four men who were shot in 1864. From 1913 to 1990, the electric chair was used in each execution, except one hanging in 1930. From 1990 on, lethal injection has been the primary method, according to state statute 5-4-617(a)(1); however, Arkansas provides for an election for electrocution. Twenty jurisdictions provide for "alternative methods of execution," including Arkansas and Missouri. "Contingent upon the choice of the inmate, the date of the execution or sentence, or the possibility of the method being held unconstitutional,"[12] an alternative may be available. The location of death row in Arkansas for men is Grady and for women is Pine Bluff.

The method of execution in Missouri from 1810 to 1937 was hanging, except one man who was shot in 1864. The gas chamber was prevalent there from 1938 to 1965. There were no executions from 1965 to 1989. The primary death sentence method from 1989 to the present has been lethal injection (state statute 546.720); however, the alternative in Missouri is lethal gas. The location of Missouri's death row for men is Mineral Point and for women is Fulton.

The methods used to inform the public of a death penalty and its outcome include national and local media and government and private agencies, and their websites. Whether the trial's outcome involved deterrence or retribution, past executions were public affairs. As Banner wrote on page one of his book, "[T]he death penalty was understood as something that had to be seen in order to have its maximum effect." They were even considered family affairs and "especially wholesome for the children" to see the outcome of a criminal life, according to Banner's eighteenth-century colonial entries. Public

display, the execution, and the prolonged showing of the corpse were intended as preventative measures to potential criminals.[13] Public executions were commonplace in Arkansas and Missouri, also.

The events were meant to draw attention to the crime, the criminal, and the justice for law-abiding citizens. "People occasionally propose modifying the ceremony to make it even more frightening—for instance, by staging the ceremony at night."[14] Banner pointed out that changing popular attitudes occurred in the beginning of the nineteenth century involving the public exhibitions of state-sponsored killing. The upper and middle classes became embroiled in many cultural changes at this time, which included the emerging technologies of the industrial age, a more refined societal expectation, and decidedly American public image awareness. Discussions and actions concerning public executions, as Banner illuminates, point out the disparity between northern and southern attitudes toward the death penalty. "Between 1830 and 1860, every northern state moved hangings from the public square into the jail yard." Most southern hangings and shootings were kept in public view until much later, into the 1900s.[15]

Banner placed part of the blame for the South's deliberate sluggishness regarding change in death penalty venues on its desire to control the slave population. The Civil War era saw all public executions in the North becoming private and taken into the jail yard for a private audience. Adroitly revealing that crowds probably wouldn't need to witness an execution to prevent them from committing a crime, the focus on capital punishment's existence switched to retribution. Missouri had stopped public executions, along with several other chiefly border states as well as Louisiana, by the beginning of the twentieth century, but Arkansas continued to hold executions publicly except for rape.[16]

Since most of the general public was not allowed to view executions, news and proof of the criminal's demise needed to be disseminated. American mass newspaper readership was treated to tawdry tales of murder, mayhem, and then execution. Many stories were deemed sordid and displeasing to sensibilities. The newspaper stories, combined with the carnival-like atmosphere of the execution sites they were thought to have created made the Fourth Estate's attendance at executions in New York illegal in 1888. Other states including Arkansas "barred journalists from describing hangings." The laws were difficult to enforce, however, and the public liked the news.[17]

The venue for executions changed because of public demand, in an effort to be more humane, less painful, and less public. Public hangings made private, for selected crowds, and firing squads with shooters not knowing whose guns had live ammunition, exemplified some of the changing standards in the death penalty. "The later executions were attacked in the northern press, which saw them as evidence of southern backwardness." Stories of the proceedings included descriptions of partying, drinking, and general rowdiness. A Massachusetts newspaper in 1901 described a recent Arkansas execution as resembling a "sideshow" with exhibitions doing business. Arkansas moved its capital punishments inside that same year.[18]

The gallows became a symbol of barbarity. "Between 1888 and 1913 fifteen states adopted the electric chair as their means of executions." As noted earlier, Arkansas used the electric chair at different times. "By 1950, eleven more states plus the District of Columbia had followed. Another new device, the gas chamber, was first adopted by Nevada in 1921 and then by ten other states by 1955." Missouri also used the gas chamber. Societal standards changed and more humane methods and locations were used for executions.

Eventually the gas chamber was questioned when several inmates were left gasping for breath and the death penalty's existence was called into question.[19]

These times marked a departure from the days of public whipping, flogging, burning at the stake, and dismemberment. "The debate over capital punishment that engulfed the northern states in the first half of the nineteenth century," Banner told us, "was virtually absent from the South." Banner deduced that "the difference was a product of slavery." The Southern state laws were harsher on slaves for everyday crimes than whites, and one of the reasons for the civil rights movement was this incongruity of the law, which continued in some areas long after the Civil War. Banner also pointed out the pamphleteering and crowd gathering that might lead to slave revolts was a capital crime, "a practice largely limited to blacks."[20]

Proliferation of sectional and regional differences in sentencing between Northern and Southern states, Banner declared, suggested through statistical analysis that the South was more inclined to the death penalty. "The South's retention of capital punishment for blacks was surely a direct result of slavery." Whites were a minority in three Southern states and made up less than two-thirds of the population of five Southern states before the Civil War. Capital punishment had long been a subject for debate in the North during the Civil War, but not in the South.[21]

Banner's writing expanded from discussing the South's aggressive pursuit of justice through capital punishment's active use to the discussion of rape cases, a capital offense in eighteen Southern states as late as 1954, with the majority executed being black. He continued that "five states, all Southern, still retained the death penalty for arson," which included Arkansas. And robbery was a capital offense in nine states, all Southern, including Missouri.[22] Banner asserted the regional and racial discrepancy with capital crime in the South helped fuel the civil rights movement in the 1950s.

Several African American organizations yearly call for the repeal of the death penalty. The National Association for the Advancement of Colored People posts anti-capital-punishment articles on its websites dealing with the demographics of the death row population in the United States and the likelihood of minority and low-income prisoners being executed. The NAACP Legal Defense and Educational Fund quarterly report as of January 1, 2007, broke down, among other statistics, Arkansas and Missouri death row prisoners by race. Arkansas had thirty-seven death row inmates, fourteen white and twenty-three African American. Missouri had fifty-one death row inmates, thirty white and twenty-one African American.[23]

Another active anti-death-penalty organization is Amnesty International. Their website has stated a deterrence argument against the death penalty, citing that "scientific studies have constantly failed to find convincing evidence that the death penalty deters crime more effectively than other punishments." The group listed figures with the number of executions over a recent two-year period. In 2006, there were sixty executions in the United States, with one in Arkansas and five in Missouri. In 2007 as of October 11, there were sixty executions, with none in Arkansas or Missouri. The website also mentioned possible innocent prisoners on death row. "Since 1973, 123 U.S. prisoners have been released from death row after evidence emerged of their innocence of the crimes for which they were sentenced to death. . . . [T]he state of Florida has the highest number of exonerations."[24]

The fear about the possibility of innocents being executed has been debated for years. The death penalty debate has brought to light exonerations for death row inmates that were later found not to have committed the crime because of new DNA evidence, because the sentence was disproportionate to the crime committed, or as a result of flawed testimony. Since 1976, the year the death penalty was reinstated in the United States marking the end of the national death penalty moratorium, 231 clemencies have been granted, including two Missouri death row inmates and one from Arkansas. During the national moratorium on executions from 1968 to 1976, various governors from Arkansas, Illinois, Ohio, and New Mexico commuted all death sentences in their respective states. Before the moratorium, governors from Massachusetts, Oklahoma, Oregon, and Tennessee granted clemencies to death row prisoners.[25]

The clemencies in Missouri and Arkansas are worth noting. The 1999 clemency in Arkansas showed a juror didn't believe in the sentence. The 1999 Missouri clemency was granted during Pope John Paul II's visit, and the 1993 clemency stated that the prisoner had varying degrees of retardation.[26]

According to the Center on Wrongful Convictions at Northwestern Law School, there have been nineteen exonerations from Arkansas since 1923 and twenty-three from Missouri where the case years were not listed. The website indicated roughly half of the death penalty convictions were overturned from faulty eyewitness information.[27]

New evidence or recanted testimony had been the elements that have brought reprieve from a death sentence countless times in the past. But if this information becomes known after a death sentence has been carried out, it would be difficult for the justice system, whose aim is to protect and defend citizens, for the lawyers involved, and for the prisoners' families. And reopening cases after the fact is an anti-death-penalty advocate argument. In the case of Dr. Hawley Harvey Crippen, who was executed in 1910 for the murder and the dismemberment of his wife, reopening the case is possible since "there is evidence that Crawley may not have committed the crime." The American doctor living in London was the recent subject of a History International Channel episode on reopened cases.[28]

A more recent example involved a case from 1995. The St. Louis *Post-Dispatch* cited on July 14, 2005, "a new report saying Larry Griffin was innocent of a drive-by shooting . . . for which Griffin was executed 10 years ago."[29] An article in the *New York Times* online archives from June 22, 1995, stated, "Mr. Griffin's lawyers said the sole witness to the shooting, now in the Federal witness protection program, had recanted. They said another federally protected witness had admitted" to the killing.[30] "When death penalty advocates appear before Congress, they often justify their position by saying no innocent person has ever been executed in the United States." The article continued with the Griffin story and a quote from prosecutor and National District Attorney Association board member Joshua Marquis, that "opponents of capital punishment have been unable to locate any case in which an innocent person has been executed. If they did, I'm sure it would have a profound impact on the discussion."[31] A local headline from July 12, 2007, summed up the possibilities. "Reopening Griffin Case May Sway Debate Over Executions–Terry Ganey."[32]

There have been many exoneration stories which have revealed some of the complexities the justice system and suspects face. A 1978 rape conviction was overturned as "the product of both a mistaken eyewitness identification" and hair analysis that was held under scrutiny with more recent DNA analysis. The prisoner was the two-hundred-seventh person aided with the DNA technology.[33]

The technology's existence broadens the power of enforcement agencies to apprehend and convict criminals and "exonerate those who may be wrongfully convicted." The Missouri General Assembly passed Senate Bill 100 in 2004 to require felons and sex offenders to give DNA samples. "Once all existing offenders have samples collected and analyzed," the state will have over 100,000 offenders catalogued.[34]

Statistical interpretation is at the heart of the death penalty debate. Anti-death-penalty advocates quote the homicide rate per 100,000, the crime associated with receiving the death sentence, and the number of executions from 1990 forward to state the death penalty does not change the murder rate. The U.S. Department of Justice figures show in 1990 there were twenty-three executions and the homicide rate was 10.0 per 100,000, with a steady increase in executions to ninety-eight by 1999, with a homicide rate of 6.2 per 100,000. The year 2000 listed eight-five executions and the homicide rate at 6.1, showing a steady decline in both sets of numbers.

Pro-death-penalty groups show a more dramatic ratio of executions and homicides in the United States, listing the moratorium years of 1968 to 1976 with no executions and the homicide rate rising from 7.3 in 1968 to 10.1 in 1974, then staying around 9.0 in 1976, with a slight increase the next two years, before going to the historical high of 10.8 in 1980, a year in which there were no executions.[35] Interpreting statistics requires disclosing outside information that would be considered pertinent to a true understanding of the figures in a final analysis. Therefore it is important to note the average amount of time on death row is twelve years,[36] which impacts the meaning of any graph presentation of homicide rates and execution numbers. For example, the U.S. execution rate from 1930 to 1949, the depression and World War II years, was never under 119, varying between 119 and 195, while the homicide rate was between 8.8 and 9.7 through the depression and 5.0 to 6.8 during the wartime era—at face value a comparatively high execution rate, more than double today's rate, with about an equivalent homicide rate.

Banner attributed the increase in death sentences in the last third of the twentieth century to a lack of governor commutations. A quick basic summary was offered in a death penalty tome. "20,000 murders in the United States annually . . . average of 300 people are sentenced to death . . . 55 are executed each year. Only 19 states actually carried out executions between 1976 and 2002. 86% [of the executions in the U.S. were] . . . in the South . . . two states—Texas and Virginia—carried out 45 of them."[37]

Arkansas statistics from 1960 forward indicate a similar pattern, with only one execution in Arkansas from 1961 to 1989, and a homicide rate that declined from 11.2 to 8.1 in that same almost-forty-year period. More recent figures show a homicide rate of 12.0 with five executions in 1994, then steady decreases to a 5.2 homicide rate with zero executions in 2002, and a 7.3 rate and zero executions in 2006. Missouri was similar to Arkansas with zero executions from 1966 to 1989, not using the death penalty until thirteen years after the federal reinstatement, and a similar homicide increase rate during those years, peaking in 1978–1980 with rates per 100,000 of 10.4, 11.2, and 10.4, respectively. Anti-death-penalty groups point out after the death penalty resumed in Missouri, there was a spike in homicides with double digits in 1991–1994, while pro-death-penalty groups will list 1995–2006 as years when the homicide rate decreased from the previous high with an increase in executions.[38]

Death penalty cases in the United States have fueled many questions, not just from Americans, but from people abroad. Many times the people who question America's death penalty process are political and diplomatic partners. One such question Yale Law School's Avalon Project has made available. Shortly after the September 11th attacks on the World Trade Center, there was a news conference with U.S. Ambassador William Farish and Attorney General John Ashcroft.

At that December 21, 2001, London conference, the attorney general was asked a variety of questions that related to national security and international terrorist rumors. A reporter asked about someone's concern that "if British troops were to capture Osama Bin Laden that they wouldn't hand him over to the United States unless they had assurance that he wouldn't face the death penalty." The reporter then asked Ashcroft if the death penalty will be a problem if there are guarantees the "extradited would not face the death penalty." Attorney General Ashcroft responded that the United States has death penalty laws and suspects are dealt with on a "case by case basis."[39]

The idea of cases being decided on their own merits has influenced both anti- and pro-death-penalty groups. Amnesty International opens their website through the University of Arkansas with a question and response. "Why does Amnesty International oppose the death penalty in all cases? The death penalty violates the right to life and security of the person as proclaimed in the Universal Declaration of Human Rights." The statement of purpose continues that death is final and eventually capital punishment will claim an innocent person.[40] The Amnesty International USA website lists Missouri with three local groups and twenty-six student groups, and Arkansas with two local groups and five student groups.

Another website declaring itself to be a "Pro Death Penalty Webpage" gives this statement of purpose: "This webpage is dedicated to the innocent victims of murder, may they always be remembered." A supporting statement mentions the argument that if executions have failed to stop murders, then we should close all the prisons, too. Bureau of Criminal Justice data and graphs are referenced to indicate rising murder rates when execution rates were falling, and quotes Texas homicide rates and executions with the preface "the most striking protection of innocent life has been seen in Texas."[41]

The interpreted facts and figures are the current method of trials and executions made public. Not exactly a gallows in the town square, but information because of the people's right to know. Banner surmises privately held executions in the late eighteenth century "would have seemed vaguely tyrannical." He then quotes a Georgia legislator in 1859 who didn't want a Bastille in his home state, and if trials are public, then executions should be public.

Arkansas and Missouri have both been involved with lawsuits, each with different outcomes, on the current private nature of executions. Arkansas had a local chapter of the American Civil Liberties Union file a lawsuit concerning the public-versus-private argument and nature of death penalty proceedings. The lawsuit seems to mirror the opinion of the aforementioned Georgia legislator. The ACLU's executive director stated, "America is an open society, and we do not carry on trials or carry out executions in secret." The Arkansas News Bureau article "Lawsuit Filed to Open Execution Process" said the suit was filed for an Arkansas branch of professional journalists to allow journalists access to death penalty proceedings.[42] The U.S. Court of Appeals in Missouri ruled in 2004 against a religious group's lawsuit to allow recording equipment to show an execution. The New Life Evangelical Center group, which owns radio and television stations in Arkansas and Missouri, stated that they wanted "to show the immorality of lethal injections." The ruling upheld Missouri's Department of Corrections ban on filming, which does allow reporters to "carry pen and paper to observe lethal injections in Missouri."[43]

The last public execution in the United States was in 1936. Rainey Bethea was hanged in Owensboro, Kentucky, before a crowd of twenty thousand. "In a frenzy of irresponsible journalism, the newspapers falsely reported that the crowd was an outrageous mob out of control. . . . Public

outrage resulted," and public executions were outlawed in Kentucky, while the other states followed the example.[44]

Banner opines that "hangings could turn criminals into heroes," and there is no opportunity for redemption.[45] Timothy McVeigh was convicted of terrorism in the Oklahoma City bombing of a federal building, which killed 168 people in 1995. Three hundred people witnessed the execution, some on closed-circuit monitors. The federal government has ruled that public executions are illegal.

The legality of the death penalty for juveniles is under heavy scrutiny. Among the topics discussed at a symposium at Cornell University, with former alumnus and U.S. attorney general Janet Reno, included "why the United States refuses to sign international covenants against the juvenile death penalty."[46] As another topic under the death penalty umbrella for discussion, it is contentious in the United States, as one of five countries in the world that executes juvenile offenders. Countries other than the United States that include juveniles with capital crime sentences are China, the Democratic Republic of Congo, Iran, and Pakistan.[47] Both Arkansas and Missouri have laws in place that specify the minimum execution age at sixteen.

The constitutionality of federal and state laws has been called into question repeatedly over the years. Federal decisions both in favor of and against the juvenile death penalty are in the flex stage. The *Legal Times* article from Law.com reported "the Supreme Court, in *Eddings v. Oklahoma* (1982), reversed the death sentence of a 16-year-old tried as an adult." The decision was based on the premise that at this age, the prisoner was not yet mentally or emotionally developed, and being tried as an adult would be cruel and unusual punishment, wording included in the Eighth Amendment traditionally used for death penalty defense. The Court did not include in its ruling whether the death sentence on the sixteen-year-old was illegal. A case involving a fifteen-year-old in 1988 concurred with the Supreme Court's statement that capital punishment for a juvenile was unconstitutional, and in 1989, the *Stanford v. Kentucky* ruling stated there is not cruel and unusual punishment with juvenile death penalties.[48]

The case of *Roper v. Simmons* was decided in favor of sparing the life of a then seventeen-year-old Missouri boy who robbed a house with two friends, tied up the resident, and threw her off a bridge. "The Supreme Court on Tuesday ruled 5–4 that executing juvenile offenders is no longer constitutional, a dramatic reversal of precedent that laid bare angry divisions among the justices." In 2005, the Court again ruled giving a juvenile the death penalty. "Juveniles are different, and those differences make the death penalty a cruel and unusual punishment for them," said American Bar Association president Robert Grey Jr. It reiterated the ruling from the case of *Atkins v. Virginia* in 2002 that here was another ruling against juvenile executions. The judges' majority and dissenting opinions summarized much of the controversy about responsibility for actions, accountability, and whether any age should be held up to adult standards.[49]

Simmons was judged ineligible for parole with life in prison. The judgment upheld *Atkins v. Virginia* and concerned the Eighth Amendment inclusiveness of prohibition of the death penalty for someone deemed mentally retarded. The judgment included a dissenting judge's comment regarding an international consensus on juvenile execution, which referred at least partially to the United Nations Convention on the Rights of the Child, Article 37. The November 20, 1989, article states that "the death penalty may not be pronounced on a protected person who was under 18 years of age at the time of the offence."[50] Every nation has ratified the article except the United States and Somalia.

The Eighth Amendment is used as the most common capital punishment defense, particularly because of the phrase "cruel and unusual punishment," which was taken from the English Bill of Rights. And its interpretation has much to do with the legal rulings involving not only juveniles, but capital punishment in general. The argument appears to involve the original intent of the Constitution's framers in 1791, and the idea that there are evolving standards of beauty, as written in the 1958 case *Trop v. Dulles*. The changing standard usually wins, which partially accounts for most of the juvenile death penalties which have been overturned. Stanley Adelman observed, "Adding the 18 states that have a death penalty but exclude juveniles from it to the 12 states that do not have any capital punishment, the majority tabulated 30 states that do not permit the execution of juveniles."[51] There are currently twelve states whose laws set a minimum age of sixteen or younger as allowable for capital punishment, four states that hold seventeen-year-olds accountable as adults, and seven states that don't specify an age for full societal accountability. State statutes for this article, Arkansas Ark. Code Ann. §5–4-615 (Michie 1997) (no express age) and Missouri Mo. Rev. Stat. Ann. § 565.020 (1999) (minimum age of sixteen), are included.[52] Twenty-two death row inmates who were juveniles when they committed a capital crime were executed between 1976 and 2003, one from Missouri.[53]

The changing standards of the death penalty, court proceedings, and the meaning of the Eighth Amendment's cruel and unusual punishment clause also affect the always changing national attitudes on the death penalty. According to Banner, "By the end of the twentieth century, capital punishment would be back with a vengeance. The annual number of death sentences would be close to three hundred, a figure higher than at any time since the Justice Department began keeping count in the 1930s . . . after nearly a century of declining popularity" and mostly not used through most of the 1960s. The Gallup Poll indications of the public's opposition to the death penalty changed in the early 1970s from 50 percent to 65 percent in favor in 1976, possibly from some well-publicized murders and serial killers. It is generally believed that Michael Dukakis sealed his doom in his presidential bid in 1988 when he voiced his opposition to capital punishment.[54] Then-Arkansas governor Bill Clinton took a break from the presidential campaign trail in 1992, to oversee a death sentence back in his home state. By 1994, public support for capital punishment had risen to 80 percent.[55] The surge in popularity continued through the 1990s in the midst of urban gang wars, when there were ninety-eight executions in 1999, the most since 1951 with 105. "According to Gallup's latest update on public support for the death penalty, 65% favor it as the penalty for someone convicted of murder, while 31% oppose it," Gallup's website reported. However, 56 percent of African Americans oppose the death penalty.[56]

Americans' affinity for the death penalty was present even when the death penalty's outcome wasn't what was expected. Throughout the changes in appropriateness, then venues, rulings as to age, and different technologies, not all new devices worked as planned. Banner recounted several apparatuses that used the prisoner's weight for the execution. And whether it was flowing water filling a container or the weight from shotgun shot tripping a scale and hauling the prisoner upward to asphyxiation, the new methods were meant to be more humane. These new methods, and some of the standard ones, didn't always accomplish the desired effect. Banner told of prisoners who were hung and came back to life,

either naturally or surreptitiously. Companions would use various concoctions, alcohol, or artificial resuscitation to bring someone back to life. Or they would be scratching from the inside of their coffin, whereby the capital punishment had to be repeated. And there was the Arkansas man Joe Bogard who "went into hiding" after coming back to life. Whether revival after execution involved the use of brandy, a battery, and ammonia spirits on North Carolina's Jack Lambert, or involved naturally regaining consciousness, it occurred enough to warrant a New York newspaper to suggest using the guillotine. [57]

Some latter-day examples of Arkansas and Missouri botched lethal injection executions, as told on the deathpenaltyinfo.com website, are worth noting. The execution problems involved finding suitable veins for the three-drug cocktail to enter the system, which delayed Arkansas resident Rickey Rector's 1992 death. In another execution the chemicals stopped flowing, which lengthened the death pronouncement to thirty minutes after Missourian Emmitt Foster's 1995 execution began. In Arkansas in 2000, Christina Riggs's execution was delayed to allow the staff to find usable veins. And in 2000, Missourian Bert Hunter had a reaction to the drugs designed to end his life. His body jerked as he heaved his chest in convulsions, and he reportedly died painfully.[58]

Among those against the death penalty are medical professional groups. They may be the most influential, as we have already seen in the Kentucky lethal injection case that has produced a wave of state-sponsored moratoriums on executions. Three of the groups involved in a moratorium of their own are the American Society of Anesthesiologists, the American Medical Association, and the Association of Emergency Medical Technicians. Together they perform various medical procedures during the death sentence process, including mixing and administering the drugs for the injection, and the death pronouncement.

Dr. Orin Guidry, president of the forty-thousand-member ASA, issued a statement after U.S. district judge Fernando Gaitan Jr. halted Missouri executions because of lethal injection issues. Guidry advised anesthesiologists to steer clear of executions, because it involved ending a life. The death penalty is against the oath sworn to protect life. The lethal injection process, said Guidry, also involves pain, suffering, and cruel and unusual punishment.[59] With professional anesthesiologists' nonparticipation in executions, prisons were forced to rely on their own staff. "Many of the personnel involved lack formal training or clinical experience in providing sedation or anesthesia care to patients," Guidry said. The Missouri court had ruled that a professional must be present, and "clearly an anesthesiologist complying with the Missouri ruling would be violating the AMA position which the ASA has adopted." He agreed a professional does need to be present, but ASA members should not shirk their oath to their patients.[60]

With those words, the ASA president sided with AMA president William G. Plested III, who rejected doctor participation. Involvement would "erode public confidence in their profession." The physician, Plested continued, is dedicated to saving life and the AMA Code of Ethics is designed to address the death penalty questions regarding doctors' participation. The EMT and paramedic society's press release of July 17, 2006, stated that "the NAEMT is strongly opposed to participation in capital punishment by an EMT, paramedic, or other emergency medical professional." The position statement concluded that participation in taking a life is against their oath.[61]

Politics and the death penalty have collided on more than one occasion, and in 2001 Amnesty International heavily criticized President Bill Clinton and his vow to justice for using "politics over human rights" for his actions during his presidency. The group's issues with Clinton revolved around the scheduled execution of Juan Raul Garza and Clinton's stating "his support for the death penalty" and he is "not imposing a moratorium on federal executions." The execution never took place, but the human rights organization nevertheless felt the president should have used the opportunity to "live up to the human principles he has so often claimed to support during his term in office." The online documentation entitled "President Clinton Passes the Buck on Execution" claimed that "he postponed the Garza execution until June 2001, to allow the Justice Department time to gather and properly analyze" racial and geographic disparities in the federal justice system. The group also highlighted over five hundred executions had taken place worldwide during the Clinton years, while twenty-eight countries abolished the death penalty. He even stopped his 1992 campaign in New Hampshire to oversee the death penalty on Arkansas's Rickey Rector, so his constituents could not say he was soft on crime, claimed the group.[62]

The political reporting on the death penalty's changing allegiances showcased Clinton's visit to Rickey Rector's execution, in a *New York Times* article entitled "The 1992 Campaign: Death Penalty: Arkansas Execution Raises Questions on Governor's Politics," by Peter Applebome. The question put to the reader concerned Clinton's refusal to issue an executive clemency to halt the execution of a disabled man. Printed January 25, 1992, the article's premise pondered what a Clinton presidency would be like based on his actions.[63] An article in the *New Yorker* "discusses how President Bill Clinton chose to handle the potentially politically damaging situation" of whether to stop Rector's execution. How could Rector, the article questioned, "with self-inflicted wounds (that) left him with the comprehension of a child" be allowed to die?[64]

The division of belief in the death penalty or its political fallout had an example in an article a former Clinton political advisor wrote for the *Arkansas Times*. The piece, titled "Testimonial: Former Bill Clinton Advisor against Death Penalty," told of the advisor's belief the death penalty should not exist, and how her belief was tested with a personal tragedy. When her twenty-one-year-old niece was brutalized and then murdered, she wrote that executing the assailant was not the answer. The death penalty "denies the power of Christ to redeem." The retribution of the criminal's death would be a premeditated murder and she disagreed with that sentiment.[65]

An Arkansas man who had to be drugged every day, including his execution day, made news around the world. Charles Singleton was in the headlines for the question of his sanity and medically diagnosed disabilities without drugs. Singleton's lawyer stated it was in his client's "best interest to take the medicine until the resulting sanity puts him on the path to execution." However the lawyer said when trial is set, it would be "unconstitutional to keep Singleton artificially sane." His mental state was in question throughout the trial, as it was through much of his medical history.[66] Singleton was Arkansas's longest-term death row inmate. He was convicted for killing a grocer, Mary York, who had befriended him.[67]

A CNN article printed before Singleton's January 6, 2004, lethal injection said, "Arkansas' attorney general has determined that appeals have been exhausted," making capital punishment possible. The U.S. Supreme Court ruled "the forced medication was acceptable" and the drugs aided his mental state. His twenty-five years on death row were interspersed with attempts to thwart the death penalty—an example, anti-death-penalty supporters would argue, of the high cost of execution. Sixteen hearings were listed, about one every other year. The main concern was the forced medication of a death row inmate to stand trial, and then be executed. The court said it was a successful balancing act and was justified in its decision to move forward with the execution.[68] His final words were reportedly a long religious tract.[69]

Amnesty International reported that the mentally ill were still sentenced to death. "The execution of the insane is unconstitutional in the USA, but in 2003, the US Court of Appeals for the Eighth Circuit ruled that he could be forcibly medicated" to make him eligible to stand trial.[70] Continental opinion on executing the disabled and mentally impaired was slightly different from statements about American justice in the past. "Majority public opinion in several European nations would like to apply the death penalty in certain circumstances," however politics plays a large role in an implementation such as that. And France's then President Mitterand helped the "death penalty continue to be outlawed in European countries."[71]

Another question about Charles Singleton and his forced medication was brought by Ivan Oransky's article in *Lancet*. Singleton and a Tennessee man, Stanley Deutsch, were discussed with regard to drugs. Singleton's case forced doctors to break their oaths to provide medicine for him to end his life, and Deutsch was found guilty of murder and sentenced for execution. One of the chemicals used for lethal injections, which was the execution method for both prisoners, was a recommendation of Deutsch's when he was a state medical school professor.[72]

The medical ethics question was again raised and Michael Grodin from Boston University and director of the school's medical ethics program asked the inquiries. Doctors should not be ending people's lives, Grodin affirmed; it was against the interests of the profession and the patients. He stated the American Nursing Association was against the Singleton ruling. The prisons have only the recourse of using their own trained staff, which some anti-death-penalty supporters have stated has led to executions that were cruel and unusual punishment for the prisoners.[73]

Anti-death-penalty advocates often tout the argument that the expense of the death penalty is more than life in prison. The cost of legal fees, extra guards for death row inmates, and the appeals process were listed in a Blue Springs, Missouri, attorney's article to the local newspaper. Entitled "Death Sentence Carries Hidden Costs," attorney Ken Garten asked how an inmate charged with rape, murder, and abduction can receive a fair trial.

Garten said a "grand standing District Attorney" was having press conferences, and it takes more things like proof of the crime for a guilty verdict. Then he got to the point of his essay, the expense of death penalty proceedings. His points are well taken, since they include presumably his firsthand knowledge of proceedings.

The Blue Springs attorney states that execution costs are "many times more than incarcerating them for the rest of their lives," then asks how this could be so. He argued that death penalty cases invariably go to trial, with no plea bargain, that the defense fights every way possible, then the two-trial process with testimony from many professionals. Next the cost of the appellate court process is figured, with its endless appeals. Then he supplied examples from other states. "Texas determined that the cost of housing a prisoner at the very highest level of security for 40 years was one-third the total cost of the average execution." Kansas and Florida also were quoted as having studied the cost of life in prison versus execution and found the death penalty more expensive.[74]

The argument over monetary costs involved with the death penalty encompasses other areas of the process. In a 1998 article, a writer for the Biloxi *Sun Herald* reported that Mississippi would give up the gas chamber. The reason was it would save twenty thousand dollars every year in upkeep. And lethal injection was considered more humane. "The bill now goes to the Senate. Similar legislation is pending in the House." Senator Ron Farris also questioned the time change for executions, since the new time makes overtime mandatory.[75]

With the most recent news from the Gallup Poll that for the first time, a majority of those polled are in favor of life imprisonment over the death penalty, there seems to be another change of attitudes and therefore a change of public opinion.

The current moratorium that seems to be in place on executions will have an effect, one way or another, on capital punishment opinions. And coupled with the current exclusive use of lethal injection in death penalty cases, while the professional medical societies are discouraging their members from participating, a change in the death penalty process is definitely possible in the foreseeable future.

Timothy R. Finch is a member of the American Historical Association. He is also a member of the Society for the History of Authorship, Reading and Publishing, and Phi Alpha Theta.

Notes

1. Stuart Banner, *The Death Penalty: An American History* (Cambridge, Mass.: Harvard University Press, 2003), 3.
2. Banner, 216.
3. http://www.clarkprosecutor.org/html/death/dpusa.htm (July 3, 2007).
4. http://www.deathpenaltyinfo.org/article/php?scod =8&dod=1110 (Oct. 1, 2007).
5. Banner, 222, 266.
6. *New York Times*, October 17, 2007.
7. http://www.ashleycountyledger.com/articles/2007 /09/22/news/h16fo82y.txt (Sept. 22, 2007).
8. http://mydjconnection.com/articles2997/09/21/news/ doc46f47b8255961916593609.txt (Sept. 22, 2007).
9. http://www.ojp.usdoj.gov/bjs/pub/ascii/ep05.txt (Oct. 1, 2007).
10. http://www.ojp.gov/bjs/pub/press/cp93.pr (August 7, 2007).
11. http://www.clarkprosecutor.org/html/death/usexecute. htm (Oct. 30, 2007).
12. http://www.clarkprosecutor.org/html/death/methods. htm (Oct. 30, 2007).
13. Banner, 1, 28, 70–73.
14. Ibid., 12.
15. Ibid., 146.
16. Ibid., 155.
17. Ibid., 163.
18. Ibid., 155.
19. Ibid., 155, 163, 201.
20. Ibid., 113, 154.
21. Ibid., 142–143.
22. Ibid., 228.
23. http://www.naacpldf.org/pdf/pubs/drusa/DRUSA_win ter_2007.pdf (Oct. 8, 2007).
24. http://amnestyusa.org/abolish/listpending.do?value =2007 (Oct. 11, 2007).
25. http://www.deathpenaltyinfo.org/article.php?did=126 &scid=13 (Oct. 31, 2007).
26. http://www.deathpenaltyinfo.org/article.php?did=126 &scid=13 (Oct. 31, 2007).
27. http://www.law.northwestern.edu/depts/clinic/wrong ful/exonerations/Arkansas.htm (Oct. 6, 2007).
28. *History International Channel* (Sept. 7, 2007).
29. St. Louis *Post-Dispatch*, from http://www.exonerations. com (Oct. 6, 2007).
30. http://query.nytimes.com/gst/fullpage.html?res=990C E2D71F3AF931A15755C0A963958260 (Oct. 31, 2007).
31. St. Louis *Post-Dispatch*, from http://www.exonerations. com (Oct. 6, 2007).
32. http://www.stltoday.com/stltoday/news/stories/nsf/ laworder/story/ d1f01c75b2e7ae238625731500723 384? opendocument (Sept. 13, 2007).
33. http://www.exonerate.org/2007/120 (Sept. 8, 2007).
34. http:www.doc.mo.gov/pdf/DNA_info.pdf (Sept. 17, 2007).
35. http.www.ojp.usdoj.gov/bjs/glancetables/exetab.htm (Oct. 2, 2007).
36. http://www.ojp.usdoj.gov/bjs/pub/ascii/ep05.txt (Oct. 1, 2007).
37. *Debating the Death Penalty: Should America Have Capital Punishment? The Experts on Both Sides*, Hugo Adam Bedau and Paul G. Cassel, eds. (Oxford, U.K.: Oxford University Press, 2005), 153.
38. http:www.disastercenter.com/crime/mocrime.htm (Oct. 15, 2007).
39. Avalon Project interview transcripts, from http://www. yale.edu/lawweb/avalon/sept_11/ashcroft_005.htm (June 17, 2007).
40. http://comp.uark.edu/~amnesty/faqs.html (Sept. 15, 2007).
41. http://www.wesleylowe.com/cp.html (Oct 1, 2007).
42. Rob Moritz, "Lawsuit filed to open execution process," *Arkansas News Bureau*, Oct. 12, 2007, from http://www. arkansasnews.com/archive/2007/07/26/news/342862. htm (Oct. 12, 2007).
43. Davin White, "Missouri Law is Constitutional," *Quill* 92, no. 7, p. 17.
44. Perry Ryan, *The Last Public Execution in America*, from http://geocities.com/lastpublichangpreface.htm (Sept. 3, 2007).
45. Banner, 148, 155.
46. http://www.news.cornell.edu/releases/Oct03/juvenile. justice.ssl.html (Oct. 31, 2007).
47. http:www.amnestyusa.org/abolish/juveniles.html (Sept. 15, 2007).
48. Office of Juvenile Justice and Delinquency Prevention Report: Juveniles in Corrections, from http://www.ncjrs. gov/html/ojjdp/202885/page16.html (Aug. 14, 2007).
49. Tony Mauro, "Legal Times," March 2, 2005, from http:// www.law.com/jsp/article.jsp?id=1109597699575 (Oct. 31, 2007).
50. http://www.unicef.org/emerg/files/HSNBook.pdf (Sept. 29, 2007).
51. Stanley Adelman, *Corrections Today* 67, no. 5 (Aug. 2005), from http://web.ebscohost.com.lib—proxy.fuller ton.edu/ehost/detail?vid= (Oct. 6, 2007).
52. http:www.law.cornell.edu/supct/html/03–633.ZO.html (Sept. 29, 2007).
53. http://www.deathpenaltyinfo.org/article.php?scid =27&did=882 (Oct. 31, 2007).
54. Banner, 267, 268.
55. Michael L. Radelet and Ronald L. Akers, "Deterrence and the Death Penalty: Views of the Experts," in *The Journal of Criminal Law and Criminology* (1973–), Vol. 87, No. 1, (Northwestern University School of

Law), (Autumn 1996), 1, from http://links.jstor.org (Sept. 17, 2007).

56. http://www.galluppoll.com/content/?ci=28243&pg=1 (Sept. 14, 2007).

57. Banner, 174–75.

58. http://www.deathpenaltyinfo.org/article.php?scid=8&did=478 (August 23, 2007).

59. *Los Angeles Times*, July 2, 2006.

60. http://www.asahq.org/news/asanews063006.htm (Sept. 3, 2007).

61. http://www.deathpenaltyinfo.org/article.php?did=1849&scid=64 (July 18, 2007).

62. http://web2.amnesty.org/library/index/ENGAMR 511832000?open (Oct. 1, 2007).

63. http://topics.nytimes.com/top/reference/timestopics/people/c/bill_clinton/index.html?query=RECTOR%20Rickey%20Ray&field=per&match=exact (Sept. 29, 2007).

64. http://xerxes.calstate.edu.lib-proxy.fullerton.edu/fullerton/metasearch (Sept. 29, 2007).

65. http://www.arktimes.com/articles/articleviewer.aspx?articleid=8419c363-dd38–4a8e859f—cce4f42e9fd7 (August 29, 2007).

66. http://www.cnn.com/2003/LAW/11/04/execution.insanity.ap/ (Sept. 18, 2007).

67. http://www.prodeathpenalty.com/pending/04/jan04.htm (Sept. 18, 2007).

68. http://wwwcnn.com/2003/law/02/27/findlaw.analysis.colb.drugs.execution (Sept. 18, 2007).

69. http://clarkprosecutor.org/html/death/US/singleton887.htm (Sept. 18, 2007).

70. http://web.amnesty.org/library/index/engamr511 492003 (Sept. 18, 2007).

71. John O. McGinnis and Ilya Somin, "Should International Law Be Part of Our Law," in *Stanford Law Review* 59, no. 5, footnote 163, 1208, from http://www.unesco.org/courier/2000_10/etique.htm (Sept. 18, 2007).

72. Ivan Oransky, "Who—and How—to Kill Are Focus of US Death Penalty Cases," *Lancet* 362, no. 9392 (10/18/2003), 1287, from http://web.ebscohost.com.lib-proxy.fullerton.edu (Oct. 7, 2007).

73. Ibid.

74. Ken Garten, Eastern Jackson County (Independence, Mo.) *Examiner*, from http://examiner.net/stories/080107/leg_188361722.shtml (August 14, 2007).

75. http://legalminds.lp.findlaw.com/list/deathpenalty/msg00583.html (Sept. 5, 2007).

CHAPTER 19

Capital Punishment and Corporal Punishment in the California Gold Mines

Andrea McDowell

CAPITAL PUNISHMENT carried out by private citizens independently of the courts is usually called murder, if it is executed by an individual, and lynching, if it is the work of a crowd. During the California gold rush, however, the tens of thousands of miners in the foothills of the Sierra Nevada found themselves in a peculiar position: there was at first no government, then a government but no courts, and then for some time a court system so inadequate to the circumstances as to leave the mining population in legal limbo.[1] The men in the mining camps believed that under these conditions, they had a legal right to try and to punish criminals, just as they assumed the right to pass their own mining regulations.[2]

Early in the gold rush, it seemed possible that another system of criminal law might emerge, namely, that elected judges would preside over trials. In the fall of 1848, a group of miners caught a suspected thief and named Kimball Dimmick "judge" to try the case.[3] Dimmick, a member of the New York bar and a former army officer, organized a court and held "a fair trial conducted on common law principles."[4] The accused was found guilty and sentenced to forfeit all of his property and was banished from the mines. The next day,

the court tried and convicted two thieves; it sentenced one to fifty lashes on his bare back and the other to twenty-five lashes. For a while, Dimmick said, he "ruled these 'diggins,' meting out Justice and making the laws." After a month or two, however, he resigned his office and moved to San Jose.[5] Talented, respected individuals could do better for themselves than serving as a judge in the goldmines.

In the town of Marysville, an *alcalde* or justice of the peace tried civil and criminal matters long after lynch trials had become the norm in the mines. Stephen Field was elected to the office on January 18, 1850.[6] Since the new state constitution of California had just gone into effect, Field was officially appointed to the post. As one would expect from a future chief justice, Field ran a model court. "In criminal cases," he wrote, "when the offence was of a high grade, I went through the form of calling a grand jury, and having an indictment found; and in all cases I appointed an attorney to represent the people, and also the accused, when necessary."[7] Field said that the population generally recognized his fairness and sustained his decisions. When it came to punishing a convicted thief, however, Field had to bow to the community's sense of justice.[8] He could not send the prisoner to San Francisco to be put in the chain gang because transportation was too expensive, and he could not release the prisoner because the crowd would not have allowed it. Therefore, to save the criminal's life, and although it was repugnant to his own feelings, Field ordered the man to be given fifty lashes in public and banished from the vicinity. Field privately instructed a physician to observe and see to it that the whipping was not unnecessarily severe.[9]

Dimmick and Field were able to control a criminal trial because they had the necessary moral authority and willingness to punish, but they were in the minority among alcaldes. In most accounts, alcaldes are described as weak or corrupt, and when a crime was committed, the miners replaced the alcalde with a temporary judge elected from the crowd.[10] In other words, the miners resorted to lynch law.

Especially in the first years of the gold rush (1848–1850), the miners tried to see that justice was done. Their lynch trials were relatively formal and provided most of the common-law procedural safeguards, such as a jury and a defendant's right to counsel. That these trials were not merely pro forma is suggested by the substantial number of acquittals. Also, the crowd frequently reduced an initial sentence of hanging to a less severe form of corporal punishment, often after heated debate. Executions, when they did occur, can therefore fairly be called capital punishment rather than murder. Over time, however, as official courts were created and asserted their authority, miners sped up their proceedings, and these increasingly disintegrated into lynchings as we know the term.

That the miners ever managed to hold orderly trials and punishments seems implausible at first. America has a long history of extrajudicial punishments, from tarring and feathering in the colonial period to lynching as a form of racial domination.[11] The actors in every case justified themselves on

the grounds that the courts were unwilling or unable to act. It is well known that the readiness to take the "law" into their own hands has done Americans more harm, sometimes much more harm, than good, and that the consequences are still with us today.[12] The trials and punishments in the gold rush are exceptionally well documented, however, and there is good evidence that early trials in particular were surprisingly formal and fair. They were similar to criminal trials on the Overland Trail documented by John Philip Reid, which should come as no surprise since many of the overland emigrants were on their way to the gold mines.[13]

Confusingly for us, the miners called their trials "lynchings" and their criminal law, "lynch law." Today, lynching denotes racist executions by a mob, but that meaning became standard only after the Civil War.[14] Before then, the word had been applied to extrajudicial punishment of crime, usually on the frontier beyond the reach of the courts. It often involved some kind of trial, and the punishment was usually flogging. Not until the 1840s did lynchings result in hanging. This is not to say that lynching was accepted practice in the antebellum period; most Americans, especially in the Northeast, opposed lynching, and the California miners were defensive about the practice in newspaper articles intended for an eastern public and in letters home. But lynchings were not yet as horrific as they later became. This article will use the terms *lynching, lynch trial,* and *lynch law* as the Californians did, and as other Americans would have understood them, to mean trial and punishment in the absence of official courts.

Criminal Procedure

The crimes punished by "lynch law" were principally theft and murder. Trials took place in public and, ideally, involved a sheriff, a judge, a twelve-man jury, a prosecutor, defense counsel, and witnesses. Defendants who were acquitted were released; those found guilty were sentenced by a majority vote of the miners who attended the trial. Needless to say, some lynchings disregarded some or all of these formalities, and hasty executions became more frequent over time. Defenders of lynch law, however, regarded these breakdowns as departures from lynch law and degenerations into mob law. "Judge Lynch has done some things badly in his day," said the editors of the *Daily Alta California*, "but suffers more from his counterfeit rival Mob Law, than from any act of his own."[15] Critics of the institution regarded orderly lynchings and summary executions as all of a piece and denounced them all as mob law. The miners were more likely to be apologists than critics, however.

The rules of lynch law were seldom written, unlike those governing mining claims.[16] Only two mining codes are known to have included criminal provisions, namely, those of Mariposa and Jacksonville.[17] The latter is the most comprehensive; it contemplates two crimes, theft and murder, and two penalties, banishment and death:

ARTICLE XII. Any person who shall steal a mule, or other animal of draught or burden, or shall enter a tent or dwelling, and steal therefrom gold-dust, money, provisions, goods, or other articles, amounting in value to one hundred dollars or over, shall, on conviction thereof, be considered guilty of felony, and suffer death by hanging. Any aider or abettor therein shall be punished in like manner.

ARTICLE XIII. Should any person willfully, maliciously, and premeditatedly take the life of another, on conviction of the murder, he shall suffer death by hanging.

ARTICLE XIV. Any person convicted of stealing tools, clothing, or other articles, of less value than one hundred dollars, shall be punished and disgraced by having his head and eye-brows close shaved, and shall leave the encampment within twenty-four hours.[18]

This list of crimes is clearly not complete; for instance, it includes burglary but not money stolen at gunpoint. That it does not mention claim jumping is not an oversight, however. Claim jumping was not an offense in itself; in fact, the term meant taking over a claim that had been abandoned. If there was a dispute about the status of the claim, that was a civil matter and not a crime.[19]

The Jacksonville Code also spells out the proper procedure for a criminal trial. It directs that criminal cases should be tried to a jury of eight American citizens, to be increased to twelve if the accused so desires. The jury is to be sworn by the alcalde and to try the case according to the evidence. For the rest, "the rule of practice shall conform, as near as possible, to that of the United States, but the forms of no particular state shall be required or adopted."[20] The convicted criminal was required to pay the costs of the trial, unless he had no money, in which case the jurors and officials had served for free.[21] We are not told who, if anyone, paid the jurors if the accused was acquitted.

Although the Jacksonville Code is unique as a written document, it is clear from many reported cases that the procedures it describes represented "best practice" throughout the mines. Joseph Warren Wood, writing at the relatively late date of 1852, said that in all cases of lynch law or mob law that he witnessed, "[t]he form of a court most dear to Americans has always been adopted, and the prisoners have been allowed the widest construction of the privileges usual on such occasions."[22] Executions without trial did happen, as discussed below, though Wood was fortunate not to have witnessed them; but most lynchings did involve some semblance of a trial by judge and jury, no matter how defective they might be in other ways.

The judge and jury were selected by the onlookers from amongst themselves. They generally allowed the accused to have counsel, though this question and other points of procedure might be put to a vote.[23] After hearing the evidence, the jury pronounced the verdict. Occasionally, particularly in the early years, this was an acquittal for lack of evidence or because the accused acted in self-defense. Theodore Taylor Johnson wrote in 1849 that he had met a man who was generally believed to have committed murder in the preceding winter. He was tried twice "under the forms of lynch law." The first jury could not reach a verdict, and the second acquitted him.[24] Several other miners were accused of stealing money, but acquitted for lack of evidence.[25] Juries also acquitted a murder suspect whom they believed to be guilty but against whom there was insufficient evidence,[26] a miner who mistook his partner for a thief and shot him,[27] another who killed in self-defense.[28] Acquittals were rare but they did happen. If the verdict was guilty, the jury often suggested a sentence, but the final decision on this matter was decided by the majority vote of all the miners present.

Theft

The majority of trials in the mines were for theft, which under the Jacksonville Code carried a penalty of death. The word among newcomers to the mines was also that thieves would be hanged. On his arrival in San Francisco in 1849, for instance, Charles Randall told his parents, "As regards trouble or safety give yourselves no uneasiness[.] a man here is hung for stealing."[29] In practice, however, hanging was not the rule; it seems that roughly a third of convicted thieves were executed. The number may be even less, because

reports of executions are often vague and may have originated in rumors.[30]

Detailed reports of sentencing often describe disagreements over the proper punishment, with part of the crowd voting for hanging and others arguing for a lesser penalty such as flogging. For example, a man caught in the act of stealing three thousand dollars was tried and convicted by a jury and sentenced to hang. There was "some opposition to taking his life," however, and the sentence was reduced to a "milder punishment," namely, whipping, cropping his ears, shaving his head, and banishing him from the vicinity.[31] In another case, when the crowd could not decide between the options of hanging a convicted thief, on the one hand, or whipping and branding, on the other, it submitted the question to a committee. On the committee's recommendation, the man was given fifty lashes, branded with an "R," and banished from the camp.[32] In yet a third example, a sailor from Ohio was sentenced to death for stealing more than five thousand dollars; but there was some objection to taking his life and the sentence was indeed changed to one hundred lashes, cropping his ears, and shaving his head.[33]

Notably, a single individual or a group of friends could galvanize opposition to hanging. Vincente Rosales, by his own account, actually managed to persuade a group of miners to release a Chilean whom, he said, they had sentenced to death.[34]

On the other hand, a significant number of thieves were indeed hanged, sometimes over the objections of a part of the crowd. The execution of Jim Hill was particularly contentious.[35] A unanimous jury convicted Hill of stealing an iron safe and five thousand dollars. "It was then voted"—by the jury or the crowd, the text is not clear—to hang him. Hill pleaded for mercy. When the question was put to the people, "Shall he be hung?" the vote was split. "Immediately some hundreds of pistols were drawn and a universal stampede occurred. Horsemen plunged through the crowd and over them, and the people ran in every direction."[36] The miners who wanted to see Jim Hill dead managed to get their hands on him and did the deed themselves.

Another thief was sentenced to hang an hour after he was convicted, though men "more mildly disposed" managed to have that extended to three hours. Everyone was surprised that he was actually executed; even those who hanged him thought that "at the last moment the jury would release the prisoner and substitute a milder punishment."[37] Possibly the many commuted sentences led jurors and others to think that a sentence of death would not, in fact, be carried out. Finally, a motion for trial by jury was once hooted down, and a rival motion to hang the prisoner at once passed and carried into effect.[38] Observers might have called this last case "mob law" rather than lynch law because there was no trial. Nevertheless, it is clear that those who opposed hanging were not always able to stop it.

The miners' letters and diaries seldom specify who applied the punishment. Those that provide this detail name the sheriff[39] or the marshal[40] as doing the flogging. Cutting off the convicted man's ears was work for a specialist. In one case, a doctor took on the task; in another, lots were drawn for who was to do the job, but the man himself begged a doctor who was present to do it instead and the doctor complied.[41] Hanging will be discussed in the next section.

Murder

Most murders were committed as part of a robbery; a thief reduced his risk of capture substantially by killing his victim. Ruthless and efficient highway robbers preyed on miners traveling with their gold from the mines to the cities. The criminals attacked their victims at night when they were sleeping, decapitating them or crushing their skulls with axes or stones.[42] Those murderers and thieves who were apprehended were amateurs by comparison; they were miners or cooks or other members of the mining community and acted more or less on impulse. The frustration about the many unsolved murders added to the community's passion with respect to the killers on whom they did manage to get their hands.

Lynch law provided only two possible outcomes for a murder trial; acquittal or execution. The lesser forms of corporal punishment were not considered. For this reason, too, the stakes were higher when the prisoner was accused of murder rather than theft.

As mentioned earlier, some murder suspects were acquitted, showing that not every lynching was a rush to execution. But, as one would suspect, other crowds and juries were fueled by anger, prejudice, or self-interest. John Hovey's account of the Iowa Log Cabins incident provides an example of such a flawed lynch trial.[43] Hovey was one of a group of Americans who wanted to expel a party of Chileans from their mining claims. The Chileans were alleged to have shot some American miners in their cabins in retaliation. The surviving Americans "empanelled a jury to set on the bodys [sic], and returned a verdict accordingly that they came to their Death, by the hands of the Chileans, to us unknown."[44] To make a long story short, fourteen suspects were taken and a jury of twelve from Hovey's group tried and convicted them of murder in the first degree.[45] Sentencing was postponed until the next day.

Then something extraordinary happened. In the morning, some ninety men from the neighboring Moquelumne came over to take part in the proceedings. Clearly they were concerned about the justice being meted out to the defendants. There was a new vote on what to do with the accused, and it was decided "to empanel a jury and give them a fair trial, from Disinterested persons and cappable [sic] men from the other River."[46] The newcomers also provided the defendants with "a young and smart Lawyer from the City of Boston, by the name of Melville." Two defendants whom the first jury had convicted were now released without trial, one of whom was a boy who had "turned State Evidence." The jury found nine of the remainder to be peons acting under orders from their masters. These were sentenced to one hundred lashes and to have their heads shaved. One also had his ears cut off. Only the three masters were sentenced to death.[47] In short, the population of neighboring diggings managed to take the lynching out of the hands of the interested parties and give the accused something more like a fair trial. Hovey, who was hostile to the Chilean defendants, reports all of this without criticism, perhaps because he was satisfied with the terrible punishment.

Individual miners sometimes protested against breakdowns in procedure at murder trials, but without success. Edward Gould Buffum described his helplessness at the lynching of three men for attempted murder and robbery. The accused had no counsel and could not even follow the proceedings because they did not know English. "I mounted a stump," Buffum said, "and in the name of God, humanity, and law, protested against such a course of proceeding; but the crowd, by this time excited by frequent and deep potations of liquor from a neighboring groggery, would listen to nothing contrary to their brutal desires, and even threatened to hang me if I did not immediately desist from any further remarks."[48] Another deeply flawed lynching was that of the Downieville woman known as Juanita. Some thought she had been guilty of murder, others believed she had killed in self-defense, but in any case, the proceedings were chaotic.[49] Following a jury trial that lasted a full day, she was hanged "with the hungriest, craziest, wildest mob standing about that

ever I saw anywhere," wrote David Barstow.[50] The mob then "turned on" a certain Dr. Aiken because he had tried to defend her, though it is not said to have hurt him.[51]

The most chaotic lynchings happened when the miners clashed with the new legal authorities. State courts became active in the fall of 1850 and wanted to take over the trial and punishment of murderers.[52] Very few suspects held by the authorities were brought to trial, however, let alone punished; the court system was simply not equal to the problems posed by California's peculiar circumstances.[53] The criminal courts sat only in major population centers and only six times per year, and there were few jails, so that it was almost impossible to hold suspects for trial. Marysville, for instance, a moderately sized town, had no jail until January 1851.[54] Even then, jailbreaks were frequent; on June 5, 1851, for instance, ten prisoners escaped when their guard was away from his post.[55] Defense counsel often requested postponements and by the time the case came to trial, it was difficult or impossible to get the necessary witnesses, especially since they were not paid to attend.[56] In short, it was extremely difficult to get a suspected murderer to trial.

As if that were not enough, the judges and sheriffs were notoriously incompetent and corrupt.[57] The grand jury of Tuolumne County made a presentment on the disrespect for the laws, which it blamed, in part, on "failures, neglects, and incompetency of public officers."[58] It was widely believed that surrendering the prisoner to the authorities was practically the same as releasing him. As one miner wrote, the chances of escape afforded by the slow process of law "created a disposition to inflict summary punishment on the offender rather than allow him the chances of escape afforded by the slow process of the law."[59]

The miners' suspicions resulted in battles over the prisoner's person, with the officers and the miners who supported them attempting to get the man safely in jail or keep him in jail and others fighting to get their hands on him and hang him on the spot. In a typical example, a man in Hangtown was to be tried for murder, but was instead merely examined before the judge and the sheriff and, presumably, remanded for trial. At that point, "the mob raised the cry 'Bring him out! [H]ang him!'" and made a rush for the prisoner.[60] He "was seized by the hair and dragged a short distance to an oak tree a rope was put around his neck and over the limb of the tree and some men took hold of the end and hoisted him up as they would a hog to be dressed where he hung until he was dead."[61] In another affair, a crowd that had hanged one man for theft decided to keep going. Two other prisoners, both from Sydney, were in the jail. Once the "mob" had hanged the thief, someone shouted, "Let's hang the Sydney Convicts."[62] The excited crowd rushed over to the jail, pushed in the door, brought the men out, and hanged them on the same tree as the thief.

And yet even under these conditions the miners sometimes managed to hold a quick trial. William Binur wrote that "[t]he Officers have got a way of letting Criminals off and the people wont [sic] stand it so they take them from the Shireff [sic] choose a Jury try them and have them strung up in an hour or two which is the only wae [sic] to do it in these parts."[63] Although Binur makes the hearing sound like a mere formality, in fact a number of trials of prisoners taken from the authorities were as elaborate as any reported from the mines. For instance, Jesus Sevaras, also known as Charley the Bullfighter, was alleged to have been involved in the gruesome murder of Jacob Mincer.[64] He was in the courtroom being tried by the civil authorities when the "five or six hundred miners standing round" decided to try him themselves.[65] They wrested him from the sheriff and took him to the edge of town. There they selected twelve jurymen and "a justice named A.J. Lowell, of St. Louis Council, administered the oath."[66]

A string of witnesses testified that Charley had been seen in the area about the time of the murder and identified the knife found at the scene as Charley's.[67] The jury retired briefly, returned a verdict of guilty, and "asked the people to pass the sentence. Several hundred rose to their feet & declared he should be hung in one hour," which he was.[68] Other descriptions of such trials contain less detail but follow the same pattern.[69]

On the other hand, those in favor of handing over the prisoner to the proper authorities did sometimes win the day, as when a man named Simmons shot and killed a certain Elmendorff who was paying unwanted attentions to Simmons's wife. The victim's friends wanted to hang Simmons without trial, but through the interference of others he was indicted and jailed to await trial in Sonora.[70] Just as the more "mildly disposed" argued that a thief should be whipped rather than hanged, they or men like them urged their fellow miners to cooperate with the sheriff rather than execute suspected murderers on their own authority. For instance, when a baker in Grass Valley shot an acquaintance over a trifling matter, a crowd took the baker with the intention of hanging him. "[B]ut a little delay occurring in getting a rope, objections were made to the proceedings by some of the bystanders, and it eventually ended by handing Doyle over to the officers of the law, and he was sent off to jail."[71] The sheriff and his supporters even managed to win some tussles over prisoners.[72]

The physical details of execution are often recorded. "Men were hung in the readiest way which suggested itself—on a bough of the nearest tree, or on a tree close to the spot where the murder was committed."[73] The act itself was sometimes carried out by driving a wagon or a horse out from under the condemned man, leaving him hanging,[74] or by kicking out from under him the box on which he stood.[75] At other times, a group of men pulled the rope that strung up the prisoner. For instance, the Swede William Brown was hanged by the jury with the assistance of "all who felt disposed to engage in so revolting a task."[76] The amateur hangmen often bungled their job.[77] When Jesus Sevaras was executed, for instance, he hung gurgling and quivering for some time and "the people began to turn away & leave the horable [sic] & painful sight." Sevaras was only put out of his misery "when a rough looking Customer drew his revolver stepd [sic] up & shot the swinging Man through the body."[78]

At least one execution was by firing squad. The three men sentenced to death in the Iowa Log Cabins incident were executed at their campground by a line of twenty men.[79] Ten members of the squad had blank cartridges, and ten had bullets.

What finally put an end to lynching was the growth of stable communities with a long-term interest in the state.[80] Order and respectability were strengthened, Bancroft says, "by the presence of woman, when she came, as well as of churches, schools, lyceums and piano-fortes."[81] David Shaw put the end of "trial by the people" at 1856.[82]

Miners' Attitudes toward Lynching

What we know about lynch law is derived from first-person accounts, and many of the descriptions above reveal the writers' feelings about what they saw. There is more to be said on this subject, however. In general, miners accepted lynching as necessary or even praiseworthy under the circumstances, but many were concerned about some particular lynching they had witnessed or found the punishments painful to watch.

As to why the authors of preserved accounts attended lynchings in the first place, some went because they were asked to be present,[83] others because they had never seen a lynching and were

curious.[84] Most of them wrote as observers rather than participants,[85] using the third person, writing "they" gave him thirty lashes rather than "we" gave him thirty lashes. A miner called "Sam" attended a trial and execution, but he himself "refrained from participating in all of the proceedings . . . and only voted with the citizens once, and that was in the affirmative on the second proposition to give him a lawyer."[86] This remark suggests that at least some miners in the crowd did not take part in the trial. It may even have been the case that the lynching was carried out mainly by one portion of the population and that those "more mildly disposed" got involved only when it seemed that the accused would be hanged.

With respect to lynching as an institution, feelings were mixed. The lynchings themselves are evidence that many miners thought it was justified; moreover, it was often said that lynch law was bad, but better than no law.[87] Some writers were unsure, torn between the self-evident problems of lynching and the lack of alternatives.[88] There were also those who thought lynch law was simply and always wrong.[89] In other words, feelings about lynching ran the gamut. All writers were aware that the population in the East would disapprove of lynching; however, the tone of letters and newspaper articles alike is defensive or apologetic.

When it came to the actual infliction of punishment, many were revolted by whipping and mutilation; indeed, spectators appear to have found them more gruesome than hanging.[90] David Shaw, admittedly writing long after the event, stated that some men convicted of stealing horses and mules were sentenced to have their heads shaved, to be branded on the right cheek with the letter "R," to receive one hundred lashes on the bare back, and to be banished from the mines. But "[a]fter administering 50 lashes the committee decided to remit the balance, as the men were unable to bear the torture," Shaw wrote. "It looked cruel and inhuman, and not all eyes among the spectators were tearless."[91] Kimball Dimmick, as judge, sentenced two thieves to fifty and twenty-five lashes respectively. He wrote his wife, "I never saw men so severely whipped before, and never wish to again."[92]

Dame Shirley did not see two Spaniards being whipped near her home, but could not help hearing the process and was badly shocked. "I had heard of such things, but heretofore had not realized that in the nineteenth century men could be beaten like dogs, much less that other men not only could sentence such barbarism, but could actually stand by and see their own manhood degraded in such disgraceful manner."[93] One of the two, "a very gentlemanly young Spaniard," begged to be killed rather than suffer the vile "convict's punishment" to which he had been sentenced.[94] When whipping was combined with branding and cutting off the ears, the sight—and the experience—must have been ghastly.[95]

Finally, one must not forget the nature of our sources. The diaries, letters, and newspaper articles on which this article is based of course give the perspective of the writing population. The authors are literate and have family in the East with whom they want to keep in touch and to whom they intend to return. Most of the letters were sent to relatively settled parts of the United States; very few were from frontiersmen whose loved ones were in Missouri or Texas. Almost

certainly, therefore, the rougher, more footloose portion of the population is not represented in the sources.

That said, we can draw some conclusions about majority attitudes toward corporal and capital punishment. Most miners opposed capital punishment for theft. If a convicted thief was sentenced to death, the crowd was usually persuaded to reduce the punishment to whipping. On the other hand, Stephen Field and others who thought that even whipping was too harsh believed that this was the lightest practicable penalty given the passion of the crowd. Which leads to another question about whether the miners' views on criminal punishment were representative of Americans generally: would the punishments have been as harsh if half of those present had been women? Bancroft thought not, that the appearance of women changed the tone of society. Perhaps, then, the history of the mining camps at most reflects the views of American men of the mid-nineteenth century regarding criminal law and the execution of corporal and capital punishment.

Andrea McDowell is a Professor of Law at Seton Hall Law School. She has written three articles on law in the California gold rush and is currently writing a book on the same subject. McDowell has also written extensively on law in Ancient Egypt.

Suggested Bibliography

Johnson, David A. "Vigilance and the Law: The Moral Authority of Popular Justice in the Far West," *American Quarterly* 33 (1981): 558.

McDowell, Andrea. "Criminal Law beyond the State: Popular Trials on the Frontier," *Brigham Young University Law Review* (2007): 327.

Reid, John Phillip. *Policing the Elephant: Crime, Punishment, and Social Behavior on the Overland Trail* (San Marino: Huntington Library Press, 1997).

Waldrep, Christopher. *The Many Faces of Judge Lynch: Extralegal Violence and Punishment in America* (New York: Palgrave Macmillan, 2002).

Williams, Mary Floyd. *History of the San Francisco Committee of Vigilance of 1851*. University of California Publications in History 12 (Berkeley: University of California Press, 1921; republished New York: DaCapo Press, 1969). Available on books.google.com.

Notes

1. Gary Lawson and Guy Seidmen, The Hobbesian Constitution: Governing without Authority, 95 NW. U. L. REV. (2001), 581, 585–590 (noting that from May 30, 1848, to December 12, 1849, California had only a de facto military government, not authorized by Congress); Andrea McDowell, "Criminal Law beyond the State: Popular Trials on the Frontier," *Brigham Young University Law Review* (2007), 327, 335 (showing that the state court was not in a position to hear criminal cases until late August 1850 at the earliest).

2. Earlier studies of criminal law in the goldmines include David A. Johnson, *Vigilance and the Law: The Moral Authority of Popular Justice in the Far West*, 33 Am. Q. (1981), 558, 564 (discussing accounts of lynchings as a ritual carried out by a nameless and faceless crowd); Mary Floyd Williams, *History of the San Francisco Committee of Vigilance of 1851*, University of California Publications in History 12 (1921), 142–147, available on books.google.com; and McDowell, *Criminal Law beyond the State*, 327.

3. Kimball Hale Dimmick, Letter to Sarah (wife) (Oct. 26, 1848) (unpublished manuscript in the Bancroft Library, catalogued at C-B 847).

4. Id.

5. Dimmick, Letters to Sarah dated January 1, 1849, San Francisco (stating that he had resigned his office and was now "free to attend to my own matters and not to settle the disputes of others"). In San Jose, Dimmick became chief judge, but was also able to deal in land. *Ibid*, letter dated May 1, 1849, Pueblo San Jose.

6. Stephen J. Field, *Personal Reminiscences of Early Days in California* (1893; DaCapo Press reprint ed., 1968), 23–26, available at http://memory.loc.gov/ammem/cbhtml.

7. Ibid., 31–31.

8. Ibid., 33.

9. Id.

10. Dame Shirley (Mrs. Louise Amelia Knapp Smith Clappe), The Shirley Letters from California Mines in1851–52 (Thomas C. Russell, ed., 1922), 123, available at http://memory.loc.gov/ammem/cbhtml/cbhome.html (letter written October 29, 1851) (stating that the miners of Indian Bar set aside the justice of the peace and voted in their own president and jury to try a man accused of theft). See also James H. Carson, *Recollections of the California Mines* (1852; Joseph A. Sullivan, ed., Biobooks, 1950), 36 (stating that "trifling disputes" were submitted to the alcalde, but the miners themselves tried those accused of theft or murder).

11. Richard Maxwell Brown, *Strain of Violence: Historical Studies of American Violence and Vigilantism* (1975).

12. See Christopher Waldrep, *The Many Faces of Judge Lynch: Extralegal Violence and Punishment in America* (2002).

13. John Phillip Reid, *Policing the Elephant: Crime, Punishment, and Social Behavior on the Overland Trail* (1997).

14. Waldrep, *Many Faces, passim*.

15. Editorial, Judge Lynch, *Daily Alta Cal.*, Oct. 13, 1850, 2. See also Judge Lynch, Daily Alta Cal., Oct. 18, 1850, reprinting an article from the *Placer Times* but adding, "The *Times* does 'Judge Lynch' wrong by the heading of the following article. It was Mob Law, not Lynch Law. His Honor never proceeds to punishment without some evidence of guilt."

16. Much has been written on the mining codes. The first published collection of such codes was Clarence King, *The United States Mining Laws and Regulations Thereunder* (Washington, D.C.: Government Printing Office, 1885) (compiled as part of the tenth census of the United States in 1880).

17. The Mariposa Law Code of March 1, 1851, was signed by 215 individuals. Jean-Nicolas Perlot, *Gold Seeker: Adventures of a Belgian Argonaut During the Gold Rush Years* (1985), 104–105 (stating also that the code was passed to "replace the missing laws of the United States," that is, laws not yet promulgated in California); Jacksonville Code of January 20, 1850, reprinted in Daniel B. Woods, *Sixteen Months at the Gold Diggings* (1851; Ayer Co. Publishing, 1973), 125, available at http://memory.loc.gov/ammem/cbhtml/ cbhome.html.

18. Daniel Woods, Sixteen Months, 128–129.

19. See, e.g., Andrea McDowell, "Real Property, Spontaneous Order, and Norms in the Gold Mines," 29 *Law & Social Inquiry* (2004), 771, 780.

20. Ibid., Article V, 126.

21. Ibid., 129.

22. Joseph Warren Wood, Diaries of Crossing the Plains in 1849 and Life in the Diggings from 1849 to 1853 (June 25, 1852) (unpublished manuscript in the Huntington Library).

23. Letter from Sam to Willie dated Feb. 27, 1851, Sacramento City. Bancroft Mss C-B 547 Pt. I:53 (stating that he participated in a vote to allow the accused to have

counsel); Daniel W. Kleinhans, Memoirs 13 (unpublished transcript in the Bancroft Library, catalogued at ts. C-D 5056) (stating that there was discussion on whether a jury member could be a witness).

24. Theodore T. Johnson, *Sights in the Gold Region, and Scenes by the Way* (New York: Baker and Scribner, 1849), 185, available at http://memory.loc.gov/ammem/cbhtml.

25. Shirley, Letters, 152 (stating that a man accused of stealing $1,800 from his partner at Indian Bar in December 1850 was tried and acquitted for lack of evidence); Kimball Webster, *The Gold Seekers of '49* (Manchester, N.H.: Standard Book Company, 1917), 177–178 (jury reported that the accused was probably guilty, but as there was a little doubt, he was entitled to the benefit of that doubt and should be released).

26. Johnson, *Sights in the Gold Region*, 185 (the first trial resulted in a hung jury, the second in the defendant's acquittal); *Stockton Times*, October 25, 1850 (Mexicans accused of murdering an American were released for lack of evidence); Shirley, Letters, 160–161 (Letter dated December 15, 1852, describing case of two men arrested for murder but released without trial for lack of evidence).

27. "A Most Melancholy Death," *Placer Times*, November 10, 1849 (a jury of miners found that A. N. Kent killed his partner Kendall by accident at Dry Creek on October 25, 1849; those present passed a resolution of sympathy).

28. "Fatal Affray," *Daily Alta Cal.*, May 3, 1849 (describing the incident and naming the victim as Rodrick M. Morrison and the killer as Henry J. Freund).

29. Charles Henry Randall, Letter to Parents, September 12, 1849, in William Benemann, *A Year of Mud and Gold: San Francisco in Letters and Diaries, 1849–1850* (2003), 14; see also Letter from Charles Henri Doriot to Victor Doriot (July 12, 1851) (unpublished manuscript in the Bancroft Library, catalogued at MSS 85 70 C, saying of the miners, "they make their oan laws theives and murderers they generally mob them").

30. E.g., William Jackson Barry, *Up and Down: Or, Fifty Years' Colonial Experiences* (S. Low, Marston, Searle & Rivington, 1879), 102, available at http://books.google.com (stating that Hangtown got its name because Mormons hanged two men for stealing there in 1848); Theodore Johnson, *Sights in the Gold Region*, 185 (stating that "a score" of men were hanged for theft and other offenses in 1848); Carson, *Recollections*, 36 (reporting that an unidentified French man stole a horse in 1848 and was hanged—but the same author mentions this incident in Peter Browning, *Bright Gem of the Western Seas* (1991), 139, where he says the man was whipped).

31. David Augustus Shaw, *Eldorado: Or, California as Seen by a Pioneer, 1850–1900* (1900), 143.

32. Letter from Jacob H. Engle to Brother (June 3, 1852) (manuscript, on file with the Huntington Library; this letter is also reproduced in Jane B. Grabhorn, *A California Gold Rush Miscellany* [1934], 34–35).

33. William Redmond Ryan, *Personal Adventures in Upper and Lower California*, in 1848–9 vol. 2 (London: W. Shoberl, 1850), 62–63.

34. Vincente Pérez Rosales, "Vicente Pérez Rosales 1807–1866," in *We Were 49ers! Chilean Accounts of the California Gold Rush* 1, 64 (Edwin A. Beilhzarz & Carlos U. López, eds., 1976).

35. Enos Lewis Christman, *One Man's Gold: The Letters and Journal of a Forty-Niner* (Florence M. Christman ed., 1931), 190, available at http://memory.loc.gov/ammem/cbhtml (describing the trial of Hill for stealing a safe from a store). The same incident is described by David C. Ferson, California Correspondence, Shaw's Flat (July 10, 1851) (unpublished manuscript in the Beinecke Library, catalogued at WA MSS S-1315).

36. Christman, *One Man's Gold*, 192.

37. Shirley, Letters, 156.

38. "Lynched on the Consumnes," *Stockton Times*, March 12, 1850, reprinted from *Marysville Herald*, March 11, 1850; for another summary hanging, see Shaw, *Eldorado*, 59 (reporting on an Australian hung for stealing from a tent in August 1852).

39. Letter from Allen Varner to David Varner (Mar. 5, 1850) (unpublished manuscript in the Huntington Library).

40. Field, Personal Reminiscences, 34 ("[T]he marshal marched the prisoner out to a tree, made him hug the tree, and in the presence of the crowd that followed, began inflicting the lashes").

41. Samuel McNeil, *McNeil's Travels in 1849, to, through, and from the Gold Regions in California* (Columbus: Scott & Bascom, printers, 1850, 1957), 26–27 (describing an incident in Sacramento City in 1849); Shaw, *Eldorado*, 143–144 ("[A] doctor cut off his ears, from the stumps of which he bled freely while receiving his flogging"); Field, Personal Reminiscences, 33 (stating that he ordered a physician to be present to make sure the flogging was not unnecessarily severe).

42. For just two of many cases, see "Important from Sonora," *Stockton Times*, August 10, 1850, 2, and "Murder," *Stockton Times*, March 1, 1851, 2.

43. John Hovey, Journal of a Voyage . . . Commencing Jan. 23, 1849, and ending July 23, 1849, 79 (unpublished manuscript, on file with the Huntington Library) (describing the trial of Chileans accused of murdering Americans at Iowa Log Cabins on the night of December 27–28, 1849).

44. Hovey, Journal, 79.

45. Ibid., 80.

46. Ibid. at 81.

47. Ibid.

48. E. Gould Buffum, *Six Months in the Gold Mines: From a Journal of Three Years' Residence in Upper and Lower California, 1847-8-9*, (Philadelphia: Lea and Blanchard,

1850), 83–85, available at http://memory.loc.gov/amm em/cbhtml.

49. See William B. Secrest, *Juanita* (1967); David Pierce Barstow, *Recollections of California 1849–1850*, (1979), 21; Alexandre Jean Joachim Holinski, *La Californie et les Routes Interocéaniques* (Leipzig, 1853), 232.

50. Barstow, *Recollections* (1979), 23.

51. Dr. Aiken may be the person mentioned in "Life and Death in California—Horrors of Lynch Law—Execution of a Young Woman," *Daily Missouri Republican*, January 11, 1852, 2 ("[A] young lawyer mounted the bridge railing, and denounced the whole affair in words of more bitter justice than discretion.... A dozen hands pulled him down").

52. McDowell, *Criminal Law beyond the State*, 335.

53. See Williams, *San Francisco Committee of Vigilance*, 142–147, for a thorough discussion of the problems with the legal system in the early 1850s.

54. "The County Jail," *Marysville Herald*, Jan. 7, 1851, 2 (reporting on the new jail built at Marysville; its timbers were twelve inches thick and lined with heavy sheet iron).

55. "General Jail Delivery—Escape Extraordinary!" Marysville Herald, June 5, 1851; see also "Re-Arrest," *Marysville Herald*, May 1, 1851, 2 (reporting that two men who broke out of jail had been retaken).

56. McDowell, *Criminal Law beyond the State*, 335–336.

57. See Hubert Howe Bancroft, I, *Popular Tribunals*, 130–131 (San Francisco: The History Co. Publishers, 1887); available at books.google.com (stating that there is scarce a political office holder "who has not entered upon his duties and responsibilities as the means of making money enough to carry him home," quoting *Evening Picayune*, Aug. 1850); see also "Judge Turner," *Marysville Herald*, Aug. 6, 1850, 3 (reporting on Judge Turner and his incapacities); "San Francisco Correspondence," *Marysville Herald*, Aug. 9, 1850 ("[M]agistrates and judges are tainted with scoundrelism and corruption . . . successful crime of [every] character goes unpunished"); "The World Is Governed Too Much," *Marysville Herald*, Aug. 27, 1850, 2 (stating that an incompetent legislature had enacted useless laws).

58. "Presentment of the Grand Jury of Tuolumne County," *Sonora Herald*, Aug. 3, 1850, 1.

59. See "Serious Affray at Columbia—Great Excitement," *supra* note 62, 3; Letter from Sam [ ] to Willie, *supra* note 63 (stating that "the citizens were compelled to take the execution of justice into their own hands" because "the law has not punished one man"). Many other miners made comments along the same lines. See, e.g., Letter to the Editor (dated San Jose, Sept. 13, 1850), *Marysville Herald*, Sept. 22, 1850 (stating, with respect to horse thieves recently imprisoned, that "so little confidence is placed in the authorities . . . that it was suggested last night, by one of the best citizens of the place, to take the thieves out and call on Judge Lynch to preside"); "Tremendous Excitement in San Francisco," *Marysville Herald*, Feb. 28, 1851 (reporting that during the trial of Stewart and Wildred for the murder of Janson on February 19, 1851, a handbill was circulated stating that the law appeared to be a nonentity and that no redress was to be had but by the code of Judge Lynch). These were the same circumstances that led to the emergence of lynch law elsewhere on the frontier. Brown, *supra* note 5, 112–113.

60. Shubael Wescott Stowell, Diary (Oct. 25, 1850) (unpublished manuscript in the Shubael Stowell family papers, 1850–1930, unpublished manuscript in the Beinecke Library).

61. Id.; see also Letter from Ephriam Delano to Wife (Jan. 19, 1852) (unpublished manuscript in the Beinecke Library) (stating that a man was hanged for robbery and murder: "the authorities tried to get him but no use since the people has taken the law in their own hands").

62. Ezra Bourne, Diary of an Overland Journey to California in 1850, 32–33 (unpublished transcript in the Bancroft Library); see also George W. Allen, Diary, entry for Mar. 15, 1851 (unpublished manuscript, on file with the Beinecke Library) (stating that after Judge Frank acquitted a suspect, the miners "followed and arrested him and tryed [sic] and found him gilty [sic] and sentenced him to 200 Lashes or own up that he stole the Oro").

63. Willian Binur, Wooded up in Log Town: A Letter from the Gold Fields (1851), 12 (letter to Sarah, Mar. 8, 1851). Binur makes the outcome seem like a foregone conclusion, but this could be mere swaggering.

64. John Clark, *The California Guide*, 138–142 (entries for August 5, 9, and 10, 1853) (unpublished manuscript and transcription in the Beinecke Library).

65. Id., 140.

66. Id., 142.

67. Id.

68. Id.

69. Franklin A. Buck, *A Yankee Trader in the Gold Rush*, (Katherine A. White, ed., 1930), 110–111, available at http://memory.loc.gov/ammem/cbhtml (stating that Michael Grant, arrested for murder, was taken by the people, tried to a judge and jury, found guilty, and executed ten days later); Christman, *One Man's Gold*, 174 (Mexican suspects "were taken before the magistrate but before the hearing was gone through with, the excited people seized the prisoners, took them to the top of an adjacent hill, selected a jury under a tree, tried and found them guilty, and sentenced them to be hung"). The subsequent fight over the prisoner's fate is described in Henry Veel Huntley, *California: Its Gold and Its Inhabitants* (London, T. C. Newby 1856), 190–192, available at http://memory.loc.gov/ammem/cbhtml.

70. *Murder at Hawkins' Bar*, Alta California, September 4, 1850.

71. Huntley, *California*, 213.

72. Ibid., 190–192. Following a stabbing at Columbia in 1852, the people took the accused from the authorities and hanged him from the limb of a tree, but when the limb broke, they decided to try him to a jury. During the hearing, which lasted five or six hours, the sheriff of Sonora tried to recover the prisoner, but the miners fended him off. Huntley does not report the verdict, if any, but says that at the end of the proceedings the sheriff managed to obtain the accused and take him to Sonora. Id.

73. John D. Borthwick, *Three Years in California* (Edinburgh, London: W. Blackwood & Sons 1857), 226, available at http://memory.loc.gov/ammem/cbhtml.

74. Id.; see also Buck, *Yankee Trader*, 111 ("[A] wagon on which [the condemned man] was standing was driven out from under which caused his death by strangulation").

75. Borthwick, *Three Years*, 226.

76. Shirley, Letters, 155; Borthwick, *Three Years*, 226 ("In some instances the criminal was run up by a number of men, all equally sharing the hangman's duty; on other occasions, one man was appointed to the office of executioner").

77. Borthwick, *Three Years*, 226 ("[L]ife was only crushed out of him by hauling the writhing body up and down, several times in succession.").

78. Clark, *California Guide*, 142 (entry for Aug. 10, 1853).

79. Hovey, Journal, 82 (describing the execution on January 3, 1850).

80. Johnson, *Vigilance and the Law*, 584 (noting that after the 1850s, lynching came to be seen as a crime in itself). Lynching did not die out entirely in California or in any of the western and southern states.

81. Hubert Howe Bancroft, *Popular Tribunals* (San Francisco: The History Co. Publishers 1887), 124, available at books.google.com.

82. Shaw, *Eldorado*, 142.

83. E.g., Kleinhans, Memoirs, 5 (stating that he and his partners were asked to attend a lynch trial at Spanish Bar).

84. Henry Sturdivant, Journal, 47 (unpublished manuscript in the Huntington Library), recorded that he went to see a hanging on April 29, 1851, "determined to see a murderer die I watched him from the moment he came from prison till he was dead."

85. Buffum, *Six Months*, 83; Shubael Stowell wrote on Oct. 25th [1850], "In P.M. went to Hangtown to see a man have a trial for murder."

86. Letter from Sam to Willie dated Feb. 27, 1851, Sacramento City (unpublished manuscript in the Bancroft Library, Mss C-B 547 Pt. I:53).

87. See, e.g., James H. Carson, *Early Recollections of the Mines* (1852; republished, Tarrytown, N.J.: W. Abbatt, 1931), 35 (calling lynch law a "God-blessed evil"); Christman, *One Man's Gold*, 203 (stating that lynching was necessary and never unjust); William Taylor, *California Life Illustrated* (New York: Carlton & Porter, 1858), 296 (lynch law only punished the guilty); all available at http://memory.loc.gov/ammem/cbhtml.

88. See especially Frank Marryat, *Mountains and Molehills* (New York: Harper & Brothers, 1855), 215–216, available at http://memory.loc.gov/ammem/cbhtml (musing on whether or not lynching was justified under the circumstances). See also Buck, *Yankee Trader*, 111 (observing that lynch law punished some guilty persons, but also that "if circumstances are against you, however innocent you may be, you stand no chance. Give me a dungeon in the Tombs and all the police of New York first").

89. See McDowell, *Criminal Law beyond the State*, 360.

90. For a discussion on movements to abolish flogging as a punishment during this period, see Myra C. Glenn, *The Naval Reform Campaign against Flogging: A Case Study in Changing Attitudes toward Corporal Punishment, 1830–1850*, 35 Am. Q. 408 (1983). For a discussion on flogging as a degrading punishment, see James Q. Whitman, *Harsh Justice: Criminal Punishment and the Widening Divide between America and Europe* (2003), 175.

91. Shaw, *Eldorado*, 141–142.

92. Kimball Hale Dimmick, Letter to Sarah (wife) (Oct. 26, 1848) (unpublished manuscript in the Kimball Hale Dimmick papers, 1837–1886, in the Bancroft Library). See also Alex[ander] R Barrington, Journal, entry for July 17, 1850 (unpublished manuscript in the Huntington Museum), wrote, "Horrible scene, 25 lashes on mans back for stealing horse How the poor fellow begged!"

93. Shirley, Letters, 269.

94. Shirley, Letters, 269. See also Ryan, *Personal Adventures*, 63 (relating an anecdote he had heard about a thief who was flogged at one diggings, stole a mule from another diggings, and tried and sentenced by those miners; but when they saw the thief's back, they took pity on him and reduced the sentence to banishment).

95. Stephen Field wrote that, with such penalties, banishment "was supererogatory; for there was something so degrading in a public whipping that I have never known a man thus whipped who would stay longer than he could help, or ever desire to return." Field, Personal Reminiscences, 34.

CHAPTER 20

Vigilantism during the Gold Rush

Mary Marki and Christopher Clayton Smith

ALTHOUGH ACTS of vigilantism were common prior to the discovery of gold in California in 1848, it was the Gold Rush that rapidly transformed the territory and served as a catalyst for a new era of vigilantism.

California in the 1850s was far from a stable, law-abiding community. The United States had acquired the territory as part of the Mexican Secession in the Treaty of Guadalupe Hidalgo, which ended the war with Mexico in 1848. Ironically, John Marshall discovered gold at Sutter's Mill that same year and when the news spread, California's population exploded with droves of prospectors hoping to make their fortune in the California gold fields.

As gold seekers soon realized, California resembled not the proverbial El Dorado but more accurately a chaotic frontier, lacking even a semblance of law and order. In this chaotic atmosphere, vigilante committees emerged almost as a necessity in the absence of legal remedies, and individuals were increasingly willing to take the law into their own hands in hopes of achieving order and stability.

The term *vigilante* derives from the Latin root meaning "to watch" or "guard." A vigilante is a person who implements personal justice in the absence of legal authority.

Mexican Period

One of the first cases of a vigilante committee in California occurred in Los Angeles during the Mexican era. Vigilante acts in California during this period usually stemmed from the fact that the public perceived the judicial system as inadequate.

During the Mexican era, California government functioned under the alcalde system. The word *alcalde* derives from a Moorish term meaning "village judge." The alcalde were town mayors who acted as judges, legislatures, and executives in California. American visitors to California during the Mexican period often commented on its lack of a formal judicial system.[1]

The alcalde system did not always function to the satisfaction of the populous, which led to instances of vigilantism. Sometimes the mayors were simply not willing or able to resolve criminal cases, leaving the local population frustrated and willing to take it upon themselves to act.

The first recorded case of vigilantism in California occurred under these circumstances in Los Angeles. In 1836, a crowd of men decided to take justice into their own hands in a case involving a man and a woman accused of murdering the woman's husband. Although the local mayor had taken the couple into custody, local citizens assumed that the alcalde would not act, so they seized the couple and shot them both dead.[2]

R. H. Dana provides another account of discontent over an alcalde's indifference toward a criminal case. Dana recounts the story of a Yankee man who had moved to Los Angeles and was naturalized as a citizen of Mexico. When he was stabbed to death in his home, a group of Yankees accused a Spaniard of the murder and took him into custody. They contacted the alcalde demanding that justice be done. After the mayor refused to act, the group appointed their own impromptu judge and jury, and ultimately tried, convicted, and sentenced the man to be shot.[3]

Government and Law

A Transitional Period

From the beginning of the Mexican-American War through the signing of the peace treaty, U.S. military commanders governed California, utilizing the governmental system established under Mexican rule. A litany of experienced American military men who had long participated in military activities in California accepted the position of military governor and operated from the city of Monterey. These governors exercised equal or greater authority than the California mayors during the Mexican period because they had power to make certain modifications to the government if they deemed it necessary. Local governments continued to function under the alcalde system, but the local mayors looked to the governor for assistance from the state militia.

Vigilantism and the Gold Rush

While vigilantism was not unique to the Gold Rush, this lawless era acted as a catalyst to inspire a multitude of new vigilante groups. The influx of tens of thousands of gold seekers and the upsurge in criminal activity that followed provided an environment friendly to vigilantism. The resort to private justice is a reoccurring theme during the Gold Rush years for one primary reason. Citizens facing the anarchy of lawlessness in the wake of the multitude of newcomers that flooded the gold fields organized these committees in an attempt to control crime and establish peaceful, stable communities.[4]

As the 49ers rushed to stake their claims in the gold fields of California, the "diggings" became a crowded and dangerous place. During the peak of the Gold Rush, criminal activity was ubiquitous. According to historian John Boessenecker, the murder rate in California during the 1850s was seventeen times higher than the national rate a few short years ago. Thus, in 1852, a person settling in Los Angeles was thirty-seven times more likely to be murdered than in 1997. In the face of virtual lawlessness, residents of cities and mining camps came to administer justice themselves. Vigilantes sought out criminals and subjected them to impromptu trials, drawing on private citizens to make up the jury. They created makeshift miners' courts in order to simulate a trial-like setting and to achieve speedy justice. These courts were also responsible for delivering sentences in cases in which the accused was found guilty.[5]

Vigilante courts delivered verdicts that ranged from lashings to death. The most common cases tried involved stealing, which usually resulted in a sentence of flogging. Sometimes punishments were more severe and permanent, including branding the face, cutting off part of the ear, or shaving the head. These verdicts intended to mark the accused in order to alert others of the culprit's misdeeds. The most severe sentence delivered at these trials was, of course, death. For the most part, cases that carried death sentences involved serious charges such as murder, stealing horses, and land disputes. Death sentences were carried out primarily through the medium of hanging or shooting via a firing squad. If a criminal was sentenced to death by firing squad, twelve men were appointed by the miners' court to carry out the execution. Half of the guns contained live ammunition while the other half contained blank rounds so that no one actually knew who had delivered the fatal shot.

First Blood Is Spilled

It is somewhat ironic, and perhaps a little prophetic, that the first murder of the Gold Rush occurred at the very mill where James Marshall first discovered gold. On October 1, 1848, just eight months after Marshall made his discovery at Sutter's Mill, Peter Raymond allegedly murdered John Von Pfister. It was late in the evening when Raymond, a miner from Ireland, reportedly pounded on the door of the saw mill where several miners were sleeping. The intoxicated twenty-one-year-old demanded liquor from the sleeping occupants. John Von Pfister, hoping to calm Raymond, rose from his bed, placed a knife in his waistband, and convinced the drunken Raymond to sit down. After conversation, which included joking that the two of them would laugh at the whole episode in the morning, Von Pfister extended his hand in friendship. While accepting the gesture of peace with one hand, the younger man then unexpectedly seized the knife from Von Pfister's waistband with his other hand and stabbed him in the heart.

The miners caught Raymond as he attempted to escape, and authorities held him prisoner at Sutter's Fort in Sacramento while awaiting trial. However, Raymond never appeared before the alcalde. With the help of his mining partner, Peter Quinn, the accused murderer escaped, causing

many to criticize the ineffective system of law in California. Days after the escape, an editor of a San Francisco newspaper, *The Californian*, wrote, "This tragic event brings very forcibly to mind the present condition of California without law, without any regular authorized government of power for the protection of life and property, and yet holding out unparalleled inducements to desperadoes, escaped convicts and the scum of the Pacific to come to her shores."[6]

Despite a five-thousand-dollar bounty placed on their heads, Raymond and Quinn successfully fled south, arriving at Mission Soledad less than two months after the murder. There, three other outlaws and an Indian guide joined them. On December 4, 1848, the fugitives arrived at Mission San Miguel, a residence that William Reed had recently purchased, and in which he lived with his family and servants. Reed welcomed the six men into his home. As the outlaws transacted the sale of gold to Mr. Reed for thirty dollars an ounce, they were intrigued by his unguarded comment regarding a recent business venture in northern California which had secured him a sizable profit. Speculating that Reed had hidden the monies in the house, the greedy group decided to kill the family and steal their wealth. The following day, Raymond and his followers engaged in a vicious killing rampage in which they brutally murdered ten men, women, and children, including Reed's family and servants.

When news of the murders reached Santa Barbara on December 10, 1848, the townspeople formed a vigilante group comprised of thirty-seven men. The vigilantes discovered the outlaws on Ortega Hill and either killed or captured all of them as they attempted to flee. The vigilantes established a makeshift court and charged the three captives with murder. The temporary court sentenced each of them to death.

The public raised questions about the legitimacy of this vigilante court, leading to an appeal of the case to the military governor of Monterey, Colonel Richard B. Mason. He sent a military auxiliary team to Santa Barbara comprised of ten U.S. soldiers, who carried out the death sentences by firing squad.[7]

Sacramento

The undesirable consequences of tens of thousands of transients flooding into California were not limited to the gold fields; cities, also, experienced a tremendous influx of migrants, many of whom contributed to the escalation of crime.

Sacramento became a stopover or a destination for thousands traveling to and from the diggings. Miners visited the city to load up with supplies or spend their gold dust on entertainment in the numerous saloons and bordellos. Others found it more profitable to engage in trade, setting up stores and businesses to service the miners, rather than prospecting on their own. Still others became squatters, settling on unoccupied land, in disregard of the owner. With this constant influx of people, the city experienced a lawlessness that inspired the formation of vigilante groups, determined to bring order and stability to the territory.

In the absence of an effective law enforcement system, occasionally military governors called on citizens to form vigilante groups for support, as in the case of the Sacramento Squatters Riot of 1850. The city had been plagued with problems involving squatters. As white settlers arrived in California during the Gold Rush era, they began to challenge the ownership of land grants issued under Mexican rule. Many settlers resorted to simply squatting on unoccupied land. One case involved the famous John Sutter, of Sutter's Fort. Miners apparently felt it unfair that Sutter possessed so much land in the vicinity, and therefore it was their right to take some of it. Under the leadership of Albert W. Winn, the Sacramento City Council passed an ordinance making it illegal to squat on unoccupied land owned by another. In reaction to the anti-squatters law, a riot erupted on August 14, 1850, as forty armed squatters attempted to reclaim property they had been forced to leave. The mayor of Sacramento, Hardin Bigelow, acted as a mediator in the crisis. As the mayor urged the squatters to disarm and disband, someone in the crowd shot him, and he later died of his injuries. In addition to his position on the Sacramento City Council, Albert W. Winn also served as the appointed brigadier general of the California militia. When news of the mayor's death, as well as several other casualties, circulated, the governor of California, Peter H. Burnett, ordered Winn to use the military to put down the riot and restore peace in the city. Winn quickly instituted martial law and appealed to law-abiding citizens to form volunteer companies to help suppress the riot. The volunteer vigilante groups assisted state troops, which came from the capital at Benicia, to end the riot and maintain order in Sacramento.[8]

Citizens again delivered vigilante justice in Sacramento on February 26, 1851. A brawl broke out in a saloon over a card game among a professional gambler named Frederick Rowe and several other men. As the fist fight continued into the streets, an unfortunate bystander attempted to break up the fight. Rowe allegedly shot him in the head. Outraged citizens called for an end to the senseless violence that engulfed the city. Although some argued Rowe should be tried through normal legal channels, the unruly crowd demanded an immediate trial. Within hours, the extralegal jury reached a verdict of guilty, and the crowd seized Rowe from the custody of the deputy sheriff and spontaneously hanged him.

Less than six months later, another vigilante

committee eagerly wielded judicial responsibility. On July 9 four men allegedly assaulted and robbed another man of two hundred dollars. In response, an angry mob gathered, demanding that members of the local vigilance committee arrange an impromptu trial. The ten citizens who composed the committee accomplished their purpose, and the temporary jury found the four accused men guilty and ordered a penalty of seventy-five lashes for each.

In the wake of these events, the citizens of Sacramento formed its own Committee of Vigilance on June 25, 1851. According to the local newspaper, the *Alta California*, the committee had 213 members, which included many merchants and affluent citizens.[9]

San Francisco and the First Vigilance Committee

Prominent businessmen and landowners of San Francisco began to rally together as a result of the upsurge in crime that plagued their city. Citizens voiced frustration with the ineffective legal system and formed their own vigilante committees in order to deal more efficiently with criminals.[10]

A series of crimes in 1851 convinced local citizens they could not safely conduct business and make a living in San Francisco. The discontent began when two unidentified men attacked a local merchant and robbed him on February 19, 1851. The business community rose up in a rage, demanding that someone be arrested and pay for the crime. It is generally believed that the lack of rationality led to the misidentification of the assailants. Led by Sam Brannan, one of the most prominent businessmen of the Gold Rush era, the community rallied together and called for the two men to be peremptorily hanged. Cooler heads eventually persuaded the crowd to await the

decision of a citizens' court, but the impromptu jury was deadlocked, unable to reach a verdict.

In the early years of the California Gold Rush, the city of San Francisco suffered a series of fires in the downtown vicinity. The area was particularly vulnerable due to the extreme congestion and the fact that primitive, rapidly built structures were primarily comprised of wood or cloth, causing them to burn easily. This condition contributed to vigilantism when four major fires erupted between 1849 and 1850 and many citizens suspected arson. Citizens focused suspicion on a dubious gang of foreigners from Australia dubbed the Sydney Ducks, who, it was believed, were responsible for a variety of violent robberies that had recently occurred in San Francisco. Many citizens apparently believed the Ducks had set the fires to create a diversion in order to facilitate the looting of local businesses. When a fifth fire broke out on May 4, 1851, the anniversary of a previously devastating fire, citizens searched the gang's territory and found items they believed were stolen from fire-damaged businesses.

Justified by this evidence, Sam Brannan led citizens to establish a Committee of Vigilance in San Francisco. He worked in conjunction with merchants, businessmen, and local landowners to apprehend numerous alleged criminals. Within four months, the committee had tried a total of ninety cases. It issued four death sentences, resulting in the hanging of four members of the Sydney Ducks. In addition, the Committee of Vigilance issued sentences for one whipping and twenty-eight deportations, as well as the release of forty-one individuals. At the close of its operation, the Vigilance Committee boasted that as a result of its activities, a large number of criminals had fled the city and that crime was largely curtailed in San Francisco. The members of the committee also stated that members of the law enforcement community had become more diligent in fulfilling their duties to the public, realizing that they were under the constant scrutiny of watchful citizens.

Second Committee of Vigilance of San Francisco

A second vigilance committee emerged in 1856 as local merchants and businessmen reacted against the growing authority of the city government and an increase in taxation. While acting under the pretense of a necessity to catch criminals, in reality, prominent merchants distrusted city authorities and attempted to take control of the city themselves.

The murder of a local editor provided the impetus. King James of William of the *Daily Evening Bulletin* often used the paper as a forum for journalistic vigilantism, which he employed to attack corrupt city officials. On May 14, 1856, King published an article attacking the county supervisor, James P. Casey. The article exposed Casey's prison record in New York and accused the politician of implementing shady political practices, including ballot box stuffing. Reacting to King's scathing allegations, Casey threatened King. When someone later ambushed King and shot him on the streets of San Francisco, former members of the Vigilance Committee of 1851 called a meeting and decided to resurrect the organization. The committee operated out of a two-story brick structure on Sacramento Street that became known as "Fort Gunnybags" because of the sandbags that were stacked outside the building.

Only days after King's murder, the vigilante committee amassed a force of 2,500 armed men. Fearing the situation would fly out of control, other citizens organized an anti-vigilante group called the Law and Order Party. When the vigilantes appeared at the county jail demanding Casey's release, the sheriff consulted the Law and Order Party and decided to release to the vigilantes Casey and one other prisoner named Charles Cora. Cora was a U.S. marshal awaiting retrial for murder. The Vigilance Committee paraded the two accused men in a carriage down the street to its final destination at Fort Gunnybags. There, the self-appointed authorities conducted a trial followed by the execution of the two men by hanging them from the second floor of the building in full view of a crowd of spectators. The Law and Order Party advocated the disbanding of the Vigilance Committee, but instead the group fortified Fort Gunnybags and launched a new series of arrests. Influential members of the community felt that the vigilante committee had overstepped its bounds and, together with the Law and Order Party, urged the governor, J. Neely Johnson, to call out the state militia to put down the vigilante movement and uphold traditional authority in the city of San Francisco.

Governor Johnson arranged for a delivery of weapons from the federal armory at Benicia to the state militia through General John E. Wool. Next, he alerted General William Tecumseh Sherman, commander of the San Francisco state militia, of the gravity of the situation. The governor took action after the vigilantes refused to honor an order issued by Justice David S. Terry of the state supreme court, requiring them to release the keeper of the county jail. On June 2, 1856, the governor ordered General Sherman to mobilize the state militia to put down the uprising. On June 3, Governor Johnson declared San Francisco to be in a state of insurrection. General Wool derailed Sherman's march to San Francisco by refusing to release the arms at Benicia, causing General Sherman to resign, explaining he refused to command forces he could not arm.

Justice Terry of the state supreme court emerged as the leader and spokesperson for the anti-vigilante faction, the Law and Order Party. When the vigilantes attempted to intercept munitions intended for the state militia, a scuffle ensued between the opposing groups, and Justice Terry allegedly stabbed a member of the vigilante group. The vigilantes then arrested Justice Terry and summarily placed him on trial for assault. The justice ably defended himself, and though he was "convicted" of assault with intent to murder, he was released after members of the vigilante group disagreed about what to do next. The next day, August 8, 1856, the vigilantes agreed to disband. In the three months of its existence, the committee had hanged four men accused of murder, issued nearly three dozen deportation orders, and claimed to have forced hundreds of criminals to flee the city. However, crime rate statistics for the city during the year of 1856 do not substantiate this claim.

Vigilante Groups and Racism

Some vigilante groups seemed to be specifically formed to terrorize minority groups in California. As individuals from various ethnic backgrounds arrived in California, competition in the mines grew fierce, resulting in a backlash against nonwhites. During 1849, a group of native-born miners formed a volunteer law enforcement unit called the "Regulators," commonly called the "Hounds." Although they claimed to be maintaining public order, it appears obvious that their true purpose was to "hound out minority elements" in San Francisco.

Because the Hounds were initially perceived as helping to prevent crime, the mayor of San Francisco, Thaddeus M. Leavenworth, deputized the men as members of an official police force. However, as the gang proved to be volatile and unruly, launching drunken parades and harassing local merchants, citizens began to view them as a band of criminals. On July 15, 1849, a large group of Regulators attacked a community of Chileans in San Francisco. The gang rained violence on Little Chile, including the beating, kicking, and shooting of Chileans at random. During the mayhem, a young woman was assaulted and her mother murdered. As news of the unprovoked violence spread, many San Franciscans rallied against the Regulators and demanded that those responsible be brought to justice. Samuel Brannan gathered with the citizens of San Francisco the following morning. They organized a vigilante group to restrain the Regulators. Brannan's followers collected funds for the Chileans and hunted down those responsible for the violence. Brannan's vigilantes arrested and imprisoned a well-known member of the Hounds named Sam Roberts, along with eighteen other men, and the Regulators diminished the fervor of its racially motivated attacks.

Vigilante groups also targeted members of the Spanish-speaking community. One case involved a Mexican woman named Josefa Loaiza, who lived in the northwestern Gold Rush town of Downieville. On July 4, 1851, a miner named Frederick Cannon broke down the door of Josefa's home but did no other damage and quickly left. Later, Josefa's husband confronted the miner and an argument ensued. At one point in the quarrel, Josefa intervened, daring the man to dishonor her inside her home a second time. When Cannon followed Josefa into her house, she stabbed him in the heart. An impromptu court tried Josefa for murder. The defendant argued that she had feared Cannon intended to sexually assault her, but the jury found her argument unconvincing. David Barstow, an observer, described those conducting the trial as "the hungriest, craziest, wildest mob that ever I saw anywhere." The jury convicted Josefa and sentenced her to death by hanging. The consensus among scholars today is that the hanging of Josefa reflected the intense racial strife commonly found in Gold Rush communities in California at the time of the Gold Rush.

Maythee Rojas, a literary scholar who researched the event, has uncovered contemporary newspaper articles that portray Josefa as a woman who inherently possessed a propensity to kill because she was a Mexican.[11]

Conclusion

In the wake of the discovery of gold, citizens in California organized vigilance committees that they believed to be justified in response to crime, which they perceived as rampant and largely unpunished. However, scholars perceive a darker legacy to the vigilante movement since these committees often made a pretense of restoring law and order, while in practice instituting anti-ethnic agendas and implementing mob rule. According to recent research, the vigilance committees contributed little to genuine legal reform and severely violated basic principals of democratic government.

Mary Marki is a World Civilizations instructor at Long Beach City College. After living and teaching abroad for five years, Ms. Marki has settled in southern California where she can pursue her twin passions: teaching history and traveling the world. She continues to engage in historical research and is presently working on a second volume to her publication *Voices of World History: Antiquity to Pre-Modern Times* (2003). Her publications include: "The African American Frontier: Dearfield, Colorado," and "Chilean Migration to California during the Gold Rush," in *Encyclopedia of Immigration and Migration to the American West* (Thousand Oaks: Sage Publications 2006), with Sharon K. Evanshine and B. Carmon Hardy; *Voices of World History: Antiquity to Pre-Modern Times* (Boston: Houghton Mifflin Company, 2003), with William Haddad; "Jordan's Alliance with Israel and its Effects on Jordanian-Arab Relations," in *Israeli Affairs* (London: Frank Cass Publishers, 2003), with William Haddad; *Israel, the Hashemites and the Palestinians: The Fateful Triangle*, edited by Efraim Karsh and P. R. Kumaraswamy (London: Frank Cass Publishers, 2003); "The Woman's Club of Huntington Beach," in *Encyclopedia of Women in the West* (Thousand Oaks, CA: Sage Publications, 2003), with William Haddad; and "Chinese-Palestinian Relations," in *China and the Middle East: The Quest for Influence*, edited by P. R. Kumaraswamy (New Delhi: Sage Publications, 1999).

Christopher Clayton Smith is an undergraduate honors student majoring in history at the University of California, Los Angeles. His focus is on the relationship between the natural and cultural history of the West, specifically in California in the mid-nineteenth century.

Suggested Readings

Ayers, Colonel James J. *Gold and Sunshine: Reminiscences of Early California*. Boston: The Gorham Press, 1922. 150–157.

Boessenecker, John. *Gold Dust & Gunsmoke: Tales of Gold Rush Outlaws, Gunfighters, Lawmen and Vigilantes*. New York: John Wiley & Sons, Inc., 1999.

De La Roche, Roberta Senechal. "Collective Violence as Social Control." *Sociological Forum* 11, no. 1 (Mar. 1996).

Dana, Richard Henry. *Two Years before the Mast: A Personal Narrative of Life at Sea*. New York: Random House, 2001.

Eldredge, Zoeth Skinner, ed. *History of California: The Rise and Progress of an American State*, vol. 9. New York: The Century History Company.

Gaughey, John Walton. *Gold Is the Cornerstone*. Berkeley: University of California Press, 1948.

Gloady, Rick. "Local Professor's Research Shines Light on Hanged California Latina." Unknown newsclipping dated Friday, December 1, 2006.

Hunt, Rockwell D. *California in the Making: Essays and Papers in California History*. Caldwell, Idaho: The Caxton Printers, Ltd., 1953.

Marks, Paula Mitchell. *Precious Dust: The American Gold Rush Era: 1848–1900*. New York: William Morrow and Company, Inc., 1994.

Norton, Henry K. *The Story of California*. Chicago: A. C. McClurg & Co., 1925.

Rawls, James J., and Bean, Walton. *California: An Interpretive History*. Boston: McGraw Hill, 2008.

Richards, Rand. *Historic San Francisco: A Concise History and Guide*. San Francisco: Heritage House, 1997.

Sacramento County Historical Society. "*Sacramento Vigilantes—August 1851*." *Golden Notes* 24, no. 1. Sacramento: Sacramento County Historical Society, 1978.

Sacramento County Historical Society, "A.M. Winn: Father of City Government in Sacramento." *Golden Notes* 35, no. 3. Sacramento: Sacramento County Historical Society, 1989.

Sacramento County Historical Society, "The Squatters Riot: A Dramatic Episode in Sacramento's History." *Golden Notes* 38, nos. 3 and 4. Sacramento: Sacramento County Historical Society, 1992.

Notes

1. See David J. Langum, *Law and Community on the Mexican California Frontier: Anglo-American Expatriates and the Clash of Legal Traditions, 1821–1846* (Norman: University of Oklahoma Press, 1987). Also see Gordon Morris Bakken, "The Courts, the Legal Profession, and the Development of Law in Early California," in John F. Burns and Richard J. Orsi, eds., *Taming the Elephant: Politics, Government and Law in Pioneer California* (Berkeley: University of California Press, 2003), 74–95.

2. See Eric H. Monkkonon, "Homicide in Los Angeles, 1827–2002," *Journal of Interdisciplinary History* 36, no. 2 (2005): 167–183.

3. For this and other accounts of justice in Los Angeles, see Richard Henry Dana, *Two Years before the Mast: A Personal Narrative of Life at Sea* (Thorndike, Me.: G. K. Hall, 1840). Also see Gordon Morris Bakken, "Mexican and American Land Policy: A Conflict of Cultures," *Southern California Quarterly* 75 (Fall/Winter, 1993): 237–62.

4. See Ronald C. Woolsey, "Crime and Punishment: Los Angeles County, 1850–1856," *Southern California Quarterly* 61, no. 1 (1979): 79–98. This article is based on extensive reading of the court records of Los Angeles.

5. See John Boessenecker, *Badge and Buckshot: Lawlessness in Old California* (Norman: University of Oklahoma Press, 1988); John Boessenecker, *Gold Dust and Gunsmoke: Tales of Gold Rush Outlaws, Gunfighters, Lawmen and Vigilantes* (New York: John Wiley, 1999); John Boessenecker, ed., *Against the Vigilantes: The Recollections of Dutch Charley Duane* (Norman: University of Oklahoma Press, 1999).

6. See Boessenecker, *Badge and Buckshot*, for details. The dead man was a member of a prominent Kauai merchant family. See Malcolm Brown, *Reminiscences of a Pioneer Kauai Family* (Honolulu: Thomas McVeagh, 1918).

7. See Richard Maxwell Brown, *Strain of Violence* (New York: Oxford University Press, 1975), 101, 306–7. Hubert Howe Bancroft, *Popular Tribunals*, two volumes (San Francisco: The History Company, 1887). Bancroft details many of these events using oral history and newspapers.

8. See Albert L. Hurtado, *John Sutter: A Life on the North American Frontier* (Norman: University of Oklahoma Press, 2006).

9. See Gordon Morris Bakken, *Practicing Law in Frontier California* (Lincoln: University of Nebraska Press, 1991), 99–113; Ralph Mann, *After the Gold Rush* (Stanford: Stanford University Press, 1982), 75.

10. See Robert M. Senewicz, *Vigilantes in Gold Rush San Francisco* (Stanford: Stanford University Press, 1985). Also see Roger W. Lotchin, *San Francisco, 1846–1856: From Hamlet to City* (New York: Oxford University Press, 1974), 164–201. The text relies upon these two sources.

11. Albert L. Hurtado, *Intimate Frontiers: Sex, Gender, and Culture in Old California* (Albuquerque: University of New Mexico Press, 1999), 134–36.

CHAPTER 21

The Death Penalty in California

1857–1970

Susan Sanchez-Barnett

THE DEFINITION of murder was determined by the First Session of the California Legislature with the passage of the Criminal Practices Act of 1851. Murder was defined as the unlawful killing of another individual, with malice aforethought either expressed or implied, and "the punishment shall be death." The Criminal Practices Act of 1851 authorized legal executions in California, carried out by the sheriff within the respective county where the sentence was decreed. During this period of the Gold Rush in California, vigilantism had replaced institutionalized justice systems with swift decisions and executions outside the purview of organized law. A concise definition of murder and its consequences was decided by the state legislators, and enlarged by the end of the 1851 session to include grand larceny and bank robbery as capital offenses. By 1856 the degrees of murder were defined, and grand larceny and bank robbery were excluded under the death penalty.

By the late 1850s several executions had already taken place under the direction of county sheriffs. The counties retained autonomy in regards to executions, and in an 1858 case the governor granted the first reprieve. Jose Anastacio, a young Hispanic, was convicted of the murder of Frank Mellen, a Scotsman who had little of value to be gained by his murder. Jose Anastacio was a Carmelo Indian, who had been seen the day before the murder in the company of Mellen. When Mellen's body was discovered, Anastacio was absent from the town and a search was conducted to find him. He was located forty miles away and brought back to town for trial. Anastacio was convicted on circumstantial evidence of the murder of Mellon and sentenced to hang. Governor John B. Weller approved a reprieve for Anastacio, but incorrectly wrote his first name on the document. The sheriff halted the hanging for further clarification from the governor, but Undersheriff Thomas Pool, "backed by the people of Monterey," escorted the prisoner to the site of the murder and hanged him. A bitter exchange of letters occurred between Pool and Governor Weller, who accused Pool of "judicial murder." Seven years later, Pool himself would be convicted and hanged for murder in El Dorado County.[1]

During the 1860s the number of settlers residing in California continued to increase after the Gold Rush and the admission to statehood. The settlers' demand for new land continued to be a source of conflict between white immigrants and Native Americans. One capital case in 1863 was the conviction of five Yuki Native Americans on the charge of conspiracy to commit murder. The crime occurred when S. S. Davis reported his barn, filled with forty tons of hay, had been burned down. Davis reported that this was the work of local Indians, and that this act of arson was a signal of more intended hostilities. The Coast Yuki had been forced to live on the Nome Cult Reservation, relocated there by the state militia and vigilante groups. Davis led a group that rounded up many of the suspects, and several were shot while trying to escape. A total of ten Yuki were killed, and five remaining suspects were convicted of conspiracy and hung.[2]

By the end of the 1860s there was a three-year period when no state executions occurred in California. In 1875 there was an important capital case that involved the murder of Leander Davis by notorious outlaw Tiburcio Vasquez. This would be the first murder case in California in which a change of venue was requested. Vasquez was the leader of a band of robbers known for numerous holdups, stage robberies, and other crimes committed in northern California. When the band went to rob a hotel in Tres Pinos, it evolved into a multiple murder that led to a statewide search for the culprits. Governor Newton Booth authorized a large reward and commissioned Harry Morse, sheriff of Alameda County, to head up this posse, its actions being reported daily in the local papers. Vasquez was captured near the outskirts of Los Angeles by the local sheriff there, then transported by ship back to Monterey County. Because of fear that vigilante justice would occur, the trial was relocated to San Jose, making this the first occasion of a change of venue because of local prejudice. Tiburcio Vasquez was hanged on March 19, 1875, at San Jose. The Vasquez case has been interpreted by many historians as a representation of the continuing conflicts between native Californians and the new settlers. In an interview in 1874, Vasquez told a reporter, "A spirit of hatred and revenge took possession of me. I had numerous fights in defense of what I believed to be my rights and those of my countrymen."[3] Historian John Boessenecker states that the social banditry model does not fit this case: "Men might kill to do good, but they rarely steal to do good."[4]

Various legal changes in the late nineteenth century began to reshape the state judicial system. The system used when California became a state was that felony cases required a two-step process for indictment. A grand jury first had to indict, then a petty jury had to convict. The California judicial system changed so the first stage went to a lower-court judge who would hold a preliminary hearing. The judge listened to the evidence, and if he decided there was enough to justify a trial the case would be "bound over" and the defendant would go to a trial court. If there was not enough evidence, the defendant would be released. California authorized this in the state constitution in 1879; the grand jury was not abolished but only used in exceptional cases. In *Hurtado v. California* (1884), "The words 'due process of law' in the Fourteenth Amendment of the Constitution of the United States does not necessarily require an indictment by a grand jury in a prosecution by a State for murder." The state constitution adopted by California in 1879 provided a modified system for criminal indictment, which included capital cases. "Offenses heretofore required to be prosecuted by indictment, shall be prosecuted by information, after examination and commitment by a magistrate, or by indictment, with or without such examination and commitment, as may be prescribed by law. A grand jury shall be drawn and summoned at least once a year in each county."[5] This process added additional time to housing prisoners with serious charges filed against them. The state constitution allowed for depositions, sworn testimony by witnesses to be written and filed as official documents. A thirty-day time limit was also established for the district attorney to file charges against a prisoner.

California prisons were initially maintained by the counties, but the first state prison was established at San Quentin in 1852. It covered an area of 432 acres and contained forty-eight cells to incarcerate prisoners. During the 1850s, prison control changed between private and public control several times, until 1861 when the state retained permanent control. At this time there were over 554 inmates, including men and women. A second state prison was constructed at Folsom in 1880 due to the increased prison population.

The upkeep of prisoners was the responsibility of the county where the prisoners were convicted. It was normal practice to employ prisoners to work at an industry that would generate income for the prison. Work was also considered a way that the prisoners could redeem themselves for their crimes. The rehabilitation process of incarceration would be a topic that would be reconsidered many times in California. The competition between prison labor and organized labor became a political battle in numerous states. California also tried a leasing system for prison labor during the 1850s, which intensified animosity between prisoners and paid labor. The California constitution of 1879 would also include a law against convict labor.[6]

In 1877 the murder case against Chin Mook Sow brought up the question whether a "dying declaration" could be permissible if it involved Chinese participants. Chin Mook Sow was arrested for murdering Ye Ah Chin, for unknown reasons. Chin Mook Sow filed an affidavit stating he was a citizen of China and not a natural citizen of the United States. He requested that half of the jury be comprised of aliens, but this was denied by the judge. A dying statement was recorded by the victim before his death, placing his mark on a document that identified Chin Mook Sow as his assailant. A lengthy court discussion ensued over the cultural differences between Chinese and Americans, focusing on the Chinese disbelief in an afterlife. The defense argued this would make null and void a deathbed confession, but this suggestion was rejected by the court. Chin Mook Sow was convicted of murder, and hung on May 4, 1877, in San Francisco.[7]

In 1879 there was a scandalous trial that convicted Sacramento's public administrator, Troy Dye, of the murder of Aaron Tullis, a wealthy landowner. Shrewd detective work traced back evidence that implicated Troy and his business partner of killing Tullis. When brought into the police station for questioning, Troy confessed everything and it was recorded by a reporter of the *Sacramento Record Union*. Troy had been offered a deal that he would not hang if he confessed, the district attorney having initially believed Dye was a secondary party to the murder. But the confession stated that Troy was the leader of the group, and the report was published in the paper the next day. The district attorney afterward retracted his offer of not seeking the death penalty in this case, and the two men were sentenced to death.[8]

Jury selection was as difficult then as the present day; people would claim to be unable to serve for various reasons. To participate on a jury, a juror had to survive the process known as *voir dire*, which California codified in 1886. Challenges to the juror's capability to serve duty could be called by an attorney or prosecutor, and the prospective juror could be excused from service. In California the prosecution had five challenges, the defendant ten; these were doubled in capital cases.[9] Numerous times defendants were tried and sentenced without legal representation. In the late 1800s this was particularly true of misdemeanor charges. In 1872 in California, free legal counsel was provided for felony charges including capital cases. An example of the necessity for free legal assistance was the percentage of counsels appointed in Alameda County between 1880 and 1899. At least 25 percent of felony cases were assigned free counsel: "these lawyers received no money for their pains; many of them were apparently young lawyers who were hanging around the courtroom anyway, hoping to pick up a crumb or two of business."[10] The necessity to provide counsel from the pool of available attorneys would eventually lead to public defenders that would be selected by the trial judge.

During the nineteenth century there were several changes in the relative powers of the judge and jury. At the beginning of the century, the judge usually wrote out all instructions to the jurors before addressing them. He explained the laws they were going to debate, and the pertinence to the case they were going to decide. Sometimes these instructions were not helpful, and several important legal points would not be relayed to the jurors for their total comprehension of the legal facts. The purpose of these instructions was to shift the power away from the judge to the jury, and to decrease the number of appeals because of "error" in jury instructions. An increase in prepared jury instruction became commonplace by the beginning of the twentieth century.

A decline of trial by jury occurred during the late nineteenth century. The guilty plea gradually replaced many trials, allowing for a judgment on a lesser charge. Plea bargaining would occur when an agreement was reached between the prosecution and the defendant's attorneys, and a trial judge would preside over the issue or the plea bargain. In Alameda County in California, Friedman and Percival's study found that 14 percent of all defendants between 1880 and 1910 changed their pleas from not guilty to guilty. More than half of these guilty pleas were to a lesser charge, as a study of inmates at Folsom Prison during the 1880s suggests. When asked why they had pleaded guilty, 120 out of 330 prisoners wanted to "mitigate the penalty" and be charged on a lesser

account. One out of three prisoners responded to this, and it was an interesting trend to follow.[11]

In California, public executions were supposedly banned in the 1850s. An execution was expected to occur discreetly, but efficiently, behind the jail or prison walls. But the notoriety of capital punishment cases fascinated the public, with increasing newspaper coverage of murders and the subsequent trials. The public were active observers of the final verdict and sometimes the executions. But with some infamous personalities emblazoned in the press, the public became overly active in the process. One example was the executions of Joseph Jewel and Lloyd Majors for the murder of Archibald McIntyre. Jewel was tried and sentenced first, and became a celebrity while in jail. Sympathetic women crowded his jail cell, bringing him "Brussel carpets and pictures . . . flowers and maudlin sympathy." The editors were infuriated with this treatment, scolding the women who were "neglecting their household duties to pay respects to a red-handed murderer."[12] Jewel would testify against Majors in a second trial that would enforce the death penalty on him. Majors was tried twice, and the Santa Clara grand jury had to rule that he was not in double jeopardy for being tried and sentenced twice for the same crime. When Lloyd Majors was executed in Oakland in 1884, the spectators filled the streets. Numerous seats were taken on nearby rooftops, trying to obtain a view of the hanging inside the jail courtyard. The jail yard itself was filled to capacity with viewers, and "several boys had climbed into a tall poplar tree in front of the jail, in full view of the scaffold."[13] Newspaper accounts afterward covered the event, and executions continued to receive large coverage in the press.

In 1891 a California statute was passed requiring that future executions must take place at one of the state prison facilities, either at San Quentin or Folsom. The counties would no longer retain this responsibility; it would be the purview of the state. The first state execution was the conviction of Jose Gabriel, a Native American from San Diego who was found guilty of the murders of John and Anna Geyser. The reason for the crime remains indistinct, since robbery or revenge did not appear to be a motive. The jury remained at an impasse over the verdict, and could not reach agreement. Judge George Puterbaugh ruled that the evidence was sufficient for a jury verdict; the jury would reach the verdict and the court would decide the sentence. Historian Clare McKanna suggests that Jose Gabriel, because he was an Indian and poor, did not receive a fair trial. Distorted images of the defendant were presented to the court, and court-appointed counsel only had one week in which to prepare a defense. Jose Gabriel was executed at San Quentin on March 3, 1893, the first execution held in that facility.[14]

The first murder conviction that appealed on the change of venue for state executions was filed by Charles Bawden. Bawden had been convicted in 1891 for the murder of his former fiancée, Lily Price. When Lily moved away and married another man, Bawden followed after her and killed her in retaliation. When Bawden's appeal was sent to the California State Supreme Court, the new law about the change in venues for executions came into force. It took over two years before the United States Supreme Court decided to not hear the case. The state court's ruling remained valid, and Charles Bawden was the last person to be executed by Humboldt County.[15]

The insanity defense is probably one of the most controversial of all criminal defense strategies. The notoriety it receives today belies the fact that it has existed since the twelfth century. It was not a method for the accused to be found innocent, but a means of mitigating the sentence or receiving a pardon. The insanity plea in defense of a crime followed the parameter of the McNaughten Rule. This test was applied to the accused in order to establish if the person was sane at the time of the crime's commission, and therefore criminally responsible. It was named after Daniel McNaughten, who in 1843 attempted to assassinate England's prime minister Robert Peele, but instead killed his secretary. This defense has been used in the United States and adapted through court rulings and state legislation. An additional aspect of insanity has also been scrutinized, volitional insanity. This is defined as healthy people who become mentally unbalanced and not able to discern between right and wrong. In capital cases this defense was often used, but could be extremely difficult to prove. California expanded the legal definition of insanity in 1931 for criminal cases. When the plea was entered, the burden of proof of the crime committed still remained with the prosecution. It was assumed the defendant was sane at the time the incident occurred, so the burden of insanity rested with the defense.[16] The insanity plea occurred more often during the nineteenth century, influenced by the publication of *The Medical Jurisprudence of Insanity*, by Issac Ray. The theory itself is very controversial because insanity is difficult to define, and using it to excuse criminal behavior and responsibility will vary between authorities.

There was an increased use of the insanity defense from the 1930s to the 1960s and beyond, as capital punishment became a political issue. As journalism continued to cover more violent crimes in detail, psychological opinions about the possible punishment became more vocalized. One murder conviction that attempted to utilize an insanity plea after a guilty verdict was that of William Fredericks. Fredericks was convicted of the murder of a bank teller while robbing a bank in San Francisco. Fredericks was an experienced criminal with a lengthy lists of crimes committed before the bank robbery and murder that would lead to his death sentence. Fredericks refused to enter a plea when arraigned, so the court entered a plea of not guilty on his behalf. After his conviction, Fredericks's behavior in jail required a hearing by the Insanity Commission, an agency established by the state to investigate these pleas. The commission ruled that he was sane, and his behavior reverted to normal. Fredericks was hanged at San Quentin in 1895.[17]

The introduction of forensic evidence by the prosecution became more detailed during the late nineteenth century. With scientific advancements allowing greater certainty of evidence, murder trials were also affected by this progress. Forensic evidence was used in the trial of Fremont Smith, who was convicted of the murder of a local fisherman. The forensic evidence produced included a pair of bloodstained overalls, which Smith claimed came from slaughtering a hog. An analytical chemist testified that the blood was human, and the jury found Smith guilty based primarily on this evidence. An appeal that was filed reexamined the overalls, with two differing opinions being offered by scientists about the source of the blood. The scientists were two of the top experts in the state, and they were unable to offer incontrovertible evidence about the stain's origins. The local newspapers reported the results, illustrating that the public was interested in the scientific facts behind the trial. The blood could have been "mammalian. It might be that of a man, bear or dog, but could not be that of a fowl or hog." The original verdict remained, and Smith was executed in 1895.[18]

It was the usual procedure upon conviction under the death penalty to appeal to the state supreme court. The first case in which an appeal was not filed by defense counsel was that of Wee Tung, convicted for the murder of his uncle, Yee Lick Chung. The newspapers of the time covered sensational trials and they quickly noted that this was "the first time since the carrying out of sentences at San Quentin has been the rule, that a condemned murderer has gone to the gallows without taking an appeal to the Supreme Court."[19] Someone on Wee Tung's behalf did file an appeal, but it was turned down. Wee Tung was executed at San Quentin on March 11, 1898.

At the turn of the twentieth century, procedures for interrogation of prisoners by law enforcement officials were not codified for prisoner protection. In the murder of Antonio Ruiz, Juan Gonzalez and Jose Cota were charged with this crime in 1903. Both were convicted of first-degree murder and sentenced to be executed. Upon appeal, Cota's statements revealed that he had initially been held in the county jail for over a month before being officially charged. Cota was daily harassed by the county sheriff into producing a confession, until he broke down and agreed to the charges. When asked if any promises had been given to him by the sheriff, Cota replied, "No, he just said he'd do whatever he could for me."[20] Upon conviction, their appeal failed and both men were hung at San Quentin in 1903.

In 1899 George Suesser murdered the sheriff of Monterey, the first time a law enforcement officer had died in the line of duty. Suesser was well known for several criminal activities by the age of fourteen, and the sheriff was in the process of arresting Suesser when he was fatally shot. Public opinion was vehement against Suesser, and he was quickly found guilty at the trial held in Monterey. Upon appeal a second trial was held in Santa Clara County, where the judgment remained affirmed. Public opinion began to soften toward Suesser, and Governor Pardee was reluctant to have him executed during his stay in office. During an absence, acting governor Alden Anderson set the execution date and the sentence was carried out in 1904.

The rate of violent crime declined by the end of the nineteenth century, and the question arose whether to continue with the death penalty as a deterrent. Several organizations had been opposed to capital punishment for centuries, and new groups were formed at the turn of the twentieth century. Quaker societies had long been opposed to capital punishment, and a newly formed group of theosophists also believed a criminal should not be executed for religious reasons.

> Punishment is supposed to be for the protection of society, and for the reformation of the wrongdoer. . . . Capital punishment is a notorious failure in these respects. It does indeed remove the particular culprit from the possibility of repeating his crime; but this is of very small account in view of the fact that murder is seldom a career of repeated acts, but consists of single acts perpetrated by different individuals.[21]

The Housewives' Union of Palo Alto, California, wore black armbands when there was a state execution. Their opposition to the death penalty was recorded in several booklets during the 1910s.[22] Many states had at different times abolished the death penalty to reinstate it at a later date. Governor Hiram Johnson (1911–1917) during his tenure in office made numerous public statements opposing the death penalty. In 1911 a bill was passed by the California Assembly but rejected by the state senate to abolish capital punishment. The issue then went to referendum in 1912 but did not pass with the popular vote.

The state prisons were liable to numerous escapes and rioting due to the nature of the incarcerated prisoners. In 1905 one breakout involved fifteen prisoners from Folsom and resulted in the death of three men during the escape. One was a guard, and the other two were members of a posse sent to track down the escapees. Harry Eldrige was caught and convicted for conspiracy to murder, since he was a part of the original escape plan. Even though he did not kill anyone, the charge of conspiracy that results in a murder can result in a first-degree murder charge. Eldrige was convicted and executed in 1905.[23]

Because first-degree murder remained a charge that could be tried in a state court, it was not necessary to prosecute in a federal courtroom. In the charges against Wilbur Benjamin for the murder of Violet Gilmer, the judgment was a capital offense and he was sentenced to be hanged. The appeal filed by his attorney argued that since his client was a full-blooded Native American, these charges should have been heard in a federal court. Using *Cherokee Nation* as the basis for the appeal, the attorney reviewed the opinions of then current United States Supreme Court decisions. The judicial viewpoint was that Native Americans "had placed themselves, if at all, under federal rather than state protection."[24] This appeal was overruled, and Benjamin was executed in 1910.

In several cases at the beginning of the twentieth century, it was notable that jury deliberations over first-degree murder charges did not necessitate a lengthy time to reach a verdict. When Louis Fortine was convicted in 1916 of the murder of the Furrer family, the jury deliberated for seven minutes before returning with a guilty verdict. With the accused entering a guilty plea, the machinations of justice also continued at an accelerated pace for Moses Gibson. In 1920 Gibson pleaded guilty to the murder of a wealthy rancher. A column in the *Los Angeles Times* noted that "he was arraigned on Wednesday, pleaded guilty to the charge of criminal assault and murder and was sentenced to hang in the space of fifteen minutes."[25] The murder trial of Gregorio Chavez in 1923 for the murder of his wife was also notable for being one of the quickest convictions on record in Imperial County. The jury was selected, heard the testimony, and rendered a verdict in less than a day.[26]

There was public opposition to capital punishment during the 1910s. A pivotal case that was heard during the same time a referendum to abolish capital punishment was being presented to the voters, was the murder trial of Mark Wilkins. Wilkins was convicted for the murder of his common-law wife, Vernie Carmen. Wilkins was convicted of first-degree murder in 1908, and an appeal was sent to the California State Supreme Court, which upheld the lower court's judgment. Wilkins appealed to Governor Hiram Johnson and was granted one reprieve for consideration. The Anti-Capital Punishment League led by Sara Ehrmann applied public pressure on Governor Johnson to reprieve Wilkins until voters would have a chance to vote on the issue of capital punishment. Support for the league came in the form of letters and telegrams from many areas in southern California. Even though he had previously reprieved three other men sentenced for execution, Governor Johnson did not intervene in the Wilkins case. On the scaffold, Wilkins spoke about his "deep gratitude to those who have been active in trying to get a pardon." Wilkins was executed in 1912 at San Quentin, before the referendum was placed before the voters of California.[27]

A change in the California penal code would add additional amendments to include the consequence of the death penalty. Assault with a deadly weapon while serving a life sentence was an amendment implemented in the case of Jacob Oppenheimer. Oppenheimer was incarcerated in prison in 1895 for robbery. Violence inside prisons would result in many assaults, and additional charges would be added to increase an inmate's time to serve. Oppenheimer had already increased his sentence to life imprisonment by the murder of a fellow inmate who had testified against him at the robbery trial. In 1899, Oppenheimer assaulted one of the guards, who would recover from his injuries. Oppenheimer received an additional fourteen years on his sentence. Prison officials and law enforcement officers were displeased with this sentence, since

Oppenheimer was already serving a life sentence. Penal Code sec. 246 was amended to increase the penalty of an attack on a law enforcement officer to include the death penalty. Oppenheimer could not be charged retroactively under this law, but later he killed a fellow death row inmate and was sentenced to death in 1913. His death received notoriety when a tribute was written about him by Jack London in *The Star Rover* (1913): "And justice, with him, was a passion. The prison-killings done by him were due to this extreme sense of justice."[28]

During the 1920s there were different methods of deciding the sanity of a condemned prisoner. The Insanity Commission was now under the auspices of the state prison board. One theory for a declaration of insanity was if the prisoner had syphilitic insanity; most other types of insanity were not considered or were unknown at the time. When Alex Kels was convicted of the murder of Ed Merservey in 1923, the only test considered to diagnose his mental state was a spinal tap for syphilitic insanity. Kels received the test twice, at the urging of his family. Outspoken Governor Friend Richardson blasted the prisons for allowing the test. "The recent resolution of the Prison Board is evidently a frame-up on the part of the three directors hostile to me and my administration and intended for purposes of intimidation." Three labs submitted their results, which were negative, even though the test was not a certainty in diagnosing insanity. These were the only tests administered to Kels, and he was declared sane. Kels was executed in 1924 at Folsom Prison.

Public interest over the issue of capital punishment continued in California. During the 1920s and 1930s there was an increase in the number of capital offenses listed under first-degree murder, adding death caused by an armed robbery or burglary as a first-degree murder charge. Abolitionist activity continued during these decades, desiring to shape public opinion to encourage legislative reform of capital punishment. One case that gained notoriety during the 1920s was the murder of Charles Weingarten, who was killed during an armed robbery of his store by Clarence "Tuffy" Reid. Reid blamed his habit of daily narcotic use for his actions in committing the crimes. Several appeals were filed after his conviction, with a large public outpouring of letters and petitions signed on his behalf. One petition that was sent to the governor contained over fifty thousand names.[29] The governor did not grant clemency and the sentence of execution was carried out in 1925.

A murder trial and its subsequent decision were usually covered in the local newspapers. These materials were often read by prospective jurors, and were just as controversial during the early twentieth century. One case that used this point to file an appeal of a death sentence was the murder conviction of James Clark in the 1920s. Clark was convicted of shooting and killing an acquaintance while they were both drinking heavily. Clark pleaded not guilty, claiming he was under the influence of alcohol at the time of the shooting. The defense attorneys used this as the basis of an insanity plea that would prove unsuccessful. The newspaper carried various accounts that Clark had been faking "insanity" to receive a lighter sentence. The defense appealed the conviction based on the jury's prior prejudice of the defendant, but the State Supreme Court upheld the conviction. Clark was executed in 1921.

There was no specific law stating what day executions would be held, but it became customary for state executions to take place on Friday. Several exceptions did occur, one with the execution of Harry Garcia, convicted of murdering two fellow inmates in 1933 while serving time in Folsom Prison. When Garcia's case was appealed to the California State Supreme Court, they upheld the lower court's decision and affixed the execution for a Wednesday. This deviation from normal prison routine was duly noted in the newspapers at the time, but the execution continued on the appointed day. James Chandler in 1930 was executed on a Monday, another exception to the "normal" prison routine. Sometimes prisoners received last reprieves just to change the scheduled execution date. In 1933 Peter Farrington's last reprieve was to change the execution date which had been scheduled on a bank holiday.

Very often the system for signing and implementing reprieves were not quick enough to prevent executions from continuing. Joseph Francis Regan was convicted of first-degree murder when he killed a bank guard during the commission of a robbery. Regan was reprieved six times while on death row, and was hanged on April 18, 1933. His execution would have been halted if a phone call from the governor's office had been received only seconds earlier. Clinton Duffy, Warden James Holohan's assistant at San Quentin at this time, was on an open phone to the governor's office prior to the execution. At 9:55 a.m. he asked the governor's clemency secretary if there was a reprieve, and was instructed that the execution would take place at the assigned time. At 10:02 the secretary shouted into the phone, "Clint! Stop the execution! The governor signed another reprieve!" As Duffy called on the prison phone to halt the execution, he heard the sound of the gallows trap dropping. Duffy relayed to the secretary it was too late, that the prisoner had already been executed. The secretary responded, "This never happened, Clint. Don't ever breathe a word to anyone. I'll deny it, and so will the governor. I'm tearing up the reprieve. . . . Don't even tell the warden." Duffy recalled this experience and others in his memoirs written after serving as warden at San Quentin.[30]

Sometimes a problem occurred within the appeal process after conviction. This occurred when convicted murderer Rush Griffin, was executed before the appeal process had been completed. Griffin was convicted of first-degree murder and sent to San Quentin on January 26, 1935. He was executed before three months had passed, while his appeal was still before the California Supreme Court. Hearings were held after the execution to investigate what went wrong, and the blame was placed on the delay of paperwork from the warden's office. The Review Committee recommended an automatic appeal process when the death penalty is imposed, stating that "there are too many steps in the procedure where the possibility of human error enters and may result in the loss of the stay of execution which the appeal is intended for." This automatic appeal system remains until today, where the average process of appeals lasts around twenty years until execution.[31]

Between 1888 and 1913, fifteen states had designated the electric chair as an alternative method of execution. California never instituted this device, but continued with hanging until the introduction of the gas chamber in 1937. The choice of this option was based on the grounds that it was a less painful and more humane method of execution. But this was not the image that onlookers at California's first execution by the gas chamber recorded. On September 19, 1937, seven inmates initiated a violent takeover of Folsom prison. It occurred in Warden Larkin's office, where he was conducting interviews over a new parole board policy that the inmates were against. The inmates were in a volatile mood upon entering the warden's office, and during an ensuing melee injured Larkin and killed a prison guard. Larkin was initially expected to survive, but died five days later. Five men were sentenced by the Sacramento County grand jury for first-degree murder and sentenced to be executed by lethal gas at San Quentin. Since the gas chamber could not hold more than two people at a time, Robert Cannon and Albert Kessel were executed together on December 2, 1938. The gas used in the chamber was a chemical used extensively in Southern California, hydrocyanic acid. It was utilized to kill parasites on orange trees, and was the selected gas for the chamber because of its ability to block the body's cells from receiving oxygen. Cannon and Kessel died slowly, fighting to breathe in such a manner it horrified prison employees who had witnessed many executions by hanging. The cost to the state for the hydrocyanic acid was $1.80.

Since the introduction of the gas chamber in California, 192 men and four women have been executed by this method. It is still legally one of the alternative methods of execution that can be assigned upon conviction of first-degree murder. The gas chamber in California is located in the basement at San Quentin. It is a small, green, octagonal box six feet across and eight feet high. Two metal chairs are located inside, allowing up to two executions to occur simultaneously. The entrance is rubber sealed to prevent the gas from escaping, and a large chimney also ensures that, after use, gas remnants are filtered out of the basement. Five of the eight sides of the room contain glass windows for witnesses to the execution. A study conducted of executions at San Quentin shows that it took an average of over nine minutes for death to occur.[32]

"The death penalty is the antithesis of the rehabilitative, non-punitive, non-vindictive orientation of twentieth century penology," said Donald E. J. MacNamara, president of the American League to Abolish Capital Punishment, in 1961.[33]

During the 1950s there were several reform movements that aimed to change the forms of punishment decreed by society and the courts. Support for this movement in California mainly came from the middle class. During the 1930s, California had experienced several prison scandals that brought to public attention the severity of punishment within the penal system. The Prison Reorganization Act of 1944 tightened lax prison conditions and utilized prison labor for wartime efforts. This process became part of the rehabilitative penology that emphasized good administration, with support from trained specialists like psychologists and social workers. The Act also used the "indeterminate sentence" to decide when a prisoner was fully reformed. Several prison wardens were noted for being reformers and opponents of the death penalty. Clinton Duffy, while warden of San Quentin, was influential in making his anti-death-penalty and prison reform views known to the public. Through his published book, excerpted in *The Saturday Evening Post*, the ideal of a reformed prisoner returning to the public was idealized later by two Hollywood movies. Duffy later remained active on the state's parole board, declaring that "the rich are never executed: only the poor end up on death row."[34]

On November 21, 1941, Juanita Spinelli was the first woman executed in California. Juanita Spinelli, Mike Simeone, and Gordon Hawkins were convicted for the murder of Robert Sherrard, a member of their criminal gang. Since this was the first woman legally executed in state history, it evolved into a controversial story. Various groups were split about the decision, from arguments for commutation of her sentence to comments that she should not receive clemency because of her gender. One juror was noted for his statement to the press after the verdict. Juror G. P. Yoerk believed that Spinelli was guilty with the others convicted of first-degree murder, but added that if the sentence was commuted by the governor, "My mind would be relieved."[35] Governor Culbert Olson denied clemency to Spinelli, stating, "If she were a man, my decision not to intervene would be easier. But since the law does not provide for any preferred consideration to women, I do not feel I have the right to discriminate in the exercise of the power of executive clemency."[36] Spinelli was executed first on November 21, 1941. Hawkins and Simeone were executed the following week.

The motion picture industry narrated the life and execution of convicted murderer Barbara Graham. Graham was convicted for the murder of an elderly widow during a robbery attempt. In Robert Wise's *I Want To Live!* (MGM, 1958) the film dramatized Graham's life, but maintained her innocence of the crime. The movie was made to counteract the hostile treatment Graham had received from the newspapers and tabloids which conspicuously wrote about her association with criminal elements. The film's scenes emphasize Graham's rehabilitation since arriving at San Quentin, and questions what was the outcome for "reformed" prisoners. Direct criticism of the death penalty is evident in the closing scene that portrays Graham's final moments. There was an hour-and-a-half wait while the time of her execution was continually postponed. Graham is quoted as saying, "Why do they torture me? I was ready to go at 10 o'clock."[37] Her final words became the focus of an anti-death-penalty movement that would accelerate during the 1950s.

After World War II there was a strong abolitionist movement against the death penalty. This focused in on several California cases that would become controversial for both sides of the issue. Emerging from the earlier prison reform scandals and rising criticism from newspaper and motion picture commentaries, two cases influenced a concentrated effort by the public to respond to the topic of capital punishment. The first case was a coalition of several organizations in March 1954 that resulted in a commutation of execution for Wesley Robert Wells, an African American. Wells was sentenced to San Quentin in 1928 for theft, where he remained until 1941 and was released. During this time Wells's sentence was extended for the killing of another prisoner during a fight. Wells was arrested again for theft in 1941, and began to serve another term. Wells was subjected to physical and verbal abuse from the guards and other prisoners. During a 1947 disciplinary hearing he threw an ashtray at a guard who was taunting him. As violation of Section 4500 of the

California Penal Code, Wells was sent to death row for execution. The issue of segregation within the prisons initiated a suit filed against this practice by the Civil Rights Congress. With prisoners separated during meal times and in cells based upon race, the suit claimed the rehabilitation process was flawed. Governor Earl Warren would deny clemency, saying that "this Civil Rights Congress is Communist inspired and makes its parade to Sacramento solely for a political purpose, to involve me in the racial discrimination question." Bypassing the issue of segregation in the prisons and concentrating on the murder sentence, Warren sidestepped this political arena of the 1950s with the recurring fear of Communist influences. Continued pressure by numerous organizations resulted in Wells's execution being commuted, and he remained in San Quentin until released in the mid-1970s.[38]

Additions to what constituted a capital offense would continue to be made over the years by the state legislature. One addition was assault with a weapon while serving a life sentence. Robert Harmon was incarcerated under a life sentence at Soledad Prison for first-degree robbery. Harmon attacked another prisoner and stabbed him numerous times. Even though the victim recovered, under the current law Harmon was sentenced to death and executed in 1960. Another offense that could result in capital punishment was kidnapping for the purpose of robbery. Billy Monk was convicted on two counts, kidnapping and robbery, and received a death sentence. In the one conviction, the victim was approached by Monk in a parking lot, forced into the car, and Monk took off. The victim in fear opened the car door and jumped out, receiving several serious injuries afterward. The court held that "while the defendant did not touch (her) she was in a state of fear," and that her escape by throwing herself out of the car was due to Monk's kidnapping.[39]

The case that would cause considerable con-troversy during the 1950s was the death penalty conviction of Caryl Chessman. Chessman had been paroled from San Quentin for only a month before he was arrested again and charged with eighteen counts that would range from robbery and kidnapping to sexual assault. Known as "The Red Light Bandit," Chessman would place a red light on top of his vehicle to impersonate a police car to lure his victims to pull over in their vehicles. This case became controversial from the very beginning, with Chessman conducting his own defense at trial. The penal code at the time stipulated the death penalty as a consequence for kidnapping and robbery. The jury returned with two death sentences for each case, with the additional charges. The statute, known as the "Lindbergh Law," was revised in 1951 to eliminate the death penalty for the purpose of robbery.[40] Wells's and Chessman's paths crossed, while both were residents of death row, when a "strike" was held on November 1, 1950. The prisoners' protest involved demands for writing materials, lights to be on all night, longer exercise periods, and better food. Thirteen of the sixteen prisoners on death row participated and these actions gained the attention of the press immediately. Wells and Chessman were two of the instigators of the strike, and both were sent to solitary confinement as a consequence for this disruption in the prison routine.

With the writing materials gained from their strike, Chessman in May 1954 composed and then smuggled out a manuscript that would be published as *Cell 2455 Death Row*. The account was a success with the public and made into a movie the following year by Columbia Pictures. Warden Harley Teets had allowed Chessman to occupy his time with writing, but when the book became a "prolonged and very biased argument in favor of Chessman," he was prohibited from writing more.[41] Chessman continued to smuggle two additional books out of prison that kept his incarceration before the public attention, the themes centering on his case and appeal process. Chessman appealed the conviction based mainly on the transcripts from the trial, claiming that the documents were corrupted. The original court reporter died before the completion of the original transcript, and another court reporter had to translate the shorthand notes for the record. Based on due process, the United States Supreme Court vacated lower court judgments on the transcript issue. It would take two years for the transcripts to be corrected while Chessman awaited the appeal process.

During the twelve years Chessman spent on death row, he had eight stays of execution. He was a frequent participant in strike movements with other inmates, which continued to garner negative publicity for the prison but notoriety for Chessman. His cause would be spoken about by several famous people, including Eleanor Roosevelt, Aldous Huxley, Ray Bradbury, and others. His opponents would emphasize his previous criminal record and lack of contrition for the crimes committed. This became evident in his books and the basis of rejection for his appeals to higher courts. One victim became mentally ill after her attack and was confined to a mental hospital where she spent the rest of her life. During Chessman's time on death row, the Little Lindbergh Law under which he was convicted for kidnapping was repealed. Several inmates convicted under this law would receive parole, but Chessman would not. Chessman had his sentence upheld by Governor Edmund Brown. Brown's final stay of execution and Chessman's appeals to the California Supreme Court ran out, and he was executed in the gas chamber on May 2, 1960.

After Chessman's execution, the controversy over the death penalty continued. Media coverage was divided between opposing perspectives concerning capital punishment. The *New York Times* article on May 3, 1960, portrayed the event as the "convict-author . . . kept his ninth scheduled appointment in the gas chamber of San Quentin prison." A contrasting front-page article ran in the *Los Angeles Times*: "Caryl Chessman, 38, the infamous Red Light Bandit who terrorized Los Angeles lovers' lane in 1948, was executed this morning." Columnist Herb Caen summed up the abolitionist viewpoint: "The Man, Caryl Chessman, is no longer the issue; now he is the world-wide symbol of the farce that is capital punishment in California."[42] Worldwide response to Chessman's execution brought the topic of capital punishment in the United States to immediate attention. Angry mobs in Rio de Janeiro denounced the United States during President Eisenhower's visit, students smashed windows at the United States embassy in Lisbon, and additional protests were held against capital punishment in the United States.

The Caryl Chessman case became a symbol representing a larger movement against the death penalty. An editorial in the *New York Herald Tribune* after his execution suggested that "Chessman succeeded in making himself a world-wide symbol of the fight against the death penalty."[43] Numerous popular magazines debated the issue of capital punishment. *The Nation*, an advocate for Chessman and abolitionism, stated that this "aroused world opinion, plus intense local interest and agitation, had made Chessman the symbol of the movement to abolish capital punishment."[44] Norman Cousins from the Friends Movement wrote in the *Saturday Review* "the fact that other men are now under death sentence does not weaken the case for saving Chessman. He has become the ultimate symbol of a long-deferred question."[45] The aspect of possible rehabilitation for Chessman did not exonerate him from the crimes he committed. John Laurence observed, "California sentenced a young thug . . . it killed a man who learned law, and probably citizenship, the hard way."[46] The *Christian Century* opined, "However heinous his crimes and certain his guilt, it can now be admitted without sentimentalizing his case that the maturing Chessman has risen above his level of punishment."[47]

To liberal criminologists, journalists, and abolitionists, Chessman presented the appearance of a rehabilitated prisoner. Besides his books, Chessman wrote numerous letters to the California governors concerning his case. The dilemma with this rehabilitated persona was the crimes themselves. "Opponents of the death penalty, resting their case on Chessman, picked a precarious basis. This man stands convicted of particularly revolting crimes."[48]

The analysis of the concern during the 1950s and early 1960s over capital punishment needs to be observed through the sociopolitical climate of the time. This occurred during the Cold War with a reexamination of national values with concerns about state-sanctioned "murder." The Friends was an organization that had actively supported abolition of the institution of state executions, and this was an integral part of their belief system. The aspect of rehabilitation appealed to many of their members, as it did also to modern prison reformers. The rehabilitative aspect of imprisonment was a desired alternative to encourage an individual's eventual restoration to society. Prison reformers did not dwell long on the point that the alternative was a lifetime in prison with all of the negative connotations that implied. The question of the possible execution of an innocent prisoner was another point that gained interest among social and political groups. The latest principles of penology and rehabilitation suggested a legal change was necessary to accomplish this end of capital punishment, by excluding the death penalty as an alternative punishment.

Governor Brown received severe criticism over the Chessman execution. After Chessman's last stay of execution, Brown spoke to the state legislature for support of an abolitionist bill. In his address, Brown emphasized that "no matter

how efficient and fair the death penalty may seem in theory, in actual practice in California as elsewhere it is primarily inflicted upon the weak, the poor, the ignorant, and against racial minorities."[49] The NAACP (National Association for the Advancement of Colored People) and ACLU (American Civil Liberties Union) would respond to Brown's statement with additional support against capital punishment. Disillusionment with capital punishment and the justice system accelerated as the 1960s progressed. Chessman's execution became a rallying topic, and a major point in California politics. Governor Brown continued to allow executions with eleven occurring in California during 1962, the highest number in the United States for that year. After the Chessman execution, there was a total of twenty-four men and one woman executed under the Brown administration.

James Hooton was executed two weeks after Chessman, and did not receive the immense publicity of the former case. Hooton was arrested for the murder of police officer Thomas Scebbi, who had stopped Hooton for suspicious behavior while walking down the street. Hooton shot Scebbi, who died soon afterward at the scene. The jury found Hooton guilty and sentenced him to death. In cases that involved the shooting of law enforcement officials, there was not much negative publicity over a scheduled execution. This was also evident in the 1961 execution of Alexander Robillard, convicted for the murder of police officer Eugene Doran. Officer Doran had pulled Robillard over while driving for making an illegal U-turn, and was shot and killed. A massive manhunt had been undertaken for Robillard, with large coverage on the local news. The brutality of the officer's murder angered the public as well as law enforcement officials, and the appeal process was not lengthy.

During Pat Brown's administration, fourteen executions took place, thirteen men and one woman. Six of the men executed were African American, three were Hispanic. The discrepancy between the numbers illustrates the higher rate that minorities were executed in comparison to whites. The case involving the execution of Elizabeth Duncan was for the murder of her daughter-in-law. Duncan hired two men to kill her daughter-in-law, Olga. Duncan was an overbearing and possessive mother, and perceived Olga as a threat to her relationship with her son. This strange relationship became evident as, even after the murder of his wife, her son Frank continued to work on his mother's defense team. But the jury found Duncan and the two hired killers guilty of first-degree murder, and they were executed in 1962.

Governor Brown flip-flopped on his death penalty stance. After reelection in 1962 he began to call for a four-year moratorium on it and suggested that the convicted were "members of minority races, the poor, the friendless. . . . We are prone to minimizing (sentences) in defendants who are most like ourselves."[50] There was public support for the moratorium, with a 1963 Field Poll recording 44 percent approval. A moratorium bill passed the state assembly, but failed in the senate. Brown used his powers of executive clemency to allow no further executions during his tenure as governor.

Political support for abolition became more outspoken during the mid-1960s. Attorney General Ramsey Clark told Congress in 1966: "We favor the abolition of the death penalty. Modern penology, with its correctional and rehabilitative skills, affords greater protection to society than the death penalty, which is inconsistent with its goals."[51] This time abolition was not supported by small organizations but entered the political field. The transition and change of attitude toward the death penalty between the Brown and Reagan administrations was also mirrored throughout the nation.

Ronald Reagan was elected governor in November 1966, with law and order one of the major issues of his campaign. Reagan won by a large margin of votes, with support from both political parties. At this time there were sixty-four inmates on death row, and Brown had to decide their fate before leaving office. Several anti-death-penalty groups encouraged Brown to commute all death sentences. Brown had two possible ways to leave office and make known his abolitionist views. He could commute all death sentences, or reprieve all death sentences and allow the state legislature to vote on this issue. Brown chose neither option, instead commuting the sentences of only four of the condemned. In analyzing Brown's actions, Wallace Turner of *The New York Times* perceived this course of no action as Brown's adherence to state law. Brown would not place "himself above the laws of the state that provide(s) for the death penalty."[52] As the administration changed, it was a pertinent political point that one-third of the inmates on death row were African American.

One of the notable guidelines of the Reagan administration was the refusal to interfere with court decisions regarding capital punishment. The NAACP was very active during the mid-1960s to halt further executions. The legal battles over this issue would dominate the remaining years of the decade. California was one of the only states to consistently fight the legal battle over the death penalty between 1967 and 1972. An NAACP lawsuit halted five scheduled executions in California that were planned to take place within a twenty-day period in 1967. Reagan was reported by the *San Francisco Chronicle* as saying that he "wished there was a way to 'issue a stay of execution to those people in the days ahead who are going to be murdered.'"[53] Public support for the death penalty continued to be high in California, with the Field Poll finding a 65 percent approval for capital punishment.[54] The number of death penalty decisions decided by Californian juries remained controversial—six in 1960–1962, eleven in 1963, four in 1964, ten in 1965, seventeen each in 1966 and 1967, and twenty-one in 1968.[55]

At the same time public opinion supported the death penalty, civil rights organizations accelerated their efforts for the abolitionist cause. The NAACP Legal Defense Fund (LDF) began to question racial disparities in death sentences in southern states. They focused on the question of "cruel and unusual punishment" along with the large number of minorities on death row. The LDF began to challenge every execution, adopting the strategy Brown initiated by creating a halt in the courts as a method of preventing further executions. Continuing along these lines, the LDF hoped for the United States Supreme Court to finally rule on the constitutionality of the death penalty. Nationwide executions began to decrease by the late 1960s largely because of the LDF's efforts; only one took place in California in 1967 and one in 1968 in another state.

At the beginning of his tenure in office, Governor Ronald Reagan continued to make law and order a top priority. "Californians should be able to walk down the streets safely day and night. . . . [L]awlessness by the mob, as with the individual, will not be tolerated."[56] During his first year in office, Reagan slashed the welfare budget, made large cuts in mental health programs, and enacted a hiring freeze for state personnel. The death penalty also was brought back to the political arena. There were twelve executions scheduled to occur at San Quentin during the Reagan administration. If this took place it would be a larger number than all the other states combined. Four of the condemned were African American, and this point was actively discussed in the media. In March 1967 Governor Reagan had reached his first decision concerning a scheduled execution. Reagan refused to grant clemency to Paul LaVergne, a Black Muslim, who was sentenced for first-degree murder of a white taxi cab driver. It became a

political and racial issue, with the defense attorney calling the scheduled execution a "sacrificial killing. . . . Society has, but its deprivation of the Negro, created minds receptive to the Black Muslim ideology." The defense's appeal was based on the aspect that LaVergne "really didn't know that he did wrong."[57] The appeal to Supreme Court Justice William Douglas was successful, as he was a proponent of allowing the courts to slow down the process.

The only execution under the administration of Reagan was Aaron Mitchell in 1967. Mitchell was found guilty of the murder of a police officer in 1963. The case had been brought to the previous governor, but Brown refused to commute the sentence since it involved the death of a law enforcement official. The issue of clemency for Mitchell was actively sought by the NAACP Legal Defense Fund. Mitchell's final interview with *Ebony* magazine contained his statement, "Every Negro ever convicted of killing a police officer has died in the gas chamber, so what chance did I have? . . . I'm not bitter, I don't think. But I know that my being a Negro is a big factor in everything's that's happened to me."[58] The publicity over the execution was enormous, as this would be the only execution scheduled in the United States for 1967. Reagan did not use executive privilege and commute the sentence, and Mitchell was executed April 12.

Later that year, the execution of Calvin Thomas was scheduled. Thomas, an African American, had been convicted of the murder of a three year old, when he threw a bomb into his girlfriend's house. Thomas underwent a series of psychiatric examinations while incarcerated, and it was suggested he suffered from brain damage and mental illness. The June 21 execution date was stayed indefinitely by the California State Supreme Court. Reagan concurred with this decision, and delayed his announcement of executive clemency to coincide with a lawsuit initiated by the NAACP about the disparity in the state's use of the death penalty. Reagan commuted Thomas's sentence to life without parole. The political climate about the death penalty was becoming more active, with abolitionists becoming more vocal in their viewpoints.[59]

From the frontier justice of the 1850s, until the various abolition movements against the death penalty, capital punishment remained controversial in California. By the end of the 1960s during the Reagan administration, abolitionist views were becoming more widespread. Even with Reagan's election stance on "law and order," the death penalty became a debatable form of punishment. Nations allied with the United States had already abolished or limited death penalty convictions. The number of executions was dropping in the United States, with public support during 1966 plummeting in a Gallup Poll, with support at only 42 percent.[60]

The constitutionality of the death penalty began to be examined, with its legality challenged by the Fifth, Eighth, and Fourteenth Amendments. These amendments were still interpreted as permitting the death penalty. By the 1960s a reexamination of this consequence would be conducted, under the aspect of "cruel and unusual" punishment. The United States Supreme Court would hear *U.S. v. Jackson* (390 U.S. 570), where under the federal kidnapping statute requiring

the death penalty would be imposed only upon recommendation from the jury. The Supreme Court ruled this unconstitutional, stipulating that defendants would waive their right to a jury trial with this stipulation. Another case from 1968, *Witherspoon v. Illinois* (391 U.S. 510), concerned a juror's reservations about the death penalty. The court decided that a juror could not be disqualified from serving on a death penalty case based on their attitude toward capital punishment. In 1971 the Supreme Court would again address the role of the juror in capital cases in *Crampton v. Ohio* and *McGautha v. California*.[61] Jury decisions in capital cases could be completed in one proceeding, and multiple hearings did not have to be held. Future Supreme Court cases at the federal and state level would dramatically change the direction of capital punishment within California at the beginning of the 1970s.

Susan Sanchez-Barnett teaches for Baltimore County Public Schools and is an adjunct professor for Strayer University. She received her Ph.D. in History of Native Americans from University of California, Riverside. Susan writes in the field of Native American history and has articles published in *Treaties with American Indians, Encyclopedia of American Indian History, The City and Urban Life, Encyclopedia of Immigration and Migration into the American West*, and more.

Reading List

Sheila O'Hare, Irene Berry, and Jesse Silva. *Legal Executions in California*. Jefferson, N.C.: McFarland and Company, 2006.

Theodore Hamm. *Rebel and a Cause: Caryl Chessman and the Politics of the Death Penalty in Postwar California, 1948–1974.* Berkeley: University of California Press, 2001.

Stuart Banner. *The Death Penalty: An American History.* Cambridge: Harvard University Press, 2002.

Notes

1. Sheila O'Hare, Irene Berry, and Jesse Silva, *Legal Executions in California* (Jefferson, N.C.: McFarland and Company, 2006), 39.

2. Lynwood Carranco and Estle Beard, *Genocide and Vendetta: The Round Valley Wars of Northern California* (Norman: University of Oklahoma Press, 1981).

3. Alta California, 3/20/1875.

4. John Boessenecker, *Lawman: The Life and Times of*

Harry Morse, 1835–1912 (Norman: University of Oklahoma Press, 1998).

5. Cal. St. Const., Article I, section 8.

6. Shelley Bookspan, *A Germ of Goodness: The California State Prison System, 1851–1944* (Lincoln: University of Nebraska Press, 1994,) 2; Cal. Penal Code, secs. 1203, 1215; Laws Cal. 1903, chap. 34, 34–35.

7. Gordon Morris Bakken and Brenda Farrington, eds. *Law in the West* (New York: Garland Publishing, Inc., 2001).

8. Ibid., Legal Executions, 110–111.

9. Cal. Penal Code (1886), sec. 1070.

10. Lawrence Friedman, *Roots of Justice: Crime and Punishment in Alameda County, California, 1880–1910* (Chapel Hill: University of North Carolina Press, 1981).

11. Milton Huemann, "A Note on Plea Bargaining and Case Pressure," *Law and Society Review* 9:515, 1975.

12. San Francisco Call, 12/1/1883.

13. Friedman and Percival, *Roots of Justice*, 305–6.

14. Clare McKanna, *Race and Homicide in Nineteenth Century California* (Reno: University of Nevada Press, 2002).

15. James M. Sintic, "Last Hanging in Humboldt County," *The Humboldt Historian* 32:5 (Sep.–Oct. 1984).

16. Cal. Stats. 1931, p. 937.

17. Thomas Samuel Duke, *Celebrated Criminal Cases of America* (San Francisco: James H. Barry Company, 1910).

18. *Fresno Weekly Republican*, 1/5/1894.

19. *Los Angeles Times*, 11/30/1897, 3/12/1898.

20. *People v. Gonzalez*, 136 Cal. 666 (1902).

21. "To Abolish Capital Punishment: A Plea to the Citizens of Every Country, Point Loma, California, 1914," from *Sunrise* magazine, April/May 1998.

22. Stuart Banner, *The Death Penalty: An American History* (Cambridge: Harvard University Press, 2002).

23. J. C. Mobery, A Chronological History of Folsom State Prison, 1858–1941 Masters of Art in History thesis, California State University, Sacramento, 1994.

24. *Cherokee Nation*, 118 U.S. 375, 383.

25. *Los Angeles Times*, 7/23/1920.

26. O'Hare, 269–270.

27. Ibid., 224.

28. Ibid., 232.

29. Ibid., 240.

30. O'Shea, 346, from Clinton T. Duffy, *88 Men and 2 Women* (Garden City, N.Y.: Doubleday, 1962).

31. *Los Angeles Times*, 5/29/1935.

32. O'Shea, 400.

33. Theodore Hamm, *Rebel and a Cause: Caryl Chessman and the Politics of the Death Penalty in Postwar California, 1948–1974* (Berkeley: University of California Press, 2001), 11.

34. Ibid., 23.

35. O'Shea, 414.

36. Ibid., 415.

37. Ibid., 514.

38. Hamm, 91.

39. O'Shea, 557.

40. Ibid., 544.

41. Ibid., 545.

42. *San Francisco Chronicle*, 5/1/1960.

43. Quoted in John Laurence, *A History of Capital Punishment* (New York: Citadel Press, 1960), 15.

44. *The Nation*, 3/26/1960, 264–265.

45. *Saturday Review*, 4/23/1960, 26.

46. Laurence, 414.

47. *Christian Century*, 4/29/1960, 499–500.

48. Hamm, 36.

49. Edmund Brown, *Public Justice, Private Mercy: A Governor's Education on Death's Row* (New York: Weidenfeld & Nicolson, 1989), 52.

50. Hamm, 145.

51. Ramsey Clark, *Crime in America: Observations on Its Natures, Causes, Preventions and Control* (New York: Simon & Schuster, 1970), 332.

52. *New York Times*, 12/24/1966.

53. *San Francisco Chronicle*, 7/7/1967.

54. Field Institute, California Poll (May 22, 1969).

55. Hamm, 200.

56. "Reagan's Inaugural Talk, *Los Angeles Times*, Jan. 6, 1967.

57. *Los Angeles Times*, 3/14/1967.

58. *Ebony* 22:8 (June 1967), 121–125.

59. Hamm, 150.

60. R. Bohm, *Deathquest: An Introduction to the Theory and Practice of Capital Punishment in the United States* (Cincinnati: Anderson Publishing, 1999).

61. Consolidated under 402 U.S. 183.

CHAPTER 22

Capital Punishment Suggested Reading

Catherine Kaye

Encyclopedias

Barnes, Patricia G. *Congressional Quarterly's Desk Reference on American Criminal Justice.* Washington, D.C.: CQ Press, 2001. LC: HV9950 .B364 2001.

Bedau, Hugo Adam. "Capital Punishment." *Encyclopedia of Criminology and Deviant Behavior. Volume II: Crime and Juvenile Delinquency.* Ed. Clifton D. Bryant. Philadelphia, PA: Brunner-Routledge, 2001. 57–59. LC: HV6017 .E53 2001.

———. "Capital Punishment: Morality, Politics, and Policy." *Encyclopedia of Crime and Justice.* Ed. Joshua Dressler. Vol. 1. 2nd ed. New York: Macmillan Reference USA, 2002. 125–133. LC: HV6017 .E52 2002.

Berger, Vivian. "Capital Punishment (Update 2)," *Encyclopedia of the American Constitution.* Ed. Leonard W. Levy and Kenneth L. Karst. Vol. 1. 2nd ed. Detroit: Macmillan Reference USA, 2000. 306–307. LC: KF4548 .E53 2000.

Bessette, Joseph M., ed. *American Justice.* 3 vols. Pasadena, CA: Salem Press, 1996. LC: KF154 .A44 1996.

"Capital Punishment." *American Law Yearbook 2005.* Ed. Laurie Fundukian and Jeffrey Wilson. Detroit: Gale, 2006. 15–27. *Gale Virtual Reference Library.* Thomson Gale. LC: KF154 .W472.

"Capital Punishment." *National Survey of State Laws.* Ed. Richard Leiter. Vol. 1. 5th ed. Detroit: Gale, 2005. 75–104. *Gale Virtual Reference Library.* Thomson Gale. LC: KF386 .N38 2005.

"Capital Punishment." *West's Encyclopedia of American Law.* Ed. Jeffrey Lehman and Shirelle

Phelps. Vol. 2. 2nd ed. Detroit: Gale, 2005. 237–42. *Gale Virtual Reference Library*. Thomson Gale. LC: KF154 .W47 2005.

"Criminal Law: Death Penalty." *Gale Encyclopedia of Everyday Law*. Ed. Jeffrey Wilson. Vol. 1. 2nd ed. Detroit: Gale, 2006. 447–52. *Gale Virtual Reference Library*. Thomson Gale. LC: KF387 .G27 2006.

"Cruel and Unusual Punishment." *West's Encyclopedia of American Law*. Ed. Jeffrey Lehman and Shirelle Phelps. Vol. 3. 2nd ed. Detroit: Gale, 2005. 304–8. *Gale Virtual Reference Library*. Thomson Gale. LC: KF154 .W47 2005.

Dubber, Markus Dirk. "Cruel and Unusual Punishment." *Encyclopedia of Crime and Justice*. Ed. Joshua Dressler. 2nd ed. New York: Macmillan Reference USA, 2002. 494–98. *Gale Virtual Reference Library*. Thomson Gale. LC: HV6017 .E52.

Harmon, Talia Roitberg. "Capital Punishment." *Encyclopedia of Crime and Punishment*. Ed. David Levinson. Thousand Oaks, CA: Sage Publications, 2002. 159–61. LC: HV6017 .E524 2002.

Krantz, Sheldon. "Cruel and Unusual Punishment." *Encyclopedia of the American Constitution*. Ed. Leonard W. Levy and Kenneth L. Karst. Vol. 2. 2nd ed. Detroit: Macmillan Reference USA, 2000. 729–31. *Gale Virtual Reference Library*. Thomson Gale. LC: KF4548 .E53 2000.

Lane, Roger. "Capital Punishment." *Violence in America: An Encyclopedia*. Ed. Ronald Gottesman and Richard Maxwell Brown. New York: Scribner, 1999. 198–203. LC: HN90. V5 V5474 1999.

Lehman, Jeffrey, and Shirelle Phelps, eds. *West's Encyclopedia of American Law*. 2nd ed. Detroit: Gale, 2005. *Gale Virtual Reference Library*. Thomson Gale. LC: KF154 .W47 2005.

Mauro, Tony. *Illustrated Great Decisions of the Supreme Court*. 2nd ed. Washington, D.C.: CQ Press, 2006. LC: KF4549 .M334 2006.

Mikula, Mark, L. Mpho Mabunda, and Allison McClintic Marion, eds. *Great American Court Cases*. 4 vols. Detroit: Gale Group, 1999. LC: KF385 .A4 G68 1999.

Palmer, Louis J., Jr. *Encyclopedia of Capital Punishment in the United States*. Jefferson, N.C.: McFarland, 2001. LC: HV8694 .P35 2001.

Patrick, Leslie. "Capital Punishment." *Encyclopedia of the New American Nation*. Ed. Paul Finkelman. Vol. 1. Detroit: Charles Scribner's Sons, 2006. 242–43. *Gale Virtual Reference Library*. Thomson Gale. LC: E301 .E53 2006.

"Public Attitudes toward Capital Punishment." *Information Plus® Reference Series Spring 2004*. Ed. Paul Connors et al. Detroit: Gale, 2005. 87–92. *Gale Virtual Reference Library*. Thomson Gale.

Steiker, Carol S. "Capital Punishment: Legal Aspects." *Encyclopedia of Crime & Justice*. Ed. Joshua Dressler. Vol. 1. 2nd ed. New York: Macmillan Reference USA, 2002. 119–25. LC: HV6017 .E52 2002.

Tonry, Michael, ed. *Handbook of Crime & Punishment*. New York: Oxford University Press, 1998. LC: HV6789 .H25 1998.

Weisberg, Robert. "Capital Punishment." *Encyclopedia of the American Constitution*. Ed. Leonard W. Levy and Kenneth L. Karst. Vol. 1. 2nd ed. Detroit: Macmillan Reference USA, 2000. 299–304. *Gale Virtual Reference Library*. Thomson Gale. LC: KF4548 .E53 2000.

Zimring, Franklin, and Michael Laurence. "Capital Punishment (Update 1)." *Encyclopedia of the American Constitution.* Ed. Leonard W. Levy and Kenneth L. Karst. Vol. 1. 2nd ed. Detroit: Macmillan Reference USA, 2000. 304–6. *Gale Virtual Reference Library.* Thomson Gale. LC: KF4548 .E53 2000.

Statistics

"Capital Punishment Statistics." *Crime and Punishment: Essential Primary Sources.* Ed. K. Lee Lerner and Brenda Wilmoth Lerner. Detroit: Gale, 2006. 366–69. *Gale Virtual Reference Library.* Thomson Gale. LC: HV7419 .C743 2006.

"Capital Punishment Statistics, 1930–2007." Bureau of Justice Statistics. U.S. Department of Justice. Available at: http://www.ojp.usdoj.gov/bjs/cp.htm.

"Capital Punishment: 2006." Bureau of Justice Statistics, U.S. Department of Justice. Available at: http://www.ojp.usdoj.gov/bjs/cp.htm#publications.

"Correctional Populations in the United States: Statistical Tables." Bureau of Justice Statistics. U.S. Department of Justice. Available at http://www.ojp.usdoj.gov/bjs/abstract/cpusst.htm.

"Facts and Figures on the Death Penalty (1 January 2006)." Amnesty International USA. Available at: http://www.amnestyusa.org/us/document.do?id=ENGACT500062006.

"Federal Death Penalty." Death Penalty Information Center. Available at: http://www.deathpenaltyinfo.org/article.php?scid=29&did=147.

"Federal Death Penalty Survey System: A Statistical Survey (1988–2000)." Available at: http://www.usdoj.gov/dag/pubdoc/_dp_survey_final.pdf.

Liebman, James, Jeffrey Fagan, and Valerie West. *A Broken System: Error Rates in Capital Cases, 1973–1995* [The Liebman Study]. Washington, D.C.: Justice Project, 2000. Available at: http://www2.1aw.columbia.edu/instructionalservices/liebman/.

Passell, Peter. "The Deterrent Effect of the Death Penalty: A Statistical Test." *Stanford Law Review* 28.1 (Nov. 1975): 61–80.

Sourcebook of Criminal Justice Statistics [annual]. SuDoc: J 29.9/6. Available at: http://www.albany.edu/sourcebook/.

Articles

"Abolish Death Penalty." Editorial. *State Journal Register* [Springfield, IL] 23 Dec 2007: 14.

Acker, James R. "The Death Penalty: A 25-Year Retrospective and a Perspective on the Future." *Criminal Justice Review* 21.2 (1996): 139–60.

Allen, Charlotte Low. "Ending Abuse of Death Penalty Appeals." *Wall Street Journal* 14 May 1990, Eastern ed.: A16.

Baker, David N., Eric G. Lambert, and Morris Jenkins. "Racial Differences in Death Penalty Support and Opposition: A Preliminary Study of White and Black College Students." *Journal of Black Studies* 35 (March 2005): 201–24.

Barbour, James J. "Efforts to Abolish the Death Penalty in Illinois." *Journal of the American Institute of Criminal Law and Criminology* 9.4 (1919): 500–513.

Beckham, Crystal M., Beverly J. Spray, and Christina A. Pietz. "Jurors' Locus of Control and Defendants' Attractiveness in Death Penalty Sentencing." *Journal of Social Psychology* 147.3 (2007): 285–98.

Beiser, Vince. "The Death Penalty on Life Support; After Decades of Executions, the U.S. is Growing Queasy about Capital Punishment." *Los Angeles Times* 1 Jan. 2008, home ed.: A.15+.

Black, Lee J., and Mark A. Levine. "Ethical Prohibition against Physician Participation in Capital Punishment." Letter. *Mayo Clinic Proceedings* 83.1 (2008): 113–15.

Bohm, Robert M. "American Death Penalty Attitudes: A Critical Examination of Recent Evidence." *Criminal Justice and Behavior* 14.3 (1987): 380–96.

Brigham, John. "New Federalism: Unusual Punishment: The Federal Death Penalty in the United States." *Washington University Journal of Law & Policy* 16 (2004): 195, 210–11.

Burt, Robert A. "Disorder in the Court: The Death Penalty and the Constitution." *Michigan Law Review* 85.8 (1987): 1741–819.

Bye, Raymond T. "Recent History and Present Status of Capital Punishment in the United States." *Journal of the American Institute of Criminal Law and Criminology* 17.2 (Aug. 1926): 234–45.

Clinton, Bill. "Statement on Signing the Antiterrorism and Effective Death Penalty Act of 1996." *Weekly Compilation of Presidential Documents* 32.17 (29 Apr. 1996): 719–21. Available at: http://www.presidency.ucsb.edu/ws/print.php?pid=52713.

Coleman, James E., Jr., ed. *The ABA's Proposed Moratorium on the Death Penalty.* Spec. issue of *Law and Contemporary Problems* 61.4 (Autumn 1998): 1–298.

Crossen, Cynthia. "Use of Death Penalty Over Decades Points to Conflicted Public." *Wall Street Journal* 7 May 2007, Eastern ed.: B1+.

Cutler, Christopher Q. "Death Resurrected: The Reimplementation of the Federal Death Penalty." *Seattle University Law Review* 23 (Spring 2000): 1189–230.

Dambrun, Michaël. "Understanding the Relationship between Racial Prejudice and Support for the Death Penalty: The Racist Punitive Bias Hypothesis." *Social Justice Research* 20.2 (2007): 228–49.

Davis, David Brion. "The Movement to Abolish Capital Punishment in America, 1787–1861." *The American Historical Review* 63.1 (Oct. 1957): 23–46.

Deets, Lee Emerson. "Changes in Capital Punishment Policy Since 1939." *Journal of Criminal Law and Criminology (1931–1951)* 38.6 (1948): 584–94.

Denno, Deborah W. "The Lethal Injection Quandary: How Medicine Has Dismantled the Death Penalty." *Fordham Law Review* 76.1 (2007): 49–128. Available at SSRN: http://ssrn.com/abstract=983732.

Ewer, Phyllis A. "Eighth Amendment: The Death Penalty." *The Journal of Criminal Law and Criminology* 71.4 (Winter 1980): 538–46.

Farley, Maggie. "U.N. Adopts Death Penalty Moratorium." *Los Angeles Times* 19 Dec. 2007, home ed.: A.11+.

Fife, James. "Mental Capacity, Minority, and Mental Age in Capital Sentencing: A Unified Theory of Culpability." *Hamline Law Review* 28.2 (2005): 239–75.

Fisher, Patrick, and Travis Pratt. "Political Culture and the Death Penalty." *Criminal Justice Policy Review* 17 (2006): 48–60.

Frosch, Dan. "Executions in U.S. Decline to 13-Year Low, Study Finds." *New York Times* 19 Dec. 2007, late ed. (East Coast): A.20.

Garland, David. "The Peculiar Forms of American Capital Punishment." *Social Research* 74.2 (2007): 435–64.

Garrett, Brandon L. "Judging Innocence." *Columbia Law Review* 108.1 (Jan. 2008): 55–142.

Gibeaut, John. "Tinkering with Lethal Injection." *ABA Journal* 94.1 (Jan. 2008): 18–19.

Glaberson, William. "U.S. Said to Seek Execution for 6 in Sept. 11 Case." (Cover Story). *New York Times* 11 Feb. 2008, late ed.: A1+.

Green, William McAllen. "An Ancient Debate on Capital Punishment." *The Classical Journal* 24.4 (Jan. 1929): 267–75.

Gross, Samuel R., Kristen Jacoby, and Daniel J. Matheson. "Exonerations in the United States, 1989 through 2003." *The Journal of Criminal Law & Criminology* 95.2 (Winter 2005): 523–60.

Gurwitz, Jonathan. "Cross Country: Texas and the Death Penalty." *Wall Street Journal* 19 Jan. 2008, Eastern edition: A.12+.

Heath, Mark J. "Revisiting Physician Involvement in Capital Punishment: Medical and Non-medical Aspects of Lethal Injection." Letter. *Mayo Clinic Proceedings* 83.1 (2008): 115–18.

Hime, Adam. "Life or Death Mistakes: Cultural Stereotyping, Capital Punishment, and Regional Race-Based Trends in Exoneration and Wrongful Execution." *University of Detroit Mercy Law Review* 82.2 (Winter 2005): 181–218.

Hood, Roger. "Capital Punishment: A Global Perspective." *Punishment & Society* 3.3 (2001): 331–54.

Jacobs, David, and Stephanie L. Kent. "The Determinants of Executions Since 1951: How Politics, Protests, Public Opinion, and Social Divisions Shape Capital Punishment." *Social Problems* 54.3 (Aug. 2007): 297–318.

Johnson, Elmer H. "Selective Factors in Capital Punishment." *Social Forces* 36.2 (Dec. 1957): 165–69.

Koratsky, Kim. "Throw Them Back, Kill Them When They're Bigger." *Federal Lawyer* 55.1 (2008): 5.

LaChance, Daniel. "Last Words, Last Meals, and Last Stands: Agency and Individuality in the Modern Execution Process." *Law & Social Inquiry* 32.3 (2007): 701–24.

Lanier, William L. "Physician Involvement in Capital Punishment: Simplifying a Complex Calculus." *Mayo Clinic Proceedings* 82.9 (Sept. 2007): 1043–46.

Lewis, Neil A. "Death Sentences Decline, and Experts Offer Reasons." *New York Times* 15 Dec. 2006, late ed. (East Coast): A.28+.

Liebman, James S. "Comment: The New Death Penalty Debate: What's DNA Got to Do with It?" *Columbia Human Rights Law Review* 33 (Spring 2002): 527–54.

Lillquist, Erik. "Absolute Certainty and the Death Penalty." *American Criminal Law Review* 42.1 (Winter 2005): 45–91.

Liptak, Adam. "At 60% of Total, Texas is Bucking Execution Trend." *New York Times* 26 Dec. 2007, late ed. (East Coast): A.1+.

———. "States Hesitate to Lead Change on Executions." (Cover Story). *New York Times* 3 Jan. 2008, late ed. (East Coast): A1+.

Lithwick, Dahlia. "The Dying Death Penalty." *The Washington Post* 11 Feb. 2007, final ed.: B.2.

"A Long Time Coming." Editorial. *New York Times* 15 Dec. 2007, late ed. (East Coast): A.22.

Mannheimer, Michael J. "When the Federal Death Penalty is 'Cruel and Unusual.'" *University of Cincinnati Law Review* 74 (2006): 819+.

McAdams, John C. "Racial Disparity and the Death Penalty." *Law and Contemporary Problems* 61.4 (Autumn 1998): 153–70.

McGraw, Dan. "When is Forgiveness Unforgivable?" *U.S. News & World Report* 124.5 (9 Feb. 1998): 7.

Medwed, Daniel S. "Looking Forward: Wrongful Convictions and Systemic Reform." *American Criminal Law Review* 42.4 (Fall 2005): 1117–21.

Norrander, Barbara. "The Multi-Layered Impact of Public Opinion on Capital Punishment Implementation in the American States." *Political Research Quarterly* 53.4 (Dec. 2000): 771–93.

Otto, Charles W., Brandon K. Applegate, and Robin King Davis. "Improving Comprehension of Capital Sentencing Instructions." *Crime & Delinquency* 53.3 (July 2007): 502–17.

Peffley, Mark, and Jon Hurwitz. "Persuasion and Resistance: Race and the Death Penalty in America." *American Journal of Political Science* 51.4 (Oct. 2007): 996–1012.

Possley, Maurice, and Steve Mills. "Clemency for All; Ryan Commutes 164 Death Sentences to Life in Prison without Parole." *Chicago Tribune* 12 Jan 2003, Chicagoland final ed.: 1+. See also: "Excerpts from Ryan Speech at DePaul." *Chicago Tribune* 12 Jan 2003, Chicagoland final ed.: 16+.

Radelet, Michael L., and Hugo Adam Bedau. "The Execution of the Innocent." *Law and Contemporary Problems* 61.4 (Autumn 1998): 105–24. Available at: http://www.law.duke.edu/journals/61LCPRadelet.

Radelet, Michael L., and Marian J. Borg. "The Changing Nature of Death Penalty Debates." *Annual Review of Sociology* 26 (Aug 2000): 43–61.

Rankin, Joseph H. "Changing Attitudes toward Capital Punishment," *Social Forces* 58.1 (Sept. 1979): 194–211.

Rapaport, Elizabeth. "The Death Penalty and Gender Discrimination." *Law and Society Review* 25.2 (1991): 367–83.

"Reasonable Doubts: The Growing Movement against the Death Penalty." *American Prospect* 15.7 (July 2004): A1–A23.

"Revenge Begins to Seem Less Sweet." *Economist* 384.8544 (1 Sept. 2007): 20–22.

Robbers, Monica. "Tough-Mindedness and Fair Play: Personality Traits as Predictors of Attitudes toward the Death Penalty—An Exploratory Gendered Study." *Punishment & Society* 8.2 (April 2006): 203–22.

Roberts, W. J. "The Abolition of Capital Punishment." *International Journal of Ethics* 15.3 (April 1905): 263–86.

Rosen, Richard A. "Innocence and Death." *North Carolina Law Review* 82 (Dec. 2003): 61–113.

Sarat, Austin. "Innocence, Error, and the 'New Abolitionism': A Commentary." *Criminology & Public Policy* 4.1 (Feb. 2005): 45–54.

———. "Recapturing the Spirit of *Furman*: The American Bar Association and the New Abolitionist Politics." *Law and Contemporary Problems* 61.4 (Autumn 1998): 5–28.

Savitz, Leonard D. "A Study in Capital Punishment." *The Journal of Criminal Law, Criminology, and Police Science* 49.4 (Nov. 1958): 338–41.

Scheck, Barry. "Barry Scheck Lectures on Wrongful Convictions." *Drake Law Review* 54 (Spring 2006): 597–620.

———. "Innocence, Race, and the Death Penalty." *Howard Law Journal* 50 (Winter 2007): 445+.

Schuessler, Karl F. "The Deterrent Influence of the Death Penalty." *Annals of the American Academy of Political and Social Science* 284 (Nov. 1952): 54–62.

Sellin, Thorsten, and James C. Charlesworth, eds. *Murder and the Penalty of Death.* Spec. issue of *Annals of the American Academy of Political and Social Science* 284 (Nov. 1952): 1–238.

Sullivan, Thomas P. "Efforts to Improve the Illinois Capital Punishment System: Worth the Cost?" *University of Richmond Law Review* 41 (May 2007): 935+.

Thornburgh, Nathan. "Lethal Objection." *Time* 167.10 (6 March 2006): 50–51.

Unnever, James D., and Francis T. Cullen. "Reassessing the Racial Divide in Support for Capital Punishment: The Continuing Significance of Race." *Journal of Research in Crime & Delinquency* 44.1 (Feb. 2007): 124–58.

"USA: Breaking a Lethal Habit: A Look Back at the Death Penalty in 2007." 21 Dec. 2007. Amnesty International USA. Available at: http://www.amnestyusa.org/document.php?lang=e&id=ENGAMR511972007.

Van Dellen, Richard G. "Ethics of Capital Punishment." Letter. *Mayo Clinic Proceedings* 83.1 (2008): 118–19.

Van den Haag, Ernest. "On Deterrence and the Death Penalty." *The Journal of Criminal Law, Criminology, and Police Science* 60.2 (June 1969): 141–47.

———. "The Ultimate Punishment: A Defense." *Harvard Law Review* 99.7 (May 1986): 1662–69.

Von Drehle, David. "Death Penalty Walking." *Time* 171.2 (14 Jan. 2008): 38–41.

Vidmar, Neil, and Phoebe Ellsworth. "Public Opinion and the Death Penalty." *Stanford Law Review* 26.6 (June 1974): 1245–70.

Warden, Rob. "Illinois Death Penalty Reform: How It Happened, What It Promises." *Journal of Criminal Law & Criminology* 95.2 (Winter 2005): 381–426.

Weisberg, Robert. "The Death Penalty Meets Social Science: Deterrence and Jury Behavior Under New Scrutiny." *Annual Review of Law and Social Science* 1.1 (Dec. 2005): 151–70.

Williams, Marian R., Stephen Demuth, and Jefferson E. Holcomb. "Understanding the Influence of Victim Gender in Death Penalty Cases: The Importance of Victim Race, Sex-Related Victimization, and Jury Decision Making." *Criminology* 45.4 (Nov. 2007): 865–91.

Wood, Arthur Lewis. "Alternatives to the Death Penalty." *Annals of the American Academy of Political and Social Science* 284 (Nov. 1952): 63–72.

Wright, R. George. "The Death Penalty and the Way We Think Now." *Loyola of Los Angeles Law Review* 33 (Jan. 2000): 533–85. Available at: http://llr.lls.edu/volumes/v33-issue2/wright.pdf.

Young, Bethany, Marcus T. Boccaccini, Mary Alice Conroy, and Kristy Lawson. "Four Practical and Conceptual Assessment Issues that Evaluators Should Address in Capital Case Mental Retardation Evaluations." *Professional Psychology: Research and Practice* 38.2 (Apr 2007): 169–78.

Books

Library of Congress Subject Headings: *capital punishment, death row, discrimination in capital punishment, executions and executioners, guillotine, hanging, judicial error,* and *stoning.*

Acker, James R., Robert M. Bohm, and Charles S. Lanier, eds. *America's Experiment with Capital Punishment: Reflections on the Past, Present, and Future of the Ultimate Penal Sanction.* 2nd ed. Durham, N.C.: Carolina Academic Press, 2003. LC: HV8699 .U5 A746 2003.

Baldus, David C., George Woodworth, and Charles A. Pulaski, Jr. *Equal Justice and the Death Penalty: A Legal and Empirical Analysis* [The Baldus Study]. Boston: Northeastern University Press, 1990. [Found that after taking account of thirty-nine nonracial variables, the odds of a death sentence for those accused of killing whites were 4.3 times higher than the odds of a death sentence for those charged with killing blacks.] LC: KFG565.C2 B35 1990.

Banner, Stuart. *The Death Penalty: An American History.* Cambridge, Mass.: Harvard Univ. Press, 2002. LC: HV8699 .U5 B367 2002.

Bedau, Hugo Adam. *Death Is Different: Studies in the Morality, Law, and Politics of Capital Punishment.* Boston, Mass.: Northeastern University Press, 1987. LC: HV8699 .U5 B39 1987.

Black, Charles Lund. *Capital Punishment: The Inevitability of Caprice and Mistake.* New York: Norton, 1981. LC: HV8698 .B47 1981.

Brandon, Craig. *Electric Chair: An Unnatural American History.* Jefferson, N.C.: McFarland & Co., 1999. LC: HV8699 .U5 B69 1999.

Connors, Edward, Thomas Lundregan, Neal Miller, and Tom McEwen. *Convicted by Juries, Exonerated by Science: Case Studies in the Use of DNA Evidence to Establish Innocence After Trial.* Washington, D.C.: U.S. Dept. of Justice, National Institute of Justice, 1996. Available at: http://purl.access.gpo.gov/GPO/LPS53435. SuDoc: J 28.24/3:C 76/2.

Edelman, Bryan C. *Racial Prejudice, Juror Empathy, and Sentencing in Death Penalty Cases.* New York: LFB Scholarly Pub., 2006. LC: KF9685 .E33 2006.

Federal Death Penalty Cases: Recommendations Concerning the Cost and Quality of Defense Representation. Washington, D.C: Administrative Office of the U.S. Courts, Defender Services Division, 1998. Available at: http://purl.access.gpo.gov/GPO/LPS2760.

Federal Death Penalty System: Supplementary Data, Analysis and Revised Protocols for Capital Case Review. June 6, 2001. Available at: http://www.usdoj.gov/dag/pubdoc/deathpenaltystudy.htm. SuDoc: JU 10.2:199023301.

Friedman, Lauri S., ed. *The Death Penalty.* Farmington Hills, Mich.: Greenhaven Press, 2006. LC: HV8699 .U5 D35 2006.

Garvey, Stephen P., ed. *Beyond Repair? America's Death Penalty.* Durham, N.C.: London: Duke University Press, 2003. LC: KF9227 .C2 B485 2003.

Gillespie, L. Kay. *Dancehall Ladies: Executed Women of the 20th Century.* Rev. ed. Lanham, Md.: University Press of America, 2000. LC: HV9468 .G53 2000.

Gray, Mike. *The Death Game: Capital Punishment and the Luck of the Draw.* Monroe, Me.: Common Courage Press, 2003. LC: HV8699 .U5 G728 2003.

Hood, Roger G. *The Death Penalty: A Worldwide Perspective.* 3rd ed. New York: Oxford University Press, 2002. LC: HV8694 .H657 2002.

Kaminer, Wendy. *It's All the Rage: Crime and Culture.* Reading, Mass.: Addison-Wesley, 1995. LC: HV6789 .K36 1995.

Liebman, James S., Jeffrey Fagan, and Valerie West. *A Broken System: Error Rates in Capital Cases, 1973–1995* (2002). The Justice Project. Available at: http://www2.1aw.columbia.edu/instructionalservices/liebman/.

Lifton, Robert Jay, and Greg Mitchell. *Who Owns Death? Capital Punishment, the American Conscience, and the End of Executions.* New York: Morrow, 2000. LC: HV8699 .U5 L54 2000.

Lynch, Mona. "The Disposal of Inmate #85721: Notes on a Routine Execution." *Studies in Law, Politics, and Society.* Ed. Austin Sarat and Patricia Ewick. Vol. 20. Stamford, Conn.: JAI Press, 2000. 3–34. LC: K27.S6 R47.

Masur, Louis P. *Rites of Execution: Capital Punishment and the Transformation of American Culture, 1776–1865.* New York: Oxford University Press, 1989. LC: HV8699.U5 M36 1989.

Melusky, Joseph A., and Keith A. Pesto. *Cruel and Unusual Punishment: Rights and Liberties under the Law.* Santa Barbara, Calif.: ABC-CLIO, Inc., 2003. LC: KF9227 .C2 M42 2003.

Ogletree, Charles J., Jr., and Austin Sarat, eds. *From Lynch Mobs to the Killing State: Race and the Death Penalty in America.* New York: New York University, 2006. LC: KF9227. C2 F76 2006.

O'Shea, Kathleen A. *Women and the Death Penalty in the United States, 1900–1998.* Westport, Conn.: Praeger, 1999. LC: HV9466 .O74 1999.

Palmer, Louis J., Jr. *The Death Penalty: An American Citizen's Guide to Understanding Federal and State Laws.* Jefferson, N.C.: McFarland, 1998. LC: KF9725 .P35 1998.

Prejean, Helen. *Dead Man Walking: An Eyewitness Account of the Death Penalty in the United States.* New York: Vintage Books, 1994. LC: HV8699 .U5 P74 1994.

Radelet, Michael L., Hugo Adam Bedau, and Constance E. Putnam. *In Spite of Innocence: Erroneous Convictions in Capital Cases.* Boston: Northeastern University Press, 1992. LC: KF9756 .R33 1992.

Sarat, Austin, ed. *The Killing State: Capital Punishment in Law, Politics, and Culture.* New York: Oxford University Press, 2001. LC: KF9227 .C2 K56 2001.

———. *Mercy on Trial: What It Means to Stop an Execution.* Princeton, N.J.: Princeton University Press, 2005. LC: KFI1785 .S27 2005.

———. *When the State Kills: Capital Punishment and the American Condition.* Princeton, N.J.: Princeton University Press, 2001. LC: HV8699 .U5 S27 2001.

Schabas, William. *The Abolition of the Death Penalty in International Law.* Cambridge: Cambridge University Press, 2002. LC: K5104 .S33 2002.

Sharp, Susan F. *Hidden Victims: The Effects of the Death Penalty on Families of the Accused.* New Brunswick, N.J.: Rutgers University Press, 2005. LC: HV8699 .U5 S45 2005.

Simon, Rita James, and Dagny A. Blaskovich. *A Comparative Analysis of Capital Punishment: Statutes, Policies, Frequencies, and Public Attitudes the World Over.* Lanham, Md.: Lexington Books, 2002. LC: HV8694 .S55 2002.

Stack, Richard A. *Dead Wrong: Violence, Vengeance, and the Victims of Capital Punishment.* Westport, Conn.: Praeger, 2006. LC: HV8699.U5 S48 2006.

Streib, Victor L. *Death Penalty in a Nutshell.* Nutshell Series. St. Paul, Minn.: Thomson/West, 2003. LC: KF9227.C2 S77 2003.

United States Congress. House Committee on the Judiciary. *Racial Justice Act: Report Together with Dissenting Views* (to accompany H.R. 4017) (including cost estimate of the Congressional Budget Office). Washington, D.C.: U.S. G.P.O., 1994. SuDoc: Y 1.1/8: 103–458.

United States Congress. House Committee on the Judiciary. Subcommittee on Civil and Constitutional Rights. *Innocence and the Death Penalty: Assessing the Danger of Mistaken Executions: Staff Report.* 103d Congress, 2d session. Committee print. 1994. SuDoc: Y 4. J 89/1:IN 6.

United States Congress. Senate Committee on the Judiciary. *An Examination of the Death Penalty in the United States: hearing before the Subcommittee on the Constitution, Civil Rights, and Property Rights of the Committee on the Judiciary, United States Senate, One Hundred Ninth Congress, second session, February 1, 2006.* Washington, D.C.: U.S. G.P.O., 2006. SuDoc: Y 4.J 89/2:S.HRG.109–540. Available at: http://judiciary.senate.gov/hearing .cfm?id=1745.

United States Congress. Senate Committee on the Judiciary. *Protecting the Innocent: Proposals to Reform the Death Penalty: Hearing before the Committee on the Judiciary, United States Senate, One Hundred Seventh Congress, second session, June 18, 2002.* SuDoc: Y 4.J 89/2: S.HRG.107–917.

United States Congress. Senate Committee on the Judiciary. *Reducing the Risk of Executing the Innocent: The Report of the Illinois Governor's Commission on Capital Punishment: hearing before the Subcommittee on the Constitution of the Committee on the Judiciary, United States Senate, One Hundred Seventh Congress, second session, June 12, 2002.* Available at: http://judiciary.senate.gov/hearing.cfm?id=256. SuDoc: Y 4.J 89/2:S.HRG.107–907.

Vila, Bryan, and Cynthia Morris, eds. *Capital Punishment in the United States: A Documentary History.* Westport, Conn.: Greenwood Press, 1997. LC: HV8699 .U5 C3 1997.

Westervelt, Saundra D., and John A. Humphrey, eds. *Wrongly Convicted: Perspectives on Failed Justice.* New Brunswick, N.J.: Rutgers University Press, 2001. LC: KF220 .W76 2001.

Zimring, Franklin E. *The Contradictions of American Capital Punishment.* Studies in Crime and Public Policy. Oxford: Oxford University Press, 2003. LC: HV8699 .U5 Z563 2003.

Zimring, Franklin E., and Gordon Hawkins. *Capital Punishment and the American Agenda.* New York: Cambridge University Press, 1986. LC: HV8699 .U5 Z56 1986.

Databases

CQ Researcher. CQ Press. Fee-based database of reports on current issues with overview, background, current situation, outlook, chronology, pro/con, and bibliography. Available at: http://library.cqpress.com/cqresearcher/.

Gale Virtual Reference Library. Thomson Gale. Fee-based database of encyclopedias providing electronic access to *American Law Yearbook, Encyclopedia of the American Constitution, Encyclopedia of Crime and Justice, Gale Encyclopedia of Everyday Law, National Survey of State Laws,* and *West's Encyclopedia of American Law.* Available at: http://www .gale.com/gvrl/.

National Criminal Justice Reference Service. Free database containing abstracts and full-text documents published by the National Institute of Justice, the Office of Juvenile Justice and Delinquency Prevention, the Office for Victims of Crime, the Bureau of Justice

Statistics, and the Bureau of Justice Assistance. Available at: http://www.ncjrs.gov/App/search/AdvancedSearch.aspx.

Opposing Viewpoints Resource Center. Thomson Gale. Fee-based virtual library of full-text publications categorized by the nature of their material: viewpoints (essays), reference, statistics, magazines and newspapers, images, primary documents, and Web sites. Available at: http://www.gale.com/OpposingViewpoints/.

Oxford Reference Online. Oxford University Press. Fee-based database of encyclopedias providing electronic access to *The Oxford Companion to American Law, The Oxford Companion to the Supreme Court of the United States*, and *The Oxford Guide to United States Supreme Court Decisions.* Available at: http://www.oxfordreference.com/.

Web Sites

American Civil Liberties Union. "Death Penalty." Available at: http://www.aclu.org/capital/index.html.

Amnesty International USA. "Death Penalty." Available at: http://www.amnestyusa.org/abolish/index.do.

California Department of Corrections and Rehabilitation. "Capital Punishment." Available at: http://www.cdcr.ca.gov/Reports_Research/capital.html.

Cornell Law School. "Cornell Death Penalty Project." Available at: http://library.lawschool.cornell.edu/death/links.html

Cornell Law School. Legal Information Institute. "Death Penalty." Available at: http://www.law.cornell.edu/wex/index.php/Death_penalty.

Death Penalty Information Center. Available at: http://www.deathpenaltyinfo.org/.

Death Penalty Information Center. "State by State Information." Available at: http://www.deathpenaltyinfo.org/state/.

MegaLaw.com, LLC. "Death Penalty/Capital Punishment Law." Available at: http://www.megalaw.com/top/deathpenalty.php.

National Criminal Justice Reference Service. "Capital Punishment." Available at: http://www.ncjrs.gov/App/Topics/Topic.aspx?topicid=2.

U.S. Department of State. "Capital Punishment." Available at: http://usinfo.state.gov/dhr/human_rights/capital_punishment.html.

Juveniles & the Death Penalty

Aryanpur, Arianne. "The Nation: U.S. Is Urged to Quit Executing Youth Offenders; Crime: In Plea, Amnesty International Says the Nation Is One of Few Left to Allow Such Action." *Los Angeles Times* 26 Sept. 2002, home ed.: A.21.

Bazan, Elizabeth B. "Death Penalty for Juveniles." *CRS Review* 9:8 (Sept. 1988): 8–9. SuDoc: LC 14.19:9.

———. "Youth, Mental Retardation, and the Death Penalty." *CRS Review* 10:8 (Sept. 1989): 17–19. SuDoc LC 14.19:10.

Butler, Brooke. "The Role of Death Qualification in Capital Trials Involving Juvenile Defendants." *Journal of Applied Social Psychology* 37.3 (March 2007): 549–60.

"Children and the Death Penalty: Executions Worldwide Since 1990." Amnesty International, September 25, 2002. Available at: http://web.amnesty.org/library/Index/engACT5000720 02?OpenDocument&of=THEMES/DEATH+PENALTY.

Cothern, Lynn. "Juveniles and the Death Penalty." Coordinating Council on Juvenile Justice and Delinquency Prevention. 2000. Available at: http://www.ncjrs.gov/html/ojjdp/coord council/index.html.

Fagan, Jeffrey, and Valerie West. "The Decline of the Juvenile Death Penalty: Scientific Evidence of Evolving Norms." *Journal of Criminal Law & Criminology* 95.2 (2005): 427–97.

Hale, Robert L. *A Review of Juvenile Executions in America.* Lewiston, N.Y.: The Edwin Mellen Press, 1997. LC: HV8699 .U5 H36 1997.

Hansen, Brian. "Kids in Prison." *CQ Researcher Online* 11.16 (27 April 2001): 345–74.

Jost, Kenneth. "Rethinking the Death Penalty." *CQ Researcher Online* 11.40 (16 Nov. 2001): 945–68.

Morreale, Madlyn C., and Abigail English. "Abolishing the Death Penalty for Juvenile Offenders: A Background Paper." *Journal of Adolescent Health* 35.4 (Oct. 2004): 335–39.

Myers, Wayne. "'*Roper v. Simmons*': The Collision of National Consensus and Proportionality Review." *The Journal of Criminal Law & Criminology* 96.3 (Spring 2006): 947–94.

Park, Jennifer. "*Yarborough v. Alvarado*: At the Crossroads of the 'Unreasonable Application' Provision of the Antiterrorism and Effective Death Penalty Act of 1996 and the Consideration of Juvenile Status in Custodial Determinations." *The Journal of Criminal Law & Criminology* 95.3 (2005): 871–904.

Penn, Everette B., Helen Taylor Greene, and Shaun L. Gabbidon, eds. *Race and Juvenile Justice.* Durham, N.C.: Carolina Academic Press, 2006. LC: HV9104 .R23 2006.

Roper v. Simmons, 543 U.S. 551 (2005). Held that the Eighth and Fourteenth Amendments forbid the execution of offenders who were under the age of eighteen when their crimes were committed. Available at: http://www.law.cornell.edu/supct/html/03–633.ZS.html.

Schiraldi, Vincent. "Commentary: Abolish the Death Penalty for Youths." Editorial. *Los Angeles Times* 16 Sept. 2002, home ed.: B.11.

Sharp, Susan F., Meghan K. McGhee, Trina L. Hope, and Randall Coyne. "Predictors of Support of Legislation Banning Juvenile Executions in Oklahoma: An Examination by Race and Sex." *Justice Quarterly* 24.1 (March 2007): 133–55.

Streib, Victor L. "Adolescence, Mental Retardation, and the Death Penalty: The Siren Call of *Atkins v. Virginia*." *New Mexico Law Review* 33.2 (2003): 183–206.

———. "Prosecutorial Discretion in Juvenile Homicide Cases." *Penn State Law Review* 109.4 (2005): 1071–86.

———. "Standing between the Child and the Executioner: The Special Role of Defense Counsel in Juvenile Death Penalty Cases." *American Journal of Criminal Law* 31.1 (2003): 67–115.

Vogel, Brenda L., and Ronald E. Vogel. "The Age of Death: Appraising Public Opinion of Juvenile Capital Punishment." *Journal of Criminal Justice* 31.2 (2003): 169–83.

Pro and Con

Babcock, Sandra. "The Global Debate on the Death Penalty." *Human Rights: Journal of the Section of Individual Rights & Responsibilities* 34.2 (2007): 1–5.

Bedau, Hugo Adam, ed. *The Death Penalty in America: Current Controversies*. New York: Oxford University Press, 1997. LC: HV8699 .U5 D37 1997.

Bedau, Hugo Adam, and Paul G. Cassell, eds. *Debating the Death Penalty: Should America Have Capital Punishment? The Experts on Both Sides Make Their Best Case*. New York: Oxford University Press, 2004. LC: HV8699 .U5 D635 2004.

Cohen, Andrew I., and Christopher Heath Wellman, eds. *Contemporary Debates in Applied Ethics*. Malden, Mass.: Blackwell Pub., 2005. LC: BJ1031 .C597 2005.

The Constitution Project: Death Penalty Initiative. Available at: http://www.constitutionpro ject.org/deathpenalty/index.cfm?categoryId=2

Cooper, Mary H. "Death Penalty Update." *CQ Researcher Online* 9.1 (8 Jan. 1999): 1–24.

"Debating the Impact of the Death Penalty." *Chronicle of Higher Education* 54.16 (14 Dec. 2007): B4.

Foley, Michael A. *Arbitrary and Capricious: The Supreme Court, the Constitution, and the Death Penalty*. Westport, Conn.: Praeger, 2003. LC: KF9227 .C2 F65 2003.

Greenblatt, Alan. "The Capital Punishment Crossroads." (Cover Story). *CQ Weekly* 65.8 (2007): 530–39.

Haines, Herbert H. *Against Capital Punishment: The Anti-Death Penalty Movement in America, 1972–1994*. New York: Oxford University Press, 1999. LC: HV8699.U5.

Hanks, Gardner C. *Against the Death Penalty: Christian and Secular Arguments Against Capital Punishment*. Scottdale, Pa.: Herald Press, 1997. NetLibrary: http://www.netlibrary. com/. LC: HV8694 .H25 1997.

Henningfeld, Diane Andrews, ed. *The Death Penalty: Opposing Viewpoints*. Farmington Hills, Mich.: Greenhaven Press, 2006. LC: HV8694 .D3814 2006.

Jost, Kenneth. "Death Penalty Controversies." *CQ Researcher Online* 15.13 (23 Sept. 2005): 785–808.

Jost, Kenneth. "Sentencing Debates." *CQ Researcher Online* 14.39 (5 Nov. 2004): 925–48.

Kaufman-Osborn, Timothy V. "A Critique of Contemporary Death Penalty Abolitionism." *Punishment & Society* 8.3 (2006): 365–83.

King, Rachel. *Don't Kill in Our Names: Families of Murder Victims Speak Out Against the Death Penalty*. New Brunswick, N.J.: Rutgers University Press, 2003. LC: HV8698 .K556 2003.

Liebman, James S., Jeffrey Fagan, and Valerie West. *A Broken System: Error Rates in Capital Cases, 1973–1995*. 2002. The Justice Project, Columbia University. Available at: http:// www2.1aw.columbia.edu/instructionalservices/liebman/.

Mackey, Philip English, ed. *Voices Against Death: American Opposition to Capital Punishment, 1787–1975*. New York: B. Franklin, 1976. LC: HV8699 .U5 V64.

Masci, David. "An Impassioned Debate: An Overview of the Death Penalty in America." 19 Dec. 2007. Pew Forum on Religion & Public Life. Available at: http://pewforum.org/ docs/?DocID=270.

Martinez , J. Michael, William D. Richardson, and D. Brandon Hornsby, eds. *The Leviathan's Choice: Capital Punishment in the Twenty-first Century*. Lanham, Md.: Rowman & Littlefield, 2002. LC: HV8694 .L475 2002.

Mello, Michael. *Against the Death Penalty: The Relentless Dissents of Justices Brennan and Marshall*. Boston: Northeastern University Press, 1996. LC: KF9227 .C2 M38 1996.

———. *Dead Wrong: A Death Row Lawyer Speaks Out Against Capital Punishment*. Madison: University of Wisconsin Press, 1997. LC: KF9227 .C2 M383 1997.

National Coalition to Abolish the Death Penalty. Available at: http://www.ncadp.org/.

Pojman, Louis P., and Jeffrey Reiman. *The Death Penalty: For and Against*. Lanham, Md.: Rowman and Littlefield, 1998. NetLibrary: http://www.netlibrary.com/.

Pro-Death Penalty.com. Available at: http://www.prodeathpenalty.com/.

Simon, Rita James, and Dagny A. Blaskovich. *A Comparative Analysis of Capital Punishment: Statutes, Policies, Frequencies, and Public Attitudes the World Over*. Lanham, Md.: Lexington Books, 2002. LC: HV8694 .S55 2002.

Van Koppen, Peter J., Dick J. Hessing, and Christianne J. de Poot. "Public Reasons for Abolition and Retention of the Death Penalty." *International Criminal Justice Review* 12 (2002): 77–92.

Worsnop, Richard L. "Death Penalty Debate." *CQ Researcher Online* 5.9 (10 March 1995): 193–216.

California—Law

California Constitution, Article 1: Declaration of Rights. §§ 17, 24, 27 [prohibiting cruel or unusual punishments]. Available at: http://www.leginfo.ca.gov/.const/.article_1.

California Penal Code. *Death penalty: Pen C §§ 190 et seq. Death penalty appeals: Pen C §§ 190.6 et seq. Enhancement of punishment for sex offenses: Pen C §§ 289.5, 1170.1. Prohibition of cruel and unusual punishments: Pen C § 673. Pronouncement of judgment imposing death penalty: Pen C § 1193. Mistreatment of prisoners: Pen C §§ 2650 et seq. Execution of prisoner: Pen C § 3600 et seq.* Available at: http://www.leginfo.ca.gov/cgi-bin/calawquery?codesection=pen&codebody=&hits=20.

Witkin, B. E., and Norman L. Epstein. *California Criminal Law*. 2nd ed. San Francisco, CA: Bancroft-Whitney Co., 1988–to date. *Constitutional and Statutory Restriction: Cruel and unusual punishment: §§ 1329–1344. Death Penalty: §§ 1345–1381.* LC: KFC1100 .W5.

California—General

Alarcon, Arthur L. "Remedies for California's Death Row Deadlock." *Southern California Law Review* 80 (May 2007): 697+.

Bailey, Eric. "Legal Experts Agree Death Penalty Needs Reforms but Disagree on How." *Los Angeles Times* 11 Jan. 2008, home ed.: B.4.

California Department of Corrections. "Capital Punishment." Available at: http://www.cdc.state.ca.us/ReportsResearch/capital.html.

California Department of Corrections and Rehabilitation. "History of Capital Punishment in California." Available at: http://www.cdcr.ca.gov/Reports_Research/capital.html.

"Capital Punishment." *National Survey of State Laws*. Ed. Richard Leiter. 5th ed. Detroit: Gale, 2005. 75–104. *Gale Virtual Reference Library*. LC: KF386 .N38 2005.

Carter, Robert M., and A. Lamont Smith. "The Death Penalty in California: A Statistical and Composite Portrait." *Crime & Delinquency* 15.1 (Jan. 1969): 62–76.

Culver, John H. "Capital Punishment Politics and Policies in the States, 1977–1997." *Crime, Law and Social Change* 32.4 (1999): 287–300.

"The Death Penalty: After Tookie." *The Economist* 377 (17 Dec. 2005): 12–13.

Emmert, Craig F., and Carol Ann Traut. "The California Supreme Court and the Death Penalty." *American Politics Research* 22.1 (Jan. 1994): 41–61.

George, Ronald M. "Reform Death Penalty Appeals; Allowing State Appellate Courts to Review Cases Would Help Ease a Huge Backlog." Editorial. *Los Angeles Times* 7 Jan. 2008, home ed.: A.15.

Hamm, Theodore. *Rebel and a Cause: Caryl Chessman and the Politics of the Death Penalty in Postwar California, 1948–1974*. Berkeley: University of California Press, 2001. LC: HV8699. U5 H363 2001.

Kreitzberg, Ellen. "The Death Penalty: A Review of Special Circumstances in California Death Penalty Cases: Updated Report Jan 7, 2008." California Commission on the Fair Administration of Justice. Available at: http://www.ccfaj.org/documents/reports/dp/expert/Kreitzberg.pdf.

Lee, Catherine. "Hispanics and the Death Penalty: Discriminatory Charging Practices in San Joaquin County, California." *Journal of Criminal Justice* 35.1 (2007): 17–27.

Marcus, Michael H., and David S. Weissbrodt. "The Death Penalty Cases." *California Law Review* 56.5 (Oct. 1968): 1268–490.

Nice, David C. "The States and the Death Penalty." *Western Political Quarterly* 45.4 (Dec. 1992): 1037–48.

Steinhauer, Jennifer. "California Addresses Death Penalty Concerns." *New York Times* 16 May 2007, late ed. (East Coast): A.15+.

Stolz, Preble. *Judging Judges: The Investigation of Rose Bird and the California Supreme Court*. New York: Free Press, 1981.

"Too Harsh: California Can Sentence Criminals Under 18 to Life Without Parole. It's Cruel and Unusual Punishment." Editorial. *Los Angeles Times* 16 Jan. 2008, home ed.: A.20.

Traut, Carol Ann, and Craig F. Emmert. "Expanding the Integrated Model of Judicial Decision Making: The California Justices and Capital Punishment." *Journal of Politics* 60.4 (Nov. 1998): 1166–80.

Uelmen, Gerald F. *California Death Penalty Laws and the California Supreme Court: A Ten Year Perspective*. Sacramento: California Legislature Senate Committee on Judiciary, 1986. LC: KFC1108. C2.

Weinstein, Henry. "Death Penalty Survey Spurned; Many California D.A.s Refuse to Explain Their Decision-Making on Seeking Executions." *Los Angeles Times* 20 Feb. 2008, home ed.: B1+.

Weinstein, Henry. "High Court Takes Up Lethal Injection; States Have Kept the Execution Process Shrouded in Secrecy." *Los Angeles Times* 7 Jan. 2008, home ed.: A.1+.

Weiss, Robert, Richard Berk, Wenzhi Li, and Margaret Farrell-Ross. "Death Penalty Charging in Los Angeles County: An Illustrative Data Analysis Using Skeptical Priors." *Sociological Methods & Research* 28.1 (1999): 91–115.

White, Welsh S. "Patterns in Capital Punishment." Rev. of *Capital Punishment and the American Agenda*, by Franklin E. Zimring and Gordon Hawkins. *California Law Review* 75.6 (1987): 2165–85.

U.S. Law

U.S. Code Title 18: Crimes and Criminal Procedures. Available at: http://uscode.law.cornell. edu/uscode/html/uscode18.

United States Constitution, Eighth Amendment [Cruel and Unusual Punishment]. Available at: http://www.law.cornell.edu/constitution/constitution.table.html#amendments.

Corpus Juris Secundum: A Complete Restatement of the Entire American Law as Developed by all Reported Cases. St. Paul, Minn.: West Group, 2005. Constitutional Law, Cruel and Unusual Punishment, § 1656. Constitutional Law, Death Penalty, § 1657. Criminal Law, Death Penalty, § 1529–1543. Criminal Law, Cruel and Unusual Punishment, § 1593–1609. LC: KF105 .C62.

Supreme Court of the United States [official website]. Available at: http://www.supremecourt us.gov/.

"Supreme Court Collection: Capital Punishment." Cornell Law School. Legal Information Institute. Available at: http://www.law.cornell.edu/supct/cases/topics/tog_capital_punish ment.html.

U.S. Law & Supreme Court

American Bar Association. "Supreme Court Preview: Cases at a Glance." Available at: http:// www.abanet.org/publiced/preview/previewcaseglancehome.html.

Atkins v. Virginia, 536 U.S. 304 (2002). Held: Executions of mentally retarded criminals are "cruel and unusual punishments" prohibited by the Eighth Amendment. Available at: http://supct.law.cornell.edu/supct/html/historics/USSC_DN_0000_8452_ ZS.html.

Baldus, David C., Charles A. Pulaski, Jr., and George Woodworth. "Race Discrimination and the Death Penalty." *The Oxford Companion to the Supreme Court of the United States.* Kermit L. Hall. Oxford University Press, 2005. *Oxford Reference Online.* Oxford University Press.

Bazan, Elizabeth B. *Capital Punishment: An Overview of Federal Death Penalty Statutes: Updated January 5, 2005.* Washington, D.C.: Congressional Research Service, 2005. Available at: http://fas.org/sgp/crs/RL30962.pdf.

Bedau, H. A. "Cruel and Unusual Punishment." *Oxford Companion to the Supreme Court of the United States.* Kermit L. Hall. Oxford University Press, 2005. *Oxford Reference Online.* Oxford University Press.

Bigel, Alan I. *Justices William J. Brennan, Jr., and Thurgood Marshall on Capital Punishment: Its Constitutionality, Morality, Deterrent Effect, and Interpretation by the Court.* Lanham, Md.: University Press of America, 1997. LC: KF9227 .C2 B54 1997.

Blackmun, Harry. Dissenting Opinion: *Callins v. Collins*, 510 US 1141 (1994). In this dissenting opinion, Justice Blackmun writes that "From this day forward, I no longer shall tinker with the machinery of death." Available at: http://supct.law.cornell.edu/supct/search/ display.html?terms=callins&url=/supct/html/93–7054.ZA1.html.

Bowers, William. "Research Note: Capital Punishment and Contemporary Values: People's Misgivings and the Court's Misperceptions." *Law & Society Review* 27.1 (1993): 157–76.

Butler, Brooke. "Death Qualification and Prejudice: The Effect of Implicit Racism, Sexism, and Homophobia on Capital Defendants' Right to Due Process." *Behavioral Sciences & the Law* 25.6 (2007): 857–67.

Carter, Lief H., and Margery M. Koosed. "Capital Punishment." *The Oxford Companion to the Supreme Court of the United States*. Kermit L. Hall. Oxford University Press, 2005. *Oxford Reference Online*. Oxford University Press. LC: KF8742.A35 O93 2005.

Cornell Law School. Legal Information Institute. "Death Penalty: An Overview." Available at: http://www.law.cornell.edu/wex/index.php/Death_penalty.

Doyle, Charles. *The Death Penalty: Capital Punishment Legislation in the 110th Congress*. Washington, D.C.: Congressional Research Service, 2007. Available at: http://assets.open-crs.com/rpts/RL34163_20070907.pdf.

Foley, Michael A. *Arbitrary and Capricious: The Supreme Court, the Constitution, and the Death Penalty*. Westport, Conn.: Praeger, 2003. LC: KF9227 .C2 F65 2003.

Furman v. Georgia, 408 U.S. 238 (1972). Ruled that the death penalty, as administered, violated the Eighth Amendment's prohibition on cruel and unusual punishment. Available at: http://supct.law.cornell.edu/supct/html/historics/USSC_CR_0408_0238_ZS.html.

Greenhouse, Linda. "Justices Chilly to Bid to Alter Death Penalty." *New York Times* 8 Jan. 2008, late New York ed.: A1+.

Greer, Megan. "Legal Injection: The Supreme Court Enters the Lethal Injection Debate: *Hill v. McDonough*, 126 S. CT. 2096 (2006)." *Harvard Journal of Law & Public Policy* 30.2 (2007): 767–79.

Latzer, Barry. *Death Penalty Cases: Leading U.S. Supreme Court Cases on Capital Punishment*. Boston, Mass.: Butterworth Heinemann, 2002. LC: KF9227 .C2 L38 2002.

Liebman, James S. "Slow Dancing with Death: The Supreme Court and Capital Punishment, 1963–2006." *Columbia Law Review* 107.1 (2007): 1–130.

Lively, Donald E. *Landmark Supreme Court Cases: A Reference Guide*. Westport, Conn.: Greenwood Press, 1999. LC: KF4549 .L58 1999.

Marshall, Thurgood. "Remarks on the Death Penalty Made at the Judicial Conference of the Second Circuit." *Columbia Law Review* 86.1 (1986): 1–8.

Mauro, Tony. *Illustrated Great Decisions of the Supreme Court*. 2nd ed. Washington, D.C.: CQ Press, 2006. LC: KF4549 .M334 2006.

McCleskey v. Kemp 481 U.S. 279 (1987). Held that in all but "certain limited contexts," general statistics, without more, are insufficient to show discriminatory intent. Available at: http://supct.law.cornell.edu/supct/html/historics/USSC_CR_0481_0279_ZS.html.

Nossiter, Adam, Ralph Blumenthal, and Linda Greenhouse. "Rare Supreme Court Stay Halts a Texas Execution." *New York Times* 28 Sept. 2007, late ed. (East Coast): A.18+.

Palmer, Larry I. "Two Perspectives on Structuring Discretion: Justices Stewart and White on the Death Penalty." *The Journal of Criminal Law and Criminology* 70.2 (Summer 1979): 194–213.

"Supreme Court Justices Weigh Case that Questions Method of Lethal Injection in Executions." *Jet* 113.2 (2008): 60.

Wallace, Paul Starett, Jr. *Capital Punishment: Supreme Court Decisions of the 2005–2006 Term*. Washington, D.C.: Congressional Research Service, 2006. Available at: http://usinfo.state.gov/dhr/img/assets/5796/capitalpunishment2006.pdf.

Weisberg, Robert. "Deregulating Death." *Supreme Court Review* 1983 (1983): 305–95.

Zeisel, Hans. "The Deterrent Effect of the Death Penalty: Facts v. Faiths." *Supreme Court Review* 1976 (1976): 317–43.

Catherine Kaye is Assistant Librarian, Government Documents Section, Pollak Library, California State University, Fullerton.

Appendix

LIST OF MEN EXECUTED IN MONTANA BY MINER'S AND LEGAL COURTS 1862–2007*

1862	C. W. Spillman	Miner's Court	Powell County
1863	John Heron	Miner's Court	Beaverhead County
1863	George Ives	Miner's Court	Madison County
1864	John Doe	Miner's Court	Madison County
1865	John Keene	Miner's Court	Lewis and Clark County
1866	Leander Johnson	Miner's Court	Powell County
1866	J. L. Goones	Miner's Court	Silver Bow County
1868	George Ballou	Miner's Court	Powell County
1868	John Varley	Miner's Court	Granite County
1871	—Baker	Miner's Court	Broadwater County
1871	Chinaman	Miner's Court	Granite County
1875	William Wheatley	Legal Hanging	Lewis and Clark County
1875	William H. Sterres	Legal Hanging	Lewis and Clark County
1878	Michael McAndrews	Legal Hanging	Broadwater County
1878	Francois Joseph Robert	Legal Hanging	Madison County
1879	Joseph K. Koble	Legal Hanging	Chouteau County
1879	Orlando H. Marsh	Legal Hanging	Chouteau County
1881	Peter Pelkey	Legal Hanging	Lewis and Clark County
1881	John B. Douglas	Legal Hanging	Madison County
1883	Henry Fuhrmann	Legal Hanging	Lewis and Clark County
1883	Ah Yung	Legal Hanging	Missoula County
1883	John A. Clark	Legal Hanging	Gallatin County

* list compiled from Donovan and Raffety

1887	Thomas H. Harding	Legal Hanging	Beaverhead County
1888	John Patrick Hart	Legal Hanging	Lewis and Clark County
1888	Martin Luther Scott	Legal Hanging	Powell County
1889	George Duncan Bryson	Legal Hanging	Jefferson County
1889	W. H. "Harry" Roberts	Legal Hanging	Silver Bow County
1890	Thomas A. King	Legal Hanging	Jefferson County
1890	Antley	Legal Hanging	Missoula County
1890	Lala See	Legal Hanging	Missoula County
1890	Pascale	Legal Hanging	Missoula County
1890	Pierre Paul	Legal Hanging	Missoula County
1892	John Burns	Legal Hanging	Missoula County
1894	Robert A. Anderson	Legal Hanging	Park County
1894	John H. Osnes	Legal Hanging	Chouteau County
1894	Calvin J. Christie	Legal Hanging	Flathead County
1895	Clayberg Pugh	Legal Hanging	Jefferson County
1895	Joseph Cadotte	Legal Hanging	Chouteau County
1896	William Biggerstaff	Legal Hanging	Lewis and Clark County
1896	William Gay	Legal Hanging	Lewis and Clark County
1899	Thomas Salmon	Legal Hanging	Carbon County
1899	Joseph H. Allen	Legal Hanging	Lewis and Clark County
1899	William C. Brooks	Legal Hanging	Yellowstone County
1900	William Wallace Calder	Legal Hanging	Fergus County
1900	Joseph C. Hurst	Legal Hanging	Dawson County
1900	William Pepo	Legal Hanging	Teton County
1900	Daniel Lucy	Legal Hanging	Silver Bow County
1901	James Fleming	Legal Hanging	Powell County
1901	James Edward Brady	Legal Hanging	Lewis and Clark County
1902	Clinton Dotson	Legal Hanging	Powell County
1904	James Martin	Legal Hanging	Silver Bow County
1904	Louis H. Mott	Legal Hanging	Missoula County
1905	Herbert Henry Metzger	Legal Hanging	Meagher County
1906	Lu Sing	Legal Hanging	Gallatin County
1906	Miles Fuller	Legal Hanging	Silver Bow County
1908	George Rock	Legal Hanging	Montana State Prison
1909	William A. Hayes	Legal Hanging	Montana State Prison

1909	Frederick LeBeau	Legal Hanging	Flathead County
1917	Leslie Fahley	Legal Hanging	Meagher County
1917	Harrison Gibson	Legal Hanging	Meagher County
1917	Henry Hall	Legal Hanging	Meagher County
1918	Frank Fisher	Legal Hanging	Silver Bow County
1918	John O'Neil	Legal Hanging	Silver Bow County
1918	Sherman A. Powell	Legal Hanging	Silver Bow County
1918	Juan Cuellae	Legal Hanging	Yellowstone County
1920	Alfred Lane	Legal Hanging	Rosebud County
1921	Albert Yeik	Legal Hanging	Beaverhead County
1922	Joseph Vuckovich	Legal Hanging	Missoula County
1923	Glenna Martin Bolton	Legal Hanging	Treasure County
1923	Joseph B. Reagin	Legal Hanging	Treasure County
1923	Monte Harris	Legal Hanging	Silver Bow County
1923	William "Bill" Harris	Legal Hanging	Silver Bow County
1924	Seth Orrin Danner	Legal Hanging	Gallatin County
1925	Roy Walsh	Legal Hanging	Jefferson County
1926	Anthony Vettere	Legal Hanging	Silver Bow County
1927	Ferdinand Schlaps	Legal Hanging	Roosevelt County
1929	Rollin Davisson	Legal Hanging	Park County
1933	George Hoffman	Legal Hanging	Teton County
1935	Henry John Zorn	Legal Hanging	Custer County
1935	George Criner	Legal Hanging	Custer County
1938	Franklin Robideau	Legal Hanging	Stillwater County
1939	Lee Simpson	Legal Hanging	Golden Valley
1943	Philip J. Coleman	Legal Hanging	Missoula County
1995	Duncan Peder McKenzie, Jr.	Lethal Injection	Montana State Prison
1998	Terry Allen Langford	Lethal Injection	Montana State Prison
2006	David Thomas Dawson	Lethal Injection	Montana State Prison

Index

abolition, 6, 220–22, 224–25, 231, 235–36, 240, 269–71, 276, 286, 330–31, 335; BMA and, 295; efforts, in South, 205; in Europe, 123–24, 126–27; global, 120–26; universal, 127–31. *See also* anti-death-penalty movement

Abu-Jamal, Mumia, 5

Academy Awards, 138, 141, 150, 153, 159, 182

ACLU. *See* American Civil Liberties Union

Adams, Randall Dale, 2

Adamson v. Ricketts, 358

adultery, 216, 219

African Americans, 2, 208–9, 243, 246, 249, 254, 256, 257, 273

aggravating circumstances, 10–11, 229–30, 249, 359–60, 366

AI. *See* Amnesty International

Aiken, Earnest James, Jr., 197

AIUSA. *See* Amnesty USA

Alarcon, Arthur L., 199

Albion Ascendant (Prest), 49–50

Albion's Fatal Tree (Hay), 48–49, 53

alcalde system, 389–91, 403

Alcatraz, 154–56

Allen, Barbara, 194

Allen, Timothy, 366

All Over the Map: Rethinking American Regions (Ayers), 194

All the President's Men (film), 31

Ally MacBeal (television show), 43

Alta California, 407

Altman, Robert, 190n77

Alvarez, Francisco, 244

AMA. *See* American Medical Association

American Association on Intellectual and Developmental Disabilities, 4

American Association on Mental Retardation, 15

American Bar Association, 209

American Beauty (film), 182

American Civil Liberties Union (ACLU), 240, 332–33,

381, 426; AIUSA and, 119; Dawson and, 350; Duffy, John, and, 36; Harris, R. A., and, 333

American Convention on Human Rights, 126

American Indians. *See* Native Americans

American Indians and State Law: Sovereignty, Race, and Citizenship (Rosen), 194

American Jurist, 221

American Law Institute, 302

American League to Abolish Capital Punishment, 276, 422

American Medical Association (AMA), 14, 285, 313, 383–84

American Nursing Association, 385–86

American Psychiatric Association (APA), 310–12

American Psychological Association, 15

American Society of Anesthesiologists (ASA), 14, 383–84

American West, settlement of, 97–98

The American West: Interactions, Intersections, and Injunctions (Bakken & Farrington, eds), 1–2

Amnesty International (AI), 115, 128, 378, 380; Clinton and, 384; influence of, 129–31; mental illness and, 385; position of, 115–27

Amnesty USA (AIUSA), 118–20

Amsterdam, Anthony G., 4, 197–98

Anaya, Toney, 20, 245, 365–66

Anderson, Christopher, 188n29

Andrews, Joseph, 219–20

And the Law Says (film), 139

Angels with Dirty Faces (film), 138, 139–41

Annan, Kofi, 128

antebellum period, 204–5

Anti-Capital Punishment League, 270–71

anti-death-penalty movement, 205, 273–76, 322, 367, 378–80, 418–29

antilynching laws, 4

Antiterrorism and Effective Death Penalty Act of 1996, 366

Antley, 249, 346–47